Volume 2 Topics 7–12

Authors

Robert Q. Berry, III
Professor of Mathematics Education, Department of Curriculum, Instruction and Special Education, University of Virginia, Charlottesville, Virginia

Zachary Champagne
Assistant in Research
Florida Center for Research in Science, Technology, Engineering, and Mathematics (FCR-STEM)
Jacksonville, Florida

Eric Milou
Professor of Mathematics
Rowan University,
Glassboro, New Jersey

Jane F. Schielack
Professor Emerita
Department of Mathematics
Texas A&M University,
College Station, Texas

Jonathan A. Wray
Mathematics Supervisor,
Howard County Public Schools, Ellicott City, Maryland

Randall I. Charles
Professor Emeritus
Department of Mathematics
San Jose State University
San Jose, California

Francis (Skip) Fennell
Professor Emeritus of Education and Graduate and Professional Studies,
McDaniel College
Westminster, Maryland

Boston, Massachusetts Chandler, Arizona
Glenview, Illinois New York, New York

Mathematician Reviewers

Gary Lippman, Ph.D.
Professor Emeritus
Mathematics and Computer Science
California State University, East Bay
Hayward, California

Karen Edwards, Ph.D.
Mathematics Lecturer
Arlington, MA

Florida Reviewers

Kristine Peterfeso
Teacher Middle School Math,
Palm Beach County School District

Tamala Ferguson
Math Curriculum Coach,
School District of Osceola County

Melissa Nelson
Math Coach and Assessment
Coordinator, St. Lucie Public Schools

ISBN-13: 978-0-13-491320-9
ISBN-10: 0-13-491320-5
4 19

CONTENTS

TOPICS

DIGITAL RESOURCES

Go Online | **PearsonRealize.com**

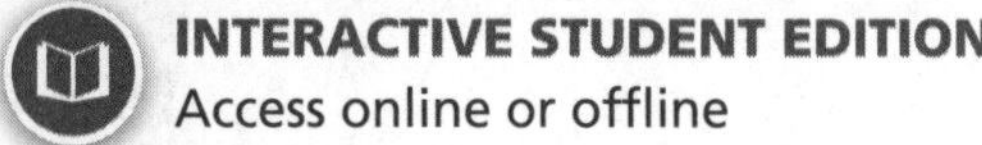

INTERACTIVE STUDENT EDITION
Access online or offline

VISUAL LEARNING
Interact with visual learning animations

ACTIVITY
Use with ***Solve & Discuss It, Explore It,*** and ***Explain It*** activities and Examples

VIDEOS
Watch clips to support ***3-Act Mathematical Modeling*** Lessons and ***enVision® STEM Projects***

PRACTICE
Practice what you've learned and get immediate feedback

TUTORIALS
Get help from ***Virtual Nerd*** any time you need it

MATH TOOLS
Explore math with digital tools

GAMES
Play math games to help you learn

KEY CONCEPT
Review important lesson content

GLOSSARY
Read and listen to English and Spanish definitions

ASSESSMENT
Show what you've learned

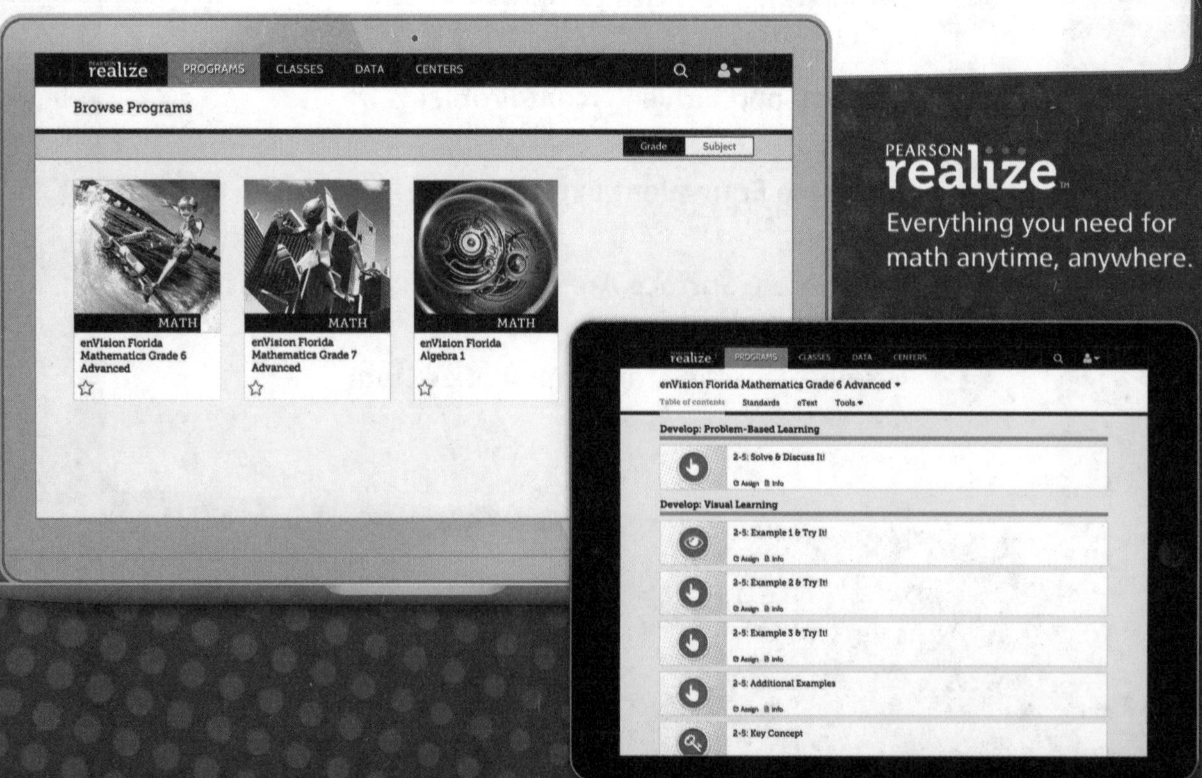

PEARSON **realize**
Everything you need for math anytime, anywhere.

Analyze and Use Proportional Relationships

TOPIC 8

Understand and Use Percent

TOPIC 9 Analyze and Solve Percent Problems

Generate Equivalent Expressions

Solve Area, Surface Area, and Volume Problems

TOPIC 12 Display, Describe, and Summarize Data

Mathematics Florida Standards (MAFS)

RATIOS AND PROPORTIONAL RELATIONSHIPS

MAFS.6.RP.1 **Understand ratio concepts and use ratio reasoning to solve problems.** (Major Cluster)

MAFS.6.RP.1.1 Understand the concept of a ratio and use ratio language to describe a ratio relationship between two quantities.

MAFS.6.RP.1.2 Understand the concept of a unit rate a/b associated with a ratio $a:b$ with $b \neq 0$, and use rate language in the context of a ratio relationship.

MAFS.6.RP.1.3 Use ratio and rate reasoning to solve real-world and mathematical problems, e.g., by reasoning about tables of equivalent ratios, tape diagrams, double number line diagrams, or equations.

MAFS.6.RP.1.3a Make tables of equivalent ratios relating quantities with whole-number measurements, find missing values in the tables, and plot the pairs of values on the coordinate plane. Use tables to compare ratios.

MAFS.6.RP.1.3b Solve unit rate problems including those involving unit pricing and constant speed.

MAFS.6.RP.1.3c Find a percent of a quantity as a rate per 100 (e.g., 30% of a quantity means 30/100 times the quantity); solve problems involving finding the whole, given a part and the percent.

MAFS.6.RP.1.3d Use ratio reasoning to convert measurement units; manipulate and transform units appropriately when multiplying or dividing quantities.

MAFS.6.RP.1.3e Understand the concept of Pi as the ratio of the circumference of a circle to its diameter.

MAFS.7.RP.1 **Analyze proportional relationships and use them to solve real-world and mathematical problems.** (Major Cluster)

MAFS.7.RP.1.1 Compute unit rates associated with ratios of fractions, including ratios of lengths, areas and other quantities measured in like or different units.

MAFS.7.RP.1.2 Recognize and represent proportional relationships between quantities.

MAFS.7.RP.1.2a Decide whether two quantities are in a proportional relationship, e.g., by testing for equivalent ratios in a table or graphing on a coordinate plane and observing whether the graph is a straight line through the origin.

MAFS.7.RP.1.2b Identify the constant of proportionality (unit rate) in tables, graphs, equations, diagrams, and verbal descriptions of proportional relationships.

MAFS.7.RP.1.2c Represent proportional relationships by equations.

MAFS.7.RP.1.2d Explain what a point (x, y) on the graph of a proportional relationship means in terms of the situation, with special attention to the points (0, 0) and $(1, r)$ where r is the unit rate.

MAFS.7.RP.1.3 Use proportional relationships to solve multistep ratio and percent problems.

THE NUMBER SYSTEM

MAFS.6.NS.1 **Apply and extend previous understandings of multiplication and division to divide fractions by fractions.** (Major Cluster)

MAFS.6.NS.1.1 Interpret and compute quotients of fractions, and solve word problems involving division of fractions by fractions, e.g., by using visual fraction models and equations to represent the problem.

MAFS.6.NS.2 **Compute fluently with multi-digit numbers and find common factors and multiples.** (Additional Cluster)

MAFS.6.NS.2.2 Fluently divide multi-digit numbers using the standard algorithm.

MAFS.6.NS.2.3 Fluently add, subtract, multiply, and divide multi-digit decimals using the standard algorithm for each operation.

MAFS.6.NS.2.4 Find the greatest common factor of two whole numbers less than or equal to 100 and the least common multiple of two whole numbers less than or equal to 12. Use the distributive property to express a sum of two whole numbers 1–100 with a common factor as a multiple of a sum of two whole numbers with no common factor.

MAFS.6.NS.3 Apply and extend previous understandings of numbers to the system of rational numbers. (Major Cluster)

MAFS.6.NS.3.5 Understand that positive and negative numbers are used together to describe quantities having opposite directions or values (e.g., temperature above/below zero, elevation above/below sea level, credits/debits, positive/negative electric charge); use positive and negative numbers to represent quantities in real-world contexts, explaining the meaning of 0 in each situation.

MAFS.6.NS.3.6 Understand a rational number as a point on the number line. Extend number line diagrams and coordinate axes familiar from previous grades to represent points on the line and in the plane with negative number coordinates.

MAFS.6.NS.3.6a Recognize opposite signs of numbers as indicating locations on opposite sides of 0 on the number line; recognize that the opposite of the opposite of a number is the number itself, e.g., $-(-3) = 3$, and that 0 is its own opposite.

MAFS.6.NS.3.6b Understand signs of numbers in ordered pairs as indicating locations in quadrants of the coordinate plane; recognize that when two ordered pairs differ only by signs, the locations of the points are related by reflections across one or both axes.

MAFS.6.NS.3.6c Find and position integers and other rational numbers on a horizontal or vertical number line diagram; find and position pairs of integers and other rational numbers on a coordinate plane.

MAFS.6.NS.3.7 Understand ordering and absolute value of rational numbers.

MAFS.6.NS.3.7a Interpret statements of inequality as statements about the relative position of two numbers on a number line diagram.

MAFS.6.NS.3.7b Write, interpret, and explain statements of order for rational numbers in real-world contexts.

MAFS.6.NS.3.7c Understand the absolute value of a rational number as its distance from 0 on the number line; interpret absolute value as magnitude for a positive or negative quantity in a real-world situation.

MAFS.6.NS.3.7d Distinguish comparisons of absolute value from statements about order.

MAFS.6.NS.3.8 Solve real-world and mathematical problems by graphing points in all four quadrants of the coordinate plane. Include use of coordinates and absolute value to find distances between points with the same first coordinate or the same second coordinate.

MAFS.7.NS.1 Apply and extend previous understandings of operations with fractions to add, subtract, multiply, and divide rational numbers. (Major Cluster)

MAFS.7.NS.1.1 Apply and extend previous understandings of addition and subtraction to add and subtract rational numbers; represent addition and subtraction on a horizontal or vertical number line diagram.

MAFS.7.NS.1.1a Describe situations in which opposite quantities combine to make 0.

MAFS.7.NS.1.1b Understand $p + q$ as the number located a distance $|q|$ from p, in the positive or negative direction depending on whether q is positive or negative. Show that a number and its opposite have a sum of 0 (are additive inverses). Interpret sums of rational numbers by describing real-world contexts.

MAFS.7.NS.1.1c Understand subtraction of rational numbers as adding the additive inverse, $p - q = p + (-q)$. Show that the distance between two rational numbers on the number line is the absolute value of their difference, and apply this principle in real-world contexts.

MAFS.7.NS.1.1d Apply properties of operations as strategies to add and subtract rational numbers.

MAFS.7.NS.1.2 Apply and extend previous understandings of multiplication and division and of fractions to multiply and divide rational numbers.

MAFS.7.NS.1.2a Understand that multiplication is extended from fractions to rational numbers by requiring that operations continue to satisfy the properties of operations, particularly the distributive property, leading to products such as $(-1)(-1) = 1$ and the rules for multiplying signed numbers. Interpret products of rational numbers by describing real-world contexts.

MAFS.7.NS.1.2b Understand that integers can be divided, provided that the divisor is not zero, and every quotient of integers (with non-zero divisor) is a rational number. If p and q are integers, then $-\left(\frac{p}{q}\right) = \frac{(-p)}{q} = \frac{p}{(-q)}$. Interpret quotients of rational numbers by describing real-world contexts.

MAFS.7.NS.1.2c Apply properties of operations as strategies to multiply and divide rational numbers.

MAFS.7.NS.1.2d Convert a rational number to a decimal using long division; know that the decimal form of a rational number terminates in 0s or eventually repeats.

MAFS.7.NS.1.3 Solve real-world and mathematical problems involving the four operations with rational numbers.

EXPRESSIONS AND EQUATIONS

MAFS.6.EE.1 Apply and extend previous understandings of arithmetic to algebraic expressions. (Major Cluster)

MAFS.6.EE.1.1 Write and evaluate numerical expressions involving whole-number exponents.

MAFS.6.EE.1.2 Write, read, and evaluate expressions in which letters stand for numbers.

MAFS.6.EE.1.2a Write expressions that record operations with numbers and with letters standing for numbers.

MAFS.6.EE.1.2b Identify parts of an expression using mathematical terms (sum, term, product, factor, quotient, coefficient); view one or more parts of an expression as a single entity.

MAFS.6.EE.1.2c Evaluate expressions at specific values of their variables. Include expressions that arise from formulas used in real-world problems. Perform arithmetic operations, including those involving whole-number exponents, in the conventional order when there are no parentheses to specify a particular order (Order of Operations).

MAFS.6.EE.1.3 Apply the properties of operations to generate equivalent expressions.

MAFS.6.EE.1.4 Identify when two expressions are equivalent (i.e., when the two expressions name the same number regardless of which value is substituted into them).

MAFS.6.EE.2 Reason about and solve one-variable equations and inequalities. (Major Cluster)

MAFS.6.EE.2.5 Understand solving an equation or inequality as a process of answering a question: which values from a specified set, if any, make the equation or inequality true? Use substitution to determine whether a given number in a specified set makes an equation or inequality true.

MAFS.6.EE.2.6 Use variables to represent numbers and write expressions when solving a real-world or mathematical problem; understand that a variable can represent an unknown number, or, depending on the purpose at hand, any number in a specified set.

MAFS.6.EE.2.7 Solve real-world and mathematical problems by writing and solving equations of the form $x + p = q$ and $px = q$ for cases in which p, q and x are all nonnegative rational numbers.

MAFS.6.EE.2.8 Write an inequality of the form $x > c$ or $x < c$ to represent a constraint or condition in a real-world or mathematical problem. Recognize that inequalities of the form $x > c$ or $x < c$ have infinitely many solutions; represent solutions of such inequalities on number line diagrams.

MAFS.6.EE.3 Represent and analyze quantitative relationships between dependent and independent variables. (Major Cluster)

MAFS.6.EE.3.9 Use variables to represent two quantities in a real-world problem that change in relationship to one another; write an equation to express one quantity, thought of as the dependent variable, in terms of the other quantity, thought of as the independent variable. Analyze the relationship between the dependent and independent variables using graphs and tables, and relate these to the equation.

MAFS.7.EE.1 Use properties of operations to generate equivalent expressions. (Major Cluster)

MAFS.7.EE.1.1 Apply properties of operations as strategies to add, subtract, factor, and expand linear expressions with rational coefficients.

MAFS.7.EE.1.2 Understand that rewriting an expression in different forms in a problem context can shed light on the problem and how the quantities in it are related.

MAFS.7.EE.2 Solve real-life and mathematical problems using numerical and algebraic expressions and equations. (Major Cluster)

MAFS.7.EE.2.3 Solve multi-step real-life and mathematical problems posed with positive and negative rational numbers in any form (whole numbers, fractions, and decimals), using tools strategically. Apply properties of operations to calculate with numbers in any form; convert between forms as appropriate; and assess the reasonableness of answers using mental computation and estimation strategies.

MAFS.7.EE.2.4 Use variables to represent quantities in a real-world or mathematical problem, and construct simple equations and inequalities to solve problems by reasoning about the quantities.

MAFS.7.EE.2.4a Solve word problems leading to equations of the form $px + q = r$ and $p(x + q) = r$, where p, q, and r are specific rational numbers. Solve equations of these forms fluently. Compare an algebraic solution to an arithmetic solution, identifying the sequence of the operations used in each approach.

MAFS.7.EE.2.4b Solve word problems leading to inequalities of the form $px + q > r$ or $px + q < r$, where p, q, and r are specific rational numbers. Graph the solution set of the inequality and interpret it in the context of the problem.

GEOMETRY

MAFS.6.G.1 Solve real-world and mathematical problems involving area, surface area, and volume. (Supporting Cluster)

MAFS.6.G.1.1 Find the area of right triangles, other triangles, special quadrilaterals, and polygons by composing into rectangles or decomposing into triangles and other shapes; apply these techniques in the context of solving real-world and mathematical problems.

MAFS.6.G.1.2 Find the volume of a right rectangular prism with fractional edge lengths by packing it with unit cubes of the appropriate unit fraction edge lengths, and show that the volume is the same as would be found by multiplying the edge lengths of the prism. Apply the formulas $V = \ell wh$ and $V = bh$ to find volumes of right rectangular prisms with fractional edge lengths in the context of solving real-world and mathematical problems.

MAFS.6.G.1.3 Draw polygons in the coordinate plane given coordinates for the vertices; use coordinates to find the length of a side joining points with the same first coordinate or the same second coordinate. Apply these techniques in the context of solving real-world and mathematical problems.

MAFS.6.G.1.4 Represent three-dimensional figures using nets made up of rectangles and triangles, and use the nets to find the surface area of these figures. Apply these techniques in the context of solving real-world and mathematical problems.

STATISTICS AND PROBABILITY

MAFS.6.SP.1 Develop understanding of statistical variability. (Additional Cluster)

MAFS.6.SP.1.1 Recognize a statistical question as one that anticipates variability in the data related to the question and accounts for it in the answers.

MAFS.6.SP.1.2 Understand that a set of data collected to answer a statistical question has a distribution which can be described by its center, spread, and overall shape.

MAFS.6.SP.1.3 Recognize that a measure of center for a numerical data set summarizes all of its values with a single number, while a measure of variation describes how its values vary with a single number.

MAFS.6.SP.2 Summarize and describe distributions. (Additional Cluster)

MAFS.6.SP.2.4 Display numerical data in plots on a number line, including dot plots, histograms, and box plots.

MAFS.6.SP.2.5 Summarize numerical data sets in relation to their context, such as by:

MAFS.6.SP.2.5a Reporting the number of observations.

MAFS.6.SP.2.5b Describing the nature of the attribute under investigation, including how it was measured and its units of measurement.

MAFS.6.SP.2.5c Giving quantitative measures of center (median and/or mean) and variability (interquartile range and/or mean absolute deviation), as well as describing any overall pattern and any striking deviations from the overall pattern with reference to the context in which the data were gathered.

MAFS.6.SP.2.5d Relating the choice of measures of center and variability to the shape of the data distribution and the context in which the data were gathered.

MATHEMATICAL PRACTICE

MAFS.K12.MP.1.1 Make sense of problems and persevere in solving them.

MAFS.K12.MP.2.1 Reason abstractly and quantitatively.

MAFS.K12.MP.3.1 Construct viable arguments and critique the reasoning of others.

MAFS.K12.MP.4.1 Model with mathematics.

MAFS.K12.MP.5.1 Use appropriate tools strategically.

MAFS.K12.MP.6.1 Attend to precision.

MAFS.K12.MP.7.1 Look for and make use of structure.

MAFS.K12.MP.8.1 Look for and express regularity in repeated reasoning.

CORRELATION TO LANGUAGE ARTS FLORIDA STANDARDS (LAFS)

LAFS.6.SL.1.1 Engage effectively in a range of collaborative discussions (one-on-one, in groups, and teacher-led) with diverse partners on grade 6 topics, texts, and issues, building on others' ideas and expressing their own clearly.

a. Come to discussions prepared, having read or studied required material; explicitly draw on that preparation by referring to evidence on the topic, text, or issue to probe and reflect on ideas under discussion.

b. Follow rules for collegial discussions, set specific goals and deadlines, and define individual roles as needed.

c. Pose and respond to specific questions with elaboration and detail by making comments that contribute to the topic, text, or issue under discussion.

d. Review the key ideas expressed and demonstrate understanding of multiple perspectives through reflection and paraphrasing.

LAFS.6.SL.1.2 Interpret information presented in diverse media and formats (e.g., visually, quantitatively, orally) and explain how it contributes to a topic, text, or issue under study.

LAFS.6.SL.1.3 Delineate a speaker's argument and specific claims, distinguishing claims that are supported by reasons and evidence from claims that are not.

LAFS.6.SL.2.4 Present claims and findings, sequencing ideas logically and using pertinent descriptions, facts, and details to accentuate main ideas or themes; use appropriate eye contact, adequate volume, and clear pronunciation.

LAFS.68.RST.1.3 Follow precisely a multistep procedure when carrying out experiments, taking measurements, or performing technical tasks.

LAFS.68.RST.2.4 Determine the meaning of symbols, key terms, and other domain-specific words and phrases as they are used in a specific scientific or technical context relevant to grades 6–8 texts and topics.

LAFS.68.RST.3.7 Integrate quantitative or technical information expressed in words in a text with a version of that information expressed visually (e.g., in a flowchart, diagram, model, graph, or table).

LAFS.68.WHST.1.1 Write arguments focused on discipline-specific content.

a. Introduce claim(s) about a topic or issue, acknowledge and distinguish the claim(s) from alternate or opposing claims, and organize the reasons and evidence logically.

b. Support claim(s) with logical reasoning and relevant, accurate data and evidence that demonstrate an understanding of the topic or text, using credible sources.

c. Use words, phrases, and clauses to create cohesion and clarify the relationships among claim(s), counterclaims, reasons, and evidence.

d. Establish and maintain a formal style.

e. Provide a concluding statement or section that follows from and supports the argument presented.

LAFS.68.WHST.2.4 Produce clear and coherent writing in which the development, organization, and style are appropriate to task, purpose, and audience.

CORRELATION TO ENGLISH LANGUAGE DEVELOPMENT STANDARDS (ELDS)

ELD.K12.ELL.MA.1 English language learners communicate information, ideas and concepts necessary for academic success in the content area of Mathematics.

ELD.K12.ELL.SI.1 English language learners communicate for social and instructional purposes within the school setting.

Math Practices and Problem Solving Handbook

The **Math Practices and Problem Solving Handbook** is available at **PearsonRealize.com**.

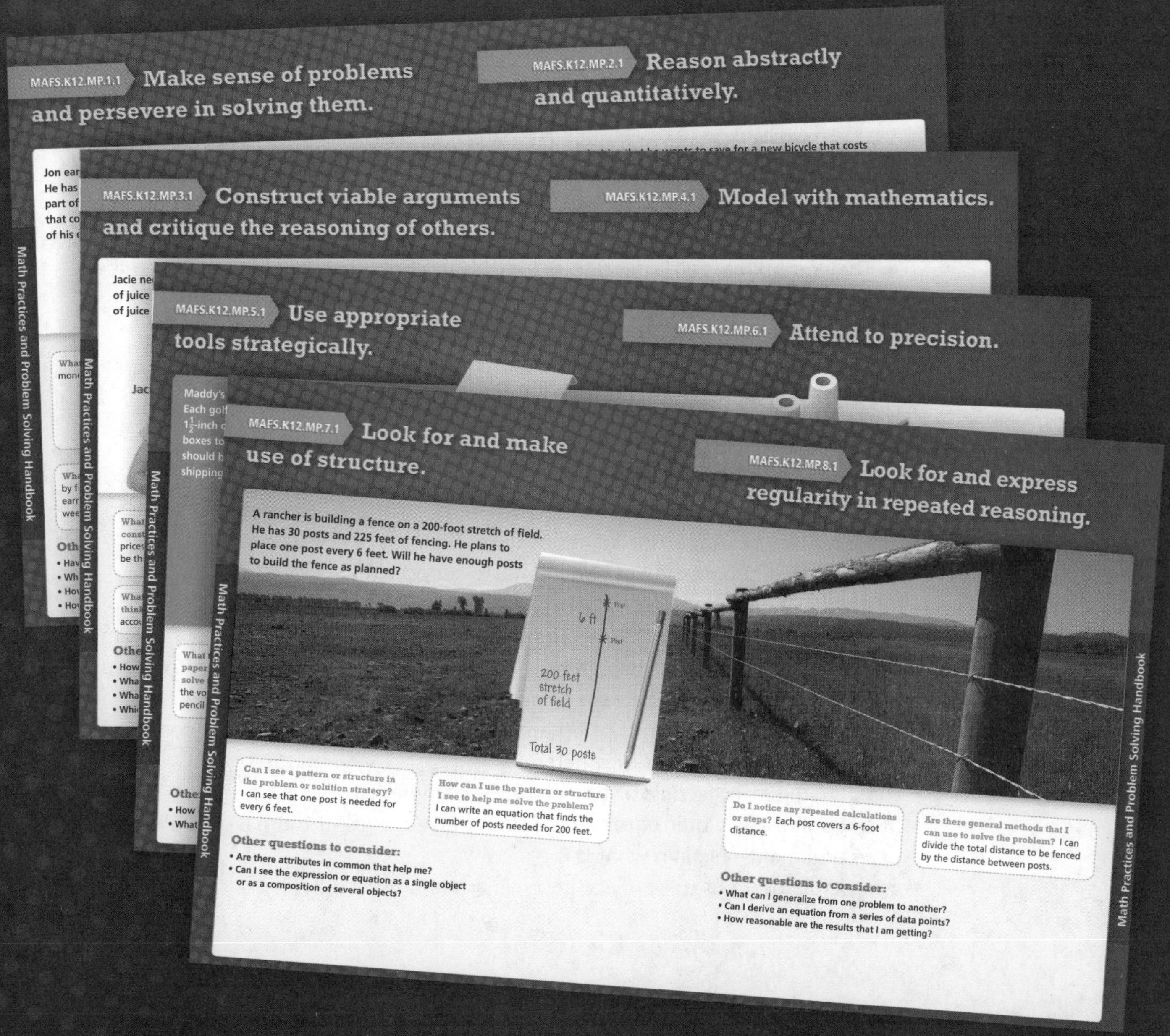

MAFS.K12.MP.1.1 Make sense of problems and persevere in solving them.

MAFS.K12.MP.2.1 Reason abstractly and quantitatively.

MAFS.K12.MP.3.1 Construct viable arguments and critique the reasoning of others.

MAFS.K12.MP.4.1 Model with mathematics.

MAFS.K12.MP.5.1 Use appropriate tools strategically.

MAFS.K12.MP.6.1 Attend to precision.

MAFS.K12.MP.7.1 Look for and make use of structure.

MAFS.K12.MP.8.1 Look for and express regularity in repeated reasoning.

A rancher is building a fence on a 200-foot stretch of field. He has 30 posts and 225 feet of fencing. He plans to place one post every 6 feet. Will he have enough posts to build the fence as planned?

6 ft
200 feet stretch of field
Total 30 posts

Can I see a pattern or structure in the problem or solution strategy? I can see that one post is needed for every 6 feet.

How can I use the pattern or structure I see to help me solve the problem? I can write an equation that finds the number of posts needed for 200 feet.

Other questions to consider:
- Are there attributes in common that help me?
- Can I see the expression or equation as a single object or as a composition of several objects?

Do I notice any repeated calculations or steps? Each post covers a 6-foot distance.

Are there general methods that I can use to solve the problem? I can divide the total distance to be fenced by the distance between posts.

Other questions to consider:
- What can I generalize from one problem to another?
- Can I derive an equation from a series of data points?
- How reasonable are the results that I am getting?

Math Practices and Problem Solving Handbook

Standards for Mathematical Practice

MAFS.K12.MP.1.1

Make sense of problems and persevere in solving them.

Mathematically proficient students:

- can explain the meaning of a problem
- look for entry points to begin solving a problem
- analyze givens, constraints, relationships, and goals
- make conjectures about the solution
- plan a solution pathway
- think of similar problems, and try simpler forms of the problem
- evaluate their progress toward a solution and change pathways if necessary
- can explain similarities and differences between different representations
- check their solutions to problems.

MAFS.K12.MP.2.1

Reason abstractly and quantitatively.

Mathematically proficient students:

- make sense of quantities and their relationships in problem situations:
    - They *decontextualize*—create a coherent representation of a problem situation using numbers, variables, and symbols; and
    - They *contextualize* – attend to the meaning of numbers, variables, and symbols in the problem situation
- know and use different properties of operations to solve problems.

MAFS.K12.MP.3.1

Construct viable arguments and critique the reasoning of others.

Mathematically proficient students:

- use definitions and problem solutions when constructing arguments
- make conjectures about the solutions to problems
- build a logical progression of statements to support their conjectures and justify their conclusions
- analyze situations and recognize and use counterexamples
- reason inductively about data, making plausible arguments that take into account the context from which the data arose
- listen or read the arguments of others, and decide whether they make sense
- respond to the arguments of others
- compare the effectiveness of two plausible arguments
- distinguish correct logic or reasoning from flawed, and—if there is a flaw in an argument—explain what it is
- ask useful questions to clarify or improve arguments of others.

MAFS.K12.MP.4.1

Model with mathematics.

Mathematically proficient students:

- can develop a representation—drawing, diagram, table, graph, expression, equation–to model a problem situation
- make assumptions and approximations to simplify a complicated situation
- identify important quantities in a practical situation and map their relationships using a range of tools
- analyze relationships mathematically to draw conclusions
- interpret mathematical results in the context of the situation and propose improvements to the model as needed.

MAFS.K12.MP.5.1

Use appropriate tools strategically.

Mathematically proficient students:

- consider appropriate tools when solving a mathematical problem
- make sound decisions about when each of these tools might be helpful
- identify relevant mathematical resources, and use them to pose or solve problems
- use tools and technology to explore and deepen their understanding of concepts.

MAFS.K12.MP.6.1

Attend to precision.

Mathematically proficient students:

- communicate precisely to others
- use clear definitions in discussions with others and in their own reasoning
- state the meaning of the symbols they use
- specify units of measure, and label axes to clarify their correspondence with quantities in a problem
- calculate accurately and efficiently
- express numerical answers with a degree of precision appropriate for the problem context.

MAFS.K12.MP.7.1

Look for and make use of structure.

Mathematically proficient students:

- look closely at a problem situation to identify a pattern or structure
- can step back from a solution pathway and shift perspective
- can see complex representations, such as some algebraic expressions, as single objects or as being composed of several objects.

MAFS.K12.MP.8.1

Look for and express regularity in repeated reasoning.

Mathematically proficient students:

- notice if calculations are repeated, and look both for general methods and for shortcuts
- maintain oversight of the process as they work to solve a problem, while also attending to the details
- continually evaluate the reasonableness of their intermediate results.

ANALYZE AND USE PROPORTIONAL RELATIONSHIPS

? Topic Essential Question

How can you recognize and represent proportional relationships and use them to solve problems?

Topic Overview

7-1 Connect Ratios, Rates, and Unit Rates
7.RP.1.1, 7.RP.1.3, MP.1.1, MP.3.1, MP.6.1, MP.7.1, MP.8.1

7-2 Determine Unit Rates with Ratios of Fractions
7.RP.1.1, 7.RP.1.3, MP.2.1, MP.3.1, MP.6.1, MP.7.1

7-3 Understand Proportional Relationships: Equivalent Ratios
MAFS.7.RP.1.2a, MP.1.1, MP.2.1, MP.3.1. MP.7.1, MP.8.1

7-4 Describe Proportional Relationships: Constant of Proportionality
7.RP.1.2b, 7.RP.1.2c, MP.2.1, MP.3.1, MP.4.1, MP.6.1, MP.8.1

7-Act Mathematical Modeling: Mixin' It Up
7.RP.1.1, 7.RP.1.2a, MP.1.1, MP.2.1, MP.3.1, MP.4.1, MP.5.1, MP.7.1, MP.8.1

7-5 Graph Proportional Relationships
7.RP.1.2a, 7.RP.1.2b, 7.RP.1.2d, MP.2.1, MP.3.1, MP.4.1, MP.7.1

7-6 Apply Proportional Reasoning to Solve Problems
7.RP.1.2, 7.RP.1.3, MP.1.1, MP.2.1, MP.5.1, MP.7.1

Topic Vocabulary

- constant of proportionality
- proportion
- proportional relationship

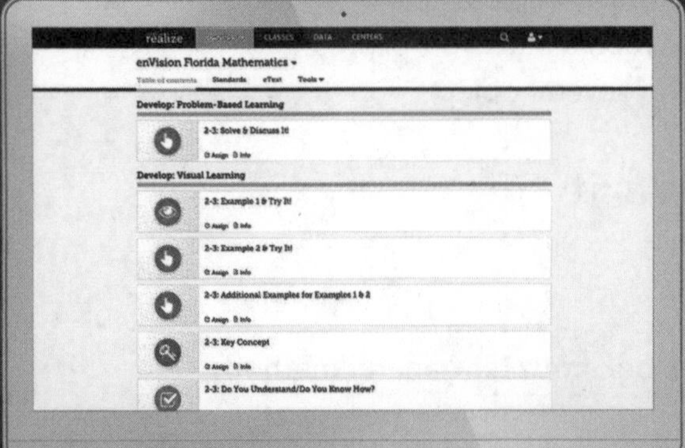

Go online | **PearsonRealize.com**

Lesson Digital Resources

INTERACTIVE STUDENT EDITION
Access online or offline.

VISUAL LEARNING ANIMATION
Interact with visual learning animations.

ACTIVITY Use with ***Solve & Discuss It, Explore It,*** and ***Explain It*** activities, and to explore Examples.

VIDEOS Watch clips to support ***3-Act Mathematical Modeling Lessons*** and ***STEM Projects.***

3-ACT MATH

Mixin' It Up

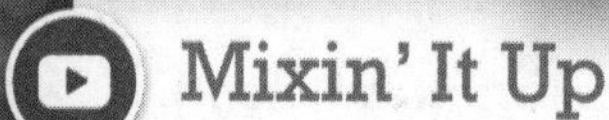

Mixin' It Up

Drinking plenty of water each day is important. Water is necessary for everything your body does. Not drinking enough water can lead to health problems. It's even easier to drink enough water if you like the taste.

There are many ways to make water more exciting. You can drink seltzer or filtered water. You can add fruit, vegetables, herbs, or flavor enhancers. You can add more or less based on what you like. Think about this during the 3-Act Mathematical Modeling lesson.

PRACTICE Practice what you've learned.

TUTORIALS Get help from ***Virtual Nerd***, right when you need it.

MATH TOOLS Explore math with digital tools.

GAMES Play Math Games to help you learn.

KEY CONCEPT Review important lesson content.

GLOSSARY Read and listen to English/Spanish definitions.

ASSESSMENT Show what you've learned.

TOPIC 7

enVision® STEM Project

Did You Know?

There are more than **326 million trillion gallons** of water on Earth.

Only a small percentage of all this water is fresh water...

...and **much of that fresh water** is locked up in ice caps and glaciers.

The United Nations says that each person needs about **50 liters** of water each day.

Each person in Africa has access to less than **20 liters** of water each day.

Many doctors recommend that each person drinks eight 8-ounce glasses of water each day.

Each person in the United States uses on average about **35–40 gallons** of water each day.

Your Task: An Essential Resource

Access to fresh, clean water is important for human survival. You and your classmates will determine how much fresh water is available on Earth for people to use. You will also explore ways in which people have developed access to clean water.

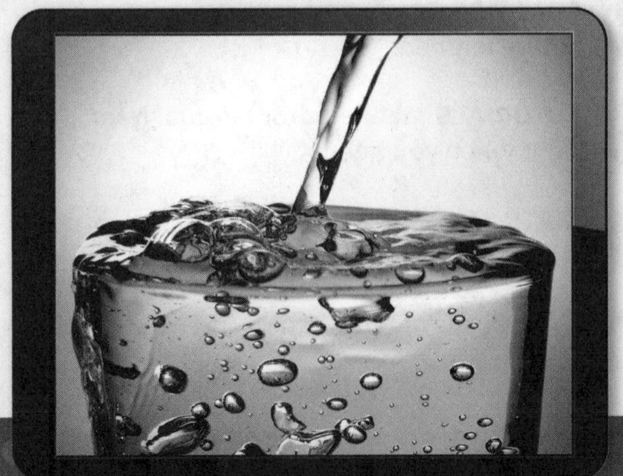

Review What You Know!

Vocabulary

Choose the best term from the box to complete each definition.

- complex fraction
- equivalent ratios
- rate
- ratio
- terms

1. The quantities x and y in the ratio $\frac{x}{y}$ are called ________________.

2. $\frac{2 \text{ dogs}}{3 \text{ cats}}$ and $\frac{10 \text{ dogs}}{15 \text{ cats}}$ are an example of ________________.

3. A(n) ________________ is a type of ratio that has both terms expressed in different units.

4. A(n) ________________ has a fraction in its numerator, denominator, or both.

Equivalent Ratios

Complete each equivalent ratio.

5. $\frac{4 \text{ boys}}{7 \text{ girls}} = \frac{8 \text{ boys}}{\square \text{ girls}}$

6. $\frac{16 \text{ tires}}{4 \text{ cars}} = \frac{\square \text{ tires}}{1 \text{ car}}$

7. $\frac{8 \text{ correct}}{10 \text{ total}} = \frac{\square \text{ correct}}{50 \text{ total}}$

8. $\frac{16 \text{ pearls}}{20 \text{ opals}} = \frac{8 \text{ pearls}}{\square \text{ opals}}$

9. $\frac{32 \text{ pencils}}{8 \text{ erasers}} = \frac{8 \text{ pencils}}{\square \text{ erasers}}$

10. $\frac{7 \text{ balls}}{9 \text{ bats}} = \frac{\square \text{ balls}}{27 \text{ bats}}$

Rates

Write each situation as a rate.

11. John travels 150 miles in 3 hours.

12. Cameron ate 5 apples in 2 days.

Equations

Write an equation that represents the pattern in the table.

13.

x	4	5	6	7	8
y	12	15	18	21	24

Build Vocabulary

Use the graphic organizer to help you understand new vocabulary terms.

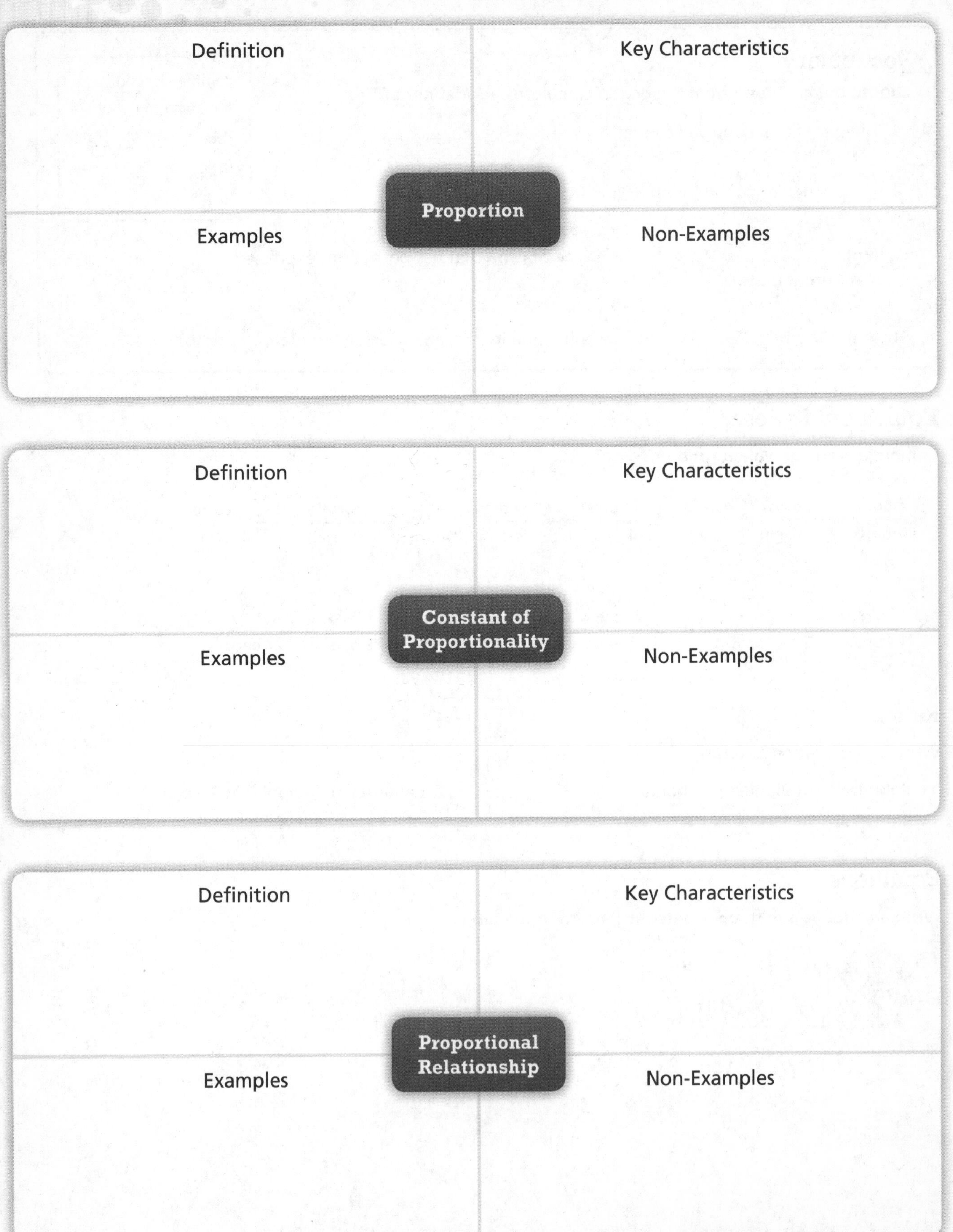

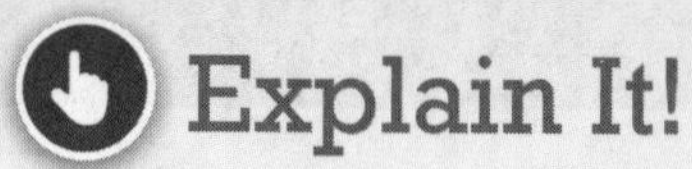

Explain It!

In a basketball contest, Elizabeth made 9 out of 25 free throw attempts. Alex made 8 out of 20 free throw attempts. Janie said that Elizabeth had a better free-throw record because she made more free throws than Alex.

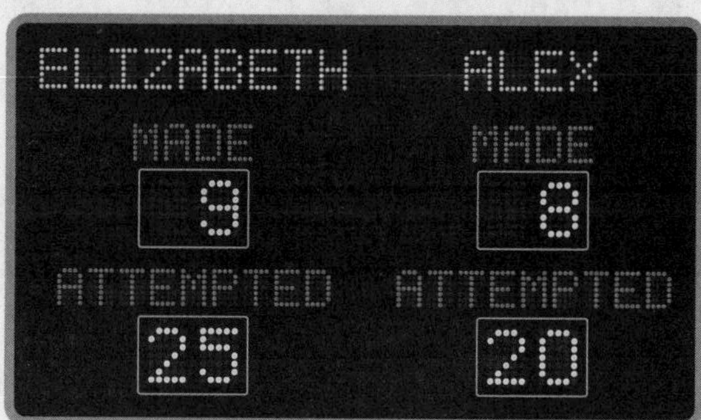

Lesson 7-1 Connect Ratios, Rates, and Unit Rates

Go Online | PearsonRealize.com

I can...
use ratio concepts and reasoning to solve multi-step problems.

MAFS.7.RP.1.1 Compute unit rates associated with ratios of fractions, including ratios of lengths, areas and other quantities measured in like or different units. Also 7.RP.1.3

MAFS.K12.MP1.1, MP.3.1, MP.6.1, MP.7.1, MP.8.1

A. Critique Reasoning Do you agree with Janie's reasoning? Explain.

B. Construct Arguments Decide who had the better free-throw record. Justify your reasoning using mathematical arguments.

Focus on math practices

Construct Arguments What mathematical model did you use to justify your reasoning? Are there other models you could use to represent the situation?

Essential Question How are ratios, rates, and unit rates used to solve problems?

EXAMPLE 1  Find Unit Rates

Scan for Multimedia  

Nathan and Dan were both hired as lifeguards for the summer. They receive their paychecks for the first week. Who earns more per hour?

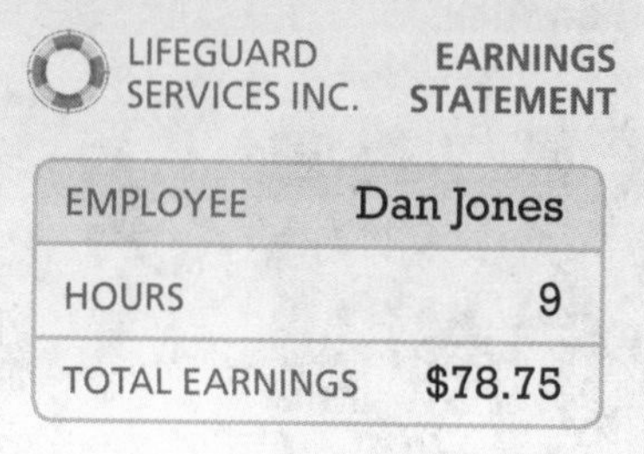

LIFEGUARD SERVICES INC.	EARNINGS STATEMENT
EMPLOYEE	Dan Jones
HOURS	9
TOTAL EARNINGS	$78.75

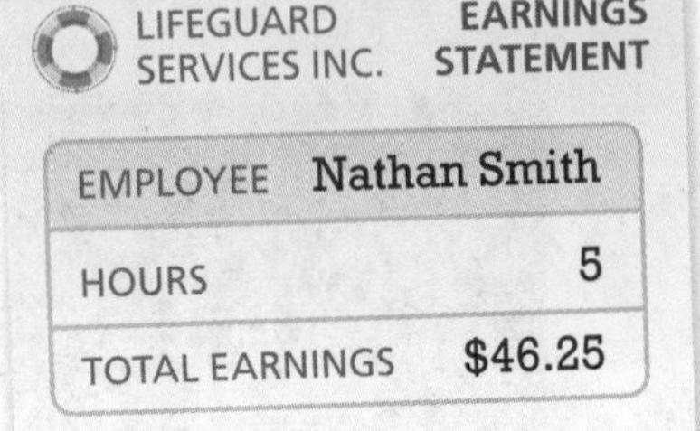

LIFEGUARD SERVICES INC.	EARNINGS STATEMENT
EMPLOYEE	Nathan Smith
HOURS	5
TOTAL EARNINGS	$46.25

Make Sense and Persevere
You can use a ratio to relate the number of hours worked and the amount earned.

Draw a model to show how the quantities are related.

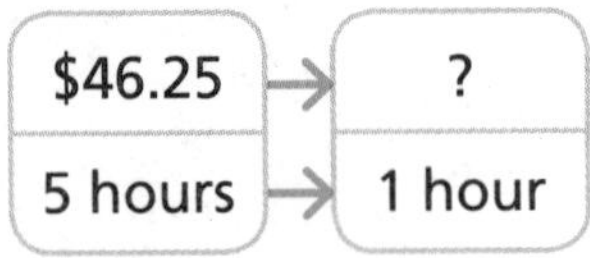

Find unit rates to determine how much each lifeguard earns each hour.

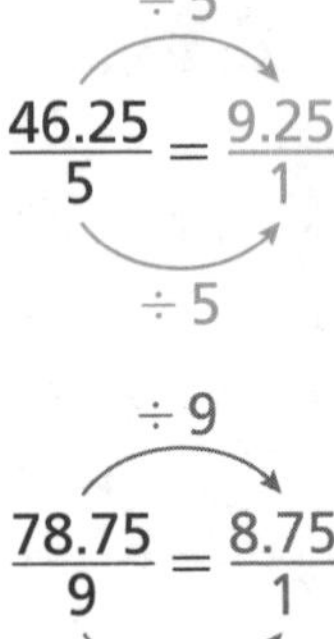

$$\frac{46.25}{5} = \frac{9.25}{1} \quad (\div 5)$$

$$\frac{78.75}{9} = \frac{8.75}{1} \quad (\div 9)$$

Nathan earns 50¢ more per hour.

Try It!

Jennifer is a lifeguard at the same pool. She earns $137.25 for 15 hours of lifeguarding. How much does Jennifer earn per hour?

Jennifer earns $ ☐ per hour.

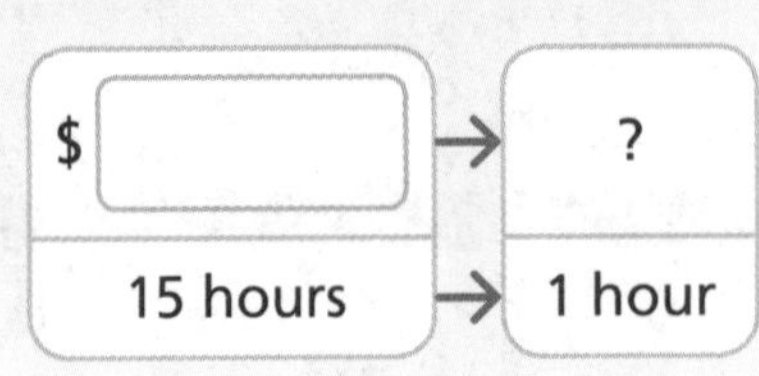

$$\frac{\square}{15} = \frac{\square}{1} \quad (\div \square)$$

Convince Me! What do you notice about the models used to find how much each lifeguard earns per hour?

EXAMPLE 2  Use Unit Rates

ACTIVITY ASSESS

Brian agrees to watch his neighbor's dogs for 7 days. His neighbor provided a 128-ounce bag of dog food. Does Brian have enough food to feed the dogs all 7 days? Explain.

STEP 1 Use unit rates to find how much each dog eats in 7 days.

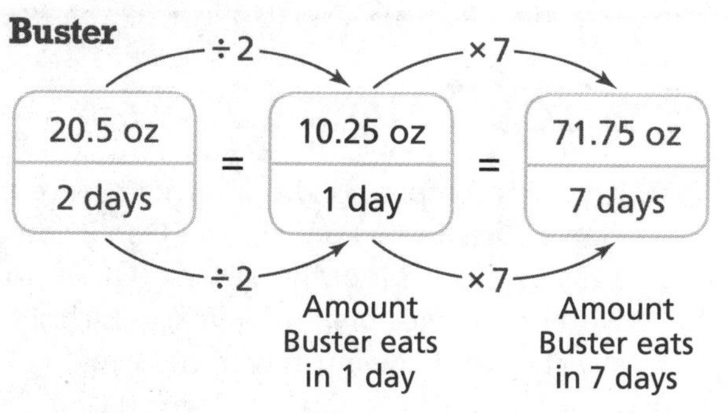

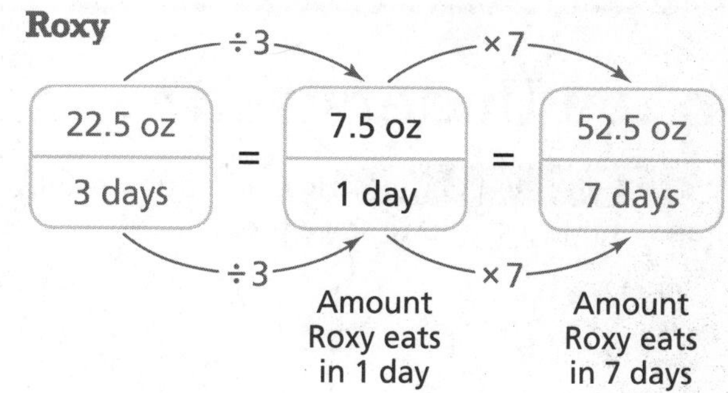

STEP 2 Find the total amount of dog food needed for 7 days. Then compare.

$71.75 + 52.5 = 124.25$ and $124.25 < 128$, so Brian has enough dog food.

EXAMPLE 3  Compare Using Rates

Suppose that each jump covers the same distance. How many jumps does it take each animal to cover the same distance?

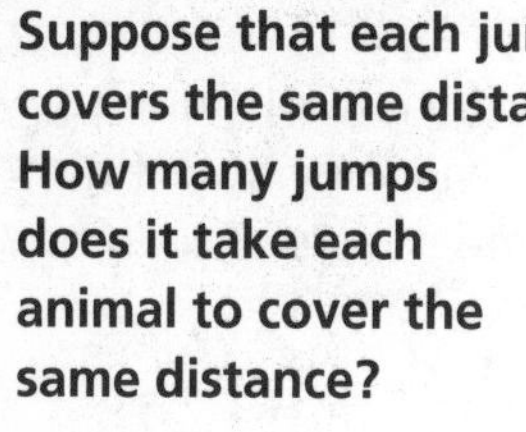

Make tables of equivalent ratios until the distance jumped is the same.

Rabbit (× 3)

Jumps	Meters
3	8
6	16
9	24

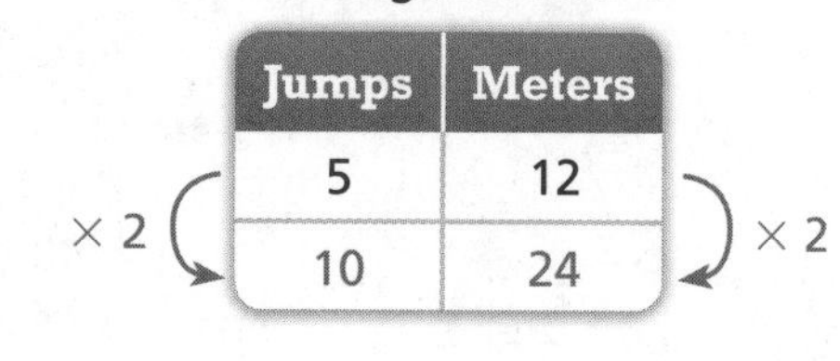

Kangaroo Rat (× 2)

Jumps	Meters
5	12
10	24

The rabbit jumps 24 meters in 9 jumps.

The kangaroo rat jumps 24 meters in 10 jumps.

Try It!

A kitchen sink faucet streams 0.5 gallon of water in 10 seconds.
A bathroom sink faucet streams 0.75 gallon of water in 18 seconds.
Which faucet will fill a 3-gallon container faster?

KEY CONCEPT

KEY CONCEPT

You can use equivalent ratios and rates, including unit rates, to compare ratios and to solve problems.

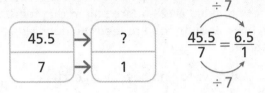

45.5	→	?
7	→	1

$$\frac{45.5}{7} = \frac{6.5}{1} \quad (\div 7)$$

Do You Understand?

1. **Essential Question** How are ratios, rates, and unit rates used to solve problems?

2. **Use Structure** Dorian buys 2 pounds of almonds for $21.98 and 3 pounds of dried apricots for $26.25. Which is less expensive per pound? How much less expensive?

   Complete the tables of equivalent ratios to help you solve.

Almonds

Cost	Weight (lb)
	2

Dried Apricots

Cost	Weight (lb)
$26.25	

3. **Generalize** How are unit rates and equivalent ratios related?

Do You Know How?

4. Krystal is comparing two Internet service plans. Plan 1 costs $34.99 per month. Plan 2 costs $134.97 every 3 months. If Krystal plans to stay with one service plan for 1 year, which should she choose? How much will she save?

5. Pam read 126 pages of her summer reading book in 3 hours. Zack read 180 pages of his summer reading book in 4 hours. If they continue to read at the same speeds, will they both finish the 215-page book after 5 total hours of reading? Explain.

6. Nora and Eli are making homemade spring rolls for a party. Nora can make 8 spring rolls in 10 minutes. Eli can make 10 spring rolls in 12 minutes. If they each make 40 spring rolls, who will finish first?

Name: ______________________________

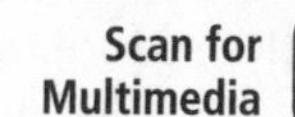

Practice & Problem Solving

Scan for Multimedia

Leveled Practice **In 7–8, complete the tables of equivalent ratios to solve.**

7. After Megan walked 5 miles, her activity tracker had counted 9,780 steps. David's activity tracker had counted 11,928 steps after he walked 6 miles. Suppose each person's step covers about the same distance. Who takes more steps to walk 1 mile? How many more steps?

[ ] takes more steps to walk 1 mile.

[ ] – [ ] = [ ] more steps for 1 mile

Meghan's Steps

Steps	Miles
9,780	[ ]
[ ]	1

David's Steps

Steps	Miles
[ ]	6
[ ]	1

8. A package of 5 pairs of insulated gloves costs $29.45. What is the cost of a single pair of gloves?

One pair of gloves costs [ ].

Price	Pairs of Gloves
[ ]	5
[ ]	1

9. Which package has the lowest cost per ounce of rice?

10. A nursery owner buys 5 panes of glass to fix some damage to her greenhouse. The 5 panes cost $14.25. Unfortunately, she breaks 2 more panes while repairing the damage. What is the cost of another 2 panes of glass?

11. Be Precise An arts academy requires there to be 3 teachers for every 75 students and 6 tutors for every 72 students. How many tutors does the academy need if it has 120 students?

12. Make Sense and Persevere In large cities, people often take taxis to get from one place to another. What is the cost per mile of a taxi ride? How much is a 47-mile taxi ride?

13. The Largo Middle School track team needs new uniforms. The students plan to sell plush toy tigers (the school mascot) for \$5. The students find three companies online that sell stuffed mascots.

a. Which company has the lowest cost per tiger?

b. If they use that company, how much profit will the students make for each tiger sold?

Company A
12 tigers for
\$33.24

Company B
16 tigers for
\$44.80

Company C
15 tigers for
\$41.10

14. A contractor purchases 7 dozen pairs of padded work gloves for \$103.32. He incorrectly calculates the unit price at \$14.76 per pair.

a. What is the correct unit price?

b. **Critique Reasoning** What error did the contractor likely make?

15. **Higher Order Thinking** A warehouse store sells 5.5-ounce cans of tuna in packages of 6. A package of 6 cans costs \$9.24. The store also sells 6.5-ounce cans of the same tuna in packages of 3 cans for \$4.68. It also sells 3.5-ounce cans in packages of 4 cans for \$4.48. Which package has the lowest cost per ounce of tuna?

Assessment Practice

16. Lena is making two dishes for an event. Each batch of her mac-and-cheese recipe calls for 6 ounces of cheese and 2 tablespoons of basil. For every two pizzas, she needs 16 ounces of cheese and 5 tablespoons of basil. 7.RP.1.3

PART A

Lena buys a 32-oz package of cheese. Does she have enough cheese to make 2 batches of mac-and-cheese and 3 pizzas? Explain.

PART B

Lena decides to make 1 batch of mac-and-cheese and 3 pizzas. How many tablespoons of basil does she need? Explain your answer.

17. It cost Irene \$58.90 to fill her car's gas tank with $15\frac{1}{2}$ gallons of gas. Select all the rates that are equivalent to \$58.90 for $15\frac{1}{2}$ gallons of gas. 7.RP.1.1

- ☐ \$41.80 for 11 gallons of gas
- ☐ \$28.80 for 8 gallons of gas
- ☐ \$26.60 for 7 gallons of gas
- ☐ \$8.55 for 2 gallons of gas
- ☐ \$3.80 for 1 gallon of gas

Solve & Discuss It!

Allison and her classmates planted bean seeds at the same time as Yuki and her classmates in Tokyo did. Allison is video-chatting with Yuki about their class seedlings. Assume that both plants will continue to grow at the same rate. Who should expect to have the taller plant at the end of the school year?

Allison's Class
2.5 inches in **5 days**

Yuki's Class
5.5 centimeters in **4 days**

Lesson 7-2
Determine Unit Rates with Ratios of Fractions

Go Online | PearsonRealize.com

I can...
find unit rates with ratios of fractions and use them to solve problems.

MAFS.7.RP.1.1 Compute unit rates associated with ratios of fractions, including ratios of lengths, areas and other quantities measured in like or different units. Also 7.RP.1.3
MAFS.K12.MP.2.1, MP.3.1, MP.6.1, MP.7.1

Look for Relationships
How can you compare the growth rates of the seedlings?

Focus on math practices

Be Precise What must the students do before they can compare the heights of the plants?

? Essential Question Why is it useful to write a ratio of fractions as a unit rate?

EXAMPLE 1 Find a Unit Rate Involving Unit Fractions

Scan for Multimedia

Sergio is training for a triathlon. His target speed is 25 miles per hour. Did he achieve his target speed for the first 7 miles of his ride?

Reasoning You can use a unit rate to describe Sergio's cycling speed.

You know that 15 minutes is equal to $\frac{1}{4}$ hour. Draw a diagram to show how the distance Sergio bikes is related to the time he bikes.

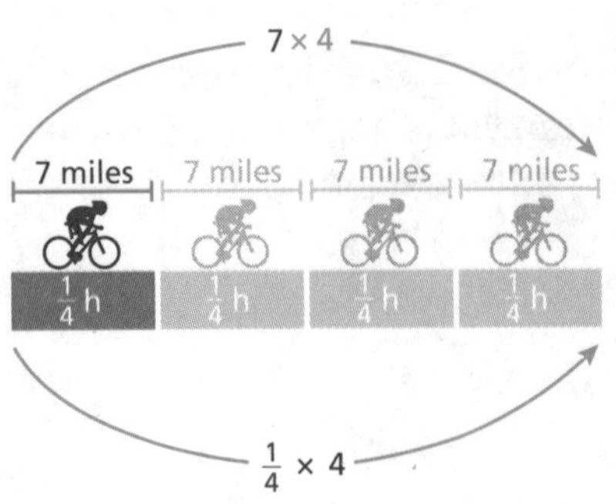

Make a table of equivalent ratios to find the unit rate.

×4

Miles	7	28
Hour	$\frac{1}{4}$	1

×4

Sergio bikes $\frac{28 \text{ miles}}{1 \text{ hour}}$, or 28 miles per hour, so he has achieved, and exceeded, his target speed.

Try It!

Sergio increases his target speed to 30 miles per hour. How many more miles does Sergio need to ride in $\frac{1}{4}$ hour to achieve this target speed?

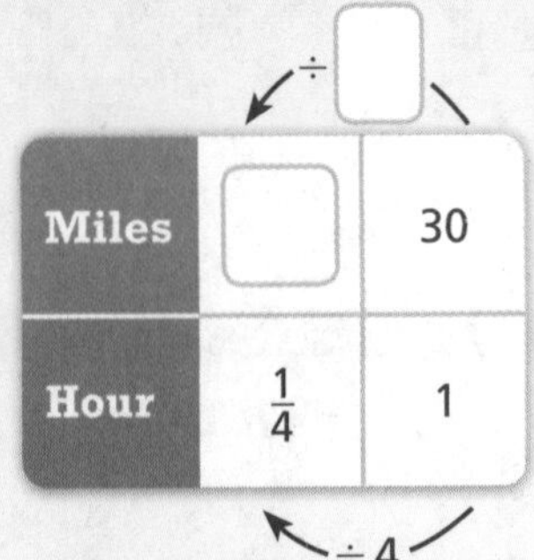

Sergio must ride ☐ miles in $\frac{1}{4}$ hour to achieve this target speed, so he needs to ride an additional ☐ mile per $\frac{1}{4}$ hour.

Convince Me! How does the unit rate describe Sergio's cycling speed? How is the unit rate helpful in determining how much farther Sergio must cycle in a given amount of time each time he increases his target speed?

EXAMPLE 2  Find and Apply a Unit Rate Involving Fractions

Bronwyn mows the lawn every other weekend. She can mow 12,000 ft^2 in $\frac{2}{3}$ hour. The lawn is 36,000 ft^2.

How long does it take her to mow the entire lawn?

$$\frac{12{,}000}{\frac{2}{3}} = \frac{12{,}000 \times \frac{3}{2}}{\frac{2}{3} \times \frac{3}{2}} = \frac{18{,}000 \text{ ft}^2}{1 \text{ h}}$$

$$\frac{18{,}000 \times 2}{1 \times 2} = \frac{36{,}000}{2}$$

Multiply each term by 2 for the area of the entire lawn.

Bronwyn mows at a rate of 18,000 ft^2 per hour. It takes her 2 hours to mow the entire lawn.

Look for Relationships How do the operations used in the table relate to the operations used in the equations at the left?

Area (ft^2)	12,000	18,000	36,000
Time (h)	$\frac{2}{3}$	$\frac{6}{6}$ or 1	2

($\times \frac{3}{2}$ from first to second column, $\times 2$ from second to third column, in both rows.)

Try It!

Every other weekend, Bronwyn's brother Daniel mows the lawn. He can mow 15,000 ft^2 in $\frac{3}{4}$ hour. Who mows the lawn in less time? Explain.

EXAMPLE 3  Solve Problems Using Unit Rates

Omar knows that his friend Chris lives $\frac{3}{5}$ mile away. How far is the school from his house?

$$\frac{\frac{3}{5}\text{ mi}}{\frac{3}{4}\text{ in.}} = \frac{\frac{3}{5} \times \frac{4}{3}}{\frac{3}{4} \times \frac{4}{3}} = \frac{\frac{4}{5}\text{ mi}}{1\text{ in.}}$$

($\div \frac{3}{4}$ applied to both terms.)

Divide both terms by $\frac{3}{4}$ to find the unit rate.

$$\frac{\frac{4}{5}\text{ mi} \times 2}{1\text{ in.} \times 2} = \frac{\frac{8}{5}\text{ mi}}{2\text{ in.}} = \frac{1\frac{3}{5}\text{ mi}}{2\text{ in.}}$$

Multiply both terms of the unit rate by 2 to find an equivalent rate.

Omar's school is $1\frac{3}{5}$ miles from his house.

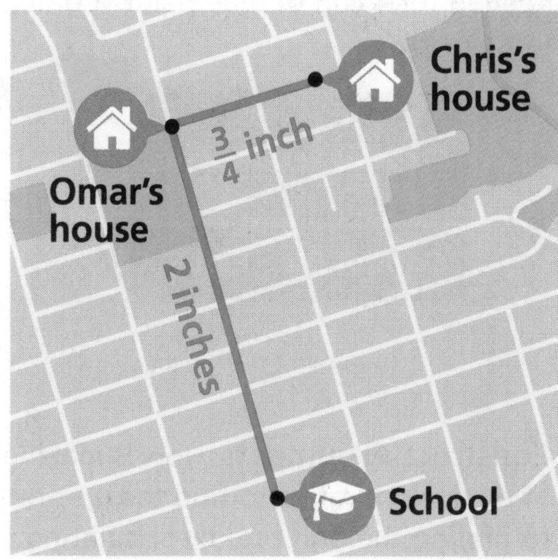

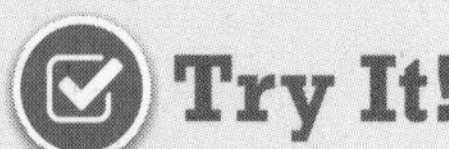

Try It!

Sonoma bikes 5 miles to Paige's house. On a map, they measure that distance as $\frac{5}{6}$ cm. The same map shows that the mall is $3\frac{1}{2}$ cm from Paige's house. What is the actual distance between Paige's house and the mall?

KEY CONCEPT 

You can use what you know about equivalent ratios and operations with fractions to write a ratio of fractions as a unit rate.

Tia skateboards $\frac{2}{3}$ mile for every $\frac{1}{6}$ hour.

$$\frac{\frac{2}{3}}{\frac{1}{6}} = \frac{\frac{2}{3} \times \frac{6}{1}}{\frac{1}{6} \times \frac{6}{1}} = \frac{4}{1} = 4$$

She skateboards 4 miles per hour.

		$\times \frac{6}{1}$
Miles	$\frac{2}{3}$	4
Hours	$\frac{1}{6}$	1
		$\times \frac{6}{1}$

Do You Understand?

1. **Essential Question** Why is it useful to write a ratio of fractions as a unit rate?

2. **Use Structure** Jacob mixes $\frac{1}{3}$ cup of yellow paint for every $\frac{1}{5}$ cup of blue paint to make green paint. How many cups of yellow paint are needed for 1 cup of blue paint? Complete the table below.

Cups of Yellow Paint	$\frac{1}{3}$	
Cups of Blue Paint	$\frac{1}{5}$	1

3. **Construct Arguments** How is making a table of equivalent ratios to find the unit rate similar to finding the unit rate by calculating with fractions? Use a specific example to explain your reasoning.

Do You Know How?

4. Claire boarded an airplane in Richmond, VA, and flew 414 miles directly to Charleston, SC. The total flight time was $\frac{3}{4}$ hour. How fast did Claire's airplane fly, in miles per hour?

5. Brad buys two packages of mushrooms. Which mushrooms cost less per pound? Explain.

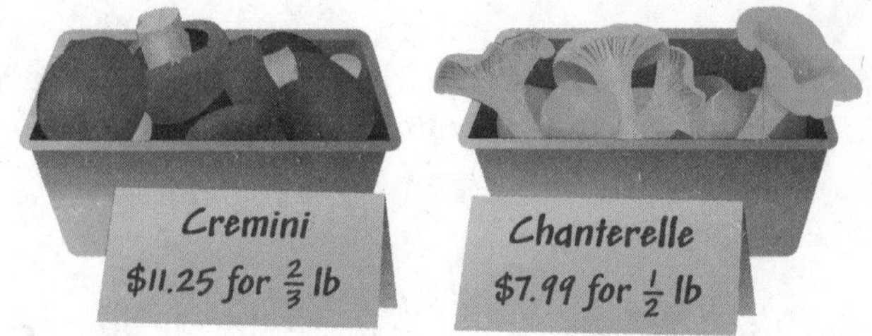

6. Jed is baking shortbread for a bake sale. The recipe calls for $1\frac{1}{4}$ cups of flour and $\frac{1}{2}$ stick of butter. How many cups of flour will Jed need if he uses 3 sticks of butter?

Name: ____________________

PRACTICE TUTORIAL

Practice & Problem Solving

Scan for Multimedia

Leveled Practice **In 7–10, fill in the boxes to find the unit rate.**

7.

Cups of Sugar	$\frac{3}{4}$	☐
Cups of Butter	$\frac{1}{8}$	☐

☐ cups of sugar for each cup of butter

8.

Miles	$\frac{3}{5}$	☐
Hours	$\frac{1}{3}$	☐

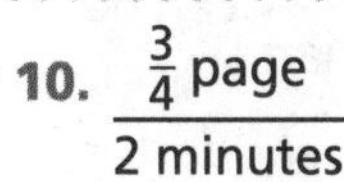 miles in 1 hour

9.

$$\frac{7\text{ mi}}{\frac{1}{3}\text{ gal}} = \frac{7 \div \square}{\square \div \square} = \frac{7 \times \square}{\square \times \square} = \frac{\square}{\square}$$

☐ miles per gallon

10. $\frac{\frac{3}{4}\text{ page}}{2\text{ minutes}}$

☐ page in 1 minute

11. Hadley paddled a canoe $\frac{2}{3}$ mile in $\frac{1}{4}$ hour. How fast did Hadley paddle, in miles per hour?

12. A box of cereal states that there are 90 Calories in a $\frac{3}{4}$-cup serving. How many Calories are there in 4 cups of the cereal?

13. A robot can complete 8 tasks in $\frac{5}{6}$ hour. Each task takes the same amount of time.

a. How long does it take the robot to complete one task?

b. How many tasks can the robot complete in one hour?

14. You are running a fuel economy study. You want to find out which car can travel a greater distance on 1 gallon of gas.

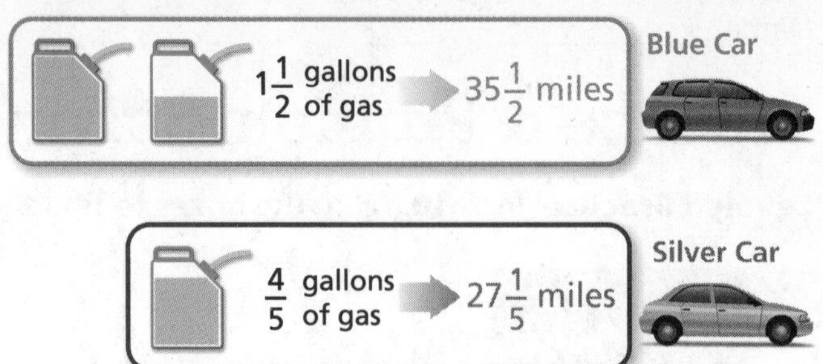

a. What is the gas mileage, in miles per gallon, for the blue car?

b. What is the gas mileage, in miles per gallon, for the silver car?

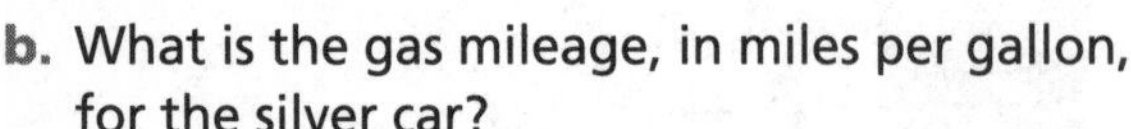

c. Which car could travel the greater distance on 1 gallon of gas?

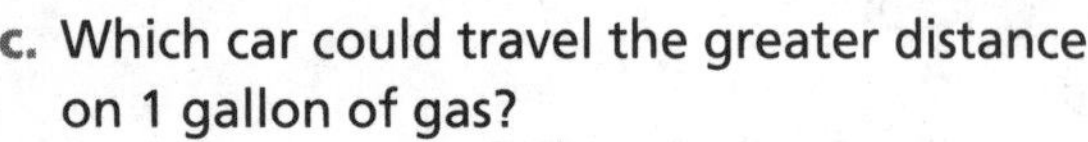

15. Henry incorrectly said the rate $\frac{\frac{1}{5}\text{ pound}}{\frac{1}{20}\text{ quart}}$ can be written as the unit rate $\frac{1}{100}$ pound per quart.

a. What is the correct unit rate?

b. **Critique Reasoning** What error did Henry likely make?

16. **Higher Order Thinking** Ari walked $2\frac{3}{4}$ miles at a constant speed of $2\frac{1}{2}$ miles per hour. Beth walked $1\frac{3}{4}$ miles at a constant speed of $1\frac{1}{4}$ miles per hour. Cindy walked for 1 hour and 21 minutes at a constant speed of $1\frac{1}{8}$ miles per hour. List the three people in order of the times they spent walking from least time to greatest time.

Assessment Practice

17. A blueprint shows a house with two fences. Fence A is $1\frac{4}{5}$ inches long on the blueprint and is to be $1\frac{1}{2}$ feet long. How long is Fence B on the blueprint? 7.RP.1.3

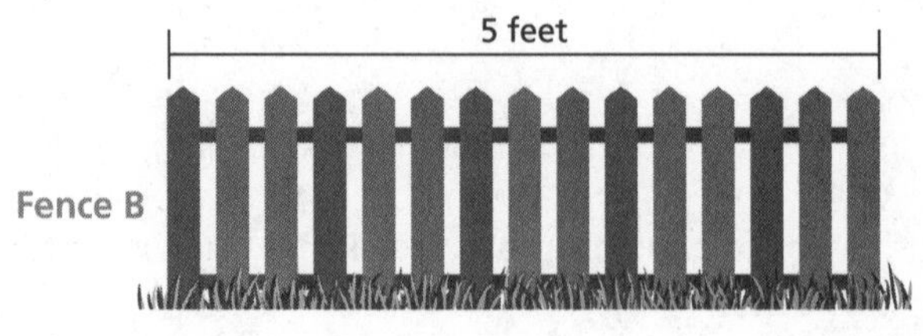

18. Leo reads 13 pages in $\frac{1}{3}$ hour. Use the table to find how many pages he reads in one hour. 7.RP.1.1

Leo reads ☐ pages in one hour.

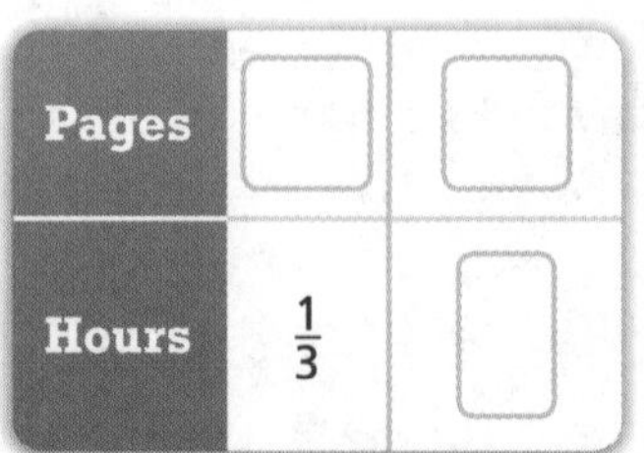

Pages	☐	☐
Hours	$\frac{1}{3}$	☐

Solve & Discuss It!

Weight is a measure of force affected by gravity. The Moon's gravity is less than Earth's gravity, so objects weigh less on the Moon than on Earth.

Using the information provided, how much do you think a cat will weigh on the Moon? Explain your reasoning.

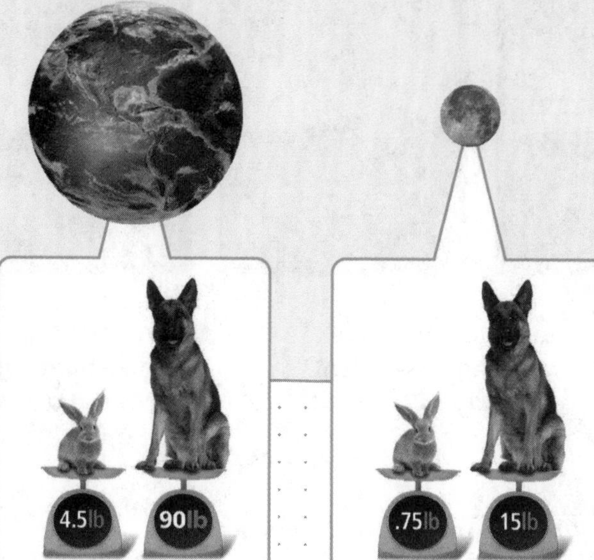

Lesson 7-3

Understand Proportional Relationships: Equivalent Ratios

Go Online | PearsonRealize.com

I can...
test for equivalent ratios to decide whether quantities are in a proportional relationship.

MAFS.7.RP.1.2a Decide whether two quantities are in a proportional relationship, e.g., by testing for equivalent ratios in a table... .
MAFS.K12.MP.1.1, MP.2.1, MP.3.1. MP.7.1, MP.8.1

Make Sense and Persevere
About how much does a cat weigh on Earth?

Focus on math practices

Generalize How could you find the approximate weight of any object on the Moon? Explain your reasoning.

Essential Question How are proportional quantities described by equivalent ratios?

EXAMPLE 1  Recognize a Proportional Relationship

Scan for Multimedia 

On Sarah's favorite mobile game, she is awarded game lives when she finds gold coins. How is the number of game lives awarded related to the number of gold coins found? Explain.

Write ratios that relate the gold coins found and the game lives awarded.

(3 coins over 9 hearts) $= \frac{3}{9}$

(2 coins over 6 hearts) $= \frac{2}{6}$

(5 coins over 15 hearts) $= \frac{5}{15}$

Make a ratio table to determine whether the ratios are equivalent.

Coins	3	2	5
Game Lives	9	6	15
$\frac{\text{Coins}}{\text{Game Lives}}$	$\frac{3}{9} = \frac{1}{3}$	$\frac{2}{6} = \frac{1}{3}$	$\frac{5}{15} = \frac{1}{3}$

Two quantities are in a **proportional relationship** if all of the ratios that relate the quantities are equivalent.

Each ratio $\frac{\text{coins}}{\text{game lives}}$ is equivalent to $\frac{1}{3}$. The number of game lives awarded is proportional to the number of gold coins found.

Try It!

Miles records the time it takes to download a variety of file types. How is the download time related to the file size? Explain.

The ratios for each pair of data are [   ], so the download time and the file size are [   ].

Type of Media	File Size (MB)	Download Time (s)	$\frac{\text{Download Time}}{\text{File Size}}$
Document	1.25	25	$\frac{25}{\square} = 20$
Song	3.6	72	$\frac{\square}{3.6} = 20$
Video	6.25	125	$\frac{125}{6.25} = \square$

Convince Me! How can you show that two quantities have a proportional relationship?

EXAMPLE 2  Decide Whether Quantities are Proportional

Is the relationship between the area and the side length of the squares proportional? Explain your reasoning.

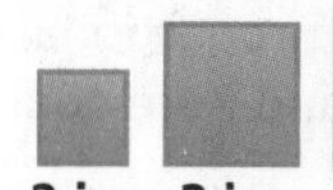
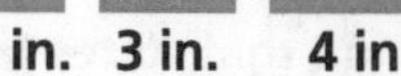

STEP 1 Make a table to organize the data. Find the ratio of area to side length for each data pair.

Side Length (x)	Area (y)	$\frac{\text{Area } (y)}{\text{Side Length } (x)}$
2	4	$\frac{4}{2} = \frac{2}{1}$
3	9	$\frac{9}{3} = \frac{3}{1}$
4	16	$\frac{16}{4} = \frac{4}{1}$

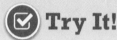

STEP 2 Compare the ratios by finding the unit rates.

$\frac{2}{1} \neq \frac{3}{1}$ $\quad \frac{3}{1} \neq \frac{4}{1}$ $\quad \frac{2}{1} \neq \frac{4}{1}$

The ratios are not equivalent so the relationship between the area and side length is NOT proportional.

Try It!

The table at the right shows information about regular hexagons. Is the relationship between the perimeter and the side length of the hexagons proportional? Explain.

Side Length (x)	Perimeter (y)
2	12
3	18

EXAMPLE 3  Use Proportions to Solve Problems

A proportion is an equation that represents equal ratios. Use the table at the right. How many times will a hummingbird beat its wings in 60 seconds?

Hummingbird Wing Beats

Seconds (x)	2	7	10
Wing Beats (y)	160	560	800

wing beat

STEP 1 Verify that the quantities are proportional.

$\frac{160}{2} = \frac{80}{1}$ $\quad \frac{560}{7} = \frac{80}{1}$ $\quad \frac{800}{10} = \frac{80}{1}$

The ratios are equivalent, so the quantities are proportional.

STEP 2 Write and solve a proportion.

$\frac{80}{1} = \frac{y}{60}$

$\frac{80}{1} \cdot 60 = \frac{y}{60} \cdot 60$

Multiply both sides by 60 to solve for y.

$4{,}800 = y$

A hummingbird beats its wings 4,800 times in 60 seconds.

Try It!

Ginny's favorite cookie recipe requires $1\frac{1}{2}$ cups of sugar to make 24 cookies. How much sugar does Ginny need to make 36 of these cookies?

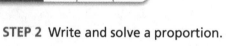

KEY CONCEPT

Two quantities x and y have a proportional relationship if all the ratios $\frac{y}{x}$ for related pairs of x and y are equivalent.

A proportion is an equation that states that two ratios are equivalent.

$\frac{3}{120} = \frac{5}{200}$

x	y	$\frac{y}{x}$
120	3	$\frac{3}{120} = 0.025$
200	5	$\frac{5}{200} = 0.025$

Do You Understand?

1. **Essential Question** How are proportional quantities described by equivalent ratios?

2. **Look for Relationships** How do you know if a relationship between two quantities is NOT proportional?

3. **Reasoning** If the ratio $\frac{y}{x}$ is the same for all related pairs of x and y, what does that mean about the relationship between x and y?

Do You Know How?

4. Use the table below. Do x and y have a proportional relationship? Explain.

x	2	3	5	8
y	5	7.5	12.5	18

5. Each triangle is equilateral. Is the relationship between the perimeter and the side length of the equilateral triangles proportional? Explain.

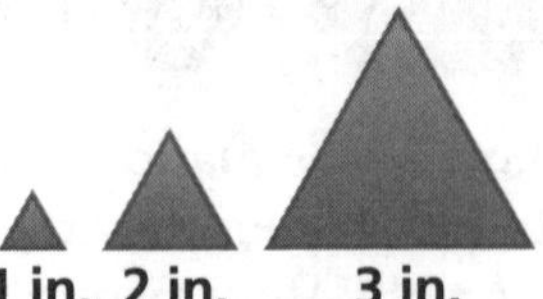

6. Is the relationship between the number of tickets sold and the number of hours proportional? If so, how many tickets were sold in 8 hours?

Hours (h)	Tickets Sold (t)
3	240
5	400
9	720

Name: ______________________________

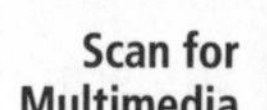

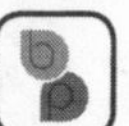

Practice & Problem Solving

Scan for Multimedia

7. The amount of seed a landscaper uses and the area of lawn covered have a proportional relationship. Complete the table.

Lawn Seed

Seed (oz)	2	3	4
Area Covered (ft^2)	50	75	100
$\frac{\text{Area Covered}}{\text{Seed}}$	$\frac{50}{2} = \frac{25}{1}$		

8. **Construct Arguments** Is the relationship between the number of slices of salami in a sandwich and the number of Calories proportional? Explain.

Calories in a Sandwich

Slices of Salami	Calories
1	66
2	96
3	126
4	156

9. **Look for Relationships** A wholesale club sells eggs by the dozen. Does the table show a proportional relationship between the number of dozens of eggs and the cost? Explain.

Cost of Dozens of Eggs

Dozen	Cost ($)
6	21
8	28
10	35
14	49

10. Does the table show a proportional relationship? If so, what is the value of y when x is 11?

x	4	5	6	10
y	64	125	216	1,000

11. Does the table show a proportional relationship? If so, what is the value of y when x is 10?

x	5	6	7	8
y	$1\frac{2}{3}$	2	$2\frac{1}{3}$	$2\frac{2}{3}$

12. The height of a building is proportional to the number of floors. The figure shows the height of a building with 9 floors.

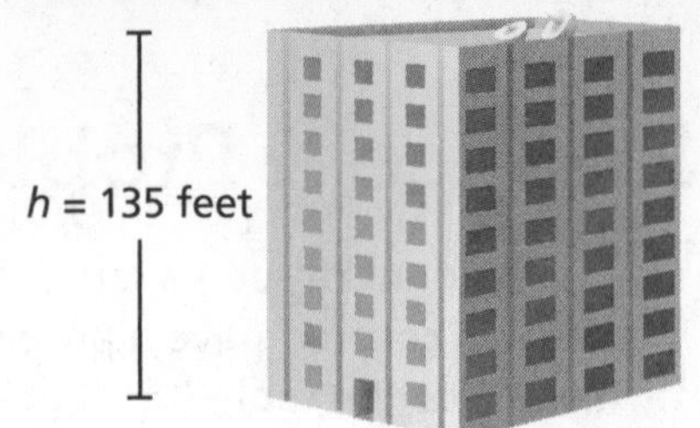

a. **Reasoning** Write the ratio of height of the building to the number of floors. Then find the unit rate, and explain what it means in this situation.

b. How tall would the building be if it had 15 floors?

13. **Higher Order Thinking** Do the two tables show the same proportional relationship between x and y? Explain how you know.

x	160	500	1,200
y	360	1,125	2,700

x	2	5	7
y	4.5	11.25	15.75

Assessment Practice

14. The table shows the number of cell phone towers a company will build as the number of its customers increases. 7.RP.1.2a

Cell Phone Towers

Customers (thousands)	Towers
5.25	252
6.25	300
7.25	348
9.25	444

PART A

Is the relationship between number of towers and number of customers proportional? Explain.

PART B

If there are 576 towers, how many customers does the company have? Write a proportion you can use to solve.

15. Select all true statements about the table at the right. 7.RP.1.2a

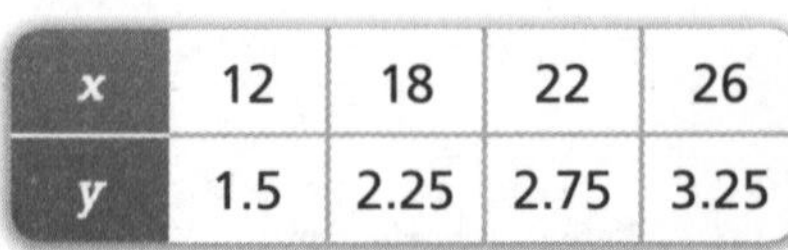

x	12	18	22	26
y	1.5	2.25	2.75	3.25

- ☐ The table shows a proportional relationship.
- ☐ When x is 20, y is 2.55.
- ☐ All the ratios $\frac{y}{x}$ for related pairs of x and y are equivalent to 8.
- ☐ The unit rate of $\frac{y}{x}$ for related pairs of x and y is $\frac{1}{8}$.
- ☐ If the table continued, when x is 30, y would be 3.75.

Lesson 7-4

Describe Proportional Relationships: Constant of Proportionality

Go Online | PearsonRealize.com

I can...
use the constant of proportionality in an equation to represent a proportional relationship.

MAFS.7.RP.1.2b Identify the constant of proportionality (unit rate) in tables, ... equations, ... and verbal descriptions of proportional relationships. Also 7.RP.1.2c

MAFS.K12.MP.2.1, MP.3.1, MP.4.1, MP.6.1, MP.8.1

Solve & Discuss It!

ACTIVITY

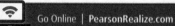

Jamal can run 1 mile in 5.05 minutes. If Jamal maintains this pace during a 5-kilometer (5K) race, he expects to break the course record of 15.25 minutes. Is Jamal's expectation reasonable? Explain.

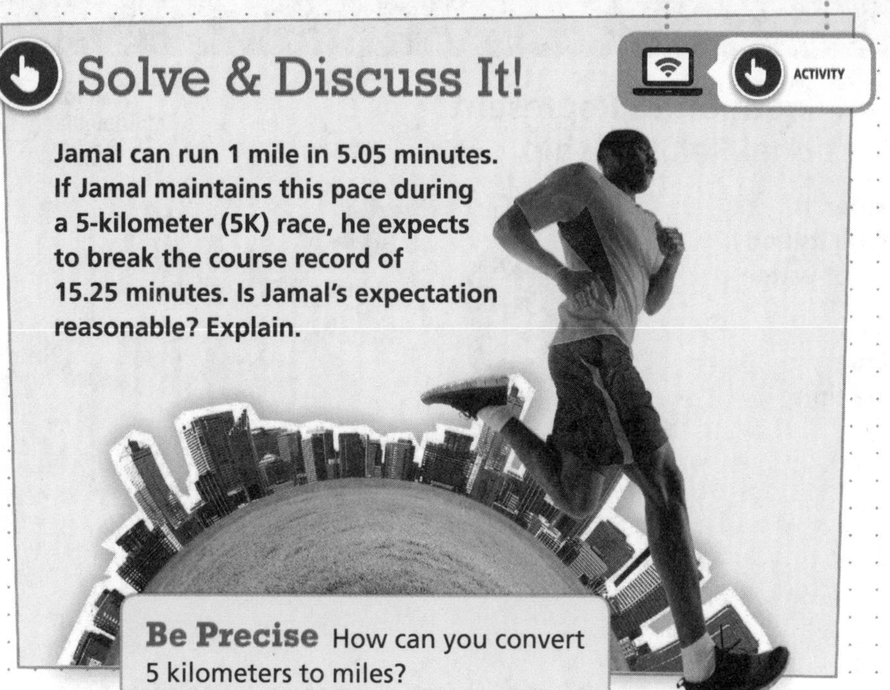

Be Precise How can you convert 5 kilometers to miles?

Focus on math practices

Reasoning Assuming that Jamal runs at a constant rate, how does his pace describe the time it takes him to finish a race of any length?

Essential Question How can you represent a proportional relationship with an equation?

EXAMPLE 1  Write an Equation to Represent a Proportional Relationship

Scan for Multimedia 

A sponge is an example of a *filter feeder*. It takes in food by filtering water through its body. The sponge maintains a constant flow of water through its body.

What is an equation that represents the proportional relationship between the time and the amount of water filtered?

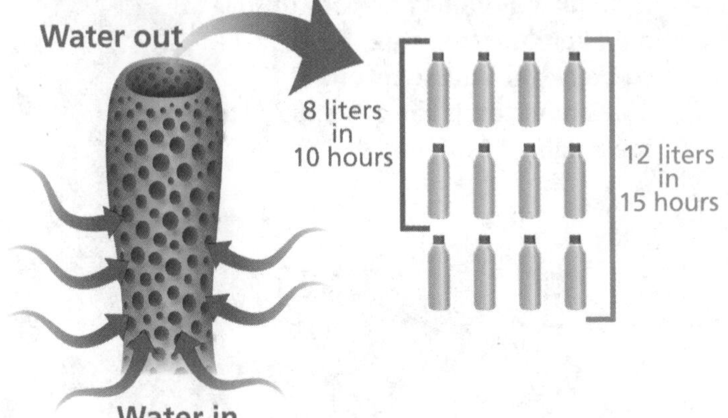

The **constant of proportionality** is the constant multiple that relates proportional quantities x and y. It is the value of the ratio $\frac{y}{x}$ and is represented by k.

Make a table to find the constant of proportionality.

Hours (x)	Liters (y)	$\frac{\text{Liters}}{\text{Hours}}\left(\frac{y}{x}\right)$
10	8	$\frac{8}{10} = 0.8$
15	12	$\frac{12}{15} = 0.8$

The constant of proportionality, k, is 0.8.

You can use k to write an equation that represents a proportional relationship.

$k = \frac{y}{x}$

$kx = y$

$y = kx$

You can use an equation in the form $y = kx$ to represent any proportional relationship.

Use the equation to represent the relationship between time and the amount of water filtered.

$y = 0.8x$

Try It!

Maria made two batches of fruit punch. The table at the right shows how many quarts of juice she used for each batch. Write an equation that relates the proportional quantities.

Apple Juice (x)	Grape Juice (y)	$\frac{\text{Grape Juice}}{\text{Apple Juice}}\left(\frac{y}{x}\right)$
5	8	
10	16	

The constant of proportionality is ☐.

An equation that represents this proportional relationship is $y =$ ☐ x.

Convince Me! How does the equation change if the amount of grape juice is the independent variable, x, and the amount of apple juice is the dependent variable, y?

EXAMPLE 2  Solve Problems Using an Equation

  ACTIVITY  ASSESS

1 inch = 2.54 centimeters. How many centimeters long is an 18-inch ruler?

STEP 1 Write an equation to represent this relationship.

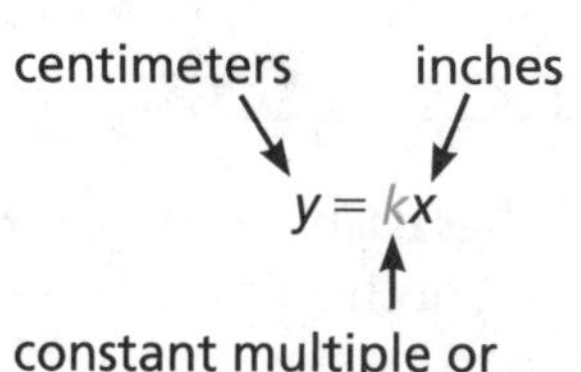

constant multiple or constant of proportionality

$y = 2.54x$

STEP 2 Use the equation to find the length of the ruler in centimeters.

$y = 2.54x$

$y = 2.54(18)$

$y = 45.72$

The ruler is 45.72 centimeters long.

 Try It!

A florist sells a dozen roses for $35.40. She sells individual roses for the same unit cost. Write an equation to represent the relationship between the number of roses, x, and the total cost of the roses, y. How much would 18 roses cost?

EXAMPLE 3  Determine Whether $y = kx$ Describes a Situation

WELCOME TO
FUN FAIR
ADMISSION: $20
EACH RIDE: $5

Can you represent the total cost, y, for admission and x rides at the amusement park using an equation in the form $y = kx$? Explain.

STEP 1 Make a table that shows the total cost.

Rides	Cost
1	$25
2	$30
3	$35

STEP 2 Compare the ratios to determine whether the relationship is proportional.

$\frac{\$25}{1} = \$25$

$\frac{\$30}{2} = \$15$

$\frac{\$35}{3} = \$11.67$

This relationship is not proportional, so it cannot be represented with an equation of the form $y = kx$.

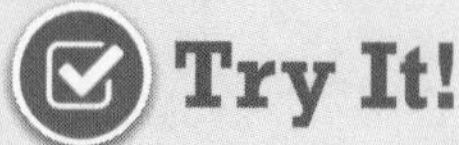 Try It!

Balloon A is released 5 feet above the ground. Balloon B is released at ground level. Both balloons rise at a constant rate.

Which situation can you represent using an equation of the form $y = kx$? Explain.

Balloon A

Time (s)	Height (ft)
1	9
2	13
3	17

Balloon B

Time (s)	Height (ft)
1	4
2	8
3	12

KEY CONCEPT 

Two proportional quantities x and y are related by a constant multiple, or the constant of proportionality, k.

You can represent a proportional relationship using the equation $y = kx$.

Do You Understand?

1. **Essential Question** How can you represent a proportional relationship with an equation?

2. **Generalize** How can you use an equation to find an unknown value in a proportional relationship?

3. **Reasoning** Why does the equation $y = 3x + 5$ NOT represent a proportional relationship?

Do You Know How?

4. Determine whether each equation represents a proportional relationship. If it does, identify the constant of proportionality.

   a. $y = 0.5x - 2$

   b. $y = 1{,}000x$

   c. $y = x + 1$

5. The manager of a concession stand estimates that she needs 3 hot dogs for every 5 people who attend a baseball game. If 1,200 people attend the game, how many hot dogs should the manager order?

6. A half dozen cupcakes cost $15. What constant of proportionality relates the number of cupcakes and total cost? Write an equation that represents this relationship.

Name: ______________________________

Practice & Problem Solving

Scan for Multimedia

7. What is the constant of proportionality in the equation $y = 5x$?

8. What is the constant of proportionality in the equation $y = 0.41x$?

9. The equation $P = 3s$ represents the perimeter P of an equilateral triangle with side length s. Is there a proportional relationship between the perimeter and the side length of an equilateral triangle? Explain.

10. **Model with Math** In a chemical compound, there are 3 parts zinc for every 16 parts copper, by mass. A piece of the compound contains 320 grams of copper. Write and solve an equation to determine the amount of zinc in the chemical compound.

11. The weight of 3 eggs is shown. Assuming the three eggs are all the same weight, find the constant of proportionality.

12. The height of a stack of DVD cases is proportional to the number of cases in the stack. The height of 6 DVD cases is 114 mm.

    a. Write an equation that relates the height, y, of a stack of DVD cases and the number of cases, x, in the stack.

    b. What would be the height of 13 DVD cases?

13. Ann's car can travel 228 miles on 6 gallons of gas.

    a. Write an equation to represent the distance, y, in miles Ann's car can travel on x gallons of gas.

    b. Ann's car used 7 gallons of gas during a trip. How far did Ann drive?

14. The value of a baseball player's rookie card began to increase once the player retired in 1996. The value has increased by \$2.52 each year since then.

a. How much was the baseball card worth in 1997? In 1998? In 1999?

b. **Construct Arguments** Why is there not a proportional relationship between the years since the player retired and the card value? Explain.

15. **Higher Order Thinking** A car travels $2\frac{1}{3}$ miles in $3\frac{1}{2}$ minutes at a constant speed.

a. Write an equation to represent the distance the car travels, *d*, in miles for *m* minutes.

b. Write an equation to represent the distance the car travels, *d*, in miles for *h* hours.

Assessment Practice

16. For every ten sheets of stickers you buy at a craft store, the total cost increases \$20.50. 7.RP.1.2b

An equation that relates the number of sheets purchased, *x*, and the total cost, *y*, of the stickers is $y =$ ☐ x.

Use the equation you wrote to complete the table.

Cost of Stickers

Number of Sheets (x)	3	☐	☐	19
Total Cost (y)	☐	\$10.25	\$26.65	☐

17. 600,000 gallons of water pass through a given point along a river every minute. Which equation represents the amount of water, *y*, that passes through the point in *x* minutes? 7.RP.1.2c

Ⓐ $x = 10{,}000y$

Ⓑ $y = 600{,}000x$

Ⓒ $y = 10{,}000x$

Ⓓ $y = 600{,}000 + x$

Name: ______________________________

MID-TOPIC CHECKPOINT

TOPIC 7

1. **Vocabulary** How do you know if a situation represents a proportional relationship? *Lesson 7-3* 7.RP.1.2a

2. Ana runs $\frac{3}{4}$ mile in 6 minutes. Assuming she runs at a constant rate, what is her speed, in miles per hour? *Lessons 7-1 and 7-2* 7.RP.1.1, 7.RP.1.3

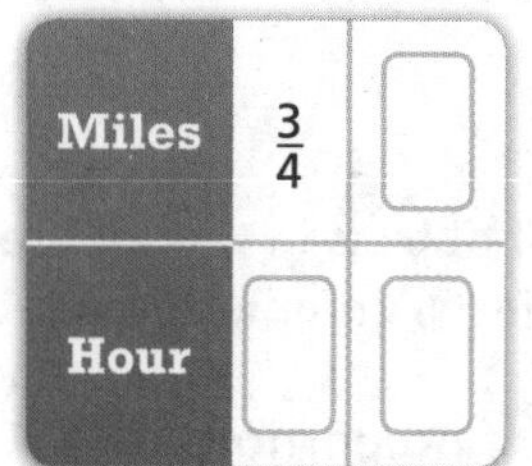

3. A trail mix recipe includes granola, oats, and almonds. There are 135 Calories in a $\frac{1}{4}$-cup serving of the trail mix. How many Calories are in 2 cups of trail mix? *Lesson 7-2* 7.RP.1.1, 7.RP.1.3

4. Does this table show a proportional relationship? If so, what is the constant of proportionality? *Lessons 7-3 and 7-4* 7.RP.1.2a, 7.RP.1.2b

x	40	50	60	70
y	8	10	12	14

Ⓐ Yes; $\frac{1}{5}$

Ⓑ Yes; 5

Ⓒ Yes; 10

Ⓓ The quantities are not proportional.

5. Janet, Rosi, and Tanya buy postcards from their favorite souvenir shop. Janet buys 3 postcards for $1.05. Rosi buys 5 postcards for $1.75. Tanya buys 8 postcards for $2.80. Are the cost, y, in dollars and the number of postcards, x, proportional? Explain your answer. Write an equation to represent this relationship, if possible. *Lesson 7-4* 7.RP.1.2a, 7.RP.1.2c

6. Four movie tickets cost $30.00. Five concert tickets cost $36.50. Does the movie or the concert cost less per ticket? How much less? *Lesson 7-1* 7.RP.1.1, 7.RP.1.3

How well did you do on the mid-topic checkpoint? Fill in the stars.

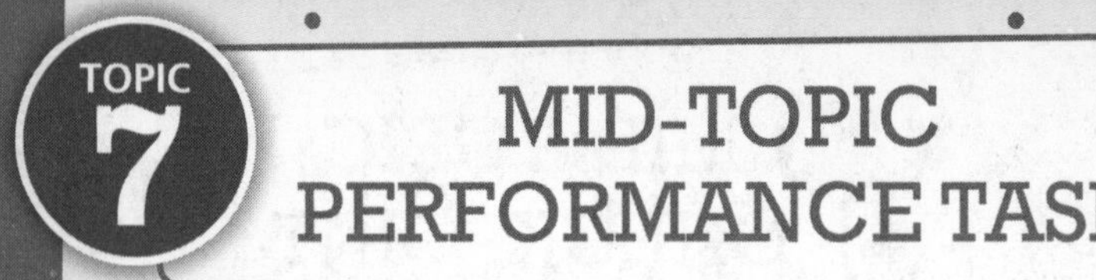

The school's theater club is building sets that will make ordinary students look like giants. The actors need a door, a table, and a stool that will make them look almost twice as tall.

PART A

The heights of objects in the set are proportional to the actual heights of objects. Complete the table. 7.RP.1.2b, 7.RP.1.3

The constant of proportionality is ☐.

	Actual Height	Height on Set
Door	80 in.	44 in.
Table	28 in.	☐
Stool	18 in.	☐

PART B

How can the stage manager use the constant of proportionality to find the dimensions of any new props the director requires? 7.RP.1.3

PART C

What should the height of a can of fruit juice used as a prop be if its actual height is 7 inches? Show your work. 7.RP.1.3

3-Act Mathematical Modeling: Mixin' It Up

Go Online | PearsonRealize.com

MAFS.K12.MP.4.1 Model with mathematics. Also MP.1.1, MP.2.1, MP.3.1, MP.5.1, MP.7.1, MP.8.1

MAFS.7.RP.1.1 Compute unit rates associated with ratios of fractions, including ratios of lengths, areas and other quantities measured in like or different units. Also 7.RP.1.2a

ACT 1

1. After watching the video, what is the first question that comes to mind?

2. Write the Main Question you will answer.

3. **Construct Arguments** Predict an answer to this Main Question. Explain your prediction.

4. On the number line below, write a number that is too small to be the answer. Write a number that is too large.

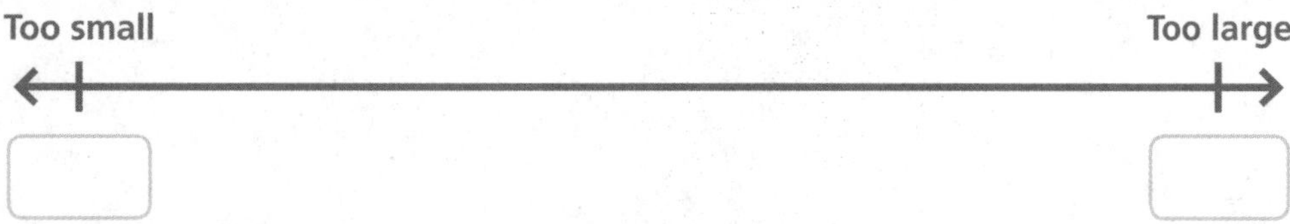

5. Plot your prediction on the same number line.

ACT 2

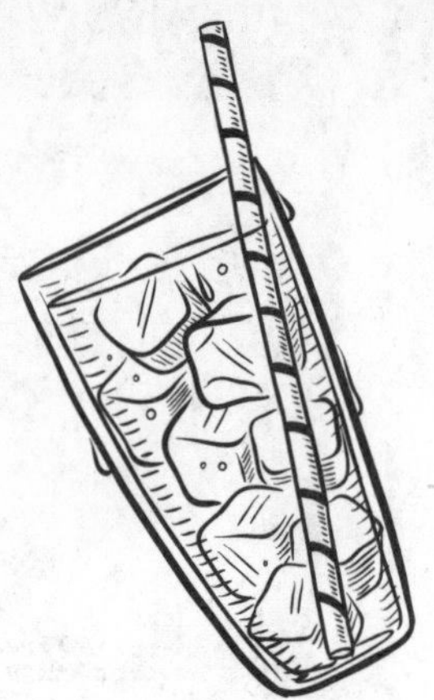

6. What information in this situation would be helpful to know? How would you use that information?

7. **Use Appropriate Tools** What tools can you use to get the information you need? Record the information as you find it.

8. **Model with Math** Represent the situation using the mathematical content, concepts, and skills from this topic. Use your representation to answer the Main Question.

9. What is your answer to the Main Question? Is it higher or lower than your prediction? Explain why.

ACT 3

10. Write the answer you saw in the video.

11. **Reasoning** Does your answer match the answer in the video? If not, what are some reasons that would explain the difference?

12. **Make Sense and Persevere** Would you change your model now that you know the answer? Explain.

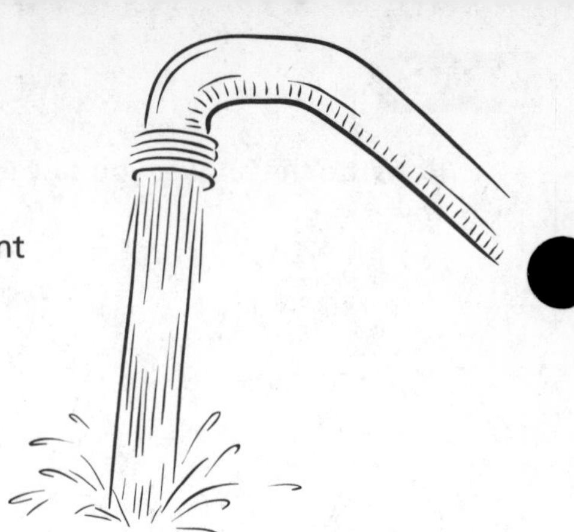

Reflect

13. Model with Math Explain how you used a mathematical model to represent the situation. How did the model help you answer the Main Question?

14. Critique Reasoning Choose a classmate's model. How would you adjust that model?

SEQUEL

15. Use Structure A classmate usually adds 6 drops to 16 ounces of water. Use your updated model to predict the number of drops she would use for the large container.

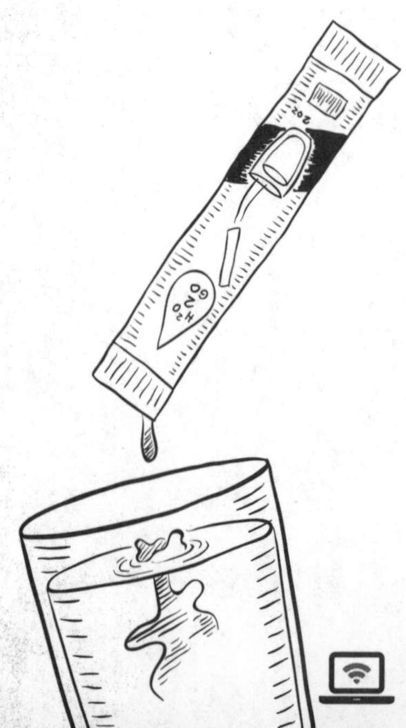

Explore It!

ACTIVITY

Lesson 7-5
Graph Proportional Relationships

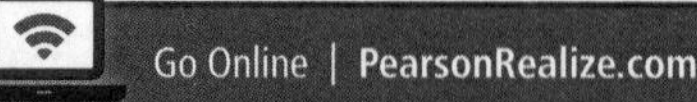

Go Online | PearsonRealize.com

The graph shows the time it takes Jacey to print T-shirts for her school's math club.

I can...
use a graph to determine whether two quantities are proportional.

MAFS.7.RP.1.2a Decide whether two quantities are in a proportional relationship, e.g., by...graphing on a coordinate plane and observing whether the graph is a straight line through the origin.
Also 7.RP.1.2b, 7.RP.1.2d

MAFS.K12.MP.2.1, MP.3.1, MP.4.1, MP.7.1

A. Use the points on the graph to complete the table. Are the quantities proportional? Explain.

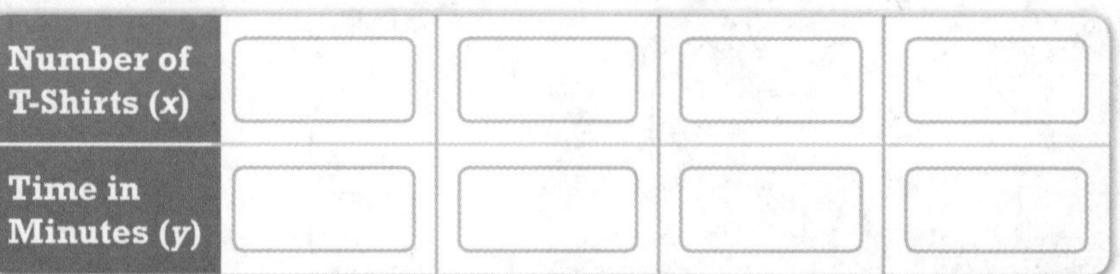

Number of T-Shirts (x)				
Time in Minutes (y)				

B. Start at (1, 5). As you move from one point to the next on the graph, how does the x-coordinate change? How does the y-coordinate change?

C. Write the points for 0 T-shirts and for 5 T-shirts as ordered pairs. Graph the points and draw the line that passes through all six points.

Focus on math practices

Reasoning Suppose that after printing 4 T-shirts it takes Jacey 4 minutes to change the ink cartridge. Would this point for 5 T-shirts lie on the line you drew in Part C? Explain.

? **Essential Question** What does the graph of a proportional relationship look like?

EXAMPLE 1  Graph to Recognize a Proportional Relationship

Scan for Multimedia 

Tanya exercised for 30 minutes. She noted the Calories burned at three times during her workout. How can Tanya use this information to find how many Calories she burned after 15 minutes of exercise?

Model with Math You can represent the situation on the coordinate plane.

STEP 1 Use a graph to display the data.

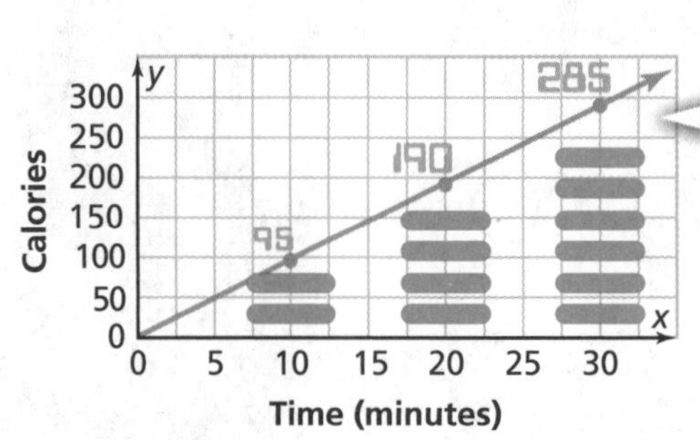

The graph is a straight line through the origin, (0, 0).

The relationship between exercise time, *x*, and Calories burned, *y*, is proportional.

STEP 2 Use the graph to find the constant of proportionality.

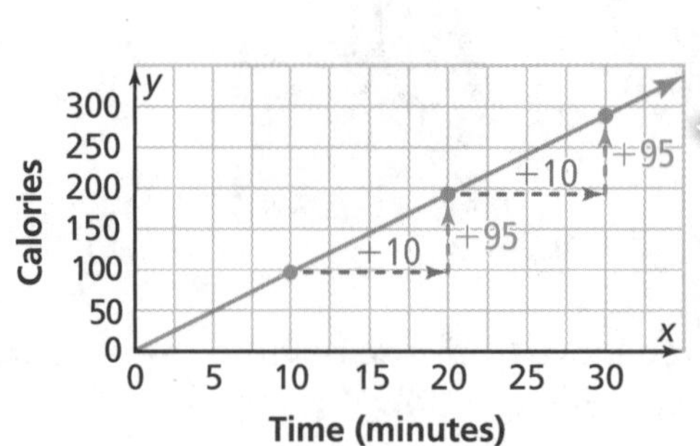

Find the differences between the coordinates of any two ordered pairs.

The constant of proportionality is $\frac{95}{10}$ or 9.5.

Tanya can use the graph and the constant of proportionality to determine that she burned 142.5 Calories in 15 minutes.

Try It!

Each $\frac{1}{4}$-cup serving of cereal has 3 grams of protein. How can you use the graph at the right to determine whether the quantities are proportional and to find how many grams of protein are in 1 cup of the cereal?

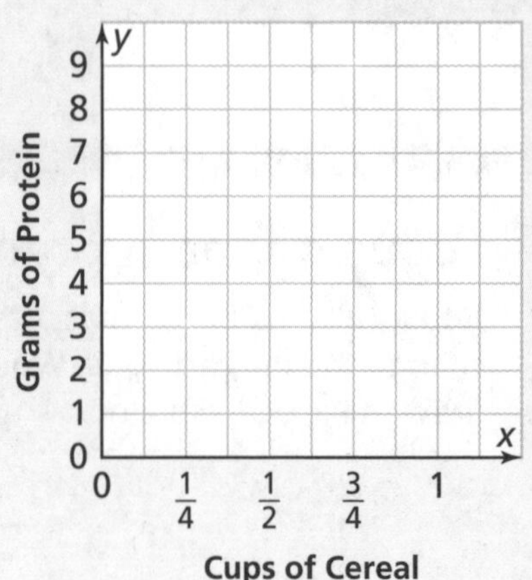

Convince Me! How can you find the constant of proportionality from the coordinates of one point on the graph?

EXAMPLE 2  Interpret the Graph of a Proportional Relationship

ACTIVITY ASSESS

The graph shows a proportional relationship between the distance and the amount of time Mr. Brown drives.

a. What does each of these points represent in this situation: (0, 0), (1, 55), and (5, 275)?

(0, 0): Mr. Brown drives 0 miles in 0 hours.
(1, 55): Mr. Brown drives 55 miles in 1 hour.
(5, 275): Mr. Brown drives 275 miles in 5 hours.

b. What is the constant of proportionality?

Find the y-coordinate when x is 1.
The constant of proportionality is 55.

c. What equation relates the distance, y, and the time, x?

$y = 55x$

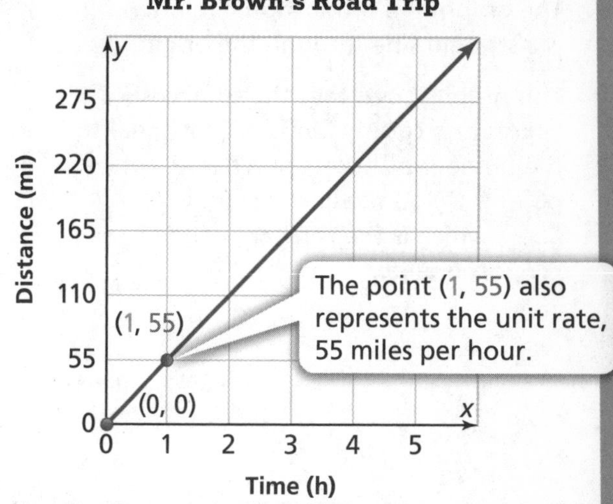

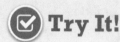

 Try It!

Suppose the graph of Mr. Brown's Road Trip is extended. Find the ordered pair with an x-coordinate of 7. What does this point represent in the situation?

If the graph is extended, it will pass through the point (7, ☐). This means Mr. Brown drives ☐ miles in ☐ hours.

EXAMPLE 3  Recognize Graphs of Proportional Relationships

Explain why each graph does or does not show a proportional relationship.

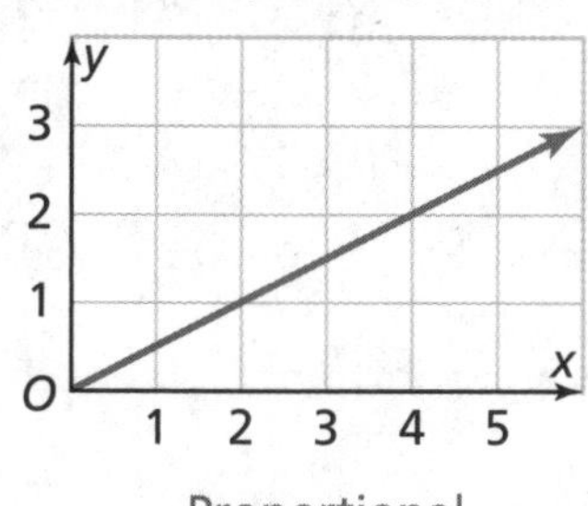

Proportional

The graph is a straight line that passes through the origin.

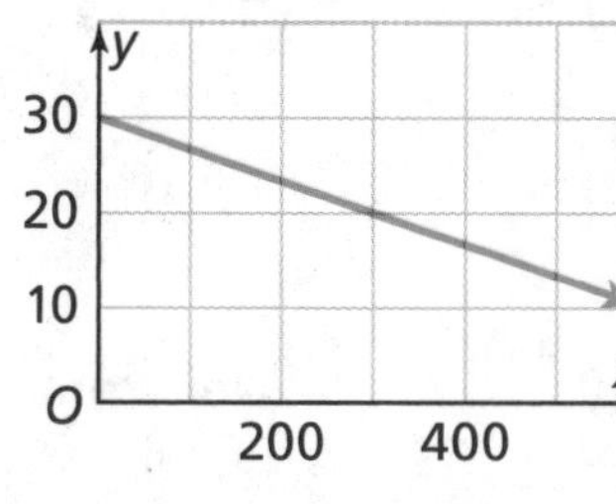

NOT Proportional

The graph is a straight line but does not pass through the origin.

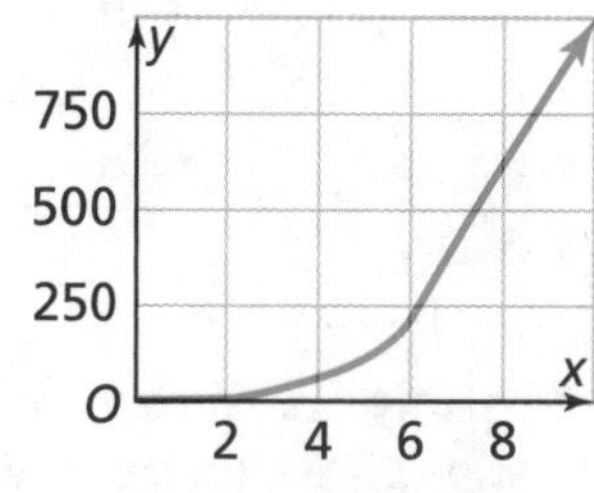

NOT Proportional

The graph passes through the origin but is not a straight line.

Try It!

Draw two graphs that pass through the point (2, 3), one that represents a proportional relationship and one that does not. Label your graphs as *Proportional* or *NOT Proportional*.

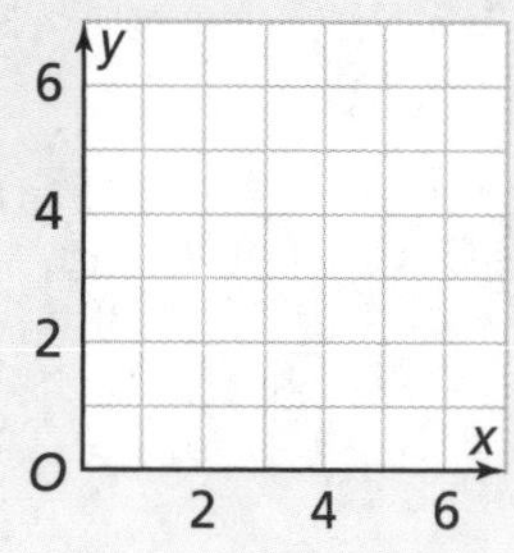

KEY CONCEPT

The graph of a proportional relationship is a straight line through the origin.

This graph shows that the total cost of tickets at a county fair is proportional to the number of tickets purchased. For each point (x, y) on the line except (0, 0), $\frac{y}{x} = 5$, which is the constant of proportionality.

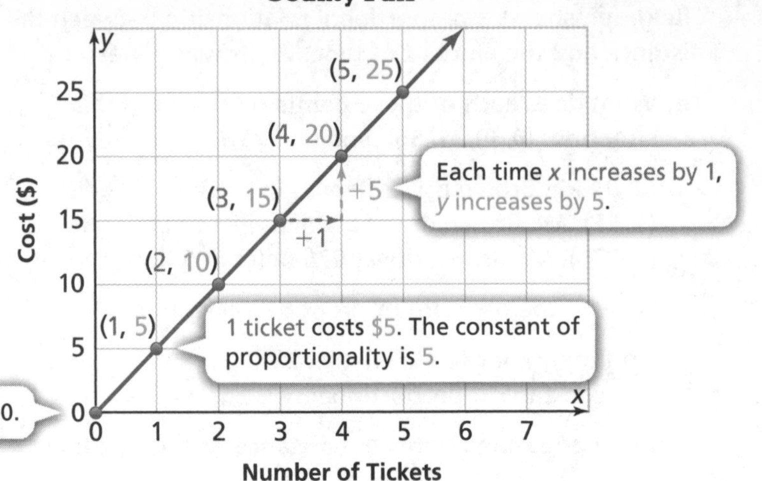

Do You Understand?

1. **Essential Question** What does the graph of a proportional relationship look like?

2. **Reasoning** Why will the graph of every proportional relationship include the point (0, 0)?

3. **Construct Arguments** Makayla plotted two points, (0, 0) and (3, 33), on a coordinate grid. Noah says that she is graphing a proportional relationship. Is Noah correct? Explain.

Do You Know How?

For 4–7, use the information below.

Martin and Isabelle go bowling. Each game costs $10, and they split that cost. Martin has his own bowling shoes, but Isabelle pays $3 to rent shoes.

4. Complete the graphs below.

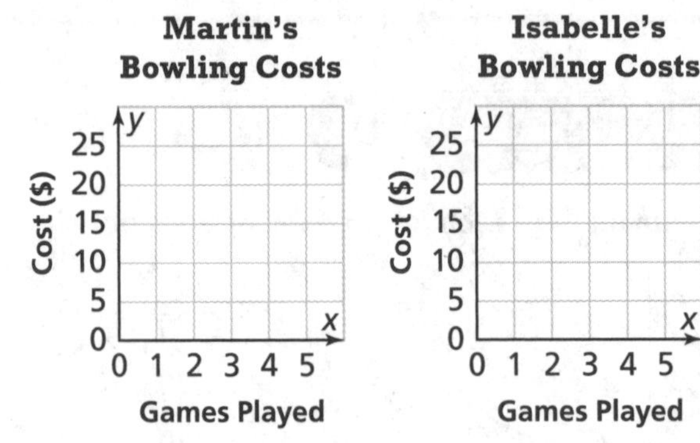

5. Which graph shows a proportional relationship? Explain why.

6. Choose one point on the graph of the proportional relationship and explain what this point means in terms of the situation.

7. What equation represents the proportional relationship?

Name: ______________________________

Practice & Problem Solving

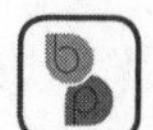

Scan for Multimedia

8. For each graph shown, tell whether it shows a proportional relationship. Explain your reasoning.

a.

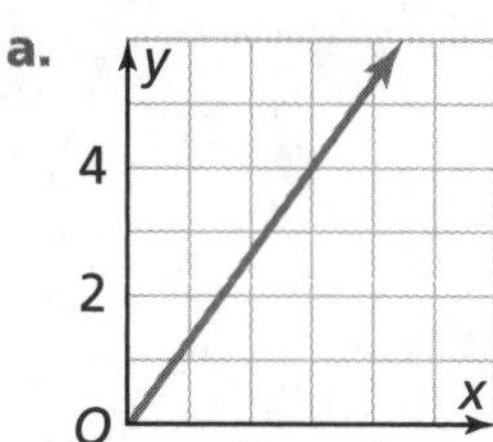

b.

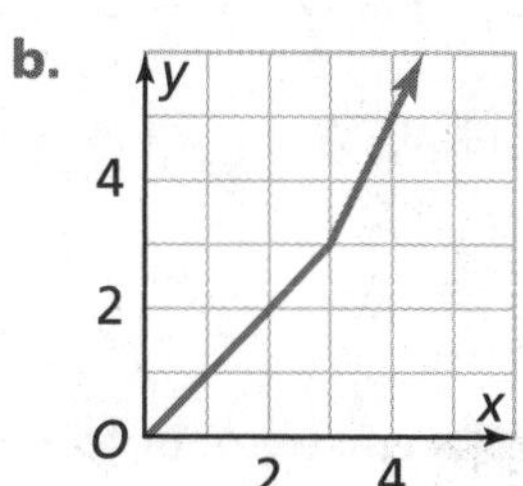

c.

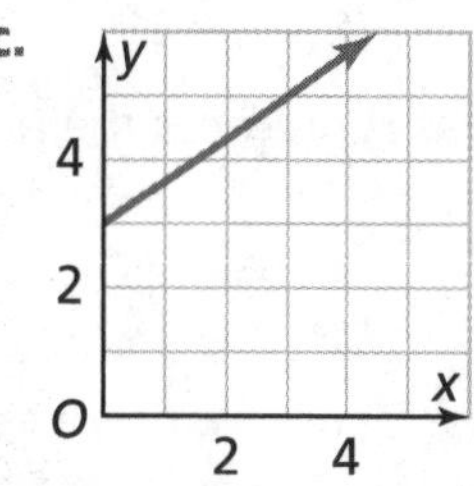

9. The graph shows the number of boxes a machine packages over time. Is the relationship proportional? How many boxes does the machine package in 4 minutes?

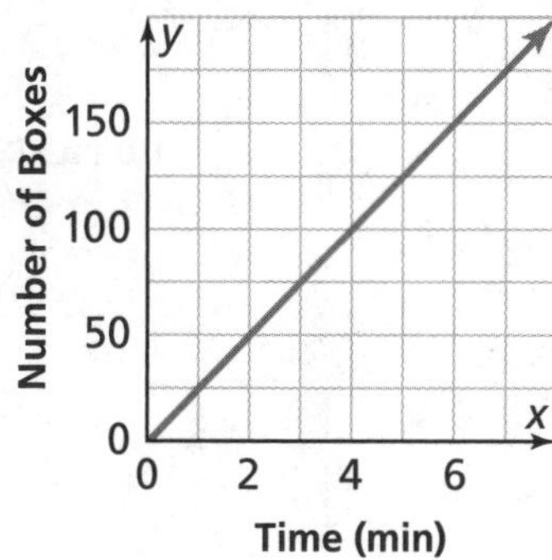

10. Does the graph show a proportional relationship? If so, use the graph to find the constant of proportionality.

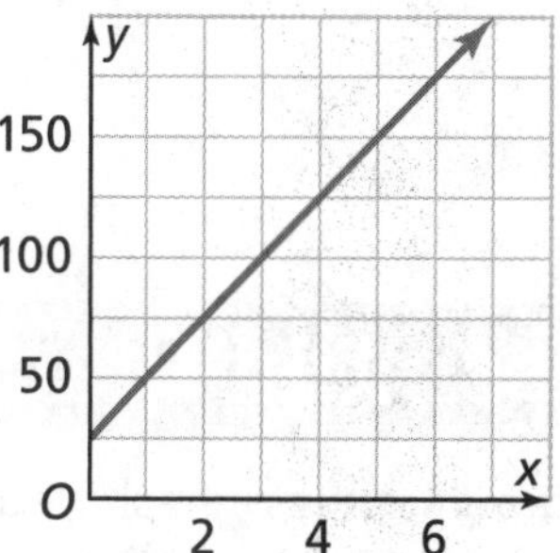

11. The graph shows a proportional relationship between the cups of flour a baker uses and the number of cookies made.

a. Use Structure What does the point (0, 0) represent in the situation?

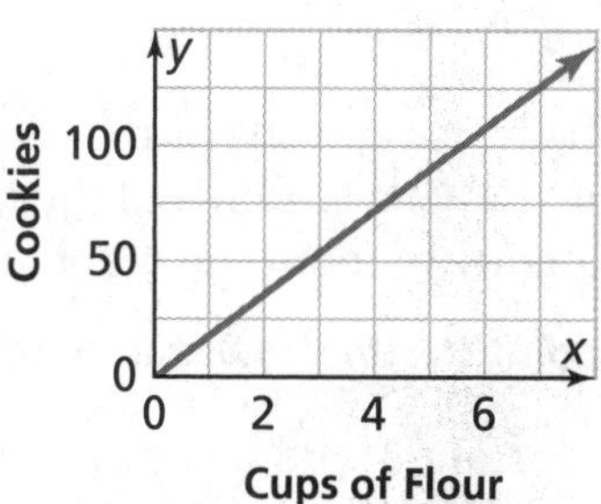

b. What does the point (1, 18) represent?

12. The points $\left(0.5, \frac{1}{10}\right)$ and $\left(7, 1\frac{2}{5}\right)$ are on the graph of a proportional relationship.

a. What is the constant of proportionality?

b. Name one more point on the graph.

c. Write an equation that represents the proportional relationship.

13. Higher Order Thinking Denmark uses the kroner as its currency. Before a trip to Denmark, Mia wants to exchange $1,700 for kroner.

a. Does Bank A or Bank B have the better exchange rate? Explain.

b. How many more kroner would Mia get if she exchanged her $1,700 at the bank with the better exchange rate?

Bank A

Dollars ($)	Kroner
80	408
100	510
120	612

Bank B

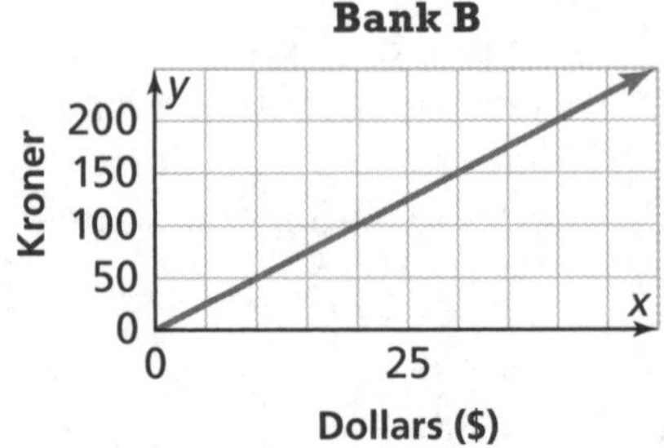

Assessment Practice

14. Does the graph at the right show a proportional relationship between x and y? Explain. 7.RP.1.2a

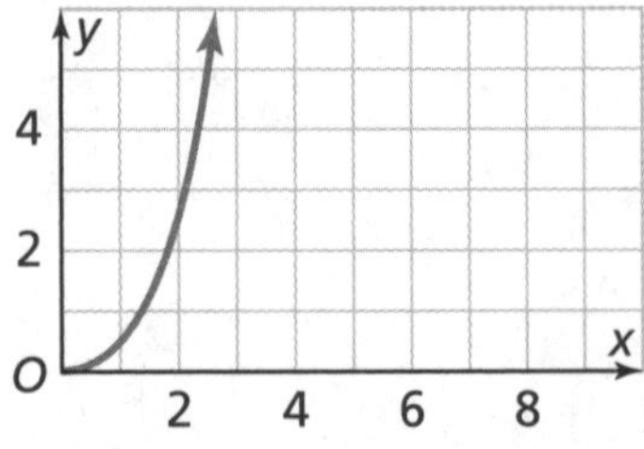

15. The graph at the right shows the relationship between rainfall during the growing season and the growth of a type of plant. Which statements about the graph are true? 7.RP.1.2a, 7.RP.1.2b

- ☐ The point (1, 10) shows the constant of proportionality.
- ☐ The constant of proportionality is $\frac{5}{7}$.
- ☐ The graph does not show a proportional relationship.
- ☐ The graph is a straight line through the origin.
- ☐ The point (28, 20) means the type of plant grows 20 mm when it rains 28 cm.

Rainfall and Plant Growth

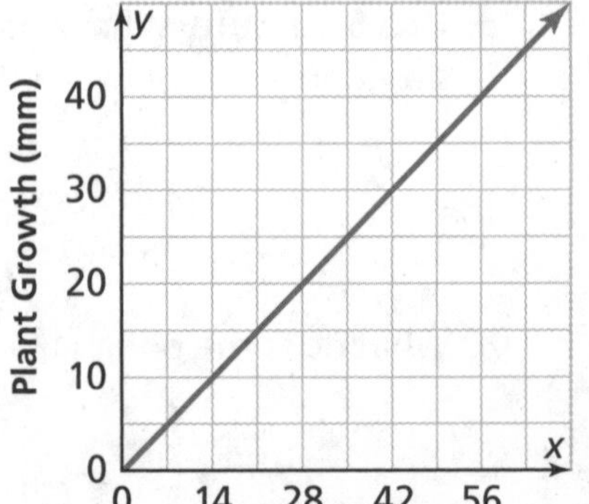

Lesson 7-6
Apply Proportional Reasoning to Solve Problems

I can...
determine whether a relationship is proportional and use representations to solve problems.

MAFS.7.RP.1.2 Recognize and represent proportional relationships between quantities. Also 7.RP.1.3

MAFS.K12.MP.1.1, MP.2.1, MP.5.1, MP.7.1

Solve & Discuss It!

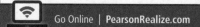

Xander and Pedro are at an ice cream social. For every scoop of ice cream, Xander uses $\frac{1}{8}$ cup of fruit topping. Pedro uses one more tablespoon of fruit topping than the number of scoops. If Xander and Pedro each use the same amount of fruit topping, how many scoops of ice cream does each use?

Look for Relationships
There are 2 tablespoons in $\frac{1}{8}$ cup.

Focus on math practices

Reasoning For which person, Xander or Pedro, is the relationship between the quantities of ice cream and fruit topping proportional? Explain.

? Essential Question How can proportional reasoning help solve a problem?

EXAMPLE 1  Use Proportional Reasoning to Solve a Problem

Scan for Multimedia 

The ratio of collectible cards DeShawn owns to cards that Stephanie owns is 5:2. Stephanie has 36 cards. How will the ratio of DeShawn's cards to Stephanie's cards change if they both sell half their cards? Explain.

DeShawn's Cards

Stephanie's Cards

> **Make Sense and Persevere**
> How can you use proportional reasoning to compare the quantities of cards?

STEP 1 Draw a diagram that represents the ratio of DeShawn's cards to Stephanie's cards. You can use the diagram to find the number of cards DeShawn owns.

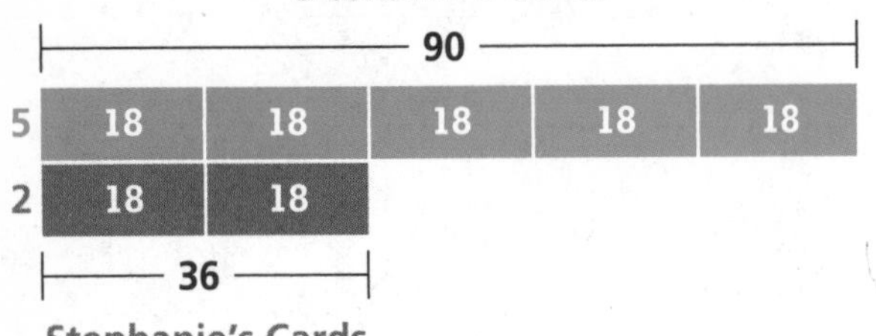

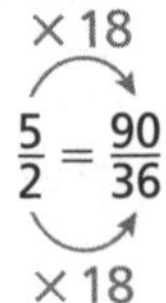

$$\frac{5}{2} = \frac{90}{36}$$

DeShawn owns 90 cards.

STEP 2 Find the ratio after they sell half their cards.

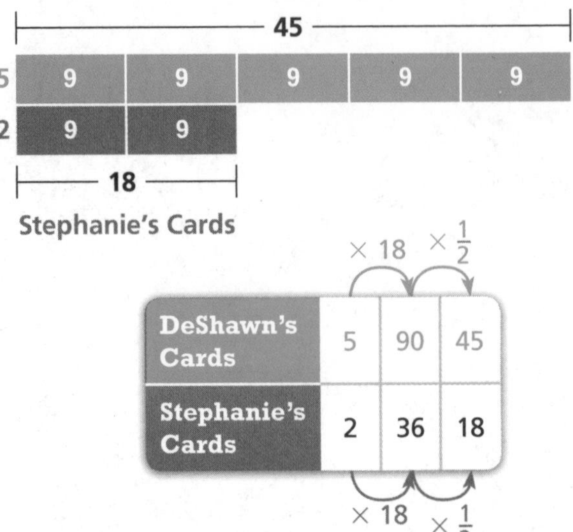

DeShawn's Cards	5	90	45
Stephanie's Cards	2	36	18

After they both sell half their cards, the ratio is $\frac{45}{18}$, or $\frac{5}{2}$. If the numbers of cards change by the same multiple, the ratio that relates them is equivalent, so it does not change.

Try It!

After selling half their card collections, DeShawn and Stephanie each buy 9 new cards. What is the ratio of the number of cards DeShawn has to the number Stephanie has?

Convince Me! Why did the ratio stay the same in the Example but change in the Try It?

EXAMPLE 2  Recognize When to Use Proportional Reasoning

Martin is 6 years old when his sister Cassandra is 3 years old. How old will Martin be when Cassandra is 6 years old?

Make a table to find Martin's age.

> **Use Structure** Look for a constant multiple to determine whether you can use proportional reasoning to solve this problem.

Martin's Age	Cassandra's Age
6	3
7	4
8	5
9	6

$\times 1.5$ (Martin's Age, 6 to 9) $\times 2$ (Cassandra's Age, 3 to 6)

There is no constant multiple so you cannot use proportional reasoning. In 3 years when Cassandra is 6 years old, Martin will also be 3 years older, or 9 years old.

EXAMPLE 3  Apply Proportional Reasoning

A video streaming service charged Bryan $143.84 for a full year of access. Bryan thinks he was not charged the correct amount. What should Bryan say when he calls customer service?

STEP 1 Write an equation to represent the situation.

The rate is $8.99 per month. So an equation that represents the cost y after x months is $y = 8.99x$.

STEP 2 Substitute the given information into the equation and solve.

Option 1

$$y = 8.99x$$
$$= 8.99(12)$$
$$= 107.88$$

Bryan should have been charged $107.88. He should ask customer service for a credit of $143.84 − $107.88 = $35.96.

Option 2

$$y = 8.99x$$
$$143.84 = 8.99x$$
$$\frac{143.84}{8.99} = \frac{8.99x}{8.99}$$
$$16 = x$$

Bryan was charged for 16 months, so he should ask customer service to give him 4 months of free online service.

Try It!

A florist makes bouquets that include 50 white flowers and 7 red flowers. If the florist orders 1,050 white flowers and 140 red flowers, there will be leftover flowers. How can the florist adjust the order so there are no leftover flowers?

KEY CONCEPT

Think about how two quantities are related before you decide to use proportional reasoning to solve a problem.

When Evie is 2 years old, Josh is 6 years old.

Josh is 4 years older than Evie.
Josh is 3 times as old as Evie.

In 2 years

When Evie is 4 years old, Josh is 8 years old.

Josh is still 4 years older than Evie.
Josh is now 2 times as old as Evie.

You cannot use proportional reasoning to solve this problem because Josh's age is not a constant multiple of Evie's age.

Do You Understand?

1. **Essential Question** How can proportional reasoning help solve a problem?

2. **Use Appropriate Tools** How can knowing how to represent proportional relationships in different ways be useful in solving problems?

3. **Reasoning** How many ways are there to adjust two quantities so that they are in a given proportional relationship? Explain your reasoning.

Do You Know How?

4. A recipe calls for 15 oz of flour for every 8 oz of milk.

   a. Is the relationship between ounces of flour and ounces of milk proportional? Explain.

   b. If you use 15 oz of milk, how much flour should you use?

5. A food packing company makes a popular fruit cocktail. To ensure a good mixture of fruit, there are 3 cherry halves for every 8 white grapes in a jar. An inspector notices that one jar has 12 cherry halves and 20 white grapes. What can be done to fix the error?

Name: ______________________________

Practice & Problem Solving

Scan for Multimedia 

In 6 and 7, determine whether you can use proportional reasoning and then solve.

6. If Hector is 8 years old and Mary is 3 years old, how old will Mary be when Hector is 16?

7. Marco needs to buy some cat food. At the nearest store, 3 bags of cat food cost $15.75. How much would Marco spend on 5 bags of cat food?

8. An architect makes a model of a new house with a patio made with pavers. In the model, each paver in the patio is $\frac{1}{3}$ in. long and $\frac{1}{6}$ in. wide. The actual dimensions of the pavers are shown.

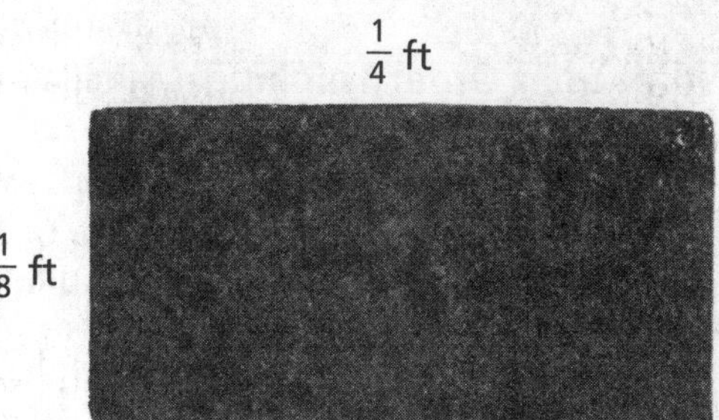

a. What is the constant of proportionality that relates the length of a paver in the model and the length of an actual paver?

b. What is the constant of proportionality that relates the area of a paver in the model and the area of an actual paver? Explain your reasoning.

9. Reasoning The table lists recommended amounts of food to order for 25 guests. Nathan is hosting a graduation party for 40 guests. There will also be guests stopping by for a short time. For ordering purposes, Nathan will count each of the 45 "drop-in" guests as half a guest. How much of each food item should Nathan order?

Party Food

Item	Amount
Fried Chicken	24 pieces
Deli Meats	$3\frac{2}{3}$ pounds
Lasagna	$10\frac{3}{4}$ pounds

10. Emily and Andy each go to a hardware store to buy wire. The table shows the relationship between the cost and the length of wire.

a. Emily needs 24 feet of wire. How much will she spend on wire?

b. Andy needs 13 yards of wire. How much will he spend on wire?

Cost of Wire

Length in Inches (x)	Cost in Dollars (y)
120	4.80
135	5.40
150	6.00
175	7.00

11. Make Sense and Persevere The weights of Michael's and Brittney's new puppies are shown in the table and graph. Whose dog gains weight more quickly? Explain.

Weight of Michael's Puppy

Age (months)	1	2	3
Weight (pounds)	8.6	17.2	25.8

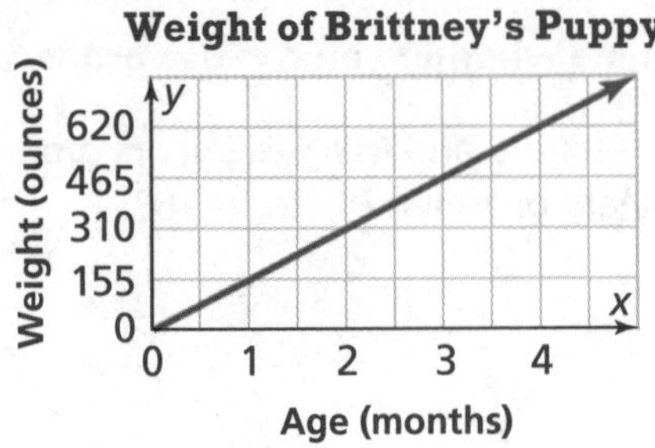

12. Higher Order Thinking Marielle's painting has the dimensions shown. The school asks her to paint a larger version that will hang in the cafeteria. The larger version will be twice the width and twice the height. Is the area of the original painting proportional to the area of the larger painting? If so, what is the constant of proportionality?

18 in.

24 in.

Assessment Practice

13. The ratio of orange juice concentrate to water that Zoe used to make orange juice yesterday was 3 : 7. She used 14 ounces of water in the juice yesterday. Today she wants to make twice as much orange juice.

PART A

Is the relationship between the amount of orange juice concentrate c and the amount of water w proportional? Explain. 7.RP.1.2

PART B

How much orange juice concentrate does she need? 7.RP.1.3

Ⓐ 6 ounces

Ⓑ 12 ounces

Ⓒ 18 ounces

Ⓓ 28 ounces

? Topic Essential Question

How can you recognize and represent proportional relationships and use them to solve problems?

Vocabulary Review

Complete each definition and then provide an example of each vocabulary word.

Vocabulary	constant of proportionality	ratio	proportion
	proportional relationship	rate	unit rate

Definition	Example
1. For two quantities x and y, if y is always a constant multiple of x, they have a(n) ______.	
2. The value of the ratio $\frac{y}{x}$ of two proportional quantities x and y is called the ______.	
3. An equation that shows that two ratios are equal is a(n) ______.	

Use Vocabulary in Writing

A sunflower grows 8 feet in 92 days. Assuming that it grows at a constant rate, explain how you could use this information to find the number of days it took for the sunflower to grow 6 feet. Use vocabulary words in your explanation.

Concepts and Skills Review

LESSONS 7-1 AND 7-2 Connect Ratios, Rates, and Unit Rates | Determine Unit Rates with Ratios of Fractions

Quick Review

A ratio is a relationship in which for every x units of one quantity there are y units of another quantity. A rate is a ratio that relates two quantities with different units. A unit rate relates a quantity to 1 unit of another quantity. You can use what you know about equivalent fractions and calculating with fractions to write a ratio of fractions as a unit rate.

Example

In 3 days, a typical robin can eat up to 42.6 feet of earthworms. Write a rate to relate the number of feet of earthworms to the number of days. Then find the unit rate.

$$\frac{42.6 \text{ feet}}{3 \text{ days}} = \frac{14.2 \text{ feet}}{1 \text{ day}}$$

A robin eats 14.2 feet of earthworms per day.

Practice

1. Mealworms are a healthy food for wild songbirds. Adam buys a 3.5-oz container of mealworms for \$8.75. Marco buys a 3.75-oz container of mealworms for \$9.75. Which container is the better deal?

2. A painter mixes $2\frac{1}{2}$ pints of yellow paint with 4 pints of red paint to make a certain shade of orange paint. How many pints of yellow paint should be mixed with 10 pints of red paint to make this shade of orange?

LESSON 7-3 Understand Proportional Relationships: Equivalent Ratios

Quick Review

Two quantities x and y have a proportional relationship if the ratios $\frac{y}{x}$ for every related pair of x and y are equivalent. You can write a proportion to show that two ratios have the same value.

Example

Does the table show a proportional relationship between x and y? Explain.

x	200	400	500
y	600	1,200	1,500

$\frac{600}{200} = \frac{3}{1}$ $\quad \frac{1{,}200}{400} = \frac{3}{1}$ $\quad \frac{1{,}500}{500} = \frac{3}{1}$

Because every ratio is equivalent, there is a proportional relationship between x and y.

Practice

In 1 and 2, use the table below that shows information about squares.

Side Length (cm)	2	4	6
Perimeter (cm)	8	16	24

1. Are the perimeter and the side length of squares proportional? Explain.

2. Write and solve a proportion to find the perimeter of a square when its side length is 12.

LESSON 7-4 Describe Proportional Relationships: Constant of Proportionality

Quick Review

The equation $y = kx$ describes a proportional relationship between two quantities x and y, where k is the constant of proportionality. $k = \frac{y}{x}$ for any related pair of x and y except when $x = 0$.

Example

The table shows the wages Roger earned for the hours he worked. What equation relates the wages, w, and the number of hours, h?

Time (h)	Wages (w)
3	\$27.00
5	\$45.00
6	\$54.00

Find the constant of proportionality, k.

$\frac{27}{3} = 9$ $\frac{45}{5} = 9$ $\frac{54}{6} = 9$

Write the equation in the form $y = kx$.

$w = 9h$

Practice

1. Sally is going on vacation with her family. In 2 hours they travel 90.5 miles. If they travel at the same speed, write an equation that represents how far they will travel, d, in h hours.

2. The table shows the weights of bunches of bananas and the price of each bunch. Identify the constant of proportionality. Write an equation to relate weight, w, to the price, p.

Weight (w)	Price (p)
3 pounds	\$1.35
3.8 pounds	\$1.71
5.2 pounds	\$2.34

LESSON 7-5 Graph Proportional Relationships

Quick Review

The graph of a proportional relationship is a straight line through the origin. You can identify the constant of proportionality, k, from the point $(1, k)$ or by dividing $\frac{y}{x}$ for any point (x, y) except the origin.

Example

Is the number of sunny days proportional to the number of rainy days? If so, find the constant of proportionality, and explain its meaning in this situation.

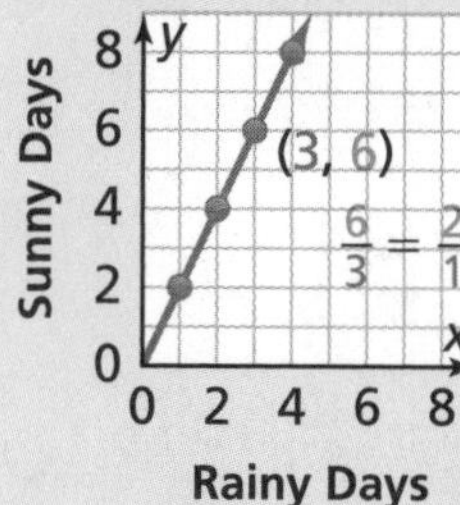

The graph is a straight line through the origin, so it shows a proportional relationship. The constant of proportionality is 2, which means for every 1 rainy day, there were 2 sunny days.

Practice

1. Does the graph show a proportional relationship? Explain.

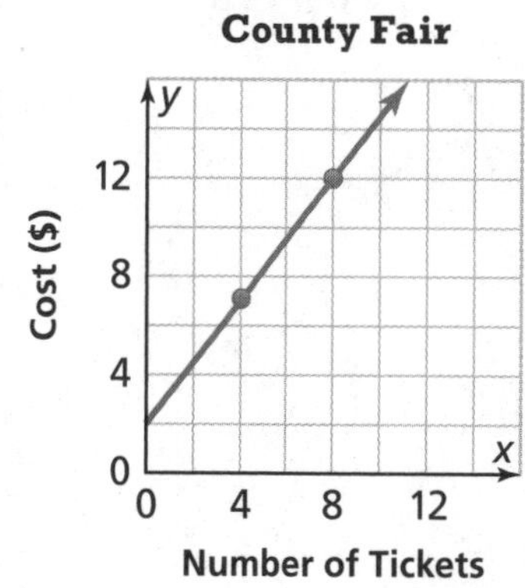

2. Sketch a graph that represents a proportional relationship.

LESSON 7-6 Apply Proportional Reasoning to Solve Problems

Quick Review

Think about how two quantities are related before you decide to use proportional reasoning to solve a problem.

Example

Ann-Marie makes gift baskets that each contain 3 pounds of gourmet cheese with every 2 boxes of crackers. She ordered 80 pounds of cheese and 50 boxes of crackers. How can she adjust her order to make 25 gift baskets, with no leftover items?

$\frac{3 \times 25}{2 \times 25} = \frac{75}{50}$

Ann-Marie can order 5 fewer pounds of cheese so that her order of 75 pounds of cheese and 50 boxes of crackers will make exactly 25 gift baskets.

Practice

Decide which problems can be solved by using proportional reasoning. Select all that apply.

☐ Yani buys 4 dozen flyers for $7.25. What is the cost of 12 dozen?

☐ First-class letters cost $0.49 for the first ounce and $0.22 for each additional ounce. What is the cost of a 5-oz letter?

☐ 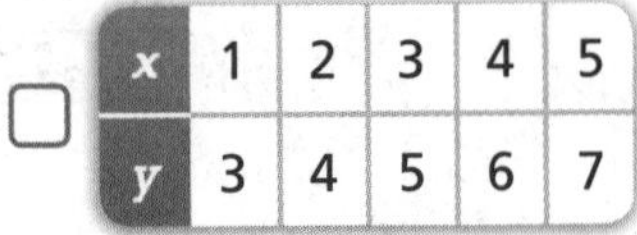

x	1	2	3	4	5
y	3	4	5	6	7

What is the value of y when $x = 8$?

☐

x	1.5	3	5.2	6.5	8
y	4.5	9	15.6	19.5	24

What is the value of y when $x = 5$?

Pathfinder

Shade a path from START to FINISH. Follow the solutions from the least value to the greatest value. You can only move up, down, right, or left.

I can...
add, subtract, multiply, and divide integers. 7.NS.1.1d, 7.NS.1.2c

START

$3 - 24$	$3 \times (-13)$	-3×14	$44 - 49$	$-48 \div 16$
$-26 + 7$	$-7 - 27$	$13 \times (-4)$	$8 - 19$	$-18 \div (-6)$
$3 \times (-5)$	$28 \div (-2)$	$(-35) \div 2$	$4 + (-25)$	$-68 \div 17$
$23 - 46$	$-2 - 11$	$15 + (-26)$	$17 - 23$	$29 - 38$
$-12 \div (-3)$	$18 + (-32)$	$11 - 29$	$-60 \div 12$	$-3 \times (-2)$

FINISH

TOPIC 8

UNDERSTAND AND USE PERCENT

? Topic Essential Question

What is the meaning of percent? How can percent be estimated and found?

Topic Overview

Topic Vocabulary

- percent

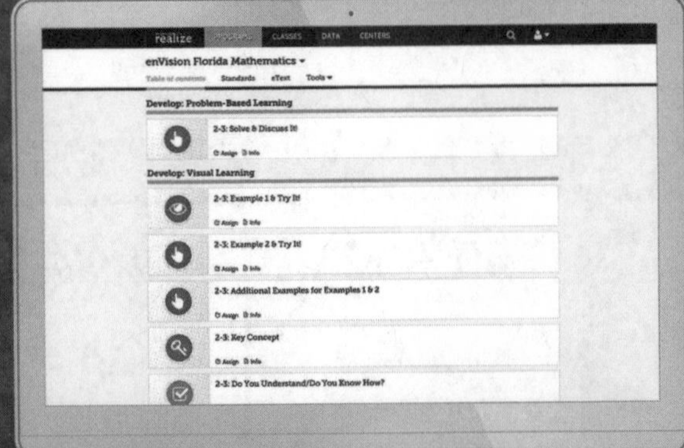

 Go online | **PearsonRealize.com**

Lesson Digital Resources

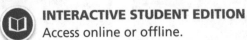

INTERACTIVE STUDENT EDITION
Access online or offline.

VISUAL LEARNING ANIMATION
Interact with visual learning animations.

ACTIVITY Use with ***Solve & Discuss It, Explore It,*** and ***Explain It*** activities, and to explore Examples.

VIDEOS Watch clips to support ***3-Act Mathematical Modeling Lessons*** and ***STEM Projects***.

Ace the Test

Ace the Test

Numbers, percents, letters—teachers use grades as a language to help explain how you are doing in class. When you know how your grade is determined, it is easier to understand your teacher's expectations. Think about this during the 3-Act Mathematical Modeling lesson.

PRACTICE Practice what you've learned.

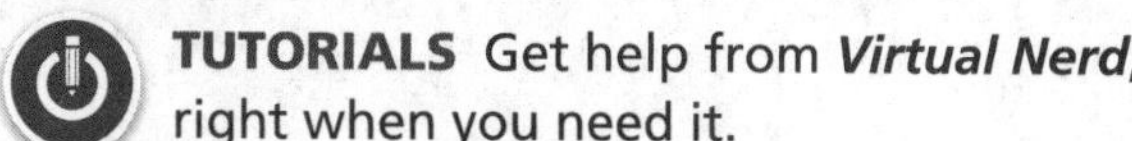
TUTORIALS Get help from ***Virtual Nerd***, right when you need it.

MATH TOOLS Explore math with digital tools.

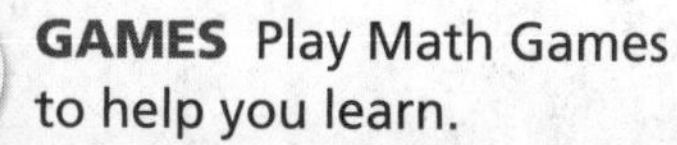
GAMES Play Math Games to help you learn.

KEY CONCEPT Review important lesson content.

GLOSSARY Read and listen to English/Spanish definitions.

ASSESSMENT Show what you've learned.

TOPIC 8

enVision® STEM Project

Did You Know?

Extinction normally occurs at a rate of about one to five species per year. The earth is now **losing species** at 1,000 to 10,000 times that rate, with dozens going extinct every day.

Polar Bears need ice floes to rest when they travel long distances to find food or migrate. Due to **melting ice**, the population will likely decrease by more than **30%** in the next three generations.

There are 1,373 species of birds identified as **threatened**.

13% of all bird species threatened

Scientists estimate that the **population** of nearly 17,000 eastern lowland gorillas has **declined** by more than **50%**.

Conservation efforts helped the total number of **black rhinos** to grow from 2,410 to 4,880 in 15 years.

According to the Chinese government, the population of wild giant pandas has reached 1,864, up from 1,596 at last count.

In **100 years**, the number of the world's tigers **declined** from 100,000 to 3,200.

Your Task: Engineering to Prevent Extinction

Engineers help to to prevent extinction with both direct and indirect solutions. Materials engineers develop wood alternatives. Mechanical and chemical engineers produce clean energy. You and your classmates will research threatened species and identify ways that engineers can help to prevent the extinction of these species.

Review What You Know!

Vocabulary

Choose the best term from the box to complete each definition.

decimal
fraction
ratio
term

1. A __________ can be written as x to y, x:y, or $\frac{x}{y}$.

2. The number 2.25 is a __________.

3. A number that can be used to describe a part of a whole is a __________.

Rates

Write an equivalent rate.

4. $\frac{60 \text{ mi}}{1 \text{ hr}} = \frac{\square \text{ mi}}{5 \text{ hr}}$

5. $\frac{8 \text{ hr}}{2 \text{ days}} = \frac{28 \text{ hr}}{\square \text{ days}}$

6. $\frac{16 \text{ limes}}{\square \text{ bags}} = \frac{40 \text{ limes}}{5 \text{ bags}}$

7. $\frac{\square \text{ cups}}{9 \text{ boxes}} = \frac{24 \text{ cups}}{4 \text{ boxes}}$

8. $\frac{\square \text{ m}}{3 \text{ s}} = \frac{135 \text{ m}}{15 \text{ s}}$

9. $\frac{36 \text{ lb}}{\$\square} = \frac{9 \text{ lb}}{\$6}$

Decimal Computation

Find each product or quotient.

10. $21 \div 0.05$

11. 18×1.25

12. $10.2 \div 1.2$

13. 150×0.625

14. $4 \div 100$

15. 0.25×0.1

Equivalent Ratios

Write three equivalent ratios for each ratio.

16. $\frac{8}{12}$

17. $\frac{15}{35}$

18. $\frac{30}{48}$

19. What are two ways to find an equivalent ratio for $\frac{10}{25}$?

Prepare for Reading Success

Before you begin this topic, read through the lessons. Outline the lessons by writing statements that you think are important about each lesson's content. After you finish each lesson, re-read the statements you wrote and correct or change anything that you had not understood.

Lesson Title	Outline Statements	Changes, If Needed
Understand Percent		
Relate Fractions, Decimals, and Percents		
Represent Percents Greater Than 100 or Less Than 1		
Estimate to Find Percent		
Find the Percent of a Number		
Find the Whole Given a Part and the Percent		

Explain It!

ACTIVITY

Tom made a vegetable pizza and a pepperoni pizza. He cut the vegetable pizza into 5 equal slices and the pepperoni pizza into 10 equal slices. Tom's friends ate 2 slices of vegetable pizza and 4 slices of pepperoni pizza.

Lesson 8-1 Understand Percent

Go Online | PearsonRealize.com

I can...
represent and find the percent of a whole.

MAFS.6.RP.1.3c Find a percent of a quantity as a rate per 100 (e.g., 30% of a quantity means $\frac{30}{100}$ times the quantity); ...
MAFS.K12.MP.2.1, MP.3.1, MP.4.1, MP.7.1

A. Draw lines on each rectangle to represent the equal slices into which each pizza was cut.

Vegetable Pizza **Pepperoni Pizza**

B. Construct Arguments Tom says his friends ate the same amount of vegetable pizza as pepperoni pizza. How could that be true?

Focus on math practices

Model with Math What if Tom's friends ate $\frac{6}{10}$ of the pepperoni pizza? How could you use the rectangles above to find an equal amount of vegetable pizza?

? **Essential Question** How can you represent a rate with 100 as the whole?

EXAMPLE 1 Represent Percents

Scan for Multimedia

What percent of people prefer Bright White Toothpaste?

A percent is a rate in which the first term is compared to 100. The percent is the number of hundredths that represents the part of the whole.

Model with Math
Decimal grids, number lines, or equivalent fractions can be used to represent percents.

ONE WAY Use a grid to represent the percent.

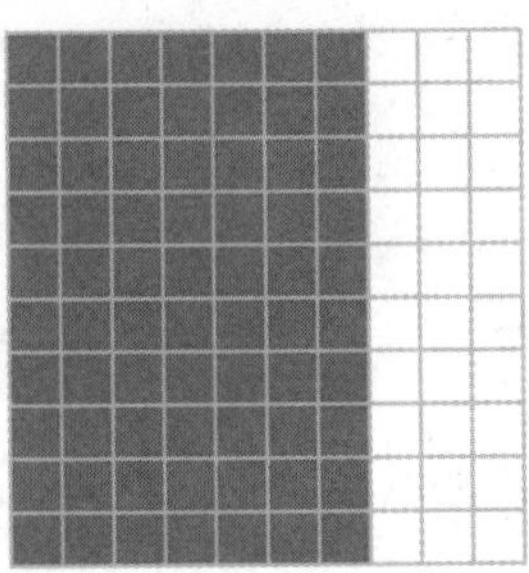

$\frac{7}{10} = \frac{70}{100} = 70\%$

You can use the % symbol to represent percent.

ANOTHER WAY Use number lines to represent the percent.

7 out of 10 is equivalent to 70 out of 100.

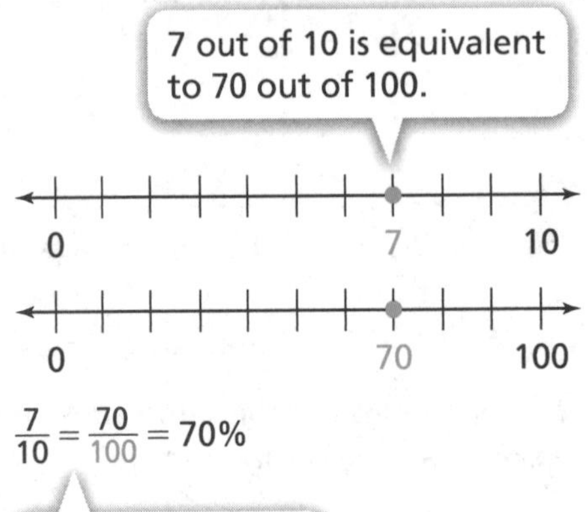

$\frac{7}{10} = \frac{70}{100} = 70\%$

Percent is always compared to 100.

ANOTHER WAY Use an equivalent fraction to find the percent.

Multiply both the numerator and the denominator by 10.

$\frac{7 \times 10}{10 \times 10} = \frac{70}{100}$

$\frac{70}{100} = 70\%$

70% of people prefer Bright White Toothpaste.

Try It!

Jane won 9 out of the 10 video games she played. What percent of the video games did Jane win?

Convince Me! When using an equivalent fraction to find a percent, why do you write 100 as the denominator?

EXAMPLE 2  Examine Percents and Wholes

Each line segment represents 100%, but the segments are not the same length. Use equivalent rates to find the percent, or part, of each line segment that points *A* and *B* represent.

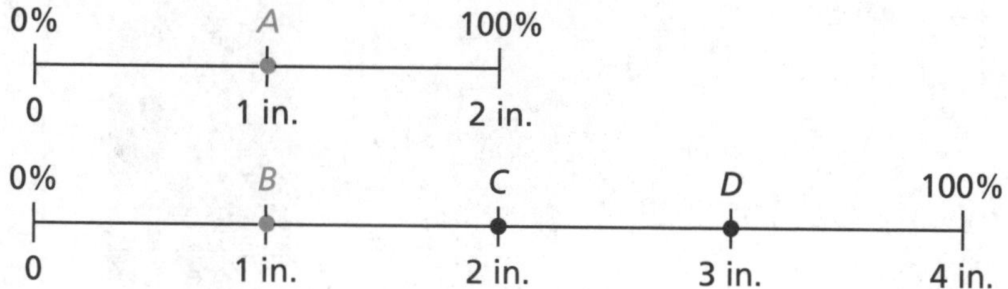

Point *A* is at $\frac{1}{2}$ of the line segment.

$\frac{1 \times 50}{2 \times 50} = \frac{50}{100} = 50\%$

2 × 50 = 100, so multiply the numerator and the denominator by 50.

Point $A = 50\%$

Point *B* is at $\frac{1}{4}$ of the line segment.

$\frac{1 \times 25}{4 \times 25} = \frac{25}{100} = 25\%$

4 × 25 = 100, so multiply the numerator and the denominator by 25.

Point $B = 25\%$

Try It!

Which point represents 50% on the second line segment? Explain.

EXAMPLE 3  Use Percents

You can use percent and mental math to find the length of a line segment.

A. If $\overline{CD}$ represents 10%, what is the length of a line segment that is 100%?

100% is 10 × 10%, so the length of the line segment is 10 × 4 inches, or 40 inches.

B. If $\overline{EF}$ represents 200%, what is the length of a line segment that is 100%?

E F

6 in.

100% is $\frac{1}{2}$ of 200%, so the length of the line segment is $\frac{1}{2}$ of 6 inches, or 3 inches.

Try It!

If $\overline{CD}$ represents 100%, what is the length of a line segment that is 25%? Explain.

KEY CONCEPT

A percent is a rate that compares a part to a whole. The second term in the rate is always 100. The whole is 100%.

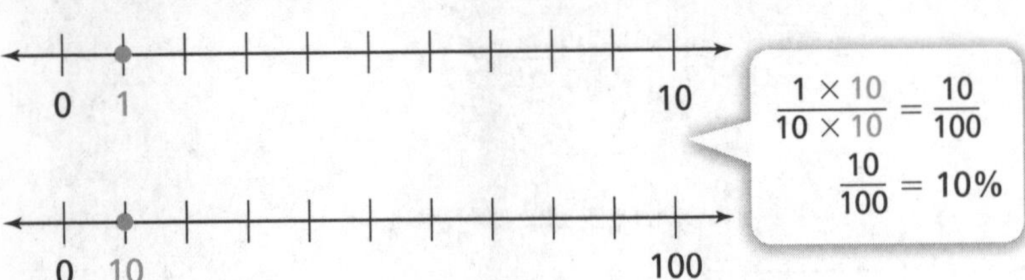

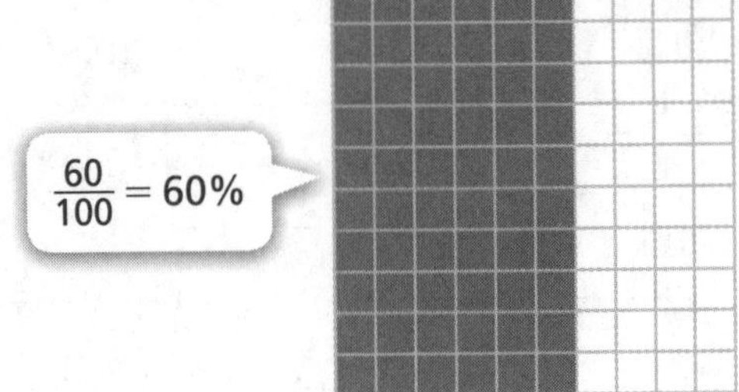

Do You Understand?

1. **Essential Question** How can you represent a rate with 100 as the whole?

2. When writing a percent as a fraction, what number do you write as the whole, or denominator?

3. Why are tenths, fifths, fourths, and halves easy to express as percents?

4. Why is the grid in Example 1 a good way to represent a percent?

5. **Look for Relationships** If $\overline{CD}$ in Example 3 represents 100%, is the length of a line segment that is 300% longer or shorter than 4 inches? Explain.

Do You Know How?

In 6 and 7, write the percent of each figure that is shaded.

6.

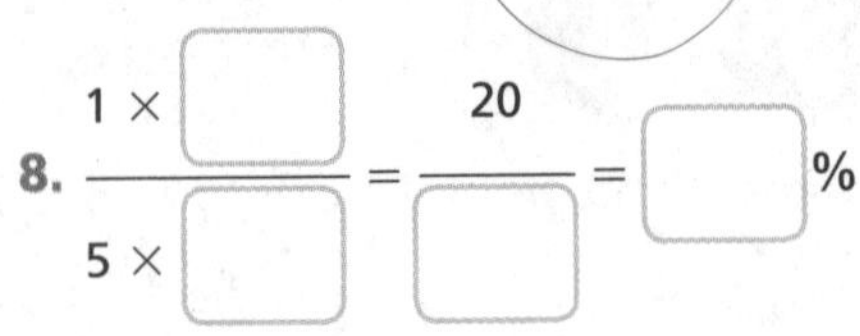

7.

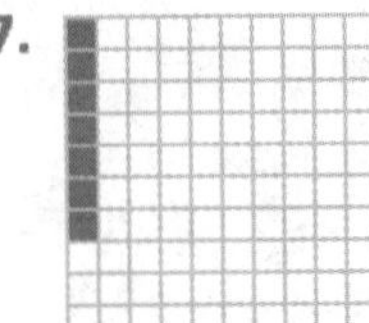

In 8–10, find the percent.

8. $\frac{1 \times \square}{5 \times \square} = \frac{20}{\square} = \square\%$

9. $\frac{3 \times \square}{10 \times \square} = \frac{30}{\square} = \square\%$

10. $\frac{11 \times \square}{20 \times \square} = \frac{55}{\square} = \square\%$

11. Find the percent of the line segment that point *D* represents in Example 2.

  PRACTICE  TUTORIAL

Name: ____________________

Practice & Problem Solving

Scan for Multimedia 

In 12 and 13, shade each model to represent the percent.

12. 14%

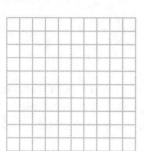

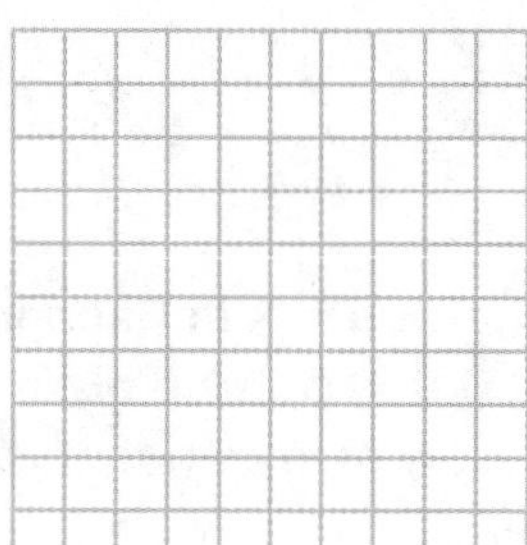

13. 20%

In **14** and **15**, use $\overline{AB}$.

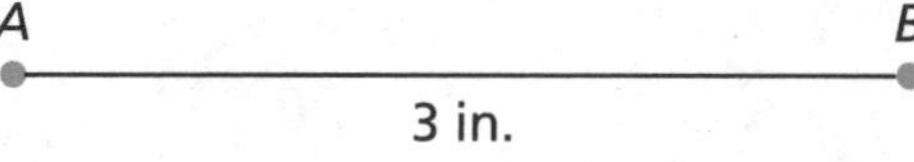

14. If $\overline{AB}$ represents 50%, what is the length of a line segment that is 100%?

15. If $\overline{AB}$ is 300%, what is the length of a line segment that is 100%?

16. Your friend shows you a coin collection. In it, $\frac{45}{50}$ of the coins are quarters. What percent of the coins are quarters?

17. Use Structure In a race, 19 out of 50 runners finished in fewer than 30 minutes. What percent of the runners finished in fewer than 30 minutes? Write an equivalent fraction to find the percent.

18. A basketball player made 63 out of 100 attempted free throws. What percent of free throws did the player make?

19. Harry kept a weather journal for September. The sun was shining on 4 out of every 5 days. On what percent of the days was the sun not shining?

In 20 and 21, use the line segment.

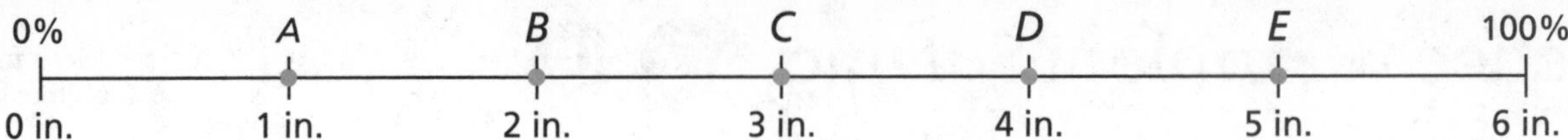

20. What percent of the line segment is 6 inches long?

21. What percent of the line segment does point *C* represent?

22. Critique Reasoning Kyle solved 18 of 24 puzzles in a puzzle book. He says that he can use an equivalent fraction to find the percent of puzzles in the book that he solved. How can he do that? What is the percent?

23. Reasoning Twenty of the students in Hannah's class, or 80% of the class, voted to have pizza for lunch every Wednesday. How many students are in Hannah's class?

24. According to a survey of workers, $\frac{2}{20}$ of the workers walk to work, $\frac{1}{20}$ bike, $\frac{4}{20}$ carpool, and $\frac{13}{20}$ drive alone. What percent of the workers walk or bike to work?

25. Higher Order Thinking From Monday through Friday, James works in the library on 2 days and in the cafeteria on another day. On Saturday and Sunday, James washes cars 50% of the days. How many days does James work in a week? What percent of the days from Monday through Friday does he work?

Assessment Practice

26. Select all the figures that are shaded to represent 20% of the whole. 6.RP.1.3c

☐ 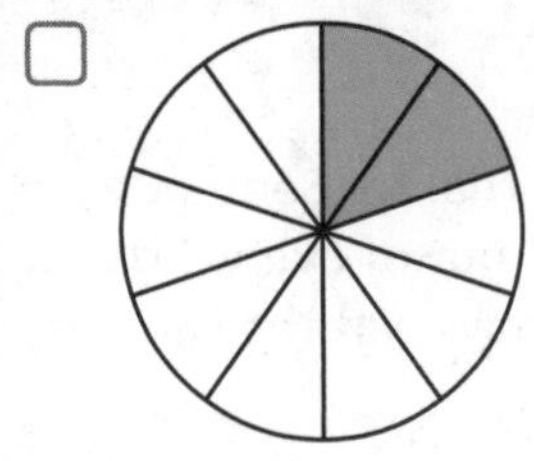

☐ 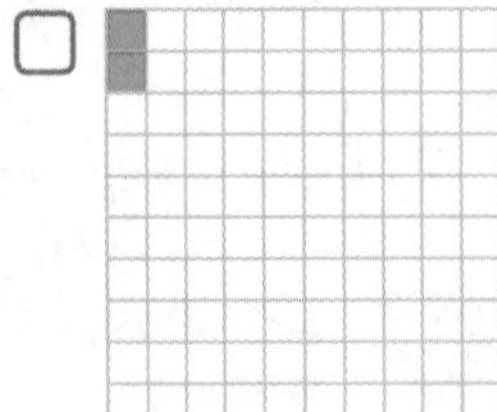

☐ 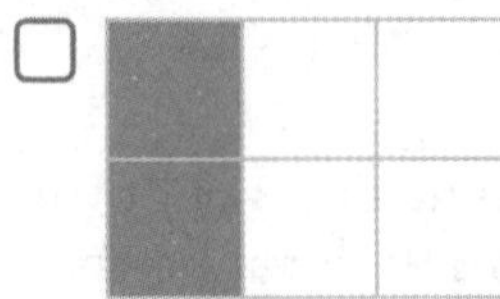

☐ 

☐ 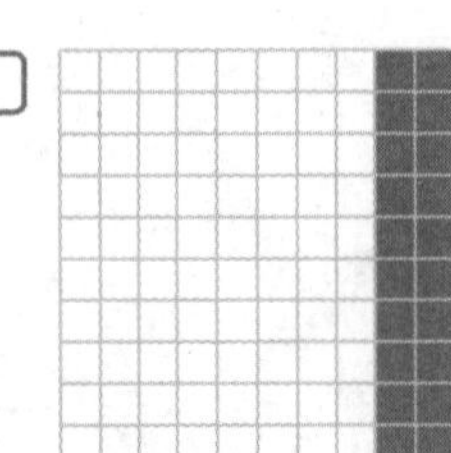

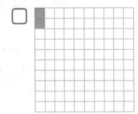

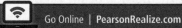

Solve & Discuss It!

The grid is shaded with blue, orange, and yellow. What part of the grid is shaded blue? What part is shaded orange? What part of the grid is shaded?

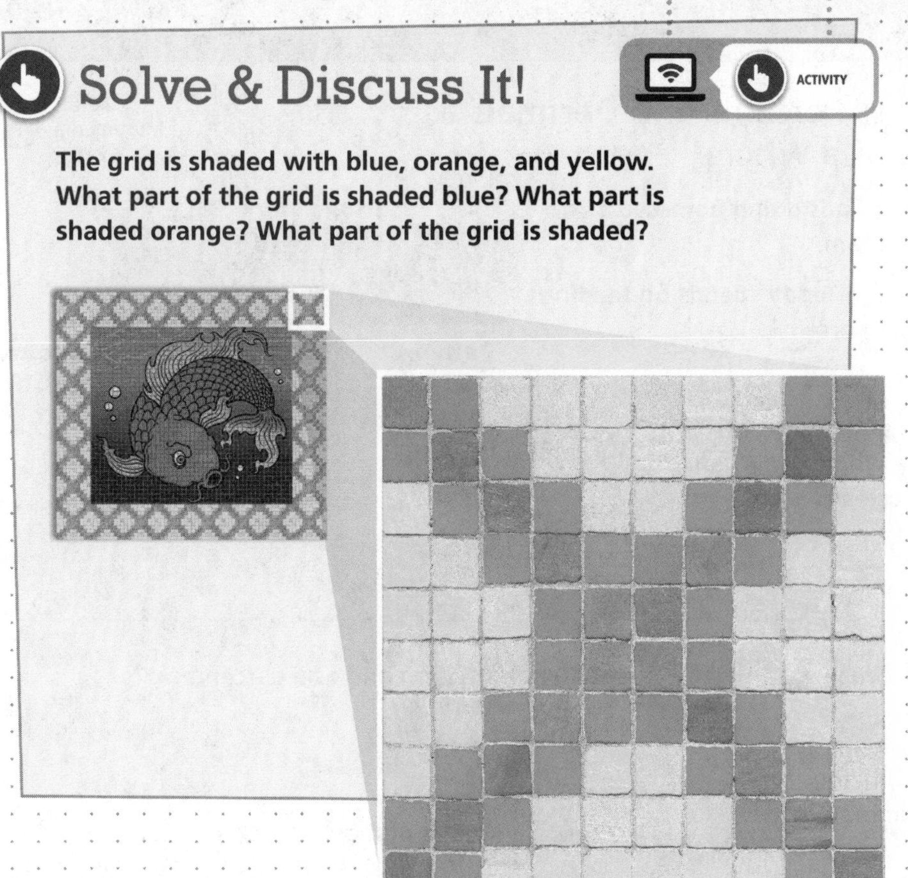

Lesson 8-2
Relate Fractions, Decimals, and Percents

Go Online | PearsonRealize.com

I can...
write equivalent values as fractions, decimals, or percents.

MAFS.6.RP.1.3c Find a percent of a quantity as a rate per 100 (e.g., 30% of a quantity means $\frac{30}{100}$ times the quantity); ...
MAFS.K12.MP.2.1, MP.3.1, MP.7.1, MP.8.1

Use Structure Look for patterns in the grid to help count parts that are shaded in blue and in orange.

Focus on math practices

Reasoning Write the part of the grid that is shaded yellow as a decimal and a percent. How are the decimal and the percent alike and how are they different?

? Essential Question How are fractions, decimals, and percents related?

EXAMPLE 1 Express Percents and Decimals as Parts of a Whole

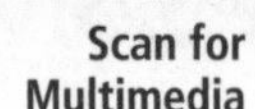

The portion of the time that Teddy spends doing homework for each subject is shown in the bar diagram.

How can you write the amount of time Teddy spends on reading or science as a fraction, decimal, and percent?

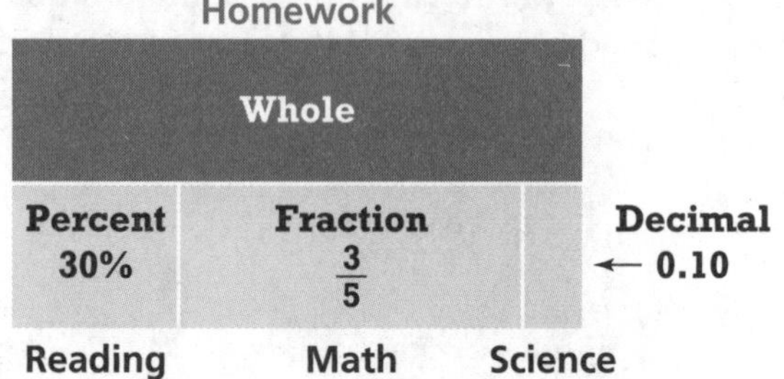

> **Reasoning** Fractions, decimals, and percents are three ways to show parts of a whole. How can you use reasoning to write quantities as a fraction, a decimal, or a percent?

Write 30% as a fraction and as a decimal.

$30\% = \frac{30}{100}$ or $\frac{3}{10}$ — Write the percent as a fraction with 100 as the denominator.

$\frac{30}{100} = 0.30$ — Write a fraction with a denominator of 10 or 100 as a decimal.

$\frac{3}{10} = 0.3$

30% can be written as $\frac{30}{100}$ or $\frac{3}{10}$ and 0.30 or 0.3.

Write 0.10 as a fraction and as a percent.

$0.10 = \frac{10}{100}$

$\frac{10}{100} = 10\%$ — The number compared to 100 is the percent.

$\frac{10 \div 10}{100 \div 10} = \frac{1}{10}$ — You can also write an equivalent fraction.

0.10 can be written as $\frac{10}{100}$ or $\frac{1}{10}$ and 10%.

Try It!

Ana spends 0.45 of her homework time reading. What is 0.45 as a percent? Explain.

Convince Me! What relationship do you see when comparing the equivalent fraction and percent?

EXAMPLE 2  Express Fractions as Parts of a Whole

Teddy spends $\frac{3}{5}$ of his homework time doing math problems. Write $\frac{3}{5}$ as a decimal and as a percent.

Homework

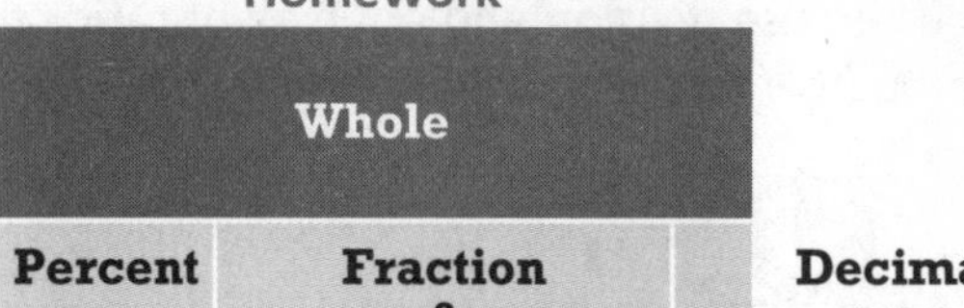

> **Look for Relationships** If the denominator of a fraction is not 100, how can you express the fraction as a decimal and as a percent?

Use division to find the decimal.

$\frac{3}{5} = 3 \div 5$

$$\begin{array}{r} 0.6 \\ 5\overline{)3.0} \\ -30 \\ \hline 0 \end{array}$$

Insert a decimal point and annex a zero to divide.

$\frac{3}{5}$ can be written as 0.6 or 0.60.

Use an equivalent rate to find the percent.

$$\frac{3}{5} = \frac{x}{100}$$

$$\frac{3 \times 20}{5 \times 20} = \frac{60}{100}$$

5 × 20 = 100, so multiply the numerator and the denominator by 20.

$$\frac{60}{100} = 60\%$$

$\frac{3}{5}$ can be written as 60%.

EXAMPLE 3  Use Division with Equivalent Rates to Express Fractions as Part of a Whole

Teddy's friend Jacob spends $\frac{5}{8}$ of his homework time doing math problems. Write $\frac{5}{8}$ as a decimal and as a percent.

Homework

Whole

$\frac{5}{8}$	$\frac{3}{8}$
Math	Science

Use division to find the decimal.

$\frac{5}{8} = 5 \div 8$

$$\begin{array}{r} 0.625 \\ 8\overline{)5.000} \\ -48 \\ \hline 20 \\ -16 \\ \hline 40 \\ -40 \\ \hline 0 \end{array}$$

Insert a decimal point and annex zeros to divide.

$\frac{5}{8}$ can be written as 0.625.

Use the decimal to find an equivalent rate.

$$0.625 = \frac{625}{1{,}000}$$

$$\frac{625 \div 10}{1{,}000 \div 10} = \frac{62.5}{100}$$

1,000 ÷ 10 = 100, so divide the numerator and the denominator by 10.

$$\frac{62.5}{100} = 62.5\%$$

$\frac{5}{8}$ can be written as 62.5%.

Try It!

Isabel spends $\frac{3}{8}$ of her homework time on reading. What is $\frac{3}{8}$ as a decimal and as a percent?

KEY CONCEPT

You can use division and equivalent ratios to express fractions, decimals, and percents in equivalent forms.

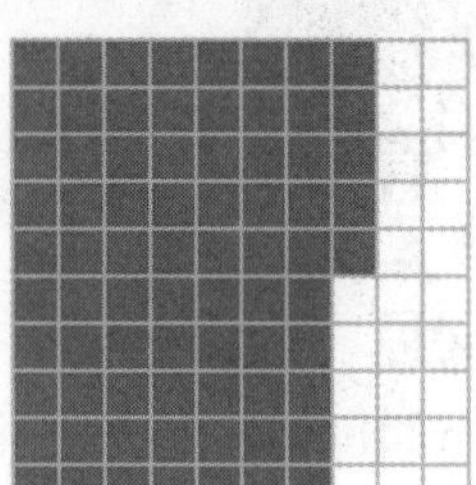

$0.75 = \frac{75}{100}$

$\frac{75}{100} = 75\%$

$0.75 = \frac{75}{100} = 75\%$

Whole

0.75

Do You Understand?

1. **Essential Question** How are fractions, decimals, and percents related?

2. Why do you use a denominator of 100 when you write a percent as a fraction?

3. **Look for Relationships** How do you use the digits in a hundredths decimal to write a percent?

4. How do you write a fraction with a denominator of 20 as a decimal?

Do You Know How?

In 5–7, write each number in equivalent forms using the two other forms of notation: fraction, decimal, or percent.

5. 27%

6. 0.91

7. $\frac{6}{100}$

8. Greek yogurt has 25% of the calcium that most people need in a day. What is 25% as a decimal?

25%
Daily
Calcium

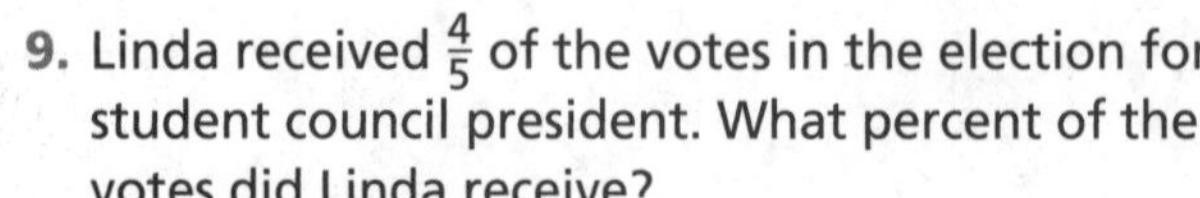

9. Linda received $\frac{4}{5}$ of the votes in the election for student council president. What percent of the votes did Linda receive?

Name: ____________________

Practice & Problem Solving

Scan for Multimedia

Leveled Practice In **10–15**, write each number in equivalent forms using the two other forms of notation: fraction, decimal, or percent.

10. 0.25

$0.25 = \frac{\square}{100} = \square\%$

$0.25 = \frac{\square \div 25}{100 \div \square} = \frac{\square}{4}$

11. $\frac{2}{2}$

$\frac{2}{2} = \frac{2 \times \square}{2 \times \square} = \frac{100}{100} = \square\%$

$\frac{2}{2} = 2 \div \square = \square.0$

12. 7%

$7\% = \frac{\square}{100}$

$7\% = \frac{\square}{100} = 0.\square$

13. 38%

14. $\frac{7}{8}$

15. 0.04

16. Devon answered 23 out of 25 problems on a math test correctly. What percent of the problems did Devon answer correctly?

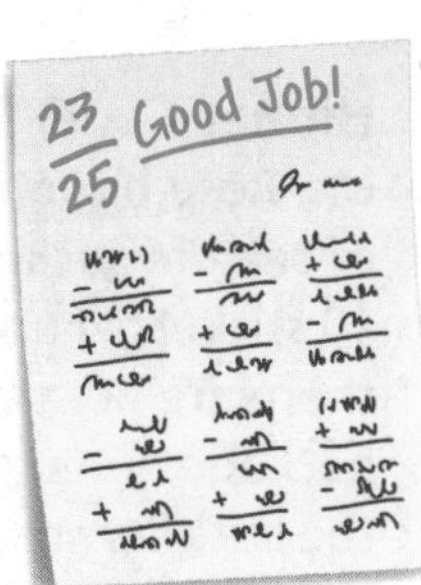

17. Reasoning How could you write $\frac{4}{8}$ as a percent without dividing?

In **18–21**, use the circle graph.

18. Many chemical elements can be found in Earth's atmosphere. What fraction of Earth's atmosphere is made up of nitrogen?

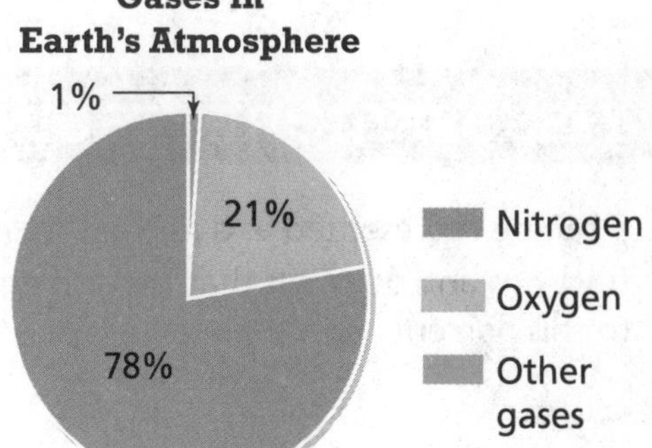

19. How much of Earth's atmosphere is made up of oxygen? Write the part as a decimal.

20. What percent of gases in Earth's atmosphere does the whole circle graph represent?

21. What fraction of the gases in Earth's atmosphere are gases other than nitrogen and oxygen?

22. **Look for Relationships** All T-shirts in a store are on sale as shown. Is this markdown greater than or less than a markdown of $\frac{1}{5}$ off the original price? Explain.

23. **Critique Reasoning** Enrollment at Jacksonville Middle School increased by 3% this year. Sofia says that the increase, written as a decimal, is 0.3. Is Sofia correct? Explain.

24. **Generalize** What are the attributes of fractions that are equivalent to 100%?

25. The cost of building a new library is 0.85 of the cost of remodeling the old library. What is the cost as a percent?

26. Nine out of every 20 people walking out of a movie theater say that they would recommend the movie to a friend. What percent of the people would recommend the movie to a friend?

27. **Higher Order Thinking** Ms. Rose bought a package of sea life stickers. Out of every 10 stickers, 4 are starfish. If there are 60 stickers in the package, what fraction of the stickers are starfish? What percent of the stickers in the package are starfish?

Assessment Practice

28. $\frac{3}{4}$ can be represented as a percent. Select all the fractions and decimals that are also equivalent to this percent. 6.RP.1.3c

- ☐ $\frac{51}{68}$
- ☐ 0.34
- ☐ $\frac{36}{50}$
- ☐ 0.75
- ☐ $\frac{39}{52}$

29. There are 110 sixth-grade students in a Florida middle school. 40% of the students enjoy playing video games on the weekends. Using the percent as a rate per 100, how many students enjoy playing video games? 6.RP.1.3c

☐

Lesson 8-3

Represent Percents Greater Than 100 or Less Than 1

Go Online | PearsonRealize.com

I can...
write percents that are greater than 100 or less than 1.

MAFS.6.RP.1.3c Find a percent of a quantity as a rate per 100 (e.g., 30% of a quantity means $\frac{30}{100}$ times the quantity); ...
MAFS.K12.MP.2.1, MP.3.1, MP.4.1, MP.7.1

Solve & Discuss It!

ACTIVITY

Marci, Bobby, and Max began their homework at the same time. Marci finished her homework in 60 minutes. Bobby finished his homework in 50% of the time it took Marci to finish. Max finished his homework in 150% of Marci's time. How long did each of them work?

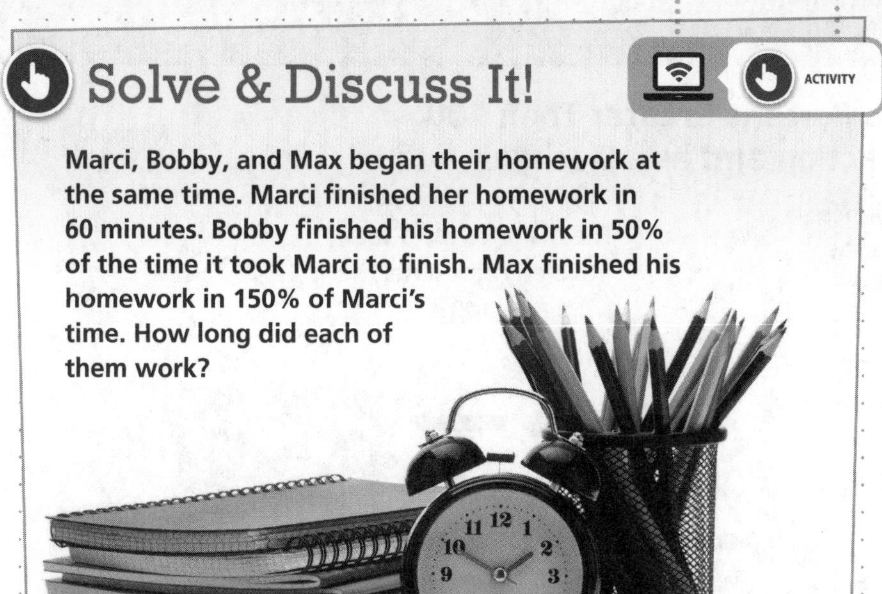

Model with Math How can you use a model to represent a part that is greater than a whole?

Focus on math practices

Reasoning Did Max spend more time or less time on his homework than Marci? Explain.

? Essential Question How can you write a percent greater than 100 or less than 1 as a fraction and as a decimal?

EXAMPLE 1  Write a Percent Greater Than 100 as a Fraction and as a Decimal

Scan for Multimedia 

Jan and Kim built model cars for a science project. Kim's car traveled 140% as far as Jan's car. How can you write 140% as a fraction and as a decimal?

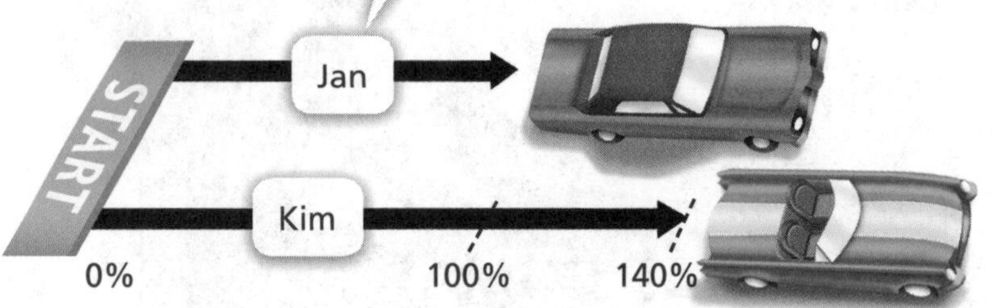

Write 140% as a fraction compared to 100.

$$140\% = \frac{140}{100}$$

Use division to write an equivalent fraction.

$$140\% = \frac{140 \div 20}{100 \div 20} = \frac{7}{5}$$

140% can be written as $\frac{140}{100}$ or $\frac{7}{5}$.

The fraction equivalent of a percent greater than 100 has a numerator greater than the denominator.

You can use reasoning or division to write 140% as a decimal.

Use reasoning.

$$140\% = \frac{140}{100}$$
$$= \frac{14}{10}$$
$$= 1.4$$

Use division.

$$\begin{array}{r} 1.4 \\ 100\overline{)140.0} \\ -100 \\ \hline 400 \\ -400 \\ \hline 0 \end{array}$$

Insert a decimal point and annex a zero to divide.

140% can be written as 1.4.

A decimal value greater than 1 will always be a percent greater than 100%.

Try It!

The area of a new movie theater is 225% of the area of the old theater. What is 225% as a fraction and as a decimal?

2.25

Convince Me! How would you write 1.75 as a percent? Give an example in which you would use a percent that is greater than 100.

175% = 1.75

EXAMPLE 2 Write a Fraction Percent Less Than 1 as a Fraction and as a Decimal

Write $\frac{1}{2}$% as a fraction and as a decimal.

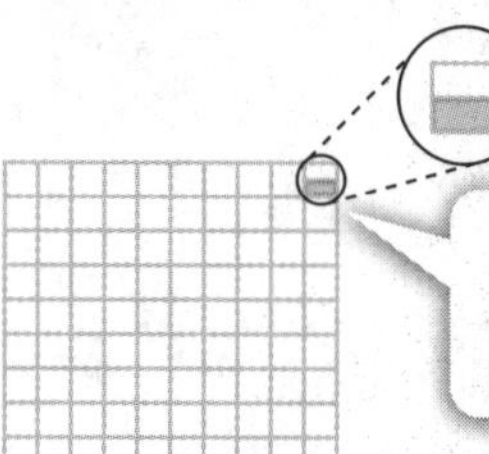

A percent less than 1 is less than $\frac{1}{100}$ of the whole.

Write $\frac{1}{2}$% as a fraction.

$$\frac{1}{2}\% = \frac{\frac{1}{2}}{100}$$

Percent means out of 100. Divide $\frac{1}{2}$ by 100.

$$= \frac{1}{2} \div 100$$

$$= \frac{1}{2} \times \frac{1}{100}$$

$$= \frac{1}{200}$$

$\frac{1}{2}$% can be written as $\frac{1}{200}$.

Write $\frac{1}{2}$% as a decimal.

$$\frac{1}{2}\% = 0.5\%$$

$$= \frac{0.5}{100}$$

$$= \frac{5}{1{,}000} = 0.005$$

$\frac{1}{2}$% can be written as 0.005.

EXAMPLE 3 Write a Decimal Percent Less Than 1 as a Fraction and as a Decimal

Write the percent of the solution that is water as a fraction and as a decimal.

0.9% of this solution is water.

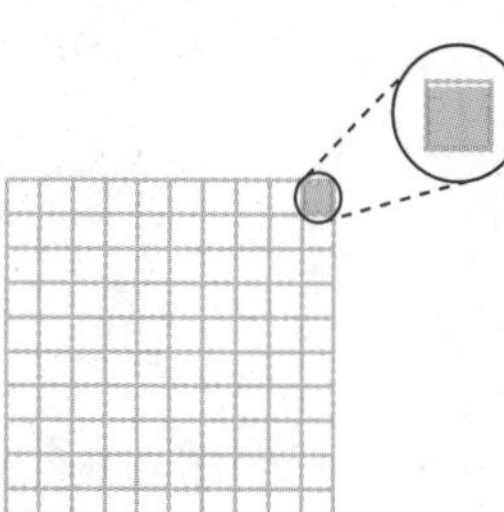

0.9% is less than 1%.

Write 0.9% as a fraction.

$$0.9\% = 0.9 \div 100$$

$$= \frac{0.9}{100}$$

$$= \frac{9}{1{,}000}$$

0.9% can be written as $\frac{9}{1{,}000}$.

Write 0.9% as a decimal.

$$0.9\% = 0.9 \div 100$$

$$\frac{0.9}{100} = \frac{9}{1{,}000}$$

$$= 0.009$$

0.9% can be written as 0.009.

Try It!

Write each percent as a fraction and as a decimal.

a. $\frac{2}{5}$%   **b.** 0.3%

KEY CONCEPT 

You can express percents greater than 100 or less than 1 in equivalent forms.

$275\% = \frac{275}{100}$

$\frac{275 \div 25}{100 \div 25} = \frac{11}{4}$

$275\% = \frac{11}{4} = 2.75$

$\frac{1}{5}\% = 0.2\%$

$\frac{0.2}{100} = \frac{2}{1{,}000}$ or $\frac{1}{500} = 0.002$

$\frac{1}{5}\% = \frac{1}{500} = 0.002$

Do You Understand?

1. **Essential Question** How can you write a percent greater than 100 or less than 1 as a fraction and as a decimal?

2. **Reasoning** Explain why $\frac{3}{4}$ is less than 100%.

3. **Reasoning** Why is the numerator greater than the denominator in a fraction that is equivalent to a percent greater than 100?

4. Explain the difference between $\frac{1}{2}$ and $\frac{1}{2}\%$.

Do You Know How?

In 5–7, write each percent as a fraction and as a decimal.

5. 150%

150% = 150/100 → 1.50

6. $\frac{3}{10}\%$

3/10 % = 30% → 0.3

7. 0.24%

0.24% = 24/100 = 24%

8. Kelly saved $\frac{4}{5}\%$ of her allowance. What is this percent expressed as a fraction and as a decimal?

fraction: 80/100 %
Decimal: 0.8%

9. Mrs. Sanchez sold her house for 250% of the amount she paid for it. What is this percent expressed as a fraction and as a decimal?

Fraction: 250/100 %
Decimal: 2.50 %

Name: ____________________

Practice & Problem Solving

Scan for Multimedia

Leveled Practice **In 10–15, write each percent as a fraction and as a decimal.**

10. $\frac{3}{5}\% = \frac{3}{5} \div \square$

$= \frac{3}{5} \times \frac{1}{\square}$

$= \frac{3}{\square} = \square$

11. $\frac{3}{4}\% = 0.\square\%$

$= \frac{\square}{100}$

$= \frac{\square}{10{,}000} = \square$

12. $0.1\% = 0.1 \div 100$

$= \frac{0.1}{\square} = \frac{1}{\square}$

$= \square$

13. $0.4\% = 0.4 \div 100$

$= \frac{0.4}{\square} = \frac{4}{\square}$

$= \square$

14. 322%

15. 210%

16. Reasoning Use the art at the right. How do you express the length of the *Queen Mary 2* as it compares to the height of the Washington Monument as a fraction and as a decimal?

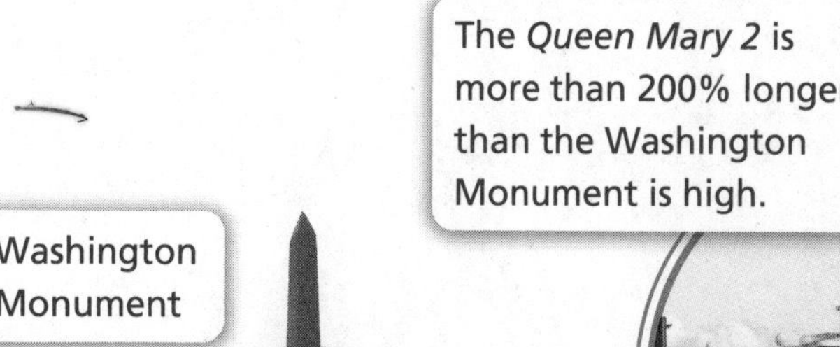

Washington Monument
The *Queen Mary 2* is more than 200% longer than the Washington Monument is high.

17. About $\frac{7}{10}\%$ of the passengers on a cruise ship swam in the ship's pool on the first day of the cruise. How would you express this number as a decimal and as a percent?

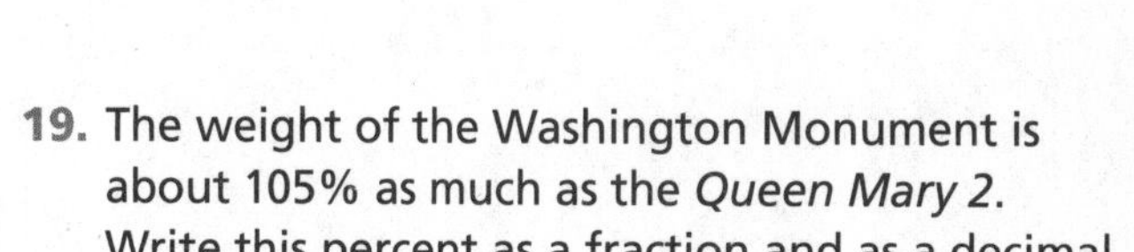

18. The fastest boat can reach speeds more than 710% as fast as the *Queen Mary 2*. How would you express this number as a fraction and as a decimal?

19. The weight of the Washington Monument is about 105% as much as the *Queen Mary 2*. Write this percent as a fraction and as a decimal.

20. Students set a goal for the number of cans to collect for the canned food drive. They reached 120% of their goal. What is 120% expressed as a fraction and as a decimal?

21. **Use Structure** Popcorn sales at a Saturday afternoon matinee were 108% of the sales at the 8:00 showing of the movie. Calvin expressed 108% as 10.8. Is Calvin correct? Explain.

22. **Construct Arguments** There are 350% more students enrolled in Spanish class than Latin class. How does expressing 350% as a decimal prove that more than 3 times as many students are enrolled in Spanish class as are enrolled in Latin class?

23. **Critique Reasoning** Free round-trip tickets to Orlando, Florida were given to 0.4% of the people staying at a hotel. Larry says that tickets were given to $\frac{4}{10}$ of the people at the hotel. What did Larry do wrong when he calculated 0.4% as a fraction? What is the correct fraction?

24. The unemployment rate decreased by $\frac{1}{10}\%$ in one month. Write $\frac{1}{10}\%$ as a fraction and as a decimal.

25. **Higher Order Thinking** A photo of a mosquito in a science book is magnified to 635% of the mosquito's actual size. If the mosquito is 16 millimeters long, what is the length of the mosquito in the picture?

? mm

Assessment Practice

26. At a Florida zoo, one adult female panther weighs 100 pounds. An adult male panther at the same zoo weighs 159% of the female panther's weight. What is the weight of the adult male panther? Show your work. 6.RP.1.3c

27. The results of a survey show that 0.32% of the people in the survey have never sent a text message. Select all the fractions and decimals that can be expressed as 0.32%. 6.RP.1.3c

- ☐ $\frac{32}{100}$
- ☐ $\frac{2}{625}$
- ☐ 0.0032
- ☐ $\frac{8}{2,500}$
- ☐ 0.032

Name: ______________________

MID-TOPIC CHECKPOINT

TOPIC 8

1. **Vocabulary** Explain how fractions, decimals, and percents are related. *Lesson 8-2* 6.RP.1.3c

2. Sarai is mixing a solution. She pours all the liquid from a full small beaker into a large beaker. The liquid fills the large beaker to 15% of its capacity. If the small beaker holds 300 mL, how much does the large beaker hold? *Lessons 8-1 and 8-3* 6.RP.1.3c

3. The Murphy family is on a road trip. On the first day, they traveled 30% of their total distance. On the second day, they traveled another $\frac{1}{4}$ of the total distance. What fraction of the total distance do they have left after the second day? What percent? *Lesson 8-2* 6.RP.1.3c

4. Complete the table. *Lessons 8-2 and 8-3* 6.RP.1.3c

Percent	Fraction	Decimal
70%		
		1.25
	$\frac{11}{20}$	
0.2%		

5. A basketball player made 17 out of 20 free throws at practice. What percent of the free throws did the player miss? *Lesson 8-1* 6.RP.1.3c

6. A section of rope 5 inches long represents 20% of the length of the entire rope. How long is the rope? *Lesson 8-1* 6.RP.1.3c

How well did you do on the mid-topic checkpoint? Fill in the stars. ☆☆☆

MID-TOPIC PERFORMANCE TASK

The students in Mr. Anderson's class conducted a survey of 1,000 people. They asked each person to name his or her favorite color. The results are shown in the table.

Color	Number
Blue	450
Red	300
Orange	50
Yellow	10
White	5

PART A

Complete the table to write each result as a fraction, a decimal, and a percent. 6.RP.1.3c

Color	Number	Fraction	Decimal	Percent
Blue	450			
Red	300			
Orange	50			
Yellow	10			
White	5			

PART B

Green was chosen by 18% of the people. Which number is equivalent to 18%? Select all that apply. 6.RP.1.3c

- ☐ $\frac{18}{1{,}000}$
- ☐ $\frac{18}{100}$
- ☐ 0.18
- ☐ 0.018
- ☐ $\frac{9}{5}$

PART C

Cecilia noticed that not all of the survey responses were recorded in the table. What percent of the responses were not recorded in the table? Explain. 6.RP.1.3c

Explore It!

Lesson 8-4
Estimate to Find Percent

Go Online | PearsonRealize.com

I can...
estimate the percent of a number using equivalent fractions, rounding, or compatible numbers.

MAFS.6.RP.1.3c Find a percent of a quantity as a rate per 100 (e.g., 30% of a quantity means $\frac{30}{100}$ times the quantity); ...
MAFS.K12.MP.1.1, MP.2.1, MP.7.1

Sarah wants to score 78% on her next test. She knows that the test will have 40 questions.

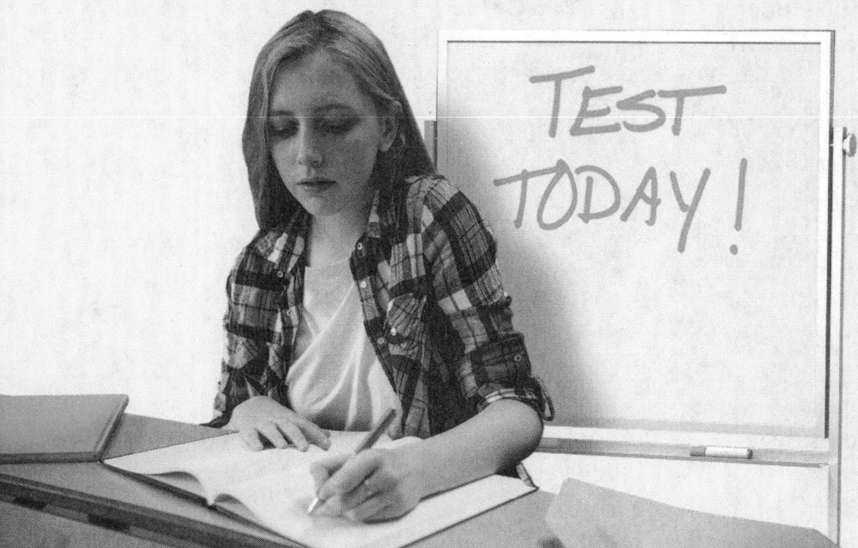

A. How can Sarah represent the situation to help her determine how many questions she needs to answer correctly?

1	2	3	4	5	6	7	8	9	10
11	12	13	14	15	16	17	18	19	20
21	22	23	24	25	26	27	28	29	30
31	32	33	34	35	36	37	38	39	40

B. How could you use the model to help solve the problem?

Focus on math practices

Use Structure On her last test, Sarah answered 82% of 60 questions correctly. About how many questions did Sarah answer correctly? Use estimation.

Essential Question How can you estimate to find the percent of a number?

EXAMPLE 1  Use Equivalent Fractions to Estimate

Scan for Multimedia 

This graph shows the eye colors among 500 students at a school. About how many students have brown eyes? About how many have blue eyes?

Use Structure How can you use what you know about percents and their fraction equivalents to estimate?

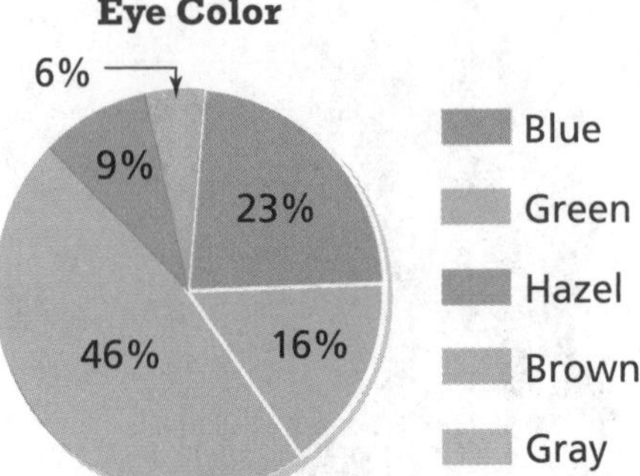

According to the graph, 46% of the students have brown eyes.

Estimate 46% of 500.

$46\% \approx 50\%$ and $50\% = \frac{1}{2}$

So, 46% of 500 is about $\frac{1}{2}$ of 500.

$$\frac{1}{2} \times 500 = 250$$

About 250 students have brown eyes.

According to the graph, 23% of the students have blue eyes.

Estimate 23% of 500.

$23\% \approx 25\%$ and $25\% = \frac{1}{4}$

So, 23% of 500 is about $\frac{1}{4}$ of 500.

$$\frac{1}{4} \times 500 = 125$$

About 125 students have blue eyes.

Try It!

Suppose the graph shows eye colors among 120 students in sixth grade. About how many sixth grade students would have green eyes? Explain how you can use estimation to find the answer.

Convince Me! How does understanding fraction equivalents help you estimate how many students in sixth grade have green eyes?

EXAMPLE 2  Use Rounding and Compatible Numbers to Estimate

  ACTIVITY  ASSESS

Use the results of the survey shown to the right. About how many high school students plan to get a summer job?

Reasoning You can use rounding or compatible numbers to find a reasonable estimate of how many students plan to get a summer job.

53% of 94 students surveyed plan to get a summer job.

ONE WAY Use rounding to estimate 53% of 94.

53% of 94 — 94 rounds to 90.

$53\% \approx 50\%$ and $50\% = \frac{1}{2}$

$\frac{1}{2} \times 90 = 45$

About 45 students plan to get a summer job.

ANOTHER WAY Use compatible numbers to estimate 53% of 94.

53% of 94 — 100 is a compatible number for 94.

$53\% \approx 50\%$ and $50\% = \frac{1}{2}$

$\frac{1}{2} \times 100 = 50$

About 50 students plan to get a summer job.

Both 45 and 50 are good estimates for the number of students who plan to get a summer job.

Try It!

Students in another survey were asked whether they plan to attend summer camp. Out of the 56 students in the survey, 44% said yes. Use rounding and compatible numbers to estimate how many students plan to attend summer camp.

Use rounding to estimate 44% of 56.

$44\% \approx 40\%$ and $40\% = \frac{4}{\square}$ or $\frac{2}{\square}$

56 rounds to $\square$.

$\frac{2}{\square} \times \square = \square$

About $\square$ students plan to attend summer camp.

Use compatible numbers to estimate 44% of 56.

$44\% \approx 40\%$ and $40\% = \frac{4}{\square}$ or $\frac{2}{\square}$

$\square$ is a compatible number for 56.

$\frac{2}{\square} \times \square = \square$

About $\square$ students plan to attend summer camp.

KEY CONCEPT 

Fraction equivalents, rounding, or compatible numbers can be used to estimate the percent of a number.

$8\% \approx 10\%$ and $10\% = \frac{1}{10}$

8% of 300,000 is about 30,000. $\frac{1}{10} \times 300{,}000 = 30{,}000$

$27\% \approx 25\%$ and $25\% = \frac{1}{4}$

300 is a compatible number for 297.

27% of 297 is about 75. $\frac{1}{4} \times 300 = 75$

Do You Understand?

1. **Essential Question** How can you estimate to find the percent of a number?

2. Is there more than one fraction you could use to estimate 27% of 200? Explain.

3. What compatible number could you use to estimate 75% of 35? Why is this number compatible with 75%?

4. **Use Structure** Out of 195 students, 9% have hazel eyes. How can you estimate the number of students with hazel eyes?

Do You Know How?

In 5–8, estimate the percent of each number.

5. 47% of 77

$47\% \approx$ [50] $77 \approx$ [80]

[50] of [80] = [40]

$\frac{5}{10} \times \frac{8}{10} = \frac{40}{100}$

6. 18% of 48

$18\% \approx$ [20] $48 \approx$ [50]

[20] of [50] = [10]

$\frac{2}{10} \times \frac{5}{10} = \frac{10}{100}$

7. 73% of 800

73 = 70 × 80 = 560

$\frac{7}{10} = \frac{80}{10}$ = 27

8. 31% of 94

31 = 30 94 = 90

$\frac{3}{10} \times \frac{9}{10} = 27$

9. Tara sent party invitations to 98 people. Eighty-two percent of the people said they will come to the party. About how many people said they will come to the party? Explain. about 80

98 = 100 82 = 80 people

$\frac{10}{10} \times \frac{8}{10} = \frac{80}{100}$

Name: ____________________

Practice & Problem Solving

Scan for Multimedia

Leveled Practice In 10–15, estimate the percent of each number.

10. 74% of 63

74% ≈ ☐ 63 ≈ ☐

☐ of ☐ = ☐

11. 8% of 576

8% ≈ ☐ 576 ≈ ☐

☐ of ☐ = ☐

12. 34% of 55

13. 27% of 284

14. 65% of 89

15. 4% of 802

16. There are about 320 million residents in the United States. If 38% of them live in the South, estimate how many live in other areas of the United States.

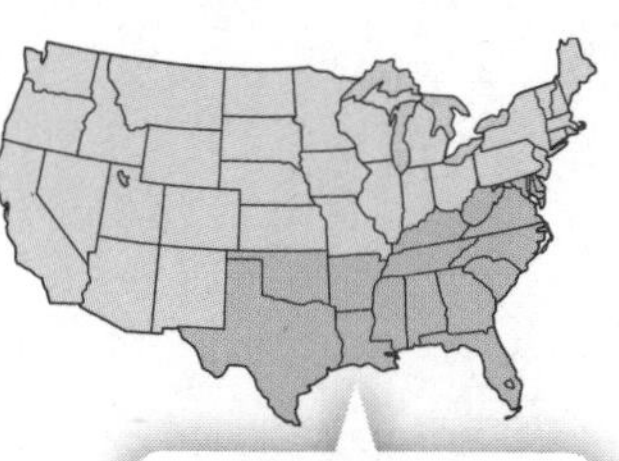

38% of the U.S. population lives in this region.

17. Lisa and Bill made 60 magnets for a craft fair. They sold 55% of the magnets. Lisa says that they sold about 30 magnets. Bill says that they sold about 36 magnets. Could they both be correct? Explain.

18. Make Sense and Persevere Roland has 180 coins in his collection. Approximately 67% of the coins are quarters. About how much money does Roland have in quarters? Explain.

19. Out of 9,799 whistles that a company manufactured, some were rejected for shipment to stores because they did not pass the quality control standards of the company. Estimate the number of whistles that did not pass.

19% of the whistles were rejected.

20. There are 8,249 people registered to vote in the town of Mayfield. About how many people voted in the election? Explain.

The
Mayfield Report
Search
Friday, 8 December 2015 11:30 AM
Home | Daily News | Sports | Business | Politics | Entertainment | Technology & Science
ELECTION NEWS:
Voter Turnout
Reaches 74%!
VOTE
HERE

21. **Higher Order Thinking** Lea spent 25% of *x* hours at her part-time job. What is *x* if 25% of *x* is about 30 hours? Explain how you estimated and which property of equality you used to find *x*.

22. **Reasoning** Vanessa scored 78% on a test with 120 questions. What benchmark fraction would you use to estimate the number of questions that Vanessa answered correctly? Explain.

23. Jason has saved 41% of what he needs to buy a skateboard. About how much has Jason saved? Explain.

Assessment Practice

24. There were 240 shoppers at an electronics store on opening day. The specials that day allowed 25% of shoppers to receive a free set of earbuds and 20% of shoppers to receive $10 off their first purchase. 6.RP.1.3c

PART A

Use an equivalent fraction to determine how many shoppers received a free set of earbuds. Show your work.

PART B

Use an equivalent fraction to determine how many shoppers received $10 off their first purchase. Show your work.

Lesson 8-5
Find the Percent of a Number

Go Online | PearsonRealize.com

I can...
solve problems involving percents.

MAFS.6.RP.1.3c Find a percent of a quantity as a rate per 100 (e.g., 30% of a quantity means $\frac{30}{100}$ times the quantity); ...
MAFS.K12.MP.1.1, MP.4.1, MP.5.1, MP.6.1, MP.8.1

Solve & Discuss It!

ACTIVITY

Lauren bought a jacket that was on sale for 60% off. She paid 40% of the original price of $75. How much did Lauren pay for the jacket?

Model with Math
How can you use a model to represent problems involving percents?

Focus on math practices

Generalize When finding the percent of a number, how can you tell whether your answer is reasonable? Will the answer be greater than or less than the original amount? Explain.

EXAMPLE 1  Estimate and Find Percent

Scan for Multimedia 

The fourth, fifth, and sixth graders at Great Oaks School are taking a field trip. Of the 575 students attending the field trip, how many are sixth graders?

Make Sense and Persevere The percents in the circle graph sum to 100%, which represents 575 total students, or the whole.

Percent of Students in Each Grade Attending the Field Trip

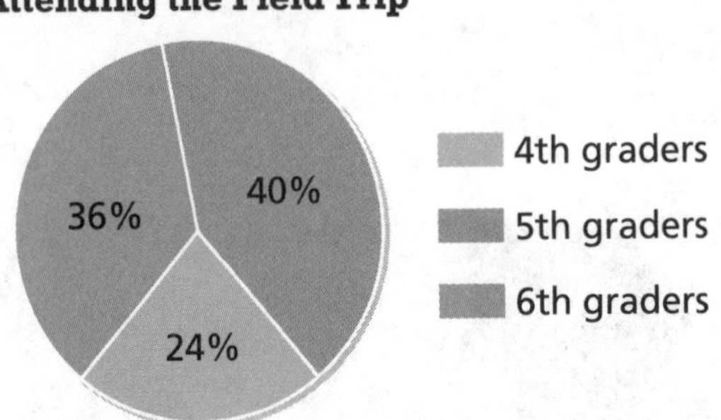

Use a double number line diagram and benchmark fraction equivalents to estimate 36% of 575.

$36\% \approx 33\frac{1}{3}\% = \frac{1}{3}$ and $575 \approx 600$

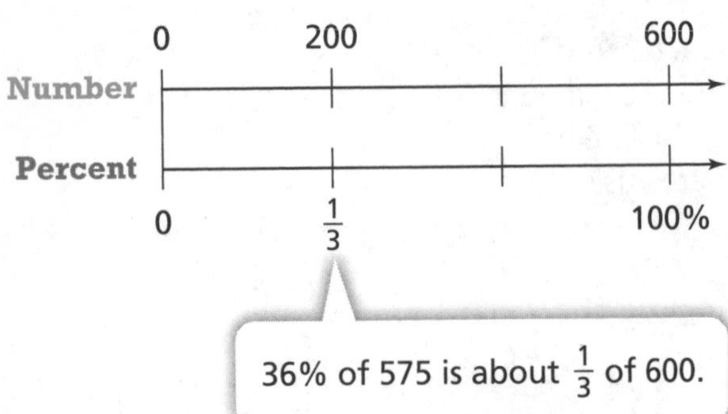

About 200 sixth graders are attending.

Use the decimal form of a percent to find 36% of 575.

The decimal form of 36% is 0.36.

$0.36 \times 575 = 207$

207 is close to 200. The answer is reasonable.

There are 207 sixth graders attending the field trip.

Try It!

Suppose 68% of the students attending the field trip were boys. How can you use the double number line diagram above to find the number of boys and to check whether your answer is reasonable?

Convince Me! In finding the percent of a number, when might you want to use the fraction form of the percent instead of the decimal form?

  ACTIVITY  ASSESS

EXAMPLE 2  Find the Part

D'wayne plans to wallpaper 72.5% of a 60-square-foot wall. How many square feet of the wall does D'wayne plan to wallpaper? Find 72.5% of 60.

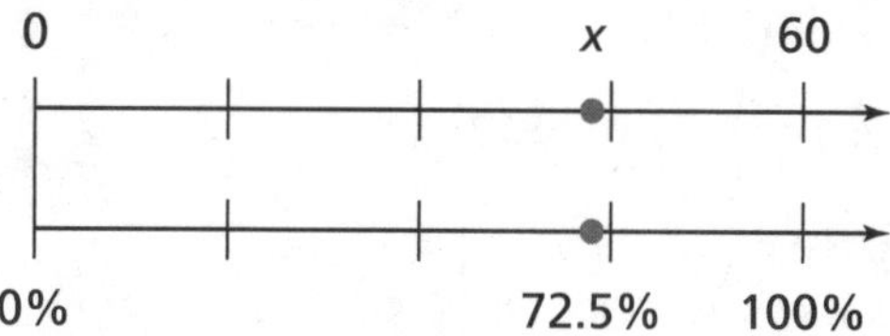

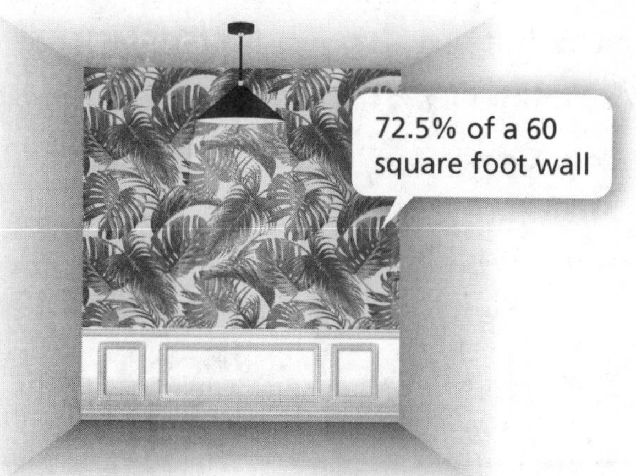

> **Model with Math** You can use a double number line diagram to help write an equation to find the part in a percent problem.

Write an equation.

$x = 0.725 \cdot 60$ — *x* represents 72.5% of 60. Multiply 72.5% by 60 to find *x*.

$x = 43.5$

So, 43.5 is 72.5% of 60.

D'wayne plans to wallpaper 43.5 square feet.

Try It!

What is 0.8% of 35?

EXAMPLE 3  Find the Percent

What percent of 92 is 11.5?

Write an equation.

$p \cdot 92 = 11.5$ — *p* represents the percent value 11.5 is of 92. Divide 11.5 by 92 to find *p*.

$92p = 11.5$

$\frac{92p}{92} = \frac{11.5}{92}$

$p = 0.125$ or 12.5%

So, 11.5 is 12.5% of 92.

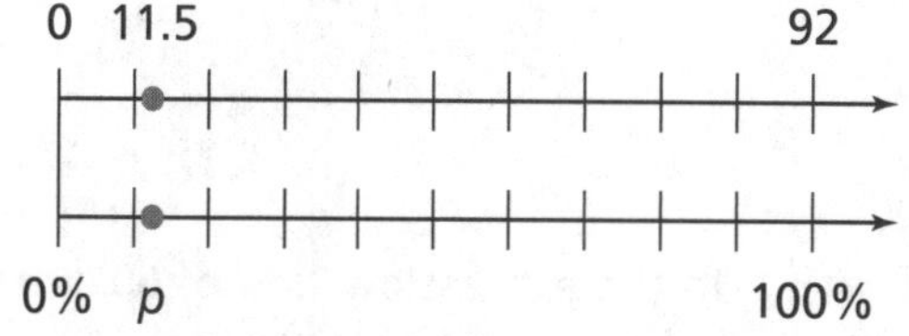

> **Model with Math** You can use a double number line diagram to help write an equation to find the percent of a number.

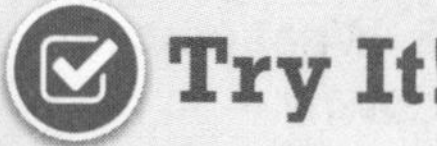

Try It!

What percent of 120 is 72?

KEY CONCEPT 

Percent equations have a part, a whole, and a percent. You can use the equation to solve for the part, the whole, or the percent.

Find the Part:

What is 12% of 6.75?

$x = 0.12 \cdot 6.75$
$x = 0.81$

12% of 6.75 is 0.81.

Find the Percent:

What percent of 6.75 is 0.81?

$p \cdot 6.75 = 0.81$
$6.75p = 0.81$
$\frac{6.75p}{6.75} = \frac{0.81}{6.75}$
$p = 0.12$ or 12%

12% of 6.75 is 0.81.

Do You Understand?

1. Essential Question How can you find percents?

2. Describe the equation you use to find the unknown part in a percent problem.

3. Describe the equation you use to find the percent value in a percent problem.

4. **Be Precise** In the expression 34% of 60, what operation does the word "of" mean?

5. **Use Appropriate Tools** How can you use a calculator to find what percent of 180 is 108?

Do You Know How?

In 6 and 7, find the part.

6. What is 26% of 50?

7. What is 2.1% of 60?

In 8 and 9, find the percent.

8. What percent of 315 is 126?

9. What percent of 120 is 28.8?

10. An electronics company has 450 employees. The company plans to increase its staff by 30%. How many new employees will the company hire?

11. The original price of a computer game is $45. The price is marked down by $18. What percent of the original price is the markdown?

Name: ______________________________

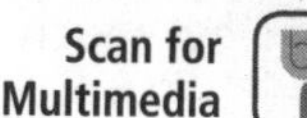

Practice & Problem Solving

Scan for Multimedia

Leveled Practice **In 12–17, find each part or percent.**

12. What is 5% of 210?

$x = \square \times 210$

$x = \square$

13. What is 8.2% of 500?

$x = \square \times 500$

$x = \square$

14. What percent of 32 is 5.6?

$p \cdot 32 = \square$

$32p = \square$

$\frac{32p}{32} = \frac{\square}{32}$

$p = \square = \square\%$

15. What is 35% of 10?

16. What percent of 75 is 33?

17. What is 2.25% of 24?

18. The meal tax at a restaurant is 5.5%. What is the meal tax on a dinner that costs $24?

Dinner $24.00
MEAL TAX, 5.5%
TOTAL
Thank You • Please Come Again

19. An electronics store donated a percentage of every sale to charity. The total sales were $7,150, of which the store donated $429. What percent of $7,150 was donated to charity?

In 20–22, use the circle graph.

There are 180 cars in a parking lot. The colors of the cars are represented in the circle graph.

20. How many blue cars are there?

21. How many red cars are there?

Cars in Parking Lot

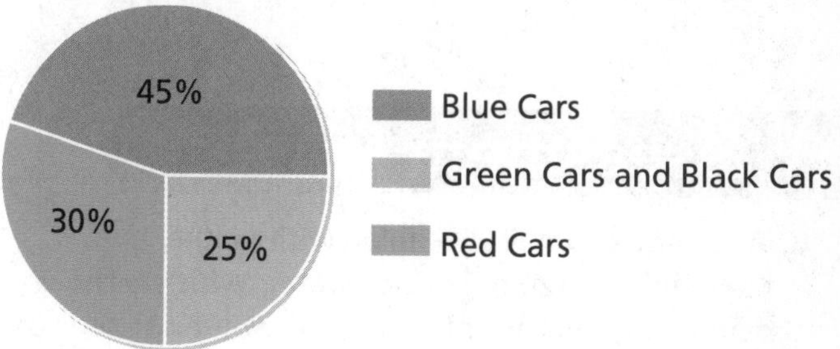

22. Reasoning There are 27 more green cars than black cars in the parking lot. What percentage of the cars in the parking lot are green? What percent are black?

23. The bank contains pennies, nickels, dimes, and quarters. There are 4 more nickels than pennies. How much money does the bank contain?

Of the 50 coins, 10% are pennies and 42% are dimes.

24. **Model with Math** How can you use the double number line diagram to find what percent of 450 is 270?

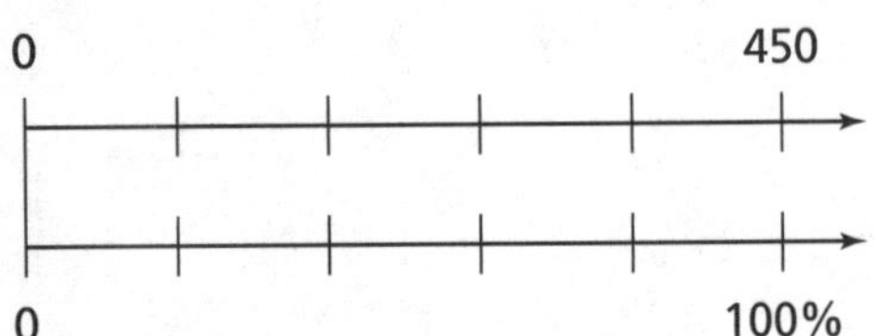

25. **Make Sense and Persevere** A movie complex is showing the same movie in three theaters. In theater A, 112 of the 160 seats are filled. In theater B, 84 seats are filled and 56 seats are empty. In theater C, 63 of the 180 seats are empty. Which theater has the greatest percent of its seats filled?

26. **Higher Order Thinking** Thomas has an album that holds 600 baseball cards. Each page of the album holds 6 cards. If 45% of the album is empty, how many pages are filled with baseball cards?

27. **Be Precise** Miguel collected aluminum cans for recycling. He collected a total of 150 cans. How many of the cans Miguel collected were not soda cans?

58% of the cans collected were soda cans.

Assessment Practice

28. Ava's aquarium is 95% filled with water. The tank holds 1,120 gallons of water. Which is the remaining number of gallons of water needed to fill the aquarium to the top? 6.RP.1.3c

Ⓐ 1,120 gallons

Ⓑ 1,010 gallons

Ⓒ 101 gallons

Ⓓ 56 gallons

29. Students set a goal of collecting 900 cans for the canned food drive. The number of cans they have collected so far is 82% of their goal. How many more cans do the students need to collect to reach their goal? 6.RP.1.3c

Ⓐ 162 cans

Ⓑ 180 cans

Ⓒ 720 cans

Ⓓ 738 cans

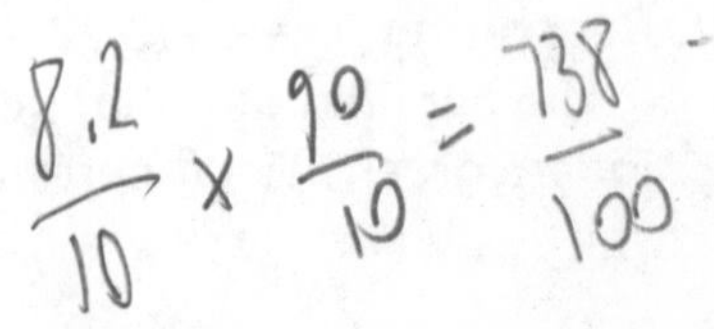

A school soccer team won 80% of its matches. The team won 40 matches. How many matches did the soccer team play?

Look for Relationships
How can you use a diagram to analyze the relationship between the quantities?

Lesson 8-6
Find the Whole Given a Part and the Percent

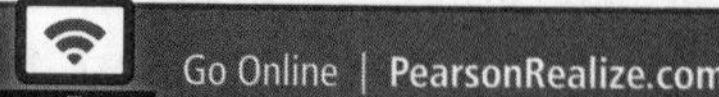

I can...
find the whole amount when given a part and the percent.

MAFS.6.RP.1.3c ... solve problems involving finding the whole, given a part and the percent.
MAFS.K12.MP.1.1, MP.2.1, MP.4.1, MP.6.1, MP.7.1

Focus on math practices

Model with Math Write an equation to find the total number of matches played by the soccer team. Let m represent the total number of matches.

Essential Question How can you find the whole in a percent problem?

EXAMPLE 1  Find the Whole in a Percent Problem

Bree scored 90% on her math test. Out of the total possible points on the test, her score was 135 points. How many points were possible on the test?

Model with Math How can you draw pictures and write equations to find the total possible points?

ONE WAY Use a double number line diagram to find the total possible points.

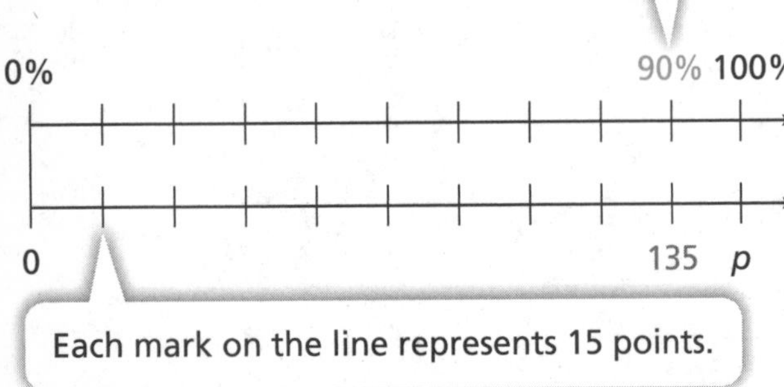

Add to find the total possible points, p.

$$135 + 15 = 150$$

There were 150 total possible points on the test.

ANOTHER WAY Use an equation to find the total possible points.

90% of *what number* is 135?

Let p = the total number of possible points.

$$90\% \cdot p = 135$$

$$90\% = \frac{90}{100} = 0.90$$

Write 90% as a decimal.

Solve the equation.

$$0.90p = 135$$

$$p = 135 \div 0.90$$

$$p = 150$$

There were 150 total possible points on the test.

Try It!

Bree took another math test and scored 152 points, which was 95% of the total possible points on the test. What was the total number of possible points?

Convince Me! How could you use a double number line diagram to check your answer?

EXAMPLE 2  Find the Whole When the Percent Is Greater Than 100

  ACTIVITY  ASSESS

The students in one classroom sold tickets to the talent show. They sold 200% of the amount of tickets that they sold last year. How many tickets did the students sell last year? Find the number of which 200% is 40.

One classroom sold a total of 40 tickets.

ONE WAY Use a double number line diagram.

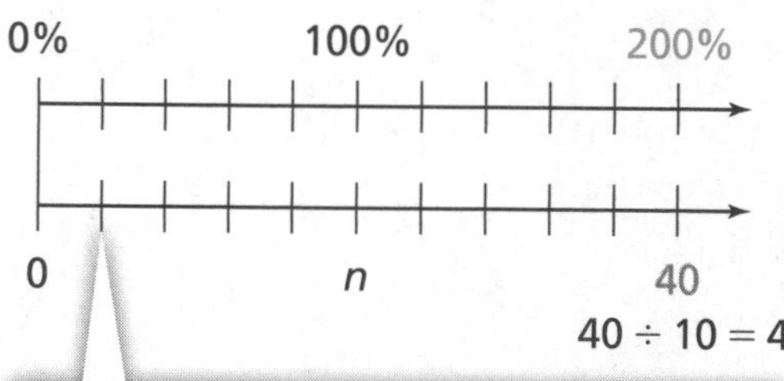

40 ÷ 10 = 4

Each mark represents an increase of 4.

So, 100% is 20.

200% of 20 is 40.

The students sold 20 tickets last year.

ANOTHER WAY Write and solve an equation.

$$200\% \cdot n = 40$$

$$2n = 40$$

$$\frac{2n}{2} = \frac{40}{2}$$

$$n = 20$$

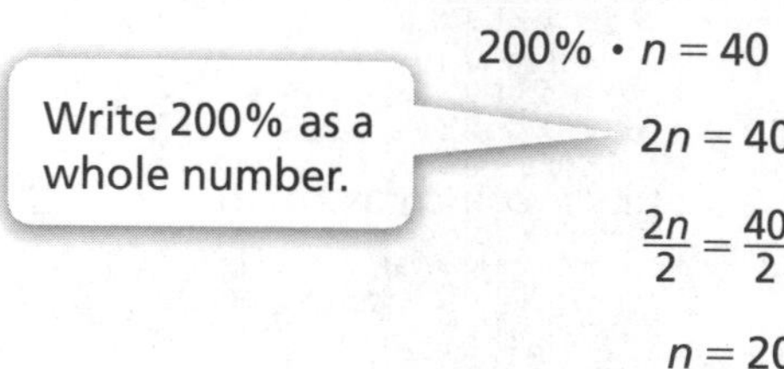

Write 200% as a whole number.

200% of 20 is 40.

200% is the same as 2 times 100%.

The students sold 20 tickets last year.

EXAMPLE 3  Find the Whole When the Percent Is a Decimal

62.5% of what number is 30?

ONE WAY Use a double number line diagram.

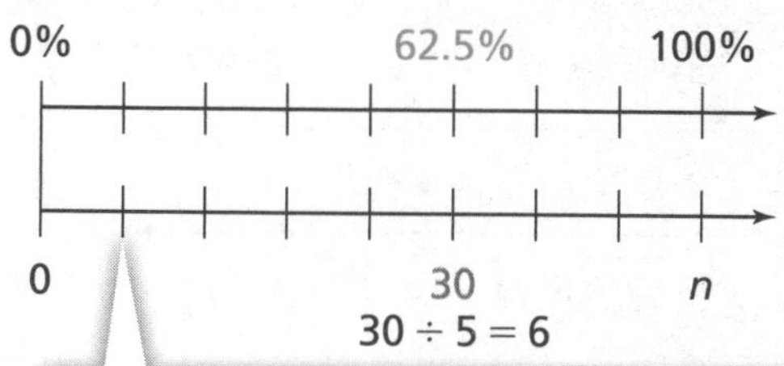

30 ÷ 5 = 6

Each mark represents an increase of 6.

62.5% of 48 is 30.

ANOTHER WAY Write and solve an equation.

$$62.5\% \cdot n = 30$$

$$0.625n = 30$$

$$\frac{0.625n}{0.625} = \frac{30}{0.625}$$

$$n = 48$$

62.5% of 48 is 30.

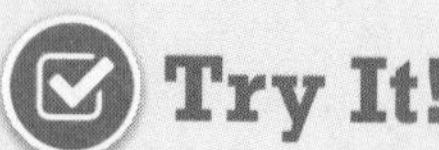

Try It!

a. 300% of what number is 180?

b. 0.3% of what number is 24?

You can use a double number line diagram or an equation to find the whole when the percent and a part are known.

Use a diagram.

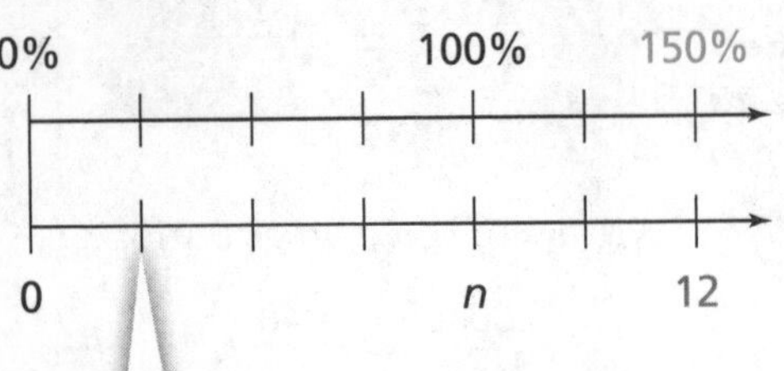

Each mark represents an increase of 2.

150% of 8 is 12.

Use an equation.

Let n = the whole.

$$150\% \cdot n = 12$$

$$1.5n = 12$$

$$\frac{1.5n}{1.5} = \frac{12}{1.5}$$

$$n = 8$$

150% of 8 is 12.

Do You Understand?

1. **Essential Question** How can you find the whole in a percent problem?

2. When you write an equation for a problem such as *300% of what number is 180*, what do you use to represent the phrase 'what number'?

what
300% of 180 is

3. When you find the whole in a percent problem in which the percent is greater than 100%, is the whole less than or greater than the part?

less

4. **Be Precise** Tony participated in 6 races, or 10% of the events. Do the 6 races represent the part, the percent, or the whole? Tell what the others represent.

6 is the whole
10% is the percent

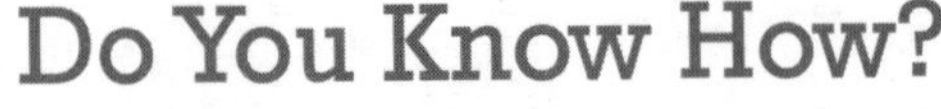

Do You Know How?

5. 40% of what number is 80?

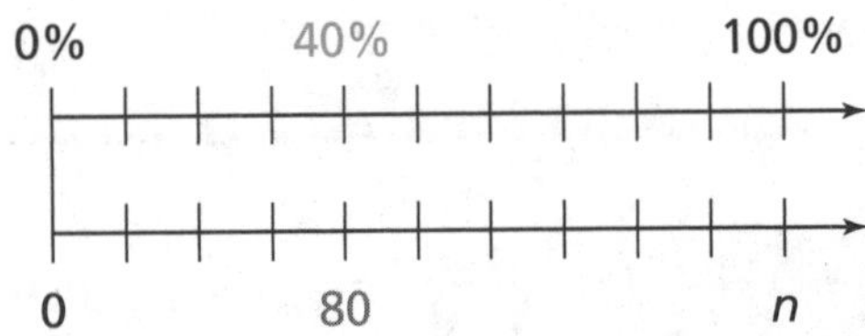

6. 300% of what number is 90?

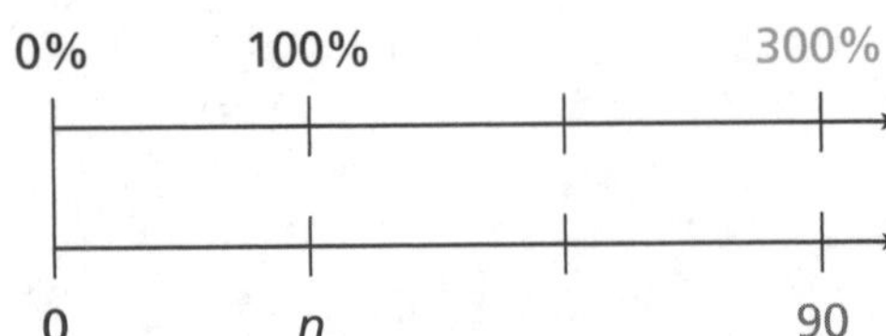

7. 70% of what number is 112?

8. 35% of what number is 28?

9. 7.5% of what number is 15?

Name: ______________________________

Practice & Problem Solving

Scan for Multimedia

Leveled Practice **In 10–15, find each whole.**

10. 35% of what number is 91?

$35\% \cdot a = 91$

$0.35a = \square$

$\frac{0.35a}{\square} = \frac{\square}{\square}$

$a = \square$

35% of ☐ is 91.

11. 125% of what number is 45?

$125\% \cdot n = 45$

$1.25n = \square$

$\frac{1.25n}{\square} = \frac{\square}{\square}$

$n = \square$

125% of ☐ is 45.

12. 87.5% of what number is 49?

$87.5\% \cdot y = 49$

$\square y = 49$

$\frac{\square y}{\square} = \frac{49}{\square}$

$y = \square$

87.5% of ☐ is 49.

13. 700% of what number is 1,540?

14. 0.7% of what number is 35?

15. 56% of what number is 14?

In 16–18, use the list of state taxes.

16. Reasoning Otis had a salad for \$4.50, a sandwich for \$6.25, and a drink at his favorite restaurant. The tax for the entire meal was \$0.54. What was the price of the drink?

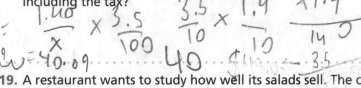

STATE TAXES	
Sales tax:	3.5%
Income tax:	5%
Meal tax:	4.5%

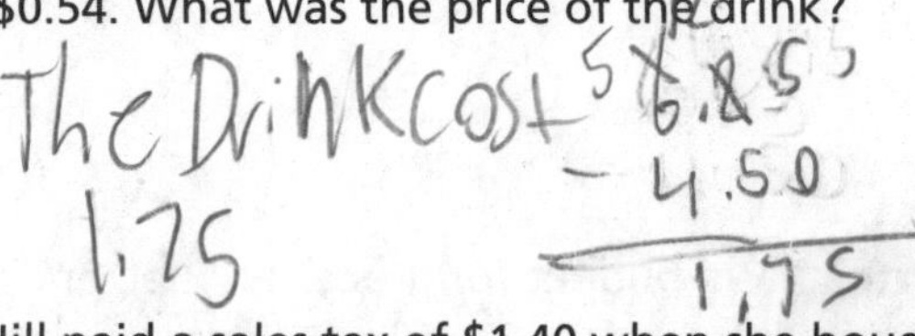

17. Jill paid a sales tax of \$1.40 when she bought a vest. What was the price of the vest not including the tax?

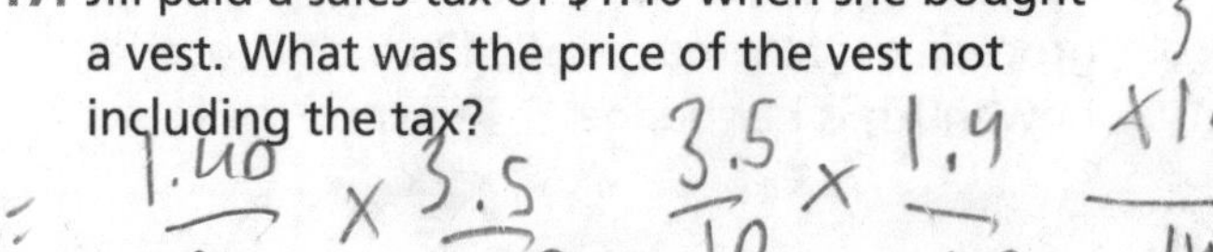

18. Rachel paid \$46 in tax for the money she earned as a camp counselor. How much money did Rachel earn?

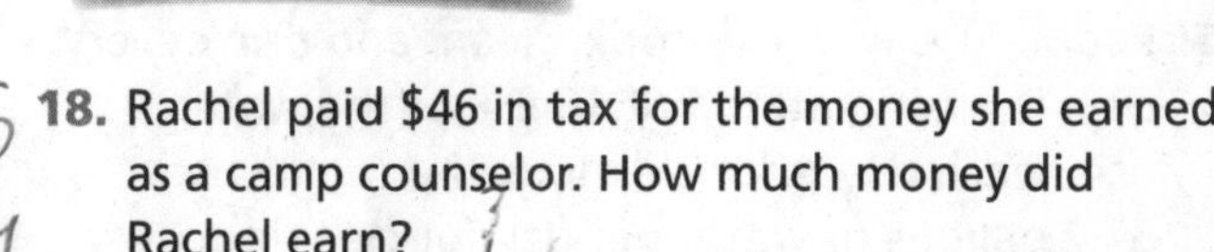

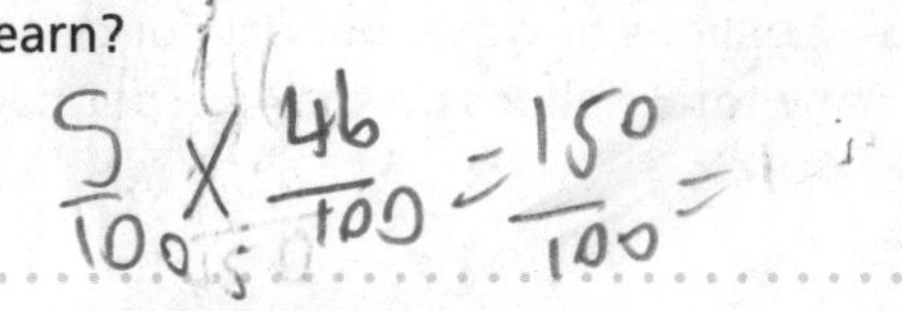

19. A restaurant wants to study how well its salads sell. The circle graph shows the sales of salads during the past few days. If 5 of the salads sold were Caesar salads, how many total salads did the restaurant sell?

Salads Sold

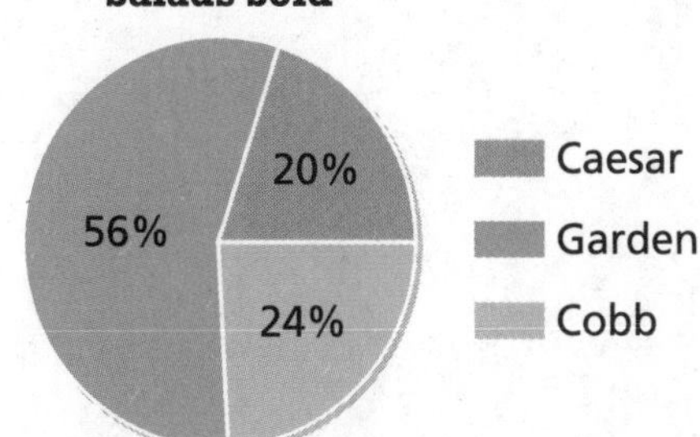

20. **Make Sense and Persevere** Sydney completed 60% of the math problems assigned for homework. She has 4 more problems to finish. How many math problems were assigned for homework?

21. **Reasoning** Carrie gave her hair stylist a \$4.20 tip. The tip was 15% of the cost of the haircut. Write an equation to find h, the cost of the haircut.

22. **Use Structure** Solve each of the number sentences and describe the pattern.

80% of what number is 80?
60% of what number is 60?
127% of what number is 127?

23. **Higher Order Thinking** An hour before show time, only 105 people have arrived for a concert. According to ticket sales, 95% of the people have yet to arrive. How many tickets were sold for the concert? Explain.

24. Nineteen students named lacrosse as their favorite sport. Explain how to use the circle graph to find the total number of students surveyed.

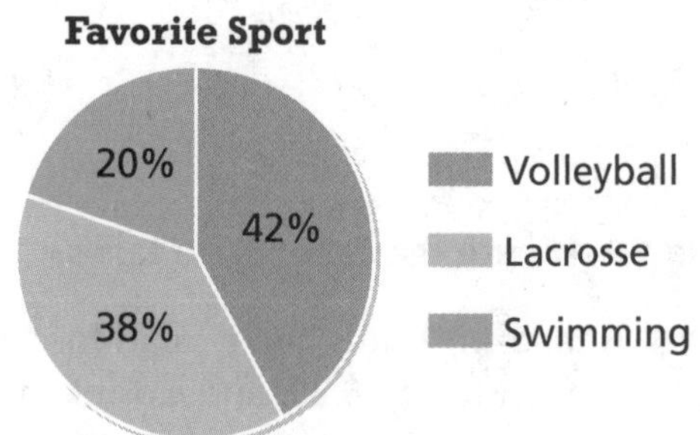

Assessment Practice

25. People use water to cook, clean, and drink every day. It is estimated that 16.8% of the water used each day is for cleaning. If a family uses 67.2 gallons of water per day for cleaning, how many total gallons do they use per day? Explain. 6.RP.1.3c

26. Martha has a budget for groceries, fuel, and utilities. She spent 20% of her budget on groceries. If Martha spent \$42.00 on groceries, how much is her budget? 6.RP.1.3c

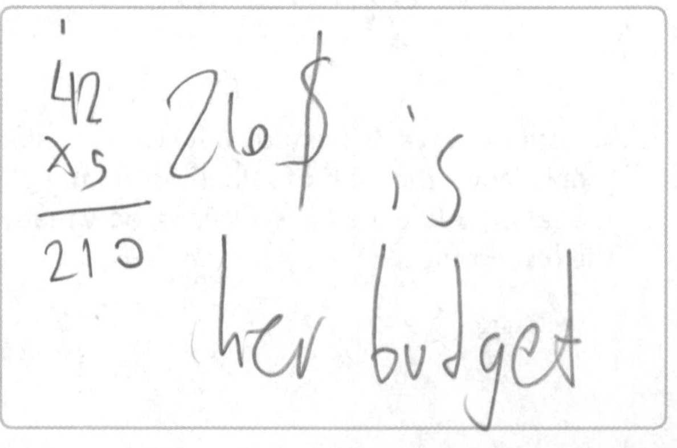

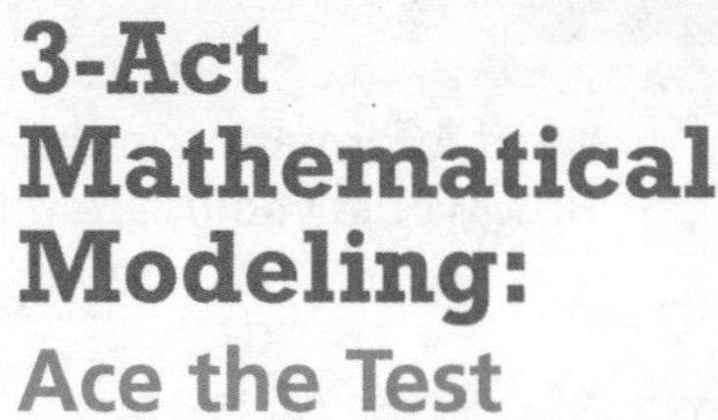

3-Act Mathematical Modeling: Ace the Test

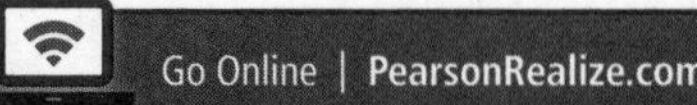

MAFS.K12.MP.4.1 Model with mathematics. Also MP.1.1, MP.2.1, MP.3.1, MP.5.1, MP.6.1, MP.7.1, MP.8.1

MAFS.6.RP.1.3c Find a percent of a quantity as a rate per 100 (e.g., 30% of a quantity means $\frac{30}{100}$ times the quantity); solve problems involving finding the whole, given a part and the percent. Also 6.RP.1.1

ACT 1

1. After watching the video, what is the first question that comes to mind?

2. Write the Main Question you will answer.

3. Predict an answer to this Main Question.

4. Construct Arguments Explain how you arrived at your prediction.

ACT 2

5. What information in this situation would be helpful to know? How would you use that information?

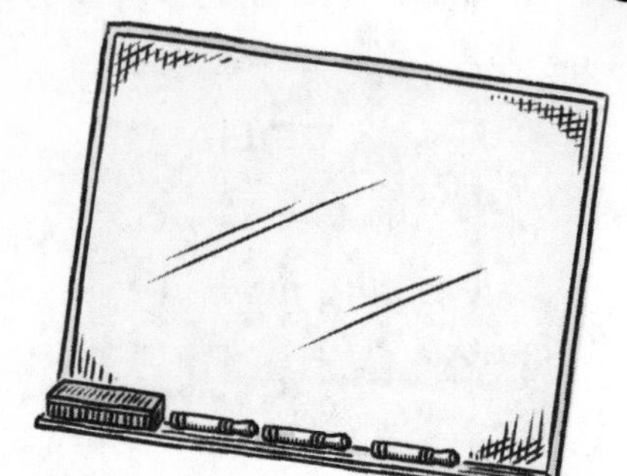

6. **Use Appropriate Tools** What tools can you use to get the information you need? Record the information as you find it.

7. **Model with Math** Represent the situation using the mathematical content, concepts, and skills from this topic. Use your representation to answer the Main Question.

8. What is your answer to the Main Question? Does it differ from your prediction? Explain.

ACT 3

9. Write the answer you saw in the video.

10. **Reasoning** Does your answer match the answer in the video? If not, what are some reasons that would explain the difference?

11. **Make Sense and Persevere** Would you change your model now that you know the answer? Explain.

ACT 3 Extension

Reflect

12. **Model with Math** Explain how you used a mathematical model to represent the situation. How did the model help you answer the Main Question?

13. **Be Precise** Why are percents more useful in this situation than the number of correct answers?

SEQUEL

14. **Reasoning** Suppose each test has 3 additional questions, and she gets 2 of them correct. How will that affect the answer?

? Topic Essential Question

What is the meaning of percent? How can percent be estimated and found?

Vocabulary Review

Complete each definition with a vocabulary word.

Vocabulary	compatible numbers	fraction	percent	ratio

1. A ratio of a quantity to 100 is a ______________.
2. A ______________ compares two numbers or the number of items in two groups.
3. ______________ are numbers that are easier to compute mentally.

Draw a line to match each *fraction*, *decimal*, or *percent* in Column A to the equivalent value in Column B.

	Column A	Column B
4.	$\frac{40}{50}$	$1\frac{3}{4}$
5.	13%	$1\frac{11}{20}$
6.	1.75	0.13
7.	155%	80%

Use Vocabulary in Writing

Out of 230 students surveyed, 11% chose gymnastics as their favorite sport. Explain how you can estimate the number of students who chose gymnastics. Use vocabulary words in your explanation.

Concept and Skills Review

LESSON 8-1 Understand Percent

Quick Review

A percent is a rate that compares a part to 100. The word *percent* means "of a hundred."

Example

Write the percent represented by the shaded part of the grid.

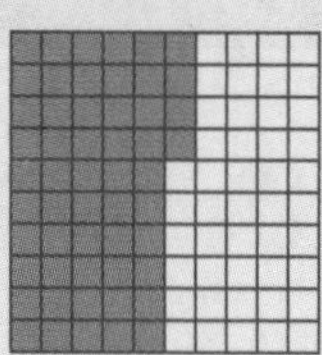

$\frac{54}{100}$ parts shaded = 54%

Practice

In 1 and 2, write the percent of each figure that is shaded.

1. 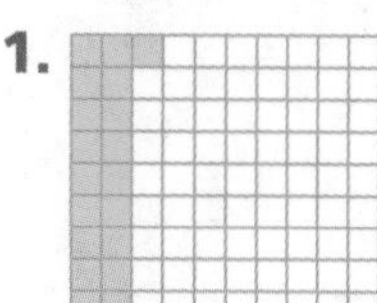

2. 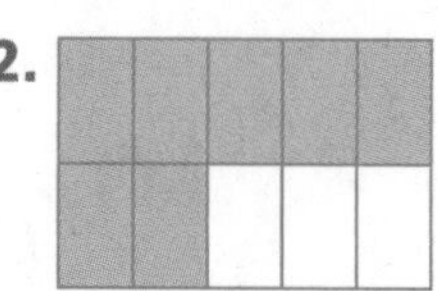

In 3 and 4, write each ratio as a percent.

3. 14 losses in 50 games

4. $\frac{4}{5}$ of the students ride a bus.

5. If $\overline{AB}$ represents 25%, what is the length of a line segment that is 100%?

A ———— B
5 ft

LESSON 8-2 Relate Fractions, Decimals, and Percents

Quick Review

Fractions, decimals, and percents are three ways to show parts of a whole. You can write a percent as a fraction with 100 as the denominator. Then you can write that fraction as a decimal.

Example

Write 35% as a fraction and a decimal.

$35\% = \frac{35}{100}$ or $\frac{7}{20}$

$\frac{35}{100} = 0.35$

Practice

In 1–6, write each number using the two other forms of notation: fraction, decimal, or percent.

1. 0.16

2. $\frac{63}{100}$

3. 27%

4. $\frac{7}{8}$

5. 0.55

6. 7%

7. One piece of wheat bread contains 2 g of fiber, or 8% of the amount of fiber that most people need in a day. What is 8% as a decimal and as a fraction?

LESSON 8-3 Represent Percents Greater Than 100 or Less Than 1

Quick Review

Percents less than 1% are less than $\frac{1}{100}$, and percents greater than 100% are more than one whole. You can express percents greater than 100 or less than 1 in equivalent forms.

Example

Write 221% as a fraction and as a decimal.

Fraction: $\frac{221}{100}$

Decimal: $\frac{221}{100} = 221 \div 100 = 2.21$

Write $\frac{1}{4}$% as a fraction and as a decimal.

Fraction: $\frac{1}{4}\% = \frac{1}{4} \div 100$

$= \frac{1}{4} \times \frac{1}{100} = \frac{1}{400}$

Decimal: $\frac{1}{4}\% = 0.25\%$

$= \frac{0.25}{100}$

$= \frac{25}{10,000}$

$= 0.0025$

Practice

In 1–6, write each percent as a fraction and as a decimal.

1. 140%

2. $\frac{7}{10}$%

3. 375%

4. 0.33%

5. 0.5%

6. 250%

7. The radius of the planet Saturn is 945% of the radius of Earth. What is 945% expressed as a fraction and as a decimal?

LESSON 8-4 Estimate to Find Percent

Quick Review

Fraction equivalents, rounding, or compatible numbers can be used to estimate the percent of a number.

Example

Estimate 24% of 83.

24% ≈ 25% and 25% = $\frac{1}{4}$

83 rounds to 80.

$\frac{1}{4} \times 80 = 20$

24% of 83 is about 20.

Practice

In 1–6, estimate the percent of each number.

1. 22% of 96

2. 38% of 58

3. 9% of 89

4. 76% of 41

5. 48% of 71

6. 27% of 62

7. Joanna wants to buy a backpack that costs $37.98. The sales tax rate is 8.75%. Estimate the amount of sales tax that Joanna will pay.

LESSON 8-5 Find the Percent of a Number

Quick Review

Percent equations have a percent value, a whole, and a part.

Example

What is 16% of 73.5?

Let x = the unknown part.

$x = 0.16 \cdot 73.5$ — Write 16% as a decimal.

$x = 11.76$

16% of 73.5 is 11.76.

What percent of 22 is 9.35?

Let p = the percent value.

$p \cdot 22 = 9.35$

$22p = 9.35$

$\frac{22p}{22} = \frac{9.35}{22}$

$p = 0.425 = 42.5\%$

42.5% of 22 is 9.35.

Practice

Find each part or percent.

1. 9% of 124

2. What percent of 20 is 3?

3. 24% of 35

4. What percent of 110 is 71.5?

5. 43% of 82

6. What percent of 30 is 24?

7. On Tuesday, 620 students attended a middle school. A survey showed that 341 students brought lunch to school that day. What percent of the students brought their lunches?

LESSON 8-6 Find the Whole Given a Part and the Percent

Quick Review

You can use an equation or a double number line diagram to find the whole when given the part and the percent.

Example

80% of what number is 96?

Let n = the whole. Write an equation, rename the percent as a decimal, and solve for n.

$80\% \cdot n = 96$

$0.8n = 96$

$\frac{0.8n}{0.8} = \frac{96}{0.8}$

$n = 120$

80% of 120 is 96.

Practice

Find each whole.

1. 140% of what number is 308?

2. 62% of what number is 186?

3. 80% of what number is 120?

4. 40% of what number is 10?

5. Desmond paid 8.5% sales tax when he bought a new phone. The sales tax was $12.75. What was the total cost of the phone, including tax?

Crisscrossed

Find each quotient. Write your answers in the cross-number puzzle below. Each digit of your answer goes in its own box.

I can…
divide multidigit numbers.
6.NS.2.2

ACROSS

A 94,070 ÷ 46

C 3,828 ÷ 22

E 46,680 ÷ 15

F 61,065 ÷ 45

J 5,136 ÷ 214

K 9,840 ÷ 48

L 2,407 ÷ 29

N 67,870 ÷ 55

Q 9,114 ÷ 62

R 8,268 ÷ 12

T 80,120 ÷ 20

DOWN

A 7,644 ÷ 28

B 22,016 ÷ 43

D 49,980 ÷ 12

G 67,704 ÷ 13

H 10,582 ÷ 143

K 4,148 ÷ 17

M 10,062 ÷ 26

P 63,860 ÷ 31

Q 4,508 ÷ 23

S 7,238 ÷ 77

ANALYZE AND SOLVE PERCENT PROBLEMS

? Topic Essential Question

How can percents show proportional relationships between quantities and be used to solve problems?

Topic Overview

Topic Vocabulary

- interest rate
- markdown
- markup
- percent change
- percent equation
- percent error
- percent markdown
- percent markup
- principal
- simple interest

Go online | **PearsonRealize.com**

Lesson Digital Resources

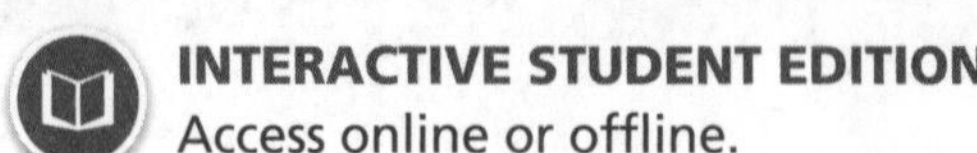

INTERACTIVE STUDENT EDITION
Access online or offline.

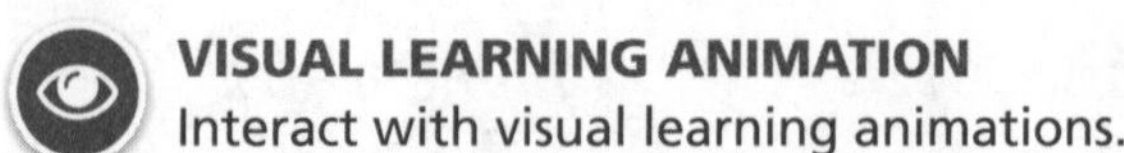

VISUAL LEARNING ANIMATION
Interact with visual learning animations.

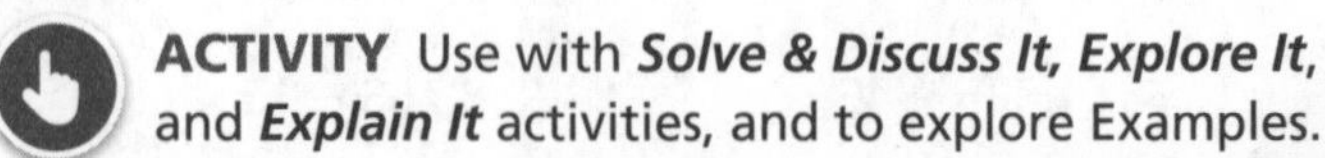

ACTIVITY Use with ***Solve & Discuss It, Explore It***, and ***Explain It*** activities, and to explore Examples.

VIDEOS Watch clips to support ***3-Act Mathematical Modeling Lessons*** and ***STEM Projects***.

3-ACT MATH

THE Smart Shopper

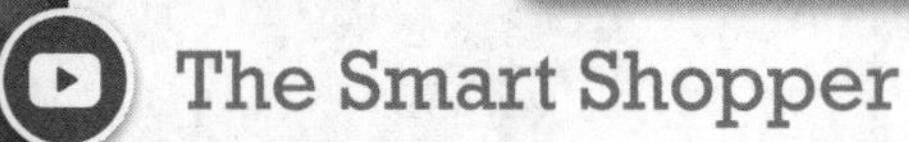

The Smart Shopper

Why do stores and manufacturers print coupons? It seems like they lose money every time you use one. Well, some coupons are designed to steer you toward a specific brand and gain your loyalty. Stores also offer coupons to get you into the store, counting on you buying other items while you are there. If you're clever, you can use multiple coupons. Think about this during the 3-Act Mathematical Modeling lesson.

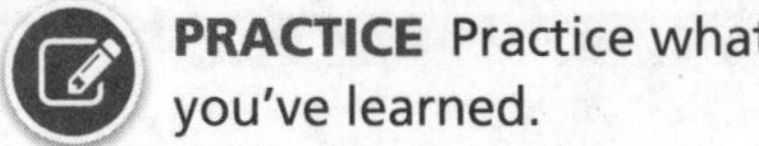

PRACTICE Practice what you've learned.

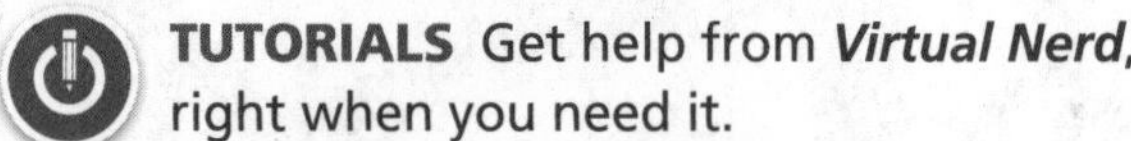

TUTORIALS Get help from ***Virtual Nerd***, right when you need it.

MATH TOOLS Explore math with digital tools.

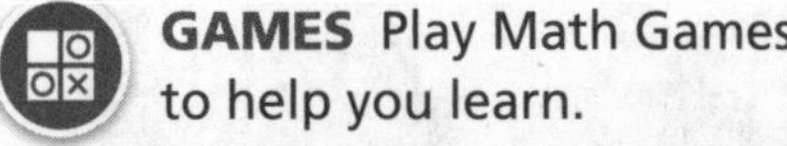

GAMES Play Math Games to help you learn.

KEY CONCEPT Review important lesson content.

GLOSSARY Read and listen to English/Spanish definitions.

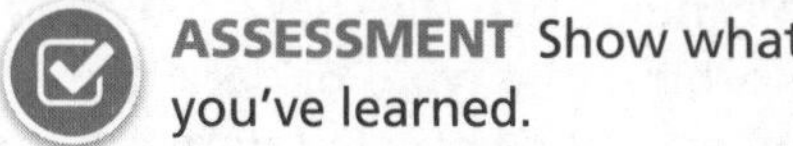

ASSESSMENT Show what you've learned.

VIDEO

Did You Know?

One of the first popular activity trackers was a pedometer, which measures number of steps taken. Some sources trace the history of the pedometer back to Leonardo da Vinci.

A pedometer called *Manpo-kei* (10,000 steps meter) was introduced in Japan in the mid-1960s. Research led by Dr. Yoshiro Hatano indicated that **10,000 steps a day is the ideal energy output** to maintain health.

Today, most activity trackers are electronic devices that can **sync to a computer or a smartphone.**

Many activity trackers are *wearable technology*. Some common places to wear activity trackers are on the wrist, arm, or chest. There are even **collar-mounted activity trackers for dogs.**

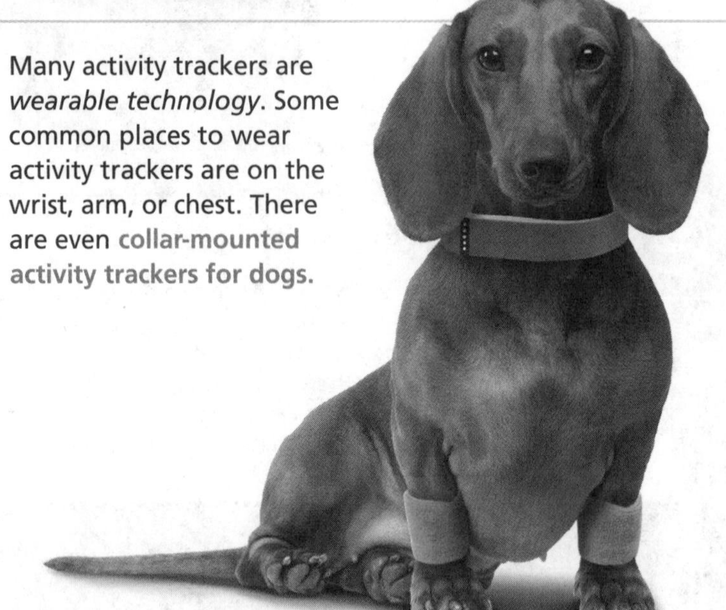

Your Task: Analyze Activity Tracker Data

Activity trackers, also called fitness trackers, have become quite popular in recent years. But is the data collected actually helpful to the user? You and your classmates will explore the types of data that an activity tracker collects, and how that data can help users reach their activity and fitness goals.

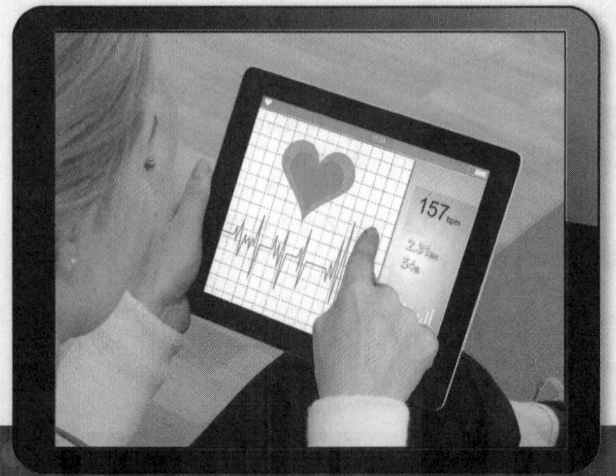

GET READY!

TOPIC 9

Review What You Know!

Vocabulary

Choose the best term from the box. Write it on the blank.

percent
proportion
rate
ratio

1. A ______________ is a ratio in which the first term is compared to 100.

2. A ratio that relates two quantities with different units of measure is a ______________.

3. A statement that two ratios are equal is called a ______________.

4. The relationship "3 students out of 5 students" is an example of a ______________.

Fractions, Decimals, and Percents

Write each number in two equivalent forms as a fraction, decimal, or percent.

5. 0.29

6. 35%

7. $\frac{2}{5}$

Proportions

Find the unknown number in each proportion.

8. $\frac{x \text{ days}}{4 \text{ years}} = \frac{365.25 \text{ days}}{1 \text{ year}}$

9. $\frac{33{,}264 \text{ feet}}{x \text{ miles}} = \frac{5{,}280 \text{ feet}}{1 \text{ mile}}$

10. A cooking magazine shows a photo of a main dish on the front cover of 5 out of the 12 issues it publishes each year. Write and solve a proportion to determine how many times a photo of a main dish will be on the front cover during the next 5 years.

Prepare for Reading Success

Before you begin Topic 9, complete the first and second columns of this table. While you work through the topic, return to complete the third column as you learn the answers to your questions from the second column.

What do I know about percents and how they are used?	What do I want to learn about how I will use percents in life?	What have I learned about how percents are used?

Lesson 9-1
Analyze Percents of Numbers

Go Online | PearsonRealize.com

I can...
understand, find, and analyze percents of numbers.

MAFS.7.RP.1.3 Use proportional relationships to solve multistep ratio and percent problems.
MAFS.K12.MP.1.1, MP.2.1, MP.3.1, MP.7.1

Jaime's older brother and his three friends want to split the cost of lunch. They also want to leave a 15%–20% tip. How much should each person pay?

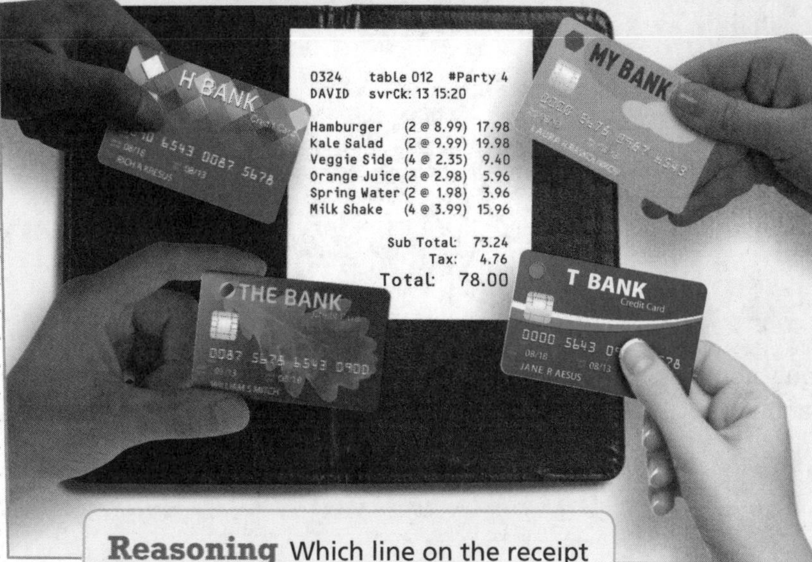

0324 table 012 #Party 4
DAVID svrCk: 13 15:20
Hamburger (2 @ 8.99) 17.98
Kale Salad (2 @ 9.99) 19.98
Veggie Side (4 @ 2.35) 9.40
Orange Juice (2 @ 2.98) 5.96
Spring Water (2 @ 1.98) 3.96
Milk Shake (4 @ 3.99) 15.96
Sub Total: 73.24
Tax: 4.76
Total: 78.00
H BANK
MY BANK
THE BANK
T BANK

Reasoning Which line on the receipt will you use to calculate the tip?

Focus on math practices

Reasoning How would the amount each person pays change if the tip is determined before or after the bill is split?

? Essential Question How do percents show the relationship between quantities?

EXAMPLE 1 Find Percents of Numbers

Scan for Multimedia

Diego starts a 12-hour road trip with his phone's battery charge at 75%. Given his normal usage, will his phone last the whole trip? Explain.

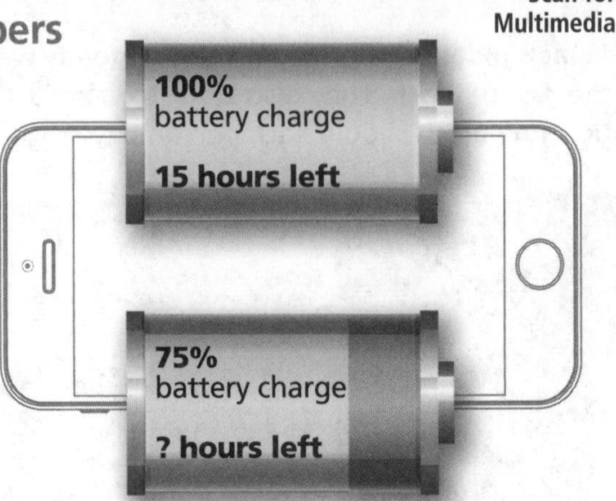

Look for Relationships How many hours will the phone last when the battery charge is at 75%?

STEP 1 Draw a bar diagram and write equivalent ratios to represent the hours remaining and the battery charge.

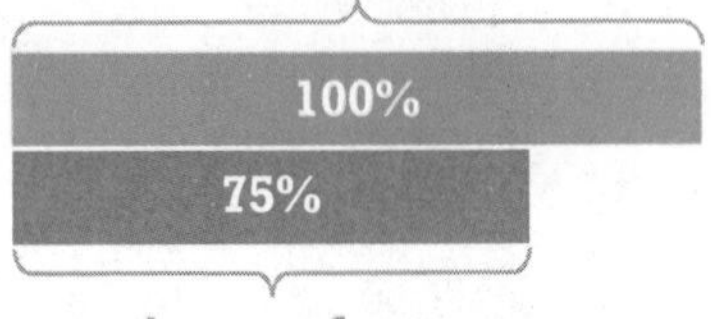

$$\frac{75}{100} = \frac{x}{15}$$

STEP 2 Use the equivalent ratios to find 75% of 15.

$$\frac{75}{100} = \frac{x}{15}$$ Solve for x.

$$\frac{75}{100} \cdot 15 = \frac{x}{15} \cdot 15$$

$$11.25 = x$$

75% of 15 is 11.25 hours.

The remaining battery life is 11.25 hours, so the phone will not last the whole 12-hour trip.

Try It!

Kita's phone had a fully charged battery. With normal usage, her phone will last 18 hours. How much time is left on Kita's phone battery with 12% charge remaining?

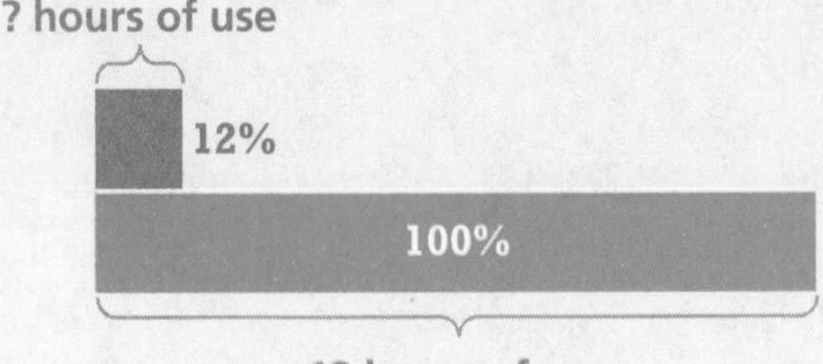

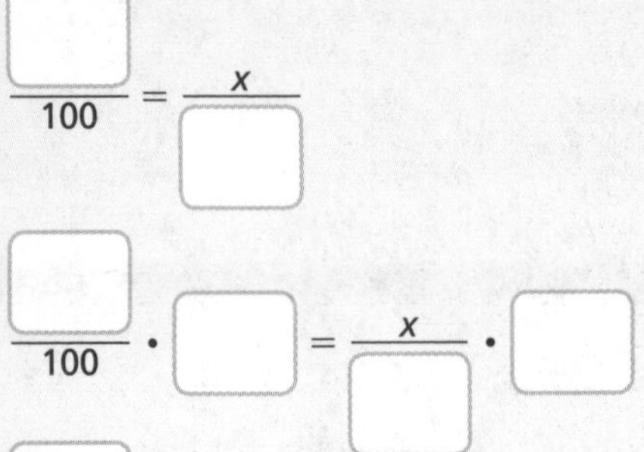

$$\frac{\square}{100} = \frac{x}{\square}$$

$$\frac{\square}{100} \cdot \square = \frac{x}{\square} \cdot \square$$

$$\square = x$$

Kita's phone battery has ☐ hours remaining.

Convince Me! Why is 51% of a number more than half of the number?

EXAMPLE 2  Use Percents Greater than 100%

ACTIVITY

ASSESS

A full set of adult teeth includes 160% as many teeth as a full set of baby teeth. How many teeth are there in a full set of adult teeth?

Use the bar diagram to write equivalent ratios. Then solve for t to find the number of adult teeth.

t adult teeth

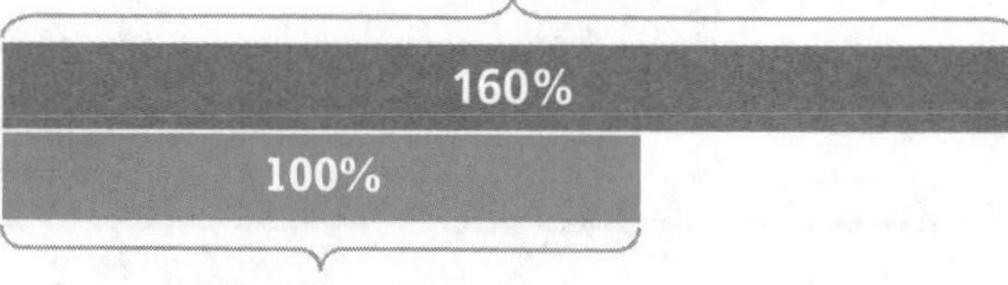

20 baby teeth

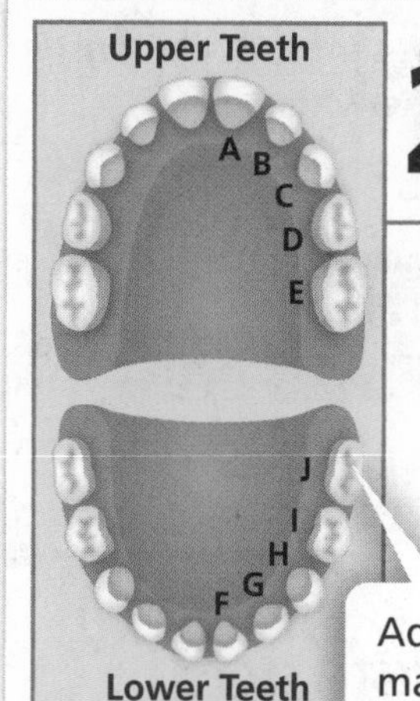

20 BABY TEETH

Types of Baby Teeth

4 central incisors (A and F)
4 lateral incisors (B and G)
4 cuspids (C and H)
4 first molars (D and I)
4 second molars (E and J)

Adults have 160% as many teeth as babies.

$$\frac{160}{100} = \frac{t}{20}$$

$$\frac{160}{100} \cdot 20 = \frac{t}{20} \cdot 20$$

$$32 = t$$

A full set of adult teeth includes 32 teeth.

EXAMPLE 3  Use Percents Less than 1%

What is the approximate distance in miles from Earth to the Moon?

STEP 1 Draw a bar diagram and write equivalent ratios.

x miles

0.27%

100%

93 million miles

93,000,000 miles

0.27% of the distance between the Sun and Earth

$$\frac{x}{93{,}000{,}000} = \frac{0.27}{100}$$

STEP 2 Solve for x.

$$\frac{0.27}{100} \cdot 93{,}000{,}000 = \frac{x}{93{,}000{,}000} \cdot 93{,}000{,}000$$

$$251{,}100 = x$$

The distance from Earth to the Moon is about 251,100 miles.

Check Your Answer Use compatible numbers to estimate the solution. 93,000,000 is approximately 100,000,000. 1% of 100,000,000 miles is 1,000,000 miles.

0.27% is about $\frac{1}{4}$ of 1%, so the distance is about $\frac{1}{4}$ of 1,000,000, or 250,000 miles.

Reasoning The exact distance is close to the estimated distance, so the answer is reasonable.

Try It!

a. Find 0.08% of 720. **b.** Find 162.5% of 200. **c.** Find 0.3% of 60.

KEY CONCEPT 

A percent is one way to represent the relationship between two quantities, generally that of a part to the whole.

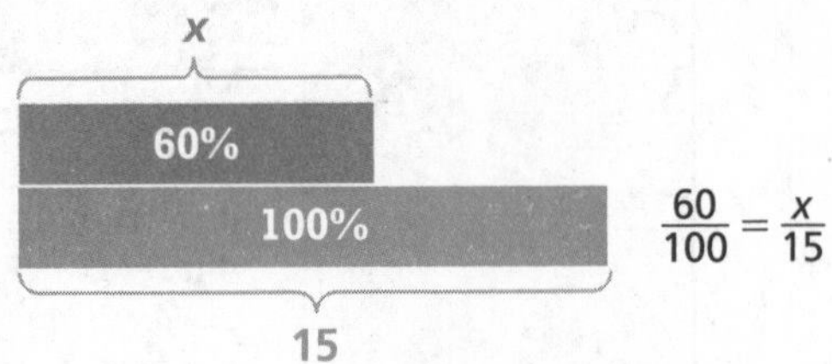

$$\frac{60}{100} = \frac{x}{15}$$

Do You Understand?

1. **Essential Question** How do percents show the relationship between quantities?

2. **Reasoning** How does a value that is greater than 100% of the original value or less than 1% of the original value compare to the original value?

3. **Construct Arguments** Gene stated that finding 25% of a number is the same as dividing the number by $\frac{1}{4}$. Is Gene correct? Explain.

Do You Know How?

4. An 8-ounce serving of apples contains 8% of your daily vitamin C. How many ounces of apples would you need to get 100% of your daily vitamin C?

5. Find the percent of each number.

   a. 59% of 640

   b. 0.20% of 3,542

   c. 195% of 568

   d. 74% of 920

6. Water is 2 parts hydrogen and 1 part oxygen (H_2O). For one molecule of water, each atom has the atomic mass unit, *u*, shown. What percent of the mass of a water molecule is hydrogen?

O 16.00 u
H 1.01 u
H 1.01 u

Name: ____________________

Practice & Problem Solving

Scan for Multimedia

Leveled Practice **In 7–8, fill in the boxes to solve.**

7. A local Little League has a total of 60 players, 80% of whom are right-handed. How many right-handed players are there?

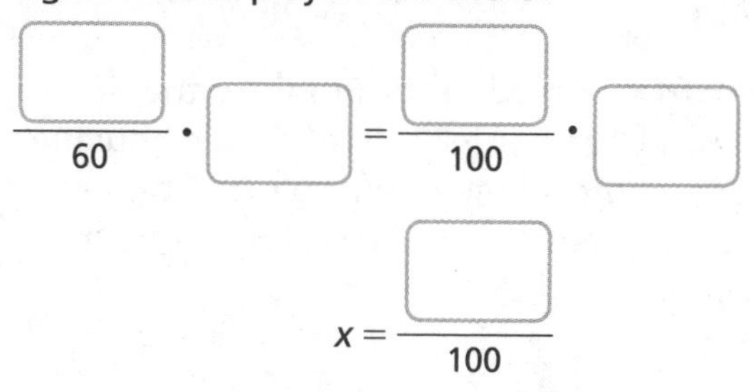

$\frac{\square}{60} \cdot \square = \frac{\square}{100} \cdot \square$

$x = \frac{\square}{100}$

$x = \square$ right-handed players

8. Sandra's volleyball team has a total of 20 uniforms. 20% are medium-sized uniforms. How many uniforms are medium-sized?

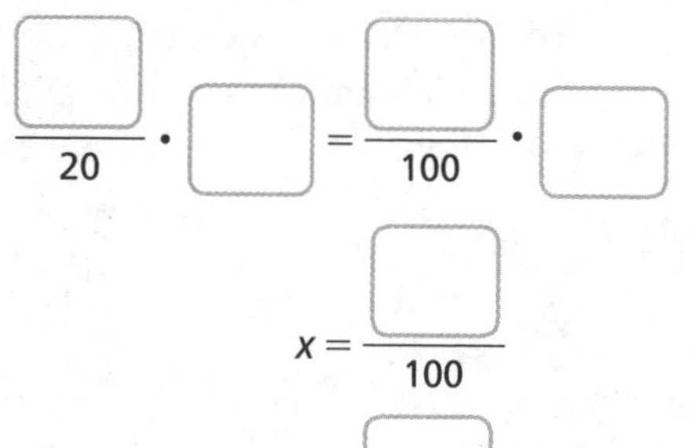

$\frac{\square}{20} \cdot \square = \frac{\square}{100} \cdot \square$

$x = \frac{\square}{100}$

$x = \square$ medium-sized uniforms

9. Meg is a veterinarian. In a given week, 50% of the 16 dogs she saw were Boxers. Steve is also a veterinarian. In the same week, 7 of the 35 dogs he saw this week were Boxers. Each wants to record the part, the whole, and the percent.

a. Does Meg need to find the part, the whole, or the percent?

b. Does Steve need to find the part, the whole, or the percent?

10. Olivia is a stockbroker. She makes 4% of her sales in commission. Last week, she sold $7,200 worth of stocks.

a. How much commission did she make last week?

b. If she were to average that same commission each week, how much would she make in commissions in a year, treating a year as having exactly 52 weeks?

11. The registration fee for a used car is 0.8% of the sale price of $5,700. How much is the fee?

12. The total cost of an item is the price plus the sales tax.

Find the sales tax to complete the table. Then find the total cost of the item.

Sales Tax

Selling Price	Rate of Sales Tax	Sales Tax
$40.00	4%	☐

13. Is 700% of 5 less than 10, greater than 10 but less than 100, or greater than 100? Explain your reasoning.

14. Is 250% of 44 less than 100, greater than 100 but less than 150, or greater than 150? Explain your reasoning.

15. The seed and skin of a typical avocado is about 30%–40% of the avocado's weight. For an 8-ounce avocado, how many ounces of edible fruit does it have?

16. A new health drink has 130% of the recommended daily allowance (RDA) for a certain vitamin. The RDA for this vitamin is 45 mg. How many milligrams of the vitamin are in the drink?

17. **Make Sense and Persevere** 153 is 0.9% of what number? Tell which equivalent ratios you used to find the solution.

18. **Construct Arguments** Brad says that if a second number is 125% of the first number, then the first number must be 75% of the second number. Is he correct? Justify your answer.

19. **Higher-Order Thinking** Mark and Joe work as jewelers. Mark has an hourly wage of $24 and gets overtime for every hour he works over 40 hours. The overtime pay rate is 150% of the normal rate. Joe makes 5% commission on all jewelry he sells. Who earns more money in a week if Mark works 60 hours and Joe sells $21,000 worth of jewelry? Explain.

Assessment Practice

20. Pamela and John work as tutors at two different test-prep companies. Pamela earns $20 per hour. John earns $65 per pupil. Pamela works 40 hours each week. John has 11 pupils. Who earns more money in a week? Explain. 7.RP.1.3

21. An Olympic-sized pool, which holds 660,000 gallons of water, is only 63% full. The pool maintenance company adds more water, filling the pool to 90% full. How many gallons of water did they add? 7.RP.1.3

Ⓐ 244,200

Ⓑ 594,000

Ⓒ 178,200

Ⓓ 415,800

Solve & Discuss It!

A florist is making flower arrangements for a party. He uses purple and white flowers in a ratio of 3 purple flowers to 1 white flower. How many flowers will he need in order to make 30 identical arrangements?

Lesson 9-2
Connect Percent and Proportion

Go Online | PearsonRealize.com

I can...
use proportions to solve percent problems.

MAFS.7.RP.1.3 Use proportional relationships to solve multistep ratio and percent problems.
Also 7.RP.1.2c

MAFS.K12.MP.1.1, MP.2.1, MP.3.1, MP.7.1

Look for Relationships
How are the number of purple flowers related to the number of white flowers?

Focus on math practices

Make Sense and Persevere If the florist can only buy white flowers in groups of flowers that have 3 white flowers and 2 red flowers, how many red flowers will the florist have to purchase? Explain your answer.

? Essential Question How does proportional reasoning relate to percent?

EXAMPLE 1  Use a Proportion to Find the Percent

Scan for Multimedia  

The basketball team statistician tracked the shots Emily made and the shots she missed during the last game. What percent of attempted shots did she make?

Draw a bar diagram and write a proportion to represent the number of shots made and the total number of shots.

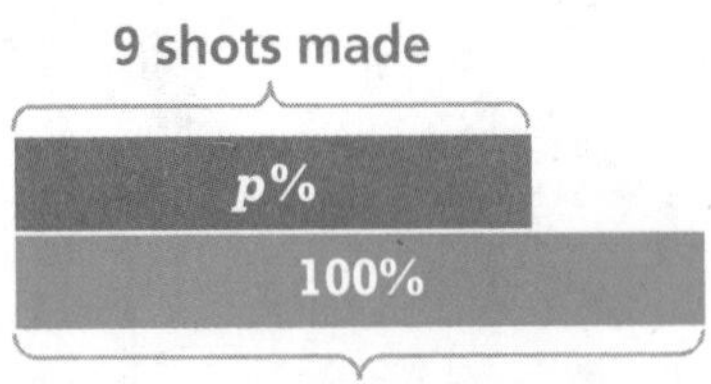

$\frac{9}{12} = \frac{p}{100}$

Solve the proportion to find the percent of shots made during the last game.

$\frac{9}{12} = \frac{p}{100}$

$\frac{9}{12} \cdot 100 = \frac{p}{100} \cdot 100$

$75 = p$

Reasoning The ratio of part to whole describes a proportional relationship.

Emily made 75% of her shots.

Try It!

Camila makes 2 of her 5 shots attempted. Is the percent of shots she made more than, less than, or the same as Emily's percent of shots?

2 shots made

p%

100%

5 attempted shots

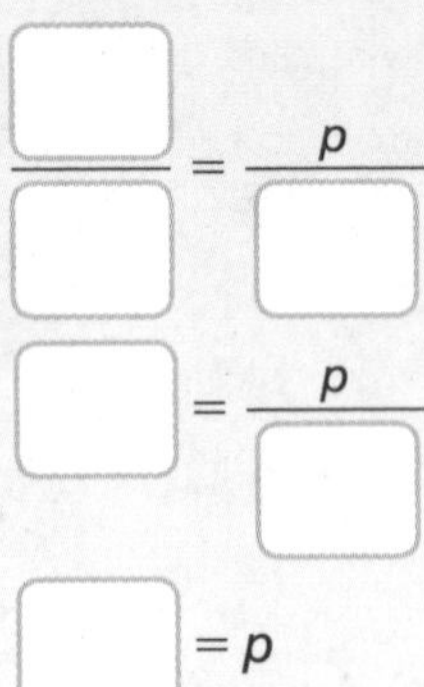

Camila made ☐ % of her shots.

Camila's percent of the shots made is ☐ Emily's.

Convince Me! A hockey goalie stops 37 out of 40 shots. What percent of attempted goals did she stop?

EXAMPLE 2  Use a Proportion to Find the Part

A plan to expand Megan's room will make the length of the room 175% of the current length. What will be the new length of her room?

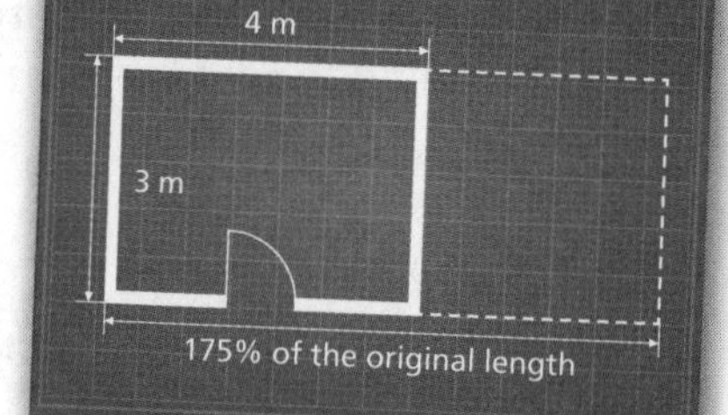

Draw a bar diagram to represent the problem and then write a percent proportion to find the new length.

$$\frac{\text{new length}}{\text{old length}} = \frac{p}{100}$$

$$\frac{n}{4} = \frac{175}{100}$$

$$\frac{n}{4} \cdot 4 = \frac{175}{100} \cdot 4$$

$$n = 7$$

The new length of the room will be 7 meters.

EXAMPLE 3  Use a Proportion to Find the Whole

The nutrition label shows the percents of the recommended daily intake for nutrients found in a serving of a soy milk. How many milligrams of calcium should you consume each day?

Write a percent proportion to find the amount of calcium.

$$\frac{\text{calcium per serving}}{\text{daily value}} = \frac{p}{100}$$

$$\frac{260}{w} = \frac{20}{100}$$

$$\frac{260}{w} \cdot w = \frac{20}{100} \cdot w$$

Multiply both sides by the variable.

$$260 = \frac{20w}{100}$$

$$260 \cdot \frac{100}{20} = \frac{20w}{100} \cdot \frac{100}{20}$$

Multiply both sides by the reciprocal.

$$1{,}300 = w$$

The daily value for calcium is 1,300 mg.

Organic
SOY MILK
SOY MILK
Nutrition Facts
Per Container 8
Calories 90 Calories from Fat 30
10% Vitamin D 2mcg
20% Calcium 260mg
45% Iron 8mg
5% Potassium 8mg

Try It!

a. Megan's room is expanded so the width is 150% of 3 meters. What is the new width?

b. Use the soy milk label in Example 3. What is the recommended amount of iron needed each day? Round your answer to the nearest mg.

KEY CONCEPT

Percent problems represent a kind of proportional relationship. You can use proportional reasoning to solve percent problems.

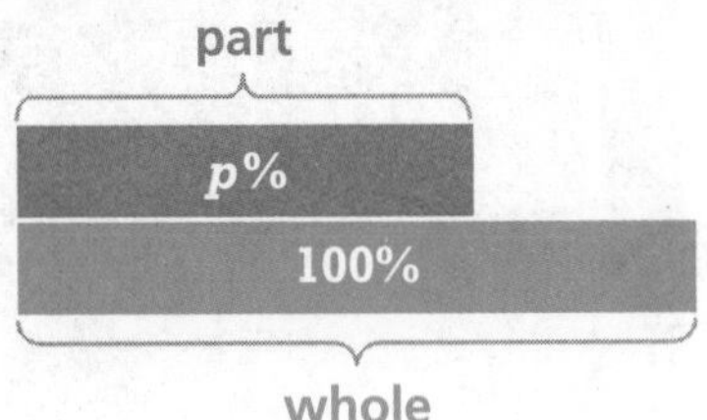

$$\frac{part}{whole} = \frac{p}{100}$$

Do You Understand?

1. **Essential Question** How does proportional reasoning relate to percent?

2. **Reasoning** Why does one of the ratios in a percent proportion always have a denominator of 100?

3. **Construct Arguments** The proportion $\frac{75}{w} = \frac{150}{100}$ can be used to find the whole, w. Use the language of percent to explain whether w is less than or greater than 75.

Do You Know How?

4. Write a percent proportion for the bar diagram shown.

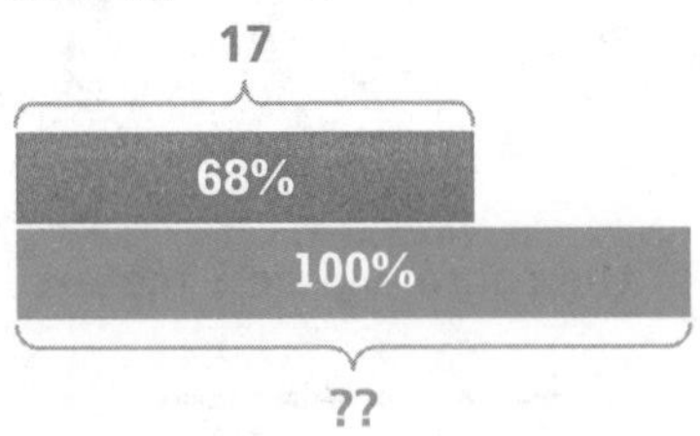

5. Use a proportion to find each value.

   a. 2% of 180

   $\frac{n}{\square} = \frac{2}{\square}$

   b. What percent is 17 out of 40?

   $\frac{\square}{\square} = \frac{p}{\square}$

6. **Construct Arguments** Gia researches online that her car is worth $3,000. She hopes to sell it for 85% of that value, but she wants to get at least 70%. She ends up selling it for $1,800. Did she get what she wanted? Justify your answer.

Name: ______________________________

Practice & Problem Solving  

Scan for Multimedia 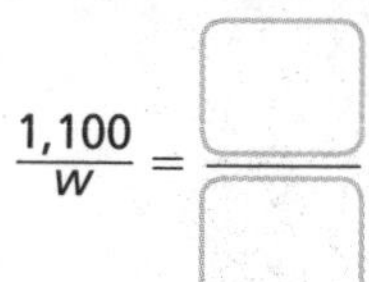

Leveled Practice **In 7–8, fill in the boxes to solve.**

7. The rabbit population in a certain area is 200% of last year's population. There are 1,100 rabbits this year. How many were there last year?

$\frac{1{,}100}{w} = \frac{\square}{\square}$

There were $\square$ rabbits last year.

8. A company that makes hair-care products had 3,000 people try a new shampoo. Of the 3,000 people, 9 had a mild allergic reaction. What percent of the people had a mild allergic reaction?

$\frac{9}{3{,}000} = \frac{p}{\square}$

Percent = $\square$ %

9. A survey was given to people who owned a certain type of car. What percent of the people surveyed were completely satisfied with the car?

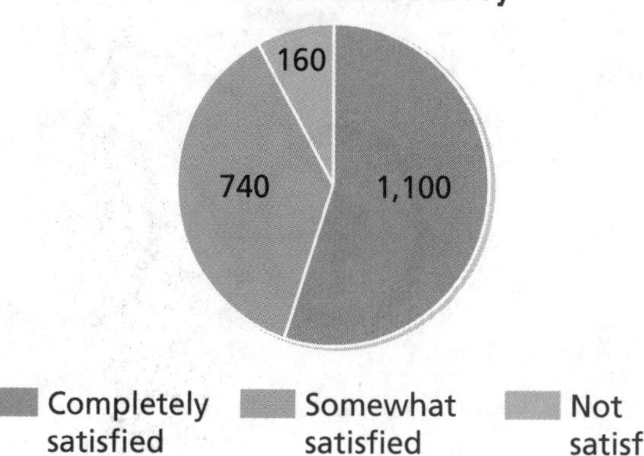

10. The Washingtons buy a studio apartment for $240,000. They pay a down payment of $60,000.

a. Their down payment is what percent of the purchase price?

b. What percent of the purchase price would a $12,000 down payment be?

11. A restaurant customer left $3.50 as a tip. The tax on the meal was 7% and the tip was 20% of the cost including tax.

a. What piece of information is not needed to compute the bill after tax and tip?

b. **Make Sense and Persevere** What was the total bill?

12. **Reasoning** What is a good estimate for 380% of 60? Explain.

13. **Critique Reasoning** Marna thinks that about 35% of her mail is junk mail. She gets about twice as much regular mail as junk mail. Is she correct? Explain.

14. Hypatia has read 13 chapters of a 22-chapter book. What percent of the chapters has she read?

15. A school year has 4 quarters. What percent of a school year is 7 quarters?

16. **Construct Arguments** A survey found that 27% of high school students and 94% of teachers and school employees drive to school. The ratio of students to employees is about 10 to 1. Roger states that the number of students who drive to school is greater than the number of teachers and employees who drive to school. Explain how Roger's statement could be correct.

17. **Higher Order Thinking** Stefan sells Jin a bicycle for $114 and a helmet for $18. The total cost for Jin is 120% of what Stefan spent originally to buy the bike and helmet. How much did Stefan spend originally? How much money did he make by selling the bicycle and helmet to Jin?

Assessment Practice

18. Last month Nicole spent $30. This month she spent 140% of what she spent last month.

Write a proportional equation to represent the situation. How much did Nicole spend this month? 7.RP.1.2c

19. Mr. Jones, the owner of a small store buys kayak paddles for $50.00 each, and sells them for 180% of the purchase price. 7.RP.1.3

PART A

A customer buys a paddle for $97.65, which includes the selling price and sales tax. What is the sales tax rate?

Ⓐ 7.65%

Ⓑ 4.7%

Ⓒ 9.75%

Ⓓ 8.5%

PART B

If Mr. Jones buys paddles for $35 instead of $50, and uses the same percent increase on price, how many paddles must Mr. Jones sell for the total paddle sales, before tax, to be at least $250? Explain your answer.

Solve & Discuss It!

Fran is shopping for a new pair of shoes. She did some research and has narrowed the options to the two pairs she likes the most. Based on buyers' reviews, which pair do you recommend that she buy? Explain your thinking.

Model with Math How can you use what you know about ratios to compare the reviews?

Lesson 9-3
Represent and Use the Percent Equation

Go Online | PearsonRealize.com

I can...
represent and solve percent problems using equations.

MAFS.7.RP.1.2c Represent proportional relationships by equations. Also 7.RP.1.3
MAFS.K12.MP.1.1, MP.2.1, MP.3.1, MP.4.1, MP.6.1, MP.7.1

Focus on math practices

Model with Math Describe another situation in which you could use ratios to make a decision.

? **Essential Question** How are percent problems related to proportional reasoning?

VISUAL LEARNING

ASSESS

EXAMPLE 1  Find the Percent

Scan for Multimedia

In science class, students compared their vertical reach and height to see if they are proportional. Maria is 60 inches tall and can reach 75 inches high. What percent of her total vertical reach is her height?

Use proportional reasoning to develop the **percent equation**.

height (part)

P%

100%

vertical reach (whole)

$$\frac{\text{part}}{\text{whole}} = \frac{p}{100}$$

$$\frac{\text{part}}{\text{whole}} = \text{percent}$$

$$\frac{\text{part}}{\text{whole}} \cdot \text{whole} = \text{percent} \cdot \text{whole}$$

$$\text{part} = \text{percent} \cdot \text{whole}$$

Use Structure The percent is a constant of proportionality that relates a *part* to the *whole*. The equation has the same form as $y = mx$.

The percent equation is part = percent • whole.

height = percent • vertical reach

$$60 = P \cdot 75$$

$$\frac{60}{75} = \frac{P \cdot 75}{75}$$

$$0.80 = P$$

To represent a decimal as a percent, multiply by 100 and add the percent symbol.

Maria's height is 80% of her total vertical reach.

Try It!

An elephant weighs 15,000 pounds on Earth and 2,500 pounds on the Moon. Assuming the weights are proportional, what percent of its weight on Earth is its weight on the Moon?

$\square = P \cdot 15,000$

$\frac{\square}{\square} = \frac{P \cdot 15,000}{\square}$

$\square \approx P$

The elephant's weight on the Moon is about $\square$ % of its weight on Earth.

Convince Me! How does the percent describe how the weights are related?

EXAMPLE 2  Find the Part

  ACTIVITY  ASSESS

Many states have a meal tax that is proportional to the total spent on food and beverages. In one state, the meal tax is 8.44%. How much tax will a customer pay if the food and beverages total $54?

Tax ($)

8.44%

100%

Total food and beverage ($)

part = percent • whole

tax = percent • bill

$t = 8.44\% \cdot b$

Use t for the tax and b for the food and beverages bill.

$t = 0.0844 \cdot 54$

Express the percent as a decimal.

$t = 4.5576$

Reasoning What does 4.5576 mean in this situation?

The customer will pay $4.56 in tax.

EXAMPLE 3  Find the Whole

Jane earns a 5.5% commission on the selling price of each home she sells. She earned $9,020 in commission on the sale of a home. What was the selling price of the home?

Be Precise Instead of a salary, some workers earn a percent of the value of a transaction, called a *commission*.

Commission ($)

5.5%

100%

Selling price ($)

part = percent • whole

$c = 5.5\% \cdot h$

Use c for the commission and h for the selling price of the home.

$9{,}020 = 0.055h$

$\frac{9{,}020}{0.055} = \frac{0.055h}{0.055}$

$164{,}000 = h$

Jane sold the home for $164,000.

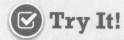

 Try It!

To make a profit, a clothing store sells board shorts at 115% of the amount they paid for them. How much did the store pay for the board shorts shown?

KEY CONCEPT

The percent equation shows how a percent relates proportional quantities. The percent is a constant of proportionality and the equation has the same form as $y = mx$.

$$\frac{\text{part}}{\text{whole}} = \text{percent}$$

$$\text{part} = \text{percent} \cdot \text{whole}$$

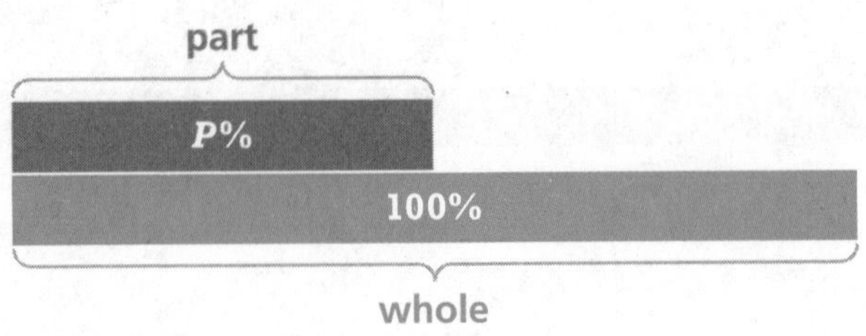

Do You Understand?

1. **Essential Question** How are percent problems related to proportional reasoning?

2. **Reasoning** A waiter at a restaurant receives $11 as a tip on a $47.20 bill. He usually receives tips that are 20% of the total bill. Is the tip amount what the waiter typically receives? Explain.

3. **Construct Arguments** Sara used an equation to solve the problem below. Justify each step of her work.

   About 11% of people are left-handed. How many people would you expect to be left-handed in a class of 30 students?

   $\ell = 0.11 \cdot 30$
   $\ell = 3.3$
   about 3 students

Do You Know How?

4. An auto insurance company pays 12% commission to its agents for each new insurance policy they sell. How much commission does an agent make on a $1,000 policy?

5. Curt and Melanie are mixing blue and yellow paint to make seafoam green paint. Use the percent equation to find how much yellow paint they should use.

6. Bill paid $35.99 in tax on a laptop that cost $449.99. About what percent sales tax did Bill pay?

Name: ______________________________

Practice & Problem Solving

Scan for Multimedia

Leveled Practice **In 7 and 8, solve each percent problem.**

7. In a survey of 500 voters, 430 said they would vote for the same candidate again. What percent of the voters would vote the same way again?

part = percent • whole

☐ = P% • ☐

☐ = P%

8. The local newspaper has letters to the editor from 40 people. If this number represents 5% of all of the newspaper's readers, how many readers, *r*, does the newspaper have?

part = percent • whole

☐ = ☐ • *r*

☐ = *r*

9. **Make Sense and Persevere** What percent of the 16-gigabyte hard drive shown is used for photos?

3.32 GB

Music	Photos	Apps	Other	Free Space

16 GB

10. A shirt that normally costs $30 is on sale for $21.75. What percent of the regular price is the sale price?

11. Complete the table.

Earning Commission

Sales	Commission Rate	Commission
$768	4%	☐

12. Complete the table.

Sales Tax

Selling Price	Tax Rate	Sales Tax
$39.98	4.5%	☐

13. A restaurant automatically charges a 20% gratuity if a party has 6 or more people. How much gratuity is added to a party of 6 on a $141 bill?

14. **Make Sense and Persevere** A large university accepts 70% of the students who apply. Of the students the university accepts, 25% actually enroll. If 20,000 students apply, how many enroll?

15. **Model with Math** There are 4,000 books in the town's library. Of these, 2,600 are fiction. Write a percent equation that you can use to find the percent of the books that are fiction. Then solve your equation.

16. A salesperson earns 4% commission on furnace sales.

a. What is the commission that the salesperson earns on the sale of $33,000 worth of furnaces?

b. Suppose the salesperson doubles his sales of furnaces. What would be true about the commission? Explain without using any calculations.

17. Heidi earns 3% commission on the jewelry she sells each week. Last week, she sold the pieces of jewelry shown.

a. How much did she make in commission?

b. **Reasoning** How much did the jewelry store take in from her sales? How do you know?

18. **Higher Order Thinking** In a company, 60% of the workers are men. If 1,380 women work for the company, how many workers are there in all? Show two different ways that you can solve this problem.

Assessment Practice

19. A salesperson starts working 40 hours per week at a job with two options for being paid. Option A is an hourly wage of $19. Option B is a commission rate of 8% on weekly sales.

How much does the salesperson need to sell in a given week to earn the same amount with each option? 7.RP.1.3

Ⓐ $9,500 Ⓑ $4,750 Ⓒ $760 Ⓓ $320

20. At a real estate agency, an agent sold a house for $382,000. The commission rate is 5.5% for the real estate agency. The commission for the agent is 30% of the amount the real estate agency gets. How much did the agent earn in commission? Explain your answer. 7.RP.1.2c

Name: ______________________

MID-TOPIC CHECKPOINT

TOPIC 9

1. **Vocabulary** Explain how the percent equation relates proportional quantities. *Lesson 9-3* 7.RP.1.2c

2. Colleen buys a movie for $20 and pays 7% sales tax. Her cousin, Brad, lives in another state. Brad buys the same movie for $22 and pays 6% sales tax. Who pays more sales tax? How much more? *Lessons 9-1 and 9-3* 7.RP.1.2c, 7.RP.1.3

3. Kamesh and Paolo each read 40 books in one year. Kamesh read 12 nonfiction books. Thirty-five percent of the books Paolo read were nonfiction. Who read more nonfiction books? How many more? *Lesson 9-2* 7.RP.1.2c, 7.RP.1.3

4. Val buys a computer for $920. If this is 115% of what the store paid for the same computer, how much did the store earn on the sale? *Lesson 9-3* 7.RP.1.3

5. For each situation, select the percent to answer the question. *Lessons 9-1, 9-2, and 9-3* 7.RP.1.2c, 7.RP.1.3

	5%	15%	20%	25%
At an auto repair shop, 14 of the 56 cars received oil changes. What percent of the cars received oil changes?	☐	☐	☐	☐
Harry pays $3.50 sales tax on a $70 item. What is the sales tax rate?	☐	☐	☐	☐
In a box of 250 paperclips, 50 are red. What percent of the paperclips are red?	☐	☐	☐	☐
Rylee saved $9 on a $60 pair of shoes. What percent did she save?	☐	☐	☐	☐

6. Explain how you can use proportional reasoning to determine the whole if you know that 21 is 60% of the whole. *Lesson 9-2* 7.RP.1.2c, 7.RP.1.3

How well did you do on the mid-topic checkpoint? Fill in the stars.

MID-TOPIC PERFORMANCE TASK

The coach of a women's basketball team wants each of her starting players to make at least 75% of the free throws attempted during regular season games. The table shows the statistics for the starting players after the first 15 games.

Player	Free Throws Attempted	Free Throws Made	Percent
Wilson	36	24	
Bartholdi	42	37	
Johnson	22	15	
Garcia	29	16	
O'Malley	14	12	

PART A

Use the table. Find the percentage of free throws made by each player. Round to the nearest whole percent. 7.RP.1.2c

PART B

Choose one of the players with a free-throw percentage less than 75%. Determine a number of free throws the player could attempt and make during the next 10 games to increase her free-throw percentage to at least 75%. 7.RP.1.3

PART C

Choose one of the players with a free-throw percentage greater than 75%. Determine the number of free throws that the player could miss during the next 10 games and still maintain an overall percentage of at least 75%. 7.RP.1.3

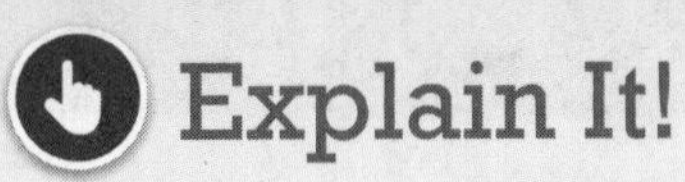

Explain It!

Lesson 9-4
Solve Percent Change and Percent Error Problems

Go Online | PearsonRealize.com

I can...
solve problems involving percent change and percent error.

MAFS.7.RP.1.3 Use proportional relationships to solve multistep ratio and percent problems.
MAFS.K12.MP.1.1, MP.3.1, MP.4.1, MP.6.1

Nadia lives in the town of Bayville. Quinn lives in the town of Portside. Nadia and Quinn each claim that her respective town's population is growing more rapidly.

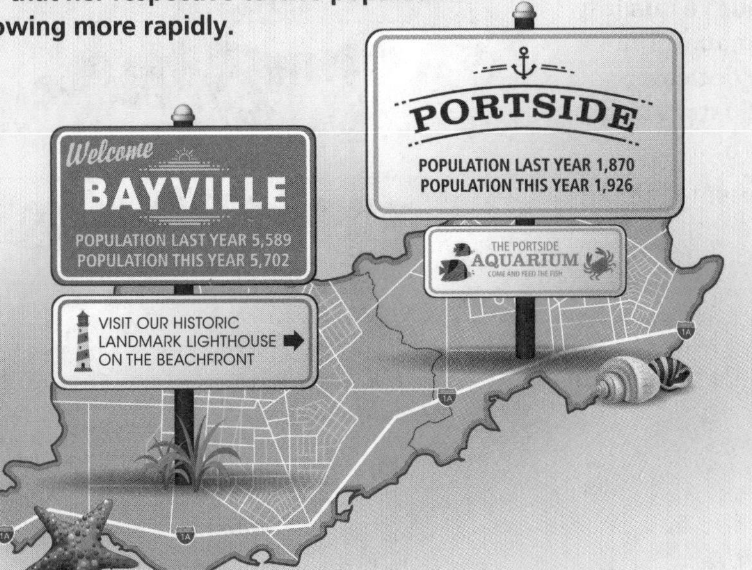

A. Write an argument to support Nadia. Why might she argue that Bayville's population is growing more rapidly?

B. Write an argument to support Quinn. Why might she argue that Portside's population is growing more rapidly?

C. Whose reasoning is more logical? Explain why.

Focus on math practices

Critique Reasoning Suppose Bayville's population is expected to grow 3% next year. Nadia says that means the population will increase by 300 people. Is Nadia's reasoning correct? Explain.

Essential Question How is finding percent error similar to finding percent change?

VISUAL LEARNING
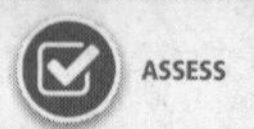
ASSESS

EXAMPLE 1  Find Percent Increase

Scan for Multimedia  

The percent change describes how much a quantity has changed relative to its original amount. The percent change can be an increase or decrease. What is the percent change of the alligator's length?

Model with Math What representation can show the change in the alligator's length?

STEP 1 Draw a bar diagram to represent the percent change from last year to this year.

The percent change is a *percent increase* because the alligator's length increased.

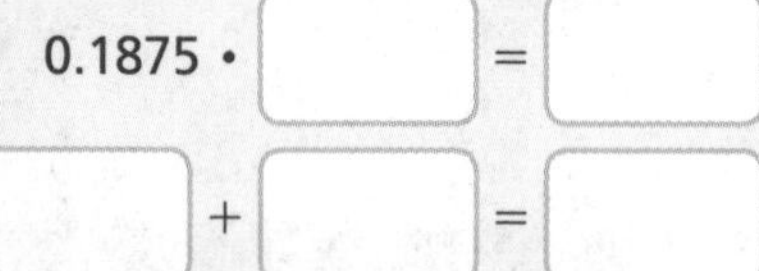

The change in length is 6 inches.

STEP 2 Use the percent equation to find the percent change.

part = percent • whole

change in length = percent change • original length

$6 = P \cdot 32$

$\frac{6}{32} = P$

$0.1875 = P$

Express the decimal as a percent by multiplying by 100.

The alligator's length increased by 18.75% this year.

Try It!

What will be the length of the alligator next year if its length changes by the same percent as it changed this year?

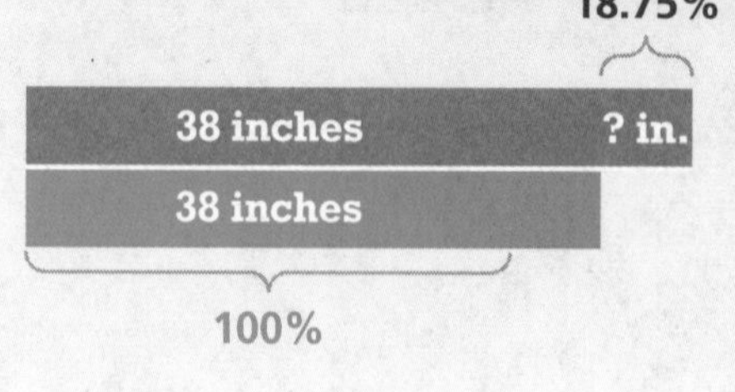

percent change • length this year = change in length

0.1875 • ☐ = ☐

☐ + ☐ = ☐

Next year, the length of the alligator will be ☐ inches long.

Convince Me! Why is the increase in the alligator's length different from year to year, even though the percent change stayed the same?

EXAMPLE 2 Find Percent Decrease

Last year, a website had 40,000 visitors and this year, it had 37,000 visitors. What is the percent change in the number of visitors to the website from last year to this year?

Find the decrease in the number of visitors. Then use the percent equation to find the percent change.

The percent change is a *percent decrease* because the number of visitors decreased.

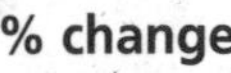

% change

37,000 visitors

40,000 visitors

100%

The change in attendance is 3,000.

change in number of visitors = percent change • number of visitors last year

$$3{,}000 = P \cdot 40{,}000$$

$$\frac{3{,}000}{40{,}000} = P$$

$$0.075 = P$$

The number of visitors decreased by 7.5% this year.

EXAMPLE 3 Find Percent Error

Shaun estimated that the attendance at a college lacrosse game was 3,000. The actual attendance was 3,296. What is the percent error of Shaun's estimate? Round to the nearest whole percent.

Percent error describes the accuracy of a measured or estimated value compared to an actual value. It is always a positive percent.

Use absolute value to find the positive difference between the estimated and actual attendance. Then use the percent equation to find the percent error.

$|3{,}000 - 3{,}296| = 296$

difference in attendance = percent error • actual attendance

$$296 = P \cdot 3{,}296$$

$$\frac{296}{3{,}296} = P$$

$$0.0898 \approx P$$

Remember to express the decimal value as a percent.

Shaun's attendance estimate has a percent error of about 9%.

Try It!

The specification for the length of a bolt is 4.75 inches. A machinist makes a bolt that is 4.769 inches long. What is the percent error of the bolt's length?

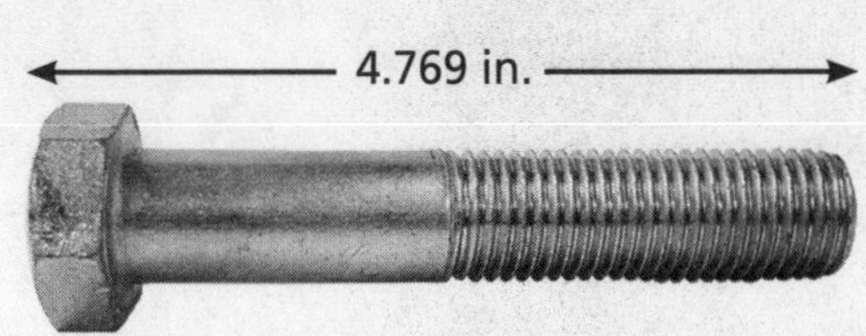

KEY CONCEPT

Percent change and percent error problems are kinds of percent problems. You can use the percent equation to solve them.

amount of change = percent change · original amount

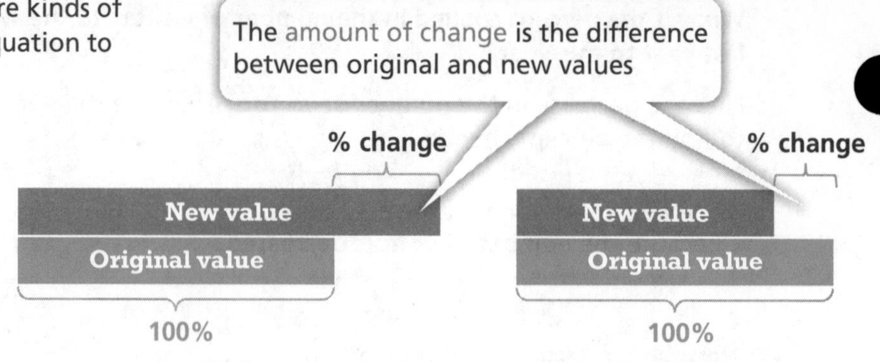

Do You Understand?

1. **Essential Question** How is finding percent error similar to finding percent change?

2. **Reasoning** Give an example of a problem in which the percent error is greater than 20%, but less than 50%. Explain how you determined the percent error.

3. **Construct Arguments** A store manager marked up a $10 flash drive by 20%. She then marked it down by 20%. Explain why the new price of the flash drive is not $10.

Do You Know How?

4. Lita's softball team won 8 games last month and 10 this month. What was the percent change in games the team won? Was it an increase or decrease?

5. What is the percent change in the price of a gallon of gas, to the nearest whole percent? Is it an increase or a decrease?

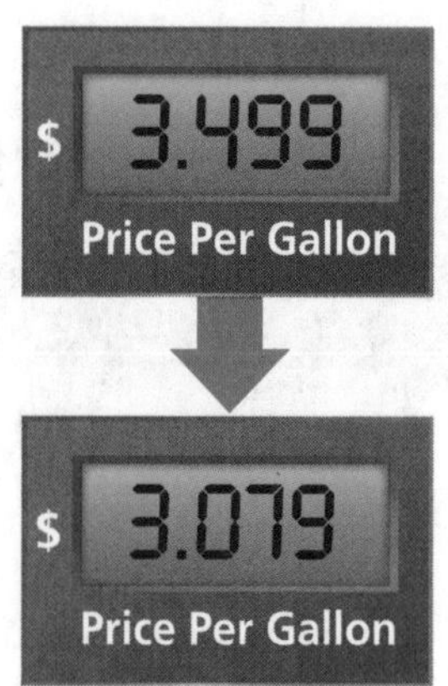

6. Several students measured a 25-mm-long nail and wrote the measurements shown in the table below. Whose measurement had the greatest percent error? Round to the nearest percent.

Student	Measurement (mm)	Percent Error
Layne	26	%
Tenicia	23	%
Juan	25	%

Name: ____________________

Practice & Problem Solving

Scan for Multimedia 

Leveled Practice **In 7–8, use the bar diagram and fill in the boxes to solve.**

7. The original quantity is 10 and the new quantity is 13. What is the percent change? Is it an increase or decrease?

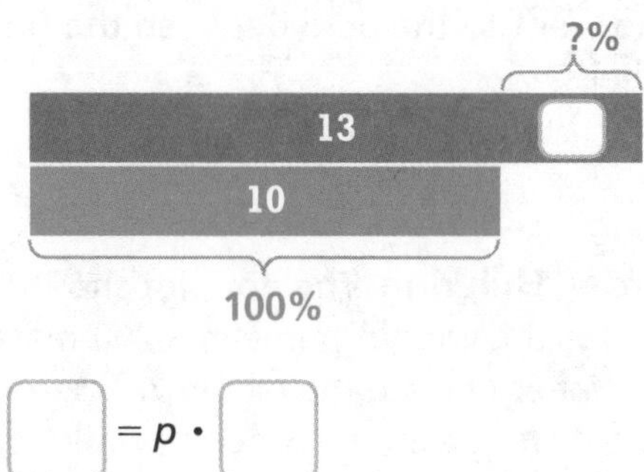

☐ = p · ☐

☐ = p

The percent increase is ☐%.

8. The original quantity is 5 and the new quantity is 3. What is the percent change? Is it an increase or decrease?

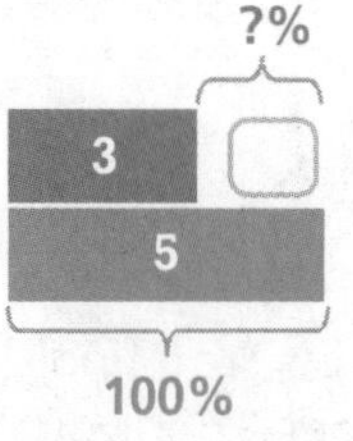

☐ = p · ☐

☐ = p

The percent decrease is ☐%.

9. At noon, a tank contained 10 cm of water. After several hours, it contained 7 cm of water. What is the percent decrease of water in the tank?

10. Craig likes to collect vinyl records. Last year he had 10 records in his collection. Now he has 12 records. What is the percent increase of his collection?

11. Carl bought an airline ticket. Two weeks ago, the cost of this flight was $300.

What is the percent increase?

12. On Monday, a museum had 150 visitors. On Tuesday, it had 260 visitors.

a. Estimate the percent change in the number of visitors to the museum.

b. About how many people would have to visit the museum on Wednesday to have the same percent change from Tuesday to Wednesday as from Monday to Tuesday? Explain your answer.

13. Rihanna has a container with a volume of 1.5 liters. She estimates the volume to be 2.1 liters. What is the percent error?

14. The label on a package of bolts says each bolt has a diameter of 0.35 inch. To be in the package, the percent error of the diameter must be less than 5%. One bolt has a diameter of 0.33 inch. Should it go in the package? Why or why not?

15. A band expects to have 16 songs on their next album. The band writes and records 62.5% more songs than they expect to have in the album. During the editing process, 50% of the songs are removed. How many songs will there be in the final album?

16. **Make Sense and Persevere** In the first week of July, a record 1,060 people went to the local swimming pool. In the second week, 105 fewer people went to the pool. In the third week, 135 more people went to the pool than in the second week. In the fourth week, 136 fewer people went to the pool than in the third week.

What is the percent change in the number of people who went to the pool between the first and last weeks?

17. **Be Precise** You have 20 quarters. You find 40% more quarters in your room. Then you go shopping and spend 50% of the total number of quarters.

a. Write an expression that represents the total number of quarters you take with you when you go shopping.

b. How much money do you have left?

18. **Higher Order Thinking** The dot plot shows predictions for the winning time in a 200-meter sprint. The winner finished the race in 22.3 seconds. Find the greatest percent error for a prediction to the nearest tenth of a percent. Justify your answer.

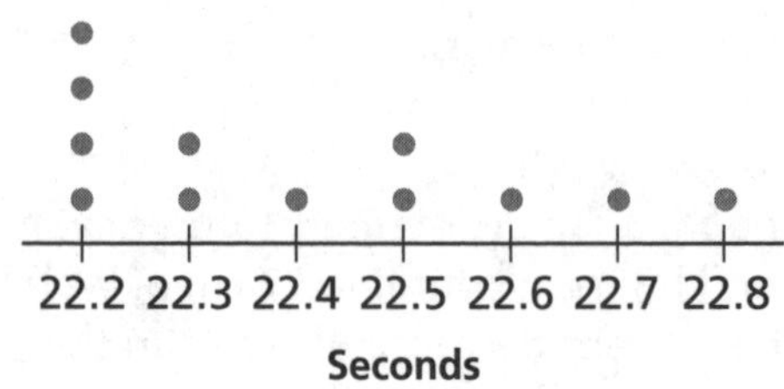

Assessment Practice

19. The amount of money in a savings account increases from \$250 to \$270 in one month. If the percent increase is the same for every month, how much money will be in the account at the end of the next month? 7.RP.1.3

Ⓐ \$291.60 Ⓑ \$295 Ⓒ \$289.60 Ⓓ \$300

20. A meteorologist predicted that there would be 1.0 inches of rainfall from a storm. Instead, there were 2.2 inches of rainfall.

Which statements are true? 7.RP.1.3

- ☐ The prediction was off by 35%.
- ☐ If the percent error should be less than 60%, the prediction was acceptable.
- ☐ The percent error of the prediction was about 55%.
- ☐ If the percent error should be less than 20%, the prediction was acceptable.
- ☐ The difference between the predicted and actual rainfall was 1.2 inches.

3-ACT MATH

3-Act Mathematical Modeling: The Smart Shopper

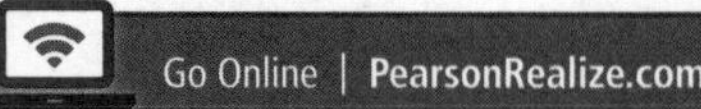

MAFS.K12.MP.4.1 Model with mathematics. Also MP.1.1, MP.2.1, MP.3.1, MP.5.1, MP.6.1, MP.7.1, MP.8.1

MAFS.7.RP.1.3 Use proportional relationships to solve multistep ratio and percent problems.

ACT 1

1. After watching the video, what is the first question that comes to mind?

2. Write the Main Question you will answer.

3. **Construct Arguments** Make a prediction to answer this Main Question. Explain how you arrived at your prediction.

4. On the number line below, write a number that is too small to be the answer. Write a number that is too large.

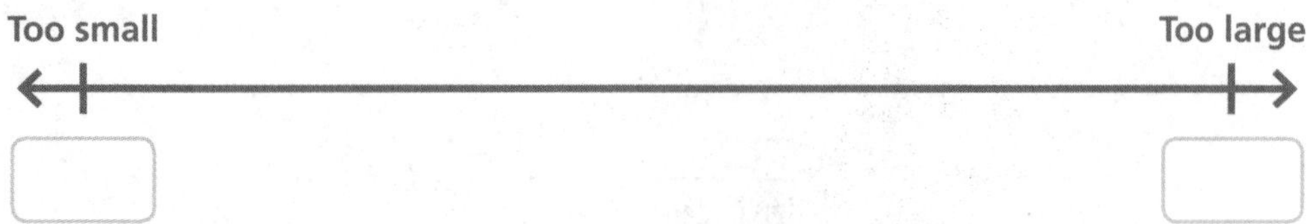

5. Plot your prediction on the same number line.

ACT 2

6. What information in this situation would be helpful to know? How would you use that information?

7. **Use Appropriate Tools** What tools can you use to get the information you need? Record the information as you find it.

8. **Model with Math** Represent the situation using the mathematical content, concepts, and skills from this topic. Use your representation to answer the Main Question.

9. What is your answer to the Main Question? Is it higher or lower than your prediction? Explain why.

ACT 3

10. Write the answer you saw in the video.

11. Reasoning Does your answer match the answer in the video? If not, what are some reasons that wouldexplain the difference?

12. Make Sense and Persevere Would you change your model now that you know the answer? Explain.

ACT 3 Extension

Reflect

13. Model with Math Explain how you used a mathematical model to represent the situation. How did the model help you answer the Main Question?

14. Be Precise Describe how you would tell the friends to use their coupons.

SEQUEL

15. Make Sense and Persevere Suppose the $20 coupon requires a purchase of $100 or more. How would that affect your solution?

Lesson 9-5 Solve Markup and Markdown Problems

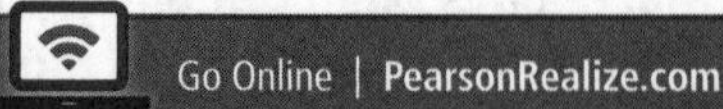

I can...
solve problems involving percent markup and markdown.

MAFS.7.RP.1.3 Use proportional relationships to solve multistep ratio and percent problems.
MAFS.K12.MP.1.1, MP.2.1, MP.4.1, MP.8.1

Solve & Discuss It!

Clare subscribes to an online music streaming service for a yearly fee of $96. Starting next month, there will be a 12% increase in the fee.

The ad for another music streaming service is shown below. Should Clare switch? Explain.

Welcome to our Music site
Log in
DIGITAL STREAMING OF MUSIC
$8.75 per month
Home | About Us | Services | FAQ | Contact Us

Model with Math
You can use the percent equation to determine the percent increase.

Focus on math practices

Make Sense and Persevere What is another problem-solving method you could use to check that your solution makes sense?

? Essential Question How are the concepts of percent markup and percent markdown related to the percent equation?

EXAMPLE 1 Find the Percent Markup

Scan for Multimedia

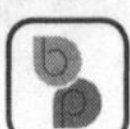

Marty buys plain cell phone cases and then decorates them to resell online at a higher price. What is the percent markup on each phone case?

Markup is the amount of increase from the cost of an item to its selling price. The markup as a percent increase from the original cost is the **percent markup**.

STEP 1 Draw a bar diagram to represent the problem and to find the markup.

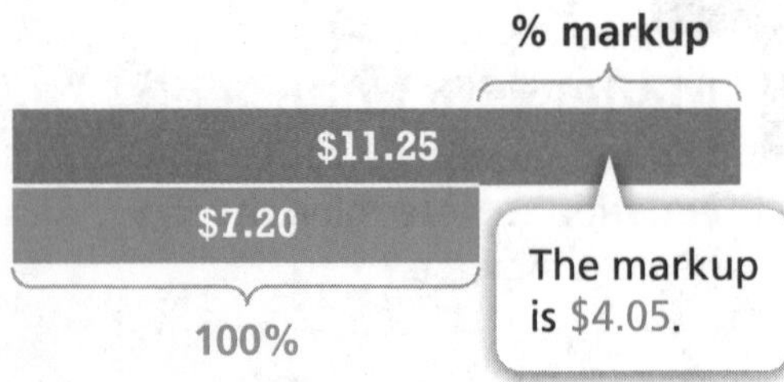

STEP 2 Use the percent equation to find the percent markup.

markup = percent markup • cost

$4.05 = P \cdot 7.20$

$\frac{4.05}{7.20} = P$

$0.5625 = P$

Remember to express the decimal value as a percent.

The percent markup on each cell phone case is about 56%.

Try It!

What is the percent markup on a $300 phone sold for $465?

markup = percent markup • cost

☐ $= P \cdot 300$

☐ $= P$

The percent markup on the phone is ☐%.

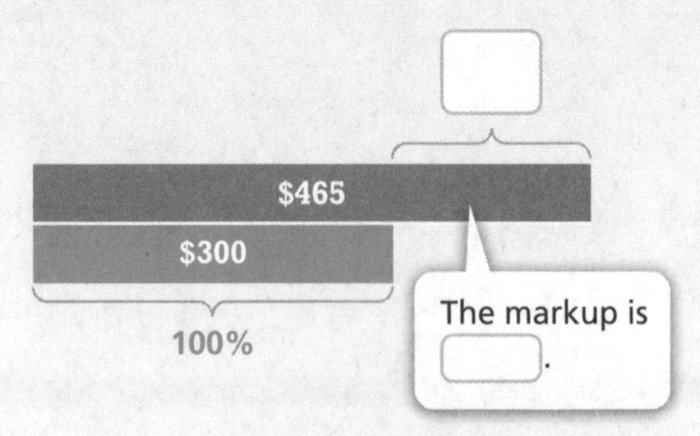

Convince Me! How does the percent equation help solve markup problems?

EXAMPLE 2  Find the Selling Price

The local furniture store pays $110 for a chest of drawers and sells it with a 40% markup. What is the selling price of the chest of drawers?

STEP 1 Draw a bar diagram to represent the problem.

40% markup

selling price

$110

100%

Amount of the markup

STEP 2 Use the percent equation to find the markup and the selling price.

$$\text{markup} = \text{percent markup} \cdot \text{cost}$$
$$a = 0.40 \cdot 110$$
$$a = 44$$

The markup is $44.

$$110 + 44 = 154$$

The selling price of the chest of drawers is $100 + $44 or $154.

 Try It!

What is the selling price for a $45 pair of shoes with a 15% markup?

EXAMPLE 3  Find Markdown and Sales Tax

Edward wants to buy a wakeboard that is on sale. If the sales tax in Edward's state is 7.5%, how much will he pay for the wakeboard?

Markdown is the decrease from the original price of an item to its sale price. The markdown as a percent decrease of the original price is the **percent markdown**.

STEP 1 Use the percent equation to find the marked down price of the wakeboard.

$$\text{markdown} = \text{percent markdown} \cdot \text{original price}$$
$$m = 0.30 \cdot 180$$
$$m = 54$$

The sale price is $180 − $54, or $126.

STEP 2 Use the percent equation to find the sales tax.

$$\text{sales tax} = \text{percent} \cdot \text{sale price}$$
$$s = 0.075 \cdot 126$$
$$s = 9.45$$

Edward will pay 126 + 9.45, or $135.45, for the wakeboard.

Try It!

Find the percent markdown for an $80 jacket that is on sale for $48.

KEY CONCEPT

You can solve markup and markdown problems using the percent equation.

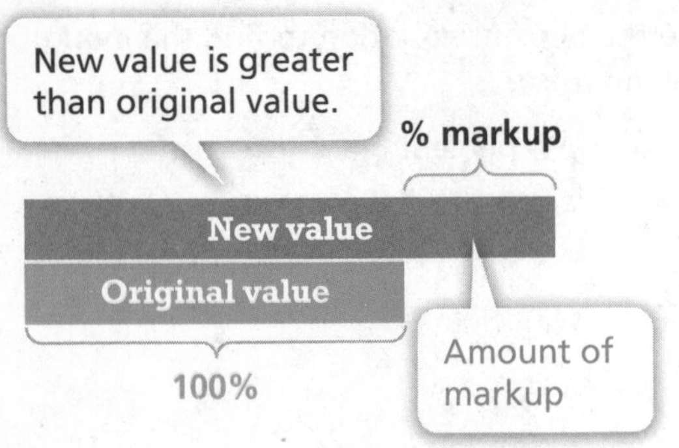

markup = **percent markup** • original value

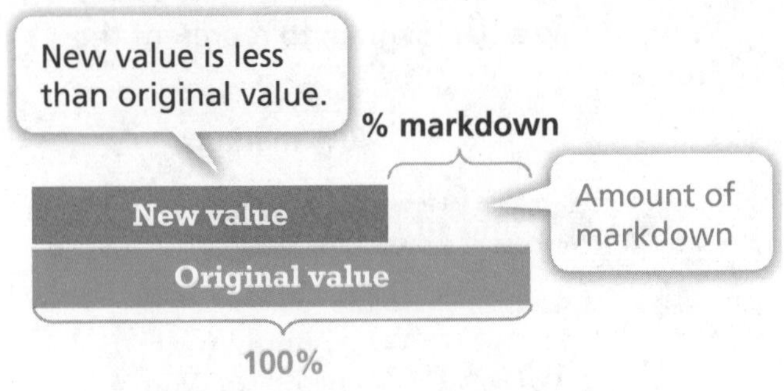

markdown = **percent markdown** • original value

Do You Understand?

1. **Essential Question** How are the concepts of markup and markdown related to the percent equation?

2. **Reasoning** What does the amount of the markup or markdown represent in the percent equation?

3. **Generalize** When an item is marked up by a certain percent and then marked down by the same percent, is the sale price equal to the price before the markup and markdown?

Do You Know How?

4. An item costs $4 before tax and $4.32 after sales tax. What is the sales tax rate?

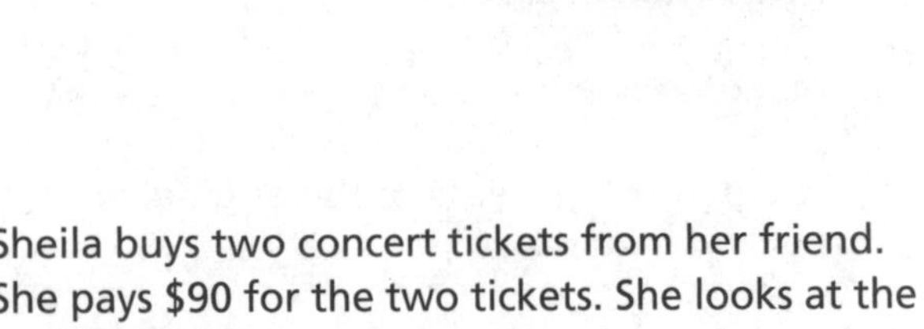

5. Sheila buys two concert tickets from her friend. She pays $90 for the two tickets. She looks at the tickets and sees that each ticket has a face value of $52.50.

   a. How much of a markdown did her friend give Sheila? Explain how you know.

   b. What was the percent markdown, rounded to the nearest whole percent?

6. Find the sale prices.

   a. $4,200 with a 35% markdown

   b. $5,000 with a 44% markdown

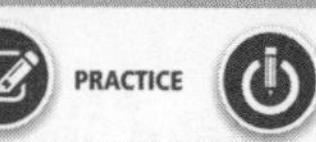

Name: ______________________

Practice & Problem Solving

Leveled Practice In 7–8, fill in the boxes to solve.

7. A \$300 suit is marked down by 20%. Find the sale price rounded to the nearest dollar.

markdown = percent markdown • original price

markdown = ☐ % • \$☐

markdown = \$☐

original price − markdown = sale price

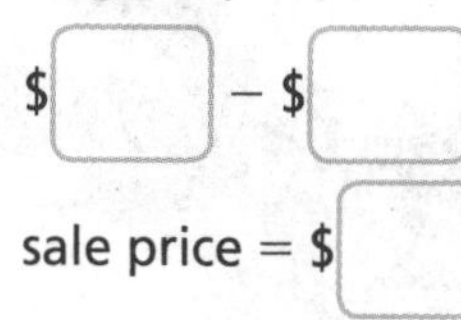

\$☐ − \$☐

sale price = \$☐

8. The selling price of an item is \$650 marked up from the wholesale cost of \$450. Find the percent markup from wholesale cost to selling price.

selling price − markup = wholesale cost

\$☐ − \$☐ = \$☐.

markup = percent markup × wholesale cost

☐ = ☐ × ☐

The percent markup is about ☐.

9. Karen purchased the DVD player shown in the sign on the right. Find the percent markdown rounded to the nearest percent.

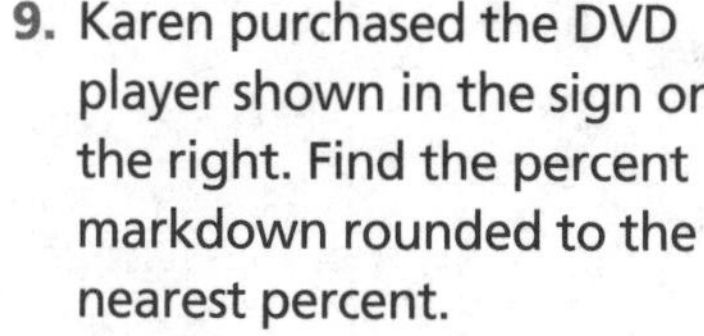

10. A store manager instructs his employees to mark up all items by 30%. A store clerk puts a price tag of \$30 on an item that the store bought for \$27. As an employee, you notice that this selling price is incorrect.

a. Find the correct selling price. Round to the nearest dollar.

b. What was the clerk's likely error?

11. Nate has \$50 to spend at the grocery store. He fills his shopping cart with items totaling \$46. At checkout he will have to pay 6% sales tax on all items in the cart. Does he have enough money to buy everything in his cart? Explain.

12. A department store buys 300 shirts at a cost of \$1,800 and sells them for \$10 each. Find the percent markup rounded to the nearest percent.

13. **Make Sense and Persevere** A computer store buys a computer system at a cost of $465.60. The selling price was first at $776, but then the store advertised a 30% markdown on the system.

a. Find the current sale price. Round to the nearest cent if necessary.

b. Members of the store's loyalty club get an additional 10% off their computer purchases. How much do club members pay for the computer with their discount?

14. **Higher Order Thinking** A sporting goods store manager was selling a kayak set for a certain price. The manager offered the markdowns shown on the right, making the one-day sale price of the kayak set $328. Find the original selling price of the kayak set.

Assessment Practice

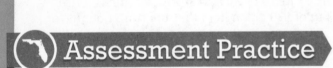

15. Eliza cannot decide which of two bicycles to buy. The original price of each is $380. The first is marked down by 50%. The second is marked down by 30% with an additional 20% off. Which bicycle should Eliza buy if the bicycles are the same except for the selling price? Explain your answer. 7.RP.1.3

16. A shoe store uses a 50% markup for all of the shoes it sells. The store also charges a 10% sales tax on all purchases. What would be the purchase price, including sales tax, of a pair of shoes that has a wholesale cost of $57? 7.RP.1.3

Lesson 9-6 Solve Simple Interest Problems

Go Online | PearsonRealize.com

Explore It!

ACTIVITY

Gerard compares the offers at two different banks to decide where he should open a savings account.

FLBUS
When you open a savings account with us, we'll add **5%** of your first deposit to the account!
New Bank
BUS STOP A1
Open a savings account – we'll add $100 to your first deposit!
Flamingo Bank

I can...
apply percent reasoning to solve simple interest problems.

MAFS.7.RP.1.3 Use proportional relationships to solve multistep ratio and percent problems.
MAFS.K12.MP.1.1, MP.2.1, MP.3.1

A. Draw a representation to show how much would be in the first savings account if Gerard's initial deposit were *d* dollars.

B. Draw a representation to show how much would be in the second savings account if Gerard's initial deposit were *d* dollars.

C. Use the two representations you drew to explain how the offers at the two banks are similar and how they are different.

Focus on math practices

Construct Arguments Gerard's first deposit is $500. Which bank should he choose? Explain.

? Essential Question How does simple interest show proportional reasoning and relate to the percent equation?

VISUAL LEARNING ASSESS

EXAMPLE 1  Find Simple Interest

Scan for Multimedia 

Victoria opens a savings account with a deposit of $300. She will earn 1.6% simple interest each year on her money. How much interest will she earn over 5 years (assuming she does not add or take out any money)?

Interest that is applied to the initial amount only is called **simple interest**.

The initial amount is called the **principal**.

0 years 1 year 2 years 3 years 4 years 5 years

STEP 1 Use the percent equation to find the amount of interest earned in one year, s.

An **interest rate** is a percent used to calculate interest on the principal.

interest amount = interest rate • principal

$s = 0.016 \cdot 300$

$s = 4.80$

The simple interest earned on the principal in one year is $4.80.

STEP 2 Multiply the interest earned in one year by 5 to calculate the total interest Victoria will earn over 5 years.

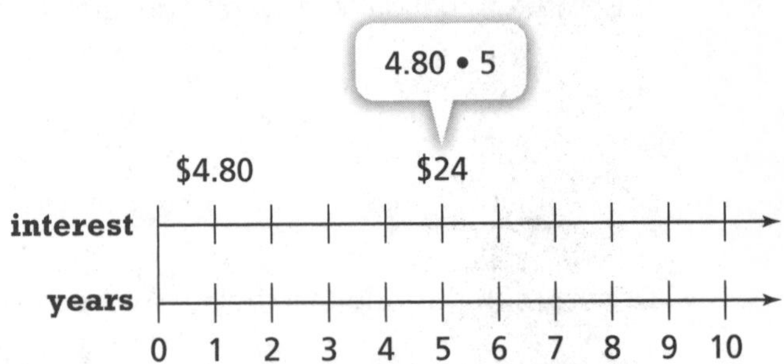

Victoria will earn $24 in interest over 5 years.

Try It!

Victoria has another account at the bank that pays $2\frac{1}{2}$% simple interest. How much interest will she earn in 8 years on an initial deposit of $250 assuming she neither adds to nor withdraws from the account?

$2\frac{1}{2}$% interest expressed as a decimal is ☐.

Interest after 1 year: s = ☐ • $☐

= $☐

Interest after 8 years: $☐ • ☐

= $☐

Victoria will earn $☐ in interest over 8 years.

Convince Me! Would the interest for the second year be the same if it were calculated on the total after the first year? Why or why not?

EXAMPLE 2  Find the Percent of Interest

  ACTIVITY  ASSESS

Maya's older sister got a loan to buy a used car for $3,400. What is the interest rate on the loan?

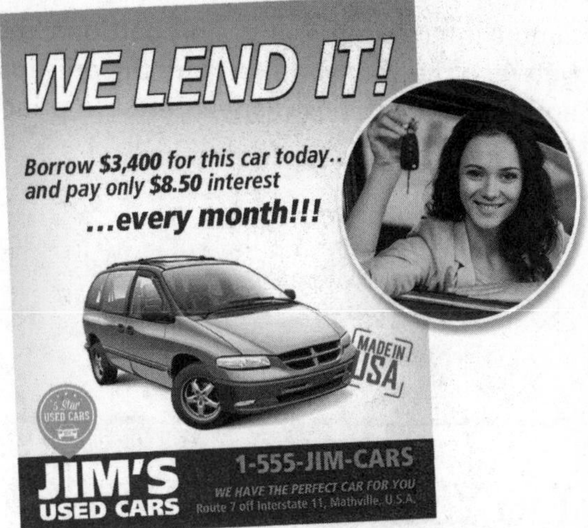

WE LEND IT!
Borrow $3,400 for this car today.. and pay only $8.50 interest
...every month!!!
MADE IN USA
JIM'S USED CARS
1-555-JIM-CARS
WE HAVE THE PERFECT CAR FOR YOU
Route 7 off Interstate 11, Mathville, U.S.A.

STEP 1 Multiply the interest amount by 12 to find the interest for 1 year.

$$8.50 \cdot 12 = 102$$

STEP 2 Use the percent equation to find the interest rate.

interest amount = interest rate • loan amount

$$102 = P \cdot 3{,}400$$

$$\frac{102}{3{,}400} = P \cdot \frac{3{,}400}{3{,}400}$$

$$0.03 = P$$

The simple interest rate is 3% for 1 year.

Try It!

Another company will lend Maya's older sister $4,000. Every month, she will pay $11.88 in interest. What is the interest rate, rounded to the nearest tenth of a percent, for 1 year?

EXAMPLE 3  Find the Principal

Jake opened a savings account that earns 1.5% interest. Jake estimates that, assuming he neither adds to nor withdraws from his account, he will earn $240 in interest after 10 years. How much did Jake deposit when he opened the account?

> **Make Sense and Persevere**
> How can using an equation help make sense of the problem situation?

First, find the amount of interest for 1 year.

$$240 \div 10 = 24$$

Then, use the percent equation to find the initial deposit or principal, d.

interest amount = interest rate • initial deposit

$$24 = 0.015 \cdot d$$

$$\frac{24}{0.015} = d \cdot \frac{0.015}{0.015}$$

$$1{,}600 = d$$

> Calculating simple interest is a good way to estimate how much interest Jake will have in the bank after 10 years.

Jake deposited $1,600.

Try It!

Katelyn's older brother borrowed money for school. He took out a loan that charges 6% simple interest. He will end up paying $720 in interest after 6 years. How much did Katelyn's brother borrow for school?

KEY CONCEPT 

Simple interest represents a proportional relationship between the yearly interest and the principal, or initial amount. The ratio of yearly interest to principal is the interest rate.

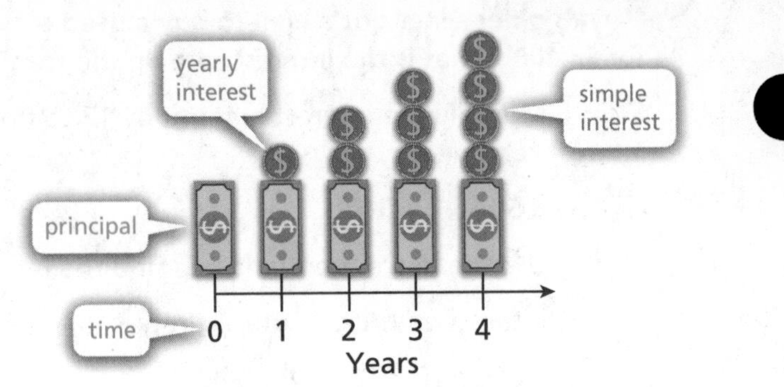

Do You Understand?

1. **Essential Question** How does simple interest show proportional reasoning and relate to the percent equation?

2. **Reasoning** If the interest earned on an account after 2 years is $15, how much would it be after 10 years? Why?

3. **Be Precise** Angelina is deciding which bank would give her the best simple interest rate on a $300 deposit. One bank says that she will have $320 in her account if she leaves the principal for 2 years. Is this enough information for Angelina to find the interest rate? Explain.

Do You Know How?

4. Find the missing value in each row. Use the percent equation.

Principal (P)	Interest Rate (r)	Time in years (t)	Interest Earned (I)
$100	5%	3	
$500	4%		$20
	10%	7	$35
$200		2	$6

5. Annika's older cousin borrowed $800 to repair her car. She will pay off the loan after 2 years by paying back the principal plus 4.5% simple interest for each year.

   a. How much will she pay in interest? Show your work.

   b. How much will she pay back altogether?

6. J.D. opened a savings account with $425. After 2 years, the total interest he earned was $10.20. What was the annual interest rate?

Name: ______________________________

Practice & Problem Solving

Scan for Multimedia

Leveled Practice **In 7–8, fill in the boxes to solve.**

7. Edward deposited \$6,000 into a savings account 4 years ago. The simple interest rate is 3%.

How much money did Edward earn in interest?

Interest = \$ ☐ • ☐ • ☐ years

Edward earned \$ ☐ in interest.

8. The interest on \$2,000 for 2 years is \$320. What is the simple interest rate?

\$ ☐ = \$2,000 • r • ☐

\$ ☐ = \$ ☐ • r

☐ = r

☐ % = r

9. Suppose you deposited \$100 in a savings account 4 years ago with a simple interest rate of 2.2%. The interest that you earned in those 4 years is \$8.80. Which of the following is true? Select all that apply.

- ☐ The interest rate is 0.022.
- ☐ The principal was \$100.
- ☐ The interest earned is \$4.
- ☐ The account was opened 8 years and 8 months ago.

10. A new bank customer with \$3,000 wants to open a money market account. The bank is offering a simple interest rate of 1.1%.

a. How much interest will the customer earn in 20 years?

b. What will be the account balance after 20 years?

11. Boden's account has a principal of \$500 and a simple interest rate of 3.3%. Complete the double number line. How much money will be in the account after 4 years, assuming Boden does not add or take out any money?

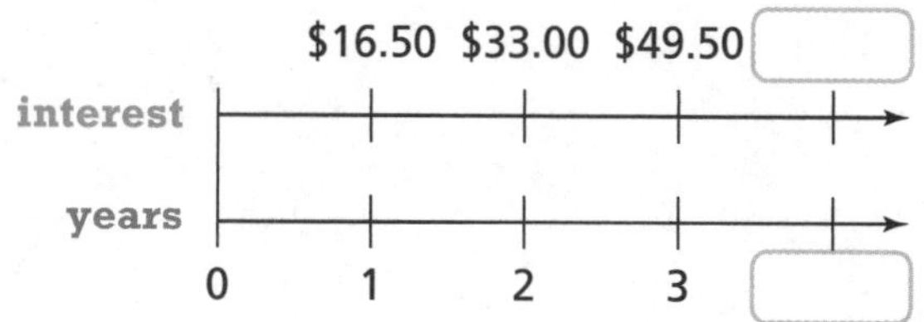

12. Critique Reasoning Monica deposits \$100 into a savings account that pays a simple interest rate of 3.4%. Paul deposits \$200 into a savings account that pays a simple interest rate of 2.2%. Monica says that she will earn more interest in one year because her interest rate is higher. Do you agree? Justify your response.

13. Construct Argument Tommy earned \$76.00 in interest after 5 years on a principal of \$400. Jane earned \$82.00 in interest after 2 years on a principal of \$1,000.

Which bank would you rather use, Tommy's or Jane's? Why?

14. **Reasoning** A bank manager wants to encourage new customers to open accounts with initial deposits of at least $3,000. He has posters made for the promotion.

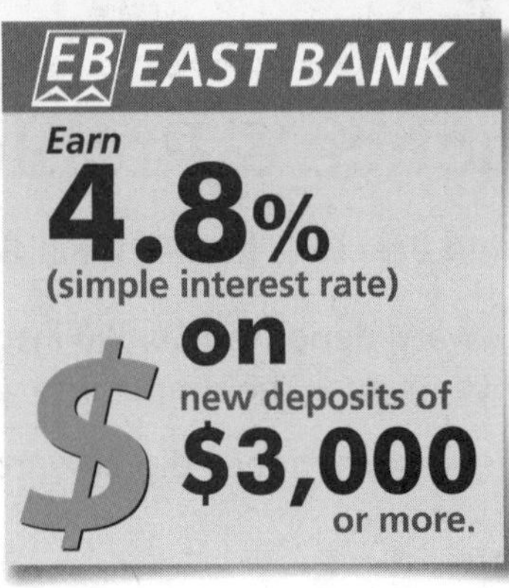
EB EAST BANK
Earn
4.8%
(simple interest rate)
on
new deposits of
$3,000
or more.

a. Under the new promotion, what is the minimum amount of interest a new account would make in one year if there were no withdrawls from the account?

b. The manager wants to add the sentence, "Open an account with $3,000 and earn at least $120 interest each year!" to the poster. Do you agree? Explain.

15. Suppose you deposit $100 in Account A with a simple interest rate of 3.4%, and $300 in Account B with a simple interest rate of 1.8%. One year later, you get a bank statement that shows the interest for Account A is $3.40 and the interest for Account B is $540.00.

a. Which account statement is incorrect?

b. What may have been the bank's error?

16. **Higher Order Thinking** You have two different savings accounts. For Account A, the interest earned after 18 months is $12.00. For Account B, the interest earned after 27 months is $27.00.

a. If the interest rate is 3.2% for Account A, how much is the principal?

b. If the interest rate is 2.4% for Account B, how much is the principal?

c. Which account earned you the most interest in the first year? Explain.

Assessment Practice

17. A certificate of deposit with principal $150 earns 4% annual interest for 2 years.

Select all the options that would earn the same amount of interest. 7.RP.1.3

- ☐ $300 at 2% for 2 years
- ☐ $150 at 6% for 18 months
- ☐ $400 at 3% for 1 year
- ☐ $100 at 1% for 8 years
- ☐ $50 at 48% for 6 months

18. Dakota earned $15.75 in interest in Account A and $28.00 in interest in Account B after 21 months. If the simple interest rate is for 3.0% for Account A and 4.0% for Account B, which account had the greater principal? Explain. 7.RP.1.3

? Topic Essential Question

How can percents show proportional relationships between quantities and be used to solve problems?

Vocabulary Review

Complete each definition and then provide an example of each word.

Vocabulary	markdown	markup	percent change
	principal	simple interest	

Definition	Example
1. The ______ is the decrease from the original price of an item to its sale price.	
2. The accuracy of a measured or estimated value compared to its actual value is described as the ______.	
3. An initial amount of money that is deposited in an account is called the ______.	
4. The ______ describes how much a quantity has changed relative to its original amount.	

Use Vocabulary in Writing

Birute deposits $500 in a savings account with a simple interest rate of 1.3%. How could you use this information to find the interest she would earn in 4 years and determine the percent change in her savings account?

Concepts and Skills Review

LESSON 9-1 Analyze Percents of Numbers

Quick Review

You can use equivalent ratios to find the percent of a number. Remember that a percent is a ratio that relates a number to 100.

Example

Find 57% of 690.

$$\frac{57}{100} = \frac{x}{690}$$

$$\frac{57}{100} \cdot 690 = \frac{x}{690} \cdot 690$$

$$393.3 = x$$

Practice

1. Find 0.8% of 1,046.

2. Find 160% of 98.

3. A company charges a shipping fee that is 4.5% of the purchase price for all items it ships. What is the fee to ship an item that costs $56?

LESSON 9-2 Connect Percent and Proportion

Quick Review

You can use proportions to solve different types of percent problems. There are three values in a percent problem—the percent, the part, and the whole. If you know two of these values, you can set up a proportion to find the third value.

Example

What percent of 19 is 4.75?

The whole is 19 and the part is 4.75. Write a proportion, and solve for the percent, p.

$$\frac{\text{part}}{\text{whole}} = \frac{p}{100}$$

$$\frac{4.75}{19} = \frac{p}{100}$$

$$\frac{4.75}{19} \cdot 100 = \frac{p}{100} \cdot 100$$

$$25 = p$$

So, 4.75 is 25% of 19.

Practice

1. 24.94 is 29% of what number?

2. On Thursday, a restaurant serves iced tea to 35 of its 140 customers. What percent of the customers order iced tea?

3. Liam puts $40 in savings in March and 175% of this amount in savings in April. How much does Liam put in savings in April?

LESSON 9-3 Represent and Use the Percent Equation

Quick Review

You can use the percent equation to solve percent problems.

part = percent • whole

Substitute two of the three values to solve for the unknown value.

Example

Michael earns a 6% commission on each house he sells. If he sells a house for $180,000, how much does he earn in commission, c?

$c = 0.06 \cdot 180{,}000$

$c = 10{,}800$

Michael earns $10,800 in commission.

Practice

1. Sharon paid $78 sales tax on a new camera. If the sales tax rate is 6.5%, what was the cost of the camera?

2. There are 45 students who play a woodwind instrument in the school band. Of these, 18 play the saxophone. What percent of these students play the saxophone?

LESSON 9-4 Solve Percent Change and Percent Error Problems

Quick Review

A percent change can be an increase or a decrease. You can use an equation to find a percent change.

change = percent change • original amount

A percent error is always a nonnegative value. You can use an equation to find a percent error.

difference = percent error • actual

Example

Juan's puppy weighed 16 pounds at the age of 2 months. The puppy weighed 60 pounds at the age of 8 months. What is the percent change in the puppy's weight?

change in pounds $= 60 - 16 = 44$

$44 = P \cdot 16$

$\frac{44}{16} = P$

$2.75 = P$

The puppy's weight increased by 275%.

Practice

1. In 2014, the attendance at Jefferson School's Fall Festival was 650. In 2015, the attendance was 575. What was the percent change in attendance from 2014 to 2015?

Round to the nearest whole percent.

2. Melissa estimated that she would read 250 pages last week. She read 290 pages. What is the percent error of Melissa's estimate? Round to the nearest whole percent.

LESSON 9-5 Solve Markup and Markdown Problems

Quick Review

You can use the percent equation to solve markup and markdown problems.

markup = percent markup • cost
markdown = percent markdown • selling price

Example

Bree buys a purse for \$90. She sells it at her store for \$135. What is the percent markup on the purse?

markup = \$135 − \$90 = \$45

$45 = P \cdot 90$

$\frac{45}{90} = P$

$0.5 = P$ — The decimal 0.5 is equivalent to 50%.

The percent markup on the purse is 50%.

Practice

1. Hank buys a used car for \$7,200 and plans to sell it on his used car lot. What is the price of the car after a markup of 15%?

2. Nya wants to buy a sweater that had an original price of \$55. The sweater is now discounted 20% and the sales tax rate is 5.5%. How much will Nya pay for the sweater?

LESSON 9-6 Solve Simple Interest Problems

Quick Review

You consider four quantities when solving problems involving simple interest.

initial amount, or principal, *p*

interest rate, *r*

time, *t*

amount of simple interest, *I*

Example

Yuni loaned \$400 to her brother. He will repay the loan by paying 2.5% simple interest for 3 years. How much will he pay in interest?

$I = 400 \cdot 0.025 \cdot 3 = \$30$

He will pay \$30 in interest.

Practice

1. Ethan put \$700 into a Certificate of Deposit (CD) account that earns 1.8% interest each year. What will the interest of the CD account be after 6 years?

2. Kelly opened a bank account that earns 1.2% simple interest each year. After 7 years, Kelly will earn \$126 in interest. How much did Kelly deposit when she opened the account?

Riddle Rearranging

Find the value of x in each unit rate. Then arrange the answers in order from least to greatest. The letters will spell out the answer to the riddle below.

I can...
find unit rates with ratios of fractions. 7.RP.1.1

K

$$\frac{\frac{3}{4}\text{ c}}{\frac{1}{3}\text{ h}} = \frac{x\text{ c}}{1\text{ h}}$$

N

$$\frac{\frac{3}{5}\text{ mL}}{\frac{2}{5}\text{ min}} = \frac{x\text{ mL}}{1\text{ min}}$$

A

$$\frac{\frac{1}{4}\text{ mi}}{\frac{5}{8}\text{ h}} = \frac{x\text{ mi}}{1\text{ h}}$$

I

$$\frac{\frac{1}{4}\text{ ft}}{\frac{3}{4}\text{ h}} = \frac{x\text{ ft}}{1\text{ h}}$$

E

$$\frac{\frac{6}{5}\text{ m}}{\frac{1}{2}\text{ s}} = \frac{x\text{ m}}{1\text{ s}}$$

Y

$$\frac{\frac{5}{6}\text{ pt}}{\frac{1}{3}\text{ min}} = \frac{x\text{ pt}}{1\text{ min}}$$

S

$$\frac{\frac{1}{4}\text{ in.}}{\frac{1}{12}\text{ min}} = \frac{x\text{ in.}}{1\text{ min}}$$

O

$$\frac{\frac{5}{3}\text{ pt}}{\frac{5}{6}\text{ h}} = \frac{x\text{ pt}}{1\text{ h}}$$

P

$$\frac{\frac{3}{10}\text{ mm}}{\frac{6}{5}\text{ s}} = \frac{x\text{ mm}}{1\text{ s}}$$

What keys cannot be put in a lock?

GENERATE EQUIVALENT EXPRESSIONS

? Topic Essential Question

How can properties of operations help to generate equivalent expressions that can be used in solving problems?

Topic Overview

10-1 Write and Evaluate Algebraic Expressions
7.EE.2.3, 7.EE.2.4, MP.2.1, MP.4.1, MP.6.1, MP.7.1

10-2 Generate Equivalent Expressions
7.EE.1.1, MP.1.1, MP.2.1, MP.3.1

10-3 Simplify Expressions
7.EE.1.1, MP.1.1, MP.2.1, MP.3.1, MP.7.1

10-4 Expand Expressions
7.EE.1.1, 7.EE.1.2, MP.1.1, MP.4.1, MP.7.1

10-5 Factor Expressions
7.EE.1.1, 7.EE.1.2, MP.1.1, MP.2.1, MP.3.1, MP.8.1

3-Act Mathematical Modeling: I've Got You Covered
7.EE.1.1, 7.EE.1.2, MP.1.1, MP.2.1, MP.3.1, MP.4.1, MP.5.1, MP.7.1, MP.8.1

10-6 Add Expressions
7.EE.1.1, 7.EE.1.2, MP.1.1, MP.2.1, MP.4.1, MP.6.1, MP.7.1

10-7 Subtract Expressions
7.EE.1.1, 7.EE.1.2, MP.1.1, MP.3.1, MP.4.1, MP.7.1

10-8 Analyze Equivalent Expressions
7.EE.1.2, MP.2.1, MP.7.1

Lesson Digital Resources

INTERACTIVE STUDENT EDITION Access online or offline.

VISUAL LEARNING ANIMATION Interact with visual learning animations.

ACTIVITY Use with ***Solve & Discuss It, Explore It,*** and ***Explain It*** activities, and to explore Examples.

VIDEOS Watch clips to support ***3-Act Mathematical Modeling Lessons*** and ***STEM Projects***.

Go online | **PearsonRealize.com**

3-ACT MATH

I've Got You Covered

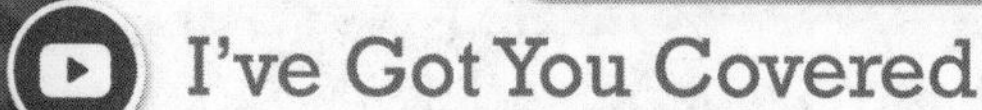

I've Got You Covered

Did you know that DIY stands for Do It Yourself? Do-it-yourself projects are a fun way to save money, learn new skills, and make your home unique.

From painting furniture to turning an old T-shirt into a pillow, there are plenty of projects for everyone.

PRACTICE Practice what you've learned.

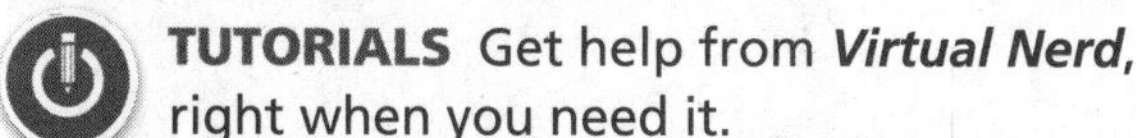

TUTORIALS Get help from ***Virtual Nerd***, right when you need it.

MATH TOOLS Explore math with digital tools.

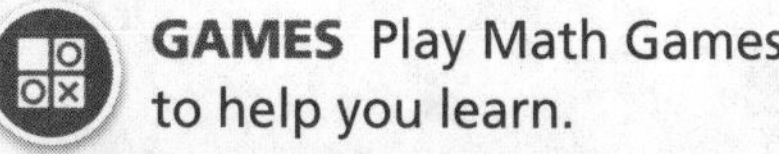

GAMES Play Math Games to help you learn.

KEY CONCEPT Review important lesson content.

GLOSSARY Read and listen to English/Spanish definitions.

ASSESSMENT Show what you've learned.

TOPIC 10

enVision® STEM Project

Did You Know?

In 2013, just over 30% of American consumers knew about activity trackers. By 2015, about **82%** recognized them.

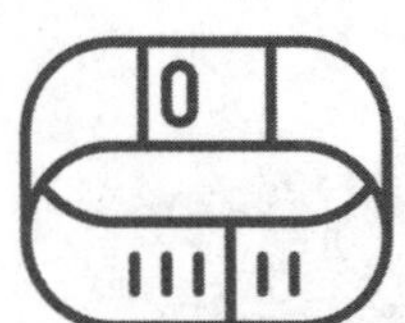

About **3.3 million** fitness bands and activity trackers were sold in the U.S. between April 2013 and March 2014.

% of people aware of activity trackers

2013
30%

2015
82%

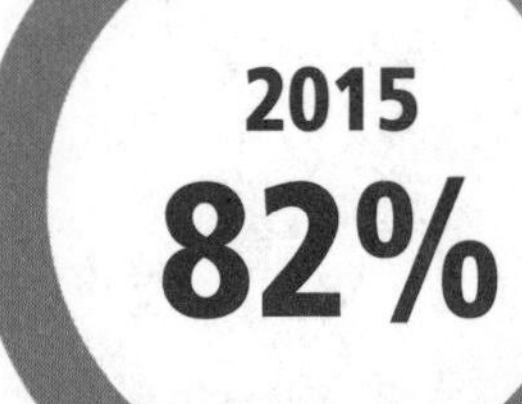

The fitness tracker industry is expected to almost **triple in value** between 2014 and 2019.

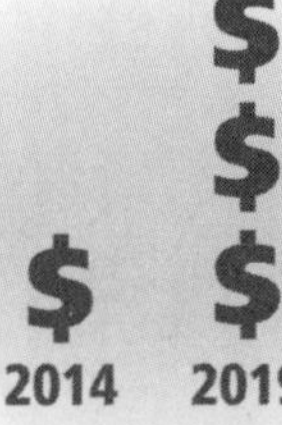

Continued research and development leads to technological advances and breakthroughs, such as the use of biosensing apparel to track activity.

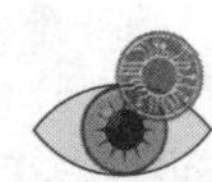

Your Task: Analyze Activity Tracker Data

The ways that data are communicated and presented to the user are just as important as the types of data collected. You and your classmates will continue your exploration of activity trackers and use data to develop models based on individual fitness goals.

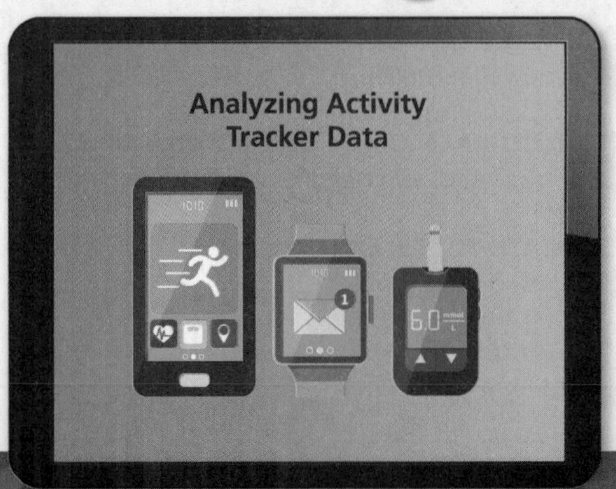

GET READY! TOPIC 10

Review What You Know!

Vocabulary

Choose the best term from the box to complete each definition.

evaluate
expression
factor
order of operations
substitute
term

1. When you ______________ an expression, you replace each variable with a given value.

2. To evaluate $a + 3$ when $a = 7$, you can ______________ 7 for a in the expression.

3. The set of rules used to determine the order in which operations are performed is called the ______________.

4. Each part of an expression that is separated by a plus or minus sign is a(n) ______________.

5. A(n) ______________ is a mathematical phrase that can contain numbers, variables, and operation symbols.

6. When two numbers are multiplied to get a product, each number is called a(n) ______________.

Order of Operations

Evaluate each expression using the order of operations.

7. $3(18 - 7) + 2$

8. $(13 + 2) \div (9 - 4)$

9. $24 \div 4 \cdot 2 - 2$

Equivalent Expressions

Evaluate each expression when $a = -4$ and $b = 3$.

10. ab

11. $2a + 3b$

12. $2(a - b)$

13. Explain the difference between evaluating $3 \cdot 7 - 4 \div 2$ and evaluating $3(7 - 4) \div 2$.

Prepare for Reading Success

Use the graphic organizer to record details you learn about equivalent expressions during Topic 10.

Write one word that describes one major idea of Topic 10.

Write two words that describe things you can do with an expression.

Write three words that describe how the Distributive Property is used.

Write four words that describe the operations that can be used with expressions.

Write five words that describe the Order of Operations.

Write six important vocabulary words.

Name seven types of problems that you solved in Topic 10.

Solve & Discuss It!

Mr. Ramirez's class was playing a game in which students need to match sticky notes that have equivalent expressions.

How can you sort the expressions into groups?

$10p - 8$

$5p + 8 + 3p$

$8p + 2p - 8$

$10p + 4 + 2p + 2$

$2(5p - 4)$

$8(p + 1)$

$4(2p + 2)$

$3p + 4p + 6 + 5p$

$3(4p + 2)$

Lesson 10-1
Write and Evaluate Algebraic Expressions

Go Online | PearsonRealize.com

I can...
write and evaluate algebraic expressions.

MAFS.7.EE.2.4 Use variables to represent quantities in a real-world or mathematical problem, and construct simple equations... to solve problems by reasoning about quantities. Also 7.EE.2.3
MAFS.K12.MP2.1, MP.4.1, MP.6.1, MP.7.1

Focus on math practices

Reasoning Is there more than one way to group the expressions? Give an example.

Essential Question How can algebraic expressions be used to represent and solve problems?

EXAMPLE 1  Write Expressions to Represent Situations

Scan for Multimedia 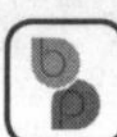

An automatic dog feeder dispenses $\frac{2}{5}$ cup of dog food each day. What expression can the dog owner use to determine the amount of food left in the feeder after d days?

Model with Math How can a bar diagram represent the situation?

Draw a bar diagram to represent the amount of food remaining in the feeder after d days.

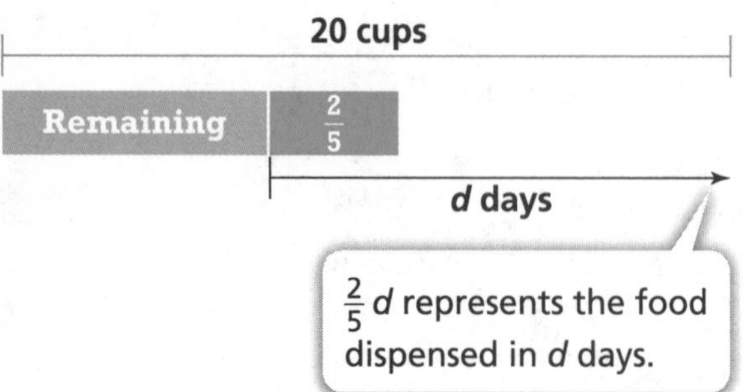

$\frac{2}{5}d$ represents the food dispensed in d days.

Use the bar diagram to write an expression to represent the amount of food remaining in the feeder after d days.

$$20 - \frac{2}{5}d$$

the number of cups of food the feeder holds

the number of cups of food dispensed in d days

The dog owner can use the expression $20 - \frac{2}{5}d$ to determine the amount of food left in the feeder after d days.

Try It!

Misumi started with \$217 in her bank account. She deposits \$25.50 each week and never withdraws any money. What expression can Misumi use to determine her account balance after w weeks?

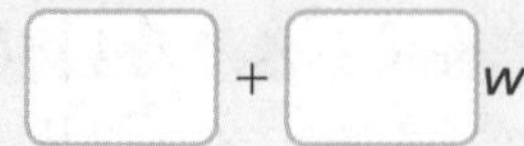

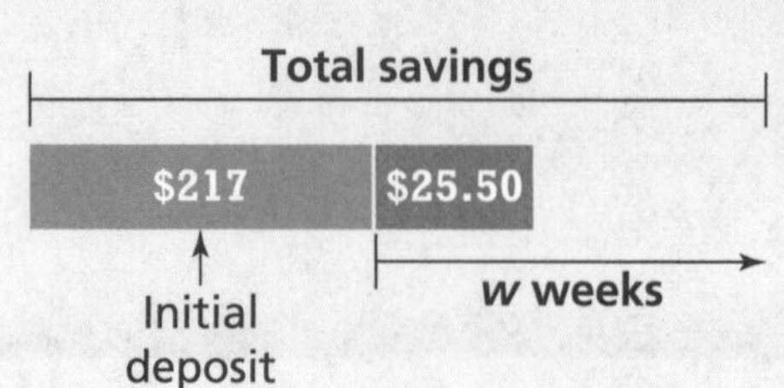

Convince Me! How did you determine which value to use for the constant and which value to use for the coefficient?

EXAMPLE 2  Evaluate Expressions

ACTIVITY ASSESS

The expression $9.99d + 12.99c$ can be used to find the total cost of d pounds of almonds and c pounds of cashews. How much does it cost to buy $1\frac{1}{2}$ pounds of almonds and $2\frac{1}{2}$ pounds of cashews?

Evaluate the expression for the given values.

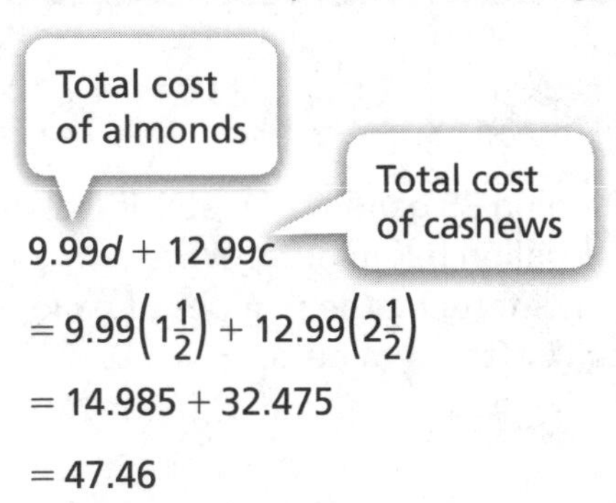

$9.99d + 12.99c$

$= 9.99\left(1\frac{1}{2}\right) + 12.99\left(2\frac{1}{2}\right)$

$= 14.985 + 32.475$

$= 47.46$

Almonds $9.99/lb

Cashews $12.99/lb

It costs $47.46 to buy $1\frac{1}{2}$ pounds of almonds and $2\frac{1}{2}$ pounds of cashews.

 Try It!

The cost to rent a scooter is $15.50 per hour and the cost to rent a watercraft is $22.80 per hour. Use the expression $15.5s + 22.8w$ to determine how much it would cost to rent a scooter for $3\frac{1}{2}$ hours and a watercraft for $1\frac{3}{4}$ hours.

EXAMPLE 3  Write and Evaluate Expressions

Malik and two friends earn m dollars in one week doing odd jobs. They split the earnings so that each friend gets $\frac{1}{3}$ of the total earnings. Malik uses $32.50 of his earnings on lunch each week. Last week, the three friends earned $963. How much money did Malik have left after paying for lunch?

Write an expression to represent how much Malik has left. Then evaluate the expression for the given value.

$\frac{1}{3}m - 32.5$

$= \frac{1}{3}(963) - 32.5$

$= 288.5$

Malik had $288.50 left after paying for lunch.

Try It!

Emelia earns $8.74 per hour plus a gas allowance of $3.50 per day at her job. How much does Emelia's job pay in a day when she works $5\frac{1}{2}$ hours? Write an expression and evaluate for $5\frac{1}{2}$ hours.

KEY CONCEPT

Algebraic expressions can be used to represent problems with unknown or variable values.

Values can be substituted for variables to evaluate the expression.

Do You Understand?

1. **Essential Question** How are algebraic expressions used to represent and solve problems?

2. **Use Structure** How is a constant term different than a variable term for an expression that represents a real-world situation?

3. **Look for Relationships** Explain why you can have different values when evaluating an algebraic expression.

Do You Know How?

4. A tank containing 35 gallons of water is leaking at a rate of $\frac{1}{4}$ gallon per minute. Write an expression to determine the number of gallons left in the tank after m minutes.

5. Write an algebraic expression that Marshall can use to determine the total cost of buying a watermelon that weighs w pounds and some tomatoes that weigh t pounds. How much will it cost to buy a watermelon that weighs $18\frac{1}{2}$ pounds and 5 pounds of tomatoes?

Watermelons $0.68 per lb

Tomatoes $3.25 per lb

6. What is the value of $\frac{3}{8}x - 4.5$ when $x = 0.4$?

7. What is the value of $8.4n - 3.2p$ when $n = 2$ and $p = 4$?

Name: ______________________________

Practice & Problem Solving

Scan for Multimedia

Leveled Practice **For 8–10, fill in the boxes to complete the problems.**

8. Evaluate $10.2x + 9.4y$ when $x = 2$ and $y = 3$.

$10.2(\square) + 9.4(\square)$

$= \square + 28.2$

$= \square$

9. Evaluate $\frac{1}{2}t + \frac{3}{8}$ when $t = \frac{1}{4}$.

$\frac{1}{2}(\square) + \frac{3}{8}$

$= \square + \frac{3}{8}$

$= \square$

10. Write an expression that represents the height of a tree that began at 6 feet and increases by 2 feet per year. Let *y* represent the number of years.

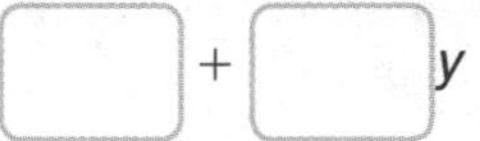

For 11–14, evaluate each expression for the given value of the variable(s).

11. $3d - 4$

$d = 1.2$

12. $0.5f - 2.3g$

$f = 12, g = 2$

13. $\frac{2}{3}p + 3$

$p = \frac{3}{5}$

14. $34 + \frac{4}{9}w$

$w = -\frac{1}{2}$

15. Model with Math What expression can be used to determine the total cost of buying *g* pounds of granola for \$3.25 per pound and *f* pounds of flour for \$0.74 per pound?

16. Model with Math Which expression can be used to determine the total weight of a box that by itself weighs 0.2 kilogram and contains *p* plaques that weigh 1.3 kilograms each?

Ⓐ $1.3p + 0.2$

Ⓑ $0.2p + 1.3$

Ⓒ $0.2 - 1.3p$

Ⓓ $1.2p$

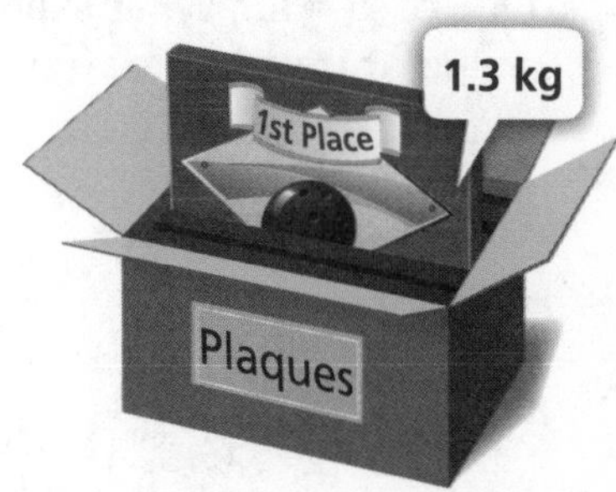

17. The expression $-120 + 13m$ represents a submarine that began at a depth of 120 feet below sea level and ascended at a rate of 13 feet per minute. What was the depth of the submarine after 6 minutes?

18. **Be Precise** A full grain silo empties at a constant rate. Write an expression to determine the amount of grain left after s seconds.

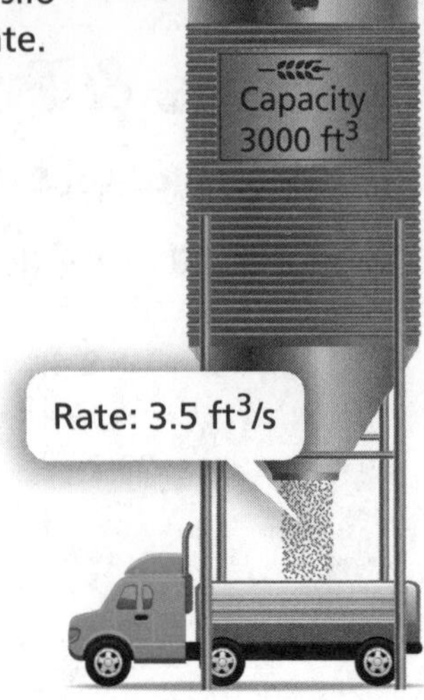

19. **Higher Order Thinking** For the expression $5 - 5x$ to have a negative value, what must be true about the value of x?

Assessment Practice

20. Joe bought g gallons of gasoline for \$2.85 per gallon and c cans of oil for \$3.15 per can.

PART A

What expression can be used to determine the total amount Joe spent on gasoline and oil? 7.EE.2.4

PART B

Joe spent \$15. He bought 2 cans of oil. About how many gallons of gasoline did he buy? 7.EE.2.3

Ⓐ 2.5

Ⓑ 3

Ⓒ 3.5

Ⓓ 4

21. The outside temperature was 73°F at 1 P.M. and decreases at a rate of 1.5°F each hour. What expression can be used to determine the temperature h hours after 1 P.M.? 7.EE.2.4

Explore It!

Lesson 10-2
Generate Equivalent Expressions

I can...
write equivalent expressions for given expressions.

MAFS.7.EE.1.1 Apply properties of operations as strategies to add, subtract, factor, and expand linear expressions with rational coefficients.
MAFS.K12.MP.1.1, MP.2.1, MP.3.1

A shipment of eggs contains some cartons with a dozen eggs and some cartons with a half-dozen eggs.

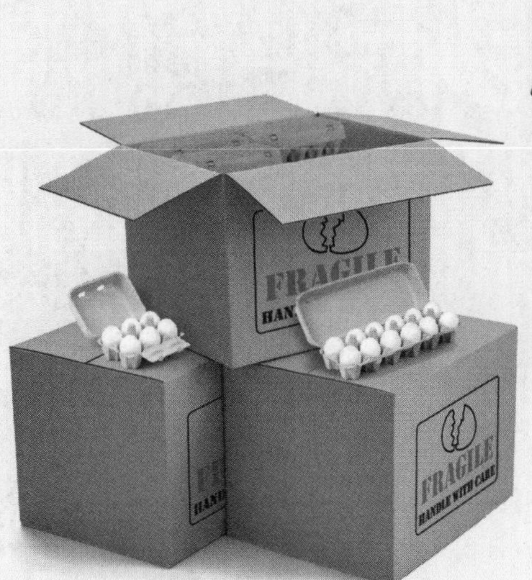

A. How can you represent the total number of eggs in the shipment using diagrams or images? Explain your diagram.

B. How can you represent the total number of eggs in the shipment using expressions? What variables do you use? What do they represent?

Focus on math practices

Construct Arguments How do the two representations compare? How are they different?

EXAMPLE 1 Use Properties of Operations to Write Equivalent Expressions

Scan for Multimedia

The student council has spent \$300 on the supplies needed to sponsor a dance concert fundraiser. Three council members wrote the following expressions to represent the total amount raised for t tickets sold. Can they all be correct? Explain.

$6t - 300$ $6(t - 50)$ $-300 + 6t$

Reasoning How can you use the properties of operations to determine whether the expressions are equivalent?

STEP 1 Verify that one of the expressions represents the amount raised for t tickets sold.

$6t - 300$

The cost of supplies

The amount made selling tickets

STEP 2 Use properties of operations to write equivalent expressions.

$6(t - 50)$

$= 6 \cdot t - 6 \cdot 50$

$= 6t - 300$

Use the Distributive Property.

$-300 + 6t$

$= 6t + (-300)$

$= 6t - 300$

Use the Commutative Property.

The council members wrote equivalent expressions. They are all correct.

Try It!

Nancy wrote the expression $3x - 12$ to represent the relationship in a table of values. Use properties of operations to write two equivalent expressions.

$3(x - \square)$

$\square + 3x$

Convince Me! What property can you use to write an equivalent expression for $-5(x - 2)$? Explain.

EXAMPLE 2 Write Equivalent Expressions by Combining Like Terms

Write equivalent expressions by combining like terms.

a. $-5x + 2y + 3x$

$-5x + 3x + 2y$ — Use the Commutative Property.

$(-5 + 3)x + 2y$ — Use the Distributive Property.

$-2x + 2y$

b. $\frac{1}{3}x + \left(\frac{1}{6}x + y\right)$

$\left(\frac{1}{3}x + \frac{1}{6}x\right) + y$ — Use the Associative Property.

$\frac{3}{6}x + y$

Look for Relationships
How can you check whether the expressions are equivalent?

Try It!

Use properties of operations to write two expressions that are equivalent to $\frac{3}{4}n + \left(8 + \frac{1}{3}z\right)$.

EXAMPLE 3 Identify Equivalent Expressions

Which of the expressions below are equivalent to $-\frac{2}{3}x - 2$?

$-\frac{2}{3}x + (-2)$

$= -\frac{2}{3}x - 2$ — Subtract the additive inverse.

The expression is equivalent to $-\frac{2}{3}x - 2$.

$2 - \frac{2}{3}x$

$= -\frac{2}{3}x + 2$ — Use the Commutative Property.

The expression is NOT equivalent to $-\frac{2}{3}x - 2$.

$-x + \left(\frac{1}{3}x + (-2)\right)$

$\left(-x + \frac{1}{3}x\right) + (-2)$ — Use the Associative Property.

$-\frac{2}{3}x + (-2)$

The expression is equivalent to $-\frac{2}{3}x - 2$.

Try It!

Write two expressions that are equivalent to $-\frac{5}{4}x - \frac{3}{4}$.

KEY CONCEPT 

You can use properties of operations to write equivalent expressions.

$-\frac{1}{2}(x+8)$

$= -\frac{1}{2}x + \left(-\frac{1}{2}\right) \cdot 8$ — Use the Distributive Property.

$= -\frac{1}{2}x + (-4)$

$= -4 + \left(-\frac{1}{2}x\right)$ — Use the Commutative Property.

The expressions $-\frac{1}{2}(x+8)$, $-\frac{1}{2}x + (-4)$, and $-4 + \left(-\frac{1}{2}x\right)$ are equivalent.

Do You Understand?

1. **Essential Question** What are equivalent expressions?

2. **Make Sense and Persevere** For which operations is the Commutative Property true?

3. How can the Associative Property be applied when writing equivalent expressions with variables?

Do You Know How?

4. Write an expression equivalent to $-3 + \frac{2}{3}y - 4 - \frac{1}{3}y$.

5. Complete the tables to determine if the expressions are equivalent. If the expressions are equivalent, name the property or properties that make them equivalent.

$3(x-5)$

x	Value of Expression
1	
2	
3	

$3x - 15$

x	Value of Expression
1	
2	
3	

6. Use the properties of operations to write an expression equivalent to $4x + \frac{1}{2} + 2x - 3$.

Name: ________________________________

Practice & Problem Solving

Scan for Multimedia

For 7–9, write an equivalent expression.

7. $-3(7 + 5g)$

8. $(x + 7) + 3y$

9. $\frac{2}{9} - \frac{1}{5} \cdot x$

10. Which expression is equivalent to $t + 4 + 3 - 2t$?

Ⓐ $t + 7$

Ⓑ $-t + 7$

Ⓒ $6t$

Ⓓ $10t$

11. The distance in feet that Karina swims in a race is represented by $4d - 4$, where d is the distance for each lap. What is an expression equivalent to $4d - 4$?

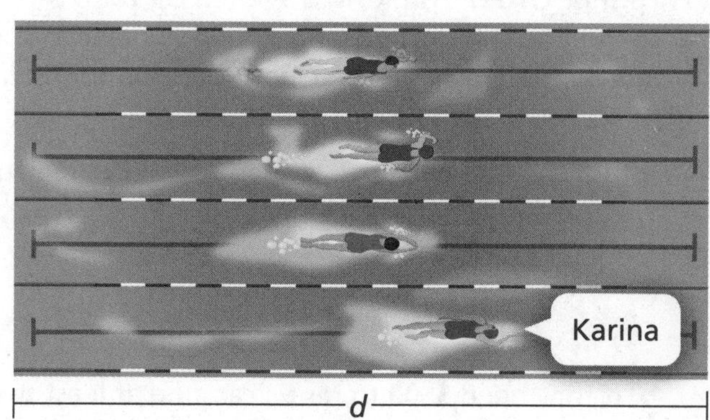

12. Use the Associative Property to write an expression equivalent to $(w + 9) + 3$.

13. Nigel is planning his training schedule for a marathon over a 4-day period. He is uncertain how many miles he will run on two days. One expression for the total miles he will run is $12 + y + 17 + z$.

Use the Commutative Property to write an equivalent expression.

Marathon Training Plan

Day	Miles to Run
1	12
2	y
3	17
4	z

14. Maria said the expression $-4n + 3 + 9n - 4$ is equivalent to $4n$. What error did Maria likely make?

15. Write an expression equivalent to $x - 3y + 4$.

16. Andre wrote the expression $-2 + 4x \div 3$ to represent the relationship shown in the table.

Write two other expressions that also represent the relationship shown in the table.

x	Value of Expression
0	−2
6	6
12	14

17. Higher Order Thinking To rent a car for a trip, four friends are combining their money. The group chat shows the amount of money that each puts in. One expression for their total amount of money is 189 plus p plus 224 plus q.

Group MMS
Travel Fund?
I've got $189.
Not sure amount yet.
I've got $224.
Get back to you!
$p
$q

a. Use the Commutative Property to write two equivalent expressions.

b. If they need $500 to rent a car, find at least two different pairs of numbers that p and q could be.

Assessment Practice

18. Select all expressions equivalent to $\frac{3}{5}x + 3$. 7.EE.1.1

- ☐ $\frac{2}{5}x + 3\frac{1}{5}x$
- ☐ $\frac{4}{5}x - \frac{1}{5}x + 3$
- ☐ $\frac{2}{5}x + 3\frac{3}{5}x - 1$
- ☐ $1 + \frac{3}{5}x + 2$
- ☐ $1 + \frac{x}{5} + 2$
- ☐ $1 + \frac{2}{5}x + 3$

Lesson 10-3
Simplify Expressions

Go Online | PearsonRealize.com

I can...
use properties of operations to simplify expressions.

MAFS.7.EE.1.1 Apply properties of operations as strategies to add, subtract ... linear expressions with rational coefficients.
MAFS.K12.MP.1.1, MP.2.1, MP.3.1, MP.7.1

Solve & Discuss It!

ACTIVITY

How can the tiles below be sorted?

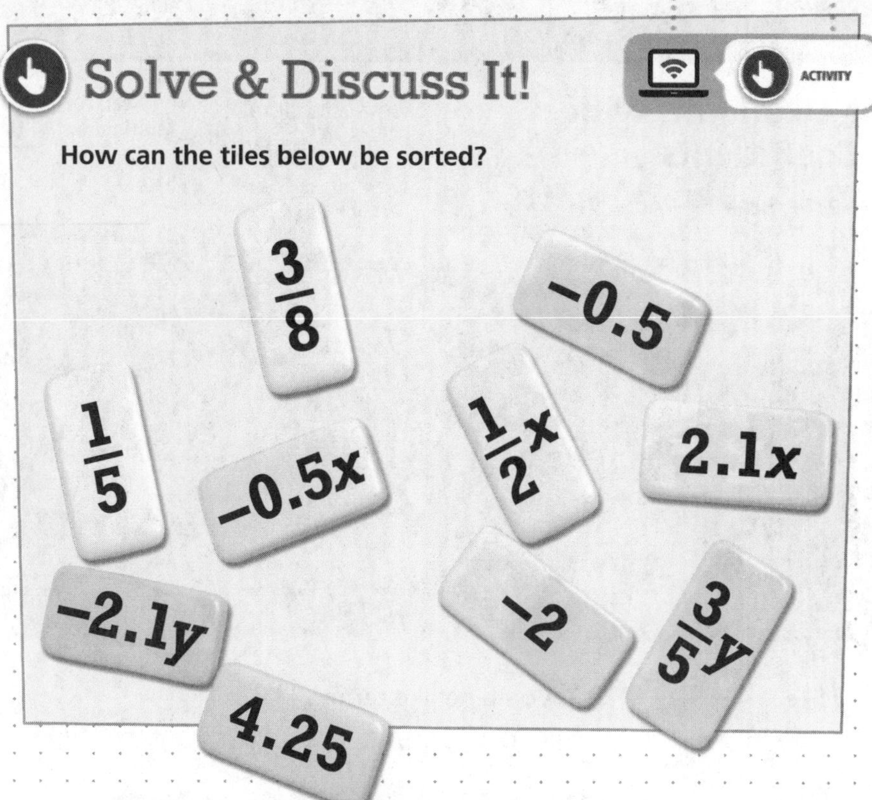

Focus on math practices

Reasoning Would sorting the tiles with positive coefficients together and tiles with negative coefficients together help to simplify an expression that involves all the tiles? Explain.

Essential Question How are properties of operations used to simplify expressions?

VISUAL LEARNING
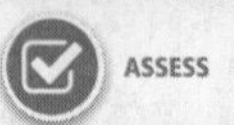
ASSESS

EXAMPLE 1  Combine Like Terms with Integer Coefficients

Scan for Multimedia 

A teacher used algebra tiles to model $-2c + 3c - 5 - 4c + 7$.

Simplify the expression.

STEP 1 Write the expression by grouping like terms together.

Use the Commutative and Associative Properties to reorder and group like terms.

$-2c + 3c - 5 - 4c + 7$

$= -2c + 3c - 4c - 5 + 7$

$= -2c - 4c + 3c - 5 + 7$

$= (-2c - 4c + 3c) + (-5 + 7)$

STEP 2 Combine like terms.

$(-2c - 4c + 3c) + (-5 + 7)$

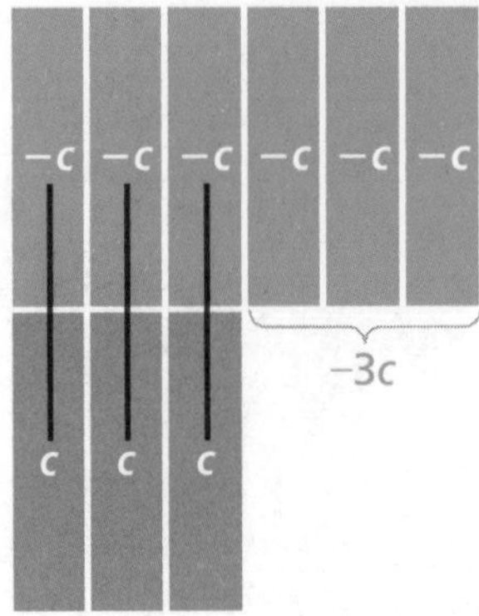

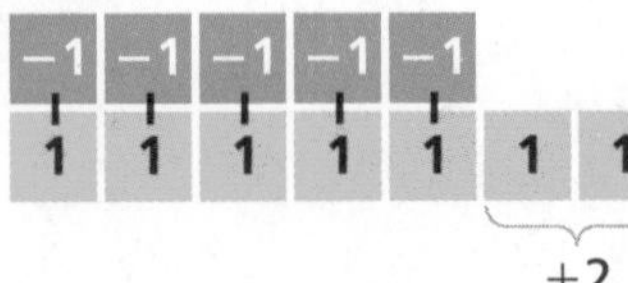

Use Structure Why can you not combine unlike terms?

The simplified expression is $-3c + 2$.

Try It!

Simplify the expression $-6 - 6f + 7 - 3f - 9$.

$\square - 3f - \square + 7 - \square$

$\square - \square$

Convince Me! How do you decide in what way to reorder the terms of an expression when simplifying it?

EXAMPLE 2  Combine Like Terms with Rational Coefficients

Simplify the expression $-3 + \frac{1}{3}x + (-4.5) - \frac{1}{5}x$.

$-3 + \frac{1}{3}x + (-4.5) - \frac{1}{5}x$

$= \left(\frac{1}{3}x - \frac{1}{5}x\right) + (-3 + (-4.5))$

Use the Commutative and Associative Properties to reorder and group like terms.

$= \left(\frac{5}{15}x - \frac{3}{15}x\right) + (-3 + (-4.5))$

$= \frac{2}{15}x + (-7.5)$

Combine like terms.

Use Structure Include the signs of terms when reordering the terms.

The simplified expression is $\frac{2}{15}x - 7.5$.

Try It!

Simplify each expression.

a. $59.95m - 30 + 7.95m + 45 + 9.49m$

b. $-0.5p + \frac{1}{2}p - 2.75 + \frac{2}{3}p$

EXAMPLE 3  Combine Like Terms with Two Variables

Simplify the expression $4a - 5b - 6 + 2b - 3a$.

$4a - 5b - 6 + 2b - 3a$

$= (4a - 3a) + (-5b + 2b) - 6$

Use the Commutative and Associative Properties to reorder and group like terms.

$= 1a - 3b - 6$

The simplified expression is $a - 3b - 6$.

Try It!

Simplify the expression $-3.7 + 5g + 4k + 11.1 - 10g$.

(☐ $- 10g) + 4k +$ (☐ $+ 11.1)$

$=$ ☐ $+ 4k +$ ☐

The simplified expression is ☐.

KEY CONCEPT

When simplifying algebraic expressions, use properties of operations to combine like terms.

To simplify the expression below, group like terms.

$\frac{3}{10}y - 3.5x - \frac{3}{8} + 0.53x + 5.25 - 2.75y - 12$

$(-3.5x + 0.53x) + \left(\frac{3}{10}y - 2.75y\right) + \left(-\frac{3}{8} + 5.25 - 12\right)$

Then combine like terms.

$-2.97x - 2.45y - 7.125$

Do You Understand?

1. **Essential Question** How are properties of operations used to simplify expressions?

2. **Make Sense and Persevere** Explain why constant terms expressed as different rational number types can be combined.

3. **Reasoning** How do you know when an expression is in its simplest form?

Do You Know How?

4. Simplify $-4b + (-9k) - 6 - 3b + 12$.

5. Simplify $-2 + 6.45z - 6 + (-3.25z)$.

6. Simplify $-9 + \left(-\frac{1}{3}y\right) + 6 - \frac{4}{3}y$.

Name: ____________________

Practice & Problem Solving

Scan for Multimedia

In 7–10, simplify each expression.

7. $-2.8f + 0.9f - 12 - 4$

8. $3.2 - 5.1n - 3n + 5$

9. $2n + 5.5 - 0.9n - 8 + 4.5p$

10. $12 + (-4) - \frac{2}{5}j - \frac{4}{5}j + 5$

11. Which expression is equivalent to $-5v + (-2) + 1 + (-2v)$?

Ⓐ $-9v$

Ⓑ $-4v$

Ⓒ $-7v - 1$

Ⓓ $-7v + 3$

12. Which expression is equivalent to $\frac{2}{3}x + (-3) + (-2) - \frac{1}{3}x$?

Ⓐ $x + 5$

Ⓑ $-\frac{1}{3}x - 5$

Ⓒ $\frac{1}{3}x - 1$

Ⓓ $\frac{1}{3}x - 5$

13. The dimensions of a garden are shown. Write an expression to find the perimeter.

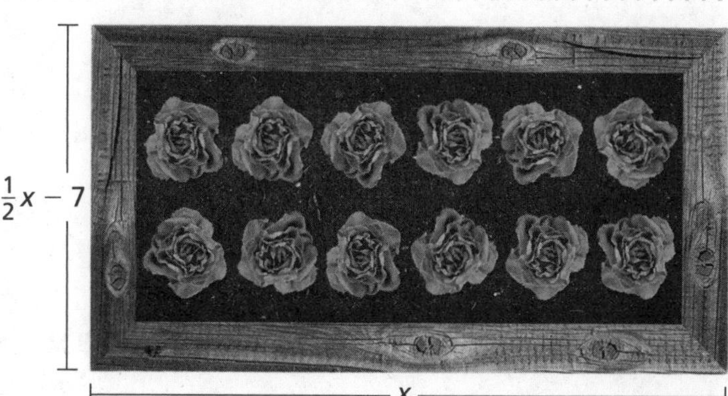

14. Simplify the expression $8h + (-7.3d) - 14 + 5d - 3.2h$.

15. Simply $4 - 2y + (-8y) + 6.2$.

16. Simplify $\frac{4}{9}z - \frac{3}{9}z + 5 - \frac{5}{9}z - 8$.

17. **Construct Arguments** Explain whether $11t - 4t$ is equivalent to $4t - 11t$. Support your answer by evaluating the expression for $t = 2$.

18. The signs show the costs of different games at a math festival. How much would it cost n people to play Decimal Decisions and Ratio Rage?

M A T H F E S T
PROBABILITY
POSSIBILITIES
Cost ($) of 1 Game: 5.5n – 3
DECIMAL
DECISIONS
Cost ($) of 1 Game: 12.70 – n + 9
RATIO RAGE!
Cost ($) of 1 Game: n/4

19. **Higher Order Thinking** In the expression $ax + bx$, a is a decimal and b is a fraction. How do you decide whether to write a as a fraction or b as a decimal?

Assessment Practice

20. Select all expressions equivalent to $-6z + (-5.5) + 3.5z + 5y - 2.5$. 7.EE.1.1

- ☐ $-8 + 5y + 2.5z$
- ☐ $-2.5z + 5y - 8$
- ☐ $-8 + 5y + (-2.5z)$
- ☐ $2.5y + (-2.5z) - 5.5$
- ☐ $5y - 8 - 2.5z$

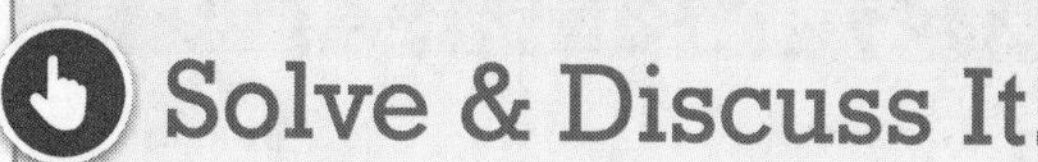

Solve & Discuss It!

Lesson 10-4
Expand Expressions

Go Online | PearsonRealize.com

I can...
expand expressions using the Distributive Property.

MAFS.7.EE.1.1 Apply properties of operations as strategies to ... expand linear expressions with rational coefficients. Also 7.EE.1.2
MAFS.K12.MP.1.1, MP.4.1, MP.7.1

The school is planning to add a weight room to the gym. If the total area of the gym and weight room should stay under 5,500 square feet, what is one possible length for the new weight room? Show your work. Are there other lengths that would work? Why or why not?

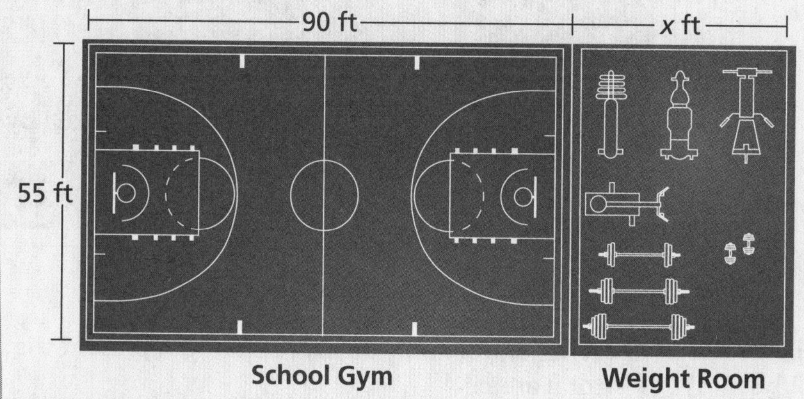

Look for Relationships What is the relationship between the areas of the gym and weight room?

Focus on math practices

Model with Math What is an expression using x that represents the total area of the gym and the weight room?

? Essential Question How does the value of an expression change when it is expanded?

VISUAL LEARNING
ASSESS

EXAMPLE 1 Expand Expressions Using the Distributive Property

Scan for Multimedia

A family farm plans to add a tomato patch to the end of their orange orchard. What is the total area of land that will be covered by the tomato patch and orange orchard?

Model with Math An area model can be used to represent the Distributive Property.

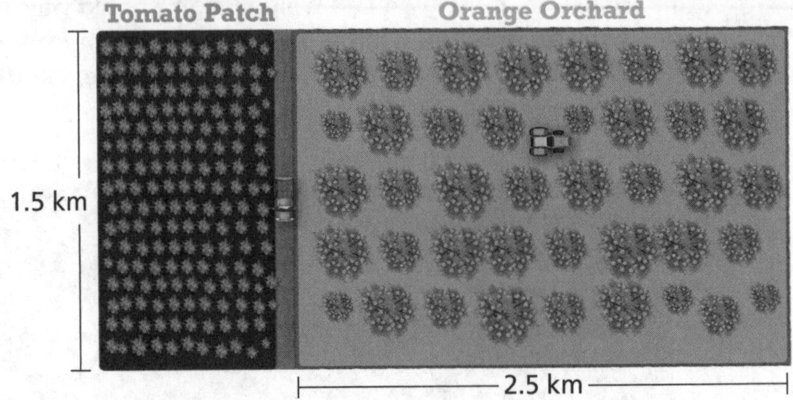
Tomato Patch
Orange Orchard
1.5 km
2.5 km

Use a diagram to represent the areas of the tomato patch and orange orchard.

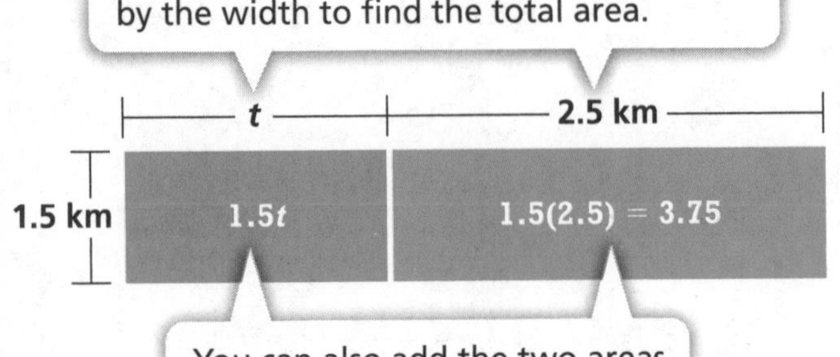
You can add the two lengths and multiply by the width to find the total area.
t
2.5 km
1.5 km
1.5t
1.5(2.5) = 3.75
You can also add the two areas to find the total area.

Write and simplify an expression to represent the total area.

$1.5(t + 2.5)$

$= 1.5t + 1.5(2.5)$

$= 1.5t + 3.75$

Use the Distributive Property to expand the expression. Multiply each term inside the parentheses by 1.5.

The expression that represents the total land area is $1.5t + 3.75$.

Try It!

What is the expanded form of the expression $3.6(t + 5)$?

$3.6(t + 5)$

$= \square t + \square \cdot 5$

$= \square + \square$

The expanded expression is $\square$.

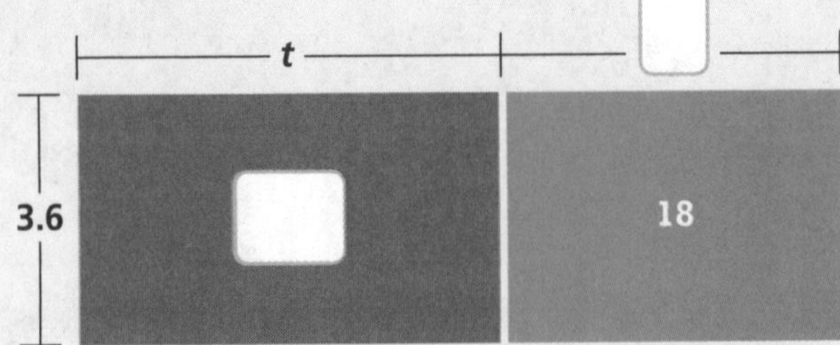
t
3.6
18

Convince Me! If you know the value of t, would the evaluated expression be different if you added the known value of t and 5 and then multiplied by 3.6? Explain.

EXAMPLE 2  Expand Expressions with a Variable

Use the Distributive Property to expand the expression $x(-2 - 0.5y)$.

$x(-2 - 0.5y)$

$= (x)(-2) + (x)(-0.5y)$ — Distribute the x to both terms inside the parentheses.

$= -2x + (-0.5xy)$

$= -2x - 0.5xy$

The expanded expression is $-2x - 0.5xy$.

Try It!

Expand the expression $t(-1.2w + 3)$.

EXAMPLE 3  Expand More Complex Expressions

Simplify the expression $-\frac{1}{3}(2 - 3x + 3)$.

ONE WAY Use the Distributive Property first to distribute the coefficient $-\frac{1}{3}$.

$-\frac{1}{3}(2 - 3x + 3)$

$= (-\frac{1}{3} \cdot 2) + (-\frac{1}{3} \cdot -3x) + (-\frac{1}{3} \cdot 3)$

$= -\frac{2}{3} + x - 1$

$= -\frac{5}{3} + x$

The simplified expression is $-\frac{5}{3} + x$.

ANOTHER WAY Simplify within parentheses first. Then distribute the coefficient $-\frac{1}{3}$.

$-\frac{1}{3}(2 - 3x + 3)$

$= -\frac{1}{3}(5 - 3x)$

$= (-\frac{1}{3} \cdot 5) + (-\frac{1}{3} \cdot -3x)$

$= -\frac{5}{3} + x$

The simplified expression is $-\frac{5}{3} + x$.

Try It!

Simplify the expression $-\frac{2}{5}(10 + 15m - 20n)$.

KEY CONCEPT

You can expand an expression using the Distributive Property.

Multiply, or distribute, the factor outside the parentheses with each term inside the parentheses.

$-7(3y - 1)$

$= (-7)(3y) + (-7)(-1)$

$= -21y + 7$

The sign of each term is included in all calculations.

Do You Understand?

1. **Essential Question** How does the value of an expression change when it is expanded?

2. **Use Structure** How does the subtraction part of the expression change when $a(b - c)$ is expanded?

3. **Make Sense and Persevere** When does expanding and simplifying $a(b + c)$ result in a positive value for ac?

Do You Know How?

4. Shoes and hats are on sale. The expression $\frac{1}{4}(s + 24.80)$ can be used to determine the discount when you buy shoes with a retail price of s dollars and a hat with a retail price of \$24.80. Write another expression that can be used to determine the discount.

5. Expand $x(4 - 3.4y)$.

6. Expand $-\frac{2}{10}(1 - 2x + 2)$.

Name: ______________________________

Practice & Problem Solving

Scan for Multimedia

Leveled Practice **For 7–8, fill in the boxes to expand each expression.**

7. $3(n + 7)$

$= (3)(\square) + (3)(\square)$

$= \square + \square$

8. $4(x - 3)$

$= \square x - \square(3)$

$= \square - \square$

For 9–14, write the expanded form of the expression.

9. $y(0.5 + 8)$

10. $4(3 + 4x - 2)$

11. $6(y + x)$

12. $-2.5(-3 + 4n + 8)$

13. $-\frac{1}{3}(y - x)$

14. $8(6x - 4)$

15. Higher Order Thinking A grocery store has a 13%-off sale on all bread. You decide to purchase 6 loaves of bread. Let b be the original price of a loaf of bread. Expand the expression $6(b - 0.13b)$. Once the expression is expanded, what do the terms represent?

16. A gardener plans to extend the length of a rectangular garden. Let x represent the garden's original length. The expression $4(x + 7)$ represents the area of the extended garden. When asked for the area of the extended portion, the gardener incorrectly said it was 11 square feet. Describe the error the gardener made.

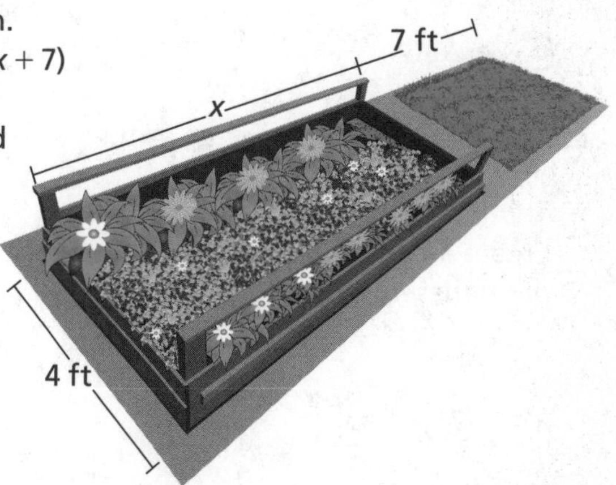

17. Find a difference equivalent to the product $11(x - y)$.

18. Use the Distributive Property to write an expression equivalent to $0.4(-5 - 7y - 13.8)$.

19. Make Sense and Persevere Use the Distributive Property to expand $7(7x - 3y) - 6$.

20. Use the Distributive Property to write an expression equivalent to $y(-3 - 8x)$.

21. An architect plans to build an extension to Meiling's rectangular deck. Let x represent the increase, in meters, of her deck's length. The expression $5(x + 8)$ represents the area of the deck, where 5 is the width, in meters, and $(x + 8)$ represents the extended length, in meters. Use the Distributive Property to write an expression that represents the total area of Meiling's new deck.

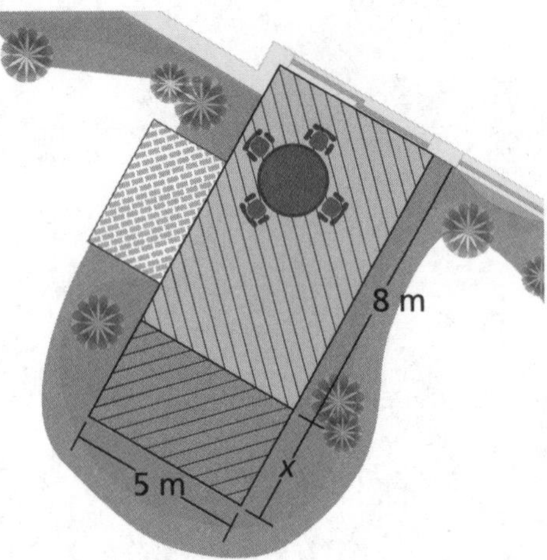

Assessment Practice

22. Select all expressions equivalent to $-\frac{1}{2}(4 - 2 + 8x)$. 7.EE.1.1

- ☐ $-4x - 1$
- ☐ $4x - 1$
- ☐ $3x$
- ☐ $-2 + 1 - 4x$
- ☐ $2 + 1 - 4x$
- ☐ $4x + 1$

23. An expression is shown. 7.EE.1.1

$\frac{1}{5}(5 - 7y + 10)$

Create an equivalent expression without parentheses.

Explain It!

Tasha is packing gift bags that include the same items. She has 72 glow sticks, 36 markers, and 24 bottles of bubbles. Tasha believes that she can pack no more than 6 bags using all of her supplies.

Lesson 10-5
Factor Expressions

Go Online | PearsonRealize.com

I can...
use common factors and the Distributive Property to factor expressions.

MAFS.7.EE.1.1 Apply properties of operations as strategies to ... factor ... linear expressions with rational coefficients. Also 7.EE.1.2
MAFS.K12.MP.1.1, MP.2.1, MP.3.1, MP.8.1

Make Sense and Persevere
How can you use what you know about common factors to solve the problem?

A. Critique Reasoning Do you agree with Tasha? Explain.

B. If Tasha creates the greatest number of gift bags, how many of each item is in each bag? Explain how you know.

Focus on math practices

Reasoning Tasha added more markers and now has a total of 48 markers. Does this change the possible number of gift bags? Explain.

? Essential Question How does the Distributive Property relate to factoring expressions?

EXAMPLE 1  Factor Expressions

Scan for Multimedia 

Kiana painted a rectangular wall blue to start an ocean mural. She used 3 cans of paint, each of which covered x square meters, and a different-sized can that covered 12 square meters. What are possible length and height dimensions of Kiana's mural?

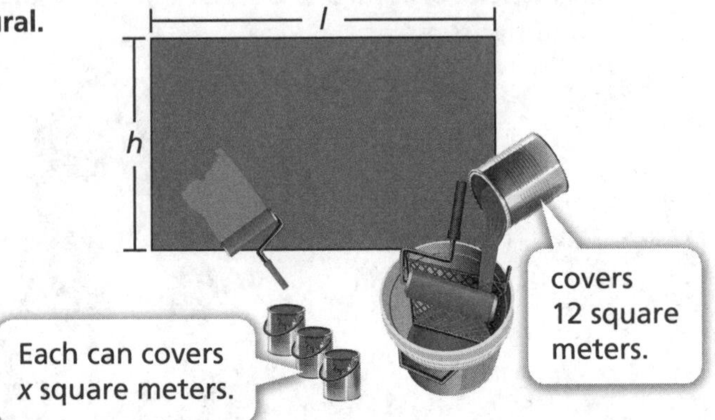

Model with Math The expression $3x + 12$ represents the area of the mural.

ONE WAY Use an area model to represent the area of the mural, $3x + 12$.

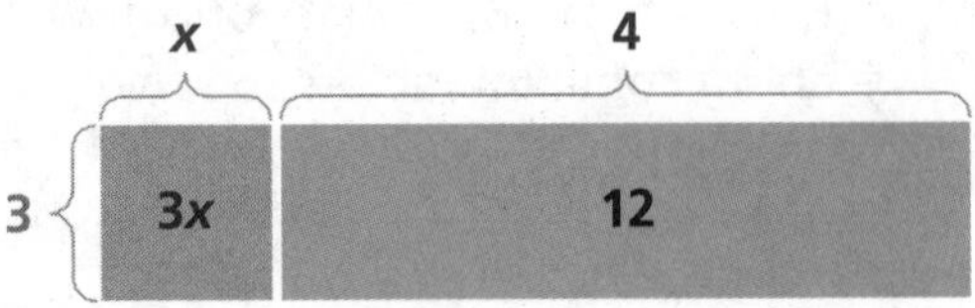

So, one possible set of dimensions of the mural could be $x + 4$ meters long and 3 meters tall.

ANOTHER WAY Use a common factor and the Distributive Property to factor the expression $3x + 12$.

$3x + 12$

$3x + (3 \cdot 4)$ — The GCF of $3x$ and 12 is 3.

$3(x + 4)$ — This represents the area of the mural as a product of two factors.

So, one possible set of dimensions of the mural could be 3 meters long and $x + 4$ meters tall.

Try It!

Use factoring to write an expression for the length of the pool with the given width.

$4x + 20 = \square(x + \square)$

So, the length of the pool is $\square$ meters.

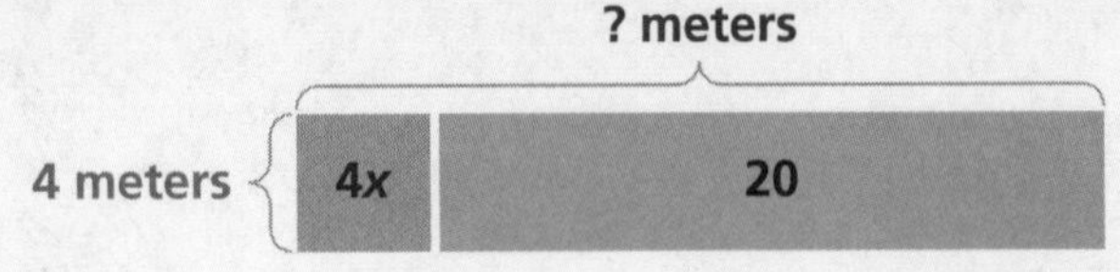

Convince Me! How can you use the Distributive Property to check the factored expression? Use the factored expression for Example 1 in your explanation.

EXAMPLE 2 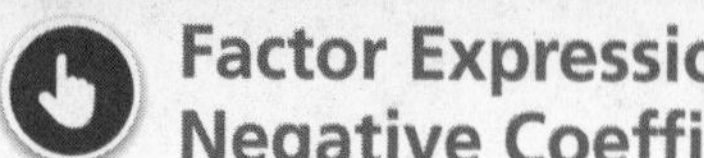

Factor Expressions with Negative Coefficients

Rodrigo and Jordan each factor the expression $-2x - 6$. Who factored the expression correctly?

Rodrigo uses a positive common factor, 2, to factor the expression.

2 is a common factor of $-2x$ and -6.

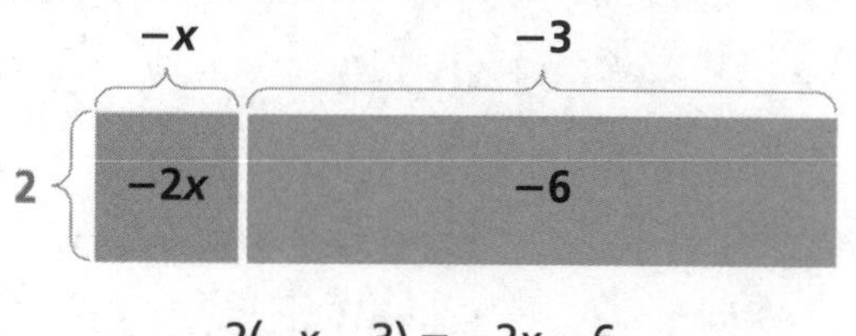

$2(-x - 3) = -2x - 6$

Jordan uses a negative common factor , -2, to factor the expression.

-2 is a common factor of $-2x$ and -6.

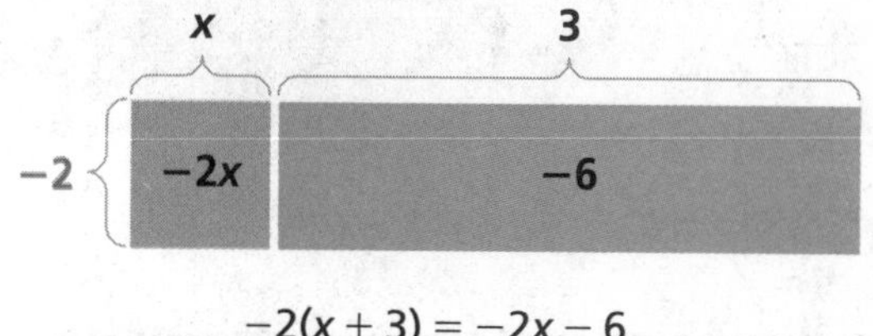

$-2(x + 3) = -2x - 6$

$2(-x - 3)$ and $-2(x + 3)$ are equivalent expressions. So, both Rodrigo and Jordan are correct.

Try It!

Show two different ways to factor $-4x - 28$.

EXAMPLE 3 

Factor Three-Term Expressions

Use the GCF to factor the expression $6x - 18 - 12y$.

STEP 1 Find the GCF of $6x$, -18, and $-12y$.

Factors of 6: 1, 2, 3, 6

Factors of 18: 1, 2, 3, 6, 9, 18

Factors of 12: 1, 2, 3, 4, 6, 12

The GCF is 6.

STEP 2 Use the GCF and the Distributive Property to factor the expression.

$6x - 18 - 12y$

$= (6)(x) - (6)(3) - (6)(2y)$

$= 6(x - 3 - 2y)$

The factored expression of $6x - 18 - 12y$ is $6(x - 3 - 2y)$.

Try It!

Write an equivalent expression for the expression above using a negative factor.

KEY CONCEPT

The greatest common factor (GCF) can be used to factor expressions.

The Distributive Property can be applied to factor an expression. Factoring an expression creates an equivalent expression.

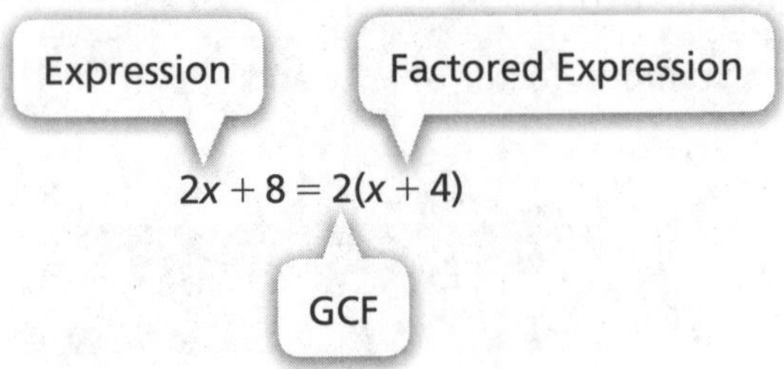

Do You Understand?

1. **Essential Question** How does the Distributive Property relate to factoring expressions?

2. Susan incorrectly factored the expression below.

$12a - 15b + 6$

$3(4a + 5b + 3)$

a. Explain any errors Susan may have made when factoring.

b. Factor the expression correctly.

Do You Know How?

3. Sahil is putting together supply kits and has 36 packs of x pencils, 12 packs of y crayons, and 24 erasers.

a. Write an expression to show the total number of items.

b. Use factoring to show many kits Sahil can make while putting every type of item in each kit.

c. Use the factored expression to find the number of each item in each kit.

4. Show two different ways to factor $-12x + 24 - 18y$.

5. How can you use the Distributive Property to factor the expression $6x + 15$?

Name: ______________________________

Practice & Problem Solving

Scan for Multimedia

Leveled Practice **In 6–9, factor the expression.**

6. $16a + 10$.

The GCF of $16a$ and 10 is 2.

$2 \times \square = 16a$ $2 \times \square = 10$

The factored expression is $\square$.

7. $-9y - 3$.

The positive GCF of $-9y$ and -3 is 3.

$3 \times \square = -9y$ $3 \times \square = -3$

The factored expression is $\square$.

8. $14x + 49$

9. $12y - 16$

10. This model shows the area of a garden. Write two expressions that represent the area.

x	x	x	x	x	1	1	1	1	1	1	1	1	1	1

11. Use the GCF to write the factored form of the expression $18x + 24y$.

12. Find the dimensions of the sports field at the right if the width is at least 60 yards.

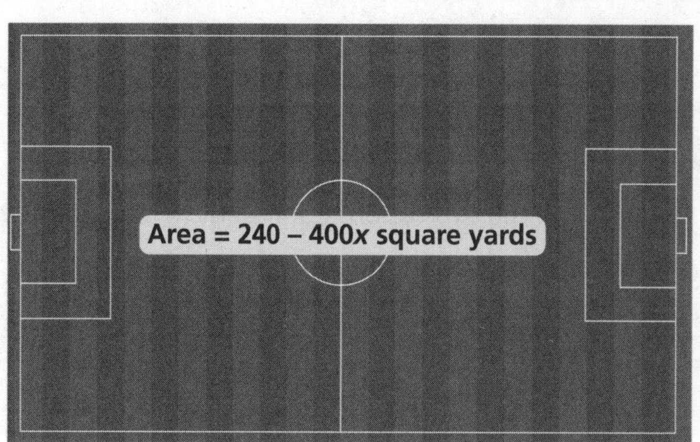

13. Your friend incorrectly factors the expression $15x - 20xy$ as $5x(3 - 4xy)$.

a. Factor the expression correctly.

b. What error did your friend likely make?

14. You are given the expression $12x + 18y + 26$.

a. **Make Sense and Persevere** What is the first step in factoring the expression?

b. Factor the expression.

15. A hotel manager is adding a tile border around the hotel's rectangular pool. Let x represent the width of the pool, in feet. The length is 3 more than 2 times the width, as shown. Write two expressions that give the perimeter of the pool.

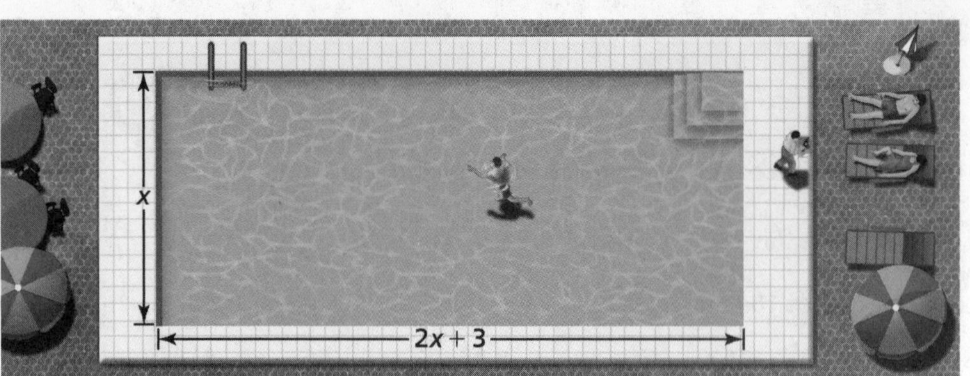

16. **Higher Order Thinking** Use the expressions below.

$14m + mn$ $\quad$ $2y + 2x + 4$

$-\frac{3}{4}m + 8m + m$ $\quad$ $4 - 3p$

$5.75t + 7.75t - t$ $\quad$ $8xy - 6xy$

a. Circle the expressions that have like terms.

b. Explain why the other expressions do not have like terms.

17. **Construct Arguments** Ryan says the expression $3 + 5y$ cannot be factored using a GCF. Is he correct? Explain why or why not.

Assessment Practice

18. Select all the expressions equivalent to $12 + 30y$. 7.EE.1.1

- ☐ $3(4 + 10y)$
- ☐ $4(3 + 10y)$
- ☐ $6(2 + 5y)$
- ☐ $2(6 + 30y)$
- ☐ $6(3 + 10y)$

19. Write an expression that is the product of two factors and is equivalent to $-2x - 10$. 7.EE.1.1

Name: ______________________

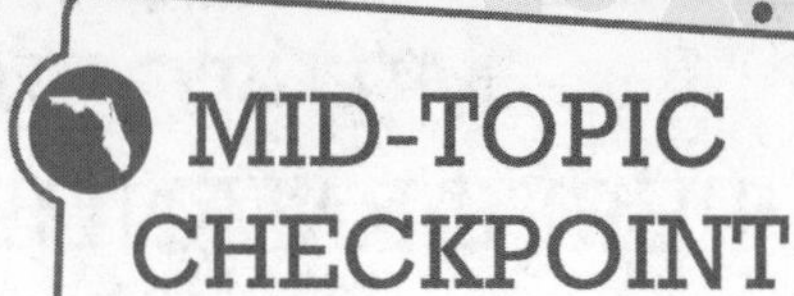

1. **Vocabulary** If you write an expression to represent the following situation, how can you determine which is the constant and which is the coefficient of the variable? *Lesson 10-1* 7.EE.2.4

   The zoo charges the Garcia family an admission fee of \$5.25 per person and a one-time fee of \$3.50 to rent a wagon for their young children.

2. An online photo service charges \$20 to make a photo book with 16 pages. Each extra page costs \$1.75. The cost to ship the completed photo book is \$5. Write an expression to determine the total cost in dollars to make and ship a photo book with x extra pages. *Lesson 10-1* 7.EE.2.4

3. Write an expression equivalent to $2a + \left(\frac{3}{4}a + \frac{1}{5}b\right)$ by combining like terms. *Lesson 10-3* 7.EE.1.1

4. Which expression is equivalent to $3.2y - \frac{1}{3} + (-7y) + \frac{2}{3}$? *Lesson 10-2* 7.EE.1.1

   Ⓐ $-10.2y + \frac{1}{3}$　Ⓑ $-3.8y + \frac{1}{3}$　Ⓒ $-3\frac{7}{15}y$　Ⓓ $-3y$

5. Ray wants to buy a hat that costs \$10 and some shirts that cost \$12 each. The sales tax rate is 6.5%. Write an expression to determine the amount of sales tax that Ray will pay on his entire purchase. Expand to simplify the expression. *Lesson 10-4* 7.EE.2.4, 7.EE.1.2

6. Factor the expression $28r + 42s - 35$. *Lesson 10-5* 7.EE.1.1

7. Describe two ways the Distributive Property can be used to write equivalent expressions. *Lessons 10-4 and 10-5* 7.EE.1.1, 7.EE.1.2

How well did you do on the mid-topic checkpoint? Fill in the stars.

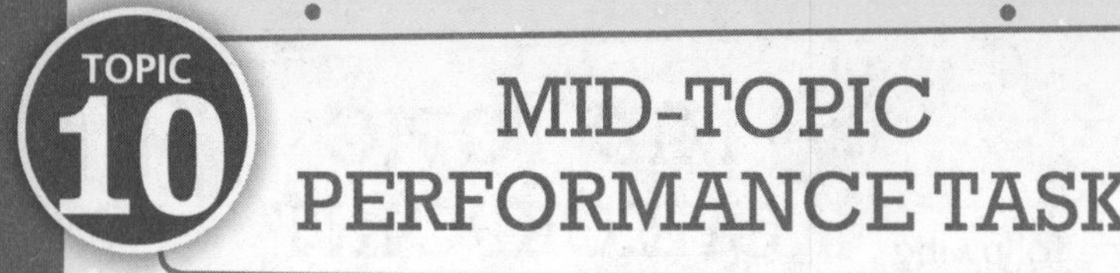

MID-TOPIC PERFORMANCE TASK

Alison is a buyer for a chain of 6 flower shops. This means that she buys flowers in bulk from a supplier and then distributes them to the 6 flower shops in the chain.

PART A

This week Alison bought 108 bunches of carnations and 96 bunches of roses from the supplier. Let *c* represent the number of carnations in each bunch, and let *r* represent the number of roses in each bunch. Write an expression to show the total number of carnations and roses that Alison bought. 7.EE.1.2

PART B

Alison wants to distribute the carnations and roses equally among the 6 flower shops. Factor the expression from Part A using 6 as the common factor. How does the factored expression help Alison determine how many carnations and how many roses each flower shop should get? 7.EE.1.1, 7.EE.1.2

PART C

There are 24 carnations in each bunch and 12 roses in each bunch. Use your answer to Part B to determine the total number of carnations and the total number of roses Alison will distribute to each flower shop this week. 7.EE.1.1, 7.EE.2.4

PART D

Jake manages one of the flower shops. He wants to use the carnations and roses to make bouquets. He wants each bouquet to have the same combination of carnations and roses, with no flowers left over. Determine a way that Jake can divide the flowers to make the bouquets. How many bouquets will there be? 7.EE.1.2, 7.EE.2.4

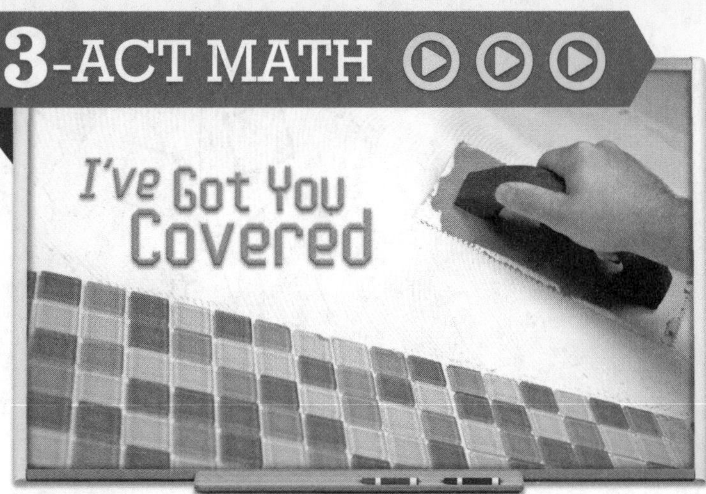

3-Act Mathematical Modeling: I've Got You Covered

Go Online | PearsonRealize.com

MAFS.K12.MP.4.1 Model with mathematics. Also MP.1.1, MP.2.1, MP.3.1, MP.5.1, MP.7.1, MP.8.1

MAFS.7.EE.1.1 Apply properties of operations as strategies to add, subtract, factor, and expand linear expressions with rational coefficients. Also 7.EE.1.2

ACT 1

1. After watching the video, what is the first question that comes to mind?

2. Write the Main Question you will answer.

3. **Construct Arguments** Predict an answer to this Main Question. Explain your prediction.

4. On the number line below, write a number that is too small to be the answer. Write a number that is too large.

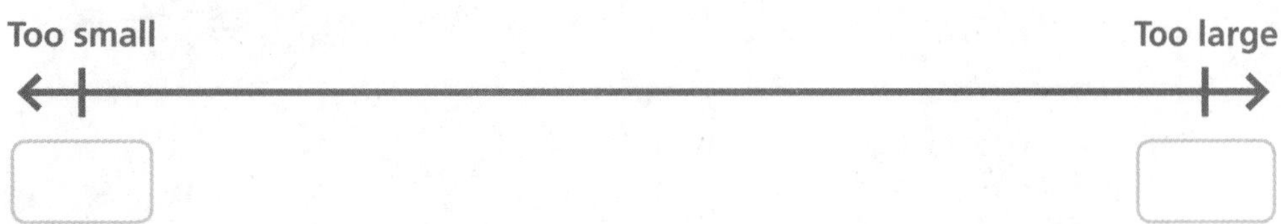

5. Plot your prediction on the same number line.

6. What information in this situation would be helpful to know? How would you use that information?

7. **Use Appropriate Tools** What tools can you use to get the information you need? Record the information as you find it.

8. **Model with Math** Represent the situation using the mathematical content, concepts, and skills from this topic. Use your representation to answer the Main Question.

9. What is your answer to the Main Question? Is it higher or lower than your prediction? Explain why.

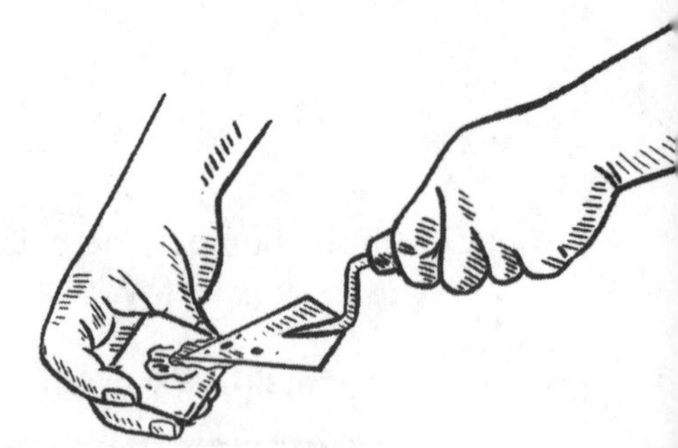

ACT 3

10. Write the answer you saw in the video.

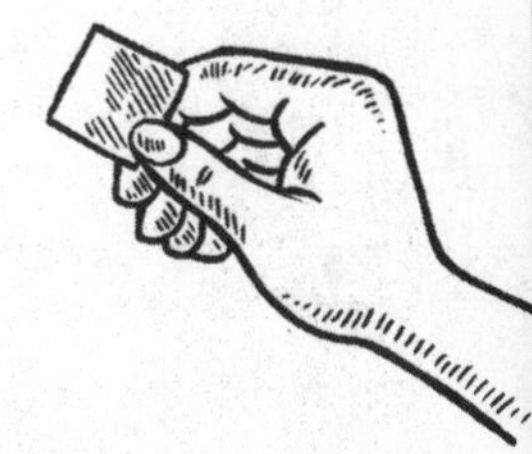

11. **Reasoning** Does your answer match the answer in the video? If not, what are some reasons that would explain the difference?

12. **Make Sense and Persevere** Would you change your model now that you know the answer? Explain.

Reflect

13. Model with Math Explain how you used a mathematical model to represent the situation. How did the model help you answer the Main Question?

14. Generalize What pattern did you notice in your calculations? How did that pattern help you solve the problem?

SEQUEL

15. Reasoning A classmate says that another object needs 512 tiles. What do you know about the dimensions of the object?

Solve & Discuss It!

The Smith family took a 2-day road trip. On the second day, they drove $\frac{3}{4}$ the distance they traveled on the first day. What is a possible distance they could have traveled over the 2 days? Is there more than one possible distance? Justify your response.

Lesson 10-6
Add Expressions

Go Online | PearsonRealize.com

I can...
add expressions that represent real-world problems.

MAFS.7.EE.1.1 Apply properties of operations as strategies to add ... linear expressions with rational coefficients. Also 7.EE.1.2
MAFS.K12.MP.1.1, MP.2.1, MP.4.1, MP.6.1, MP.7.1

Make Sense and Persevere
How are the quantities in the problem related?

Focus on math practices

Use Structure How can two different expressions be used to represent the total distance?

? **Essential Question** How can properties of operations be used to add expressions?

EXAMPLE 1  Add Expressions by Using Properties

Scan for Multimedia 

Delilah signs up for a health club and a rock-climbing gym. What expression represents her total fitness cost after *m* months?

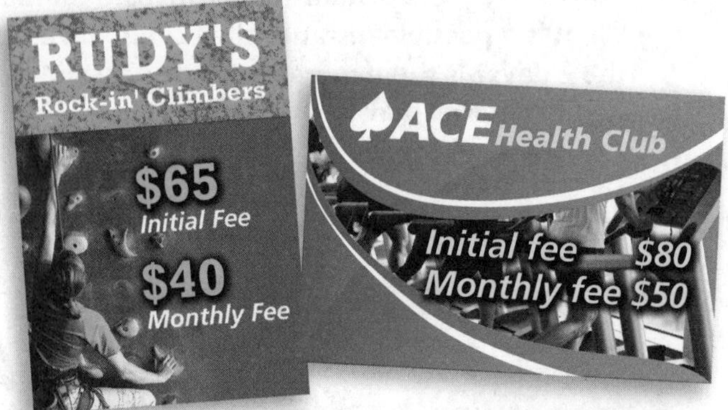

Model with Math Each bill can be represented with an expression.

Use bar diagrams to represent the situation and write an expression for the cost of each club.

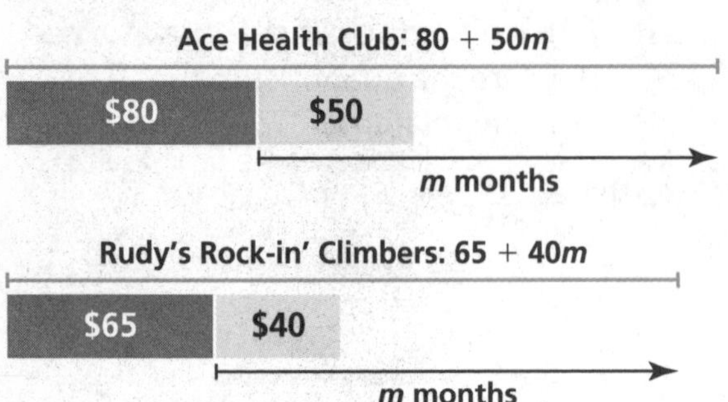

Add the expressions to find the combined cost.

$(80 + 50m) + (65 + 40m)$

$= (80 + 65) + (50m + 40m)$ — Use the Commutative and Associative Properties.

$= 145 + 90m$

The expression $145 + 90m$ can be used to determine the total cost for the health club and rock-climbing gym after *m* months.

Try It!

Sophia and Ollie each deposit $120 to open a joint account. They each make monthly deposits as shown. What expression represents the amount in the account after *m* months?

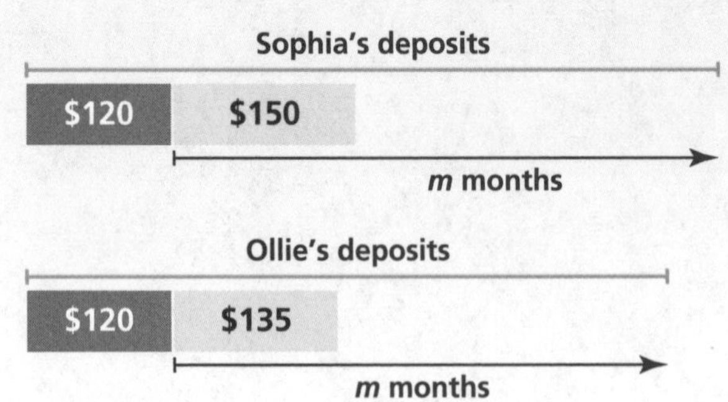

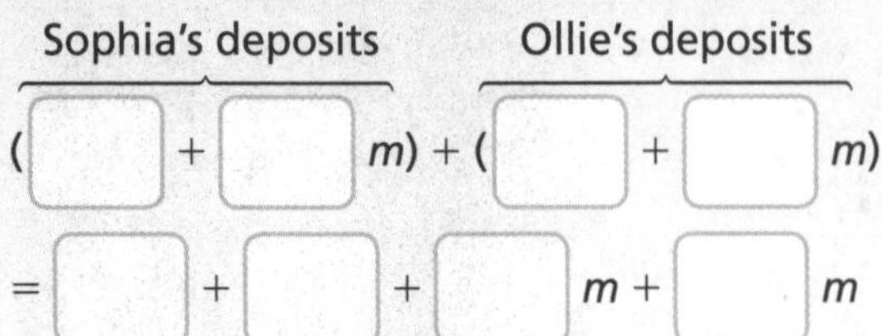

The amount of money in the joint account after *m* months is ☐ + ☐.

Convince Me! Explain why the initial deposits and monthly deposits are not combined into one term?

EXAMPLE 2  Add Expressions with More Than One Variable

Cindy spent \$125 on ingredients for muffins and \$92.40 on ingredients for bagels. Write an expression to represent Cindy's profit for *m* muffins and *b* bagels.

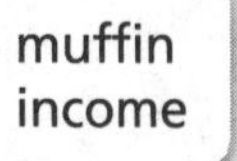

muffin income — cost of ingredients

$2.40m - 125$

bagel income — cost of ingredients

$1.80b - 92.40$

$(2.40m - 125) + (1.80b - 92.40)$

$= 2.40m + 1.80b + (-125 - 92.40)$

$= 2.40m + 1.80b - 217.4$

Use the Commutative and Associative Properties.

The expression $2.40m + 1.80b - 217.4$ represents the profit from selling the muffins and bagels.

EXAMPLE 3  Add More Complex Expressions

Add the expressions.

$\left(\frac{1}{2}x - 3 - 2y\right) + \left(\frac{1}{4}x - 2y + 5\right)$

$= \left(\frac{1}{2}x + \frac{1}{4}x\right) + (-2y + (-2y)) + (-3 + 5)$

$= \quad \frac{3}{4}x \quad + \quad (-4y) \quad + \quad 2$

$= \frac{3}{4}x - 4y + 2$

Use the Commutative and Associative Properties to reorder and group like terms.

Try It!

Find each sum.

a. $(9.74c - 250.50) + (-5.48p + 185.70)$

b. $\left(\frac{2}{11}x - 3 - 5y\right) + \left(-\frac{3}{11}x + 5y + 5.5\right)$

c. $(-14.2b - 97.35) + (6.76d - 118.7 - 3.4d)$

d. $\left(\frac{3}{8} - \frac{1}{6}m + 5t\right) + \left(\frac{7}{10}m + 9t + \frac{1}{4}\right)$

KEY CONCEPT

Adding expressions may require combining like terms.

Terms with the same variables are added together and constants are added together.

When adding terms with the same variables, the rules for adding rational numbers apply to their coefficients.

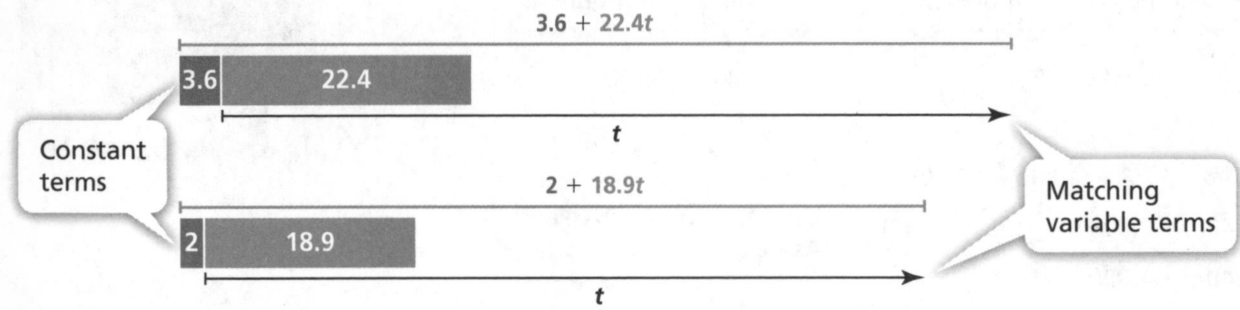

$(3.6 + 22.4t) + (2 + 18.9t) = 5.6 + 41.3t$

Do You Understand?

1. **Essential Question** How can properties of operations be used to add expressions?

2. **Reasoning** Explain whether the coefficients of two terms with different variables can be added to make one new term.

3. **Be Precise** Which properties of operations could be used to show that $(-5p + 9) + (-2 + p)$ is equivalent to $(-5p) + p + 9 - 2$?

Do You Know How?

4. Dillon says that $4b$ and $-2b$ are not like terms because $4b$ is positive and $-2b$ is negative. Is he correct? Explain.

5. Joel spent \$28 for an Internet data service and pays \$14.50 per month. He spent \$24.50 to join an online movie streaming site and pays \$13.25 per month. Write an expression to represent Joel's total cost for both memberships after m months.

6. Add $\frac{1}{3}n + \frac{2}{3}$ and $-\frac{1}{6}n + \frac{1}{6}m$.

7. Find the sum.

$(-3.5t - 4s + 4.5) + (-7.1 - 0.3s + 4.1t)$

Name: ______________________________

Practice & Problem Solving

Scan for Multimedia 

Leveled Practice **For 8–9, fill in the boxes to add the expressions.**

8. $(2a + 8) + (4a + 5)$

$= (2a + \square) + (8 + \square)$

$= \square + 13$

9. $\left(\frac{2}{7}x - 7\right) + \left(\frac{1}{7}x + 8\right)$

$= \left(\square + \square\right) + \left(-7 + \square\right)$

$= \square x + \square$

10. Find the sum.
$(8b + 7) + (6x - 4) + (5c + 8)$

11. Combine like terms.
$(-3y - 5) + (5m + 7y) + (6 + 9m)$

12. Felipe is going to plant b sunflower seeds in one garden and $5b + 10$ sunflower seeds in another. How many seeds is Felipe going to plant altogether?

13. An art class is making a mural for the school that has a triangle drawn in the middle. The length of the bottom of the triangle is x. Another side is 1 more than three times the length of the bottom of the triangle. The last side is 2 more than the bottom of the triangle. Write and simplify an expression for the perimeter of the triangle.

14. On a math test, Sarah has to identify all the coefficients and constants of the expression $4 + n + 7m$. Sarah identifies the only coefficient as 7 and the only constant as 4.

a. Identify all the coefficients of the expression.

b. Identify all the constants of the expression.

c. What error did Sarah likely make?

15. The width of a rectangle is $5x - 2.5$ feet and the length is $2.5x + 8$ feet. Find the perimeter of the rectangle.

16. Nina has x coins. Clayton has 5 fewer coins than six times the number of coins Nina has. Write an expression for the total number of coins Nina and Clayton have altogether. Then simplify the expression.

17. **Higher Order Thinking** Use the expression $(8x + 2) + (-9x + 7)$.

a. Find the sum.

b. Reasoning Explain how you know when to combine terms with variables.

18. Gabe went to the Florida Mall. He bought k model planes and spent $24 on books. Then he spent another $25 at another store.

a. Write an expression that represents the amount Gabe spent at the mall.

b. How much did Gabe spend in all if he bought 3 model planes?

Each model plane costs $14.99.

Assessment Practice

19. A middle school with x students conducted a survey to determine students' Tuesday afternoon activities.

PART A Write an expression for each activity. 7.EE.1.1

25 more than one-tenth of the students dance.	20 fewer than three-tenths of the students play soccer.	21 more than one-tenth of the students play baseball.

PART B Write a simplified expression to represent the number of students who either dance or play baseball on Tuesday afternoons. 7.EE.1.2

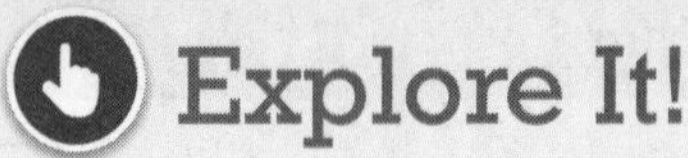

Explore It!

Lesson 10-7
Subtract Expressions

Go Online | PearsonRealize.com

I can...
subtract expressions using properties of operations.

MAFS.7.EE.1.1 Apply properties of operations as strategies to ... subtract ... linear expressions with rational coefficients. Also 7.EE.1.2
MAFS.K12.MP.1.1, MP.3.1, MP.4.1, MP.7.1

The East Side Bulldogs and the West Side Bears are playing a football game. A fan is keeping score using T for a touchdown plus extra point, worth 7 points total, and F for a field goal, worth 3 points.

	East Side Bulldogs	West Side Bears
1st quarter	TT F	FFF
2nd quarter	TT F	T FF
3rd quarter	T FF	TTT
4th quarter	TT FF	T

A. How can you represent the score of each team using expressions?

B. How can you represent the difference of the teams' scores using an expression?

C. How can you determine how many more points the winning team had than the losing team?

Focus on math practices

Look for Relationships How can looking at the coefficients help you determine which team scored the greater number of points?

? Essential Question How can properties of operations be used to subtract expressions?

EXAMPLE 1  Subtract Expressions by Using Properties

Scan for Multimedia 

Lita's family wants to put a tiled border around their swimming pool. What expression represents the total area of the border?

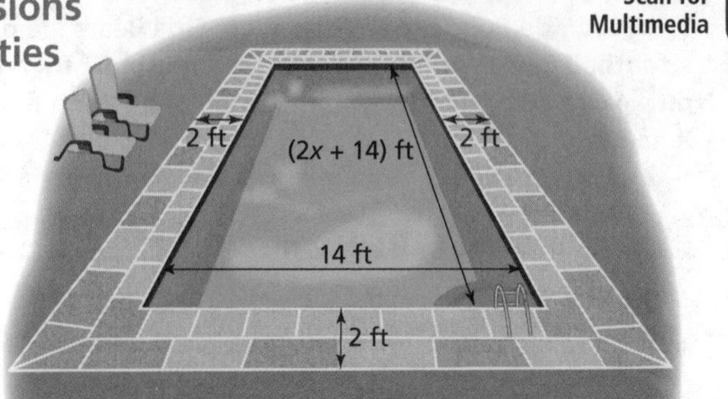

Make Sense and Persevere

How can you use subtraction to find the area of the tiled border?

Write an expression for the area of the pool only. Then write an expression for the area of the pool plus the tiled border.

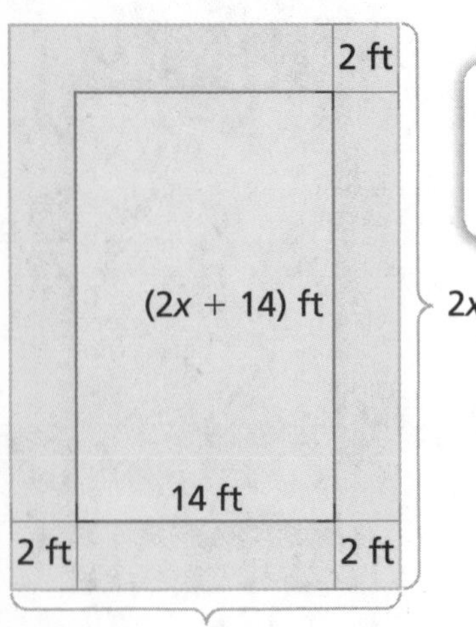

length of tiled border: $2 + (2x + 14) + 2$

$2x + 18$

18 ft

width of outer edge of walkway: $2 + 14 + 2$

Area of pool:
width • length
$14 \times (2x + 14)$ ft^2

Area of pool and tiled border:
$18 \times (2x + 18)$ ft^2

Use properties of operations to subtract the expressions.

(area of pool + tiles) − (area of pool)

$= 18(2x + 18) - 14(2x + 14)$

$= 36x + 324 - 28x - 196$

$= 36x - 28x + 324 - 196$

$= 8x + 128$

First, use the Distributive Property.

Then, use the Commutative Property.

The area of the tiled border is $8x + 128$ ft^2.

Try It!

A frame holds a picture that is 15 inches long and x inches wide. The frame border is 3 inches wide around the picture. What expression represents the area of the frame border?

Area of frame border = Area of entire frame − Area of photo = ☐ − ☐

The area of the frame is ☐ in^2.

Convince Me! Why can you choose to add or subtract when subtracting an expression?

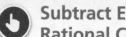

EXAMPLE 2  Subtract Expressions with Rational Coefficients

  ACTIVITY  ASSESS

Jada is comparing membership costs for two gyms. What is the difference in membership costs after *m* months if she joins Be Strong instead of Zippy Health Club?

Zippy Health Club
$49.95 to join
$19.95/month
BE STRONG
$10 off the first month!
$24.99/month

Write an expression for each membership cost for *m* months and subtract them.

(Be Strong) − (Zippy's Health Club)

$(24.99m - 10) - (19.95m + 49.95)$

$= 24.99m - 10 + (-1)(19.95m + 49.95)$

$= 24.99m - 10 + (-1)(19.95m) + (-1)(49.95)$ — Use the Distributive Property.

$= 24.99m - 10 - 19.95m - 49.95$

$= (24.99m - 19.95m) - 10 - 49.95$ — Use the Commutative and Associative Properties to reorder and group like terms.

$= 5.04m - 59.95$

Jada will pay $5.04 more each month at Be Strong, but will start with an initial savings of $59.95.

Use Structure How did the signs of the terms in the second expression change after distributing −1?

Try It!

Subtract $(0.95x - 0.04) - (0.99x - 0.13)$.

EXAMPLE 3  Subtract More Complex Expressions

Subtract the expressions.

$\left(5j - 2q + \frac{2}{5}\right) - \left(4 - 3j - \frac{1}{2}q\right)$

$= \left(5j - 2q + \frac{2}{5}\right) + \left(-4 + 3j + \frac{1}{2}q\right)$ — Distribute the minus sign, or −1, to all terms in the second expression.

$= 5j - 2q + \frac{2}{5} - 4 + 3j + \frac{1}{2}q$

$= 5j + 3j - 2q + \frac{1}{2}q + \frac{2}{5} - 4$

$= 8j - 1\frac{1}{2}q - 3\frac{3}{5}$

The simplified expression is $8j - 1\frac{1}{2}q - 3\frac{3}{5}$.

Try It!

Subtract $(17 + 4.5m + 8k) - (7.5m - 9 + 4k)$.

KEY CONCEPT

To subtract expressions, you can use properties of operations.

Write the subtraction as addition and use the Distributive Property to multiply -1 to the terms in the expression being subtracted.

$$5 - (-2x - 7)$$
$$= 5 + (-1)(-2x - 7)$$
$$= 5 + (-1)(-2)x + (-1)(-7)$$
$$= 5 + 2x + 7$$

$$5 - (-2x - 7)$$
$$= 5 + 2x + 7$$

You can use the Distributive Property to distribute the minus sign to the second expression, which changes the signs of the terms.

Do You Understand?

1. **Essential Question** How can properties of operations be used to subtract expressions?

2. **Use Structure** How is subtracting $-4x$ from $9x$ similar to subtracting -4 from 9?

3. Is adding the quantity $-12 + 8r$ to an expression the same as subtracting $-8r + 12$ from the same expression? Explain your reasoning.

Do You Know How?

4. Subtract.
   a. $(21x) - (-16 + 7x)$
   b. $(-13n) - (17 - 5n)$
   c. $(4y - 7) - (y - 7)$
   d. $(-w + 0.4) - (-w - 0.4)$

5. Jude has 5 pairs of sunglasses that cost the same in his online shopping cart, but then decides to get only 2. Each pair of sunglasses is the same price. Let p represent the cost of each pair. Write an expression for the original cost, the updated cost, and the difference in cost.

Power Shades 3000
In Stock Online
Add to Cart
Buy 3 or more, get shipping for $1.49*
*Regular shipping: $6.49

6. Subtract and simplify.

$$\frac{1}{6}m - \left(-\frac{5}{8}m + \frac{1}{3}\right)$$

Name: ____

Practice & Problem Solving

Scan for Multimedia

Leveled Practice **In 7–9, fill in the missing signs or numbers.**

7. Rewrite the expression $14m - (5 + 8m)$ without parentheses.

$14m$ ◯ 5 ◯ $8m$

8. Rewrite the expression $13d - (-9d - 4)$ without parentheses.

$13d$ ◯ $9d$ ◯ 4

9. Write an equivalent expression to $8k - (5 + 2k)$ without parentheses. Then simplify.

$8k - (5 + 2k) = 8k$ ◯ 5 ◯ $2k$

$= 8k$ ◯ $2k$ ◯ 5

$=$ ☐ k ◯ 5

10. A company has two manufacturing plants with daily production levels of $5x + 11$ items and $2x - 3$ items, respectively, where x represents a minimum quantity. The first plant produces how many more items daily than the second plant?

11. Two communications companies offer calling plans. With Company X, it costs 35¢ to connect and then 5¢ for each minute. With Company Y, it costs 15¢ to connect and then 4¢ for each minute.

Write and simplify an expression that represents how much more Company X charges than Company Y, in cents, for n minutes.

12. Make Sense and Persevere The base and height of a triangle are each extended 2 cm. What is the area of the shaded region? How do you know?

2 cm

x cm

8 cm   2 cm

13. Two friends shop for fresh fruit. Jackson buys a watermelon for \$7.65 and 5 pounds of cherries. Tim buys a pineapple for \$2.45 and 4 pounds of cherries. Use the variable p to represent the price, in dollars, per pound of cherries. Write and simplify an expression to represent how much more Jackson spent.

14. Yu's family wants to rent a car to go on vacation. EnvoCar charges \$50.50 and 8¢ per mile. Freedomride charges \$70.50 and 12¢ per mile. How much more does Freedomride charge for driving d miles than EnvoCar?

15. A rectangular garden has a walkway around it. Find the area of the walkway.

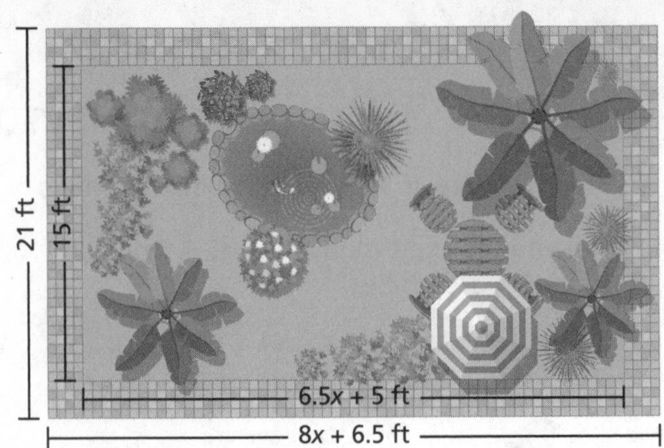

16. Critique Reasoning Tim incorrectly rewrote the expression $\frac{1}{2}p - \left(\frac{1}{4}p + 4\right)$ as $\frac{1}{2}p + \frac{1}{4}p - 4$. Rewrite the expression without parentheses. What was Tim's error?

17. Higher Order Thinking Find the difference.

$\left(7x - 6\frac{2}{3}\right) - \left(-3x + 4\frac{3}{4}\right)$

18. Each month, a shopkeeper spends $5x + 11$ dollars on rent and electricity. If he spends $2x - 3$ dollars on rent, how much does he spend on electricity?

19. Use the expression $\frac{1}{4}p - \left(1 - \frac{1}{3}p\right)$.

a. Rewrite the expression without parentheses. Simplify. Show your work.

b. Use a different method to write the expression without parentheses. Do not simplify.

Assessment Practice

20. An expression is shown. 7.EE.1.1

$(0.25n - 0.3) - (0.8n - 0.25)$

Create an equivalent expression without parentheses.

Solve & Discuss It!

How many toothpicks make a triangle? Two triangles? Write an expression that represents the number of toothpicks needed to make *x* triangles that appear side-by-side in a single row, as shown. Explain your reasoning.

Look for Relationships What do you notice about the number of toothpicks needed for more than 1 triangle?

Lesson 10-8
Analyze Equivalent Expressions

Go Online | PearsonRealize.com

I can...
use an equivalent expression to find new information.

MAFS.7.EE.1.2 Understand that rewriting an expression in different forms in a problem context can shed light on the problem and how the quantities in it are related.
MAFS.K12.MP.2.1, MP.7.1

Focus on math practices

Reasoning Can there be more than one expression that represents the total number of toothpicks needed to make *x* triangles in the arrangement shown? Explain.

Essential Question How can writing equivalent expressions show how quantities are related?

EXAMPLE 1  Write Equivalent Expressions

Scan for Multimedia 

A new box of pasta claims that it contains 25% more than the usual box. What expression shows the amount of pasta, p, in the new box?

Use Structure What expressions can you write to represent a percent greater than the original amount?

Draw a bar diagram to represent the problem situation. Then write an expression to represent the amount of pasta in the new box.

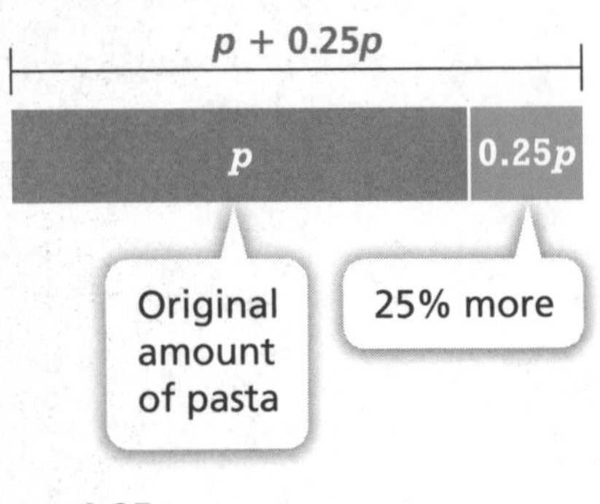

$p + 0.25p$

Combine like terms to write an equivalent expression.

The coefficient of p is 1.

$(1)p + 0.25p$

$= 1.25p$

25% more than 100% is the same as 125%.

Try It!

Joe is buying gift cards that are on sale for 15% off. He uses $c - 0.15c$ to determine the sale price of gift cards. What is an equivalent expression that Joe could also use to determine the sale price of a gift card?

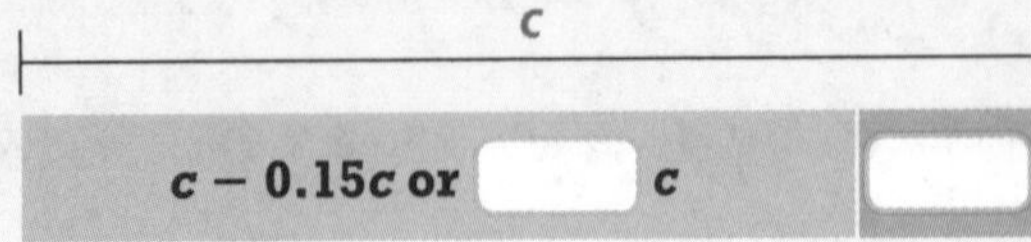

Convince Me! How do you know if an expression is describing a percent increase or a percent decrease?

EXAMPLE 2  Analyze Equivalent Expressions

Some middle school students will use 1-foot tiles to create a frame around a large square mural painting with side lengths s feet. Three students each wrote an expression to determine the number of tiles needed. Are these expressions equivalent? Explain.

$4(s + 1)$

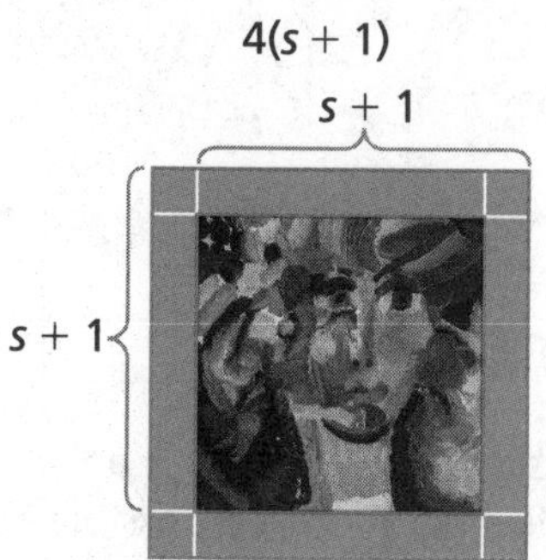

Each section requires $s + 1$ tiles and there are 4 sections.

$s + s + s + s + 4$

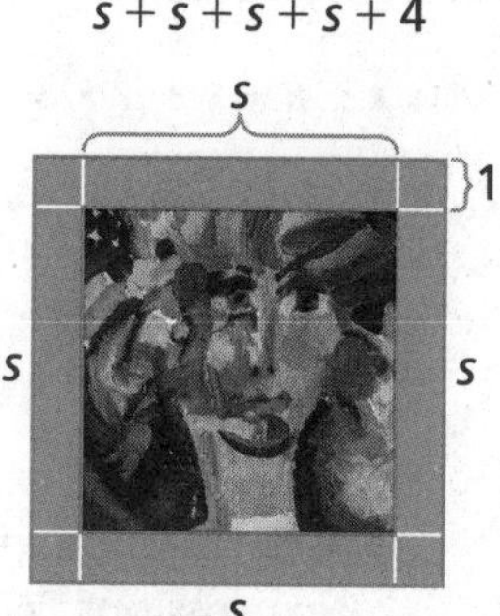

Each side requires s tiles and there are 4 sides, so $s + s + s + s$, plus 4 corner tiles.

$2s + 2(s + 2)$

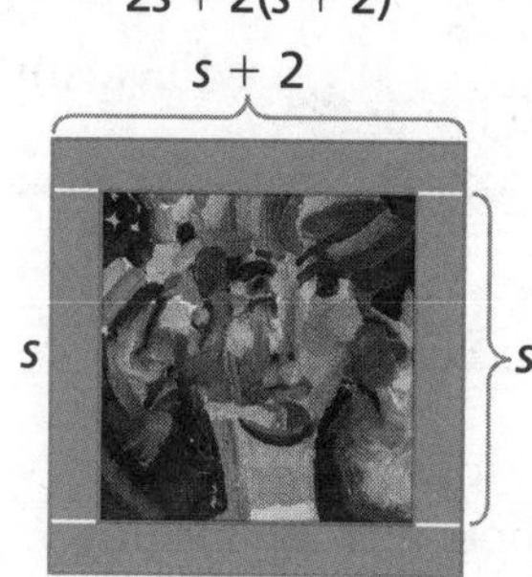

The top and bottom of the frame require $s + 2$ tiles and the two sides require s tiles.

Look for Relationships
What does each expression tell you about the relationship among quantities and variables?

The three expressions are equivalent because they each represent the number of tiles needed for the frame around the painting.

EXAMPLE 3  Interpret Equivalent Expressions

A table with a rectangular top has been extended with a table leaf as shown.

Multiply $3.5(6.5 + x)$ to write an equivalent expression for the total area of the extended table. What does each term of the equivalent expression tell you about the table?

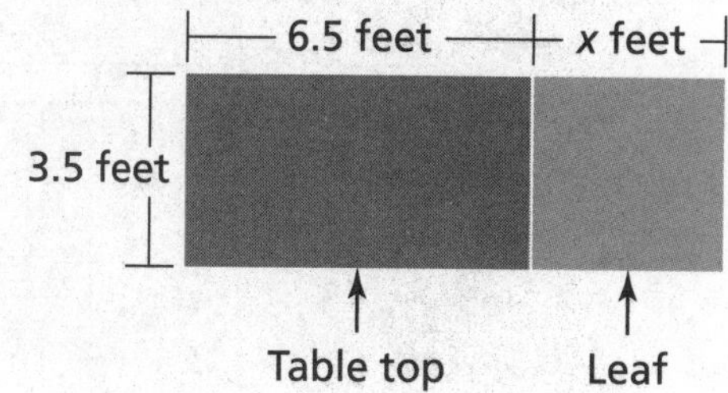

$3.5(6.5 + x)$

$= (3.5 \cdot 6.5) + (3.5 \cdot x)$

$= 22.75 + 3.5x$

Area, in ft^2, of table leaf

Area, in ft^2, of original table

Try It!

The total area, in square feet, of a rectangular stage that has been widened by x feet is represented by $1{,}900 + 76x$. Use the Distributive Property to factor the expression. What does each factor in the equivalent expression tell you about the stage?

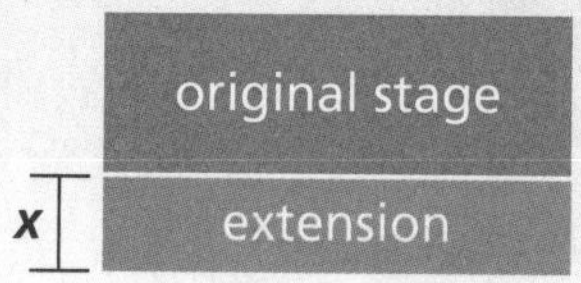

KEY CONCEPT

Rewriting expressions can clarify relationships among quantities or variables.

When you *rewrite* an expression, you are writing an *equivalent* expression.

$4x + 12$ is equivalent to $4(x + 3)$ is equivalent to $x + x + x + x + 3 + 3 + 3 + 3$

Do You Understand?

1. **Essential Question** How can writing equivalent expressions show how quantities are related?

2. **Use Structure** The total area, in square feet, of a rectangular mural that has been extended by x feet is represented by $5.5(7.5 + x)$. Expand the expression using the Distributive Property. What do each of the terms in the equivalent expression tell you about the mural?

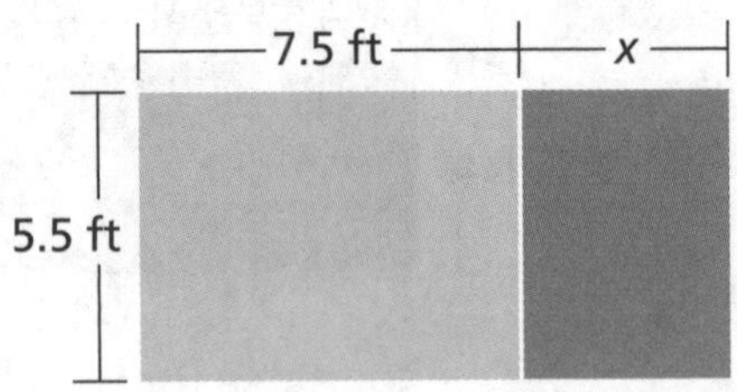

3. The expression $(2x + 6) + x$ represents the perimeter of an isosceles triangle. If x represents the length of one side of the triangle, explain how you can use the Distributive Property to find the length of each of the two equivalent sides?

Do You Know How?

4. Rewrite the expression $12x + 8$ to find an equivalent expression. Show three possible expressions. What do the rewritten expressions tell you about the relationships among the quantities?

5. A rope is used to make a fence in the shape of an equilateral triangle around a newly planted tree. The length of the rope is represented with the expression $9x + 15$.

   a. Rewrite the expression to represent the three side lengths of the rope fence.

   b. What is the length of one side?

6. The expression $(x - 0.35x)$ represents 35% off the cost of an item x. How is this equivalent to multiplying x by 0.65?

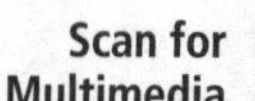

Name: ___________________________

Practice & Problem Solving

Scan for Multimedia

7. **Reasoning** Eric is planning an event at a hotel. Let g stand for the number of Eric's guests. The two expressions represent the difference between the cost of the rooms. Expression 1: $(326 + 37g) - (287 + 23g)$. Expression 2: $39 + 14g$. What can you tell about Expression 2 and Expression 1?

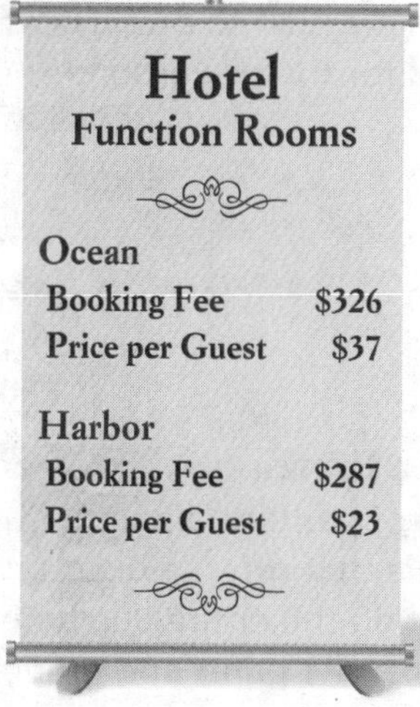

8. A student received a coupon for 17% off the total purchase price at a clothing store. Let b be the original price of the purchase. Use the expression $b - 0.17b$ for the new price of the purchase. Write an equivalent expression by combining like terms.

9. Kirana buys boxes of crackers that each have the same cost, c. She represents the cost of 3 boxes of cheese crackers, 2 boxes of poppy seed crackers, and 2 boxes of plain crackers using the expression $3c + 2c + 2c$. What equivalent expression can represent the cost?

10. A student received a coupon for 14% off the total purchase price at a clothing store. Let c be the original price of the purchase. The expression $c - 0.14c$ represents the new price of the purchase. Write an equivalent expression to show another way to represent the new price.

11. A farmer recently sold a large plot of land. The sale decreased his total acreage by 8%. Let v be the original acreage.

    a. Find two equivalent expressions that will give the new acreage.

    b. Use the expressions to describe two ways to find the new acreage.

12. An art teacher enlarged the area of a copy of a painting by 49%. Let d represent the area of the original painting. The expression $d + 0.49d$ is one way to represent the area of the new painting. Write two additional expressions that will give the area of the new painting.

13. **Use Structure** The area of a rectangular playground has been extended on one side. The total area of the playground, in square meters, can be written as $352 + 22x$.

Rewrite the expression to give a possible set of dimensions for the playground.

14. The manager of a store increases the price of the bathing suits by 7%. Let t be the original price of a bathing suit. The new price is $t + 0.07t$.

a. Find an expression equivalent to $t + 0.07t$.

b. If the original price of a bathing suit was $19.99, estimate the new price by first rounding the original price to the nearest dollar.

15. **Higher Order Thinking** A customer at a clothing store is buying a pair of pants and a shirt. The customer can choose between a sale that offers a discount on pants, or a coupon for a discount on the entire purchase. Let n represent the original price of the pants and s represent the price of the shirt.

15% OFF SALE
on all pants
SAVE 10%
OFF Entire Purchase
Cannot be combined with any other offers.
TROPICAL CLOTHES SHOP
Serving greater Orlando for over 40 years

a. Write two expressions that represent the "15% off sale on all pants" option.

b. Write two expressions that represent the "10% off her entire purchase" option.

c. If the original cost of the pants is $25 and the shirt is $10, which option should the customer choose? Explain.

Assessment Practice

16. At a college, the cost of tuition increased by 10%. Let b represent the former cost of tuition. Use the expression $b + 0.10b$ for the new cost of tuition. 7.EE.1.2

PART A

Write an equivalent expression for the new cost of tuition.

PART B

What does your equivalent expression tell you about how to find the new cost of tuition?

? Topic Essential Question

How can properties of operations help to generate equivalent expressions that can be used in solving problems?

Vocabulary Review

Complete each definition and then provide an example of each vocabulary word.

Vocabulary coefficient constant variable factor expression

Definition	Example
1. A term that contains only a number is a ______.	
2. The number part of a term that contains a variable is a ______.	
3. A ______ is a letter that represents an unknown value.	

Use Vocabulary in Writing

Membership in a digital library has a $5 startup fee and then costs $9.95 per month. Membership in a video streaming service costs $7.99 per month with no startup fee. Use vocabulary words to explain how this information could be used to write an expression for the total cost of both memberships after *m* months.

Concepts and Skills Review

LESSON 10-1 Write and Evaluate Algebraic Expressions

Quick Review

You can use an algebraic expression to represent and solve a problem with unknown values. The expression can consist of coefficients, constants, and variables. You can substitute values for variables to evaluate expressions.

Example

A farm charges $1.75 for each pound of strawberries picked and $2 for a basket to hold the strawberries. What is the total cost to pick 5 pounds of strawberries?

Write an expression to represent the total cost in dollars to pick p pounds of strawberries.

$1.75p + 2$

Substitute 5 for p.

$1.75(5) + 2 = 8.75 + 2 = 10.75$

It costs $10.75 to pick 5 pounds of strawberries.

Practice

1. Haddie makes and sells knit scarves. Next week she will pay a $25 fee for the use of a booth at a craft fair. She will charge $12 for each scarf she sells at the fair. Write an expression to determine Haddie's profit for selling s scarves after paying the fee for the use of the booth.

2. The cost to buy p pounds of potatoes at $0.32 per pound and n pounds of onions at $0.48 per pound can be determined by using the expression $0.32p + 0.48n$. How much will it cost to buy 4.5 pounds of potatoes and 2.5 pounds of onions?

LESSONS 10-2 AND 10-3 Generate Equivalent Expressions and Simplify Expressions

Quick Review

You can use properties of operations and combine like terms to simplify expressions. Like terms are terms that have the same variable part.

Example

Simplify the expression below.

$-7 + \frac{1}{3}n - \frac{4}{3} + 2n$

Use the Commutative Property to put like terms together,

$\frac{1}{3}n + 2n - 7 - \frac{4}{3}$

Combine like terms.

$2\frac{1}{3}n - 8\frac{1}{3}$

Practice

Simplify each expression below.

1. $\frac{5}{8}m + 9 - \frac{3}{8}m - 15$

2. $-8w + (-4z) + 2 + 6w + 9z - 7$

3. $-6 + (-2d) + (-4d) + 3d$

LESSON 10-4 Expand Expressions

Quick Review

The Distributive Property allows you to multiply each term inside parentheses by a factor that is outside the parentheses. This means that you can use the Distributive Property to expand expressions.

Example

Expand the expression $\frac{1}{4}(h + 7)$.

$\left(\frac{1}{4} \times h\right) + \left(\frac{1}{4} \times 7\right) = \frac{1}{4}h + 1.75$

Practice

1. Expand the expression $3.5(-3n + 4)$.

2. Simplify the expression $-\frac{3}{5}\left(-8 + \frac{5}{9}x - 3\right)$.

LESSON 10-5 Factor Expressions

Quick Review

When you factor an expression, you write it as a product of two expressions. The new expression is equivalent to the original expression. The greatest common factor (GCF) and the Distributive Property are tools that you use when you need to factor an expression.

Example

Factor the expression $12x - 9y + 15$.

The GCF of $12x$, 15, and $-9y$ is 3.

Rewrite each term using 3 as a factor.

$12x = 3 \cdot 4x$

$-9y = 3 \cdot (-3y)$

$15 = 3 \cdot 5$

Use the Distributive Property to factor the expression.

$3(4x - 3y + 5)$

Practice

Factor each expression.

1. $63a - 42b$

2. $81y + 54$

3. Which show a way to factor the expression $32t - 48$? Select all that apply.

- ☐ $2(16t - 24)$
- ☐ $4(12t - 48)$
- ☐ $6(26t - 42)$
- ☐ $8(4t - 6)$
- ☐ $16(2t - 3)$

LESSONS 10-6 AND 10-7 Add and Subtract Expressions

Quick Review

Adding and subtracting expressions may require combining like terms. This means that you must use the Commutative and Associative Properties to reorder and group terms as needed.

Example

Kerry has n markers. Rachel has 1 marker fewer than twice the number of markers Kerry has. Write and simplify an expression for the total number of markers they have.

Number of markers Kerry has: n

Number of markers Rachel has: $2n - 1$

Total number of markers:

$n + (2n - 1)$

$(n + 2n) - 1$

$3n - 1$

Practice

Add the expressions.

1. $(5.2c - 7.35) + (-3.9c + 2.65)$

2. $(6x - 2y - 5) - (-5 + 9y - 8x)$

3. Last week Jean ran 2 fewer than $4m$ miles. This week she ran 0.5 miles more than last week. Write and simplify an expression for the total number of miles Jean ran in the two weeks.

LESSON 10-8 Analyze Equivalent Expressions

Quick Review

Equivalent expressions can help to show new information about a problem. Sometimes the equivalent expression will be an expanded expression. In other cases, it will be a factored expression.

Example

The perimeter of a square is represented with the expression $84 + 44s$. What is the length of one side of the square?

A square has 4 sides, so factor 4 out of each term in the expression for the perimeter.

$84 + 44s = 4 \cdot 21 + 4 \cdot 11s = 4(21 + 11s)$

The factor within the parentheses represents the length of one side of the square.

The length of one side is $21 + 11s$.

Practice

1. Hal earns n dollars per hour. Next month he will receive a 2% raise in pay per hour. The expression $n + 0.02n$ is one way to represent Hal's pay per hour after the raise. Write an equivalent simplified expression that will represent his pay per hour after the raise.

2. The area of a garden plot can be represented by the expression $84z - 54$. The garden will be divided into six sections for planting six different vegetables. The sections will be equal in area. Write an expression that represents the area of each section.

Hidden Clue

For each ordered pair, solve the percent problems to find the coordinates. Then locate and label the corresponding point on the graph. Draw line segments to connect the points in alphabetical order. Use the completed picture to help you answer the riddle below.

I can...
represent and solve percent problems. 7.RP.1.2c

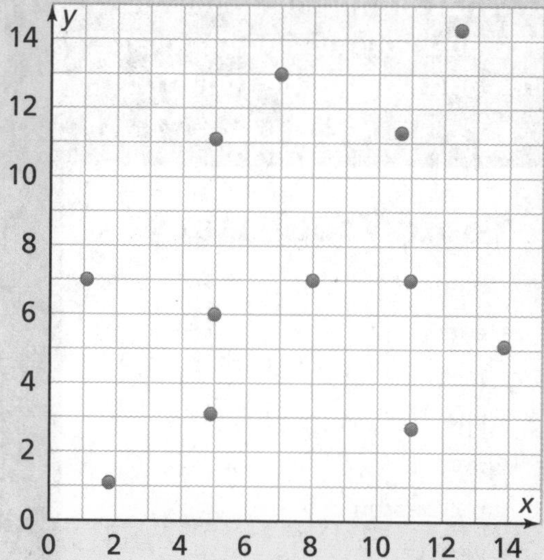

What occurs once in every minute, twice in every moment, yet never in a thousand years?

A (x is 85% of 13, 60% of 4.5 is y) ____, ____

B (x is 110% of 10, y% of 50 is 3.5) ____, ____

C (x% of 31 is 3.317, 4.407 is 39% of y) ____, ____

D (1.36 is 17% of x, 1.05 is y% of 15) ____, ____

E (x% of 60 is 3.006, 10% of 111 is y) ____, ____

F (x is 16% of 31.25, y is 24% of 25) ____, ____

G (78% of x is 3.822, y% of 8 is 0.248) ____, ____

SOLVE AREA, SURFACE AREA, AND VOLUME PROBLEMS

? Topic Essential Question

How can the areas of certain shapes be found? What are the meanings of surface area and volume and how can surface area and volume be found?

Topic Overview

Topic Vocabulary

- base
- edge
- face
- kite
- net
- polyhedron
- vertex

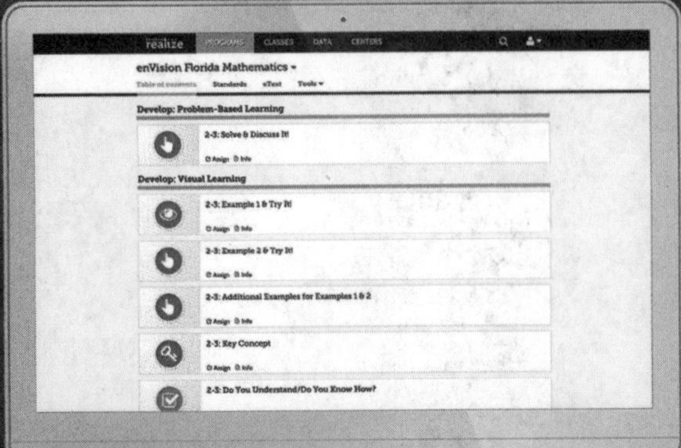

Go online | **PearsonRealize.com**

Lesson Digital Resources

INTERACTIVE STUDENT EDITION Access online or offline.

VISUAL LEARNING ANIMATION Interact with visual learning animations.

ACTIVITY Use with ***Solve & Discuss It, Explore It,*** and ***Explain It*** activities, and to explore Examples.

VIDEOS Watch clips to support ***3-Act Mathematical Modeling Lessons*** and ***STEM Projects.***

That's a Wrap

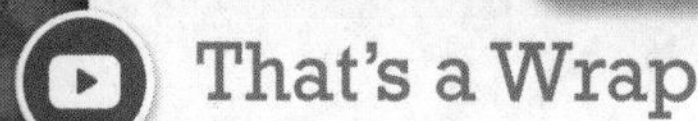

That's a Wrap

How you wrap a gift can say a lot about you. Some people conserve resources by reusing paper bags instead of purchasing wrapping paper. It may not look as nice at first, but you can unleash your crafty side and decorate the gift yourself.

No matter what you use to wrap a gift, you always need to consider the size of the object and how much paper you'll need. Think about this during the 3-Act Mathematical Modeling lesson.

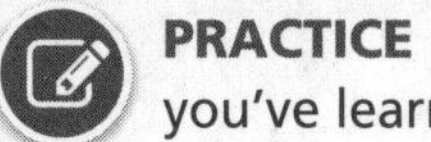

PRACTICE Practice what you've learned.

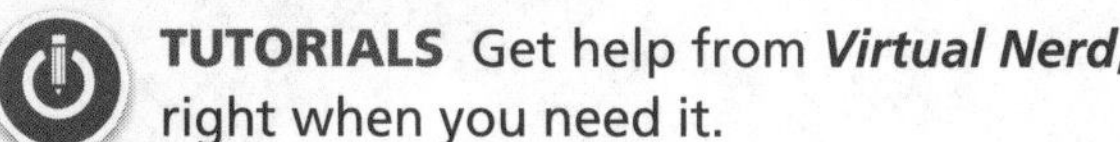

TUTORIALS Get help from ***Virtual Nerd***, right when you need it.

MATH TOOLS Explore math with digital tools.

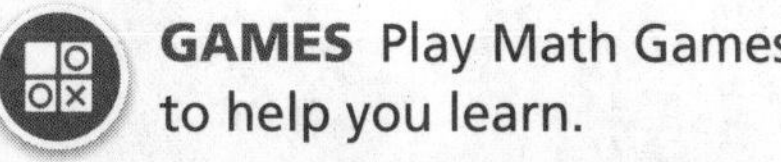

GAMES Play Math Games to help you learn.

KEY CONCEPT Review important lesson content.

GLOSSARY Read and listen to English/Spanish definitions.

ASSESSMENT Show what you've learned.

VIDEO

Did You Know?

Food packaging is designed to identify products and to attract customers. Packaging also ensures food remains fresh and free from damage and contamination.

Common types of material used for packaging are paper, cardboard, glass, steel, and aluminum. The best material to use for packaging depends on the contents—for example, soup in a paper bag could be rather messy!

Manufacturers consider several factors when designing packaging, such as cost, amount of material used, and potential environmental impact. Steel food cans are the most recycled food package in the United States.

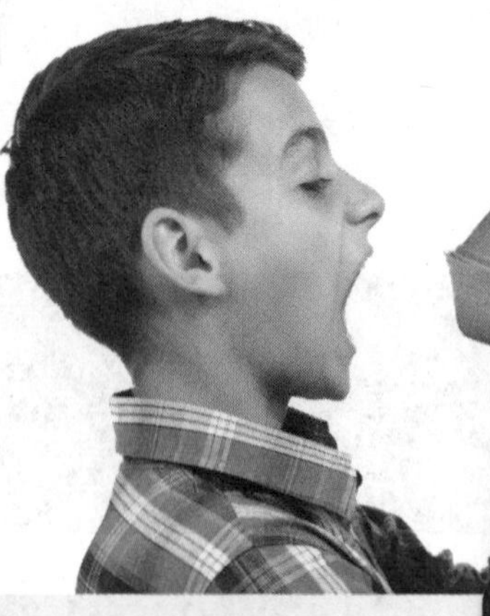

Packaging engineers consistently look for ways to innovate. Some food packaging is now self-opening, self-closing, or self-heating. Some packaging is biodegradable. Other advances include edible packaging.

Your Task: Pack It

Food packaging engineers consider many elements related to both form and function when designing packaging. How do engineers make decisions about package designs as they consider constraints, such as limited dimensions or materials? You and your classmates will use the engineering design process to explore and propose food packaging that satisfies certain criteria.

Review What You Know!

Vocabulary

Choose the best term from the box to complete each definition.

area
parallelogram
perpendicular
polygon
volume

1. A triangle is an example of a three-sided ________.
2. ________ lines form a right angle.
3. ________ is the number of cubic units needed to fill a solid figure.
4. A ________ has opposite sides that are parallel and the same length.

Evaluate Expressions

Find the value of each expression when $a = 12$, $b = 3$, $c = 4$, and $d = 9$.

5. ac
6. $\frac{1}{2}b$
7. abd
8. $0.5a$
9. $\frac{3}{4}(ad)$
10. $ab + cd$

Multiplication

Find each product.

11. 3.14×12
12. 45.8×5
13. 0.8×2.7
14. $14 \times 7.25 \times 2.5$
15. $1\frac{1}{2} \times \frac{1}{4}$
16. $2\frac{1}{3} \times 2\frac{1}{4} \times 1\frac{3}{8}$

Geometry

17. How are parallelograms and rectangles similar and how are they different?

18. How are the formulas for the area of a rectangle and the area of a triangle alike and different? Explain.

Build Vocabulary

Use the graphic organizer to help relate vocabulary terms that you studied before to the new vocabulary in this topic.

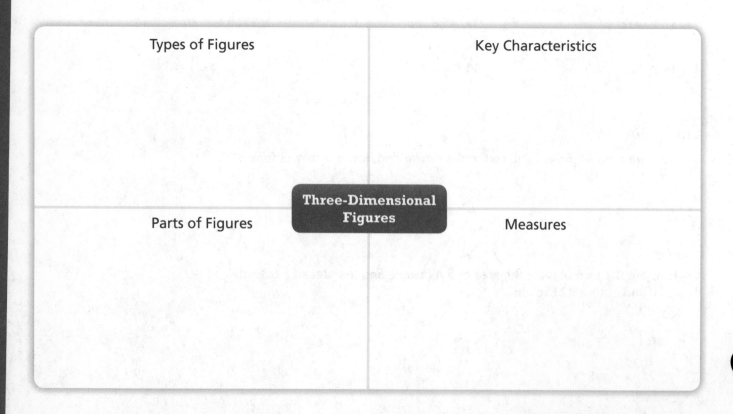

Types of Figures	Key Characteristics
Two-Dimensional Figures	
Parts of Figures	Measures

Types of Figures	Key Characteristics
Three-Dimensional Figures	
Parts of Figures	Measures

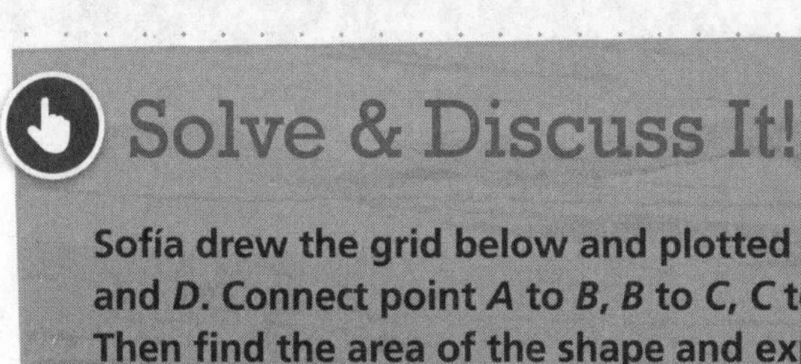

Solve & Discuss It!

Sofía drew the grid below and plotted the points *A*, *B*, *C*, and *D*. Connect point *A* to *B*, *B* to *C*, *C* to *D*, and *D* to *A*. Then find the area of the shape and explain how you found it. Using the same grid, move points *B* and *C* four units to the right. Connect the points to make a new parallelogram *ABCD*. What is the area of this shape?

Lesson 11-1
Find Areas of Parallelograms and Rhombuses

Go Online | PearsonRealize.com

I can...
use what I know about areas of rectangles to find the areas of parallelograms and rhombuses.

MAFS.6.G.1.1 Find the area of... special quadrilaterals... by composing into rectangles or decomposing into triangles... apply these techniques in the context of solving real-world and mathematical problems. Also 6.EE.1.2c
MAFS.K12.MP.2.1, MP.3.1, MP.6.1, MP.7.1, MP.8.1

Look for Relationships What relationships do you see between rectangles and parallelograms?

Focus on math practices

Generalize How can you find the area of any parallelogram?

? Essential Question How can you use the area formula of a rectangle to find the area formula of a parallelogram?

VISUAL LEARNING ASSESS

EXAMPLE 1  Find the Area Formula of a Parallelogram

Scan for Multimedia 

Look at the parallelogram below. If you move the triangle to the opposite side, you form a rectangle with the same area as the parallelogram. How can you find the area of a parallelogram?

Use Structure To compose a rectangle from a parallelogram, first decompose the parallelogram into a right triangle and a trapezoid.

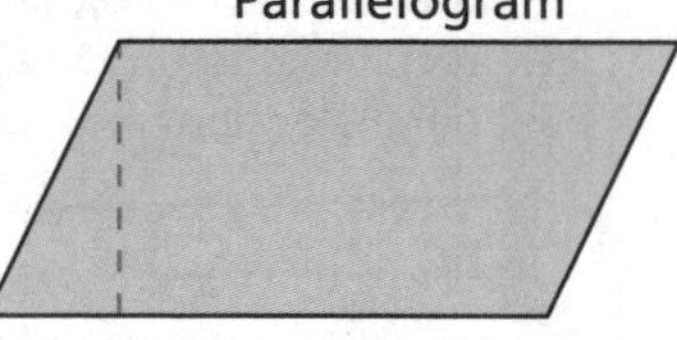

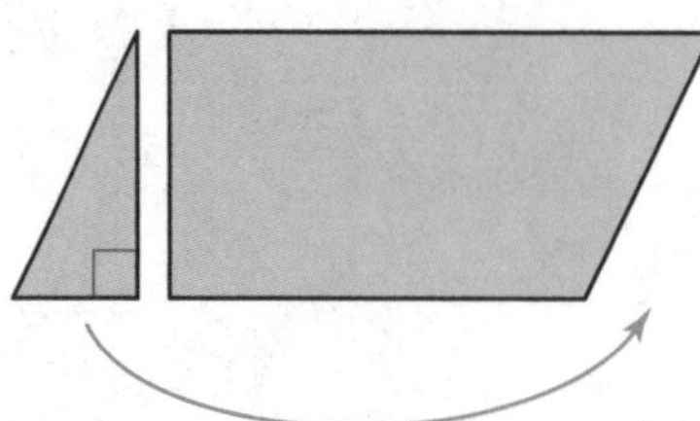

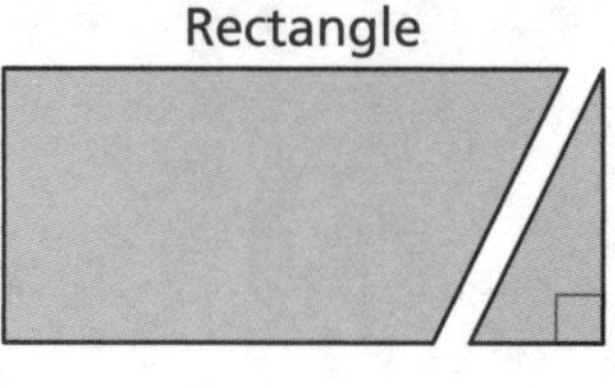

Create a rectangle.

The height of the parallelogram, h, which is perpendicular to the base, equals the width of the rectangle, w.

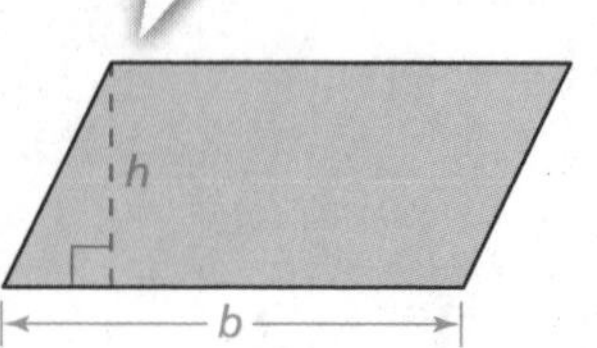

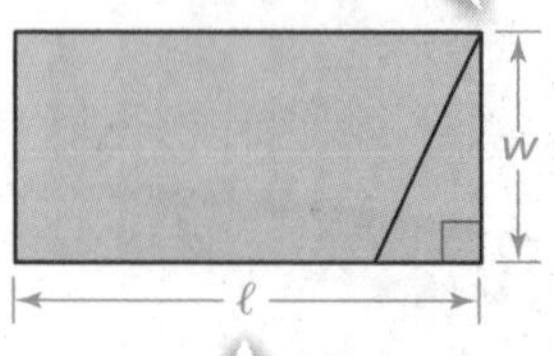

The base of the parallelogram, b, equals the length of the rectangle, ℓ.

The area of the parallelogram equals the area of the rectangle.

Area of a Rectangle $A = \ell \times w$

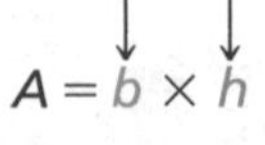

Area of a Parallelogram $A = b \times h$

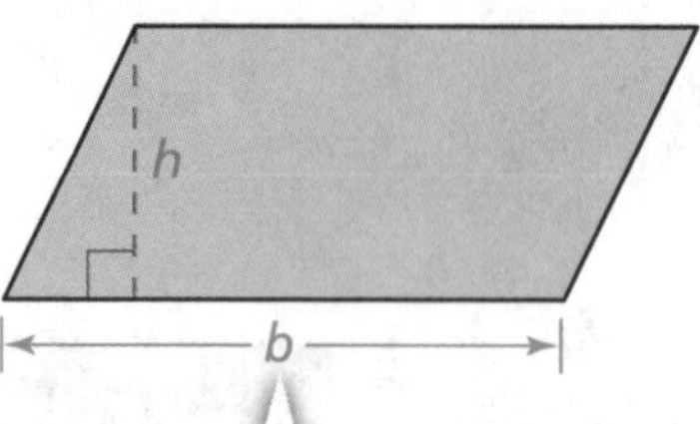

The formula for the area of a parallelogram is $A = bh$.

Try It!

Find the area of the parallelogram.

$A = \square \times h$

$A = \square \times \square$

$A = \square$

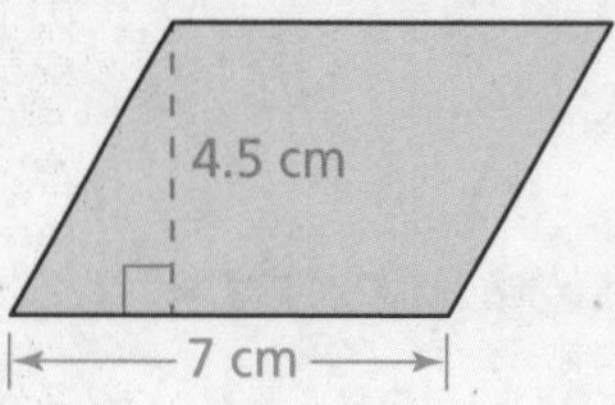

The area of the parallelogram is $\square$ cm^2.

Convince Me! Compare the area of this parallelogram to the area of a rectangle with a length of 7 cm and a width of 4.5 cm. Explain.

EXAMPLE 2 Find the Area of a Rhombus

The pendant at the right is in the shape of a rhombus. A rhombus is a parallelogram with sides of equal length. What is the area of the pendant?

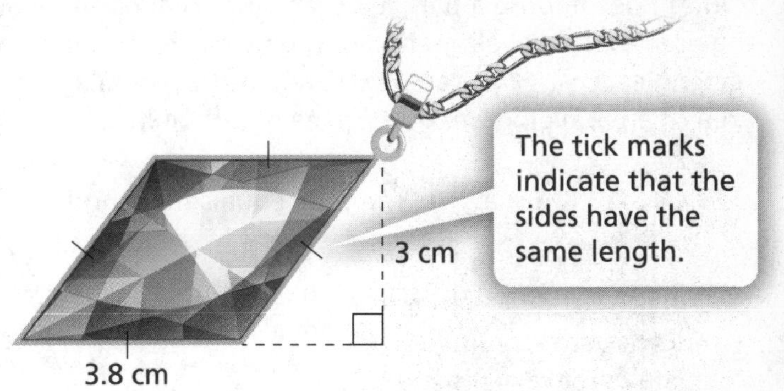

Be Precise You can use the formula for the area of a parallelogram to find the area of a rhombus. Remember to record area in square units.

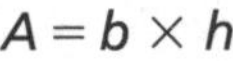

$A = b \times h$

$A = 3.8 \times 3$

$A = 11.4$

The area of the pendant is 11.4 cm^2.

EXAMPLE 3 Find the Base or Height of a Parallelogram

A. The area of the parallelogram is 72 m^2. What is the height of the parallelogram?

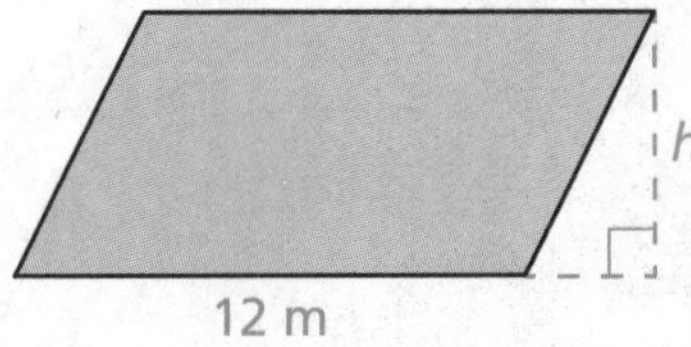

$A = b \times h$

$72 = 12 \times h$ — Substitute 72 for A and 12 for b.

$6 = h$

The height of the parallelogram is 6 m.

B. The area of the parallelogram is 135 in.^{2}. What is the base of the parallelogram?

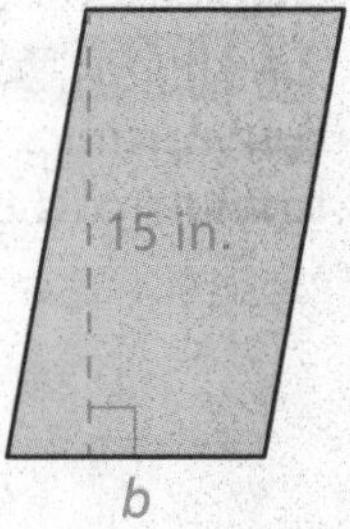

$A = b \times h$

$135 = b \times 15$ — Substitute 135 for A and 15 for h.

$9 = b$

The base of the parallelogram is 9 in.

Try It!

a. Find the area of the rhombus.

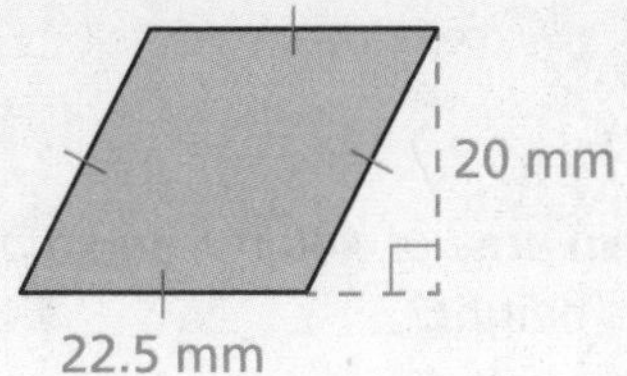

b. The area of the parallelogram is 65 ft^2. What is its height?

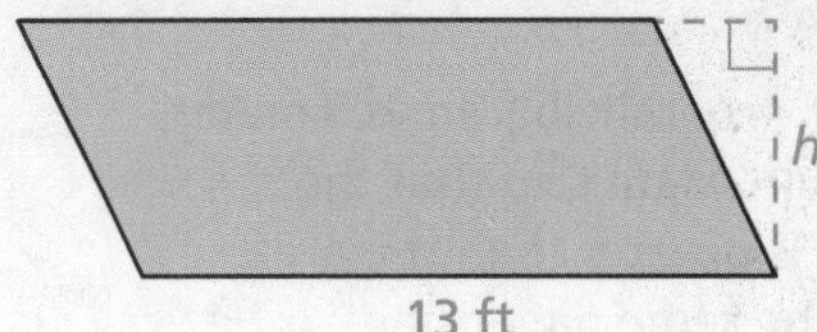

KEY CONCEPT

You can decompose a parallelogram and compose a rectangle to find the area of a parallelogram or a rhombus. The formula for the area of a rectangle, $A = \ell \times w$, can be written as the formula $A = b \times h$ to find the area of a parallelogram or the area of a rhombus.

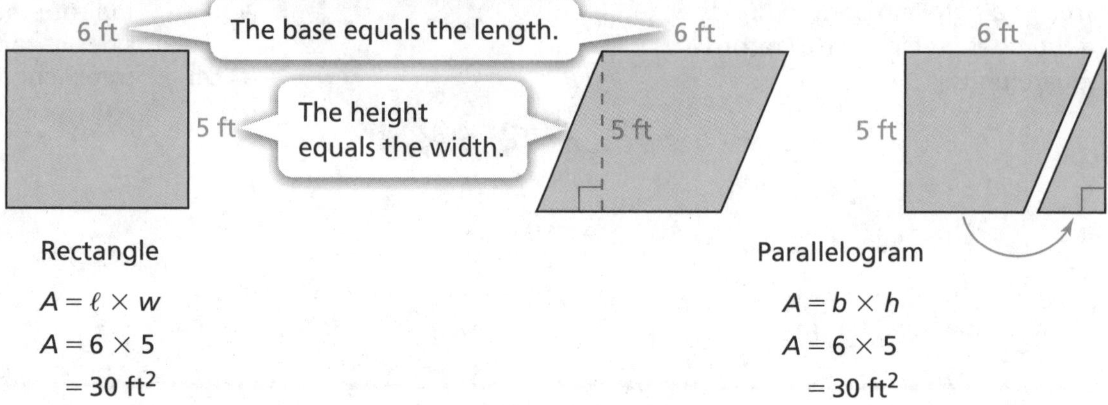

Rectangle

$A = \ell \times w$

$A = 6 \times 5$

$= 30 \text{ ft}^2$

Parallelogram

$A = b \times h$

$A = 6 \times 5$

$= 30 \text{ ft}^2$

Do You Understand?

1. **Essential Question** How can you use the area formula of a rectangle to find the area formula of a parallelogram?

2. Ken combined a triangle and a trapezoid to make a parallelogram. If the area of the triangle is 12 in.^{2} and the area of the trapezoid is 24 in.^{2}, what is the area of the parallelogram? Explain.

3. **Critique Reasoning** A parallelogram is 3 meters long and 7 meters high. Liam said that the parallelogram's area is greater than the area of a rectangle with the same dimensions. Is he correct? Explain.

Do You Know How?

In 4–6, use a formula to find the area.

4.

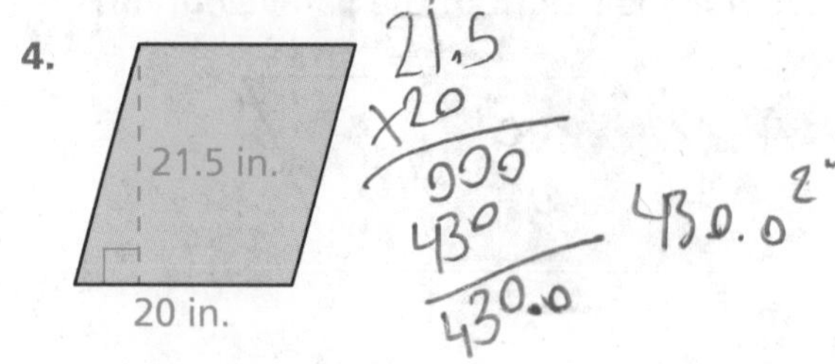

5.

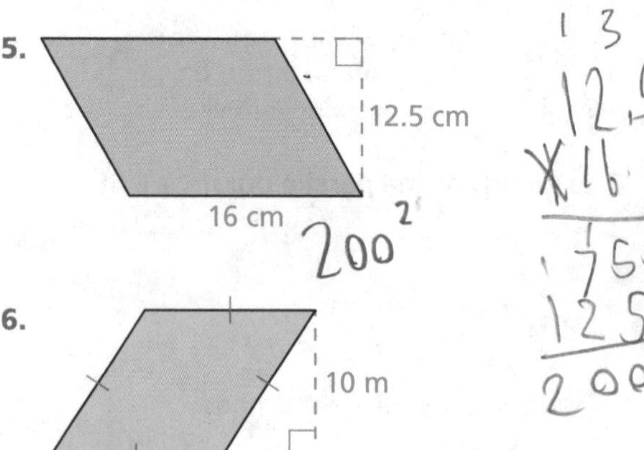

6.

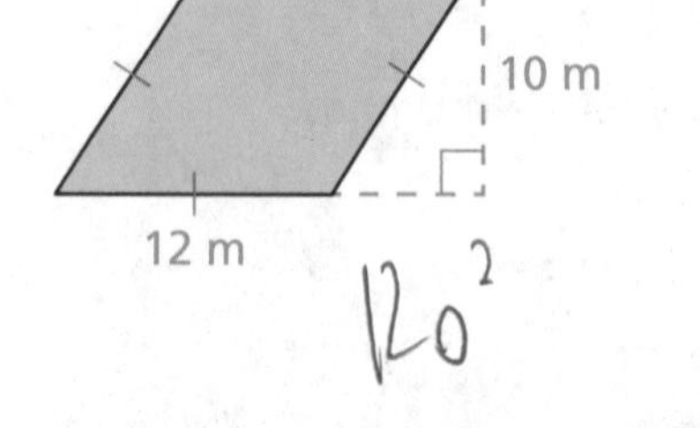

7. A rhombus has an area of 440 m^2 and a base of 22 m. What is its height?

Name: ______________________________

Practice & Problem Solving

Scan for Multimedia

Leveled Practice **In 8–11, find the area of each parallelogram or rhombus.**

8.

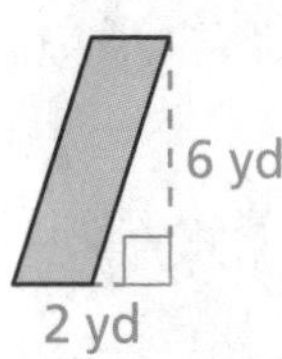

$A = b \cdot h$

$= \boxed{2} \cdot 6$

$= \boxed{12}$ yd^2

9.

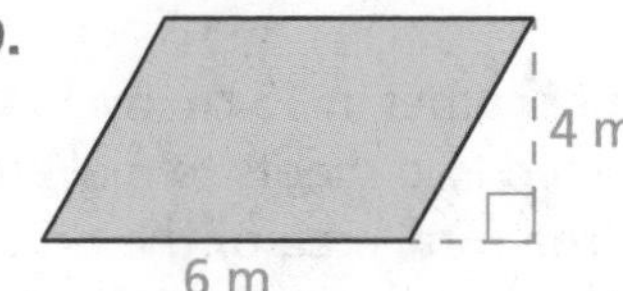

$A = b \cdot h$

$= \boxed{6} \cdot \boxed{4}$

$= \boxed{24}$ m^2

10.

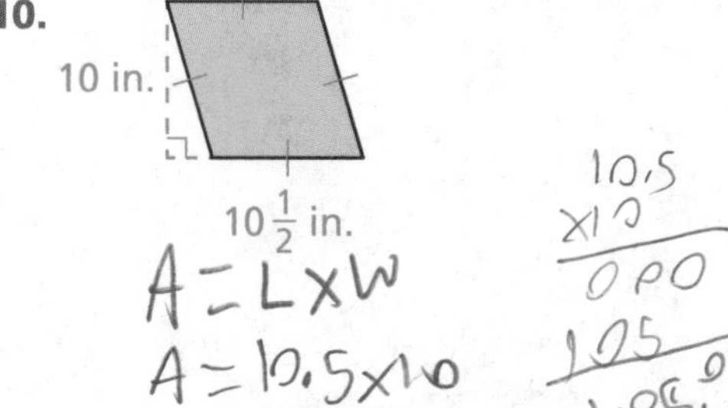

11.

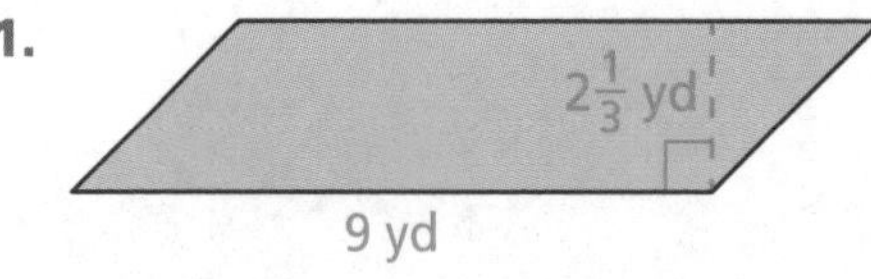

12. The area of the parallelogram is 132 in.^{2}. What is the height of the parallelogram?

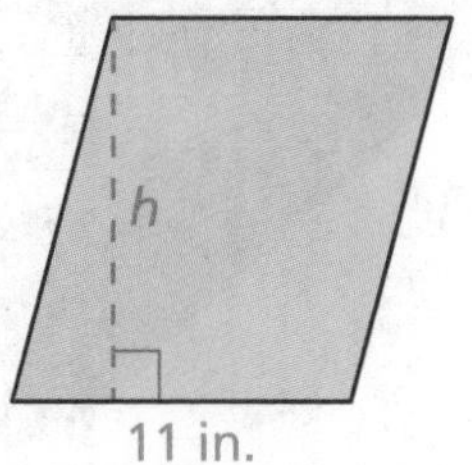

13. The area of the rhombus is 52 m^2. What is the base of the rhombus?

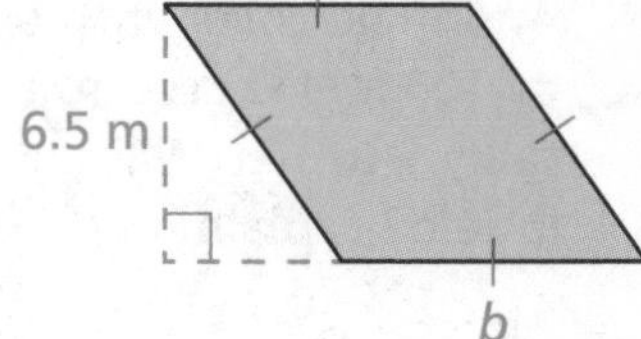

14. Micah and Jason made parallelogram-shaped stained glass windows with the same area. The height of Micah's window is 9 inches, and its base is 10 inches. The height of Jason's window is 6 inches. What is the base of Jason's window?

15. A rectangle has a length of 8 m and a width of 4.5 m. A parallelogram has a length of 6 m. The area of the parallelogram is twice the area of the rectangle. What is the height of the parallelogram?

In 16 and 17, use the picture at the right.

16. Hilary made an origami dog. What is the area of the parallelogram that is highlighted in the origami figure?

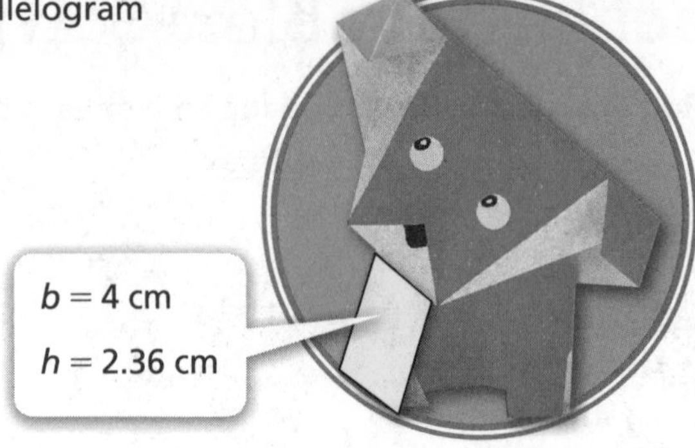

17. A type of origami paper comes in 15 cm by 15 cm square sheets. Hilary used two sheets to make the origami dog. What is the total area of the origami paper that Hilary used to make the dog?

18. Reasoning A rectangle and a parallelogram have the same base and the same height. How are their areas related? Provide an example to justify your answer.

19. Soshi's rhombus has a base of 12 in. and a height of 10 in. Jack's rhombus has base and height measures that are double those of Soshi's rhombus. Compare the area of Jack's rhombus to the area of Soshi's rhombus. Explain.

20. Higher Order Thinking The infield of a baseball diamond is in the shape of a rhombus. An infield cover with dimensions of 85 feet by 100 feet is used to protect the field during rainy weather. Will the cover protect the entire infield? Explain.

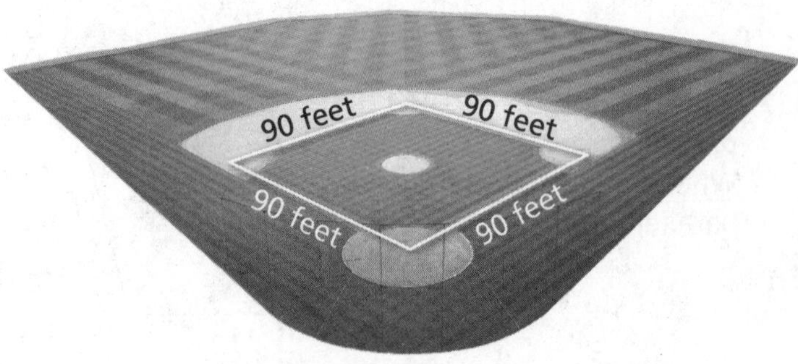

Assessment Practice

21. The parking space shown at the right has an area of 209 ft^2. A custom truck has rectangular dimensions of 13.5 ft by 8.5 ft. Can the truck fit in the parking space? Justify your answer. 6.EE.1.2c

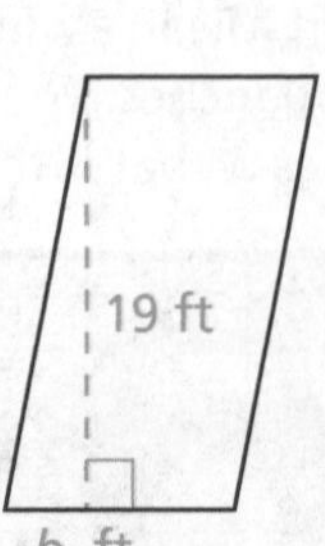

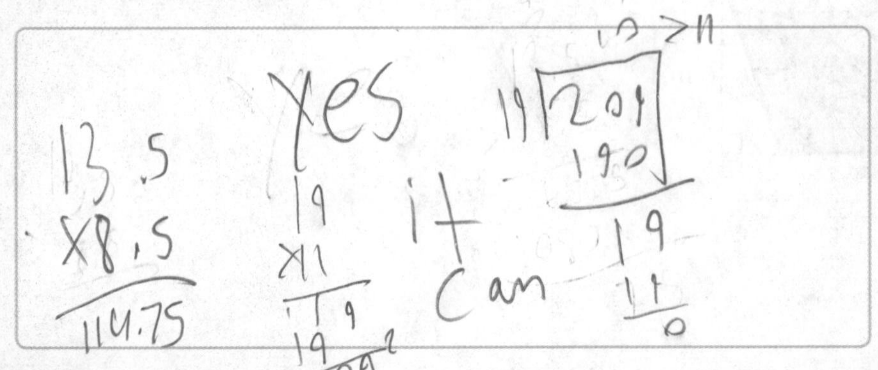

Lesson 11-2
Solve Triangle Area Problems

Go Online | PearsonRealize.com

I can...
find the areas of triangles.

MAFS.6.G.1.1 Find the area of right triangles, other triangles,... by composing into rectangles... apply these techniques in the context of solving real-world and mathematical problems. Also 6.EE.1.2c
MAFS.K12.MP.2.1, MP.3.1, MP.6.1, MP.7.1, MP.8.1

Solve & Discuss It!

ACTIVITY

Connect point *A* to *B*, *B* to *C*, *C* to *D*, and *D* to *A*. Then draw a diagonal line connecting opposite vertices in the figure and find the area of each triangle formed.

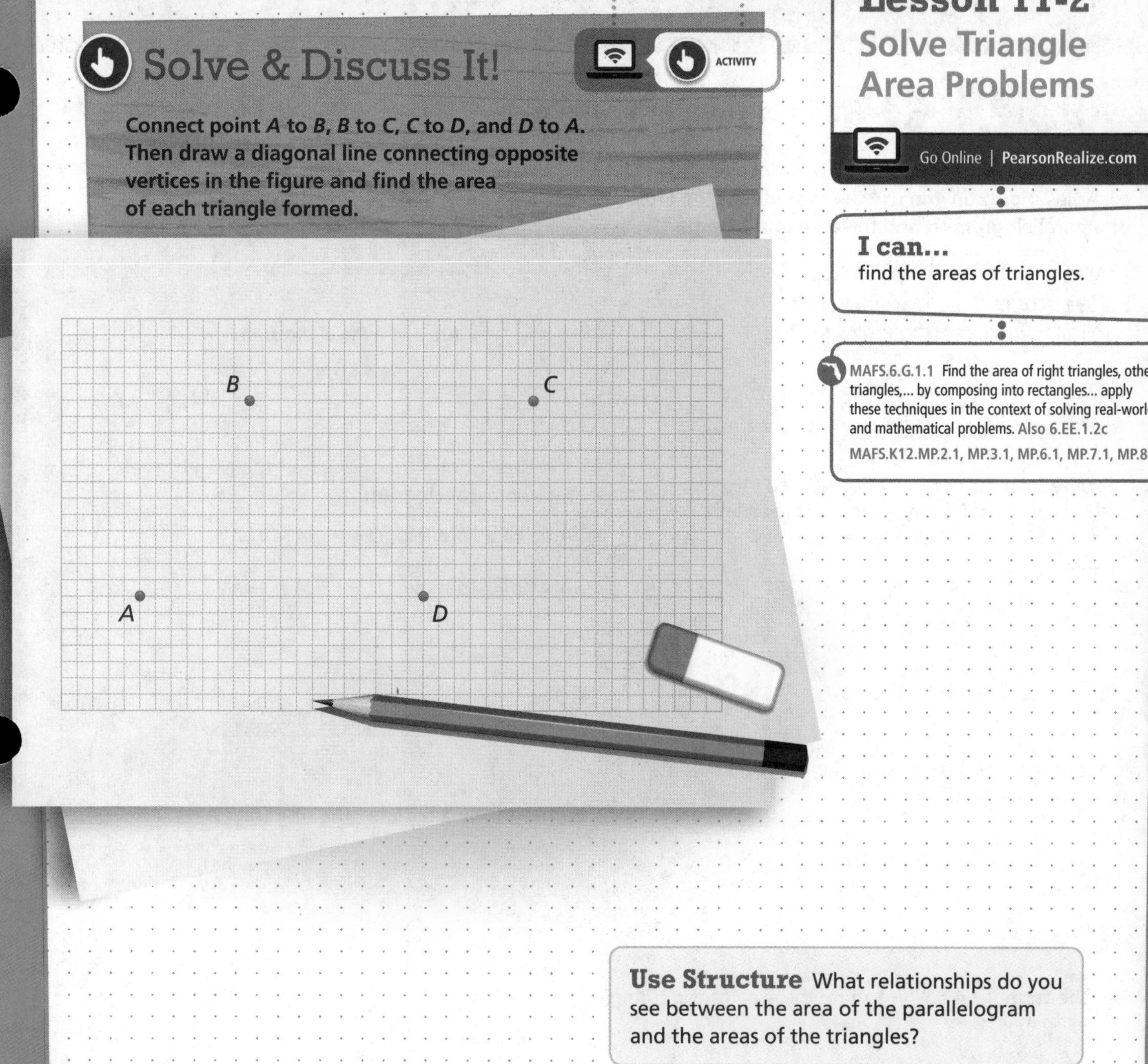

Use Structure What relationships do you see between the area of the parallelogram and the areas of the triangles?

Focus on math practices

Generalize What is a rule for finding the area of any triangle?

? **Essential Question** How can you find the area of a triangle?

EXAMPLE 1  Find the Area of a Triangle

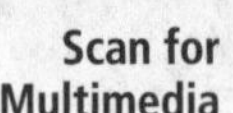

A parallelogram can be decomposed into two identical triangles. How can you use the formula for the area of a parallelogram to find the area of a triangle?

Reasoning How are the areas of parallelograms and triangles related?

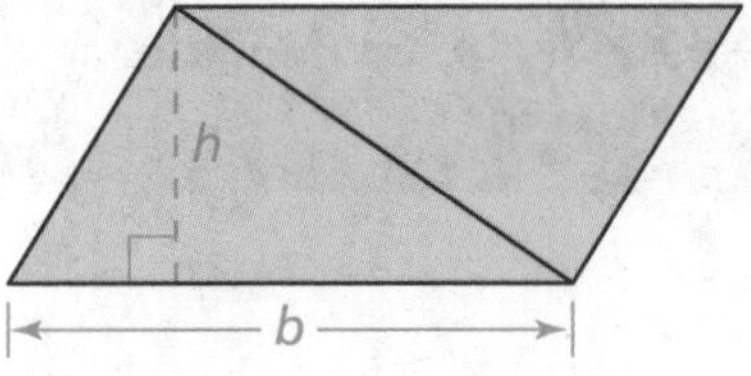

Area of a Parallelogram

$A = bh$

A parallelogram can be decomposed into two identical triangles when divided diagonally.

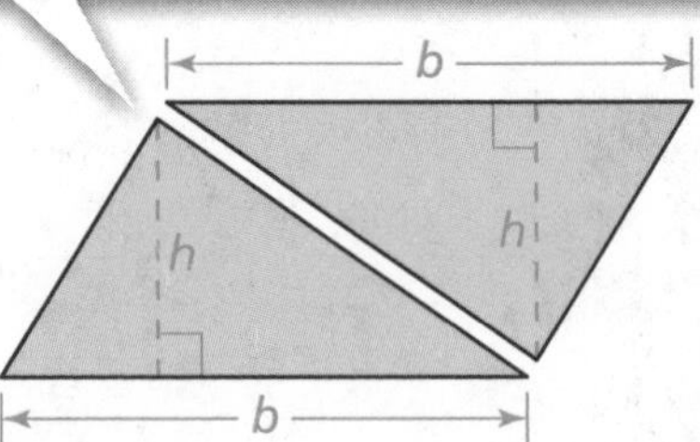

Identical triangles have the same base and height, so they also have the same area.

The area of one triangle is half the area of the related parallelogram.

Area of a Parallelogram $A = bh$

Area of a Triangle $A = \frac{1}{2}bh$

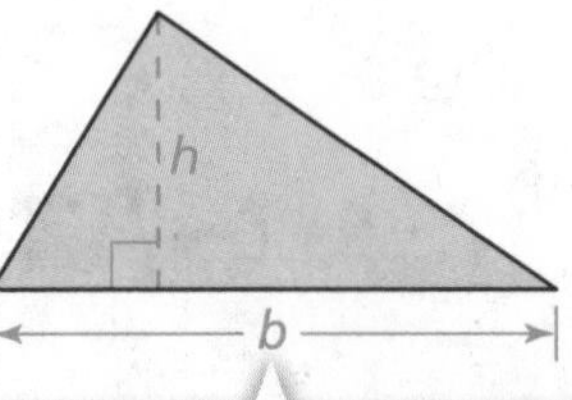

The formula for the area of a triangle is $A = \frac{1}{2}bh$.

Try It!

Use the formula $A = \frac{1}{2}bh$ to find the area of the triangle.

$A = \frac{1}{2} \times b \times h$

$A = \frac{1}{2} \times$ ☐ $\times$ ☐

$A = \frac{1}{2} \times$ ☐

$A =$ ☐

5 cm

12 cm

The area of the triangle is ☐ cm^2.

Convince Me! Two identical triangles form a parallelogram with a base of 8 inches and a height of 6 inches. What is the area of each triangle? Explain.

EXAMPLE 2  Find the Area of a Right Triangle

The side of a birdhouse is in the shape of a right triangle. What is the area of the side of the birdhouse?

Draw a triangle and compose a square.

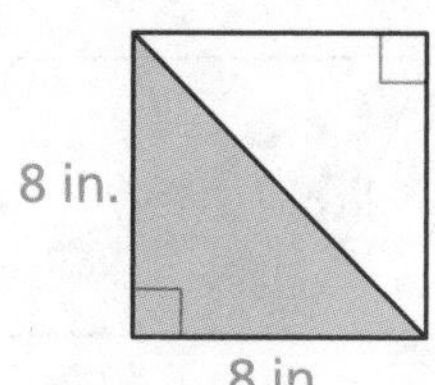

The two sides that form the right angle in a right triangle are its base and height.

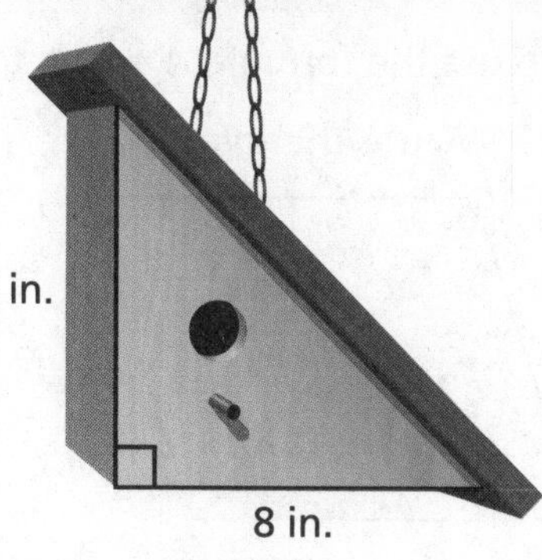

Generalize You can use the formula $A = \frac{1}{2}bh$ to find the area of *any* triangle when you know the base and height.

Find the area of the triangle.

$A = \frac{1}{2}bh$

$A = \frac{1}{2} \times 8 \times 8 = 32$

The area of the side of the birdhouse is 32 in.^{2}.

EXAMPLE 3  Identify the Corresponding Base and Height to Find the Area

Kaylan drew the triangle shown below. What is the area of the triangle?

Any side of a triangle can be its base. The height is the perpendicular distance from the base to the height of the opposite vertex.

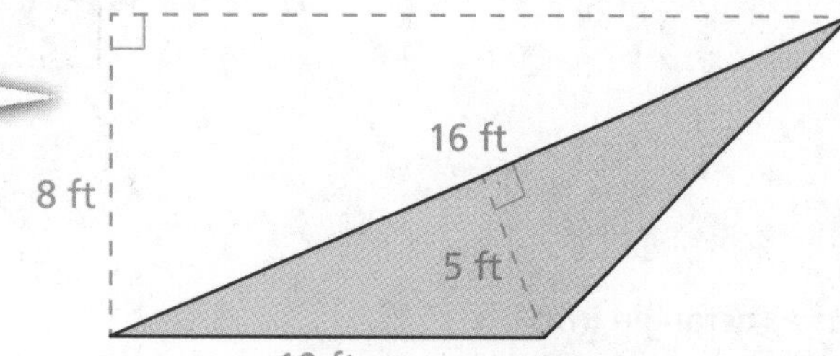

ONE WAY

$A = \frac{1}{2}bh$

$A = \frac{1}{2} \cdot 10 \cdot 8$

$A = 40$

Substitute a corresponding base of 10 ft and height of 8 ft.

The area is 40 ft^2.

ANOTHER WAY

$A = \frac{1}{2}bh$

$A = \frac{1}{2} \cdot 16 \cdot 5$

$A = 40$

Substitute a corresponding base and height.

The area is 40 ft^2.

Try It!

Find the area of each triangle.

a.

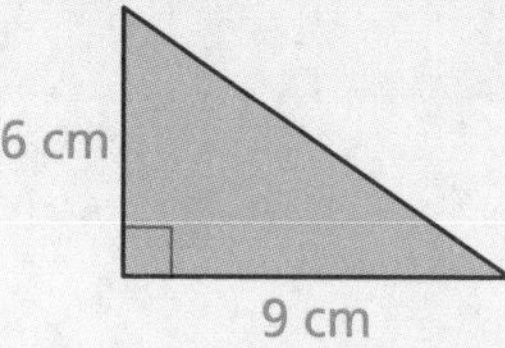

b.

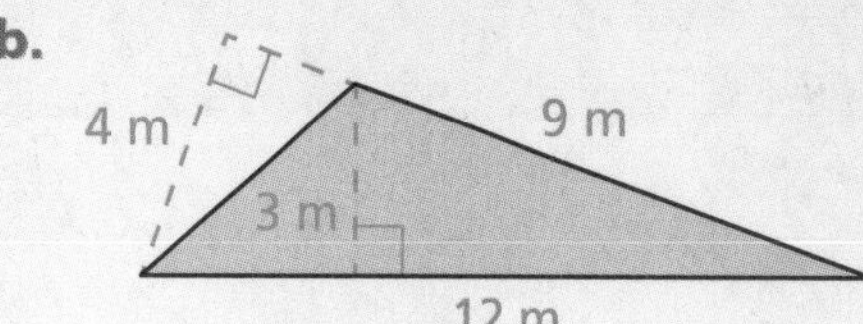

KEY CONCEPT

You can use the formula $A = \frac{1}{2}bh$ to find the area of any triangle.

Acute Triangle

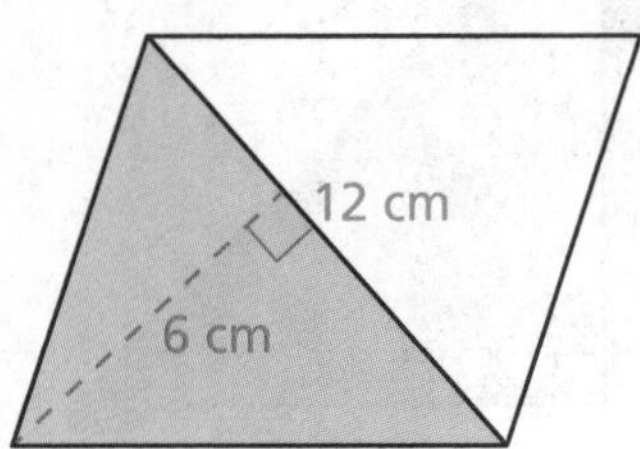

$A = \frac{1}{2}bh$

$A = \frac{1}{2} \times 12 \times 6$

$A = 36 \text{ cm}^2$

Right Triangle

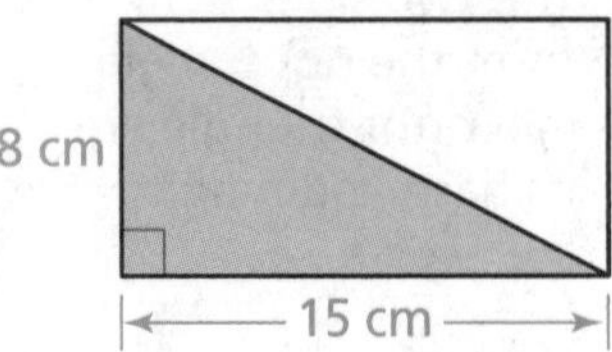

$A = \frac{1}{2}bh$

$A = \frac{1}{2} \times 15 \times 8$

$A = 60 \text{ cm}^2$

Obtuse Triangle

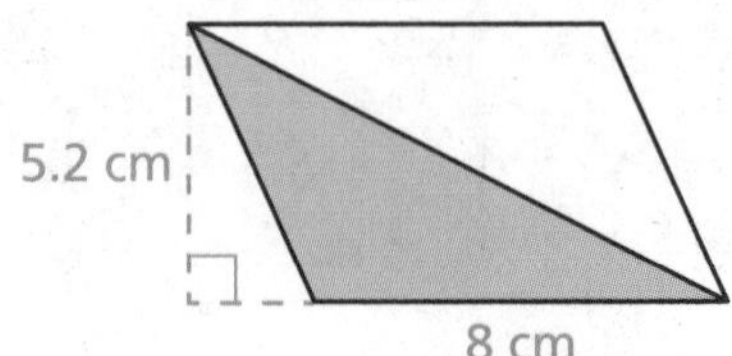

$A = \frac{1}{2}bh$

$A = \frac{1}{2} \times 8 \times 5.2$

$A = 20.8 \text{ cm}^2$

Do You Understand?

1. **Essential Question** How can you find the area of a triangle?

2. **Reasoning** If you cut a rectangle into 2 identical triangles, what type of triangles will they be?

3. **Construct Arguments** In Example 1, if the other diagonal were used to divide the parallelogram into two triangles, would the area of each of these triangles be half the area of the parallelogram? Explain.

Do You Know How?

In 4–6, find the area of each triangle.

4.

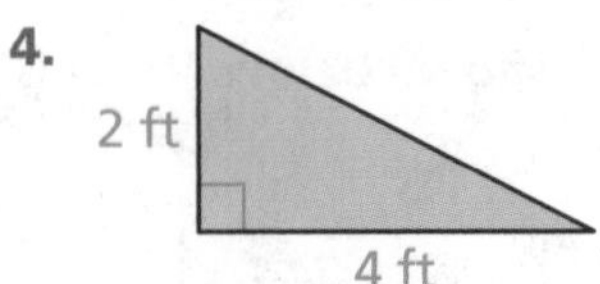

5.

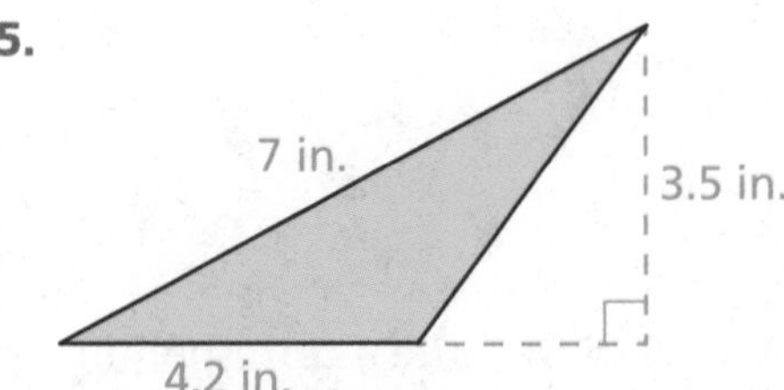

6.

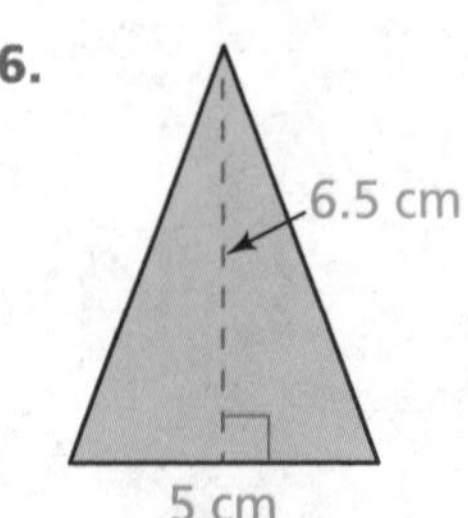

Name: ____________________

Practice & Problem Solving

Scan for Multimedia

Leveled Practice **In 7–12, find the area of each triangle.**

7.

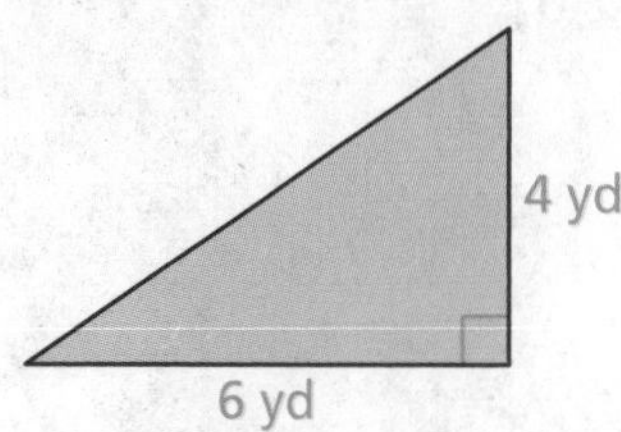

$A = \frac{1}{2}bh$

$= \frac{1}{2} \times \square \times 4$

$= \square$ yd^2

8.

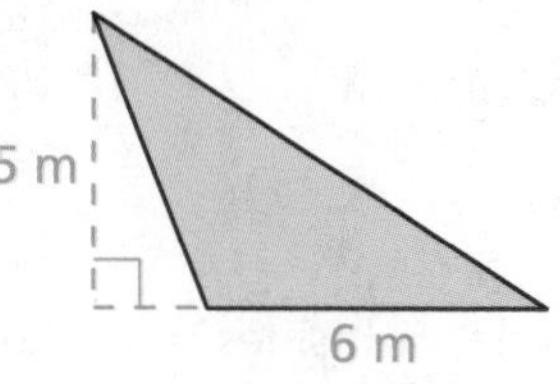

$A = \frac{1}{2}bh$

$= \frac{1}{2} \times \square \times \square$

$= \square$ m^2

9.

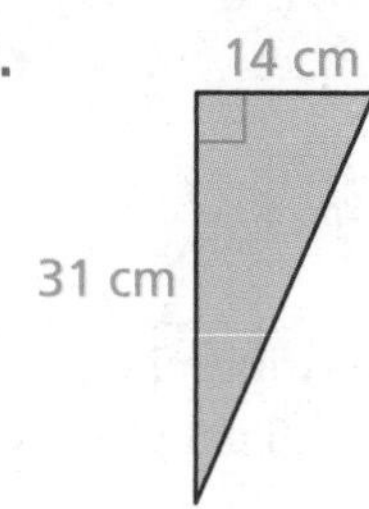

$A = \frac{1}{2}bh$

$= \frac{1}{2} \times \square \times \square$

$= \square$ cm^2

10.

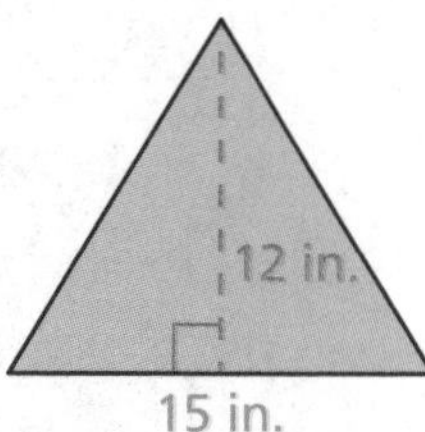

11.

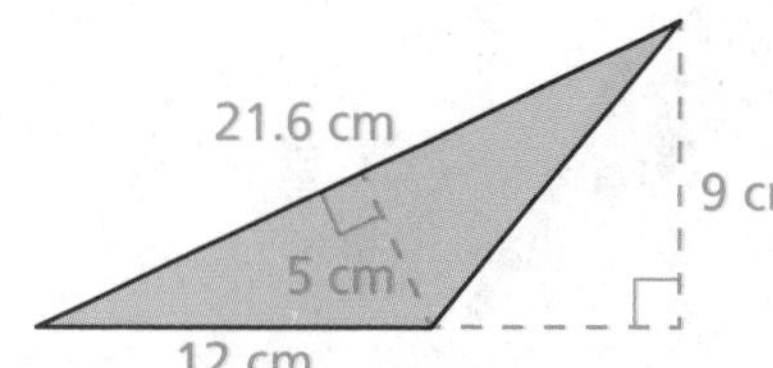

12.

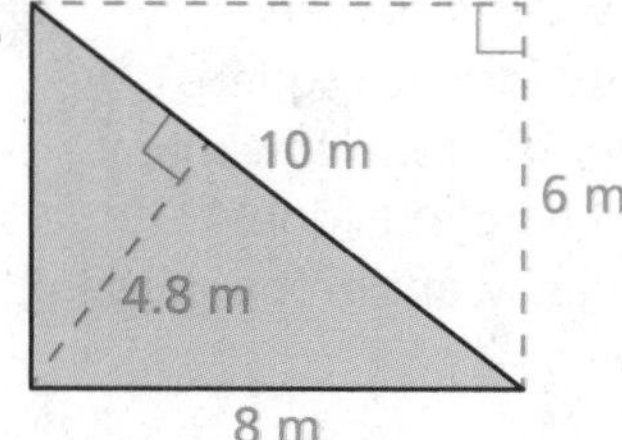

13. The vertices of a triangle are $A(0, 0)$, $B(3, 8)$, and $C(9, 0)$. What is the area of this triangle?

14. Be Precise The base of a triangle is 2 ft. The height of the triangle is 15 in. What is the area of the triangle in square inches?

15. Reasoning Ms. Lopez drew $\triangle ABC$, with a height of 6 inches and a base of 6 inches, and $\triangle RST$, with a height of 4 inches and a base of 8 inches. Which triangle has the greater area? Use an area formula to justify your answer.

16. The dimensions of the sail for Erica's sailboat are shown. Find the area of the sail.

15 ft

9 ft

In 17 and 18, use the picture at the right.

17. Be Precise What is the area in square millimeters of the yellow triangle outlined on the origami figure at the right?

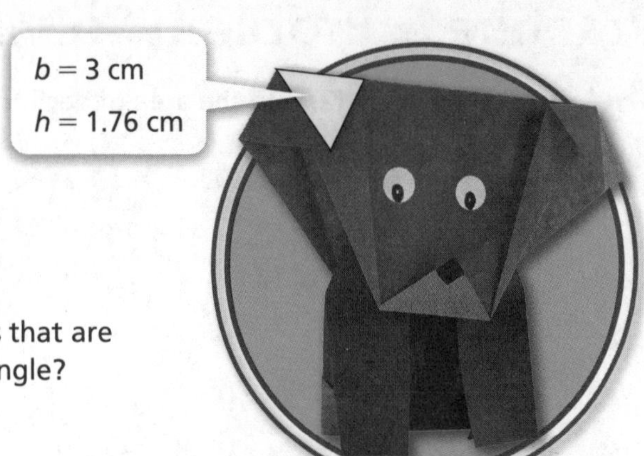

18. The nose of the origami dog is a right triangle with sides that are 2 cm, 3 cm, and 3.6 cm long. What is the area of this triangle?

19. Michael is planting a garden in the shape of a right triangle. He wants 4 tickseed plants for each square meter of area. How many tickseed plants does Michael want in the garden?

7 m
24 m
25 m

20. Higher Order Thinking If you know the area and the height of a triangle, how can you find the base?

Assessment Practice

21. Select all expressions that represent the area of the given triangle. 6.G.1.1

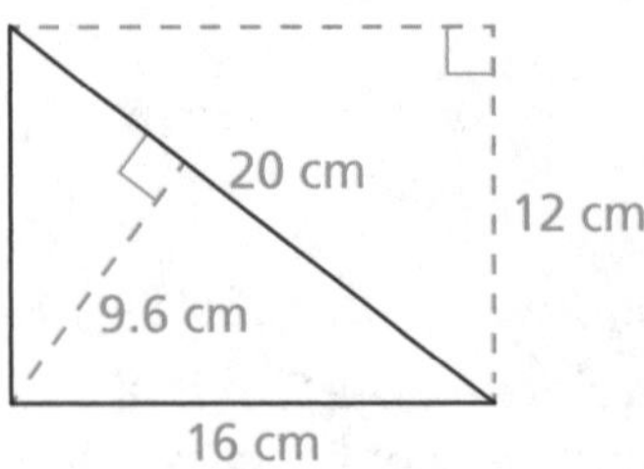

- ☐ $A = \frac{1}{2}(12 \times 16)$
- ☐ $A = 12 \times 16$
- ☐ $A = 9.6 \times 20$
- ☐ $A = \frac{1}{2}(16 \times 9.6)$
- ☐ $A = \frac{1}{2}(20 \times 9.6)$

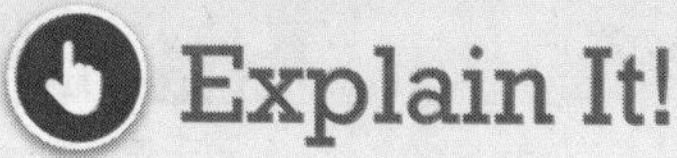

Explain It!

Lesson 11-3
Find Areas of Trapezoids and Kites

Go Online | PearsonRealize.com

I can...
find areas of trapezoids and kites.

MAFS.6.G.1.1 Find the area of... special quadrilaterals... by... decomposing into triangles and other shapes; apply these techniques in the context of solving real-world and mathematical problems. Also 6.EE.1.2c

MAFS.K12.MP.1.1, MP.3.1, MP.6.1, MP.7.1

The European basketball key was changed from a trapezoid shape to a rectangle in 2010. The diagram shows the shape of the key before 2010 outlined in blue.

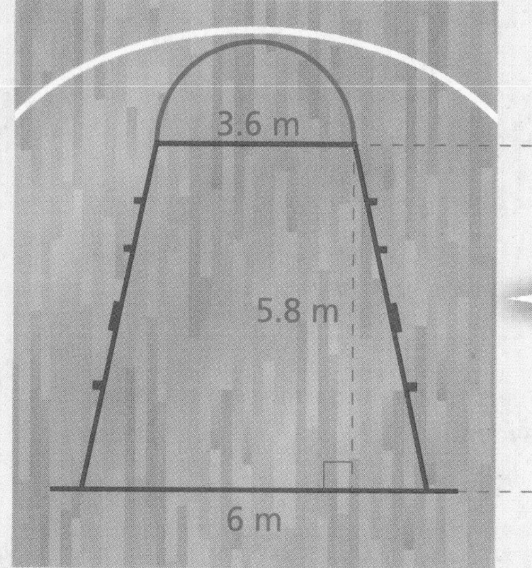

foul line

baseline

The key on a basketball court is the area between the foul line and the baseline.

A. Construct Arguments Tim finds the area of the key by multiplying the base by the height. Does his strategy make sense?

B. Use Structure How could Tim find the area of the trapezoid by decomposing it into shapes he knows? What is the area of the key?

Focus on math practices

Use Structure How can you find the area of this kite? Explain.

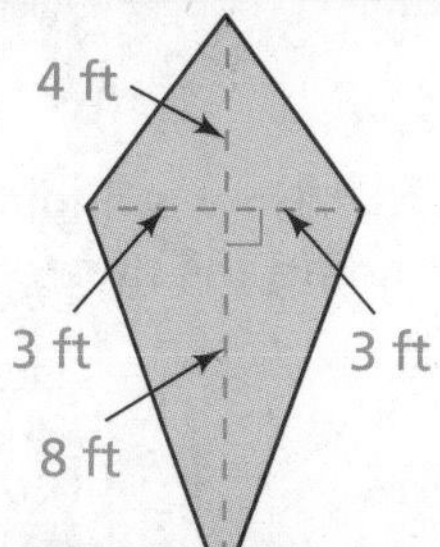

? Essential Question How can you find the areas of trapezoids and kites?

EXAMPLE 1  Find the Area of a Trapezoid

Scan for Multimedia 

The pasture is in the shape of a trapezoid. What is the area of the pasture?

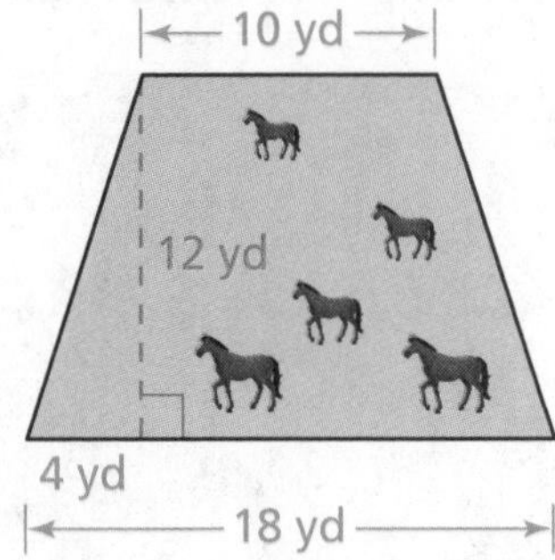

> **Be Precise** What are the properties of a trapezoid and how can they help you to find the area of a trapezoid?

Decompose the trapezoid into a rectangle and two right triangles.

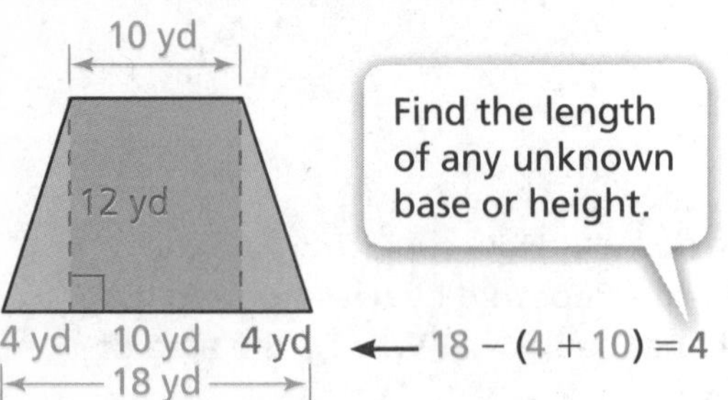

Find the area of each shape and then add the areas. The triangles are identical.

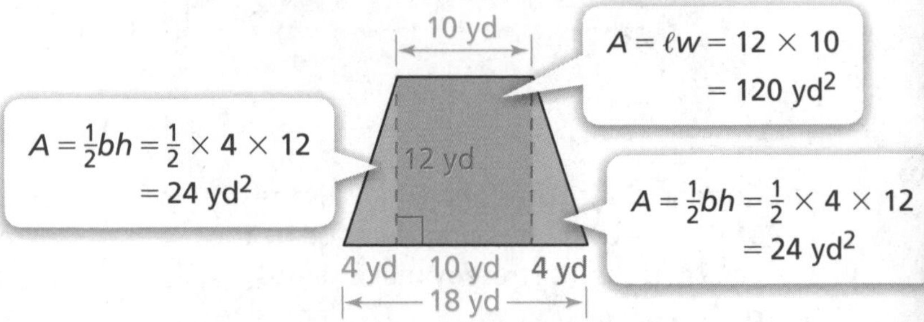

Add the areas: $24 + 120 + 24 = 168$

The area of the pasture is 168 yd^2.

Try It!

How would you decompose this trapezoid to find its area? Find the area of the trapezoid.

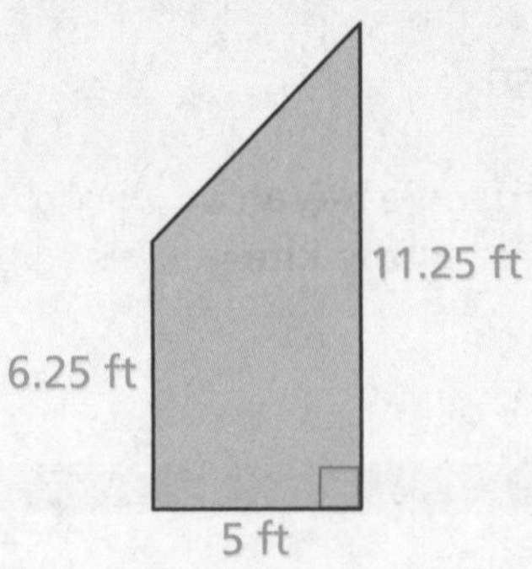

Convince Me! How is finding the area of the trapezoid in Example 1 different from finding the area of the trapezoid in the Try It!?

EXAMPLE 2  Find the Area of a Different Trapezoid

A builder needs to cut one stone in the shape of a trapezoid to fit in the space. What is the area of the front side of that stone?

> **Look for Relationships** When you decompose a trapezoid into a rectangle and two triangles, the triangles are not always identical.

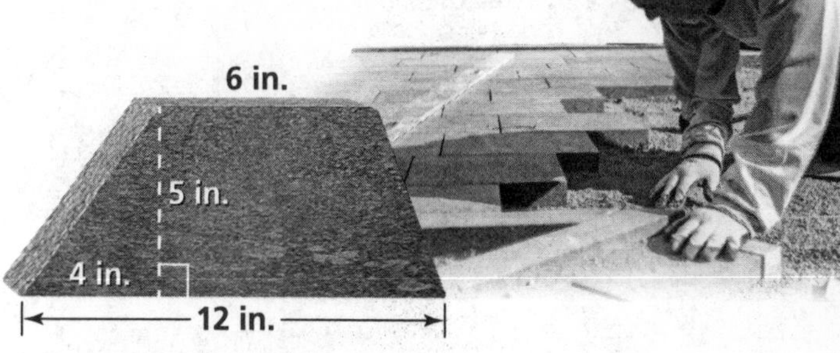

Draw lines to show the rectangle and the two triangles. Label needed measurements.

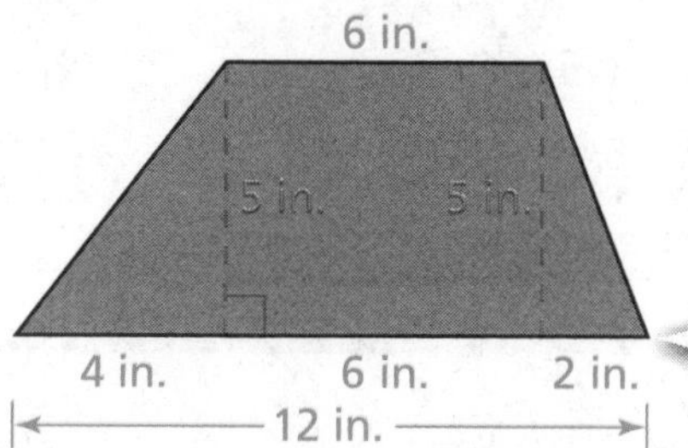

The triangles have different bases.

Find the areas:

Triangle: $A = \frac{1}{2}bh = \frac{1}{2}(4 \times 5) = 10$

Rectangle: $A = \ell w = 6 \times 5 = 30$

Triangle: $A = \frac{1}{2}bh = \frac{1}{2}(2 \times 5) = 5$

Add the areas:

$10 \text{ in.}^2 + 30 \text{ in.}^2 + 5 \text{ in.}^2 = 45 \text{ in.}^2$

The area of the side of the stone is 45 in.^{2}.

EXAMPLE 3  Find the Area of a Kite

Jackson has a rectangular piece of cloth that has an area of 298 cm^2. Does Jackson have enough cloth to make the kite shown?

> A **kite** is a quadrilateral with two pairs of adjacent sides that are equal in length.

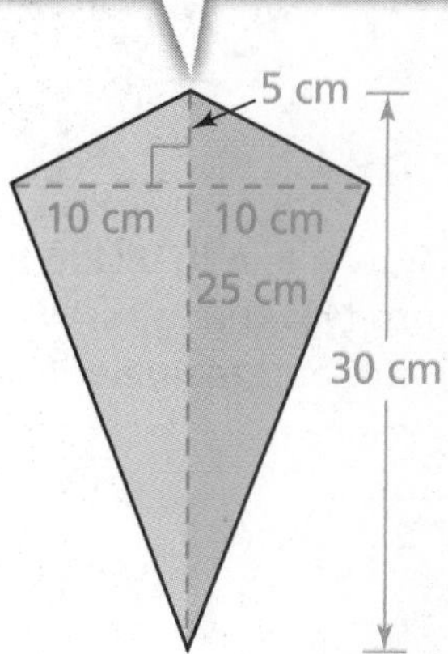

STEP 1 Decompose the kite into two identical triangles. Find the area of the triangles.

$A = \frac{1}{2}bh$

$A = \frac{1}{2} \cdot 30 \cdot 10$

$A = 150 \text{ cm}^2$

Each triangle has an area of 150 cm^2. The area of the kite is 300 cm^2.

STEP 2 Find the area of the kite. Compare the area of the kite to the area of the cloth.

$2 \times 150 \text{ cm}^2 = 300 \text{ cm}^2$

$300 \text{ cm}^2 > 298 \text{ cm}^2$

Jackson does not have enough cloth to make the kite.

Try It!

Find the area of the trapezoid and the area of the kite.

a.

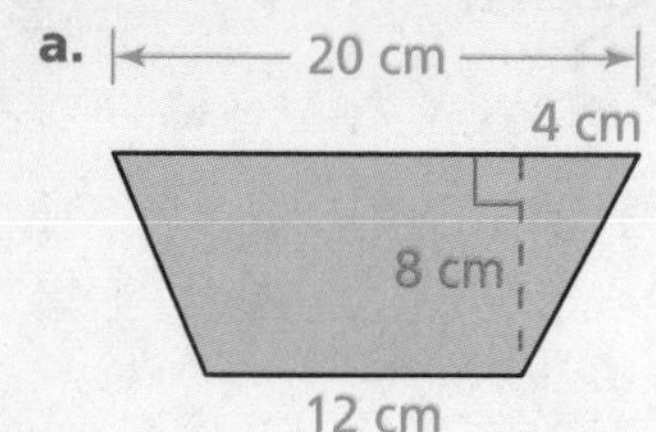

b.

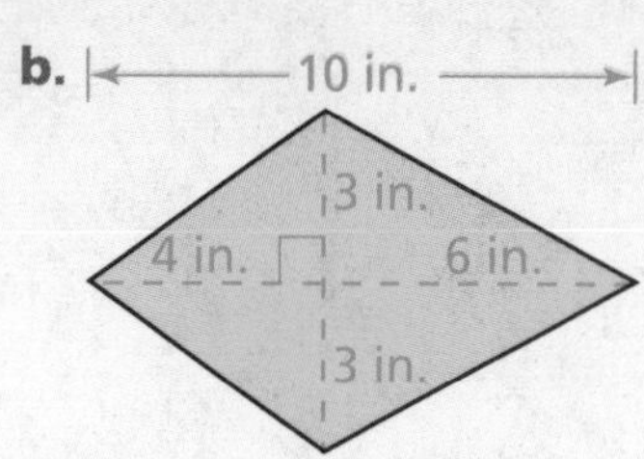

KEY CONCEPT

You can find the area of a trapezoid or a kite by decomposing the shapes into rectangles and triangles.

Trapezoid

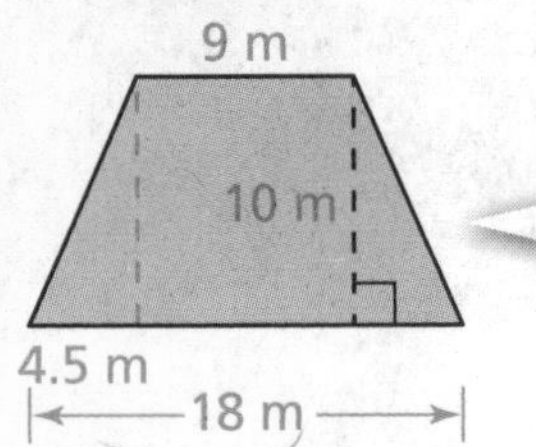

Decompose the trapezoid into two triangles and a rectangle. Find the length of the unknown triangle base.

Each triangle: $A = \frac{1}{2}(4.5)(10) = 22.5$

Rectangle: $A = 9(10) = 90$

Trapezoid: $A = 22.5 + 22.5 + 90 = 135$

The area of the trapezoid is 135 m^2.

Kite

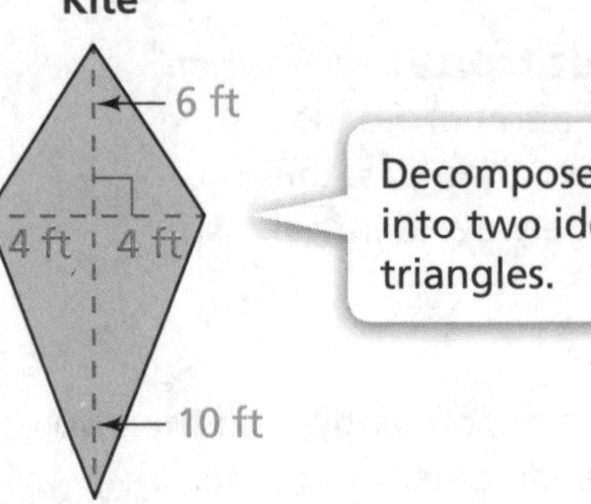

Decompose the kite into two identical triangles.

Each triangle: $A = \frac{1}{2}(16)(4) = 32$

Kite: $A = 32 + 32 = 64$

The area of the kite is 64 ft^2.

Do You Understand?

1. **Essential Question** How can you find the areas of trapezoids and kites?

2. Draw a line to divide the pasture in Example 1 into two triangles. What are the measures of the bases and the heights of the two triangles?

3. **Construct Arguments** In Example 3, how could you use 4 triangles to find the kite's area?

Do You Know How?

In 4–6, find the area of each trapezoid or kite.

4.

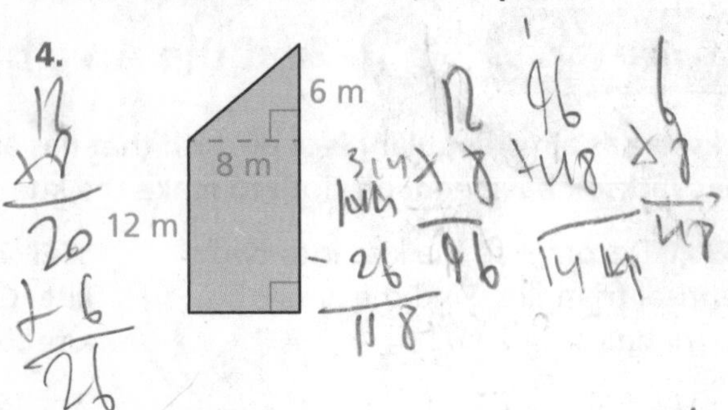

5.

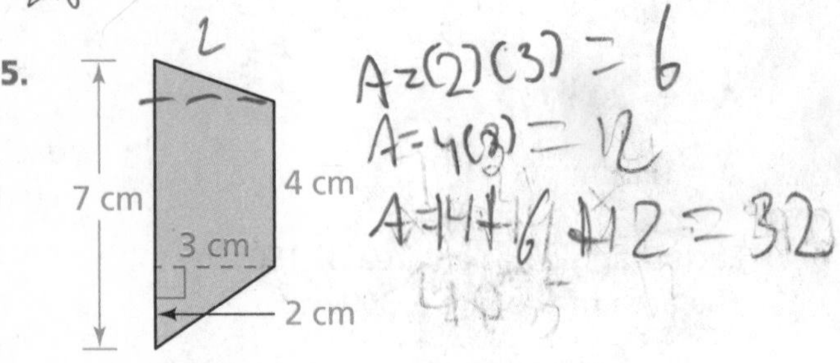

6.

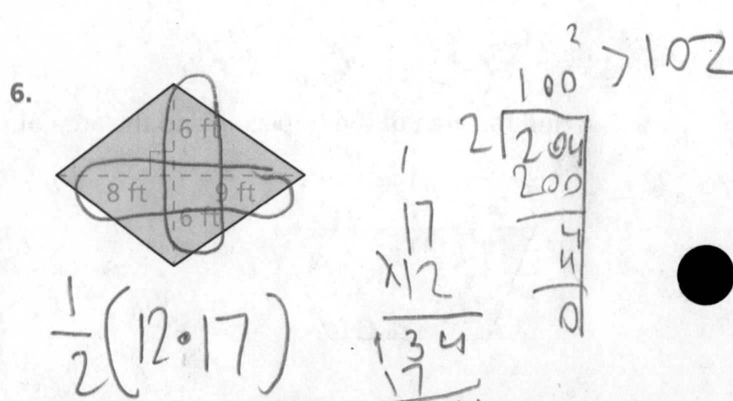

Name: ____________________

Practice & Problem Solving

Scan for Multimedia

Leveled Practice **In 7–12, find the area of each trapezoid or kite.**

7.

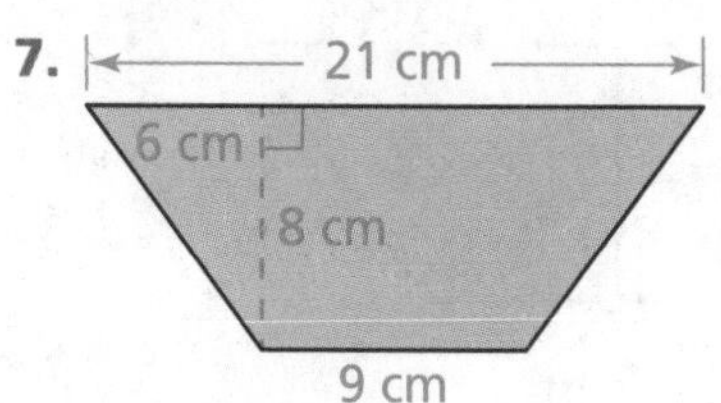

Each triangle:

$A = \frac{1}{2}bh$

$= \frac{1}{2} \times$ ___ $\times 8$

$=$ ___ cm^2

Rectangle:

$A = \ell w$

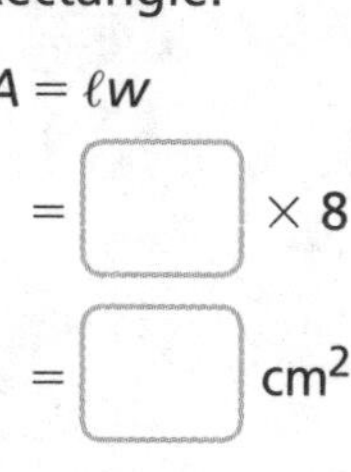

$=$ ___ $\times 8$

$=$ ___ cm^2

Trapezoid:

$A =$ ___ $+$ ___ $+$ ___ $=$ ___ cm^2

8. **9.** **10.**

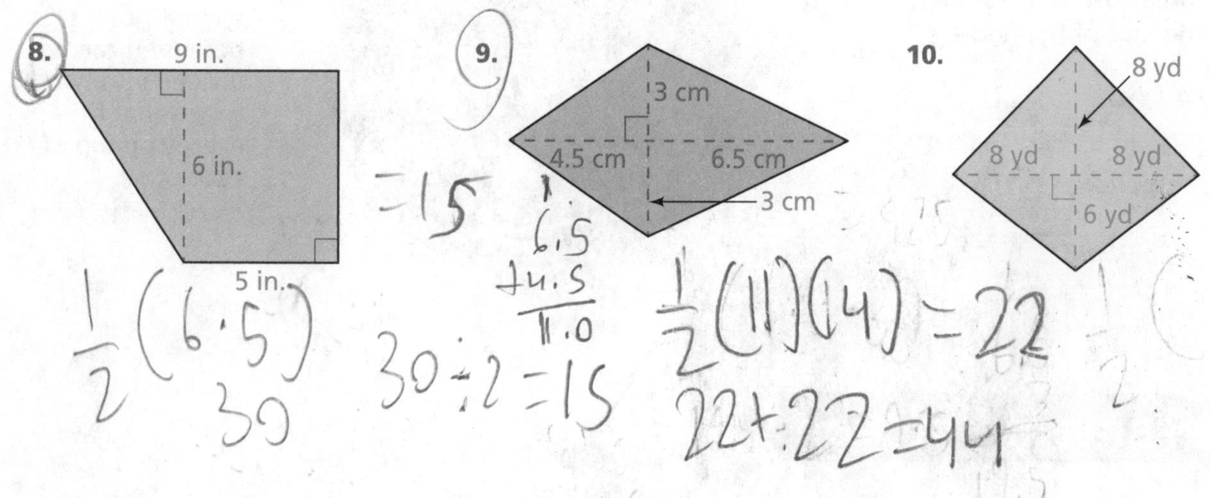

11. A sidewall of a building is shown below. What is the area of the wall?

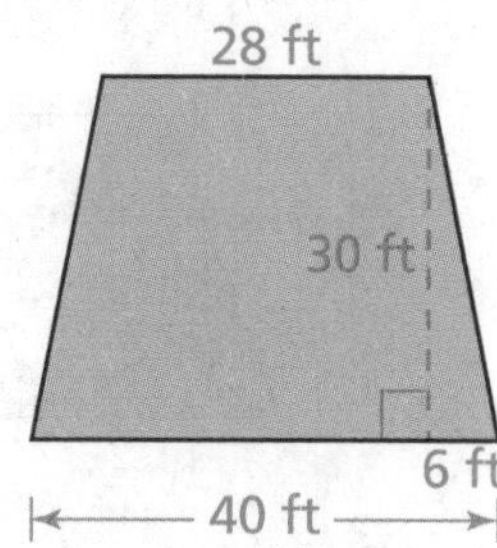

12. Be Precise The window has the shape of a kite. How many square meters of glass were used to make the window?

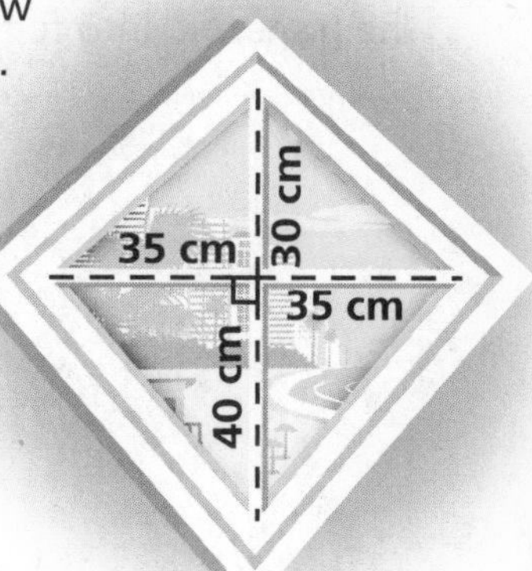

13. The area of the kite is 30 m^2. What is the value of x? Explain.

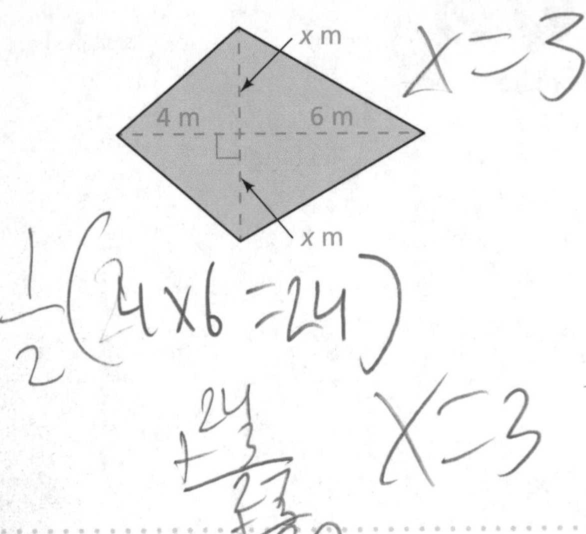

14. **Make Sense and Persevere** Hunter drew two identical trapezoids and composed them to form a parallelogram. Use the area of the parallelogram to find the area of one trapezoid. Explain.

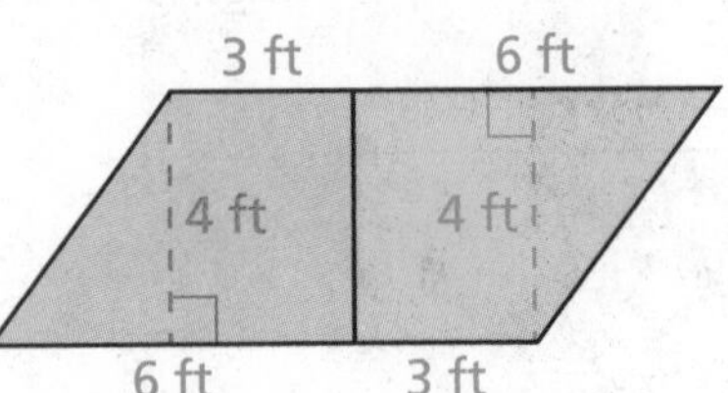

15. **Higher Order Thinking** A craftsman wants to build this symmetrical fiddle. He needs to know the area of the face of the fiddle. How could he use the measurements shown to find the area? Use your strategy to find the area of the face of the fiddle.

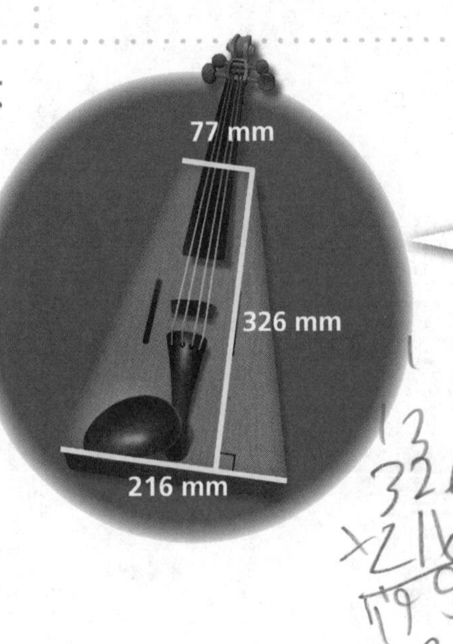

The figure is symmetrical because it can be divided into two halves that fit exactly on top of each other.

Assessment Practice

16. Marique is making a large table in the shape of a trapezoid. She needs to calculate the area of the table. The longest side of the table is twice as long as the table's width. Find the area of the table by decomposing the trapezoid into familiar shapes. Show your work. 6.G.1.1

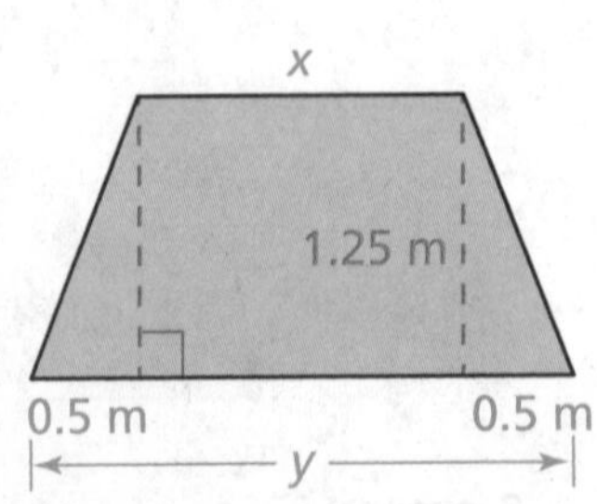

Lesson 11-4
Find Areas of Polygons

Go Online | PearsonRealize.com

I can...
find the areas of polygons.

MAFS.6.G.1.1 Find the area of... polygons by composing into rectangles or decomposing into triangles and other shapes; apply these techniques in the context of solving real-world and mathematical problems.
Also 6.EE.1.2c, 6.G.1.3, 6.NS.3.6c, 6.NS.3.8

MAFS.K12.MP.1.1, MP.4.1, MP.6.1, MP.7.1

Solve & Discuss It!

ACTIVITY

Gabrielle wants to cover the floors of a room and a hallway in her dollhouse. She measured the room and hallway and sketched the floor plan below. How much felt does Gabrielle need?

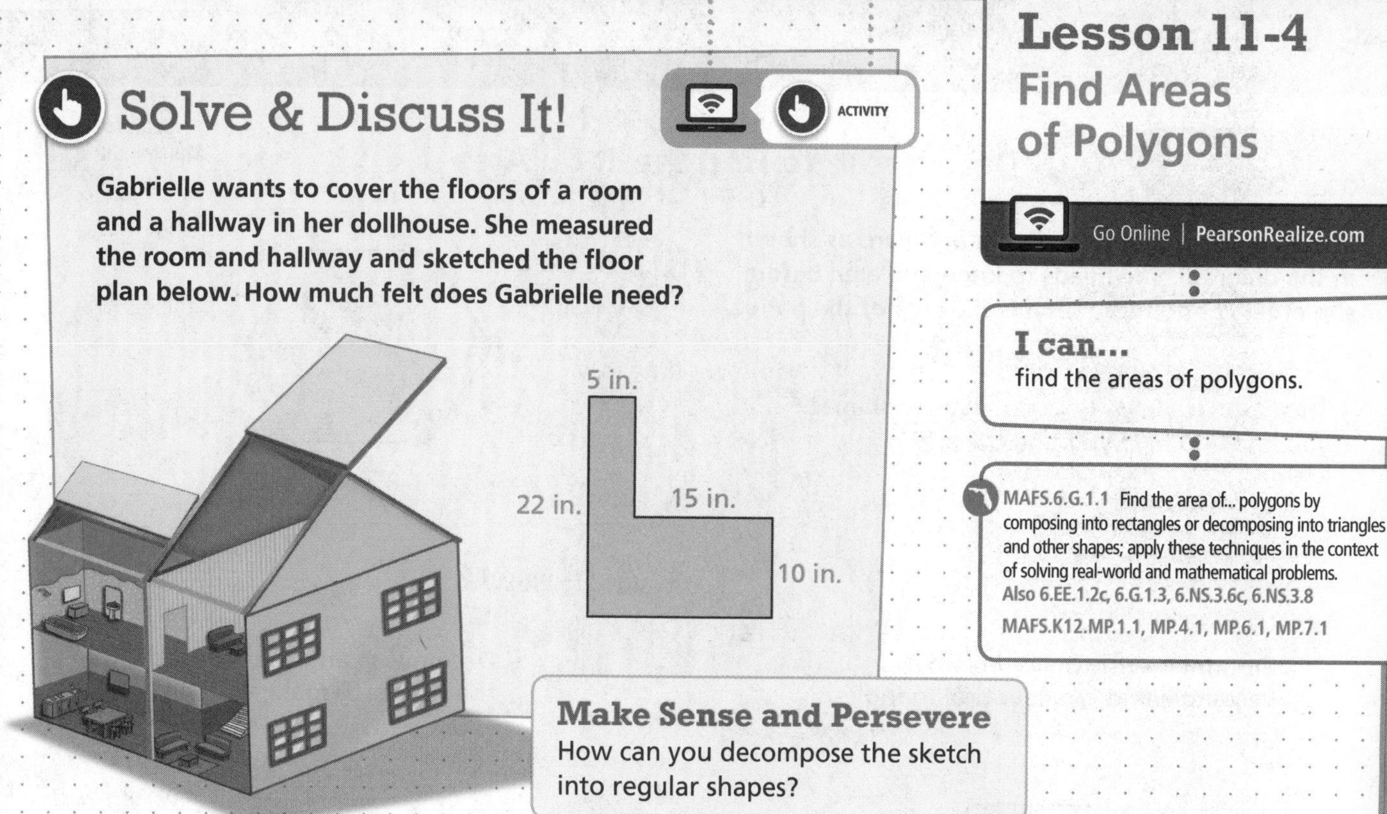

Make Sense and Persevere
How can you decompose the sketch into regular shapes?

Focus on math practices

Make Sense and Persevere Show another way to find the area of the sketch.

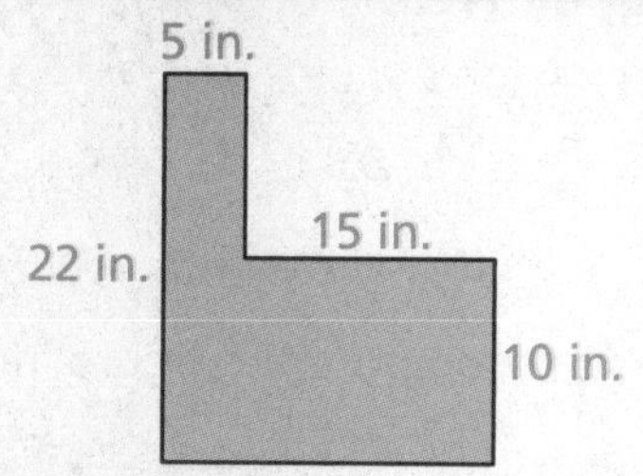

Essential Question How can you find the areas of polygons?

EXAMPLE 1  Decompose to Find the Total Area

Scan for Multimedia 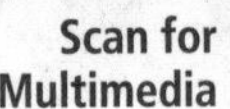 

Denise is building a patio in her backyard as shown in the diagram. She needs to know the area before she orders patio tiles. What is the area of the patio?

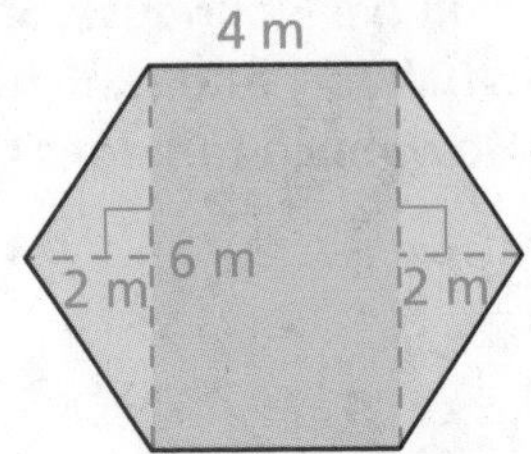

Use Structure How can you use shapes you know to help you find the area?

ONE WAY

Decompose the polygon into a rectangle and two identical triangles.

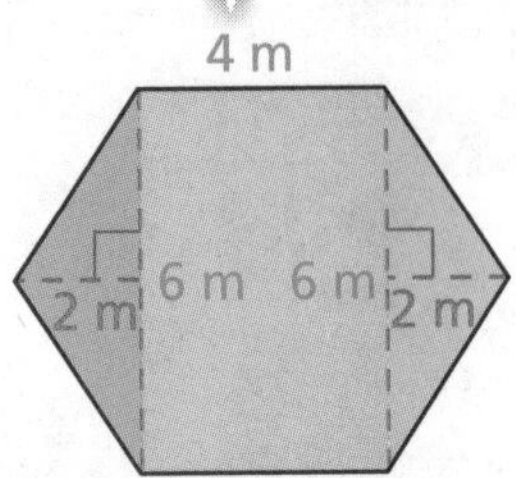

Find the area of each shape.

Each Triangle

$A = \frac{1}{2}bh$

$= \frac{1}{2}(6 \cdot 2)$

$= 6$

Rectangle

$A = \ell w$

$= 6 \cdot 4$

$= 24$

Add the areas: $6 + 6 + 24 = 36$.

The area of the patio is 36 m^2.

ANOTHER WAY

Decompose and recompose the shapes to make a square.

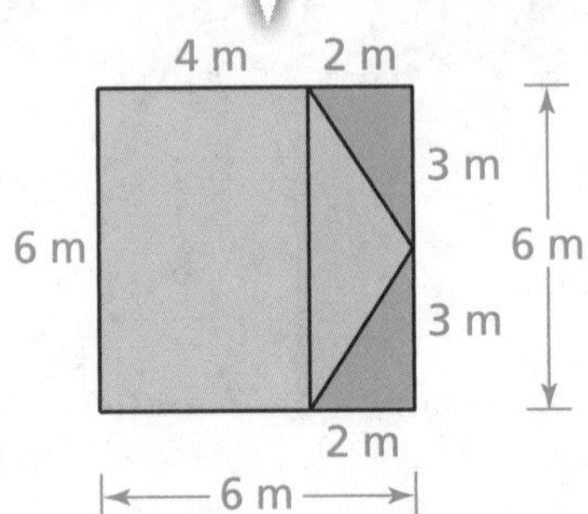

Find the area of the square.

$A = \ell w$

$= 6 \cdot 6$

$= 36$

The area of the patio is 36 m^2.

Try It!

Shari found the area of the patio by composing the shapes as shown at the right. How is Shari's strategy different?

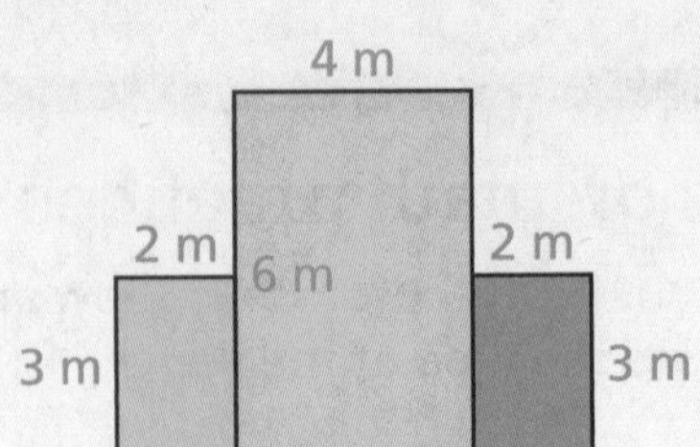

Convince Me! How could you decompose the figure in the Try It! into two rectangles?

EXAMPLE 2  Subtract to Find the Total Area

The Robinsons are planning to resurface the path that surrounds their garden, as shown. What is the area of the path?

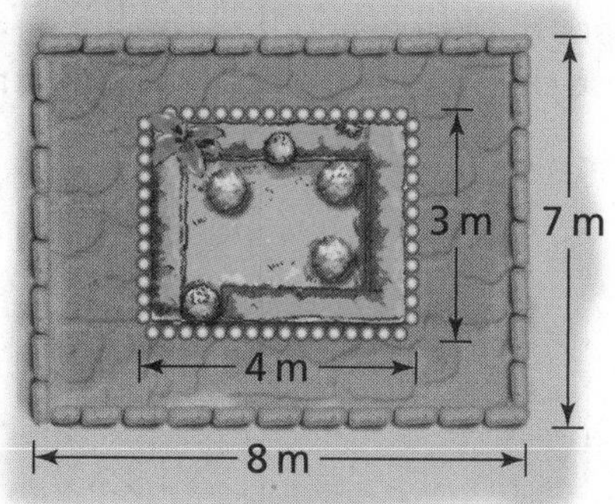

Make Sense and Persevere The area of the path can be found by subtracting the area of the garden from the total area of the garden and the path.

STEP 1 Find the total area of the garden and the path.

$A = \ell w$

$= 8 \times 7$

$= 56 \text{ m}^2$

STEP 2 Find the area of the garden.

$A = \ell w$

$= 4 \times 3$

$= 12 \text{ m}^2$

STEP 3 Subtract the area of the garden from the total area of the garden and the path.

$56 - 12 = 44$

The area of the path is 44 m^2.

EXAMPLE 3  Find the Area of a Polygon on the Coordinate Plane

The floor plan for a new stage at a school is sketched on a coordinate plane. A flooring expert recommends bamboo flooring for the stage floor. How much bamboo flooring, in square meters, does the school need?

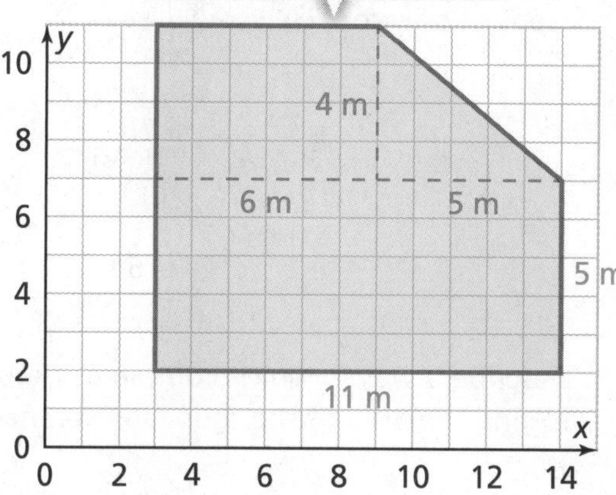

STEP 1 Decompose the polygon. Find the needed dimensions.

STEP 2 Find the area of each part.

Right Triangle

$A = \frac{1}{2}bh$

$= \frac{1}{2} \cdot 5 \cdot 4$

$= 10$

Rectangles

$A = \ell w$

$= 6 \cdot 4$

$= 24$

$A = \ell w$

$= 11 \cdot 5$

$= 55$

Add the areas: $10 + 24 + 55 = 89$

The school needs 89 m^2 of bamboo flooring.

Try It!

Find the area of the shaded region in square units.

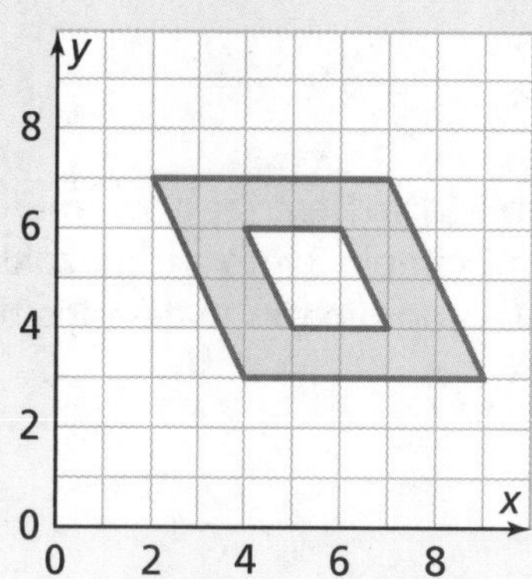

KEY CONCEPT

There are many ways to find the area of a polygon. You can decompose or compose shapes, or you can use addition or subtraction, to calculate the area.

Use Addition

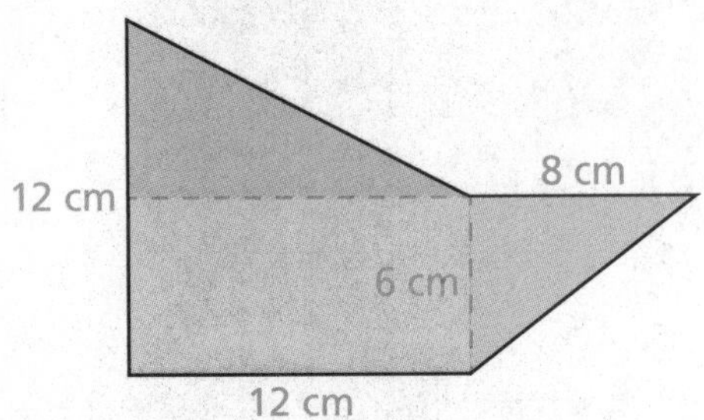

Blue triangle: $A = \frac{1}{2}(12)(6) = 36$

Green triangle: $A = \frac{1}{2}(8)(6) = 24$

Rectangle: $A = (12)(6) = 72$

$36 + 24 + 72 = 132$

The area of the polygon is 132 cm^2.

Use Subtraction

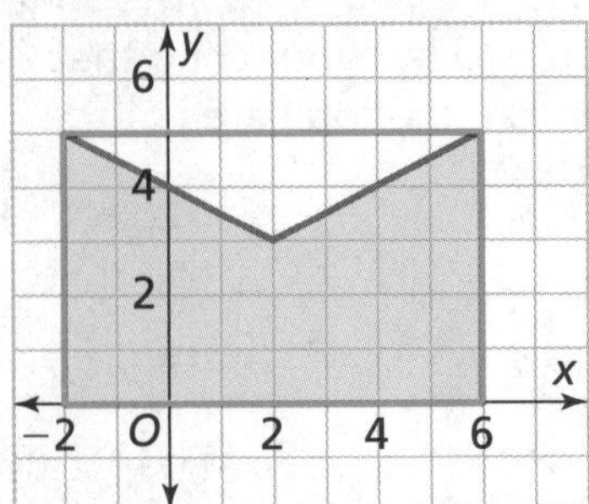

Draw a rectangle around the polygon.

Rectangle: $A = 8 \times 5 = 40$

Triangle: $A = \frac{1}{2} \times 8 \times 2 = 8$

$40 - 8 = 32$

The area of the polygon is 32 square units.

Do You Understand?

1. **Essential Question** How can you find the areas of polygons?

2. Describe a way in which you can use subtraction to find the area of the shape in Exercise 4.

3. **Model with Math** Describe how to break the floor plan in Example 3 into a trapezoid and a rectangle. Use coordinates to describe the line you can draw.

Do You Know How?

In 4 and 5, find the area of each polygon.

4.

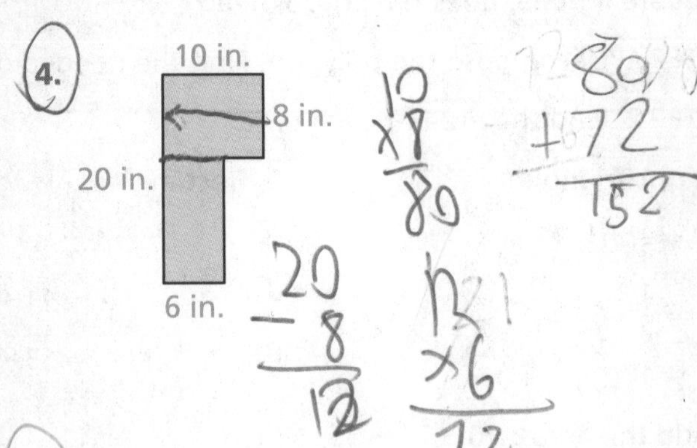

5. A polygon with vertices at (6, 2), (9, 5), (12, 2), (12, −4), and (6, −4)

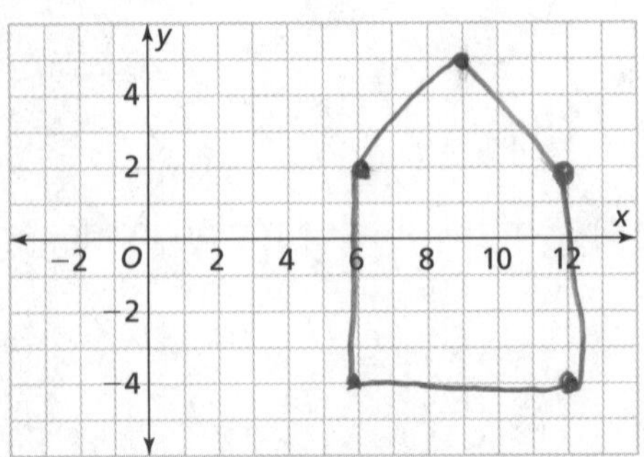

Name: ______________________________

Practice & Problem Solving

Scan for Multimedia

In 6–9, find the area of each polygon or shaded region.

6.

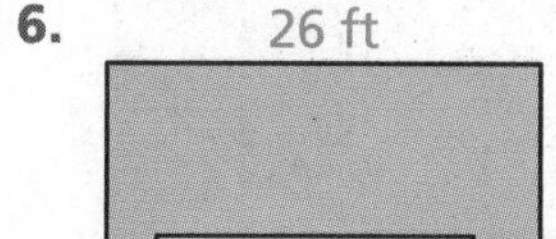

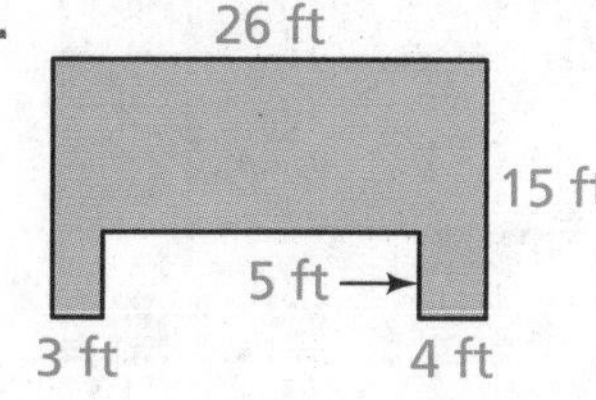

7.

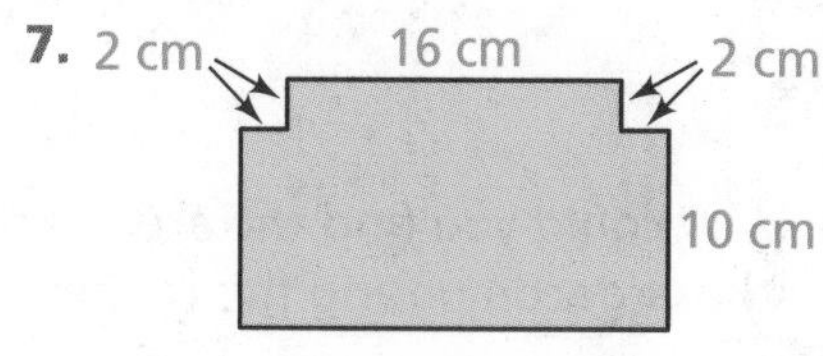

8.

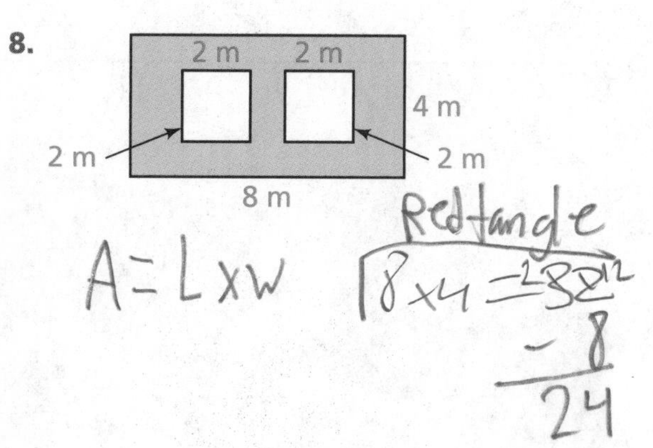

9.

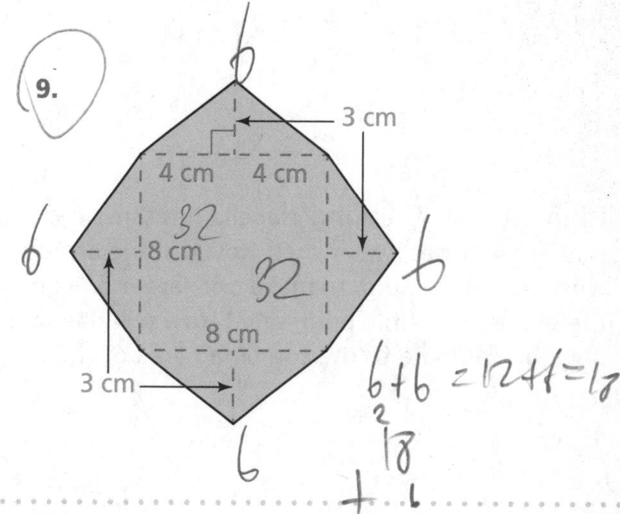

In 10 and 11, find the area in square units of each polygon.

10.

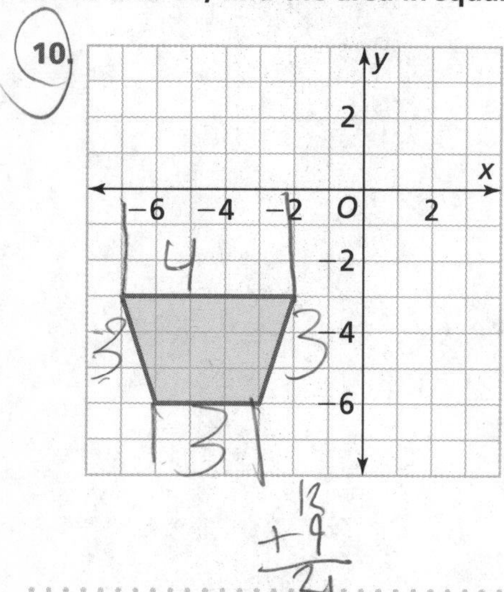

11.

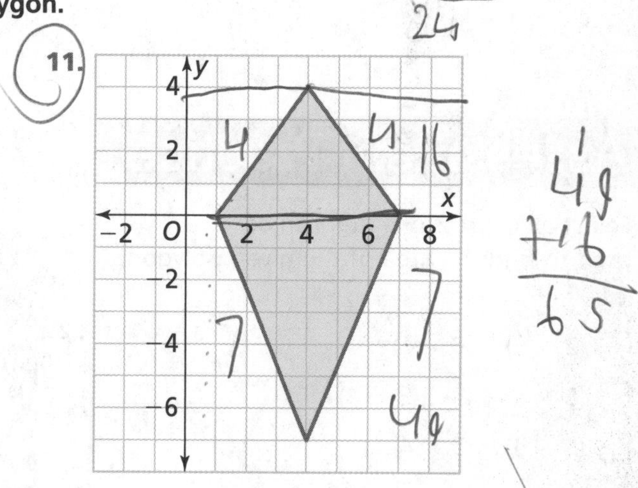

12. Be Precise Diego is designing an exercise room. How many square feet of rubber flooring will he need to cover the floor? The product is sold in whole square yards. How many square yards should Diego buy? Explain.

15 ft

14 ft

9 ft

8 ft

In 13 and 14, use the diagram at the right.

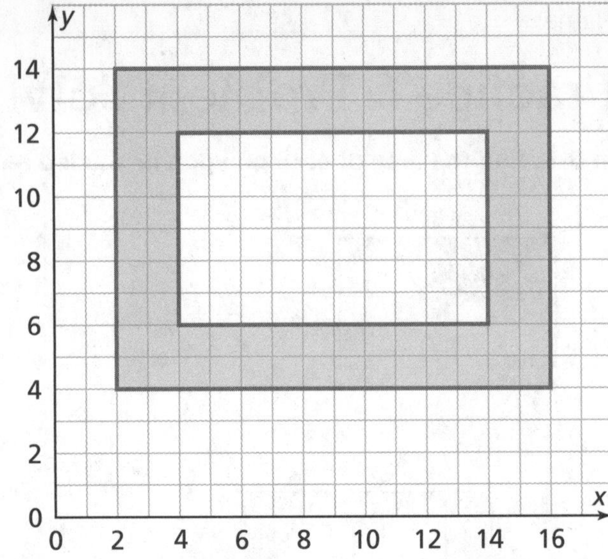

13. David drew this diagram of a picture frame that he is going to make. Each square represents 1 square inch. What is the area of the picture frame?

14. Use Structure How could you find the area of the picture frame without decomposing the frame into smaller shapes?

15. Higher Order Thinking Isabella has three rectangular cards that are 4 inches by 5 inches. How can she arrange the cards, without overlapping, to make one larger polygon with the smallest possible perimeter? How will the area of the polygon compare to the combined area of the three cards?

Assessment Practice

16. Select all expressions that can be used to find the area of the given polygon.
6.G.1.1

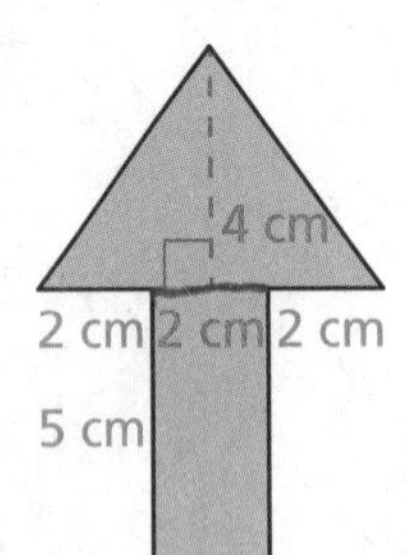

10

- ☐ $(2 \times 5) + (6 \times 4)$
- ☐ $(5 \times 2) + 2 \cdot \frac{1}{2}(3 \times 4)$
- ☐ $(6 \times 5) - (3 \times 4)$
- ☐ $(6 \times 9) - (3 \times 4)$
- ☑ 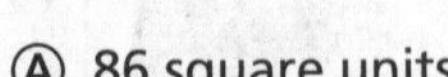 $(5 \times 2) + \frac{1}{2}[(2 + 2 + 2) \times 4]$

17. What is the area of the polygon at the right?
6.G.1.1

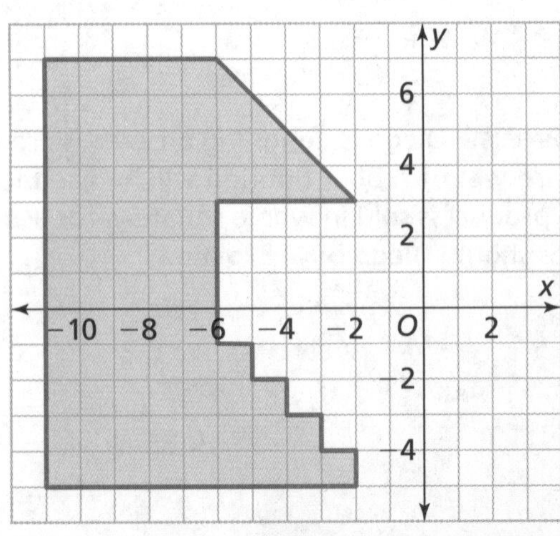

Ⓐ 86 square units

Ⓑ 78 square units

Ⓒ 70 square units

Ⓓ 68 square units

Name: ______________________________

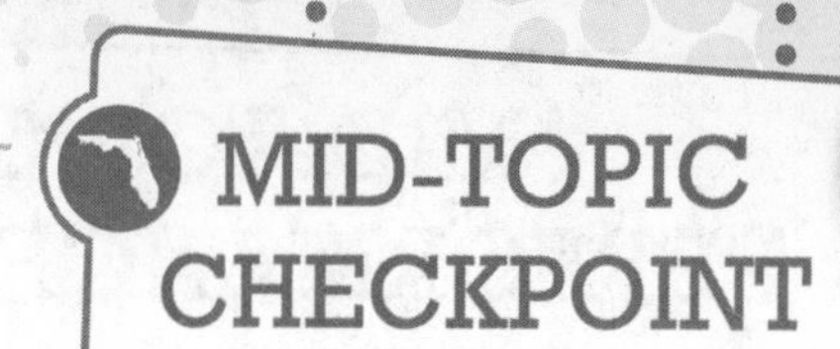

1. **Vocabulary** How many pairs of opposite sides are parallel in a trapezoid? How is this different from a parallelogram? *Lesson 11-3*
 6.G.1.1

2. Calculate the area of each figure at the right. Which figure has the greatest area? *Lessons 11-1, 11-2, and 11-3* 6.G.1.1, 6.EE.1.2c

Ⓐ triangle

Ⓑ parallelogram

Ⓒ trapezoid

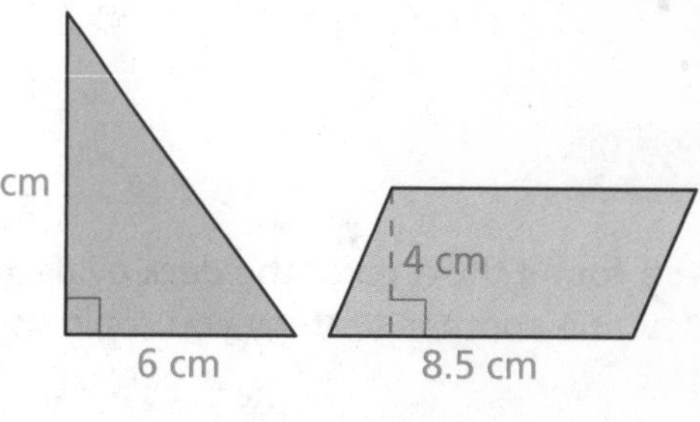

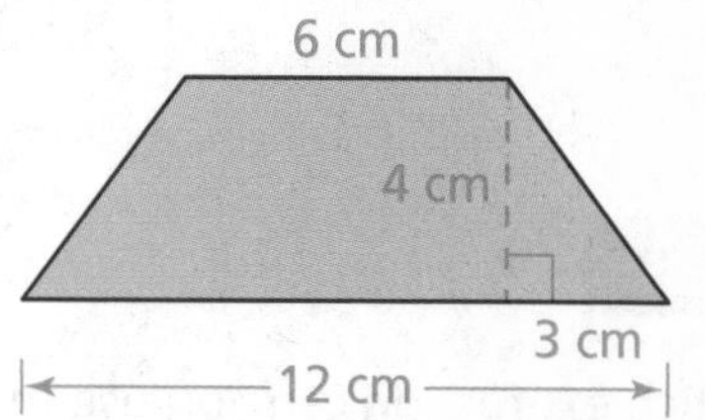

3. An earring has the shape of a rhombus. The height is 5.2 mm and the area of the earring is 39 mm^2. What is the length of each side of the earring? *Lesson 11-1* 6.G.1.1, 6.EE.1.2c

4. Shane wrapped the kite at the right with paper. How many square inches of paper did Shane use to cover the front and back? *Lesson 11-3* 6.G.1.1, 6.EE.1.2c

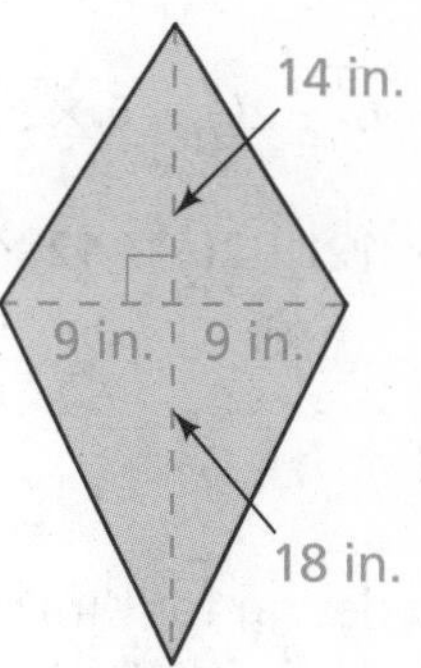

5. Explain one way to find the area of the polygon at the right. Then find the area in square units. *Lesson 11-4* 6.G.1.1, 6.EE.1.2c, 6.G.1.3

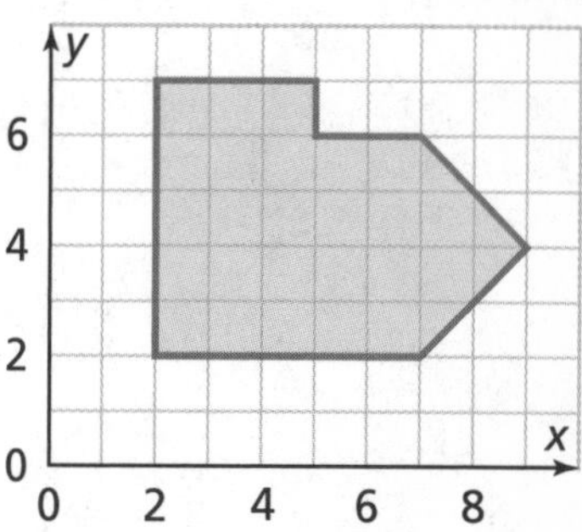

How well did you do on the mid-topic checkpoint? Fill in the stars.

MID-TOPIC PERFORMANCE TASK

Kira hires a contractor to build a new deck in her backyard. A design for the deck is shown.

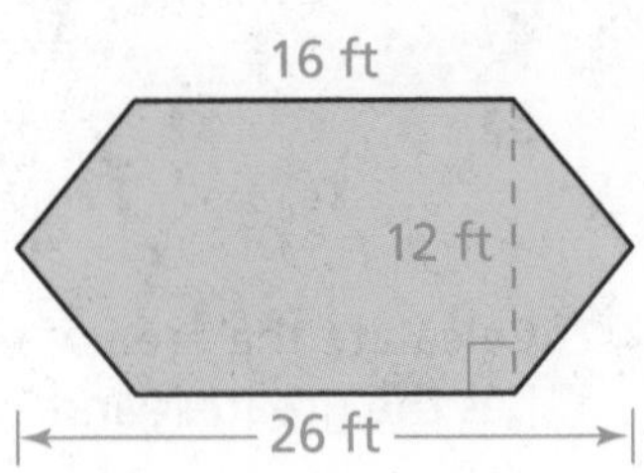

PART A

Kira found the area of the deck by decomposing it into two identical trapezoids. Describe another strategy you could use to find the area of the deck. 6.G.1.1

PART B

Which expression can you use to find the area of the deck? Select all that apply. 6.G.1.1, 6.EE.1.2c

☐ $(16 \times 12) + 2(\frac{1}{2} \times 12 \times 5)$

☐ $(26 \times 12) + 2(\frac{1}{2} \times 12 \times 5)$

☐ $(26 \times 12) - 4(\frac{1}{2} \times 6 \times 5)$

☐ $(16 \times 6) + 2(\frac{1}{2} \times 6 \times 5) + (16 \times 6) + 2(\frac{1}{2} \times 6 \times 5)$

☐ $(16 \times 12) + 2(\frac{1}{2} \times 12 \times 10)$

PART C

A second design for Kira's deck is shown at the right. Find the areas of the two deck designs. Which design will give Kira the deck with the greater area? Explain. 6.G.1.1, 6.EE.1.2c

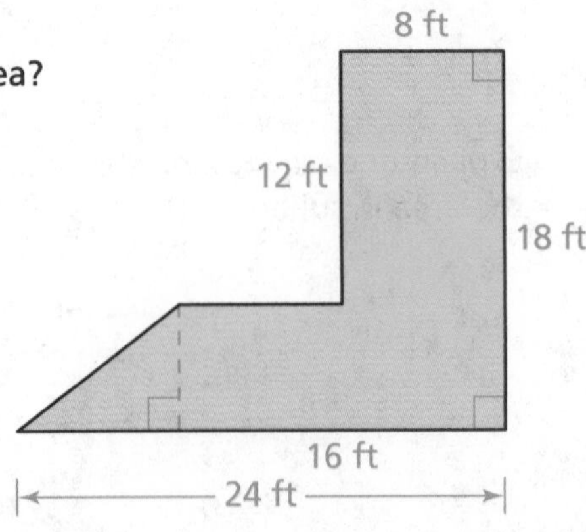

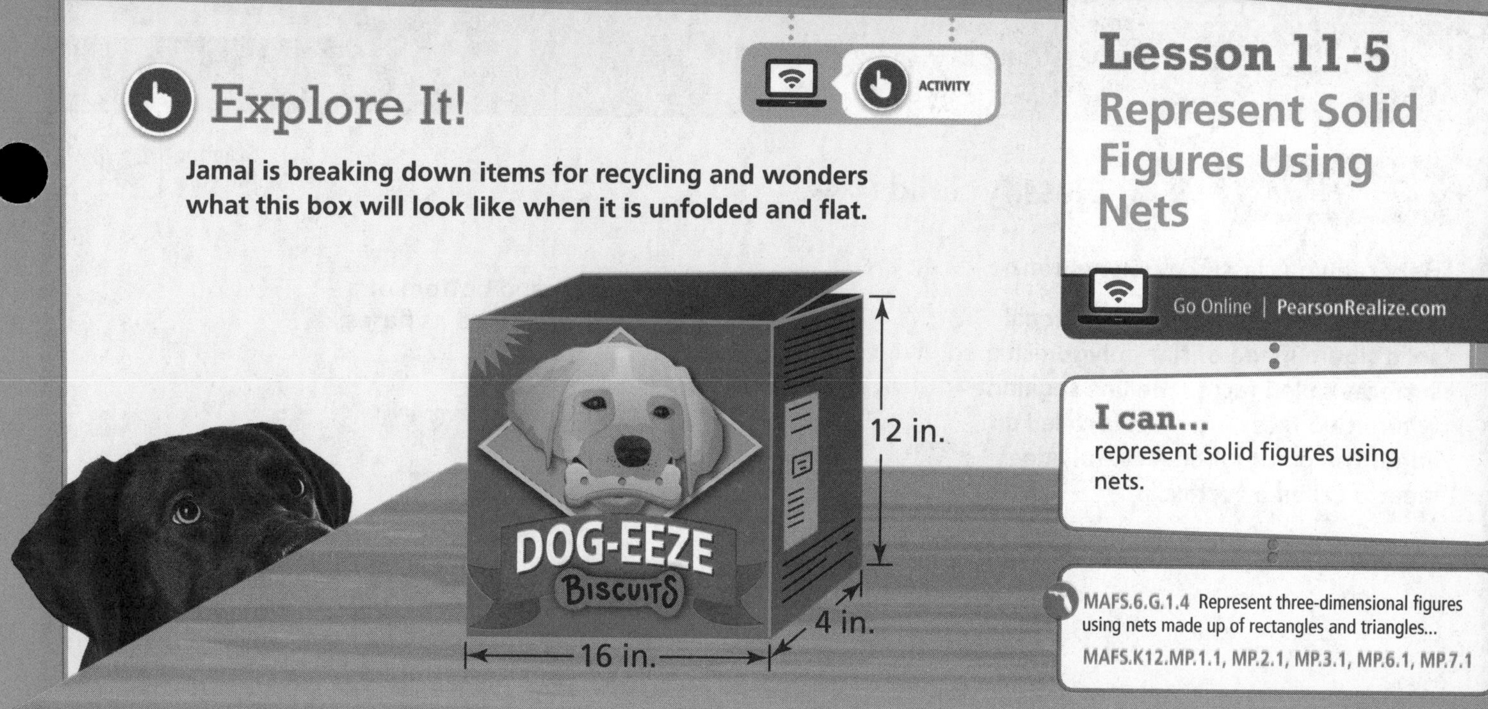

Explore It!

Jamal is breaking down items for recycling and wonders what this box will look like when it is unfolded and flat.

Lesson 11-5
Represent Solid Figures Using Nets

Go Online | PearsonRealize.com

I can...
represent solid figures using nets.

MAFS.6.G.1.4 Represent three-dimensional figures using nets made up of rectangles and triangles...
MAFS.K12.MP.1.1, MP.2.1, MP.3.1, MP.6.1, MP.7.1

A. How do the sides of the box help you think about what the unfolded box will look like?

B. How can you use the grid to represent the unfolded box?

□ = 1 square inch.

Focus on math practices

Reasoning Is there another way to represent the unfolded box on the grid? Explain.

Essential Question How do you classify and represent solid figures?

EXAMPLE 1  Classify Solids

Scan for Multimedia 

How can you classify a polyhedron?

A polyhedron is a three-dimensional solid figure made of flat polygon-shaped surfaces called faces. The line segment where two faces intersect is called an edge. The point where several edges meet is called a vertex.

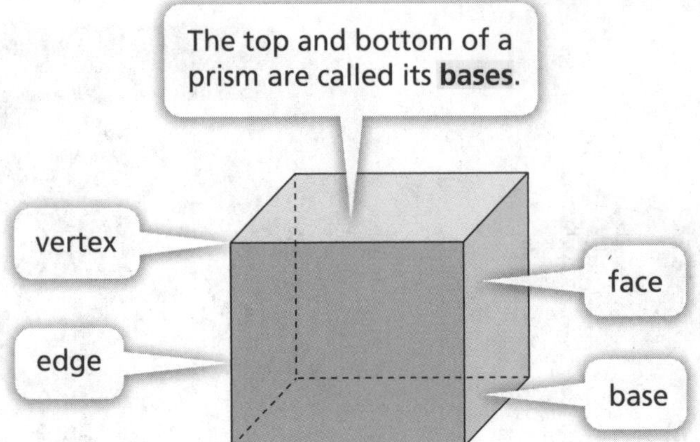

Prisms

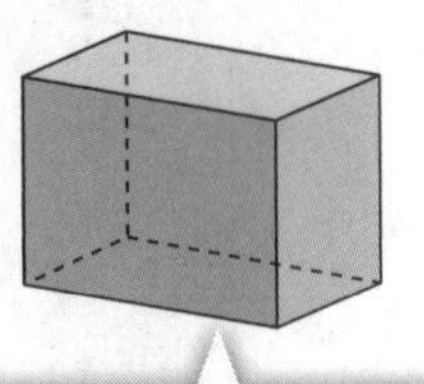

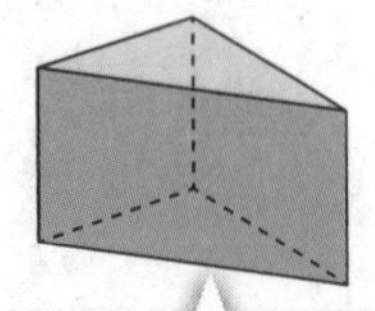

- Prisms have polygonal faces.
- Prisms have two identical, parallel, polygon-shaped bases.
- Prisms are named by the shape of their bases.

Pyramids

The base of a pyramid is the face opposite the vertex where the triangular faces meet.

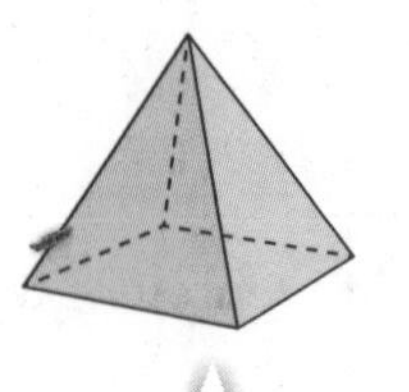

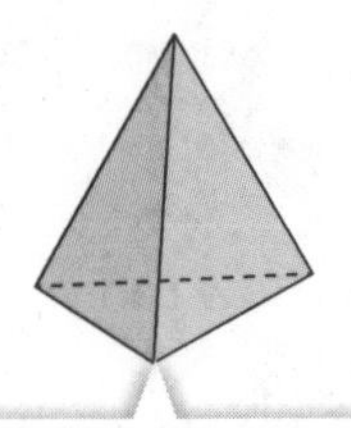

- Pyramids have one base.
- Pyramids are named by the shape of their bases.
- All other faces of pyramids are triangular.

Try It!

Classify this solid figure.

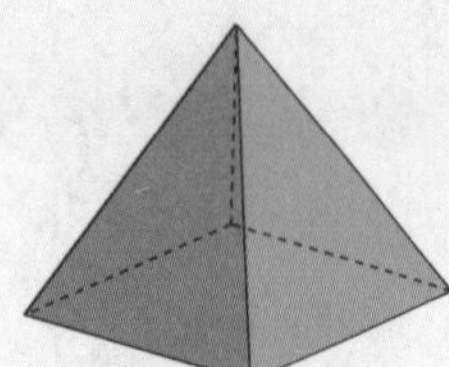

Square pyramid

Convince Me! What attributes of a solid figure should you identify to classify it as a polyhedron? face, base, vertiex

EXAMPLE 2  Identify a Solid Figure from a Net

What solid is represented by the net?

To identify a solid figure, determine the number and types of faces in the net.

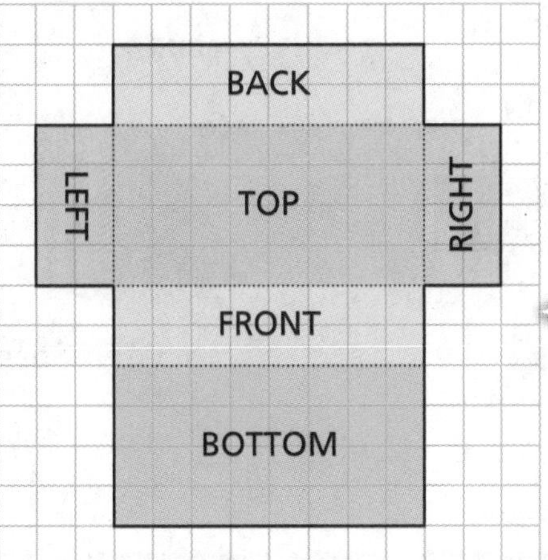

A net is a plane figure pattern which, when folded, makes a solid.

The net shows three pairs of identical rectangular faces.

Use Structure How can you use the structure of the net to identify the solid figure?

This is a net of a rectangular prism.

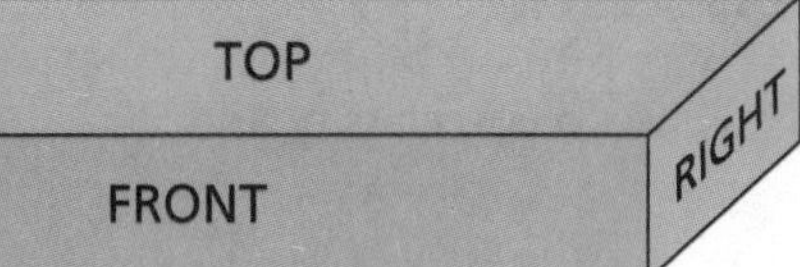

EXAMPLE 3  Draw a Net of a Solid Figure

How can you draw a net of a rectangular prism that has a height of 2 units and bases that are 4 units long and 2 units wide?

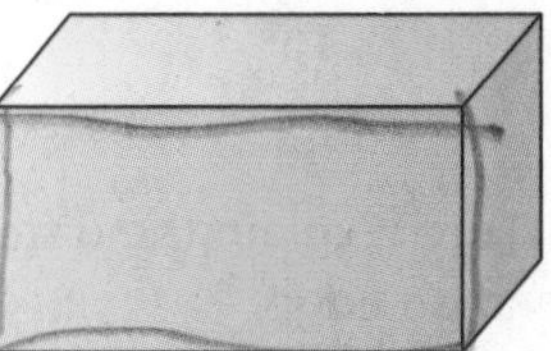

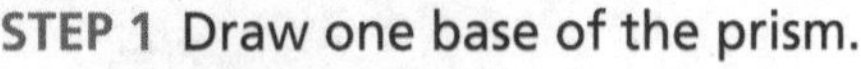

STEP 1 Draw one base of the prism.

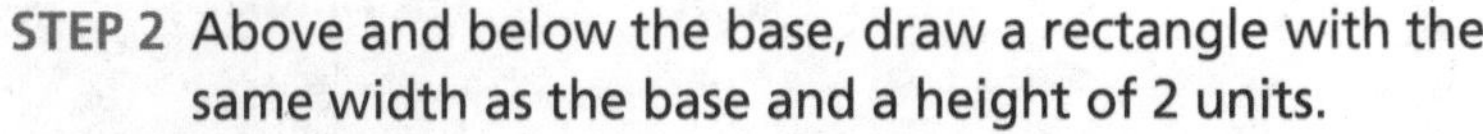

STEP 2 Above and below the base, draw a rectangle with the same width as the base and a height of 2 units.

STEP 3 Draw three additional rectangles, in line with the base, that have the same length as the base and a width of 2 units.

Step 2
Step 3 Step 3 Step 1 Step 3
Step 2

Be Precise How can you determine whether the dimensions in the net match the dimensions of the rectangular prism?

 Try It!

Identify the solid from its net.

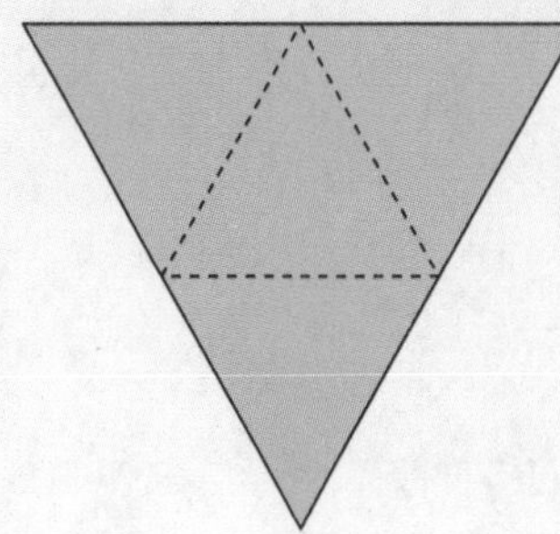

Shape of polygonal faces: 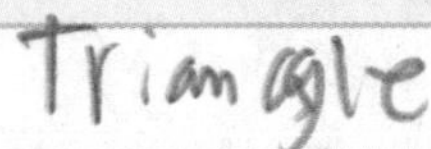 Triangles

Shape of base(s): Triangle

This is a net of a triangular pyramid.

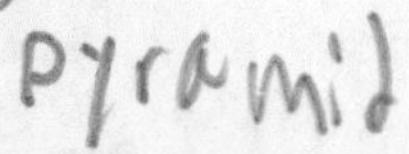

You can use nets to represent solid figures.

Prism

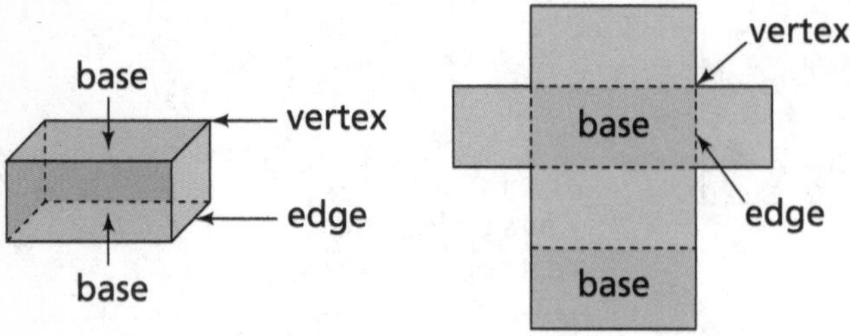

Pyramid

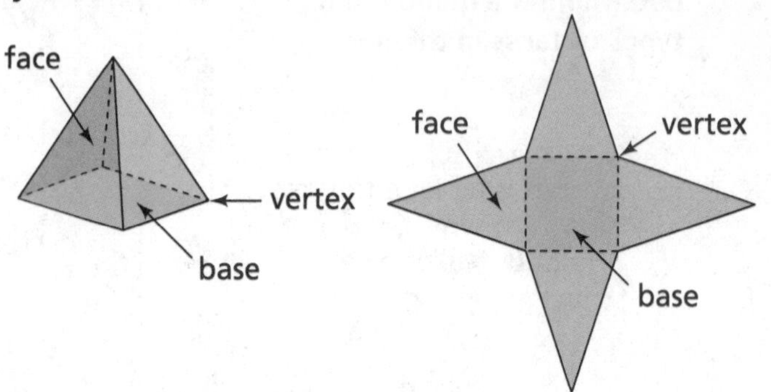

Do You Understand?

1. **Essential Question** How do you classify and represent solid figures?

2. **Use Structure** Explain the difference between a vertex and an edge.

3. **Be Precise** Explain the difference between a pyramid and a prism.

4. Describe the net of a triangular prism.

Do You Know How?

In 5 and 6, classify the solid figures.

5.

6. 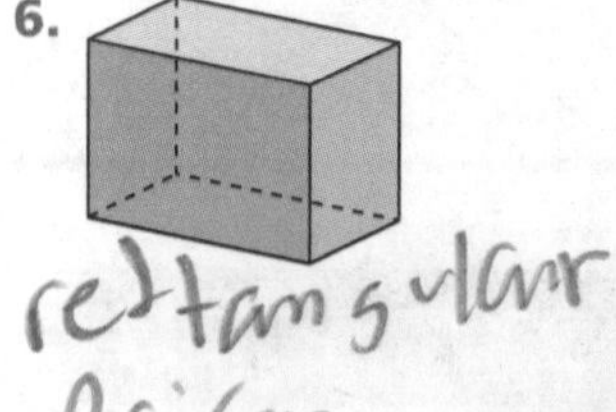

In 7 and 8, identify each solid from its net.

7.

8. 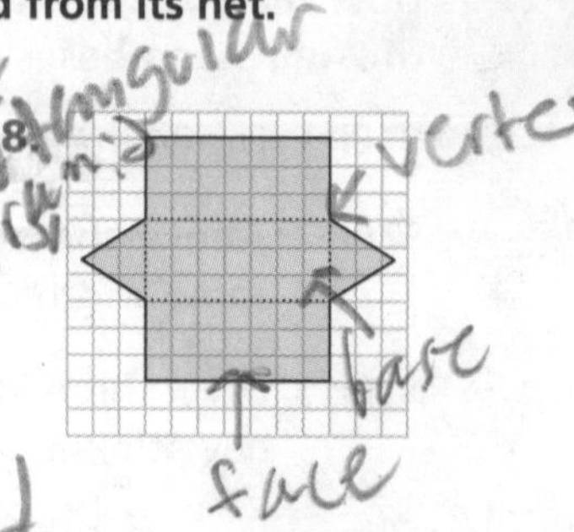

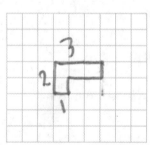

9. Draw a net of a rectangular prism that has a height of 2 units and bases that are 3 units long and 1 unit wide.

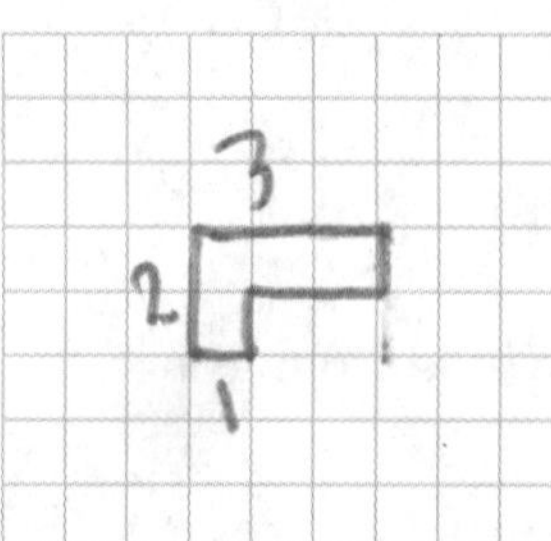

Name: ____________________

Practice & Problem Solving  

Scan for Multimedia 

In 10–12, classify the solid figures.

10.

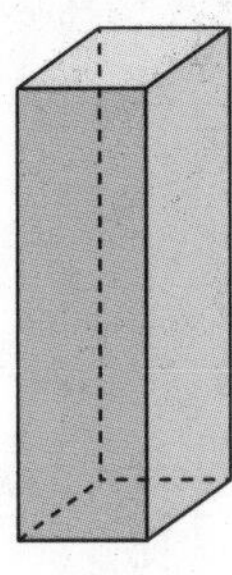

11.

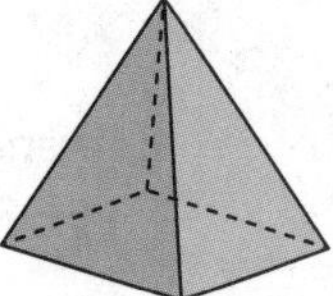

12.

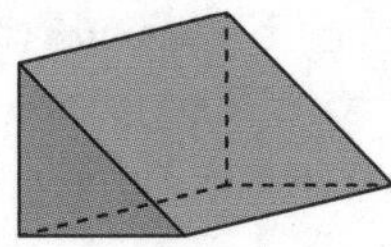

In 13–15, identify each solid from its net.

13.

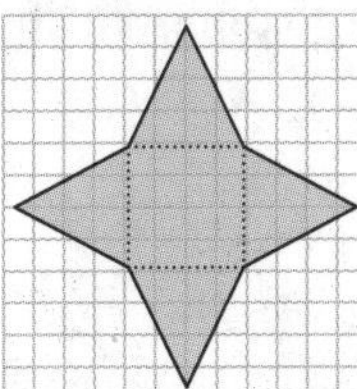

14.

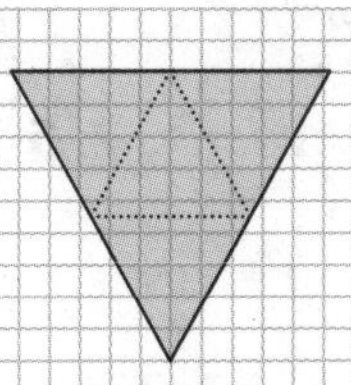

15.

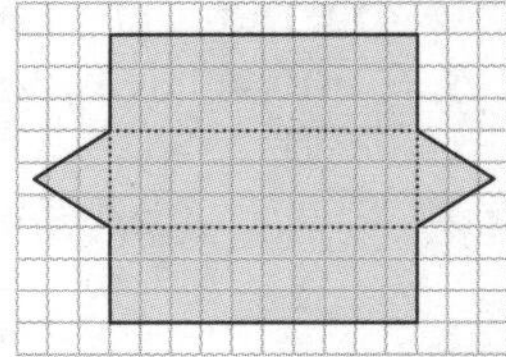

16. Ryan is going to draw a net of a rectangular prism. How many rectangles should there be in his drawing?

17. Kayla is going to draw a net of a square pyramid. How many triangles should there be in her drawing?

18. **Make Sense and Persevere** Zari folds the net below into a model of a solid figure. How many edges, faces, and vertices does the model have?

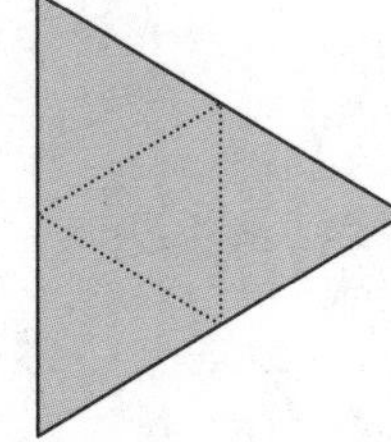

19. **Critique Reasoning** Tomas says that the net below can be folded to make a rectangular prism. Do you agree with Tomas? Explain.

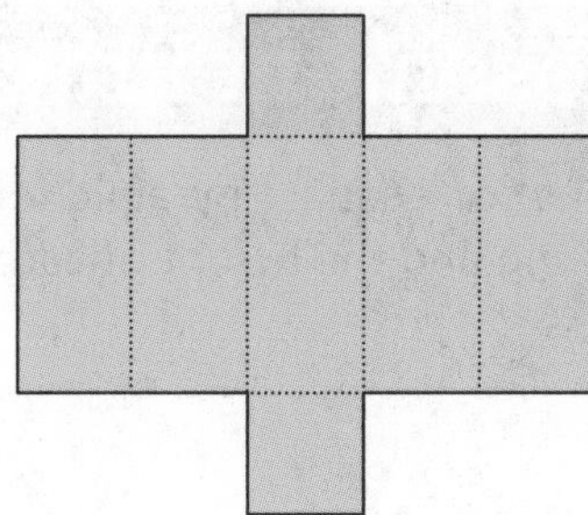

In 20–22, use the table at the right.

20. Look for Relationships The Swiss mathematician Leonhard Euler (OY-ler) and the French mathematician René Descartes (dã KART) both discovered a pattern in the numbers of edges, vertices, and faces of polyhedrons. Complete the table. Describe a pattern in the table.

Polyhedron	Faces (F)	Vertices (V)	$F + V$	Edges (E)
Triangular Pyramid				
Rectangular Pyramid				
Triangular Prism				
Rectangular Prism				

21. Higher Order Thinking Write an equation that relates the number of edges, E, to the number of faces, F, and vertices, V.

22. Use the equation that you wrote in Exercise 21 to find the number of vertices of a cube, which has 12 edges and 6 faces.

23. Corey bought the mailing tube shown at the right to mail a poster of the Gators Little League baseball team.

a. The mailing tube has the shape of which polyhedron?

b. How many faces does the mailing tube have?

c. When Corey bought the mailing tube, it was unfolded and looked like a net. What polygons would Corey have seen in the unfolded mailing tube?

Assessment Practice

24. Draw a net of a square pyramid for which the base is 2 units long and the height of each triangular face is 5 units.
6.G.1.4

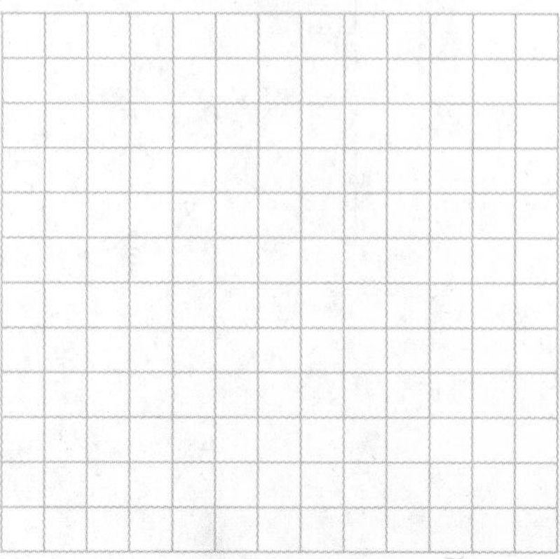

3-Act Mathematical Modeling:
That's a Wrap

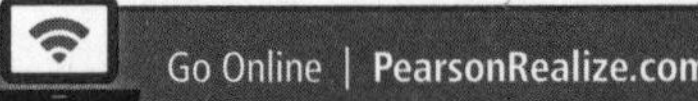

MAFS.K12.MP.4.1 Model with mathematics. Also MP.1.1, MP.2.1, MP.3.1, MP.5.1, MP.7.1, MP.8.1

MAFS.6.G.1.4 Represent three-dimensional figures using nets made up of rectangles and triangles,and use the nets to find the surface area of these figures. Apply these techniques in the context of solving real-world and mathematical problems. Also 6.EE.1.2c

ACT 1

1. After watching the video, what is the first question that comes to mind?

2. Write the Main Question you will answer.

3. **Construct Arguments** Predict an answer to this Main Question. Explain your prediction.

4. On the number line below, write a number that is too small to be the answer. Write a number that is too large.

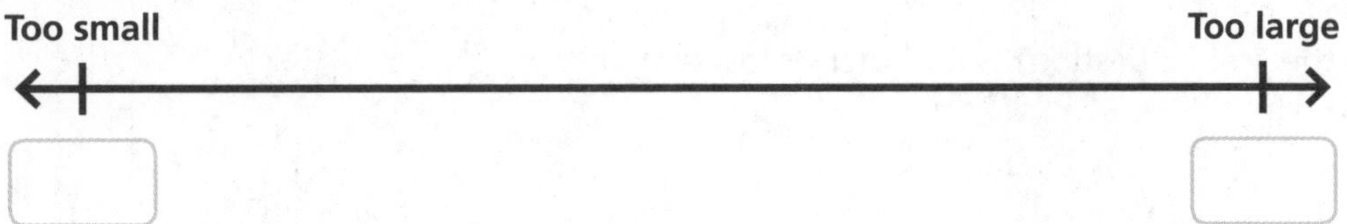

5. Plot your prediction on the same number line.

6. What information in this situation would be helpful to know? How would you use that information?

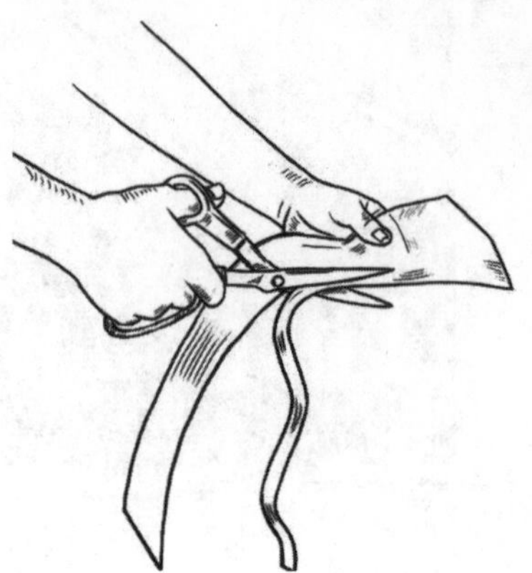

7. **Use Appropriate Tools** What tools can you use to get the information you need? Record the information as you find it.

8. **Model with Math** Represent the situation using the mathematical content, concepts, and skills from this topic. Use your representation to answer the Main Question.

9. What is your answer to the Main Question? Is it higher or lower than your prediction? Explain why.

ACT 3

10. Write the answer you saw in the video.

11. **Reasoning** Does your answer match the answer in the video? If not, what are some reasons that would explain the difference?

12. **Make Sense and Persevere** Would you change your model now that you know the answer? Explain.

ACT 3 Extension

Reflect

13. **Model with Math** Explain how you used a mathematical model to represent the situation. How did the model help you answer the Main Question?

14. **Look for Relationships** Explain how the dimensions of the gift are related to the area of its net.

SEQUEL

15. **Critique Reasoning** A classmate says that if all dimensions of the gift were doubled, you would need twice as many squares. Do you agree? Justify his reasoning or explain his error.

Lesson 11-6
Find Surface Areas of Prisms

Go Online | PearsonRealize.com

I can...
draw a net of a prism and use it to find the prism's surface area

MAFS.6.G.1.4 Represent three-dimensional figures using nets made up of rectangles and triangles,and use the nets to find the surface area of these figures. Apply these techniques in the context of solving real-world and mathematical problems. Also 6.EE.1.2a, 6.EE.1.2c, 6.EE.2.6
MAFS.K12.MP.1.1, MP.3.1, MP.5.1, MP.6.1

Solve & Discuss It!

Marianne orders boxes to pack gifts. When they arrive, she finds flat pieces of cardboard as shown below. Marianne needs to cover each face of the boxes with green paper. What is the least amount of paper needed to cover each box? Explain.

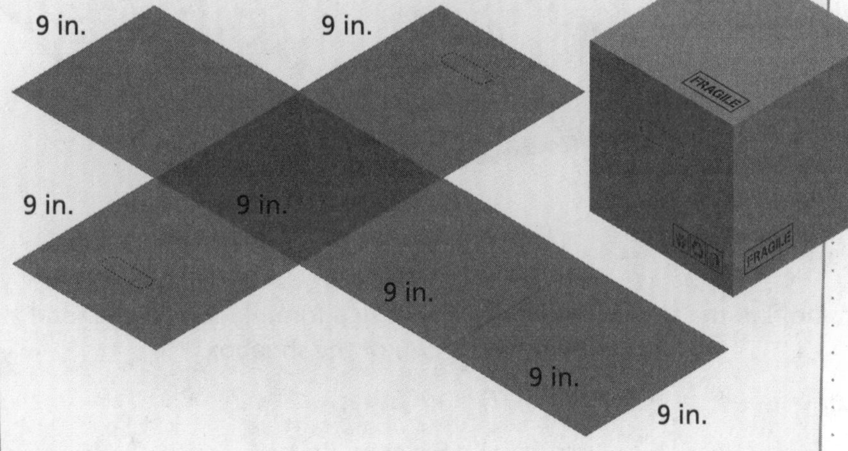

Make Sense and Persevere What solid figure does this net represent?

Focus on math practices

Make Sense and Persevere Suppose Marianne has only one large sheet of green paper that is 15 inches by 30 inches. Is the area of this sheet of paper great enough to cover all of the faces of one box? Explain.

EXAMPLE 1  Find the Surface Area of a Rectangular Prism

Kelly wants to cover a shoebox with decorative paper without overlapping the paper. How much paper will she need to cover the box?

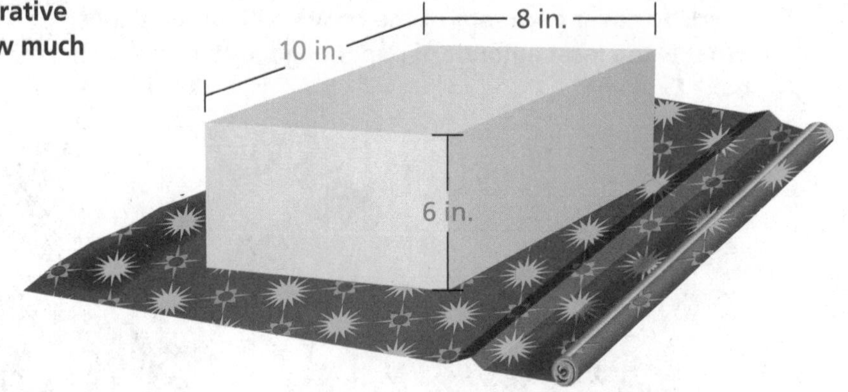

> **Use Appropriate Tools** Would a net help you find the surface area (*SA*) of the rectangular prism?

ONE WAY Draw a net of the shoebox and find the area of each face.

$8 \times 6 = 48$

$10 \times 6 = 60$ | $10 \times 8 = 80$ | $10 \times 6 = 60$ | $10 \times 8 = 80$

$8 \times 6 = 48$

Add the areas. Kelly needs 376 square inches of paper to cover the box.

ANOTHER WAY Use a formula to find the total surface area (*SA*) of the shoebox.

length (**ℓ**) = 10 inches

width (**w**) = 8 inches

height (**h**) = 6 inches

$SA = 2(\ell w) + 2(wh) + 2(\ell h)$

$= 2(10 \cdot 8) + 2(8 \cdot 6) + 2(10 \cdot 6)$

$= 2(80) + 2(48) + 2(60)$

$= 376$

> The area of each face in the net is calculated in the formula.

Kelly needs 376 square inches of paper to cover the box.

Try It!

Use the net and the formula to find the surface area of the prism.

$SA = 2(\ell w) + 2(wh) + 2(\ell h)$

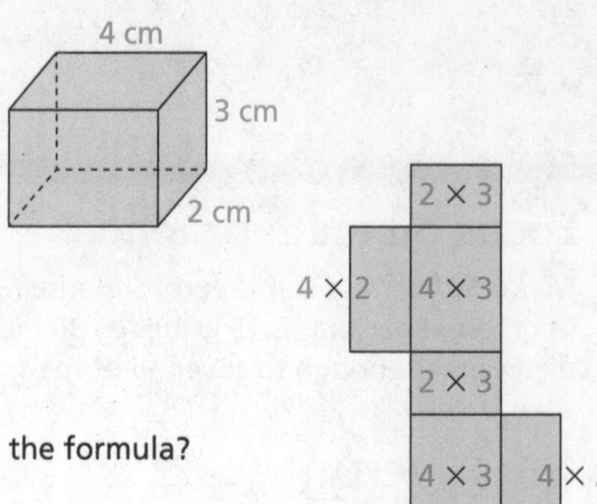

Convince Me! Why are ℓw, wh, and ℓh each multiplied by 2 in the formula?

EXAMPLE 2  Find the Surface Area of a Cube

Sam built a storage cube out of plywood. How many square meters of plywood did Sam use for the cube?

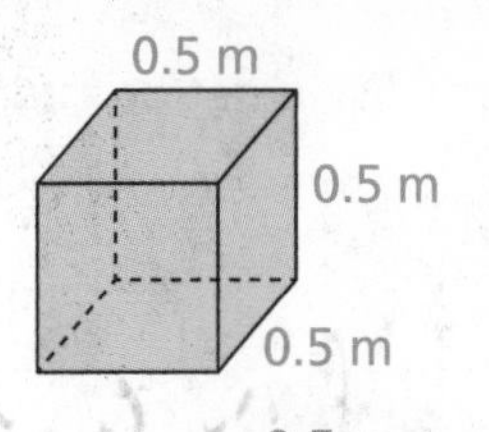

Be Precise Remember to express surface area in square units.

Draw a net of the cube.

The formula for the area of one square is $A = s^2$. Because there are 6 equal squares in the net, the formula for the surface area of a cube is $SA = 6s^2$. Use the formula to find the surface area.

$SA = 6(0.5)^2$

$SA = 6(0.25)$

$SA = 1.5$

Sam used 1.5 m^2 of plywood to build the cube.

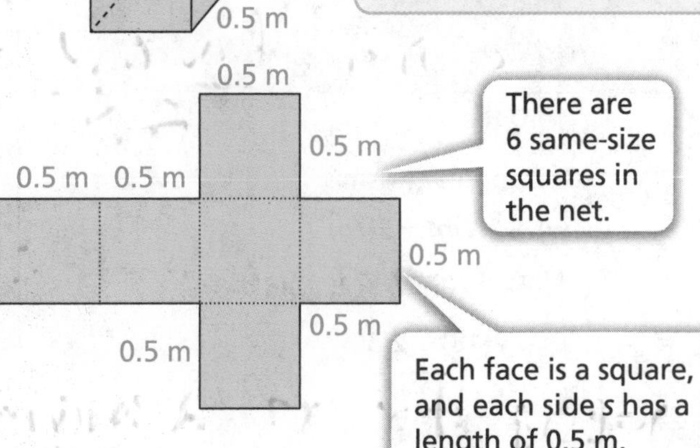

There are 6 same-size squares in the net.

Each face is a square, and each side s has a length of 0.5 m.

EXAMPLE 3  Find the Surface Area of a Triangular Prism

Find the surface area of the triangular prism.

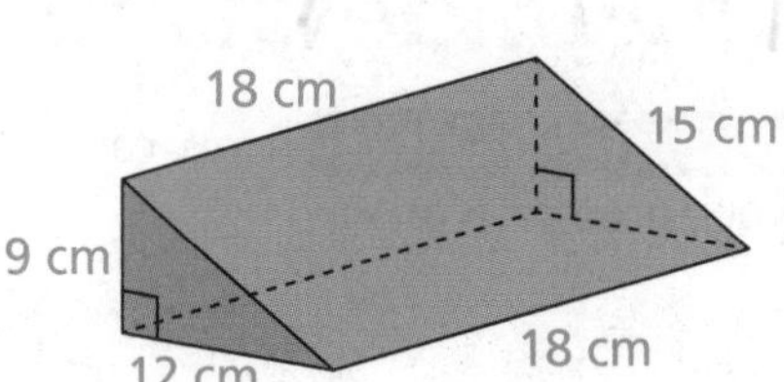

Use the net to find the area of each face of the prism. Then add the areas.

Area of triangular bases: $A = \frac{1}{2}bh = \frac{1}{2}(12)(9) = 54$

There are 2 triangular bases.

Area of bottom: $A = \ell w = 12(18) = 216$

Area of back: $A = \ell w = 9(18) = 162$

Area of sloped face: $A = \ell w = 18(15) = 270$

$SA = 2(54) + 216 + 162 + 270 = 756$

The surface area of the triangular prism is 756 cm^2.

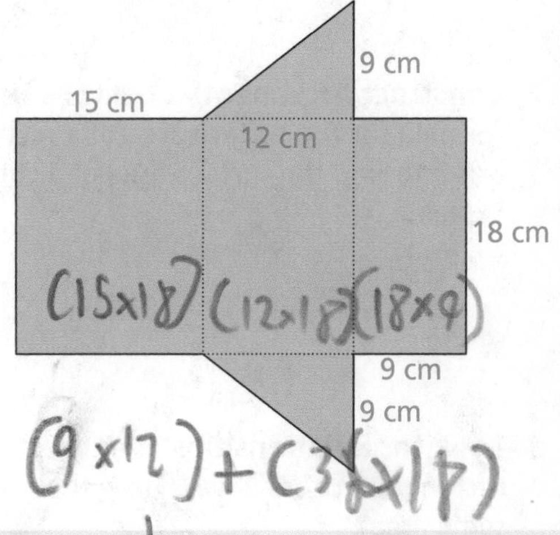

Try It!

Find the surface area of each prism.

a.

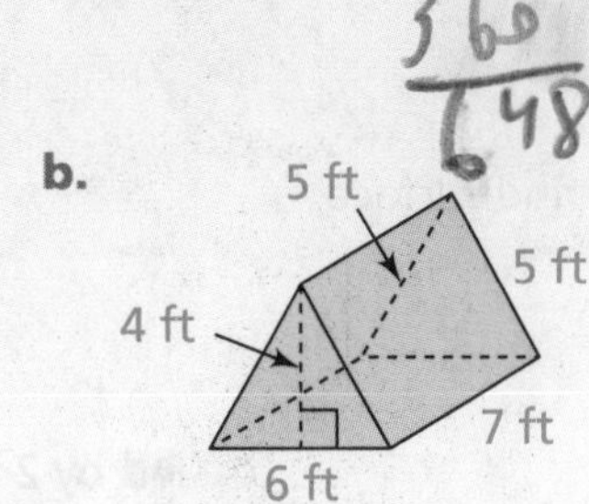

b.

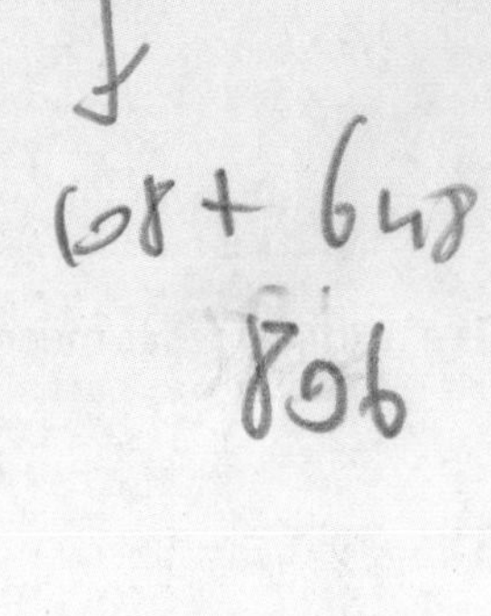

KEY CONCEPT

To find the surface area of a prism, use a net or a formula.

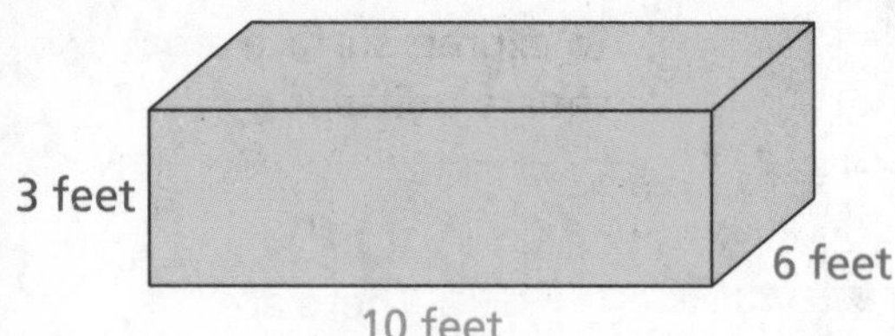

Rectangular Prism

$SA = 2(\ell w) + 2(wh) + 2(\ell h)$

$= 2(10)(6) + 2(6)(3) + 2(10)(3)$

$= 2(60) + 2(18) + 2(30)$

$= 216$

The surface area is 216 ft^2.

$6 \times 3 = 18$

$10 \times 3 = 30$ | $10 \times 6 = 60$ | $10 \times 3 = 30$ | $10 \times 6 = 60$

$6 \times 3 = 18$

Do You Understand?

1. **Essential Question** How can you find the surface area of a prism?

2. **Construct Arguments** Could you use the formula for the surface area of a rectangular prism to find the surface area of a cube? Explain.

3. **Look for Relationships** Which faces of a rectangular prism always have the same area?

4. **Generalize** What does it mean to find surface area?

Do You Know How?

In 5–7, find the surface area of each prism.

5.

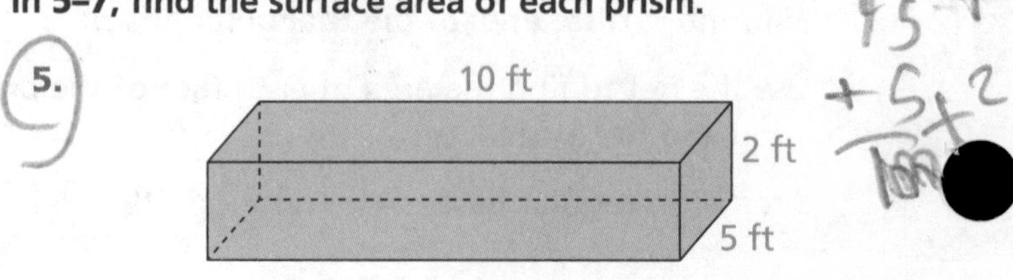

6.

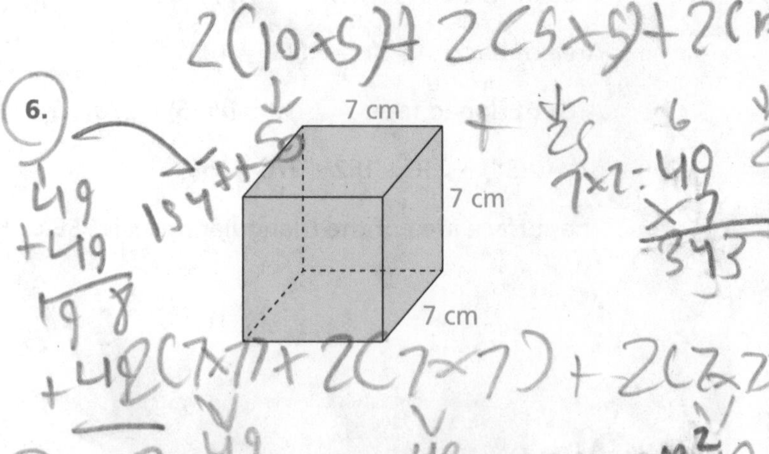

7.

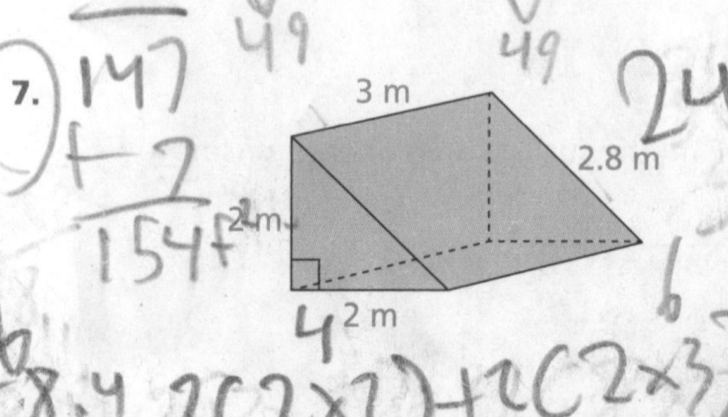

Name: ______________________________

Practice & Problem Solving

Scan for Multimedia 

In 8–13, find the surface area of each prism.

8.

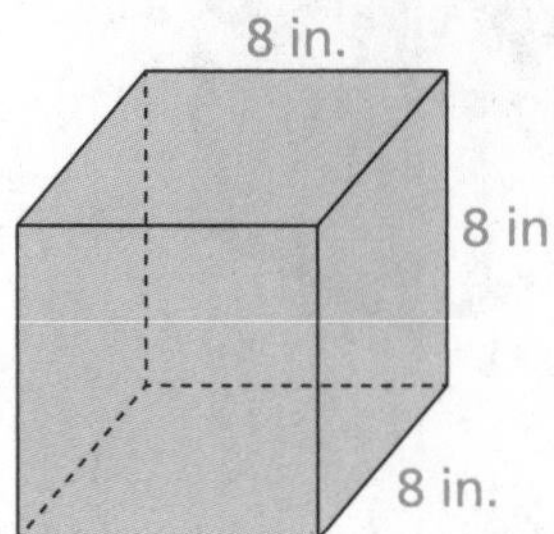

9.

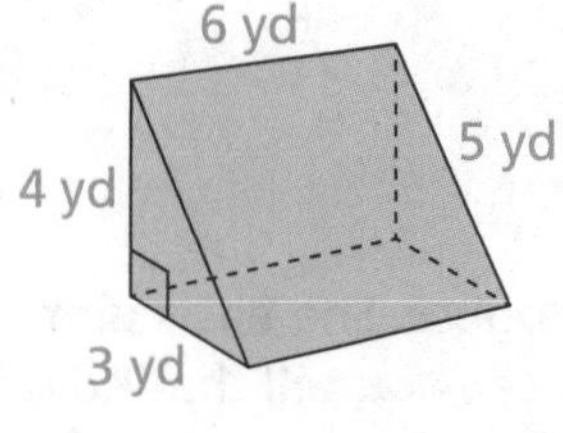

10.

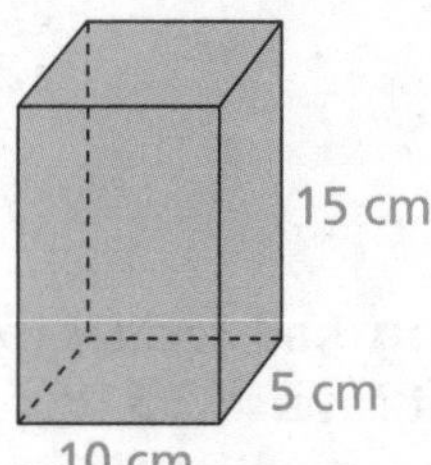

11.

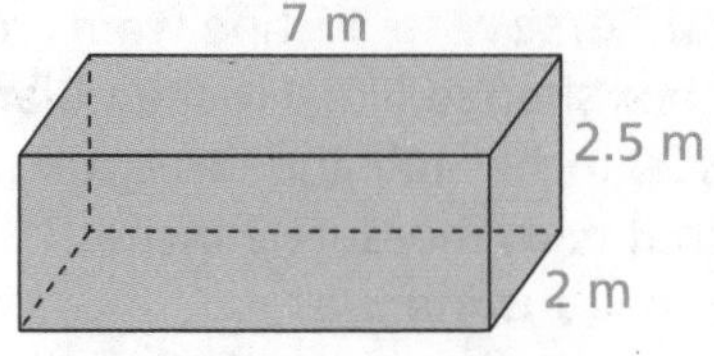

12.

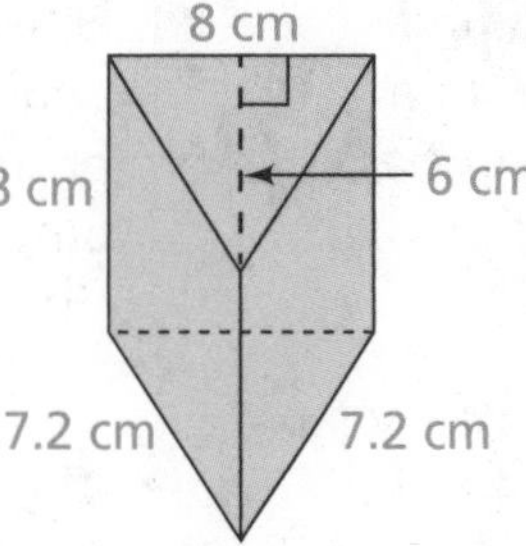

13.

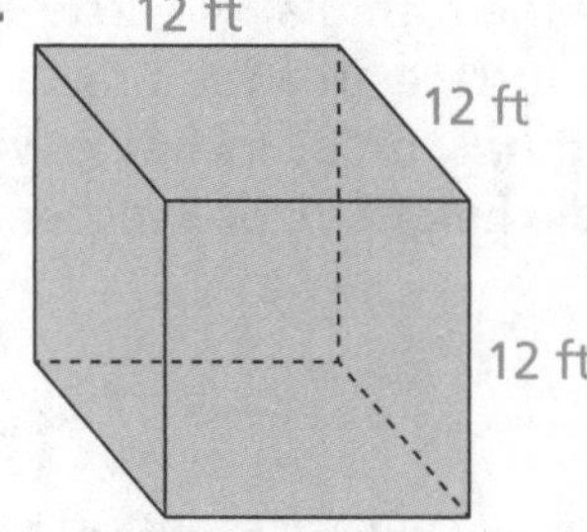

14. Critique Reasoning Jacob says that the surface area of the cube is less than 1,000 cm^2. Do you agree with Jacob? Explain.

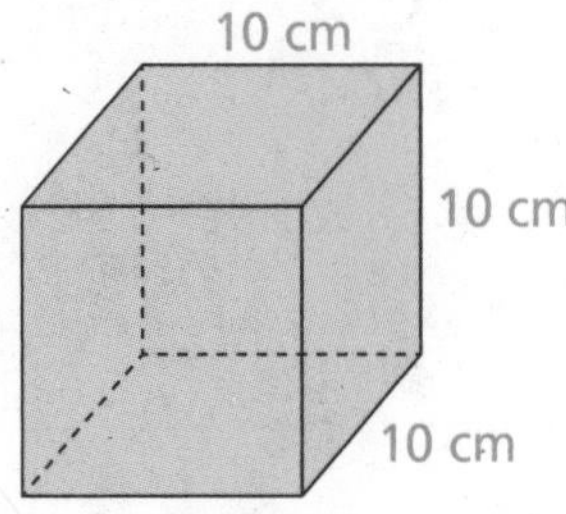

15. You want to wrap a paperweight shaped like the triangular prism shown. How many square inches of wrapping paper do you need to completely cover the prism?

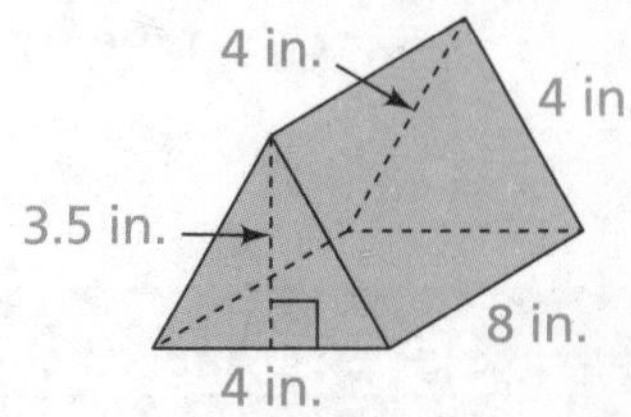

16. Sasha has 2 blocks of clay shaped like the rectangular prism below. She joins them to form a rectangular prism with a length of 12 inches. What is the surface area of the larger prism?

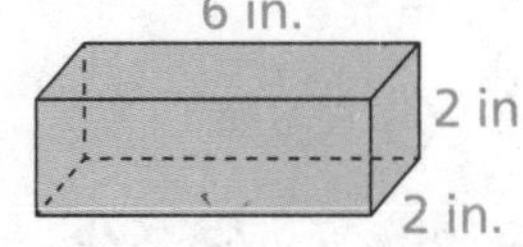

17. A rectangular prism has a length of 12 cm, a height of 6 cm, and a width of 4 cm. Use the formula $SA = 2(\ell w) + 2(wh) + 2(\ell h)$ to find the surface area of the rectangular prism.

In 18 and 19, use the diagram of the birdhouse.

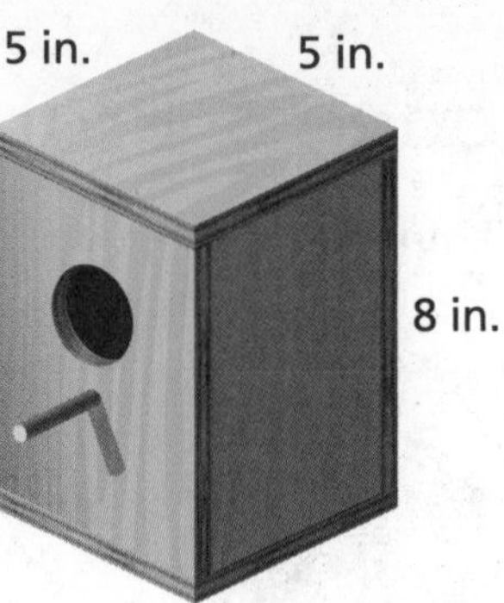

18. Kali wants to build this birdhouse. She bought a 24-inch by 48-inch sheet of plywood. Does Kali have enough wood to make the birdhouse? Explain.

19. Reasoning Kali decides to paint the birdhouse. She has a pint of paint that covers 32.5 ft^2 of surface. How can you tell that Kali has enough paint without calculating?

20. Use the formula $SA = 2\ell w + 2\ell h + 2wh$ to find the surface area for a rectangular prism with a length, ℓ, of 2.3 inches; a width, w, of 1.1 inches; and a height, h, of 3 inches.

21. Make Sense and Persevere Justine wants to wrap a shipping box shaped like a rectangular prism. The box is 28 inches tall and has a square base with sides that each measure 2 inches. How much paper will Justine use?

22. Higher Order Thinking Margaret wants to cover a footrest in the shape of a rectangular prism with cotton fabric. The footrest is 18 inches by 12 inches by 10 inches. Margaret has 1 square yard of fabric. Can she completely cover the footrest? Explain.

23. A cube has a surface area of 486 $in.^2$. Can the length of each side of the cube be 11 in.? Explain.

Assessment Practice

24. Using nets, find the surface area, in square feet, of a rectangular prism with a height of 2 feet, a length of 4.2 feet, and a width of 2.5 feet. 6.G.1.4

25. The surface area of a cube is 273.375 square feet. The net of the prism is shown. 6.G.1.4

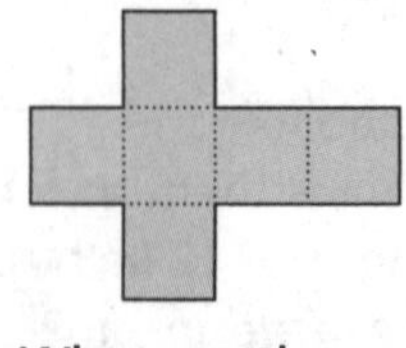

What are the possible dimensions of the cube in feet?

Ⓐ 6, 6, 6

Ⓑ 6, 6.75, 6.75

Ⓒ 6.5, 6.5, 6.5

Ⓓ 6.75, 6.75, 6.75

Lesson 11-7
Find Surface Areas of Pyramids

Go Online | PearsonRealize.com

I can...
draw a net of a pyramid and use it to find the pyramid's surface area.

MAFS.6.G.1.4 Represent three-dimensional figures using nets made up of rectangles and triangles, and use the nets to find the surface area of these figures. Apply these techniques in the context of solving real-world and mathematical problems. Also 6.EE.1.2a, 6.EE.1.2c, 6.EE.2.6
MAFS.K12.MP.2.1, MP.3.1, MP.5.1, MP.7.1

Solve & Discuss It!

ACTIVITY

The fence in Marci's front yard has decorative tops, in the shape of square pyramids, every 6 feet. Marci paints each face of each top a different color before attaching the tops to the fence. What is the total surface area that she paints on each decorative top?

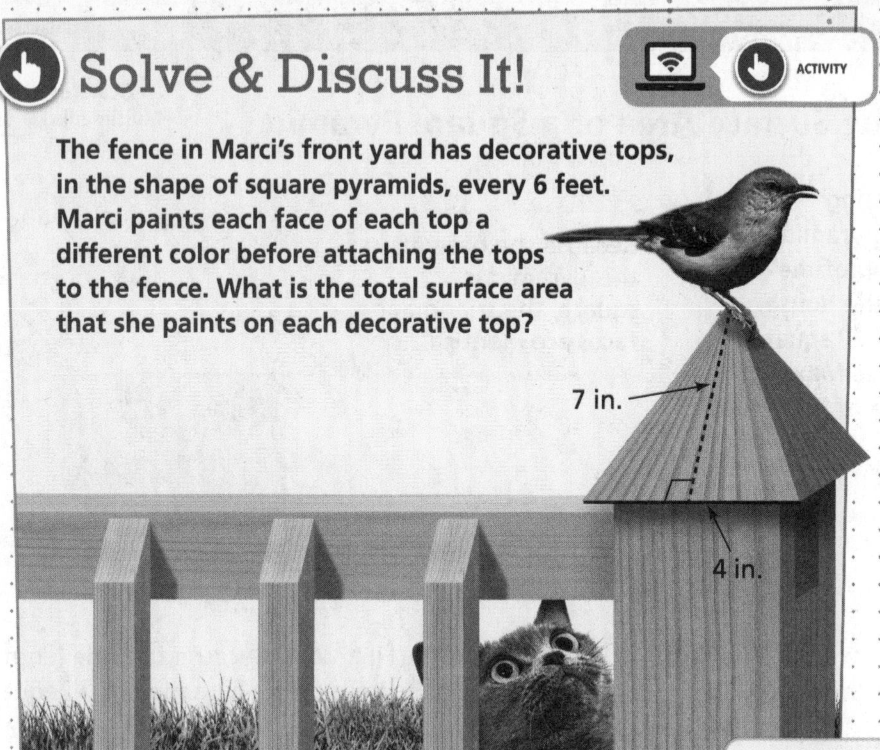

Use Appropriate Tools
What tools can you use to help solve this problem?

Focus on math practices

Use Structure Suppose the side lengths of the square base of each decorative top are increased by 2 inches. What is the total surface area of each top?

? Essential Question How can you find the surface area of a pyramid?

EXAMPLE 1  Find the Surface Area of a Square Pyramid

Scan for Multimedia 

Maxwell made a model of a house using a cube for the bottom and a square pyramid for the top. He wants to paint the top of the house blue to match the bottom of the house. One tube of craft paint covers about 20 square inches. How many tubes of paint does Maxwell need to cover all the faces of the top of his model?

Because the base of this pyramid is a square, the triangular faces are identical.

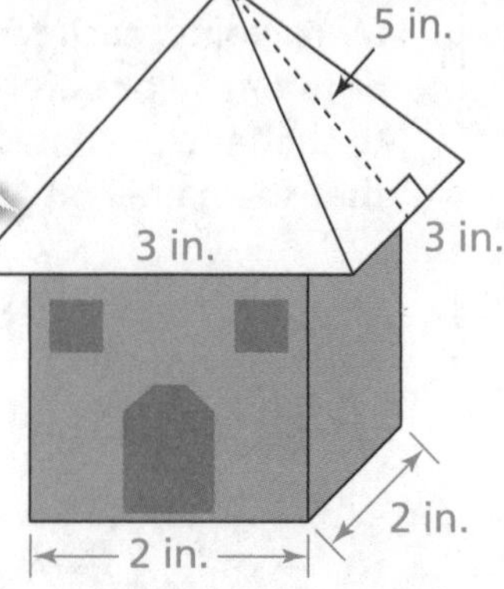

ONE WAY Draw a net of the square pyramid. Then find the sum of the areas of the base and the faces.

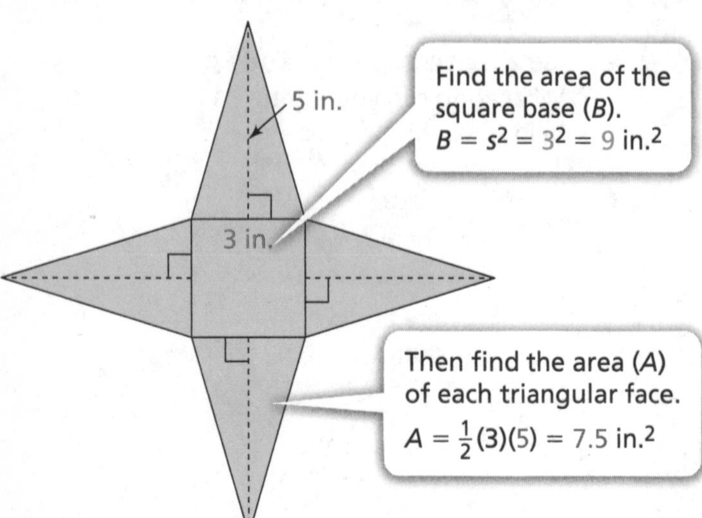

Find the area of the square base (B).
$B = s^2 = 3^2 = 9$ in.^{2}

Then find the area (A) of each triangular face.
$A = \frac{1}{2}(3)(5) = 7.5$ in.^{2}

$SA = 9 + 7.5 + 7.5 + 7.5 + 7.5 = 39$

The surface area is 39 in.^{2}, so Maxwell needs 2 tubes of craft paint.

ANOTHER WAY Because the side lengths of the base of the pyramid are all equal, you can use the formula $SA = B + (nA)$ to find the surface area (SA).

B = area of the base of the pyramid, 9

n = number of faces, 4

A = area of each triangular face, 7.5

$SA = B + (n \times A)$

$SA = 9 + (4 \times 7.5)$

$SA = 39$

The formula finds the sum of the areas of the base and each face in the net.

The surface area is 39 in.^{2}, so Maxwell needs 2 tubes of craft paint.

Try It!

Find the surface area of the square pyramid. Draw a net to find the areas of the base and each face of the pyramid.

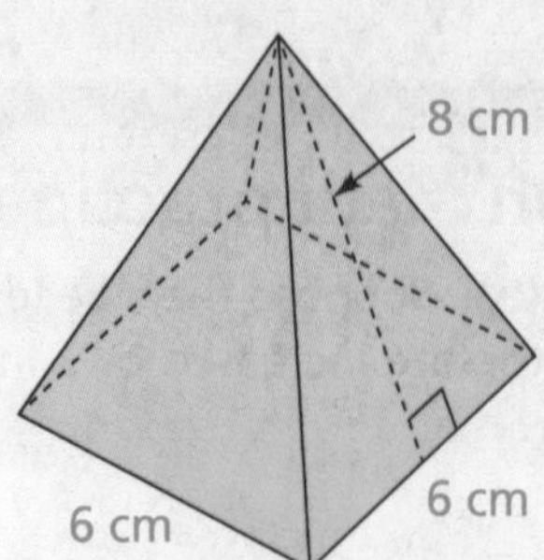

Convince Me! For the pyramid in the Try It!, what values would you use for B, n, and A in the formula $SA = B + (nA)$?

EXAMPLE 2  Find the Surface Area of a Triangular Pyramid

Tamara made a small gift box that has the shape of a triangular pyramid. The faces of the box are identical equilateral triangles. How many square centimeters of cardboard did Tamara use for the box?

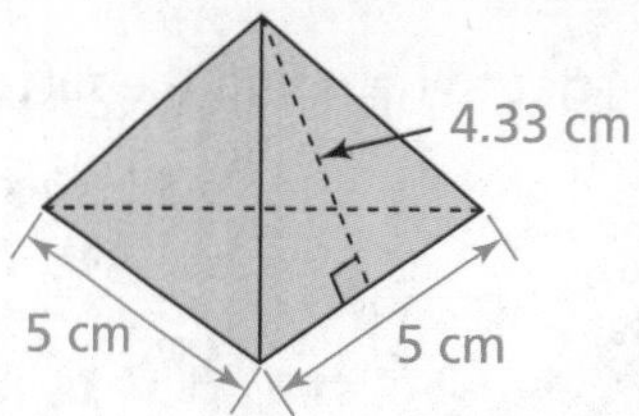

STEP 1 Draw a net.

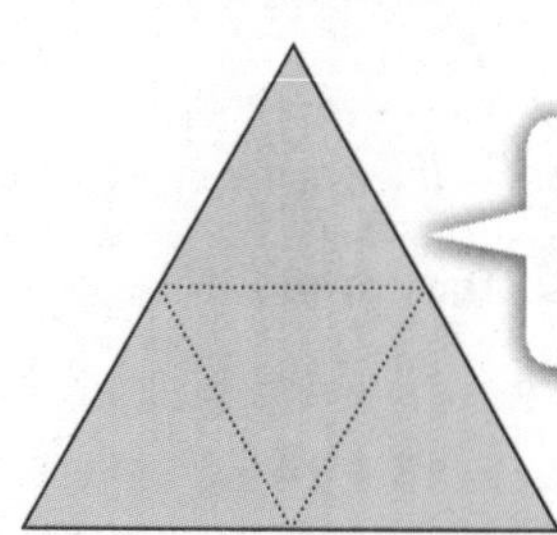

The faces of the triangular pyramid are 4 identical equilateral triangles.

STEP 2 Find the area (T) of each equilateral triangle.

$T = \frac{1}{2}bh$

$T = \frac{1}{2}(5)(4.33)$

$= 10.825 \text{ cm}^2$

STEP 3 Find the surface area (SA) of the triangular pyramid.

$SA = 4T$

$SA = 4 \times 10.825$

$= 43.3 \text{ cm}^2$

Tamara used 43.3 cm^2 of cardboard for the box.

Reasoning If you know the faces are identical equilateral triangles, then you just find the area of one triangle and multiply by 4.

 **Try It!**

Draw a net and find the surface area of the triangular pyramid.

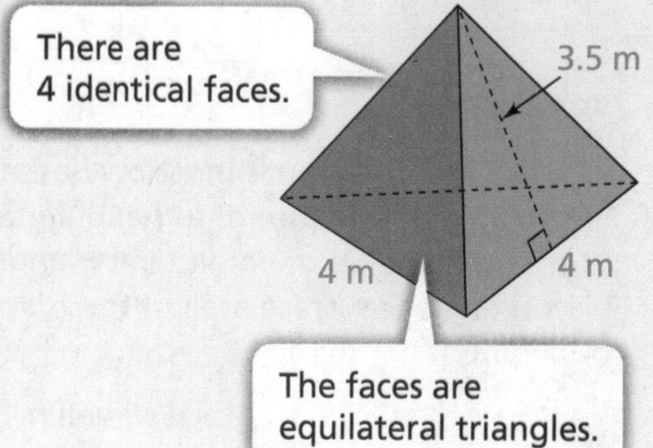

Find the area (T) of each equilateral triangle.

$T = \frac{1}{2}bh$

$T = \frac{1}{2} \times \square \times \square$

$= \square$

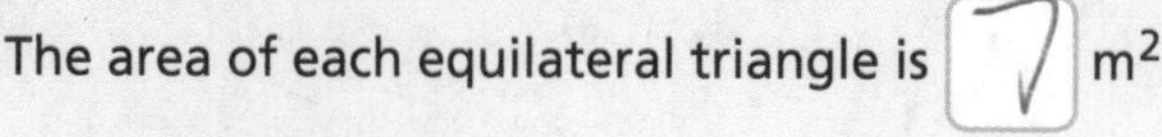

The area of each equilateral triangle is $\square$ m^2.

Find the surface area (SA) of the triangular pyramid.

$SA = 4T$

$SA = \square \times T$

$SA = 4 \times \square$

$= \square$

The surface area of the triangular pyramid is $\square$ m^2.

KEY CONCEPT

You can use a net to help find the surface area of a pyramid.

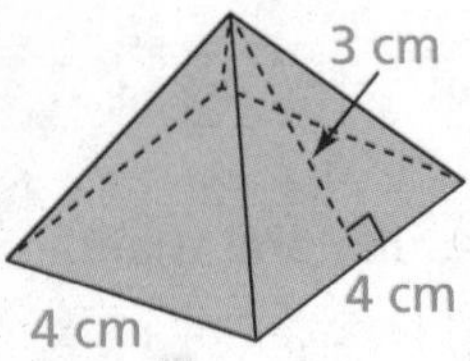

Use the dimensions shown on the pyramid to draw an accurate net.

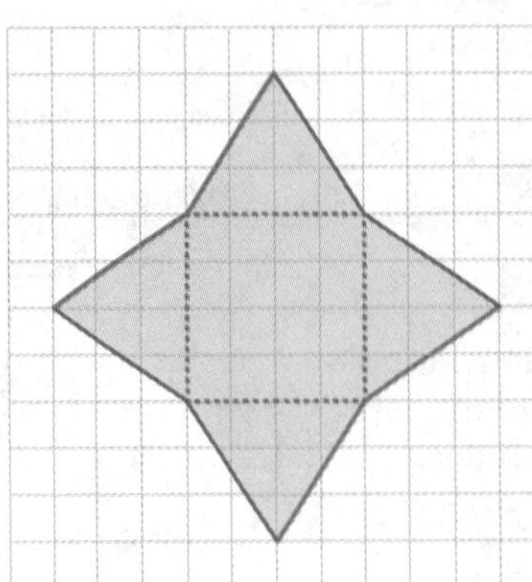

Square base:

$B = s^2$

$= 4 \cdot 4 = 16$

Each triangular face:

$A = \frac{1}{2}bh$

$= \frac{1}{2} \cdot 4 \cdot 3 = 6$

Surface area:

$SA = 16 + 4 \times 6$

$= 16 + 24$

$= 40$

The surface area is 40 cm^2.

Do You Understand?

1. **Essential Question** How can you find the surface area of a pyramid?

2. **Look for Relationships** How does finding the area of one face of a triangular pyramid that is made up of equilateral triangles help you find the surface area of the triangular pyramid?

3. **Make Sense and Persevere** In the formula $SA = 4T$, for the surface area of a triangular pyramid in which the faces are equilateral triangles, what does the variable T represent?

Do You Know How?

4. Each side of the base of a square pyramid is 4 inches and the height of each triangular face is 3 inches. Draw a net for this pyramid and find its surface area.

5. The faces of this triangular pyramid are equilateral triangles. Draw a net of the pyramid and use it to find the surface area.

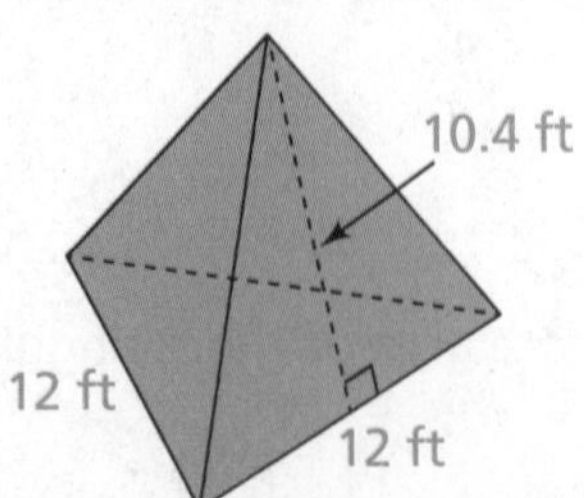

Name: ______________________________

Practice & Problem Solving 

Scan for Multimedia 

Leveled Practice **In 6 and 7, find the surface area of each pyramid. The faces of each triangular pyramid are equilateral triangles.**

6.

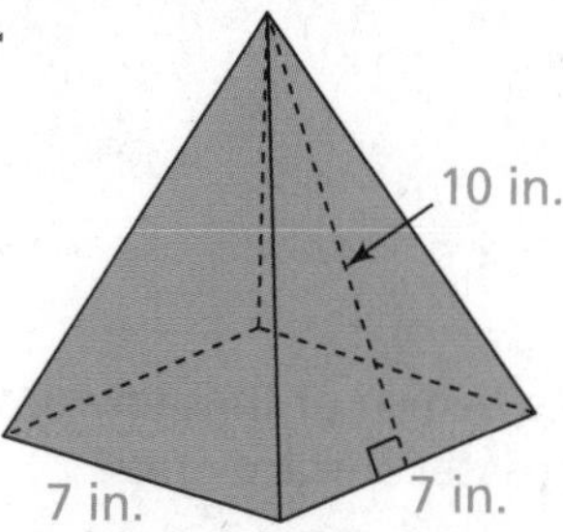

Area of base, B: $7 \times 7 =$ ☐

Area of each triangular face, A:

$\frac{1}{2} \times 7 \times$ ☐ $=$ ☐

Number of triangular faces, n: ☐

$SA = B + (n \times A)$

$SA =$ ☐ $+ ($☐ $\times$ ☐$) =$ ☐

The surface area is ☐ in.^{2}.

7.

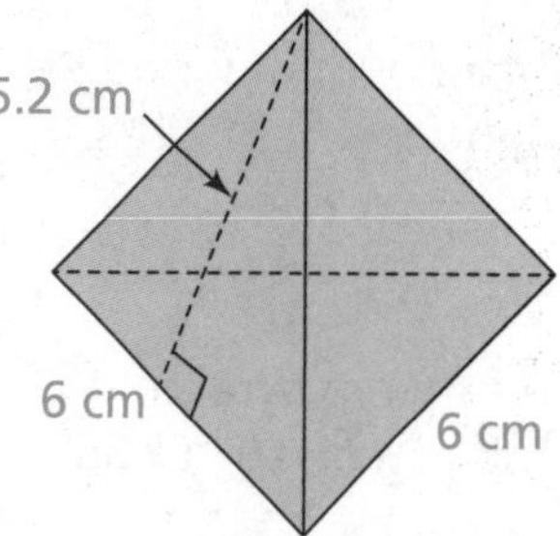

Area of each triangular face, T:

$\frac{1}{2} \times$ ☐ $\times$ ☐ $=$ ☐

$SA = 4T$

$SA = 4 \times$ ☐

$SA =$ ☐

The surface area is ☐ cm^2.

8. Complete the net at the right to find the surface area of this triangular pyramid. The faces of the pyramid are equilateral triangles.

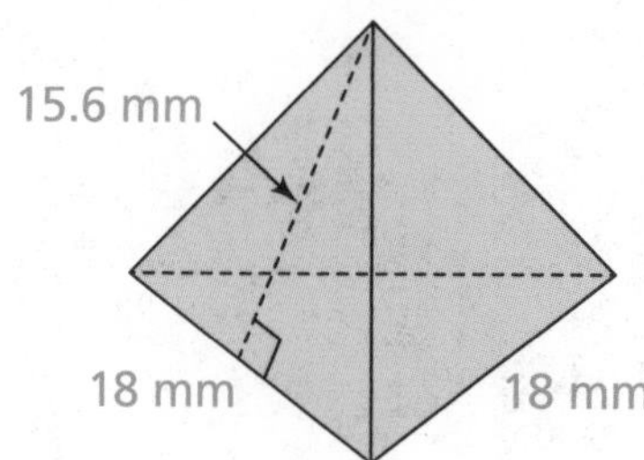

☐ mm^2

☐ mm^2

☐ mm^2

☐ mm^2

9. Simone is designing a piece of artwork in the shape of a square pyramid for a hotel. She wants to cover the pyramid with decorative glass. How many square feet of glass does Simone need to cover the entire pyramid?

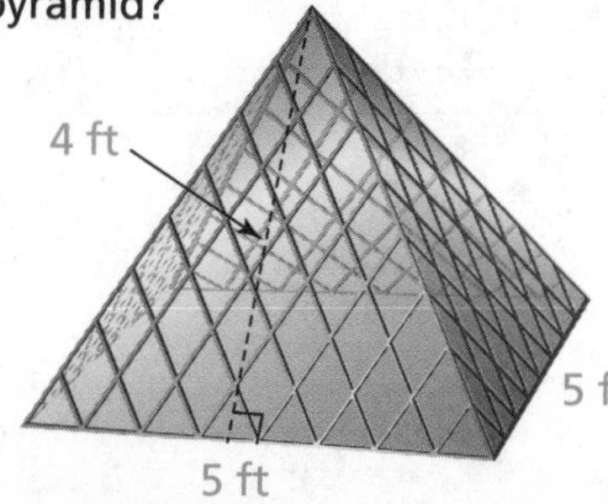

10. Critique Reasoning Kurt says that the surface area of this triangular pyramid with faces that are equilateral triangles is 173 cm^2. Do you agree with Kurt? Explain.

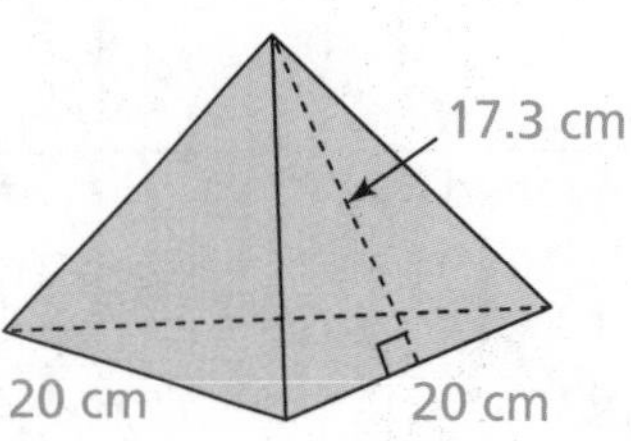

In 11 and 12, use the pyramid and net shown.

11. Model with Math Ken drew a square pyramid and its net to represent a doghouse that he is building. Complete the net by filling in the missing measures.

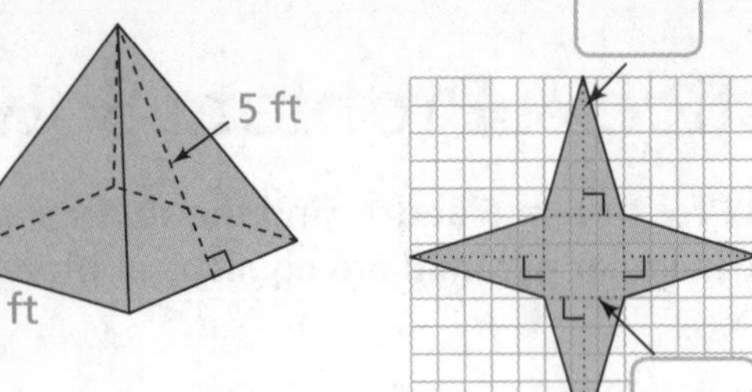

12. Use the net to find the amount of wood Ken needs to make the doghouse.

13. The surface area of this square pyramid is 644 ft^2. Can the value of x be 20? Explain.

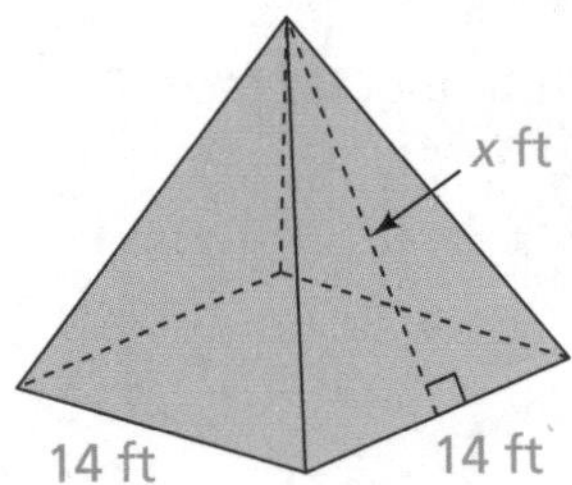

14. Construct Arguments Which of these pyramids do you think has the greater surface area? Explain.

- Square pyramid: The base is 10 cm by 10 cm and the triangular faces have a height of 8.66 cm.
- Triangular pyramid: All the faces are equilateral triangles with a base of 10 cm and a height of 8.66 cm.

15. Higher Order Thinking The base of a pyramid can be any polygon. How many faces does a pentagonal pyramid have? Describe the shapes of the faces.

16. Vocabulary What is the term used to describe a point where three or more edges of a solid figure meet?

Assessment Practice

17. Which net represents the pyramid with the greatest surface area? 6.G.1.4

Ⓐ

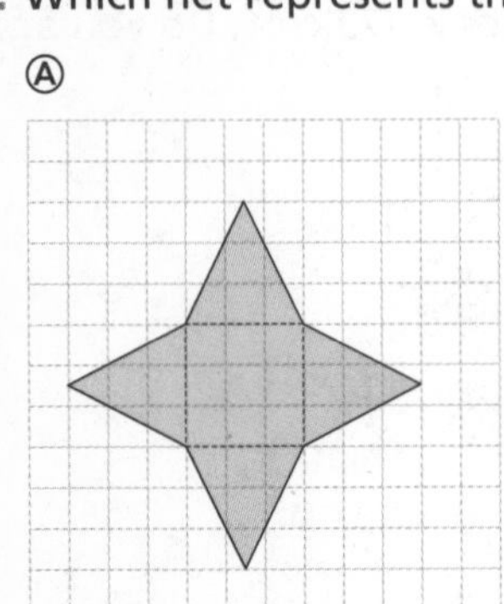

Ⓑ

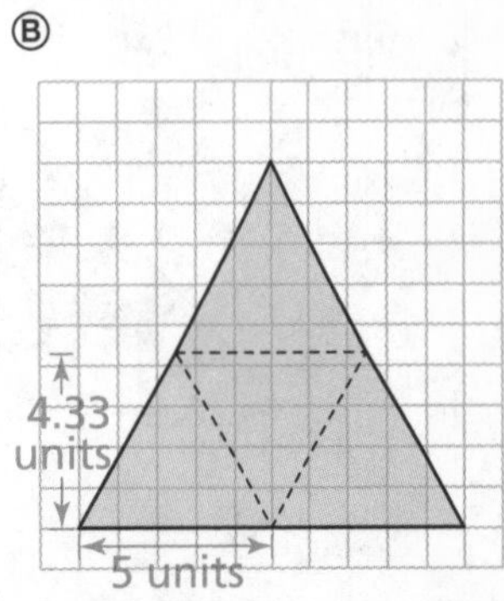

Ⓒ

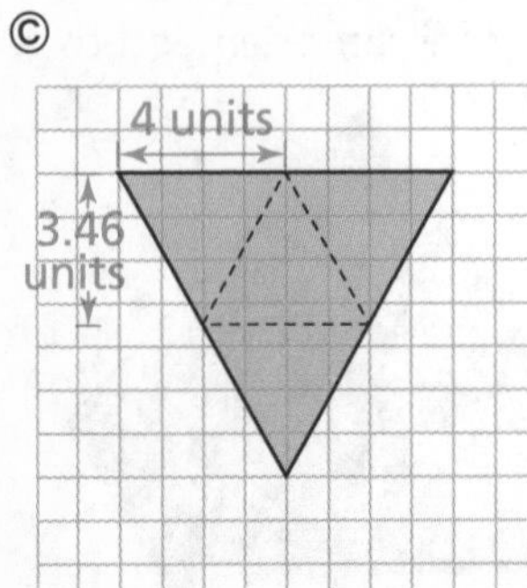

Ⓓ

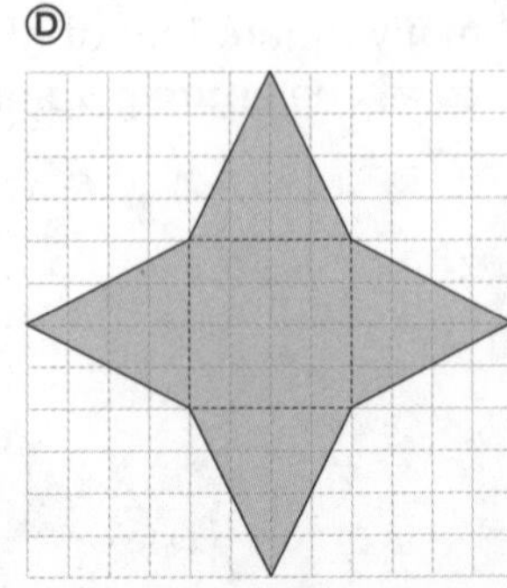

Lesson 11-8
Find Volume with Fractional Edge Lengths

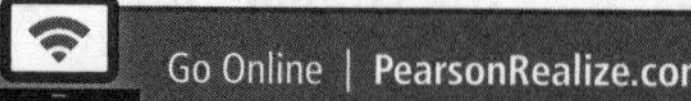

I can…
find the volume of a rectangular prism with fractional edge lengths.

MAFS.6.G.1.2 Find the volume of a right rectangular prism with fractional edge lengths by packing it with unit cubes of the appropriate unit fraction edge lengths, and show that the volume is the same as would be found by multiplying the edge lengths of the prism. Apply the formulas $V = lwh$ and $V = bh$ to find volumes of right rectangular prisms with fractional edge lengths in the context of solving real-world and mathematical problems.
Also 6.EE.1.2a, 6.EE.1.2c, 6.EE.2.6
MAFS.K12.MP.1.1, MP.3.1, MP.6.1, MP.7.1

Solve & Discuss It!

ACTIVITY

A rectangular prism has the dimensions shown. What is the volume of this rectangular prism?

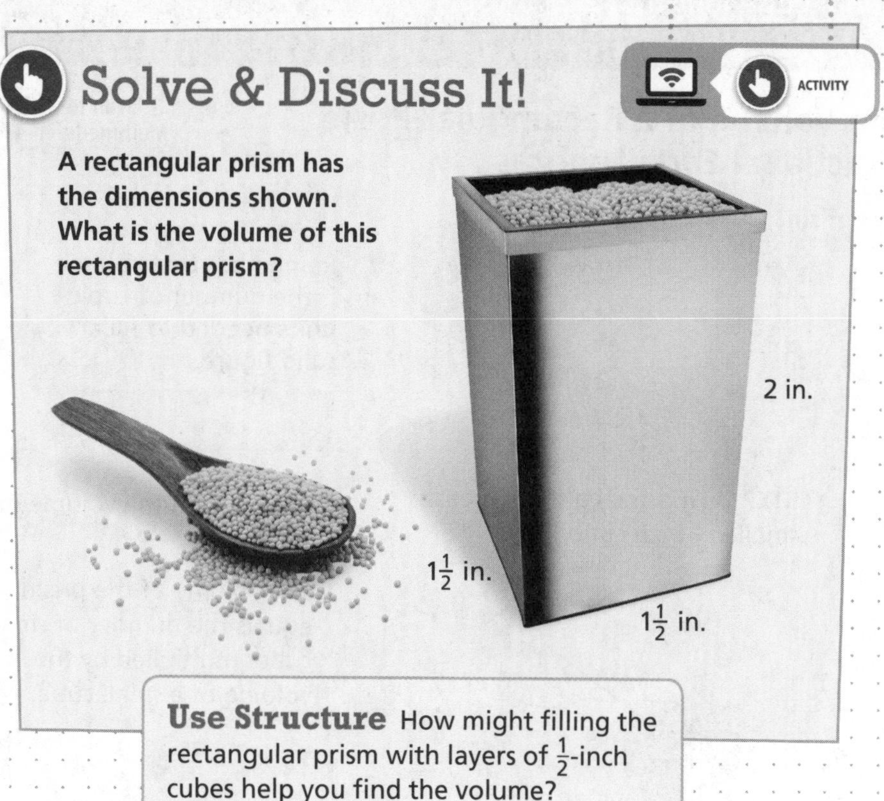

Use Structure How might filling the rectangular prism with layers of $\frac{1}{2}$-inch cubes help you find the volume?

Focus on math practices

Look for Relationships You know how to use the formula $V = \ell wh$ to find the volume of a rectangular prism. How might you use the formula to find the volume of the prism above?

? Essential Question How can you find the volume of a rectangular prism with fractional edge lengths?

VISUAL LEARNING ASSESS

EXAMPLE 1  Find the Volume of a Rectangular Prism with Fractional Edge Lengths

Scan for Multimedia 

What is the volume of the rectangular prism?

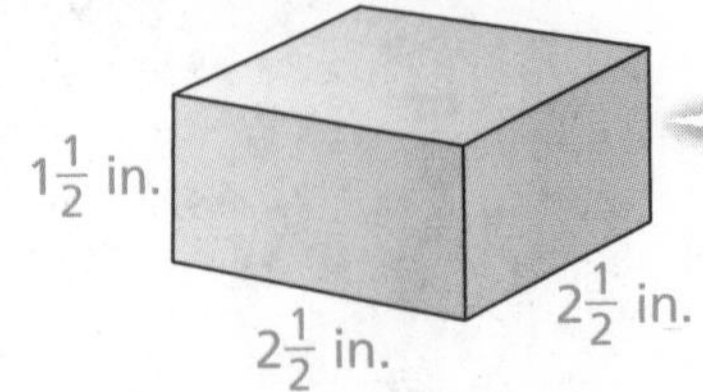

Remember that volume is the number of cubic units needed to fill a solid figure.

STEP 1 Find the number of $\frac{1}{2}$-inch cubes that will fill the prism.

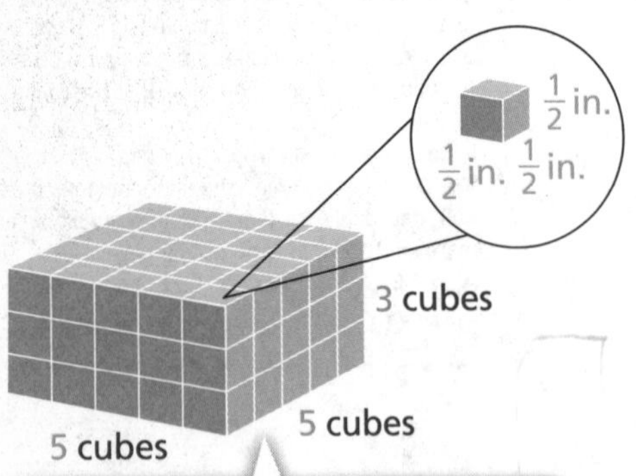

Five $\frac{1}{2}$-inch cubes fit along each $2\frac{1}{2}$-inch edge of the prism.

The bottom layer has 5×5, or 25 cubes.

The prism is 3 cubes high, so there are 25×3, or 75, cubes in the prism.

STEP 2 Find the volume of each smaller $\frac{1}{2}$-inch cube.

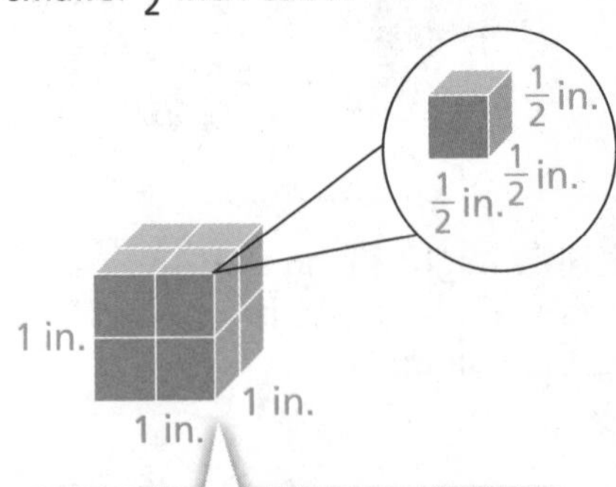

There are 4 smaller cubes on the bottom layer of the unit cube, and the unit cube is 2 smaller cubes high.

There are 4×2, or 8, smaller cubes in the unit cube. So each $\frac{1}{2}$-inch cube has $\frac{1}{8}$ the volume of a unit cube, or $\frac{1}{8} \times 1 \text{ in.}^3 = \frac{1}{8} \text{ in.}^3$.

STEP 3 Find the volume of the prism.

The volume of the prism equals the number of small cubes multiplied by the volume of a small cube.

$75 \times \frac{1}{8} = \frac{75}{8}$ or $9\frac{3}{8}$

Number of small cubes

Volume of small cube

Be Precise Use the correct units to describe area and volume.

The volume of the prism is $9\frac{3}{8}$ in.^{3}.

Try It!

Find the volume of the rectangular prism built from $\frac{1}{2}$-inch cubes.

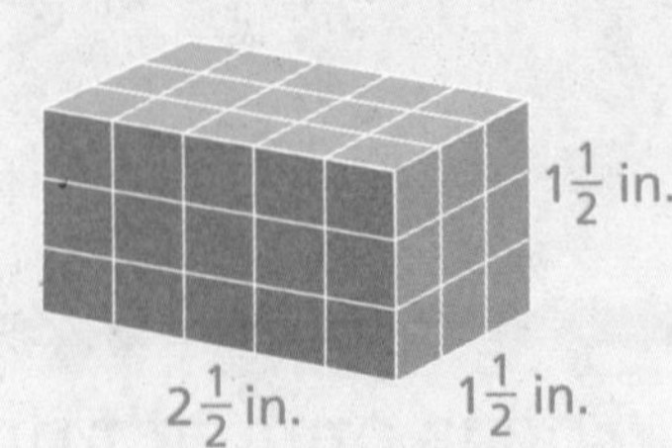

The bottom layer has ☐ cubes. The prism is ☐ cubes high. There are a total of ☐ cubes in the prism. Each cube has a volume of ☐ in.^{3}.

Volume of prism = ☐ × ☐ = ☐ in.^{3}.

Convince Me! Suppose that the length of the rectangular prism in the Try It! were $3\frac{1}{2}$ inches instead of $2\frac{1}{2}$ inches. How many cubes would there be in the prism? What would be the volume of the prism?

EXAMPLE 2  Use a Formula to Find the Volume of a Rectangular Prism

ACTIVITY

ASSESS

Sean bought the fish tank shown. What is the volume of Sean's fish tank?

Look for Relationships The volume V of any prism equals the area of the base, B, times the height of the prism, h. $V = Bh$. In a rectangular prism, $B = \ell \times w$.

Use the formula $V = \ell wh$ to find the volume of the fish tank.

$V = 3\frac{1}{3} \times 1 \times 1\frac{1}{3}$

Substitute the values for the length, width, and height. Rename mixed numbers as fractions to solve.

$V = \frac{10}{3} \times \frac{1}{1} \times \frac{4}{3}$

$V = \frac{40}{9}$ or $4\frac{4}{9}$

The volume of the fish tank is $4\frac{4}{9}$ ft^3.

EXAMPLE 3  Use a Formula to Find the Volume of a Cube

Adah has a ring box in the shape of a cube. What is the volume of Adah's ring box?

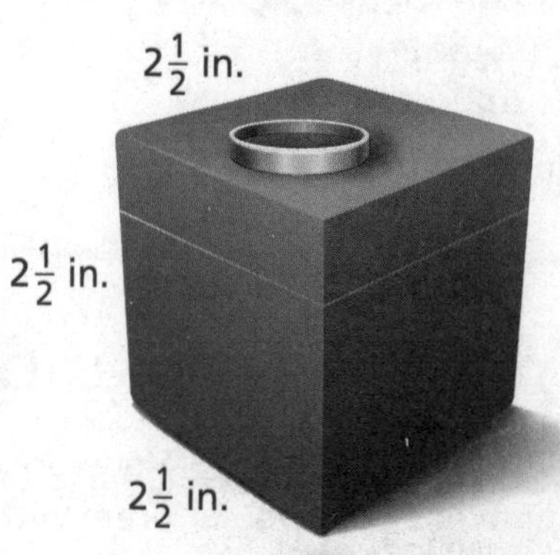

The length, width, and height of a cube are the same.

Because a cube is a rectangular prism, its volume is also the product of its length, width, and height. Since the length, width, and height of a cube are equivalent, let s represent the length of each edge.

Volume $= s \times s \times s = s^3$

$V = \left(2\frac{1}{2}\right)^3 = 2\frac{1}{2} \times 2\frac{1}{2} \times 2\frac{1}{2}$

Rename mixed numbers as fractions to solve.

$V = \frac{5}{2} \times \frac{5}{2} \times \frac{5}{2}$

$V = \frac{125}{8}$ or $15\frac{5}{8}$

The volume of the ring box is $15\frac{5}{8}$ in.^{3}.

Try It!

Find the volume of each rectangular prism.

a.

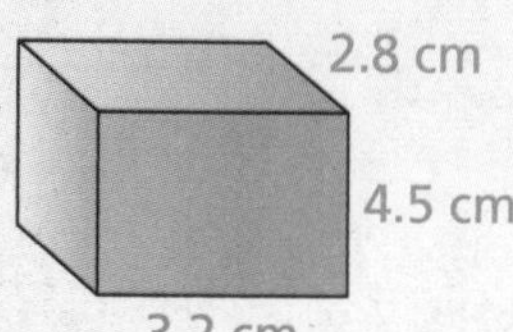

b.

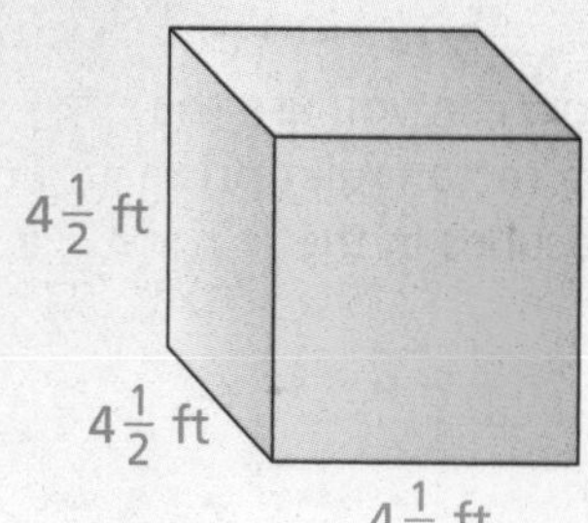

KEY CONCEPT

You can find the volume of a rectangular prism with fractional edge lengths by determining the number of same-sized cubes with unit fraction edge lengths needed to completely fill the prism, then multiplying that number of cubes by the volume of each cube. You can also apply a formula.

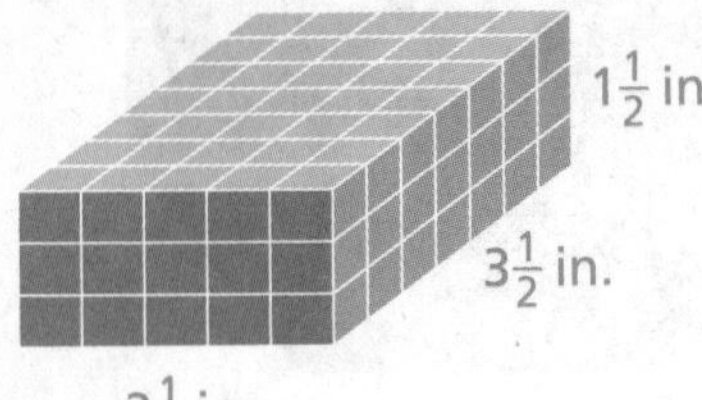

Each $\frac{1}{2}$-inch cube has a volume of $\frac{1}{8}$ in.^{3}.

Prism Dimensions:

Five $\frac{1}{2}$-inch cubes wide

Seven $\frac{1}{2}$-inch cubes long

Three $\frac{1}{2}$-inch cubes tall

$5 \times 7 \times 3 =$ One hundred five $\frac{1}{2}$-inch cubes

$V = 105 \times \frac{1}{8} = 13\frac{1}{8}$

The volume of the prism is $13\frac{1}{8}$ in.^{3}.

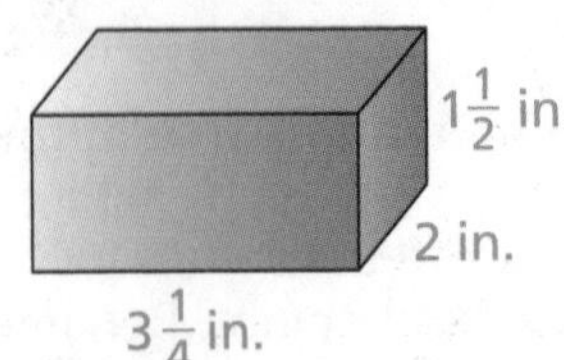

$V = \ell wh$

$V = 3\frac{1}{4} \times 2 \times 1\frac{1}{2}$

$V = \frac{13}{4} \times \frac{2}{1} \times \frac{3}{2}$

$V = \frac{78}{8}$ or $9\frac{3}{4}$

The volume of the prism is $9\frac{3}{4}$ in.^{3}.

Do You Understand?

1. **Essential Question** How can you find the volume of a rectangular prism with fractional edge lengths?

2. How is finding the volume of a rectangular prism with fractional edge lengths similar to finding the volume of a rectangular prism with whole number edge lengths?

3. **Construct Arguments** How can you use the number of $\frac{1}{2}$-inch cubes in a rectangular prism to find the number of unit cubes in the rectangular prism?

Do You Know How?

In 4 and 5, tell how many of each size of cube can fill a 1-inch cube.

4. Edge = $\frac{1}{3}$ inch

5. Edge = $\frac{1}{4}$ inch

In 6–9, find the volume of each rectangular prism.

6.

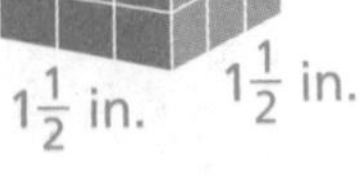

7.

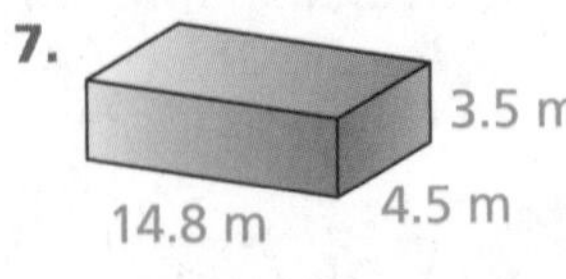

8.

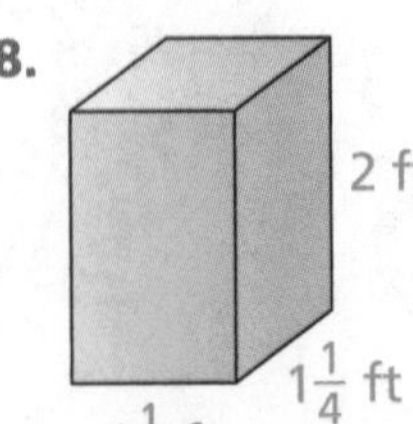

9.

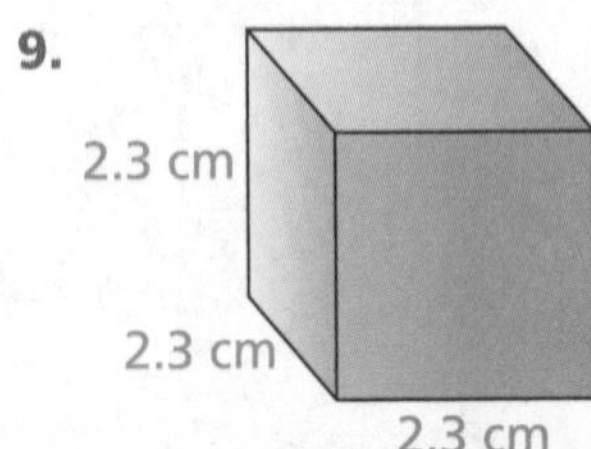

Name: ____________________

Practice & Problem Solving

Scan for Multimedia

In 10–13, find the volume of each rectangular prism.

10.

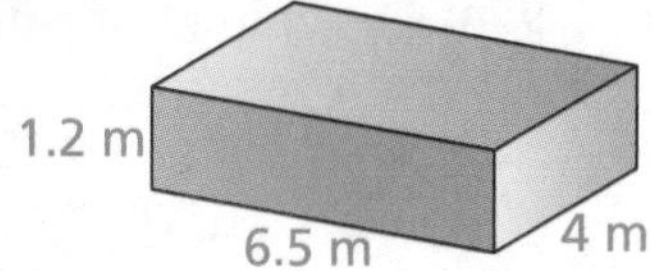

11.

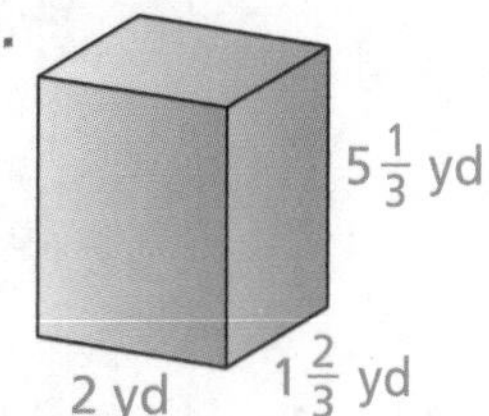

12.

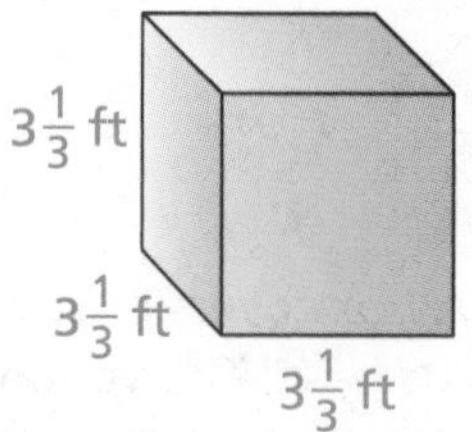

13.

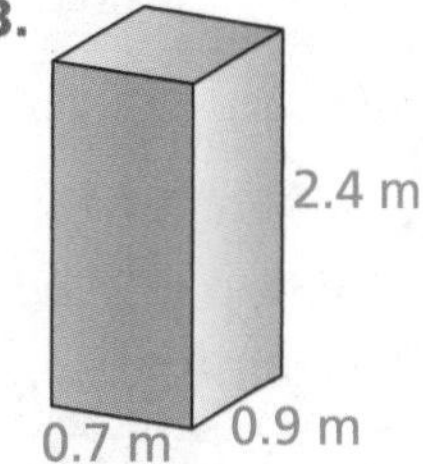

14. A clear box has the shape of a rectangular prism and is filled with sand. Find the volume of the box.

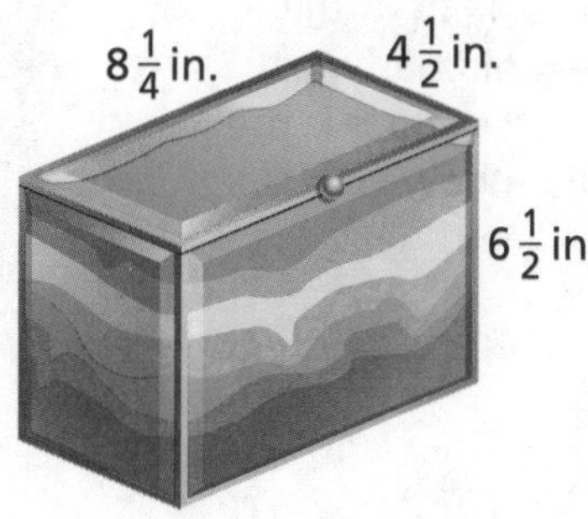

15. Use Structure A rectangular prism has a length of $2\frac{1}{2}$ yd, a width of $1\frac{1}{2}$ yd, and a height of $1\frac{1}{2}$ yd. You use cubes with fractional edge lengths of $\frac{1}{2}$ yd to find the volume. How many cubes are there for each of the length, width, and height of the prism? What is the volume of the prism?

16. A gift box has the shape of a cube. The length of each side is 10.5 cm. What is the volume of the gift box?

17. A school locker has a length of 1 ft, a width of 18 in., and a height of $2\frac{1}{2}$ ft. What is the volume of the locker in cubic feet?

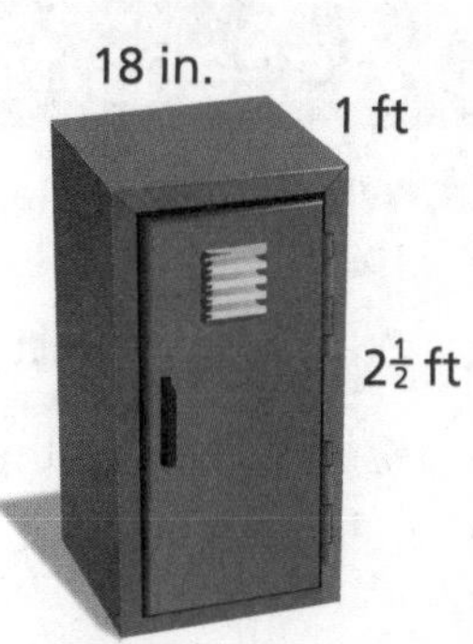

In **18** and **19**, use the table.

18. Use Structure Sandy has two boxes with the dimensions shown. She wants to use the box with the greater volume to ship a gift to her friend. Which box should Sandy use? Explain.

	Length	Width	Height
Box A	$7\frac{1}{2}$ in.	2 in.	$11\frac{1}{2}$ in.
Box B	9 in.	$2\frac{1}{4}$ in.	$8\frac{1}{2}$ in.

19. Sandy finds a third box, box C, that has a length of 8 inches, a width of $2\frac{3}{4}$ inches, and a height of $10\frac{1}{2}$ inches. If Sandy wants to use the box with the greatest volume, should she use box C? Explain.

20. The volume of a large crate is 84 yd³. It is $2\frac{2}{3}$ yd wide and $4\frac{2}{3}$ yd high. What is the length of the crate?

21. Higher Order Thinking A box covers an area of $8\frac{3}{4}$ in.² when resting on its base. The volume of the box is $74\frac{3}{8}$ in.³. Can you find the surface area of the box? Explain.

22. Make Sense and Persevere A gold bar is similar in shape to a rectangular prism. A standard mint bar is approximately 7 in. × $3\frac{5}{8}$ in. × $1\frac{3}{4}$ in. If the value of gold is $1,313 per ounce, about how much is one gold bar worth? Use the formula $w \approx 11.15n$, where w is the weight in ounces and n is the volume in cubic inches, to find the weight in ounces. Explain how you found your answer.

Assessment Practice

23. Which rectangular prism with the given dimensions has the same volume as the prism shown? 6.G.1.2

Ⓐ 1 in., 3.5 in., 4.25 in.

Ⓑ 1.25 in., 3.5 in., 4 in.

Ⓒ 1.75 in., 3 in., 3.5 in.

Ⓓ 2 in., 2.25 in., 4 in.

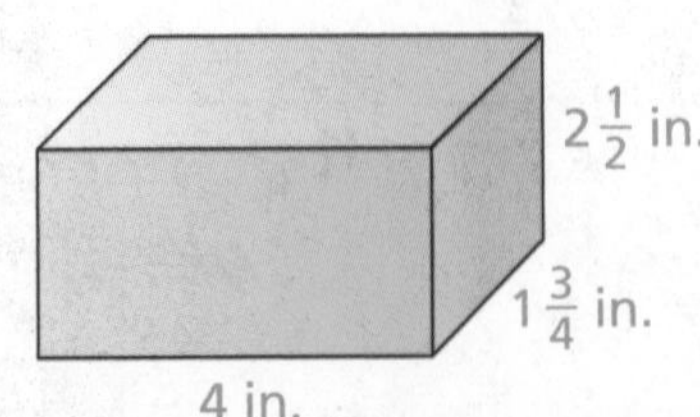

? Topic Essential Question

How can the areas of certain shapes be found? What are the meanings of surface area and volume and how can surface area and volume be found?

Vocabulary Review

Write the vocabulary term that best represents each item.

Vocabulary	net	rhombus	trapezoid	vertex	volume

1. The measure of the space this solid figure occupies.

2.

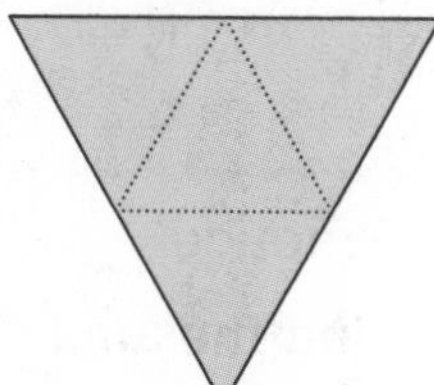

3.

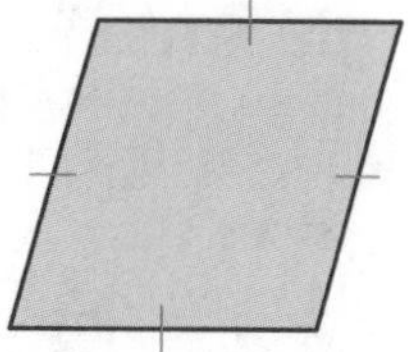

4. Point *A*

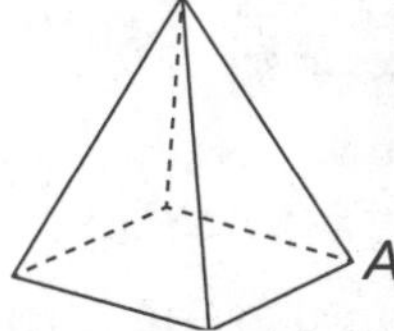

Use Vocabulary in Writing

Describe how to find the area of the quadrilateral. Use vocabulary words in your explanation.

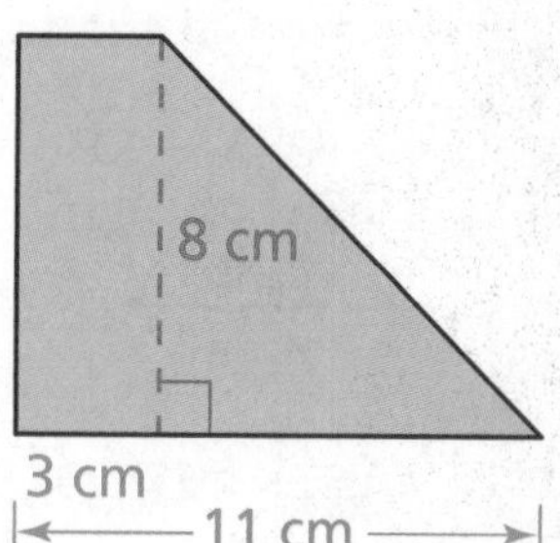

Concepts and Skills Review

LESSON 11-1 Find Areas of Parallelograms and Rhombuses

Quick Review

You can use the formula $A = bh$ to find the area of a parallelogram or a rhombus.

Example

Find the area of the parallelogram.

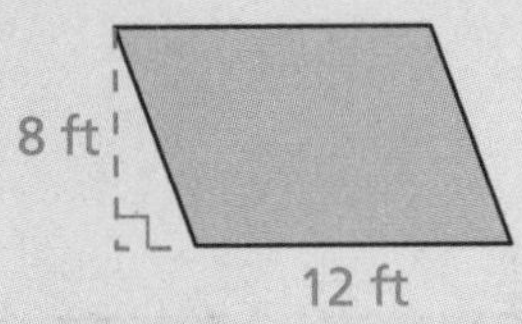

$A = bh$

$A = 12 \times 8$

$A = 96$

The area of the parallelogram is 96 ft^2.

Practice

In 1–4, find the area of each parallelogram or rhombus.

1.

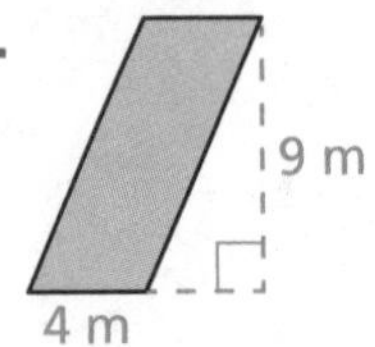

2.

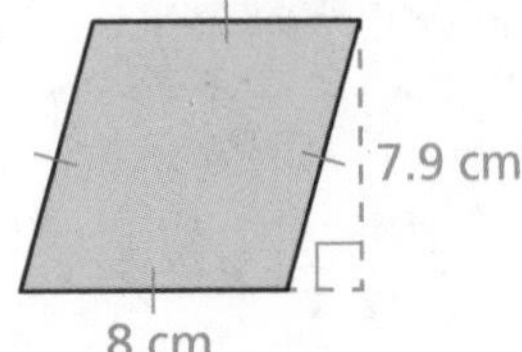

3. Rhombus
$b = 14$ in.
$h = 9$ in.

4. Parallelogram
$b = 12$ ft
$h = 8.5$ ft

5. A rhombus has an area of 375 mm^2 and a base of 25 mm. What is its height?

LESSON 11-2 Solve Triangle Area Problems

Quick Review

You can use the formula $A = \frac{1}{2}bh$ to find the area of any triangle.

Example

Find the area of the triangle.

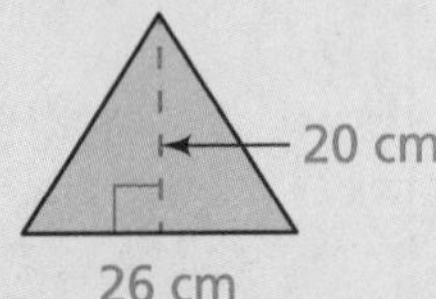

$A = \frac{1}{2} \times (26 \times 20)$

$A = 260$ cm^2

Practice

Find the area of each triangle.

1.

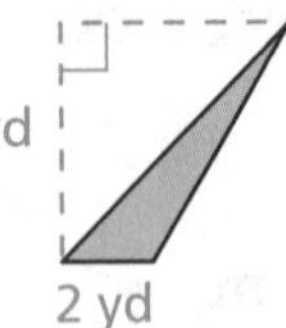

2.

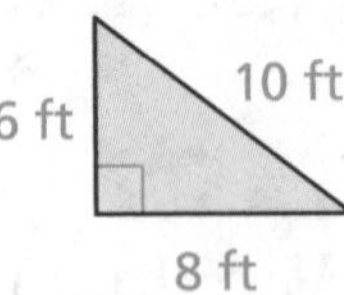

3. $b = 12.4$ cm
$h = 18$ cm

4. $b = 3.5$ m
$h = 6$ m

LESSON 11-3 Find Areas of Trapezoids and Kites

Quick Review

You can find the area of a trapezoid by decomposing it into a rectangle and one or more triangles. You can find the area of a kite by decomposing it into triangles.

Example

Find the area of the trapezoid and the kite.

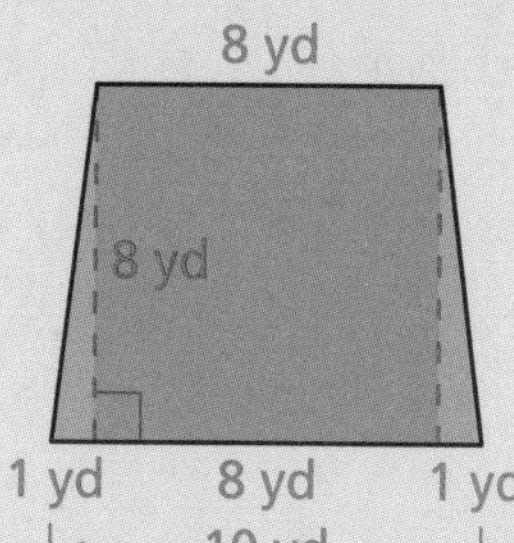

$\frac{1}{2}(1 \times 8) = 4$

$\frac{1}{2}(1 \times 8) = 4$

$8 \times 8 = 64$

$4 + 4 + 64 = 72 \text{ yd}^2$

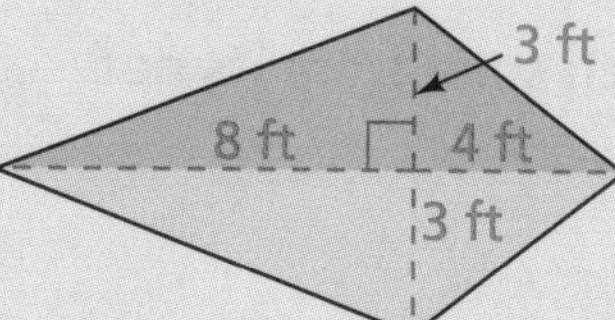

$\frac{1}{2}[(8 + 4) \times 3] = 18$

$\frac{1}{2}[(8 + 4) \times 3] = 18$

$18 + 18 = 36 \text{ ft}^2$

Practice

Find the area of each trapezoid or kite.

1.

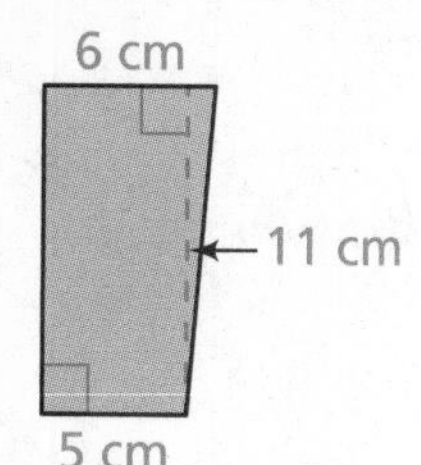

2.

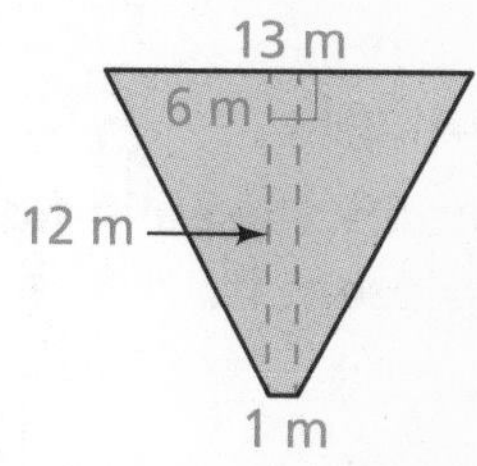

3.

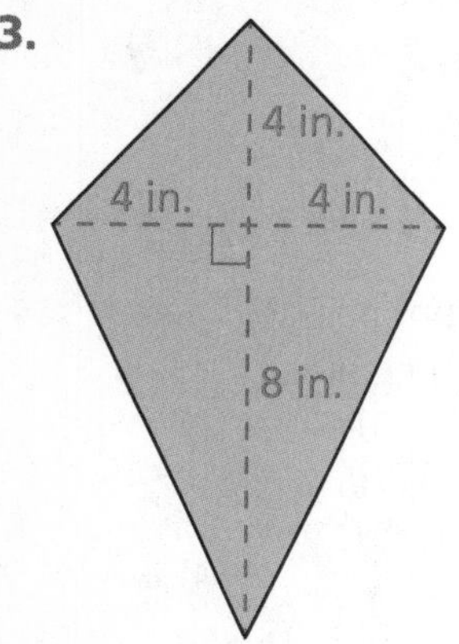

4.

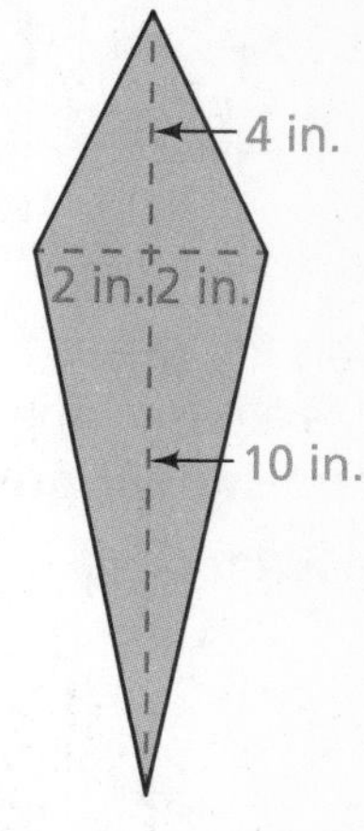

LESSON 11-4 Find Areas of Polygons

Quick Review

To find the area of a polygon, you can decompose or compose shapes, then use addition or subtraction to calculate the area.

Example

Find the area of the polygon.

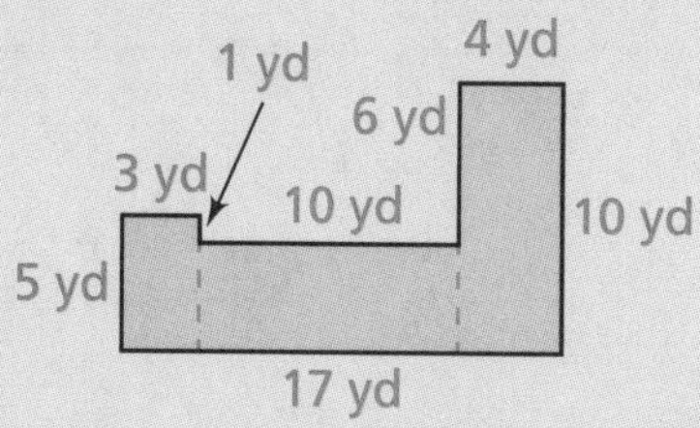

$\text{Area} = (3 \times 5) + (10 \times 4) + (4 \times 10)$

$= 15 + 40 + 40 = 95$

The area of the polygon is 95 yd^2.

Practice

1. Find the area of the polygon.

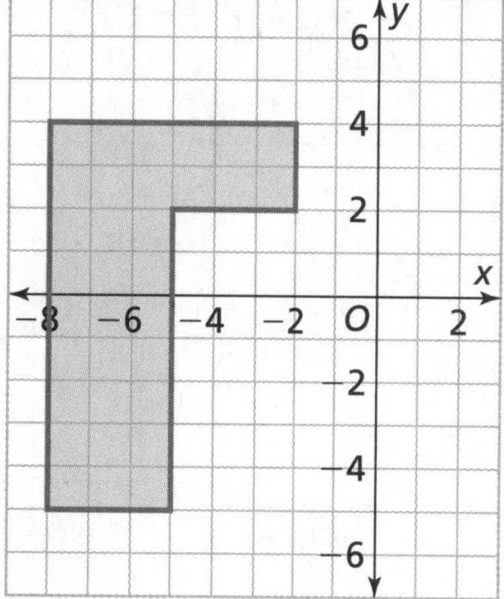

LESSON 11-5 Represent Solid Figures Using Nets

Quick Review

You can use nets to represent solid figures.

Example

Classify the solid figure and draw a net to represent it.

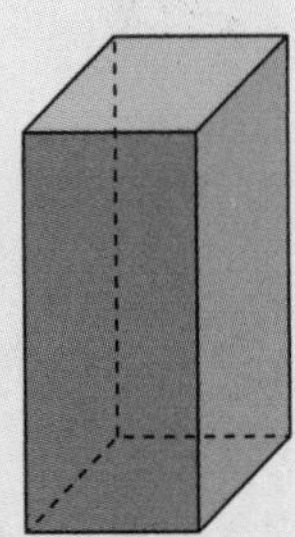

This figure has two congruent parallel bases, so it is a prism. The bases are rectangles, so it is a **rectangular prism**.

Net of rectangular prism:

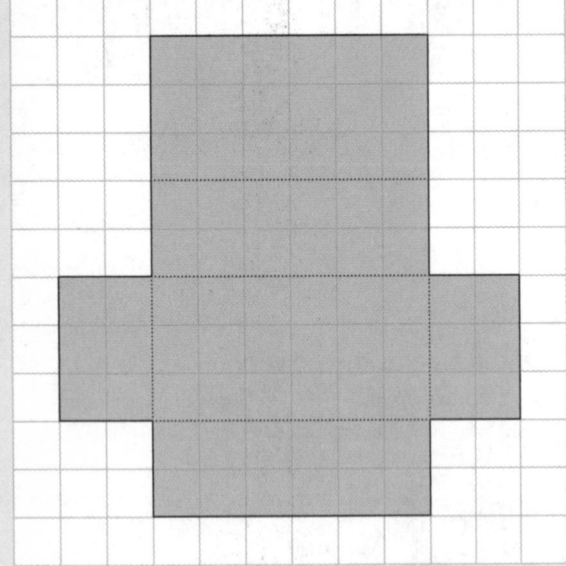

Practice

In 1 and 2, classify the solid figures.

1.

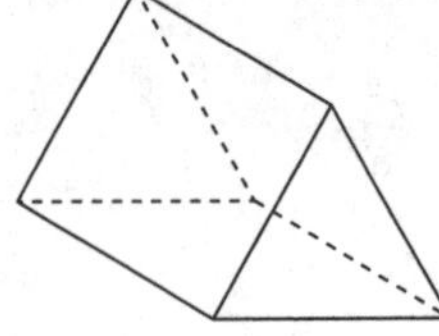

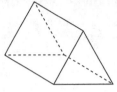

2.

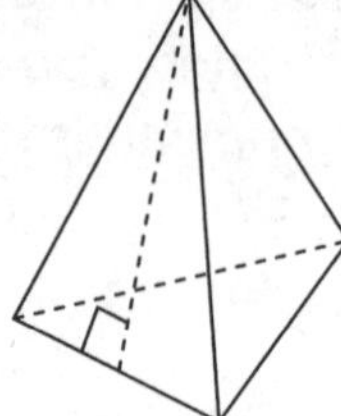

3. Draw a net of the pyramid shown.

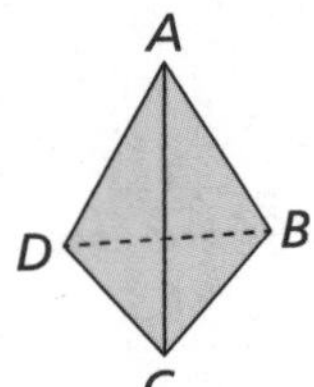

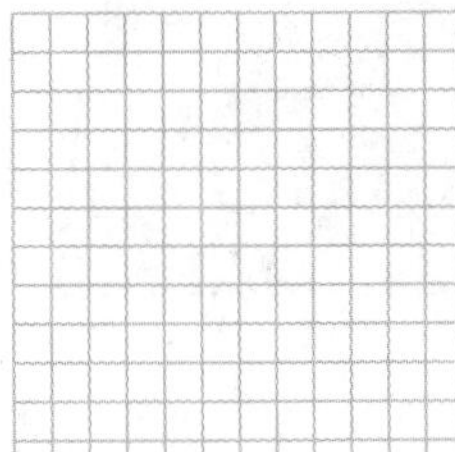

In 4 and 5, identify each solid from its net.

4.

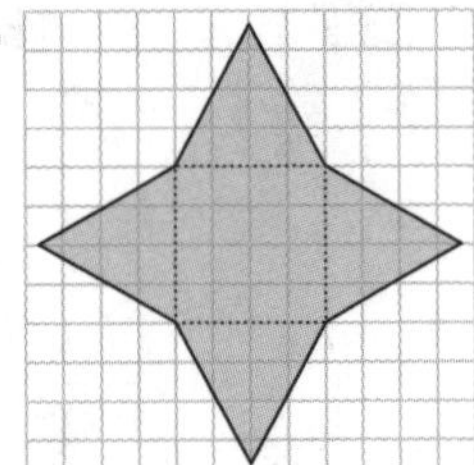

5.

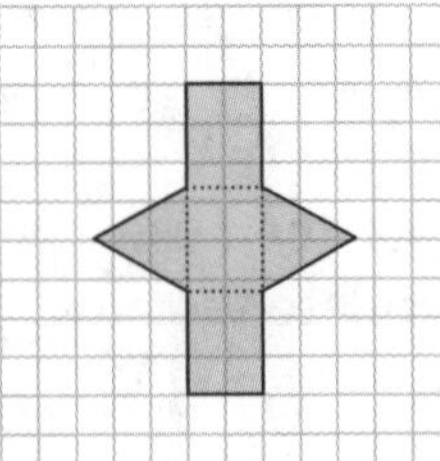

LESSON 11-6 Find Surface Areas of Prisms

Quick Review

You can use a net or a formula to find the surface area of a prism.

Example

Find the surface area.

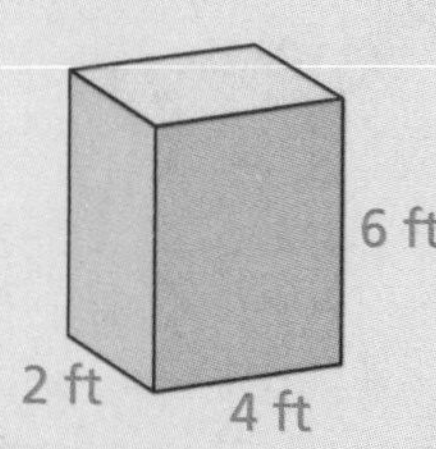

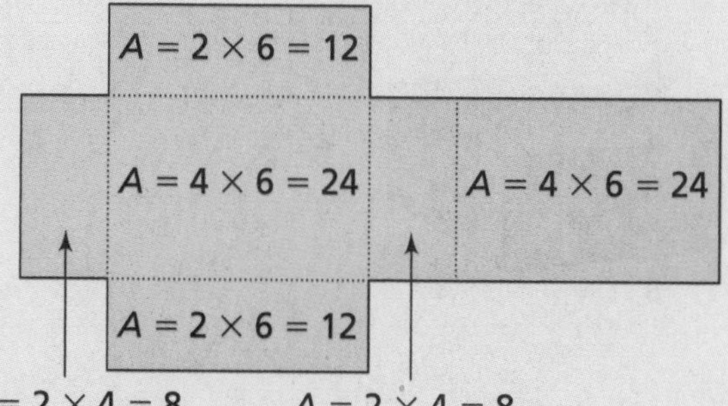

$SA = 2(8) + 2(12) + 2(24) = 88 \text{ ft}^2$

Practice

Find the surface area of each prism.

1.

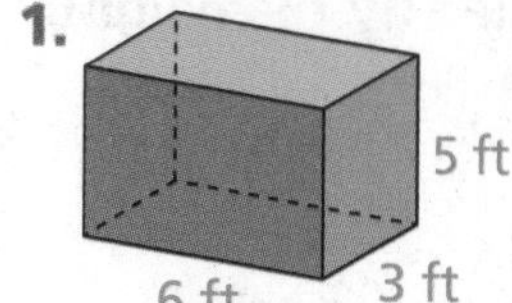

2.

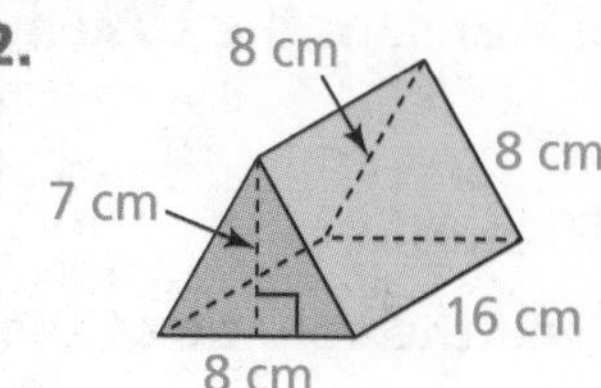

3. Cube
$s = 9.4$ m

4. Cube
$s = 7$ cm

5. Rectangular prism
$\ell = 12$ in.
$w = 7$ in.
$h = 3$ in.

6. Rectangular prism
$\ell = 5$ cm
$w = 6$ cm
$h = 7$ cm

LESSON 11-7 Find Surface Areas of Pyramids

Quick Review

You can use a net or a formula to find the surface area of a pyramid.

Example

Find the surface area.

8.7 m
10 m
10 m

Area of one triangle:

$T = \frac{1}{2} \times 10 \times 8.7 = 43.5$

$SA = 4T$
$= 4 \times 43.5$
$= 174$

The surface area of the pyramid is 174 m^2.

Practice

In 1 and 2, find the surface area of each pyramid.

1.

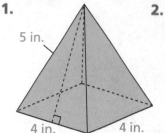

5 in.
4 in.
4 in.

2.

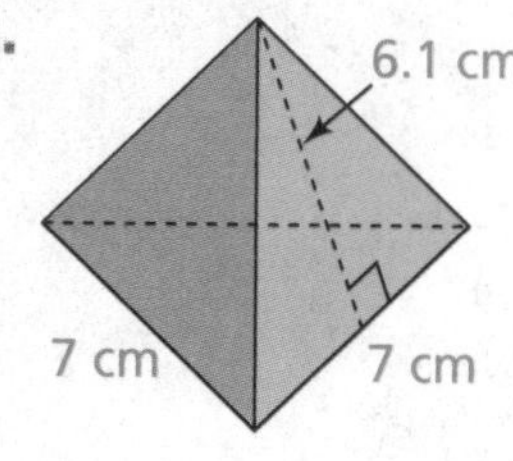

3. Each side of the base of a square pyramid is 10 ft and the height of each triangular face is 7 ft. Find the surface area of the pyramid.

LESSON 11-8 Find Volume with Fractional Edge Lengths

Quick Review

The volume of a rectangular prism is equal to the area of the base multiplied by the height.

Example

Find the volume of the rectangular prism.

STEP 1 Find the number of small $\frac{1}{4}$-in. cubes that will fill the prism.

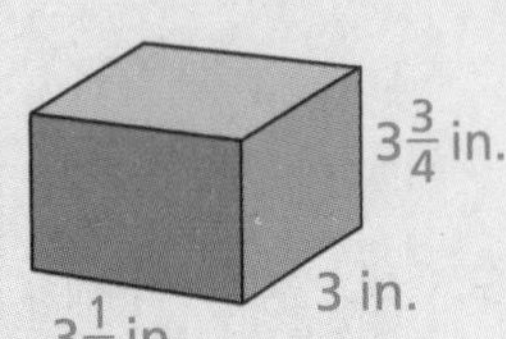

14 small $\frac{1}{4}$-in. cubes fit along the $3\frac{1}{2}$ in. side.

12 small $\frac{1}{4}$-in. cubes fit along the 3 in. side.

15 small $\frac{1}{4}$-in. cubes fit along the $3\frac{3}{4}$ in. side.

$14 \cdot 12 \cdot 15 = 2{,}520$ small $\frac{1}{4}$-in. cubes fill the prism.

STEP 2 Find the volume of each small $\frac{1}{4}$-in. cube.

$V = \ell wh = \frac{1}{4}\text{ in.} \cdot \frac{1}{4}\text{ in.} \cdot \frac{1}{4}\text{ in.} = \frac{1}{64}\text{ in.}^3$

STEP 3 Find the volume of the prism.

$2{,}520 \cdot \frac{1}{64}\text{ in.}^3 = 39\frac{3}{8}\text{ in.}^3$

You can also use a formula.

$V = \ell wh = 3\frac{1}{2}\text{ in.} \times 3\text{ in.} \times 3\frac{3}{4}\text{ in.} = 39\frac{3}{8}\text{ in.}^3$

Practice

Find the volume of each rectangular prism.

1.

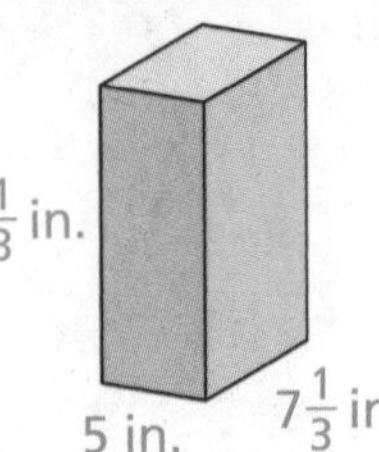

2.

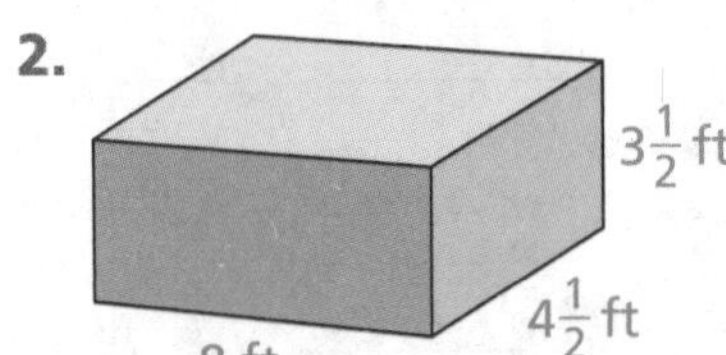

3.

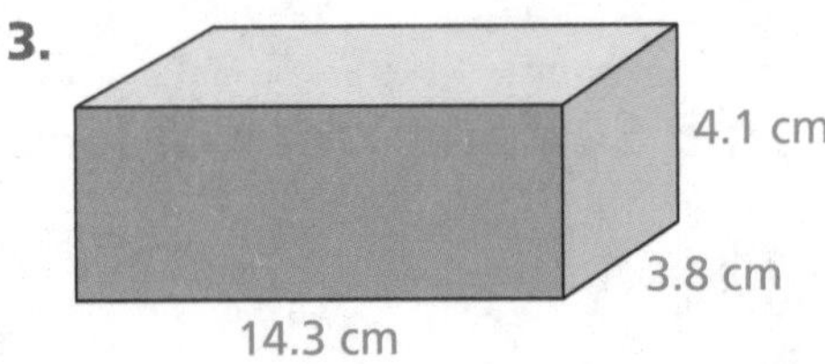

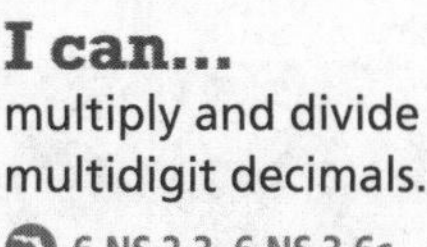

Hidden Clue

For each ordered pair, simplify the two coordinates. Then locate and label the corresponding point on the graph. Draw line segments to connect the points in alphabetical order. Connect *L* to *E* to complete the picture, then use the completed picture to help answer the riddle below.

I can...
multiply and divide multidigit decimals.
6.NS.2.3, 6.NS.3.6c

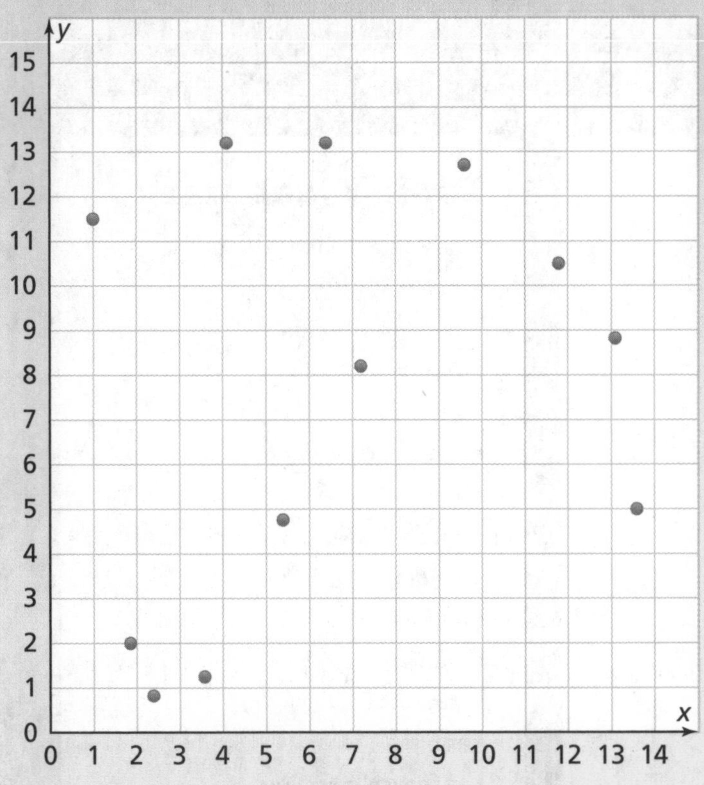

A $(1.2 \times 1.55, 2.7 \div 1.35)$ ____ , ____

B $(1.25 \times 1.92, 0.48 \div 0.6)$ ____ , ____

C $(5.04 \div 1.4, 0.5 \times 2.5)$ ____ , ____

D $(2.16 \times 2.5, 11.9 \div 2.5)$ ____ , ____

E $(16.56 \div 2.3, 5.125 \times 1.6)$ ____ , ____

F $(6.12 \div 0.45, 6.25 \times 0.8)$ ____ , ____

G $(2.62 \times 5, 12.32 \div 1.4)$ ____ , ____

H $(29.5 \times 0.4, 3.675 \div 0.35)$ ____ , ____

I $(12.48 \div 1.3, 10.16 \times 1.25)$ ____ , ____

J $(20 \times 0.32, 59.4 \div 4.5)$ ____ , ____

K $(7.79 \div 1.9, 40 \times 0.33)$ ____ , ____

L $(25 \times 0.04, 48.3 \div 4.2)$ ____ , ____

DISPLAY, DESCRIBE, AND SUMMARIZE DATA

? Topic Essential Question

How can data be described by a single number? How can tables and graphs be used to represent data and answer questions?

Topic Overview

Topic Vocabulary

- absolute deviation
- box plot
- data distribution
- frequency table
- histogram
- interquartile range (IQR)
- mean
- mean absolute deviation (MAD)
- median
- mode
- outlier
- quartile
- range
- statistical question

Go online | **PearsonRealize.com**

Lesson Digital Resources

INTERACTIVE STUDENT EDITION
Access online or offline.

VISUAL LEARNING ANIMATION
Interact with visual learning animations.

ACTIVITY Use with ***Solve & Discuss It, Explore It***, and ***Explain It*** activities, and to explore Examples.

VIDEOS Watch clips to support ***3-Act Mathematical Modeling Lessons*** and ***STEM Proje***

Vocal Range

Vocal Range

Have you ever disagreed with the judge on a reality TV show? Reality TV competitions rely on the different opinions of the judges to make the show more exciting. There are lots of factors to consider when comparing two contestants on a show. Think about this during the 3-Act Mathematical Modeling lesson.

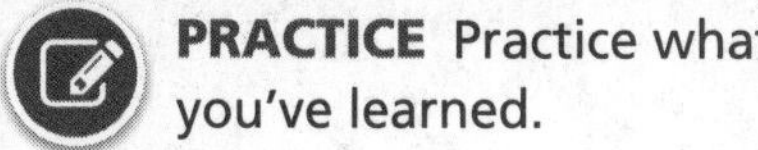

PRACTICE Practice what you've learned.

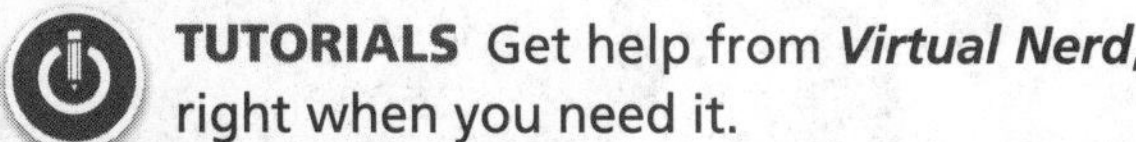

TUTORIALS Get help from ***Virtual Nerd***, right when you need it.

MATH TOOLS Explore math with digital tools.

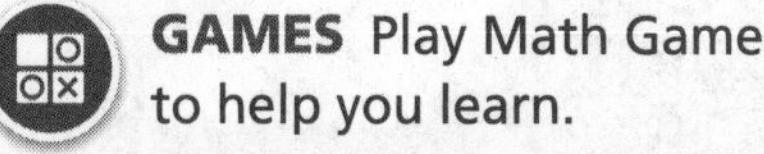

GAMES Play Math Games to help you learn.

KEY CONCEPT Review important lesson content.

GLOSSARY Read and listen to English/Spanish definitions.

ASSESSMENT Show what you've learned.

TOPIC 12

enVision® STEM Project

VIDEO

Did You Know?

Earthquakes are caused by the sudden release of energy in the Earth's crust when friction between tectonic plates causes rocks to break along fault lines.

RING OF FIRE

PACIFIC OCEAN

Nearly 80% of Earth's largest earthquakes occur along the "Ring of Fire." Many tectonic plates meet in this horseshoe-shaped region around the Pacific Ocean.

The 1964 Alaskan earthquake magnitude of 9.2 was the strongest recorded in North America. It sent tsunamis as far away as Peru, New Zealand, and Japan.

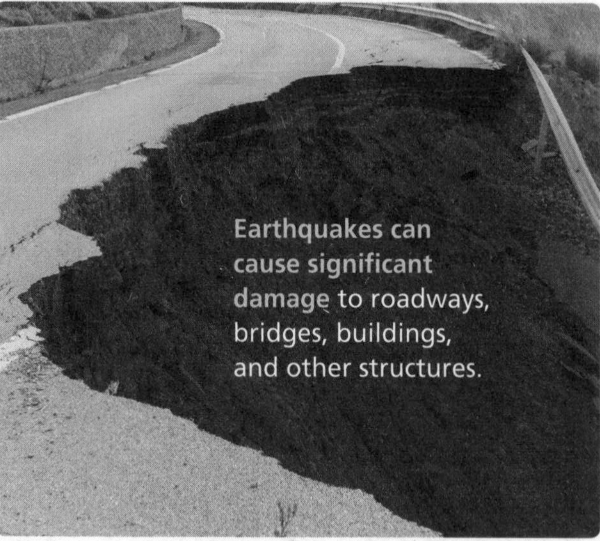

Earthquakes can cause significant damage to roadways, bridges, buildings, and other structures.

The shape of a pagoda is known for resisting damage from earthquakes.

Your Task: Shake It Up

Engineers design sturdy bridges, buildings, dams and other structures that can withstand earthquakes. They also devise detection devices to predict earthquakes. You and your classmates will gather and display data about earthquake frequency and magnitude. You will analyze the data and determine what constraints engineers must consider when designing roadways, bridges, homes, and other structures.

Review What You Know!

Vocabulary

Choose the best term from the box to complete each sentence.

bar graph
data
dot plot
tally chart

1. ________ are pieces of gathered information.
2. Display data as marks above a number line in a ________.
3. Use the lengths of bars to show and compare data in a ________.

Summarize Data

Use the number of text messages Henry sent each day: 6, 12, 2, 6, 3, 4, 2, 5, 6.

4. What is the least value?
5. What is the greatest value?
6. What numbers are repeated?
7. How many text messages did Henry send in all?

Display Data

8. The table shows the time students spend doing chores each day. Draw a dot plot to show the data.

Minutes Doing Chores Each Day
20, 25, 45, 20, 30, 40, 30, 25, 20, 15, 35, 40

Analyze Data

Use the graph to answer the questions about a student's test performance.

9. How many more points were earned on Test 3 than on Test 1?
10. Which two tests have the least difference in score? What is the difference?
11. What is the greatest difference between two scores? How do you know?

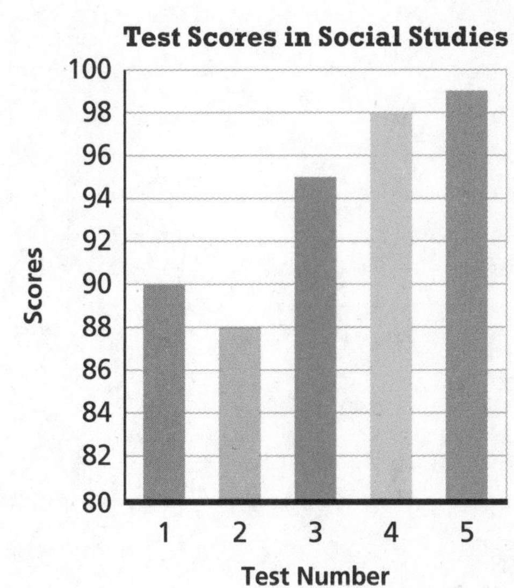

Build Vocabulary

Complete the graphic organizer by writing the definition of each measure.

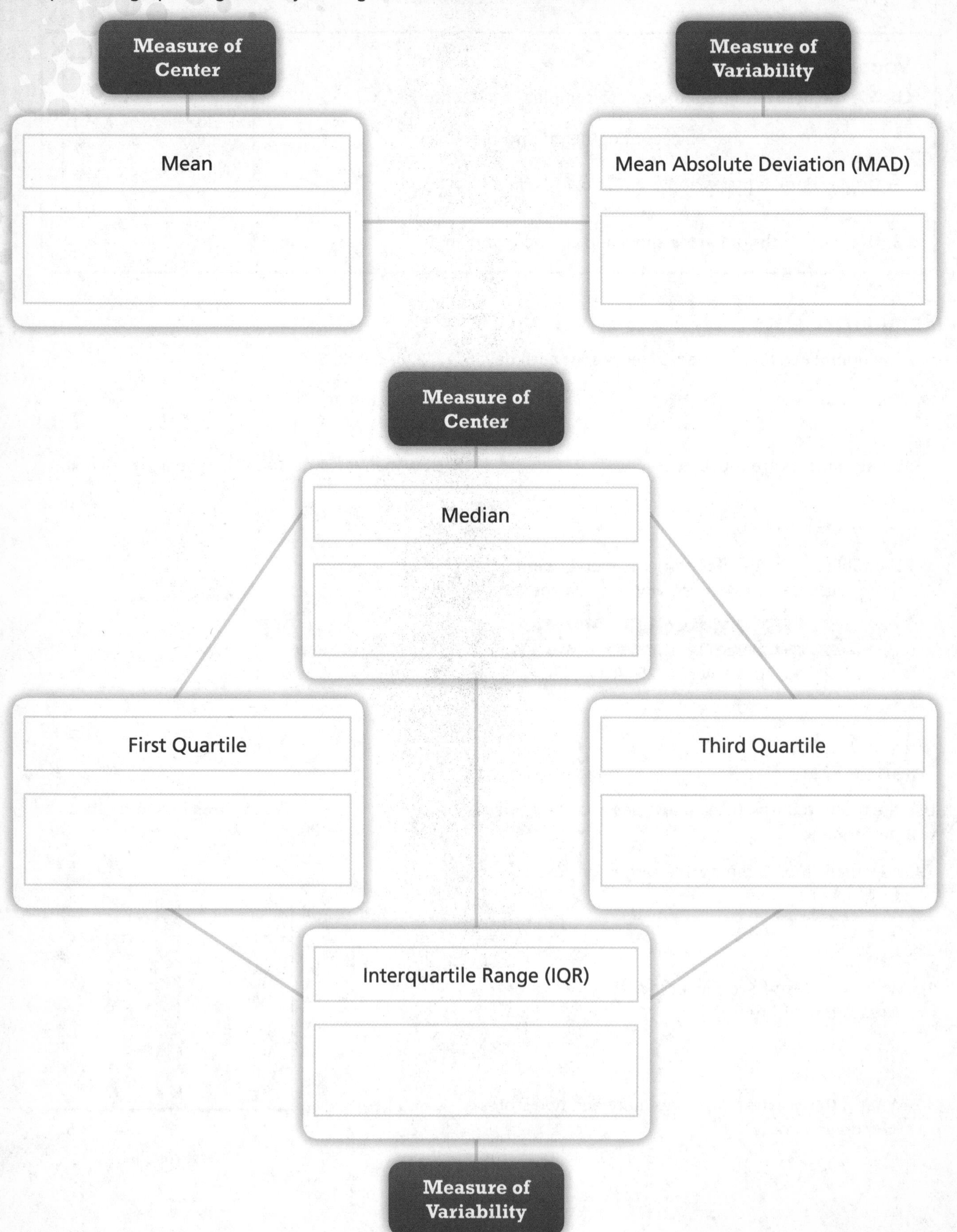

Solve & Discuss It!

Ms. Jackson wrote a question on the board. Then she collected student responses to the question and recorded them in a tally chart. What question could she have asked? Is there more than one possible response to the question? Explain.

Books	
0	III
1	~~IIII~~
2	~~IIII~~ I
3	IIII
4	II
5	I

Make Sense and Persevere
What other questions could you ask that would result in a variety of numerical answers?

Lesson 12-1
Recognize Statistical Questions

Go Online | PearsonRealize.com

I can...
identify and write statistical questions.

MAFS.6.SP.1.1 Recognize a statistical question as one that anticipates variability in the data related to the question and accounts for it in the answers. ... Also 6.SP.2.4

MAFS.K12.MP.1.1, MP.2.1, MP.4.1, MP.8.1

Focus on math practices

Reasoning Suppose Ms. Jackson wants to know the amount of time her students spent outdoors the previous afternoon. What question might she ask each student to gather the data?

Essential Question How are statistical questions different from other questions?

EXAMPLE 1  Recognize a Statistical Question

Scan for Multimedia 

Mr. Borden asked his students a question and recorded the data in a table. What question did Mr. Borden ask?

- **What is the area of an $8\frac{1}{2}'' \times 11''$ sheet of notebook paper?**
- **How many sheets of paper did you use last week?**
- **Did Bill use notebook paper to write his book report?**

Make Sense and Persevere How does thinking about possible answers to the questions help you determine which questions are statistical?

Sheets of Paper Used Last Week

Number of Sheets	Number of Students
5	I
10	I
15	II
20	IIII
25	~~IIII~~ I
30	~~IIII~~

A **statistical question** always has variability in the responses. This is, it has a range of responses.

The question *How many sheets of paper did you use last week?* can have a range of answers so it is a statistical question.

The questions *What is the area of an $8\frac{1}{2}'' \times 11''$ sheet of notebook paper?* and *Did Bill use notebook paper to write his book report?* have only one answer, so they are not statistical questions.

Mr. Borden asked, *How many sheets of paper did you use last week?*

You can display the answers to Mr. Borden's question in a bar graph.

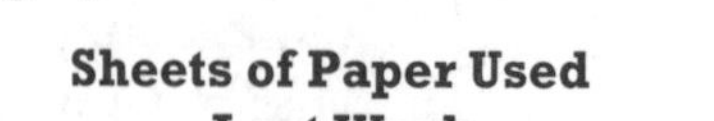

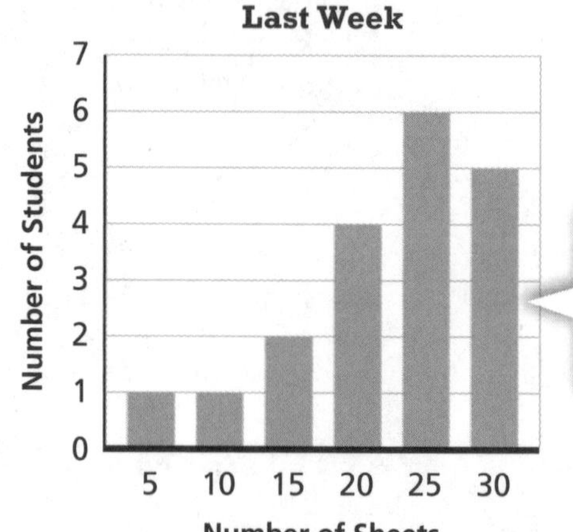

The bar graph shows that there is a range of possible answers to Mr. Borden's question.

Mr. Borden's question is a statistical question.

Try It!

Is the question *What was the high temperature on March 8 of last year?* a statistical question? Explain.

Convince Me! How could you change the question above to make it a statistical question?

EXAMPLE 2

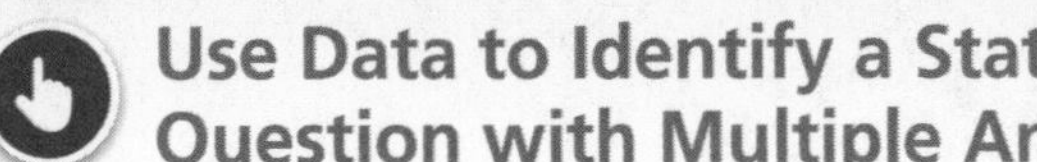

Use Data to Identify a Statistical Question with Multiple Answers

Lucia surveyed the students in her class and made a dot plot of the results. What question could Lucia have asked?

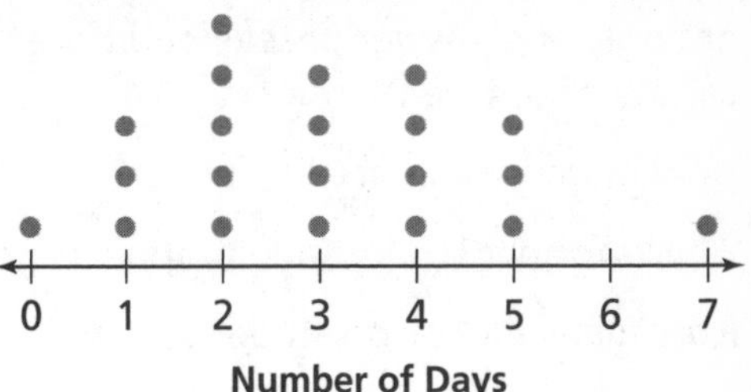

Look at the title and labels on the dot plot.

> **Model with Math** A dot plot can be used to display the answers to a statistical question.

The dot plot shows the number of days different students exercise each week. The statistical question Lucia could have asked is *How many days do you exercise each week?*

Try It!

What is another statistical question Lucia might ask about the exercise the students in her class do each week?

EXAMPLE 3

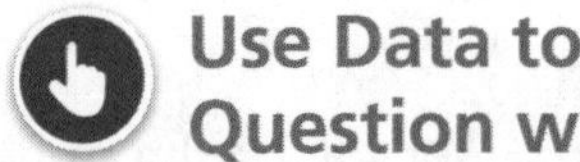

Use Data to Identify a Statistical Question with Two Answers

Dante surveyed students to see how they feel about a proposal to choose a new school mascot. The frequency table shows the results. What question did Dante likely ask? Is this a statistical question?

Dante likely asked a question such as *Do you want a new mascot?* There are only two answers, Yes or No. Because there is more than one possible answer, this is a statistical question.

Yes	~~||||~~ ~~||||~~ ~~||||~~ ~~||||~~ ||	22
No	~~||||~~ ~~||||~~ ~~||||~~ |||	18

Try It!

How could Dante change his statistical question so that there would be more than two possible answers?

KEY CONCEPT

To recognize and write statistical questions, determine whether the question has only one answer or several different answers. Statistical questions have a variety of different answers.

How many nickels are in a dollar?	Not statistical
Which former U.S. president appears on a nickel?	Not statistical
How many nickels do students carry in their backpacks?	Statistical

Do You Understand?

1. **Essential Question** How are statistical questions different from other questions?

2. **Generalize** How does examining the answers to a question help you determine if the question is a statistical question?

3. Write a question about movies that your classmates saw last month. Is the question you wrote a statistical question? Justify your response.

4. Choose which is a statistical question: *What are the ages of the students in this class?* or *How many pennies equal 1 dollar?* Explain.

Do You Know How?

5. Determine which of the questions below are statistical questions.

   a. In which months are the birthdays of everyone in your class?

   b. Does Sue wear glasses?

   c. Who is the current president of the United States?

   d. How tall are the students in Grade 6?

   e. What is the least populated state?

   f. How many fish are in the pond?

6. Mr. Borden asked his students, *How far from school do you live?* Is his question a statistical question? Explain.

7. Mr. Borden also asked his students, *How do you get to school each day?* Is this question statistical? Explain.

Name: ______________________________

Scan for Multimedia

Practice & Problem Solving

In 8 and 9, write a statistical question that you could ask to gather data on each topic.

8. Number of pets classmates own

9. Heights of different household plants

10. Kim asked her classmates, *How many siblings do you have?* She collected the following responses: 0, 1, 2, 1, 2, 0, 3, 1, 0, 5, 5, 1, 3, 1, 0, 2, 4, 1, 3, 0. Make a dot plot to display the data.

11. Sergei asked his classmates, *Will you take Spanish or French next year?* He collected these responses: 15 classmates chose Spanish and 13 chose French. Make a frequency table to display the data.

12. Is the following a statistical question? Explain. *How many plays do students see in a year?*

13. Is the following a statistical question? Explain. *How do shoppers in a town pay for groceries?*

In 14 and 15, use the dot plot at the right.

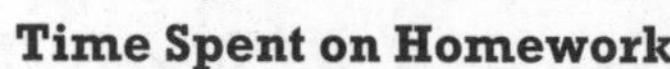

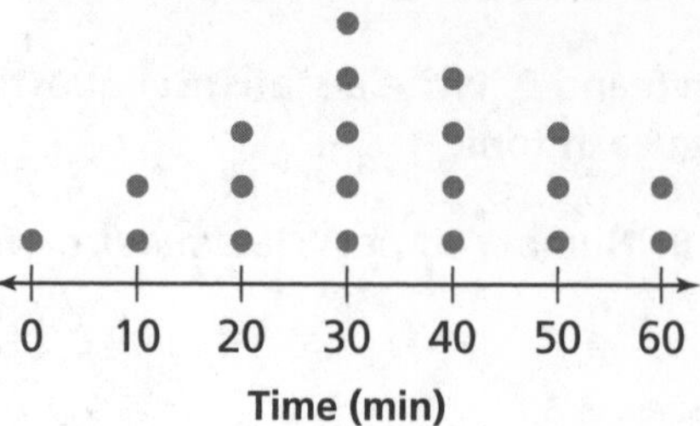

14. **Make Sense and Persevere** What statistical question could have been asked to collect the data shown in the dot plot?

15. **Higher Order Thinking** If the data in the dot plot show how many minutes students spent on homework the previous night, how many hours in all did these students spend doing homework? Did a typical student from this group spend more or fewer than 20 minutes on homework?

16. **Vocabulary** Wyatt says that a *statistical question* must have a numerical answer. Do you agree with Wyatt? Explain.

17. **Reasoning** Ms. Miller asks parents, *Do you support switching to a new lunch vendor for our school program?* How many different responses could she get? Is this a statistical question?

Assessment Practice

18. Ms. Williams asked each student in her class these two questions:

    - *How many digits are in a phone number, including the area code?*
    - *In a typical week, on how many days do you spend some time watching television?*

    Which of the questions that Ms. Williams asked is a statistical question? Explain. 6.SP.1.1

19. Select all of the statistical questions. 6.SP.1.1

    - ☐ What is your favorite color?
    - ☐ Does Carmen wear braces?
    - ☐ How many books did you read last week?
    - ☐ Which U.S. state has the largest land area?
    - ☐ Should the basketball team purchase new uniforms?

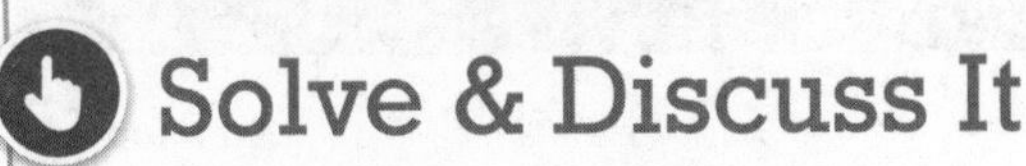

Solve & Discuss It!

Eight students were surveyed about the number of hours they spend each week reading for fun. Order their responses from least to greatest values. What do you notice about the number of hours these students spent reading each week?

Lesson 12-2
Summarize Data Using Mean, Median, Mode, and Range

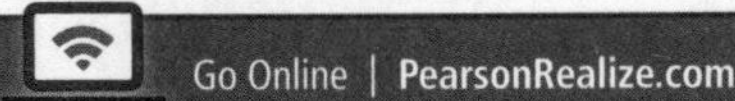

I can...
identify the mean, median, mode, and range of a data set.

MAFS.6.SP.1.3 Recognize that a measure of center for a numerical data set summarizes all of its values with a single number, while a measure of variation describes how its values vary with a single number. Also 6.SP.2.5c

MAFS.K12.MP.2.1, MP.3.1, MP.7.1, MP.8.1

Look for Relationships
How does ordering the responses from least to greatest help you analyze the data set?

Focus on math practices

Critique Reasoning Jamal says that the middle value in a data set is the number that occurs most often. Evan disagrees. Why does Jamal say what he says and why does Evan disagree? Explain.

Essential Question How can you use a single measure to describe a data set?

EXAMPLE 1  Use the Mean to Describe a Data Set

Scan for Multimedia 

Carla is in a bowling league. The league is ranking the teams by average score. What is the mean, or average, final score of the five bowlers on Carla's team?

The **mean**, or average, is the sum of all the values in a data set divided by the total number of data values in the set.

> **Generalize** You can summarize a data set by using a mean.

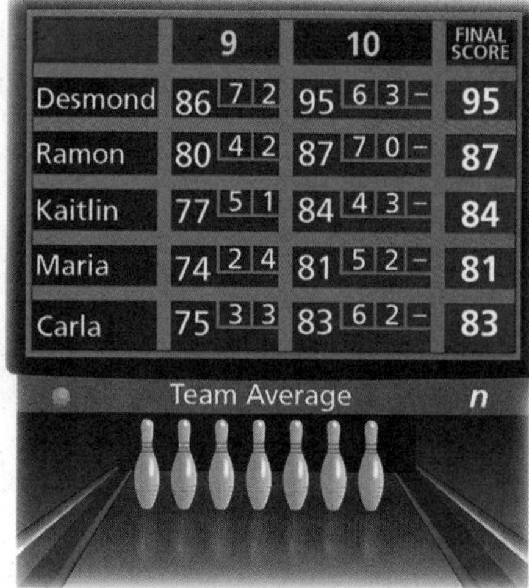

9
10
FINAL SCORE
Desmond 86 7 2 95 6 3 – 95
Ramon 80 4 2 87 7 0 – 87
Kaitlin 77 5 1 84 4 3 – 84
Maria 74 2 4 81 5 2 – 81
Carla 75 3 3 83 6 2 – 83
Team Average n

To find the mean, equally share the final scores among the five bowlers.

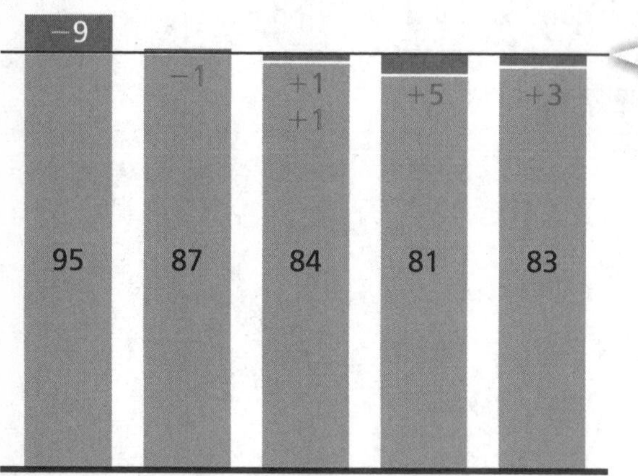

A mean is a measure of center. A measure of center summarizes a data set with a single value.

To calculate the mean, add the scores in the data set. Then divide the sum by the number of values in the data set.

$$\begin{array}{r} \overset{2}{9}5 \\ 87 \\ 84 \\ 81 \\ +\,83 \\ \hline 430 \end{array} \qquad \begin{array}{r} 86 \\ 5\overline{)430} \\ -\,40 \\ \hline 30 \\ -\,30 \\ \hline 0 \end{array}$$

The mean, or average, final score is 86.

Try It!

The next week, Maria bowls a 151-point game. The other bowlers match their scores. What is the new mean final score for the team? Explain.

Convince Me! How did the mean final score change from the Example to the Try It!?

EXAMPLE 2  Use the Median to Describe a Data Set

Trey and Sarah each download songs to their music libraries. Their players list each type of music and the total playing time in minutes for each type. How can Trey and Sarah each summarize their data sets using the median?

The **median** is a measure of center. It is the middle data value. To find the median, order the values from least to greatest, then find the middle value.

Trey's Music Library

Music Type	Minutes
Blues	62
Classical	72
Country	61
Gospel	67
Jazz	67
Movie Soundtrack	63
Popular	59

Sarah's Music Library

Music Type	Minutes
Rock	37
Rap	42
Hip Hop	38
Bluegrass	46
New Age	51
Opera	35

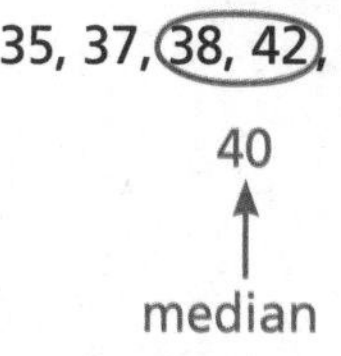

Find the median for Trey's data set.

59, 61, 62, 63, 67, 67, 72

median: 63

Trey's median playing time is 63 minutes.

Find the median for Sarah's data set.

35, 37, 38, 42, 46, 51

median: 40

The median is the average of the two middle values.

Sarah's median playing time is 40 minutes.

EXAMPLE 3  Use the Mode to Describe a Data Set

Look at Trey's and Sarah's music libraries. How can Trey and Sarah each summarize their data sets using the mode?

The **mode** is a measure of center. It is the value that occurs most often. A data set can have one mode, no mode, or more than one mode.

Find the mode for Trey's data set.

59, 61, 62, 63, 67, 67, 72

mode

The value 67 appears twice. Every other value only appears once.

Trey's mode playing time is 67 minutes.

Find the mode for Sarah's data set.

35, 37, 38, 42, 46, 51

No values repeat in Sarah's data set.

There is no mode playing time in Sarah's data set.

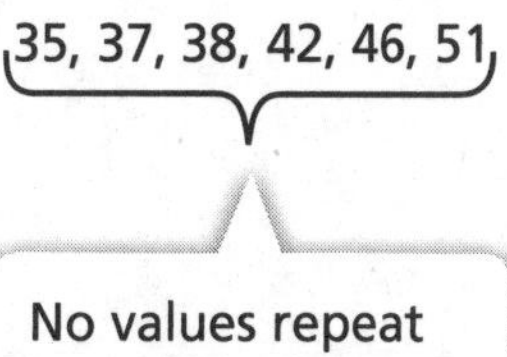 Try It!

Nadia's grades on four quizzes were 95, 75, 85, and 95. Find the mean, median, and mode for Nadia's grades.

EXAMPLE 4 Use the Range to Describe a Data Set

Look at Trey's and Sarah's music libraries. What is the range of the playing times in each of their data sets?

The **range** is a measure of variability. A measure of variability describes how the values in a data set vary with a single number. The range is the difference of the greatest value and the least value.

Trey's Music Library

Music Type	Minutes
Blues	62
Classical	72
Country	61
Gospel	67
Jazz	67
Movie Soundtrack	63
Popular	59

Sarah's Music Library

Music Type	Minutes
Rock	37
Rap	42
Hip Hop	38
Bluegrass	46
New Age	51
Opera	35

Find the range for Trey's data set.

least value → (59), 61, 62, 63, 67, 67, (72) ← greatest value

72 − 59 = (13) ← range

The range of playing times is 13 minutes.

Find the range for Sarah's data set.

least value → (35), 37, 38, 42, 46, (51) ← greatest value

51 − 35 = (16) ← range

The range of playing times is 16 minutes.

EXAMPLE 5 Use the Mean, Median, Mode, and Range to Describe a Data Set

Seven people waited in line for the "Whirl and Twirl" carnival ride. Find the mean, median, mode, and range of the wait times for the carnival ride. What do the mean, median, and mode tell you about the wait times? What does the range, as a measure of variability, tell you about the wait times?

Carnival Ride Wait Times

Person	Wait time (min.)
A	12
B	12
C	15
D	10
E	14
F	15
G	13

Mean: 13

Median: 13

Modes: 12 and 15

Range: 5

The mean, median, and mode each give a measure of the typical wait time for the ride. The mean and median wait times were 13 minutes. Two pairs each waited 12 or 15 minutes. The range uses a single number to describe how the wait times vary. The wait times vary by 5 minutes.

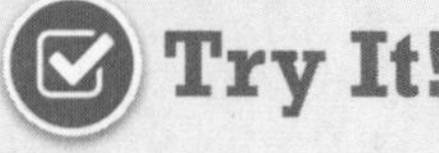

Try It!

Find the mean, median, mode, and range for the following set of data.

4, 6, 8, 3, 2, 1, 0, 12, 9

KEY CONCEPT 

You can summarize a set of data using a measure of center, such as the mean, median, or mode, or a measure of variability, such as the range.

Mean

$(7 + 10 + 16 + 9 + 12 + 21 + 14 + 8 + 13 + 15) \div 10 = 12.5$

Median

7, 8, 9, 10, 12, 13, 14, 15, 16, 21

$(12 + 13) \div 2 = 12.5$

Mode

7, 8, 9, 10, 12, 13, 14, 15, 16, 21

There is no mode.

Range

(7), 8, 9, 10, 12, 13, 14, 15, 16, (21)

$21 - 7 = 14$

The average number of hours of TV watched each week is 12.5 hours. The range of hours watched is 14 hours.

Number of Hours of TV Watched in a Week	
Juan	7
Tyrone	10
Abigail	16
Lateisha	9
Helen	12
Albert	21
Tim	14
Josh	8
Anita	13
Henry	15

Do You Understand?

1. **Essential Question** How can you use a single measure to describe a data set?

2. Maddie scored 3 goals, 2 goals, and 4 goals during her last three soccer games. How can you find the mean, or average, number of goals Maddie scored?

3. **Use Structure** Why is it important to order the data when finding the median?

Do You Know How?

The table shows data about the students in three classes.

Teacher	Boys	Girls
Ms. Green	15	14
Mr. Nesbit	12	12
Ms. Jackson	12	16

4. What is the mean number of boys in the three classes? What is the mean number of girls in the three classes?

5. What is the mode of the number of girls in the three classes?

6. What is the median number of students in the three classes?

Name: ______________________________

Practice & Problem Solving  

Scan for Multimedia

In 7–10, use the data shown in the table to find each mean.

7. Technical marks from judges

8. Presentation marks from judges

9. Find the combined marks, or total score, awarded by each of the 7 judges. Record your answers in the table.

10. What is the mean total score awarded by the judges?

A U.S. Figure Skater's Scores

Judge	Technical Marks	Presentation Marks	Total Score
A	5.9	5.4	
B	5.8	5.7	
C	5.8	5.6	
D	5.6	5.3	
E	5.9	5.5	
F	5.6	5.3	
G	6.0	5.7	

In 11–14, use the data in the table.

States Traveled To or Lived In
1, 3, 5, 2, 5, 2, 10, 7, 1, 2, 4, 1, 2, 7, 12

11. Order the data from least to greatest.

12. What are the median, mode, and range of the data?

13. Use Structure The student who traveled to 3 states visited 3 new states during a vacation. Does increasing the 3 to 6 change the median? If so, how?

14. Look for Relationships Does increasing the 3 to 6 change the mode? If so, how?

In 15–17, use the data table.

15. What is the average low temperature forecasted for the five days?

16. What is the average high temperature forecasted for the five days?

17. The forecast for Wednesday is later changed to a high of 70°F. Without calculating the new mean, describe how this changes the mean high temperature for the 5 days.

Forecasted Temperatures

Day	Low (°F)	High (°F)
Monday	42	55
Tuesday	44	57
Wednesday	45	60
Thursday	34	45
Friday	40	50

18. Vocabulary What term is used to describe the difference between the greatest and the least values of a data set?

19. Critique Reasoning Lewis thinks that since the data 5, 0, 4, 0, 0 has a mode of 0, the data has no mode. Critique Lewis's reasoning.

20. Chester scored 84, 88, and 80 on his first 3 math tests. How can you find Chester's mean, or average, score on these tests?

21. Reasoning Use the information in Exercise 20. Suppose Chester scores a 90 on his next test. Without doing any calculations, will Chester's mean score increase, decrease, or stay the same? Explain.

22. On Monday, Jeremiah collects data on the number of cars that pass through an intersection each hour from 6 A.M. to 10 A.M. He records the following data: 15, 27, 37, 29, and 12. If Jeremiah removes the 12 from his data set, will the mean change? Explain.

23. On Tuesday, Jeremiah finds the mean number of cars that pass through the same intersection from 6 A.M. to 10 A.M. was 22. Using the data from Exercise 22, how many fewer cars passed through the intersection on Tuesday?

In 24–26, use the data table.

24. What are the median, mode, and range of these data?

Known Number of Moons of the Planets	
Mercury	0
Venus	0
Earth	1
Mars	2
Jupiter	50
Saturn	53
Uranus	27
Neptune	13

25. What is the mean number of moons for the 8 planets, rounded to the nearest whole number?

26. If you include Pluto's moons in the data, the median is 5.

a. How many moons does Pluto have? Explain.

b. Would including Pluto affect the range of the data? Explain.

27. Higher Order Thinking Is the median always, sometimes, or never one of the data values? Explain.

28. Critique Reasoning Maria says the mean of the scores 7, 8, 3, 0, 2 is 5, because she added the scores and divided by 4. Is she correct? Explain why or why not.

Assessment Practice

29. The cost of 8 different sets of golf clubs is shown in the data table. A new brand of golf clubs for $533 is now being sold at the shop. Which of the following statements about the data is true? 6.SP.1.3

Ⓐ The mean cost will decrease.

Ⓑ The range of the costs will increase.

Ⓒ The mean cost will stay the same.

Ⓓ The range of the costs will stay the same.

Price of Golf Clubs (dollars per set)
265
237
325
281
265
252
494
273

Solve & Discuss It!

To track how many raisins are needed for packaging, a quality control inspector at a food processing plant collected data for the number of raisins in small boxes. Describe the data, including minimum value, maximum value, and median. Then describe what you notice about the values between the minimum and the median, and between the median and maximum.

Lesson 12-3
Display Data in Box Plots

Go Online | PearsonRealize.com

I can...
make and interpret box plots.

MAFS.6.SP.2.4 Display numerical data in plots on a number line, including... box plots.
MAFS.K12.MP.1.1, MP.2.1, MP.3.1, MP.4.1

Reasoning How can ordering the numbers of raisins in small boxes from least to greatest help you find the median?

Focus on math practices

Construct Arguments The median of the first half of the data is 26.5, and the median of the second half of the data is 30.5. Why would this information be helpful and what do those medians show? Explain.

? **Essential Question** Why is a box plot useful for representing certain types of data?

EXAMPLE 1  Make a Box Plot

Scan for Multimedia 

Helen wants to display the lengths of 15 fish she caught this year to compare to the lengths of fish she caught last year. How can she use the data to make a box plot?

A **box plot** is a diagram that shows the distribution of data values using the median, quartiles, minimum value, and maximum value on a number line.

Length of Fish (in.)		
7	9	10
7	13	13
10	15	15
18	11	13
22	14	17

Find the minimum, median, and maximum values of the data.

(7), 7, 9, 10, 10, 11, 13, (13), 13, 14, 15, 15, 17, 18, (22)

Minimum: 7 Median: 13 Maximum: 22

Find the median for each half.

7, 7, 9, (10), 10, 11, 13, (13), 13, 14, 15, (15), 17, 18, 22

First Quartile (Median of 1st Half): 10
Second Quartile (Median): 13
Third Quartile (Median of 2nd Half): 15

Quartiles are values that divide a data set into four equal parts.

Draw the box plot.

Show a number line with an appropriate scale, a box between the first and third quartiles, and a vertical segment that shows the median.

Draw segments that extend from the box to the minimum value and to the maximum value.

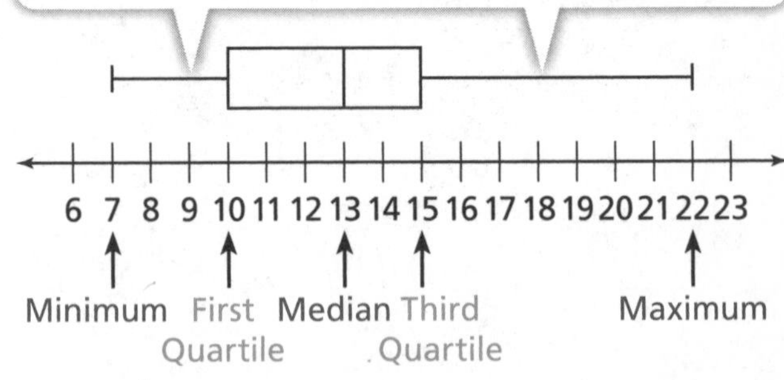

Try It!

The lengths in inches of 11 fish that Helen caught last year are listed below.

7, 8, 12, 12, 12, 13, 14, 15, 16, 17, 22

Circle the first quartile, median, and third quartile.

Convince Me! How is the distribution of Helen's data this year different from Helen's data last year? Draw a box plot of last year's data and use it to support your answer.

EXAMPLE 2  Make a Box Plot When the Number of Values Is Even

The Earth Club collected enough donations online to build compost bins. How can the club record the donation information in a box plot?

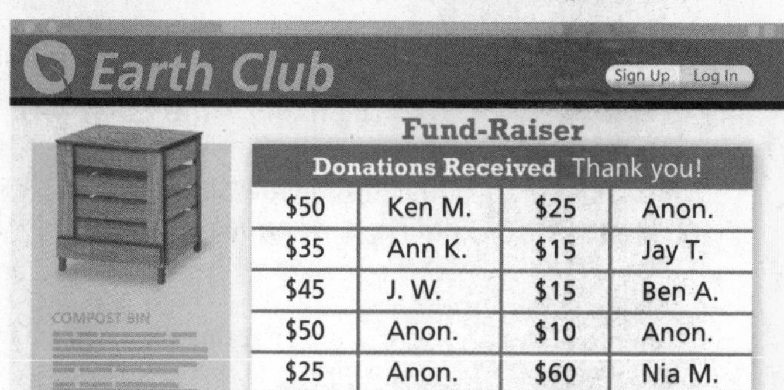

Fund-Raiser

Donations Received		Thank you!	
$50	Ken M.	$25	Anon.
$35	Ann K.	$15	Jay T.
$45	J. W.	$15	Ben A.
$50	Anon.	$10	Anon.
$25	Anon.	$60	Nia M.
$25	Hal K.	$45	Anon.

Model with Math A box plot is helpful when analyzing a data set because it visually represents the data set by dividing it into four equal parts. A data table does not visually show the division of data.

STEP 1 Find the minimum, median, and maximum values as well as the first and third quartiles.

There are 12 values. So, the median is the average of the two middle numbers.

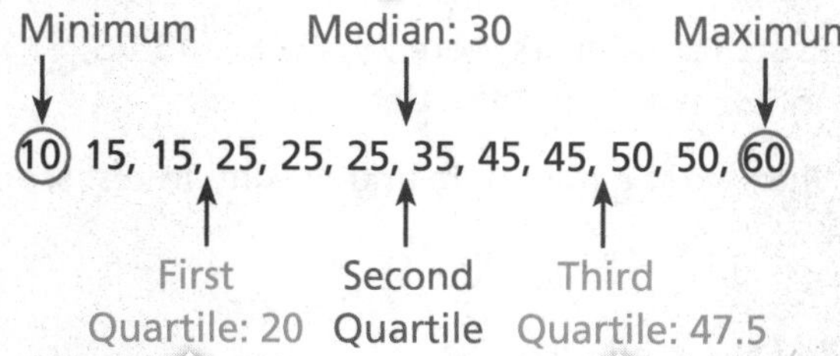

There are 6 values in each half. The quartiles are the averages of the two middle numbers in each half.

STEP 2 Draw a box plot.

The donation values range from $10 to $60, in $5 increments. So, a good scale for the number line is $5 to $65, numbered by 5s.

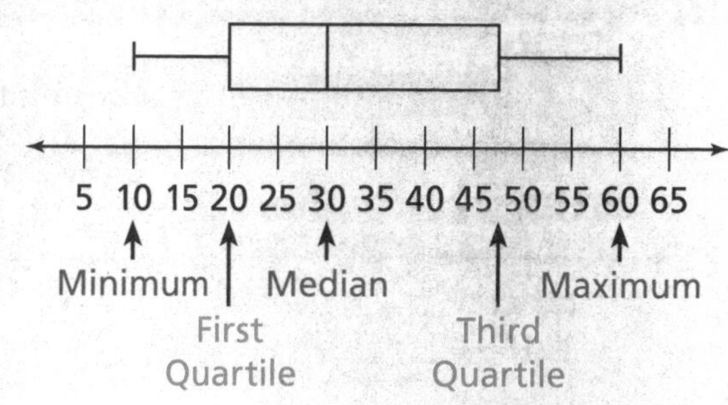

EXAMPLE 3  Interpret a Box Plot

The box plot shows the distribution of the weights, in pounds, of bags of donated clothing. What information do you know from the box plot?

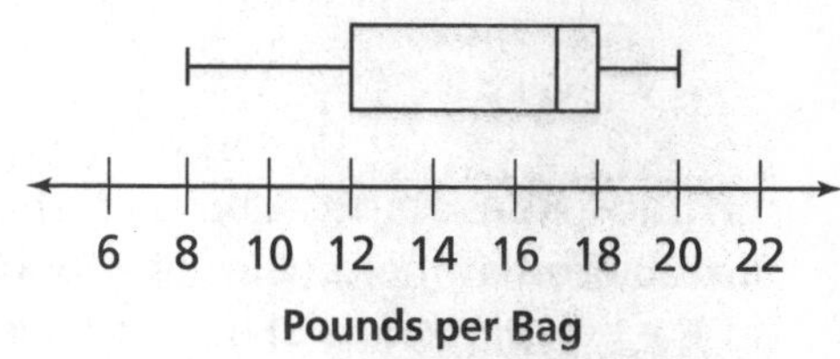

The minimum is 8, so the lightest bag weighs 8 pounds.

The maximum is 20, so the heaviest bag weighs 20 pounds.

The median weight for the bags is about 17 pounds.

The first quartile weight is 12 pounds, and the third quartile weight is 18 pounds.

Try It!

The ages of 12 volunteers participating in a beach clean-up are shown:

15, 27, 9, 15, 21, 9, 21, 9, 15, 21, 21, 24

Record the ages in a box plot.

KEY CONCEPT

A box plot shows a distribution of data values on a number line. A box plot visually represents a data set divided into four equal parts.

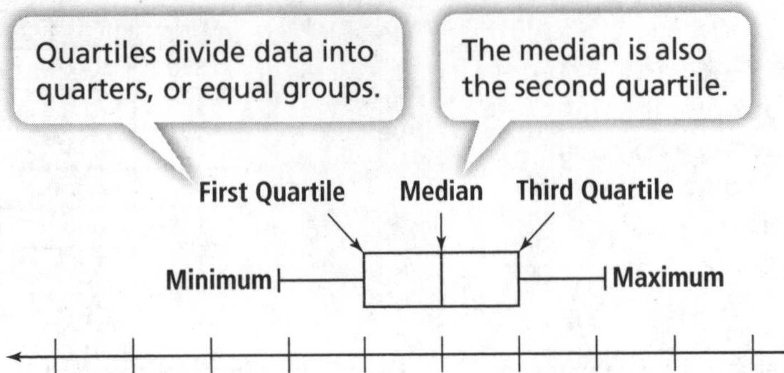

Do You Understand?

1. **Essential Question** Why is a box plot useful for representing certain types of data?

2. What values are included inside the box of a box plot?

3. **Critique Reasoning** A box plot shows the distribution of the costs of used books. The box of the box plot starts at $2 and ends at $5. Alex says this means that about one-quarter of the books cost between $2 and $5. Is Alex correct? Explain.

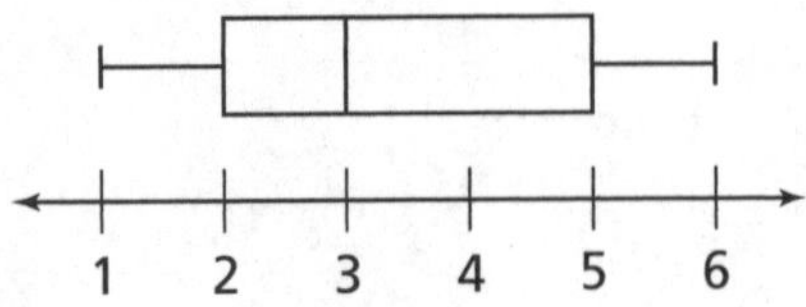

Do You Know How?

Sarah's scores on tests were 79, 75, 82, 90, 73, 82, 78, 85, and 78. In 4–8, use the data.

4. What are the minimum and maximum test scores?

5. Find the median.

6. Find the first and the third quartiles.

7. Draw a box plot that shows the distribution of Sarah's test scores.

8. Eric is in Sarah's class. This box plot shows his scores on the same nine tests. How do Eric's scores compare to Sarah's?

Eric's Tests

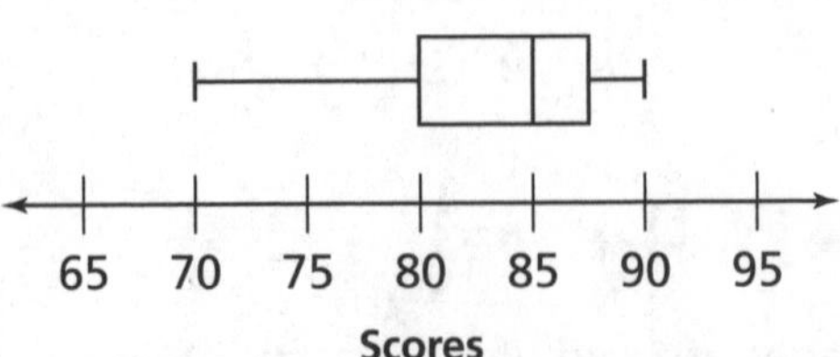

Name: ______________________

Practice & Problem Solving

Leveled Practice In 9 and 10, use this data set, which shows how many minutes Enzo practiced violin each day for 10 days.

40, 25, 45, 55, 30, 25, 30, 50, 30, 40

9. Find the statistical measures that you need to make a box plot of Enzo's practice times.

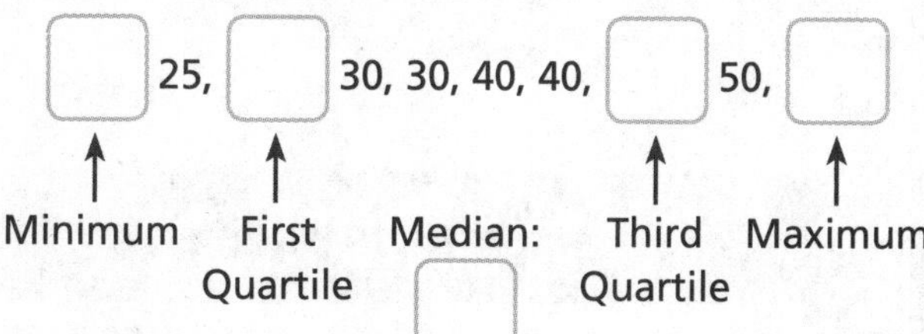

10. Complete the box plot to represent Enzo's practice times.

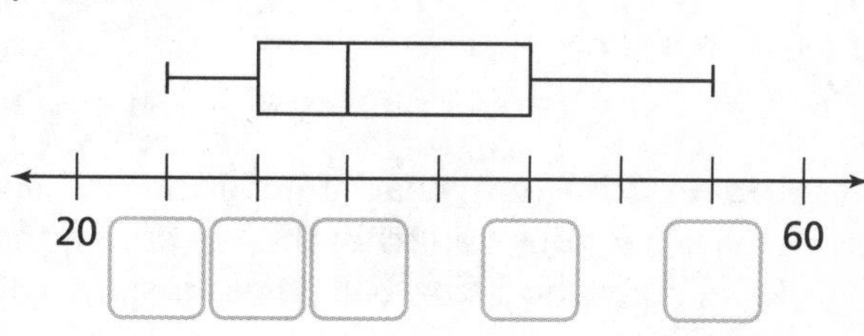

In 11 and 12, use this data set, which shows the prices, in dollars, of tickets to 10 plays at the community theater.

14, 22, 8, 14, 16, 8, 20, 14, 10, 18

11. Find the minimum, maximum, median, and quartile ticket prices.

Minimum: 8

First Quartile: 9

Median: 12

Third Quartile: 12

Maximum: 22

12. Make a box plot to display the ticket prices.

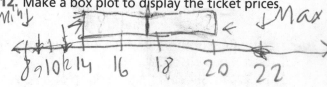

In 13 and 14, draw box plots using the data provided.

13. The sprint times, in seconds, of students who tried out for the track team:

44, 40, 40, 42, 49, 43, 41, 47, 54, 48, 42, 52, 48

14. Scores earned on science tests:

73, 78, 66, 61, 85, 90, 99, 76, 64, 70, 72, 72, 93, 81

In 15 and 16, use the box plot to answer the question.

15. How many words per minute does the fastest keyboarder type?

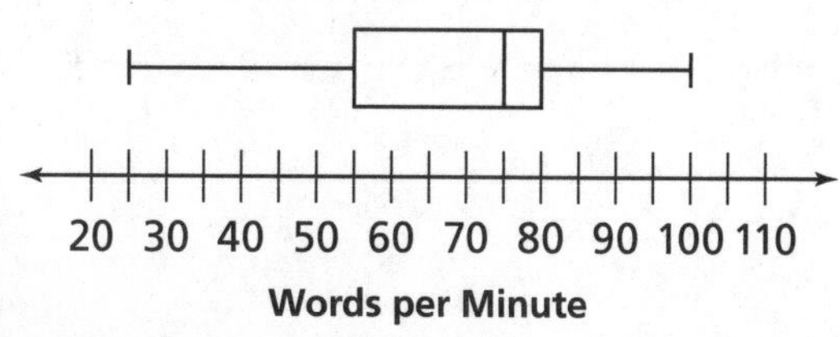

16. How many words per minute do the fastest 50% of keyboarders type?

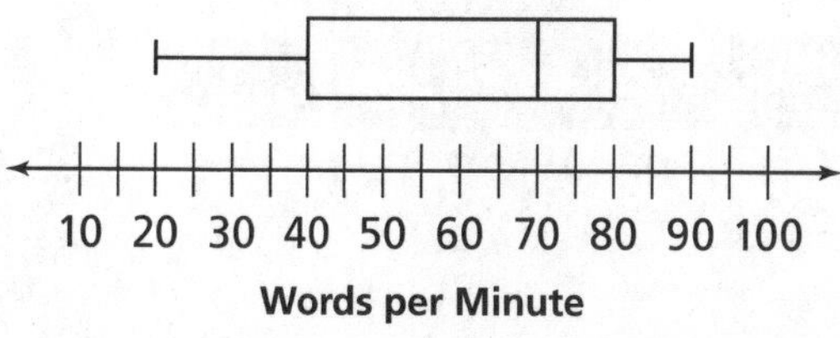

17. Reasoning The price per share of Electric Company's stock during 9 days, rounded to the nearest dollar, was as follows: \$16, \$17, \$16, \$16, \$18, \$18, \$21, \$22, \$19.

Use a box plot to determine how much greater the third quartile's price per share was than the first quartile's price per share.

18. Make Sense and Persevere The temperature forecast for Topeka, Kansas, for the next 8 days is shown. Use a box plot to determine the range for the lower half of the temperatures.

DAILY HIGH TEMPERATURES

SUN	MON	TUE	WED	THU	FRI	SAT	SUN
29°	31°	24°	26°	29°	35°	27°	32°

19. Model with Math Coach Henderson clocked the speeds in miles per hour of pitches thrown during the first inning of a middle school baseball game, as shown at the right.

Draw a box plot to display the data and write two conclusions about the data shown in the box plot.

Speeds of Pitches Thrown (in miles per hour)								
45.3	47	48.1	51.3	55.8	61.1	48.5	60.7	49

20. Critique Reasoning Tanya recorded the ages of 10 local babysitters: 20, 16, 18, 13, 14, 13, 12, 16, 22, 18. She says that the box plot below shows the distribution of ages. What error did she make?

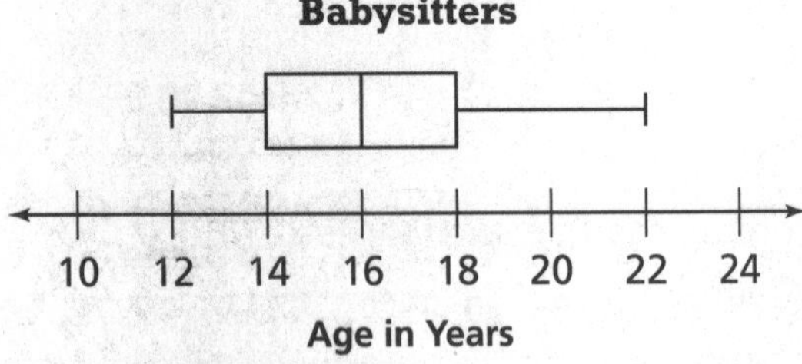

21. Higher Order Thinking Alana made this box plot to represent classroom attendance last month. Without seeing the values, what conclusions can you make about whether attendance was mostly high or low last month? Explain.

Assessment Practice

22. Use the data given to complete the box plot.

The ages in years of the students in Caryn's gymnastics class are shown in the table.

6.SP.2.4

Ages of Students in Years										
12	11	9	18	10	11	7	16	14	11	6

Complete the box plot to show the distribution of the students' ages.

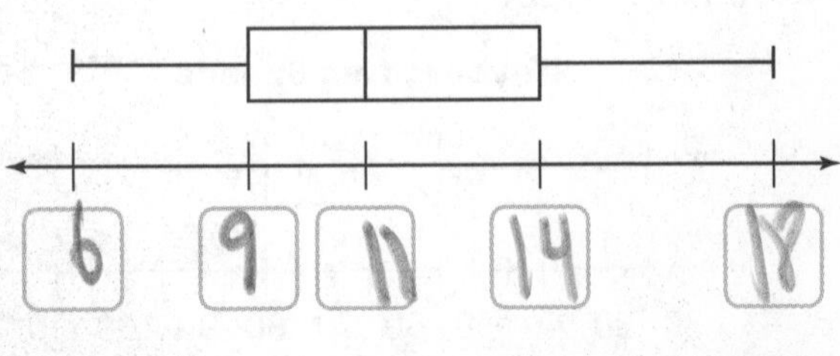

Explore It!

Lesson 12-4
Display Data in Frequency Tables and Histograms

Go Online | PearsonRealize.com

I can...
make and analyze frequency tables and histograms.

MAFS.6.SP.2.4 Display numerical data in plots on a number line, including... histograms... . Also 6.SP.2.5a
MAFS.K12.MP.2.1, MP.4.1, MP.6.1, MP.7.1, MP.8.1

The students in a sixth-grade class recorded the number of letters in their first and last names combined.

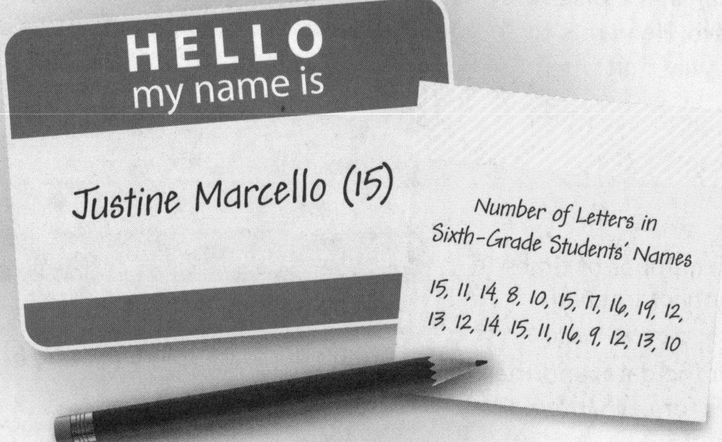

HELLO
my name is
Justine Marcello (15)
Number of Letters in Sixth-Grade Students' Names
15, 11, 14, 8, 10, 15, 17, 16, 19, 12,
13, 12, 14, 15, 11, 16, 9, 12, 13, 10

A. How can the data be organized? Describe one way to organize the data.

B. Describe another way to organize the data.

C. Compare the two ways. What do you notice about the data in each way?

Focus on math practices

Generalize What generalization can you make about the data set?

? Essential Question How can a frequency table or histogram help you organize and analyze data?

EXAMPLE 1  Make a Frequency Table and a Histogram

Scan for Multimedia 

Mr. Maxwell timed the cross-country team in a 2-mile run and recorded the times in the table shown. He wants to analyze the runners' times. What is one way that Mr. Maxwell can organize the data?

Team Times					
16:45	14:25	18:40	16:03	15:12	19:15
17:14	14:02	16:52	15:18	17:49	17:55

A **frequency table** shows the number of times a value occurs in each category or interval.

Mr. Maxwell can set up time intervals for the data, and then count the number, or frequency, of times for each interval.

Running Times	Tally	Frequency
14:00–15:59	||||	4
16:00–17:59	~~||||~~ |	6
18:00–19:59	||	2

Then he can use the frequency table to make a histogram.

Display the data by drawing a bar for each interval.

Look for Relationships How is a histogram similar to and different from a bar graph?

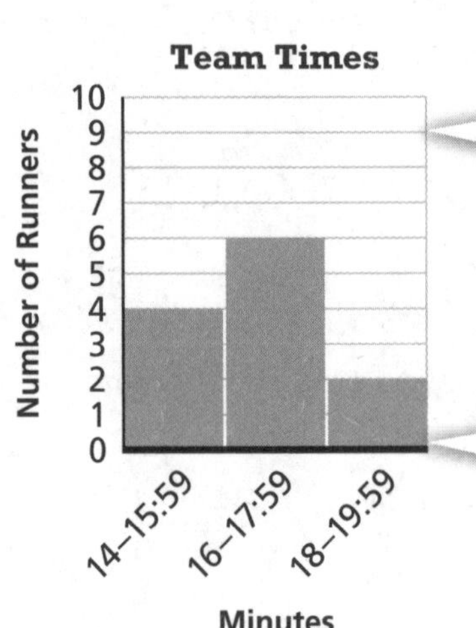

A **histogram** is a graph that uses bars to show the number of values in each category or interval.

The bars of a histogram always touch.

Try It!

This histogram shows a different way to represent Mr. Maxwell's data. Fill in the boxes with appropriate times and shade the bars for the last three intervals. How have the intervals changed?

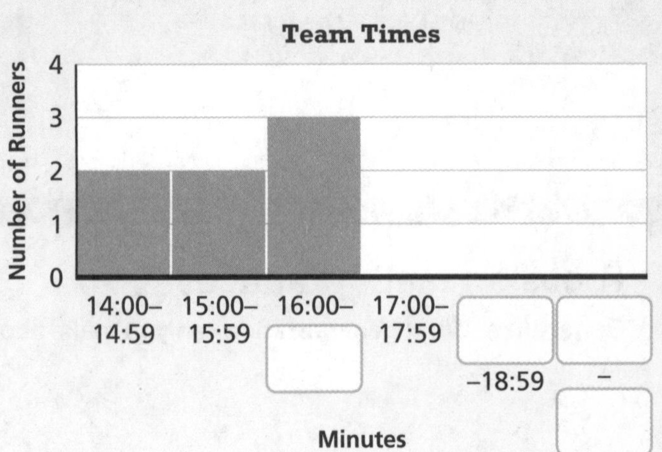

Convince Me! How is the analysis of the information displayed different between the two histograms?

EXAMPLE 2 Use a Frequency Table to Solve Problems

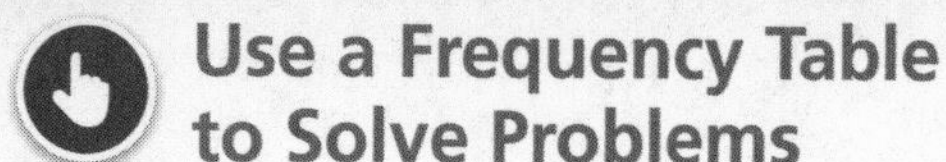

Zack surveys a group of middle school students and asks them how many texts they sent yesterday. The table shows the results.

Number of Texts	Tally	Frequency
0–19	𝍸	5
20–39	||||	4
40–59	𝍸 𝍸	10
60–79	𝍸 𝍸 |	11
80–99	𝍸 |||	8

a. Is the greatest number of texts sent between 60 and 79?

The greatest frequency is 11, which corresponds to students who sent 60–79 texts. However, the greatest number of texts sent is between 80 and 99.

b. Is the lowest number of texts sent between 20 and 39?

The lowest frequency is 4, which corresponds to students who sent 20–39 texts. However, the lowest number of texts sent is between 0 and 19.

Try It!

How many students sent between 20 and 59 texts?

EXAMPLE 3 Use a Histogram to Solve Problems

The histogram shows the number of points that Kendra scored during each basketball game she played last season.

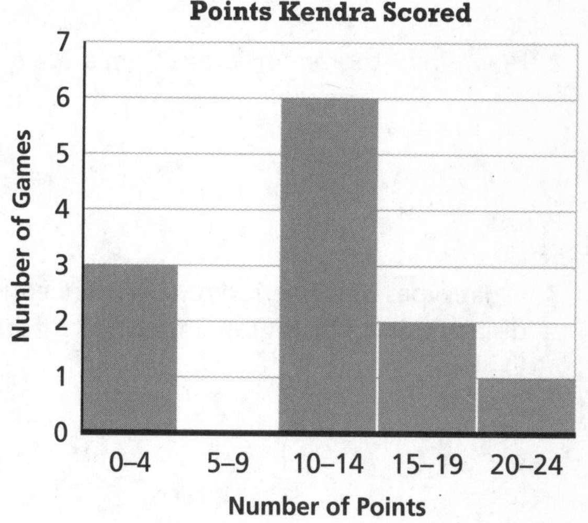

a. How many games did Kendra play last season?

The total number of games can be found by adding the number of games shown by each bar.

$3 + 0 + 6 + 2 + 1 = 12$

Kendra played 12 games.

b. In how many games did Kendra score from 5 to 9 points?

There is no bar on the histogram for 5–9 points. Kendra did not score 5–9 points in any games last season.

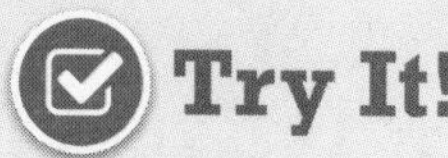

Try It!

Does the histogram show the mode of the number of points Kendra scored in the games? Explain.

KEY CONCEPT

Data displays can be used to help make sense of data.

Bags of Popcorn Sold Each Day
62, 65, 58, 31, 64, 58, 66, 68, 56, 67, 68, 51

You can organize data in a frequency table.

Bags	Tally	Frequency
30–39	|	1
40–49		0
50–59	||||	4
60–69	~~||||~~ ||	7

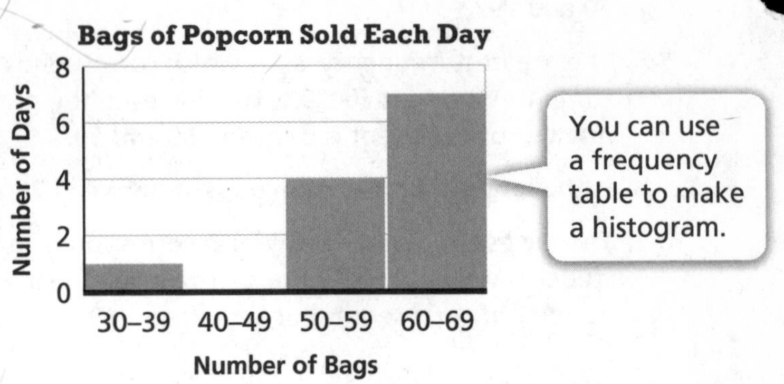

Do You Understand?

1. **Essential Question** How can a frequency table or histogram help you organize and analyze data?

2. How is a histogram different from a bar graph?

3. What types of numerical data sets are easier to display using a histogram instead of a dot plot? Explain.

4. **Reasoning** How are frequency tables and histograms alike and how are they different?

Do You Know How?

5. A data set contains ages ranging from 6 to 27.

6, 11, 9, 13, 18, 15, 21, 15, 17, 24, 27, 12

Complete the frequency table and histogram.

Ages	Tally	Frequency
6–10		
11–15		
16–20		
21–25		
26–30		

Ages in Data Set

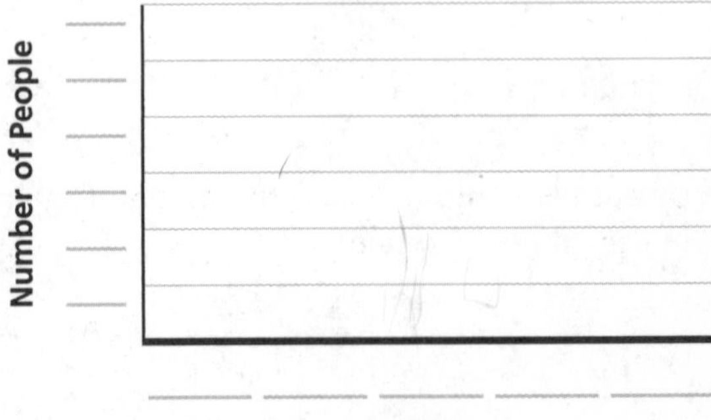

Ages

Name: ______________________________

Practice & Problem Solving  

Leveled Practice In **6–11**, use the data in the chart.

Number of Songs on Phones
125, 289, 115, 203, 192, 178, 256, 248, 165, 233, 147, 209, 225, 184, 156, 201, 143, 125, 263, 210

6. Complete the frequency table below for the number of songs stored on phones.

Song Range	Tally	Frequency
100–149		
150–199		
200–☐		
☐–☐		

7. Use your frequency table to complete the histogram.

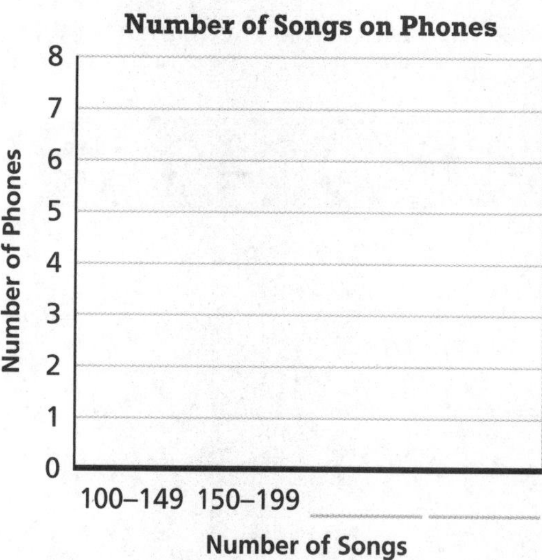

8. How many people have between 150 and 199 songs stored on their phones?

9. Do more than half of the phones have fewer than 149 songs stored on them?

10. Is the greatest number of songs stored on phones between 200 and 249 songs?

11. Are there more phones that have between 200 and 249 songs stored on them than have between 150 and 199 songs?

In **12–14**, use the data in the histogram.

12. How many students in Ms. Gioia's class took the science test?

13. How many more students had scores that were 80 or lower than had scores that were higher than 90?

3

14. Be Precise Can you tell from the histogram how many students scored 83 on the test? Explain.

No one

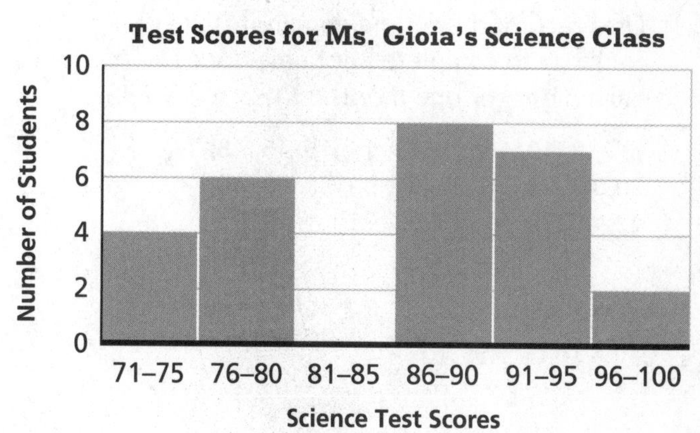

In **15–17**, use the data in the chart.

Bicycle Stopping Times (in seconds)
15, 25, 11, 8, 10, 21, 18, 23, 19, 9, 14, 16, 24, 18, 10, 16, 24, 18, 9, 14

15. Reasoning Todd wants to know how many people took 20 seconds or more to stop a bike safely. Would a frequency table or a histogram be the better way to show this? Explain.

16. Higher Order Thinking When organizing the data, what interval should Todd use? Explain.

17. Model with Math Make a frequency table and histogram for the data.

Time (in seconds)	Tally	Frequency

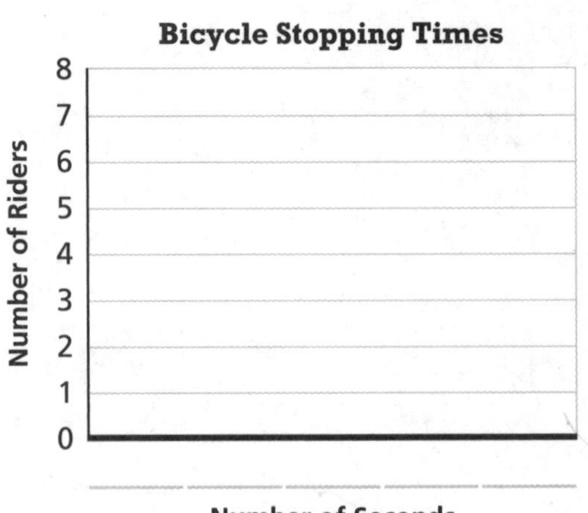

Assessment Practice

18. Use the data given to complete the histogram.

Lissa recorded the time, in minutes, it took her to complete her homework each night for one month. 6.SP.2.4

5, 7, 8, 10, 10, 11, 13, 14, 15, 15, 18, 19, 20, 20, 25, 26, 29, 31, 33, 35, 38, 40, 40, 42, 48, 50, 51, 55, 58, 71

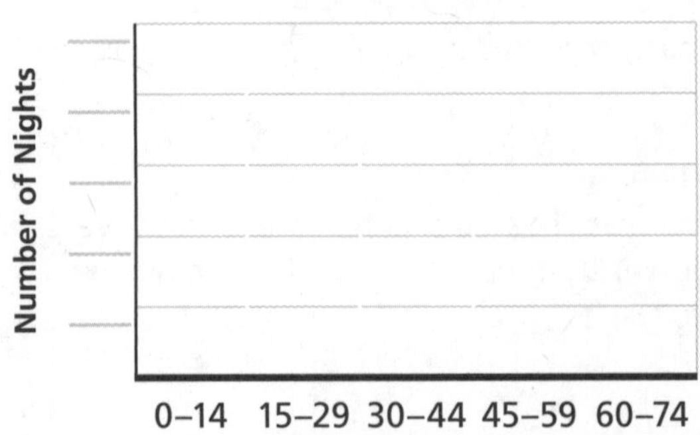

Name: ______________________________

MID-TOPIC CHECKPOINT

TOPIC 12

1. **Vocabulary** Which of the following describes the mean of a data set? *Lesson 12-2* 6.SP.1.3

Ⓐ The data value that occurs most often

Ⓑ The middle data value

Ⓒ The sum of the data values divided by the total number of data values

Ⓓ The difference of the greatest and least data values

2. A P.E. teacher recorded how many sit-ups the students in her class did in one minute. Select all the statements that describe the data. *Lesson 12-4* 6.SP.2.4, 6.SP.2.5a

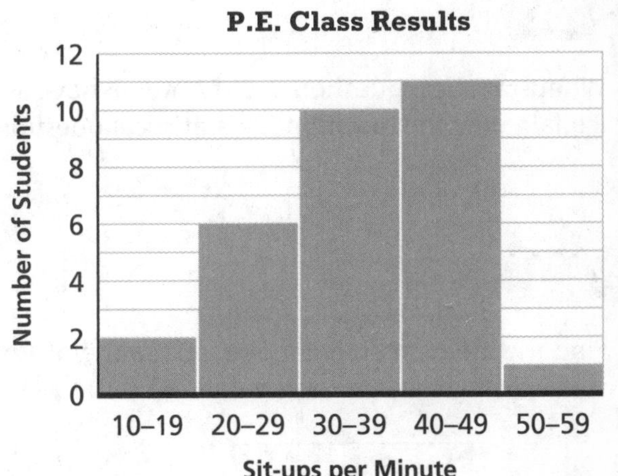

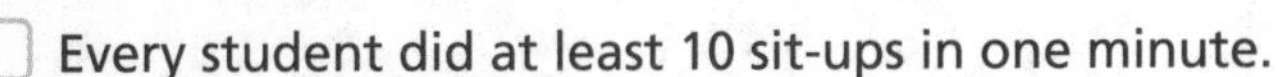

☐ Every student did at least 10 sit-ups in one minute.

☐ Two students did 50 or more sit-ups in one minute.

☐ Eight more students did 30 to 39 sit-ups than did 10 to 19 sit-ups.

☐ More than half of the students did 40 or more sit-ups in one minute.

☐ There are 30 students in the class.

In 3 and 4, determine whether each question is *statistical* or *not statistical*. Explain.

3. How many pages did Liz read yesterday? *Lesson 12-1* 6.SP.1.1

4. How many books did each of the students in grade 6 read last year? *Lesson 12-1* 6.SP.1.1

In 5 and 6, use the table of cousins' ages at a family reunion.

Cousins' Ages (years)
10, 9, 10, 14, 21, 11, 16, 10, 16

5. Make a box plot of the ages. *Lesson 12-3* 6.SP.2.4

6. One 8-year-old cousin could not make it to the reunion. Select all the ways the measures of center of the data set change if she had attended the reunion. *Lesson 12-2* 6.SP.1.3, 6.SP.2.5c

☐ The median increases by 1

☐ The mode decreases by 1

☐ The mean increases by 0.5

☐ The mean decreases by 0.5

☐ The median decreases by 0.5

How well did you do on the mid-topic checkpoint? Fill in the stars. ☆☆☆

MID-TOPIC PERFORMANCE TASK

Antonia surveys a group of students entered in a school science fair. Her results are shown.

Hours Spent on Project
8, 12, 10, 5, 2, 10, 17, 20, 14, 22

PART A

What statistical question could Antonia have asked to gather these data? Explain why the question is a statistical question. 6.SP.1.1

PART B

Find the mean, median, mode, and range of Antonia's data. Draw lines to match each measure to its value. 6.SP.1.3, 6.SP.2.5c

mean	10 hours
median	11 hours
mode	12 hours
range	20 hours

PART C

Choose reasonable intervals and then make a frequency table and a histogram to show Antonia's data. 6.SP.2.4

Hours	Tally	Frequency

Hours Spent on Project

Number of Students

Total Number of Hours

Lesson 12-5

Summarize Data Using Measures of Variability

Go Online | PearsonRealize.com

I can...
use measures of variability to describe a data set.

MAFS.6.SP.2.5c Summarize numerical data sets in relation to their context, such as by: Giving quantitative measures of... variability (interquartile range and/or mean absolute deviation), as well as describing any overall pattern and any striking deviations from the overall pattern with reference to the context in which the data were gathered.
Also 6.SP.2.4
MAFS.K12.MP.2.1, MP.3.1, MP.4.1

Solve & Discuss It!

ACTIVITY

Suppose you collected data from 11 people about the number of pieces of fruit they have eaten in the past week. The median number is 6 pieces of fruit.

Make two possible dot plots that could be used to display the data—one in which the data vary a little and one in which the data vary a lot. Explain how you created your dot plots.

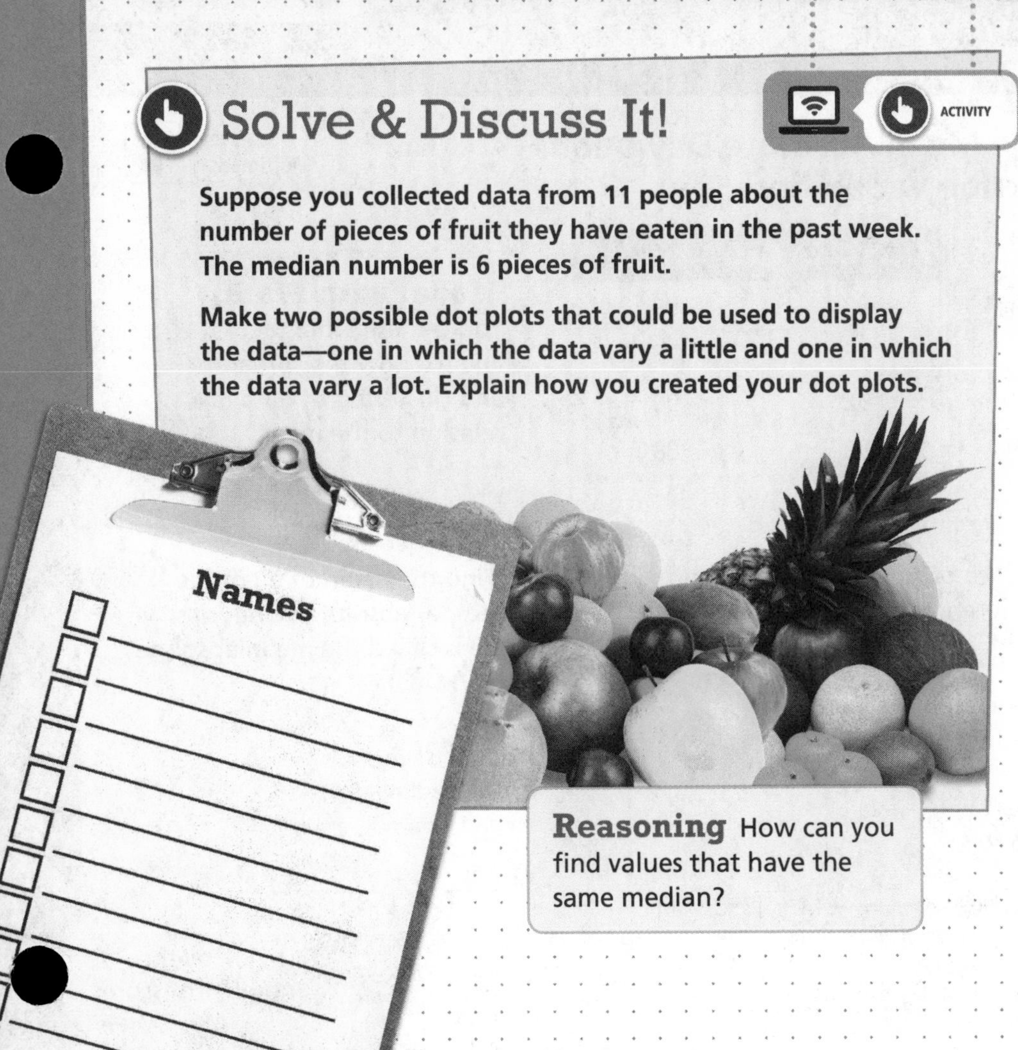

Reasoning How can you find values that have the same median?

Focus on math practices

Critique Reasoning Jackline says that only 3 people surveyed ate more than six pieces of fruit in the past week. Do you agree? Explain why or why not.

? Essential Question How can the variability of data be described using a single number?

EXAMPLE 1  Find the Mean Absolute Deviation to Describe Variability

Scan for Multimedia 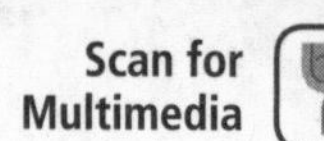

Ann is looking at her math quiz scores for one grading period. She wants to know how much her scores varied. She knows that her average (mean) score is 86%. How can Ann determine how much her scores varied during this grading period?

Ann's Math Quiz Scores (%)	
82	99
76	73
92	90
88	88

Model with Math
You can use a number line to show the spread and clustering of data in relation to the mean.

STEP 1 Find the differences between each of Ann's quiz scores and her mean (average) score. Show all differences as positive integers.

The **absolute deviation** is the absolute value of the difference between a value and the mean.

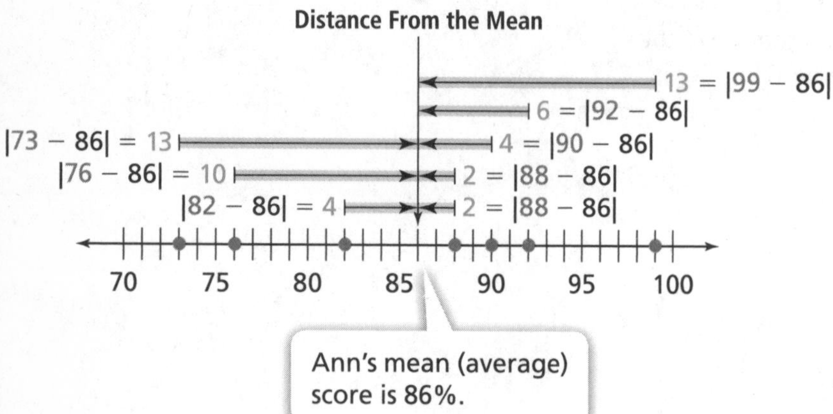

Ann's mean (average) score is 86%.

STEP 2 Find the mean of all of the differences, or absolute deviations. This value is called the **mean absolute deviation (MAD)**.

Add all of the absolute deviations.

$$\frac{13 + 10 + 4 + 2 + 2 + 4 + 6 + 13}{8}$$

$$= \frac{54}{8} \text{ or } 6.75$$

Divide by the number of scores.

Ann can find the mean absolute deviation (MAD) to determine how much her math quiz scores varied during this grading period.

Her scores varied by an average of 6.75 points.

Try It!

Ann's vocabulary quiz scores are 75, 81, and 90. The mean score is 82. What is the mean absolute deviation?

Score	Absolute Deviation
75	|82 − 75| = ☐
81	|☐ − ☐| = ☐
90	|☐ − ☐| = ☐

Convince Me! Can the mean absolute deviation ever have a negative value? Explain.

EXAMPLE 2  Find the Interquartile Range (IQR) to Describe Variability

The dot plot shows Ann's science quiz scores. How can Ann determine the variability in her science quiz scores?

78 79 80 81 82 83 84

Ann's Science Quiz Scores (%)

Draw a box plot to determine the interquartile range.

The **interquartile range (IQR)** is a measure of variability. It represents the difference between the third quartile and the first quartile.

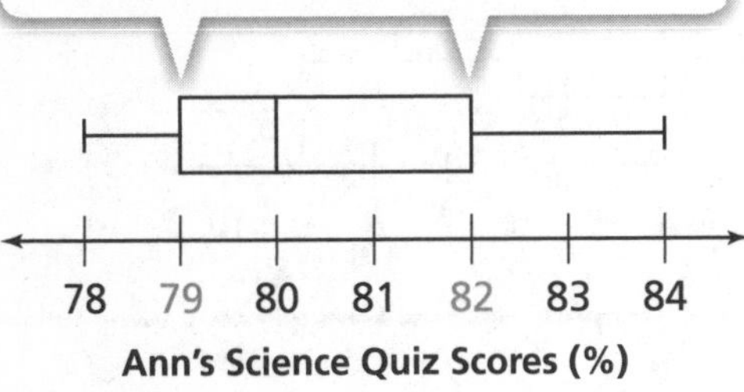

The interquartile range is $82 - 79 = 3$.
So, at least half of Ann's science quiz scores were within 3 points.

 Try It!

The dot plot shows the distribution of Ann's health quiz scores. How can the IQR describe her scores?

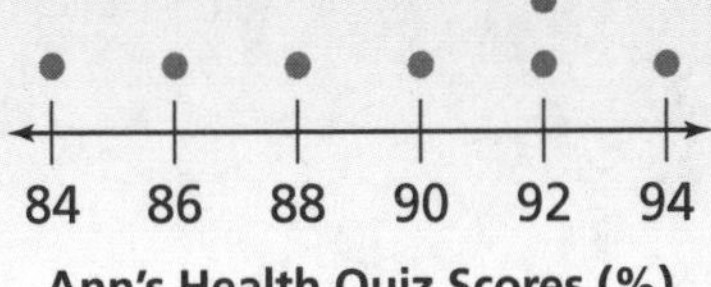

EXAMPLE 3  Use the Mean Absolute Deviation (MAD) to Find the Variability of a Data Set

Jonah recorded the points his team scored during its last nine basketball games. The mean number of points scored was 42 and the MAD was $4.\overline{4}$. How can Jonah use these measures to describe the variability of the points his team scored during the last nine games?

The MAD shows that the scores generally varied greatly from the mean. The scores were mostly less than 38 ($42 - 4.4 = 37.6$) or greater than 46 ($42 + 4.4 = 46.4$).

 Try It!

Jonah's team scored 36, 37, 38, 38, 41, 46, 47, 47, and 48 points in the last nine games. Find the IQR and range of the points Jonah's team scored in its last nine games. Are these good measures for describing the points scored?

KEY CONCEPT

The mean absolute deviation and the interquartile range each use a single number to describe the variability, or spread, of a data set. The **mean absolute deviation (MAD)** tells you how far the data are spread out from the mean. The **interquartile range (IQR)** tells you how far the middle of the data is spread out from the median.

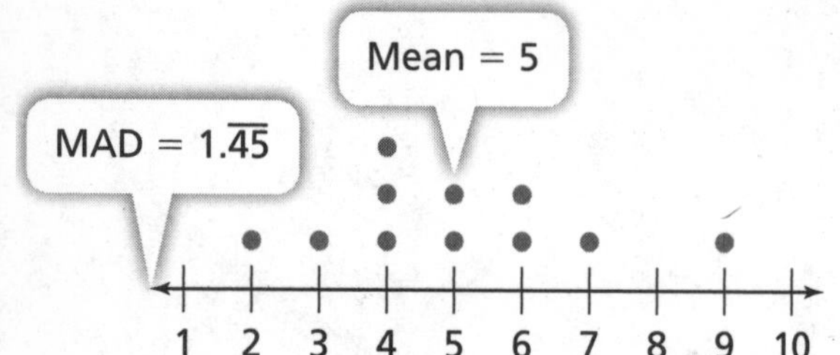

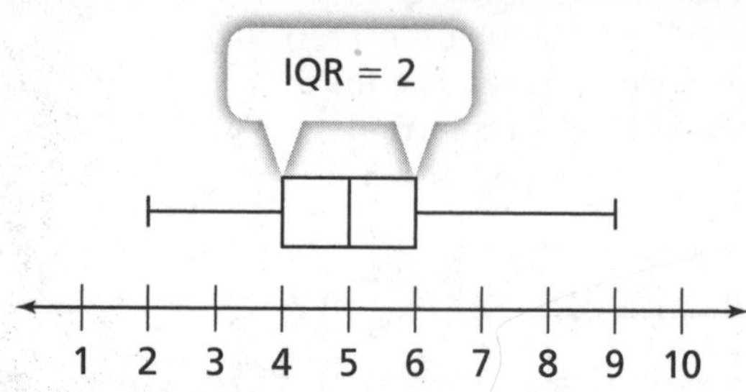

Do You Understand?

1. **Essential Question** How can the variability of data be described using a single number?

2. What does the IQR show that the range does not show?

3. **Reasoning** Two data sets have the same mean, 8. However, the MAD of Data Set A is 2 and the MAD of Data Set B is 4. What does this indicate about the variability of the data sets?

Do You Know How?

In 4–7, use these data.

Davita works at a shoe store. She measured the feet of nine customers and found that their shoe sizes were 4, 5, 5, 6, 7, 8, 8, 10, and 10.

4. Find the mean.

5. Find the sum of the absolute deviations from the mean.

6. Find the mean absolute deviation. Explain how you found the MAD.

7. Find the range and IQR. How is each calculated?

Name: ______________________________

Practice & Problem Solving

8. **Leveled Practice** The mean of the data set is 3. Find the absolute deviation of each of the green values.

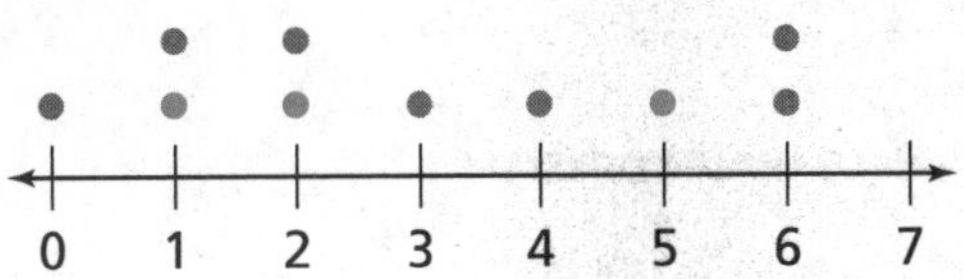

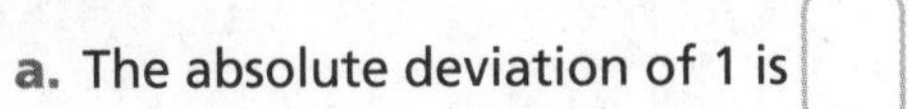
a. The absolute deviation of 1 is ☐.

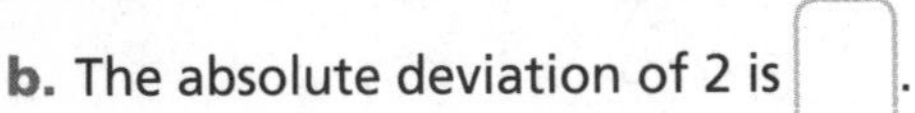
b. The absolute deviation of 2 is ☐.

c. The absolute deviation of 5 is ☐.

In 9 and 10, use the data table showing the number of miles that Jill biked on 9 days.

9. Find the mean.

Miles Biked		
5	9	11
10	8	6
7	12	4

10. Find the MAD of this data set. What does this tell you about the number of miles that Jill biked?

In 11 and 12, use the data shown in the dot plot.

10, 10, 11, 11, 12, 16, 17, 17, 18, 18

11. What are the mean and the MAD?

Mean: 14, Mad: 16

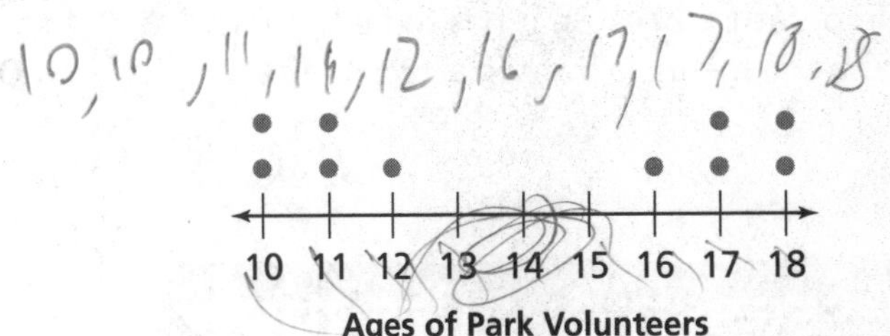

12. Describe the variability of the data.

In 13 and 14, use the data shown in the box plot.

13. What are the range and the IQR?

Range = 10

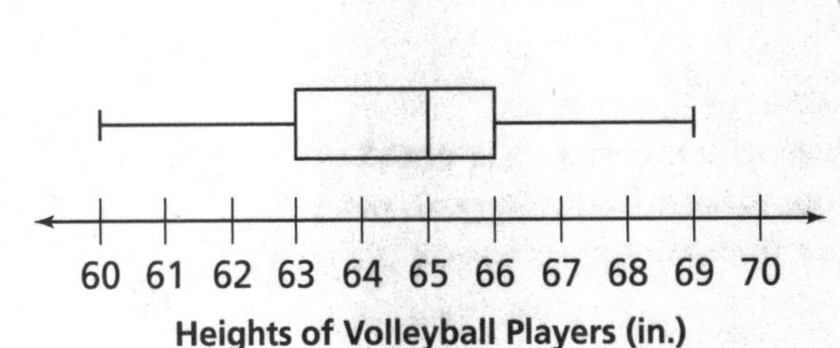

14. Describe the variability of the data.

15. The data set shows prices for concert tickets in 10 different cities in Florida.

City	Price ($)	City	Price ($)
Q	45	V	36
R	50	W	24
S	35	X	25
T	37	Y	27
U	29	Z	43

a. Find the IQR of the data set.

b. How do prices vary within the middle 50%?

16. **Reasoning** The MAD of the data set in the table is about 6.7. Does the value 4 deviate more or less than most of the values in the table? Explain.

4	28	25
19	7	13
16	22	10

In 17–19, use the data set shown in the table.

Temperatures (°C)			
11	17	20	16
19	16	15	22

17. **Vocabulary** What is the term used to describe the range of the middle half of the data set? Find that value for this data.

18. **Critique Reasoning** Dina said that the greatest absolute deviation will be found from the highest temperature because it has to be the farthest from the mean. Is she correct? Explain.

19. **Higher Order Thinking** What is the MAD for the data and what does it tell you about the temperatures?

Assessment Practice

20. Harlo recorded the tide, in feet, every hour during an 8-hour period as shown in the table. 6.SP.2.5c

Tide (ft)
3, 7, 11, 15, 20, 31, 39, 42

PART A

What is the MAD for the data set?

PART B

Select all the statements that best describe the IQR, MAD, and variability of the data set.

☐ The middle 50% of the data is spread out more than the average variation.

☐ The IQR is greater than the MAD.

☐ The middle 25% of the data is spread out more than the average variation.

☐ The IQR is less than the MAD.

☐ The MAD shows that the tides generally varied greatly from the mean.

Solve & Discuss It!

The prices in dollars of athletic shoes in one store are shown below. Does the mean, median, or mode best describe the typical price for shoes at this store?

Lesson 12-6

Choose Appropriate Statistical Measures

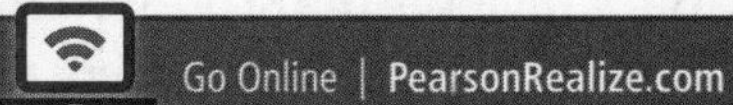

I can...
select and use appropriate statistical measures.

MAFS.6.SP.2.5d Summarize numerical data sets in relation to their context, such as by: Relating the choice of measures of center and variability to the shape of the data distribution and the context in which the data were gathered. Also 6.SP.2.5c
MAFS.K12.MP.1.1, MP.2.1, MP.3.1, MP.7.1

Look for Relationships
How can you use the spread and clustering of data to help decide which statistical measures to use?

Focus on math practices

Construct Arguments Which measure would the store most likely use in its advertising? Explain why this measure should be used.

Essential Question Why is one statistical measure more useful than another to describe a given situation?

EXAMPLE 1  Choose the Best Measure of Center to Describe a Data Set

Scan for Multimedia 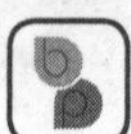

Gary reviews the scores on his weekly quizzes. What measure should Gary use to get the best sense of how well he is doing on his weekly quizzes?

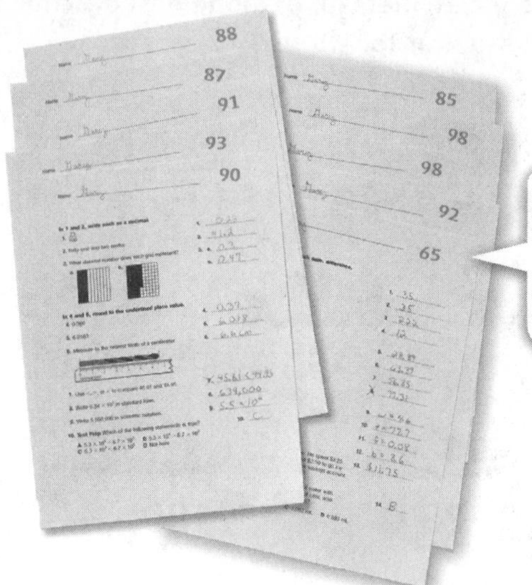

An **outlier** is a data value that is very different from the other values.

Make Sense and Persevere
What does the distribution of the data in a dot plot tell you about the shape of the data?

Display Gary's scores on a dot plot. Describe the shape of the data. Then find the mean, median, and mode of the data set.

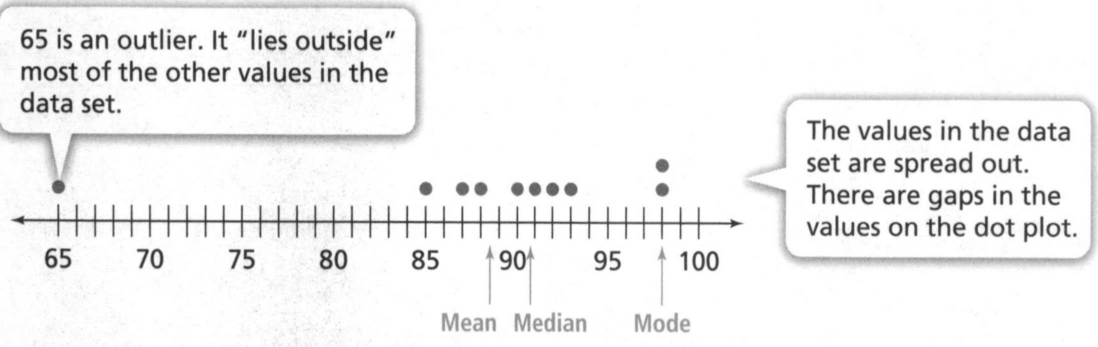

The outlier causes the mean to be less than the values of largest group of data. The best measure to use is the median because the outlier does not affect the median.

Try It!

If Gary scored a 70 on his next weekly quiz, how would that affect his mean score?

Convince Me! Gary says that he usually scores 98 on his weekly quiz. What measure of center did Gary use? Explain.

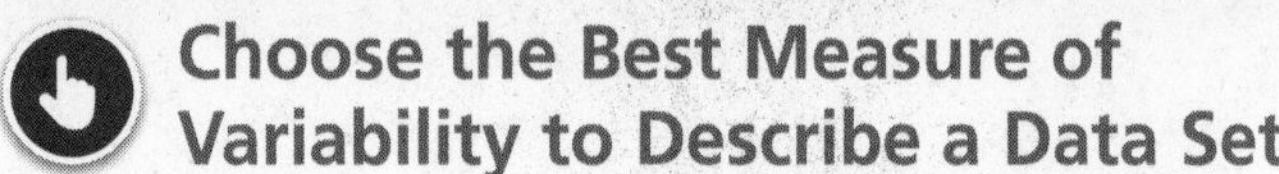

John and Yoshi are computer lab partners. During a spreadsheet project, they decide to enter their French quiz scores on their shared tablet.

A. Choose a measure of variability and use it to describe John's quiz scores.

John's scores contain an outlier, 65, so the median is a better measure of center for his data than the mean.

Use the IQR when the median is the appropriate measure of center.

First Quartile = 87 Third Quartile = 93

IQR = 93 − 87 = 6

At least half of John's quiz scores are between 87 and 93. This accurately describes how his scores are clustered.

B. Choose a measure of variability and use it to describe Yoshi's quiz scores.

Yoshi's scores range from 80 to 88, so there is no outlier. The mean, 84, is a good measure of center for her data.

Use the MAD when the mean is the appropriate measure of center.

$$\text{MAD} = \frac{4+4+2+2+0+0+2+2+4+4}{10} = \frac{24}{10} = 2.4$$

Yoshi's scores are typically within 2.4 points of her mean score of 84.

Quiz Scores

	A	B
	John	Yoshi
1	65	80
2	87	80
3	87	82
4	88	82
5	90	84
6	91	84
7	92	86
8	93	86
9	93	88
10	93	88

Try It!

Suppose the French teacher says that she will drop each student's lowest quiz score. Would the MAD now be a good measure of variability for John's quiz scores? Calculate the MAD without John's lowest score and use it to justify your answer.

John's lowest score is ☐.

Without the lowest score, John's mean score is ☐.

$$\text{MAD} = \frac{\square + \square + \square + \square + \square + \square + \square + \square + \square}{9}$$

$$= \frac{\square}{9} = \square$$

KEY CONCEPT

The statistical measure that is most appropriate to describe the center and variability of a data set should be chosen based on an analysis of the spread, clustering, and outliers in the data set.

The **mean** is a good choice to describe the center of a data set when the data are clustered together.

When the mean is used, the **mean absolute deviation (MAD)** is a good choice to describe the variability.

The **median** is a good choice to describe the center of a data set when the data contain an outlier.

When the median is used, the **interquartile range (IQR)** is a good choice to describe the variability.

The **mode** is sometimes a good choice to describe the center of a data set if the data is not numeric or does not fall in intervals.

The median and mode are the same, 30. Both describe the center of the data set.

The outlier will increase the mean. The mean and MAD are *not* the best choices.

24 26 28 30 32 34 36 38 40

Number of Points

The middle half of the data is clustered together. The IQR is a good measure of the variability of the data set because it uses the median.

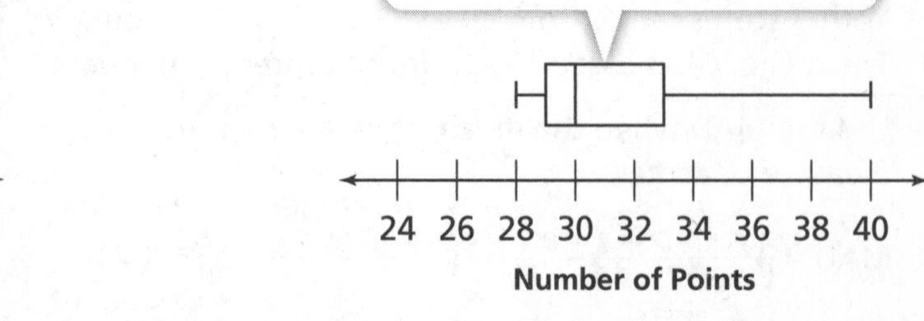

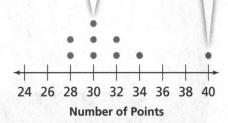

Do You Understand?

1. **Essential Question** Why is one statistical measure more useful than another to describe a given situation?

2. **Reasoning** You cannot find a good measure of center for a data set. What is probably true of the data set?

Do You Know How?

In 3–5, use the basketball team's scores for one season: 44, 43, 42, 40, 42, 45, 39, 38, 18.

3. Find the mean, median, and mode of the scores.

4. Is the median or mean the best measure of center for these data? Explain.

5. Find the measure of variability that best describes the data set.

Name: ______________________________

Practice & Problem Solving

Scan for Multimedia

In 6–8, use the data to answer the questions.

Each of five different stores sell a quart of milk for one of the following prices: $1.50, $1.55, $1.80, $1.70, $1.50.

6. What are the mean, median, and mode of the data?

7. Which measure of center best describes these data? Which measure of variability?

8. Find the best measure of variability for these data. Describe the variability.

In 9–11, use the dot plot at the right.

The dot plot shows the hourly wages of cashiers at a supermarket.

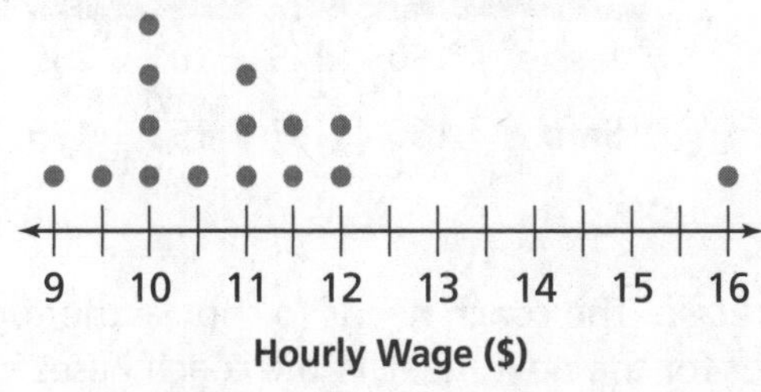

9. a. Is the median, mean, or mode the best measure of center for these data? Explain.

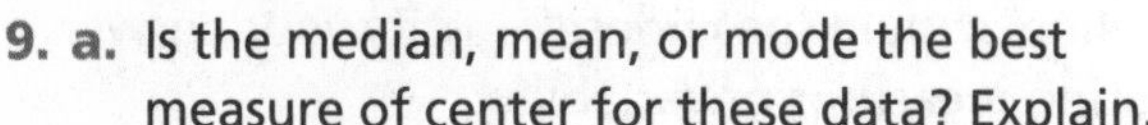

b. Find that measure of center.

10. Identify a good measure of variability for these data. Find the value.

11. Write a sentence describing the variability of the wages.

12. Critique Reasoning Hayden looks at the dot plot. He believes that the data set contains outliers and argues that the best measure of variability is the IQR because the median is a good measure to describe a data set that contains outliers. Is Hayden correct? Explain.

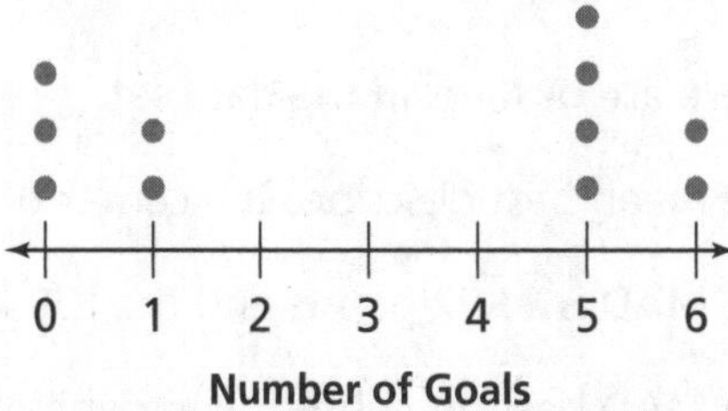

In 13–16, use the table at the right.

The table shows measures of center based on 5 data points for attendance at a national skateboarding competition.

Mean	Median	Mode
14,000	13,000	12,500

13. **Vocabulary** What is the term and the value of the middle number of the data set?

14. **Make Sense and Persevere** Which value in the data set occurs at least twice? Can it occur 3 times? Explain.

15. **Reasoning** Why must the other two numbers in the data set be greater than or equal to 13,000?

16. **Model with Math** What must be the sum of the two remaining numbers, x and y? Write an equation to show how to find this sum.

In 17 and 18, use the table.

Game Scores for the Bravo Bowling Team									
Jessie	150	145	181	235	196	211	204	221	185
Sam	186	187	192	195	194	157	157	162	200

17. **Be Precise** The coach needs to choose the top bowler for the next meet. If the coach bases her decision on the player with the best average, whom should she choose? Justify your answer using measures of center.

18. **Higher Order Thinking** If the coach bases her decision on the player who is most consistent, whom should she choose? Justify your answer using measures of variability.

Assessment Practice

19. The table at the right shows the winning bowling scores during the last five bowling events. Select the statements that best describe the data. 6.SP.2.5d

Winning Scores				
121	159	146	132	149

- ☐ There are outliers in the data set.
- ☐ The mean best describes the center of the data.
- ☐ The MAD is 11.92 points and the IQR is 27.5 points.
- ☐ The MAD best describes the variability.
- ☐ The IQR best describes the spread.

Explain It!

Lesson 12-7
Summarize Data Distributions

Go Online | PearsonRealize.com

I can...
summarize numerical data sets.

MAFS.6.SP.1.2 Understand that a set of data collected to answer a statistical question has a distribution which can be described by its center, spread, and overall shape.
Also 6.SP.2.4, 6.SP.2.5b, 6.SP.2.5c
MAFS.K12.MP.3.1, MP.4.1, MP.8.1

George tosses two six-sided number cubes 20 times. He records his results in a dot plot.

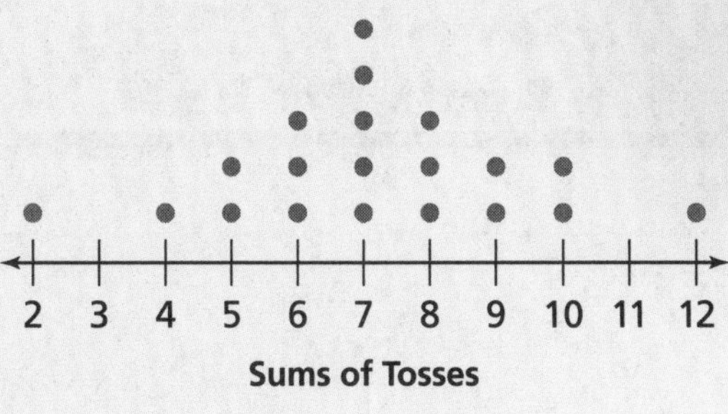

A. Describe the shape of the data distribution.

B. Critique Reasoning George says that he expects to roll a sum of 11 on his next roll. Do you agree? Justify your reasoning.

Focus on math practices

Construct Arguments Suppose George tossed the number cubes 20 more times and added the data to his dot plot. Would you expect the shape of the distribution to be different? Construct an argument that supports your reasoning.

EXAMPLE 1  Summarize a Distribution That Is Symmetric

Scan for Multimedia 

A science class is testing how different types of fertilizer affect the growth of plants. The dot plot shows the heights of the plants being grown in the science lab. How can you describe the data?

STEP 1 To describe a **data distribution**, or how the data values are arranged, look at the overall shape.

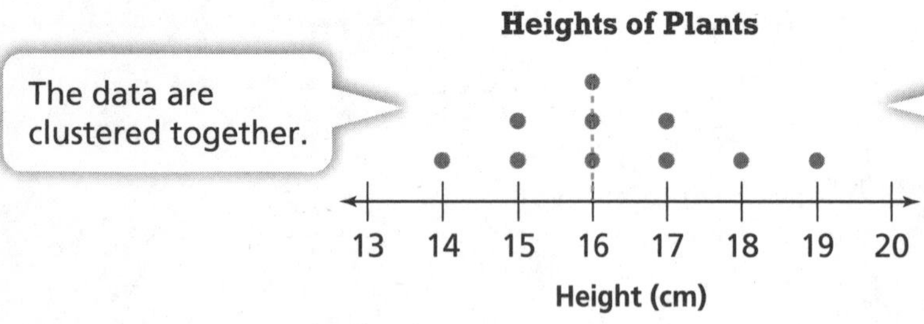

STEP 2 Since the data are roughly symmetric, the mean is the best measure of center.

$$\frac{14 + 15 + 15 + 16 + 16 + 16 + 17 + 17 + 18 + 19}{10} = 16.3$$

The mean height is 16.3 cm.

Find the mean absolute deviation (MAD).

$$\frac{2.3 + 1.3 + 1.3 + 0.3 + 0.3 + 0.3 + 0.7 + 0.7 + 1.7 + 2.7}{10} = 1.16$$

The mean absolute deviation is 1.16 cm, so a typical height is about 1.16 cm from the mean.

Generalize Since the mean is the best measure of center, the MAD is the best measure of variability.

Try It!

Does the shape of the distribution match what you found when you used measures of center and variability? Explain.

Convince Me! What are some factors that might explain why some plants grew more or less than others in the science lab?

EXAMPLE 2  Summarize a Distribution Shown in a Dot Plot

ACTIVITY

ASSESS

The fat content, in grams, was measured for one slice ($\frac{1}{8}$ pizza) of 24 different 12-inch pizzas. The data are displayed in the dot plot. How can the data be used to describe the fat content of a slice of pizza?

STEP 1 Look at the distribution of the data in the dot plot.

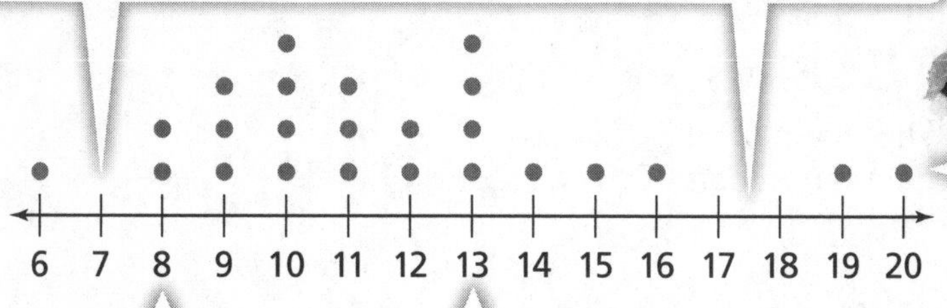

There are gaps between 6 and 8, and between 16 and 19.
6 7 8 9 10 11 12 13 14 15 16 17 18 19 20
The data are not symmetric. They are more spread out to the right.
Most data points are grouped between 8 and 13.

STEP 2 Because the data are not symmetric, the mean is not the best measure of center. Use the median and the IQR to describe the data distribution.

Median = 11 IQR = 13 − 9.5 = 3.5

The fat content of at least half of the slices is between 9.5 g and 13 g. The typical slice of pizza has a fat content of 11 g.

EXAMPLE 3  Summarize a Distribution Shown in a Box Plot

The box plot displays data for the number of days the temperature was above 80°F for the month of July. The data were collected over a ten-year period. How can you summarize these data?

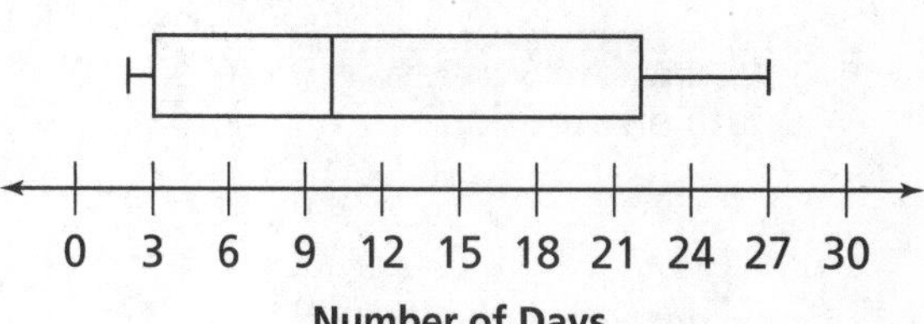

First, look at the overall shape. Then find measures of center and variability.

- The data are spread out to the right.
- The median is the center of the data.
- The first quartile is 3 and the third quartile is 22. At least half of the data fall between 3 days and 22 days. The interquartile range is 19 days.
- 25% of the years, the number of days with temperatures above 80°F in July was 3 days or less.

Model with Math You can select a box plot, dot plot, or other method to display data. You can use that display to help describe the data set.

Try It!

Why does it make sense to look at the overall shape before deciding which measures to use?

KEY CONCEPT

To describe a set of data, look at the shape and observe how the data are clustered or spread out.

A distribution can be symmetric and clustered in the center. When the data are symmetric, use the mean and mean absolute deviation (MAD) to describe the data.

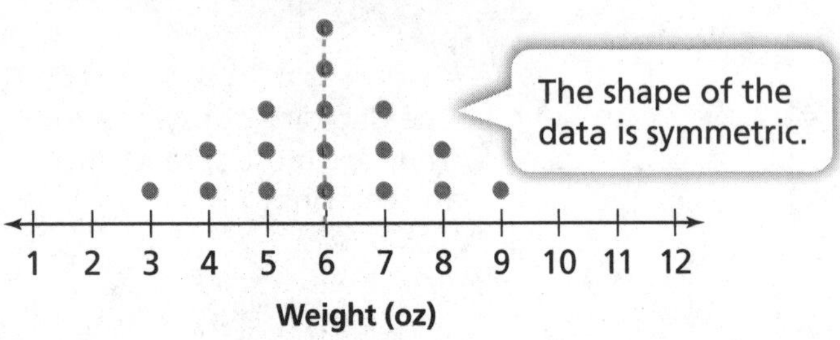

A distribution can show gaps, clusters, or outliers. It may spread out more to one side. When the data are not symmetric, use the median and interquartile range (IQR) to describe the data.

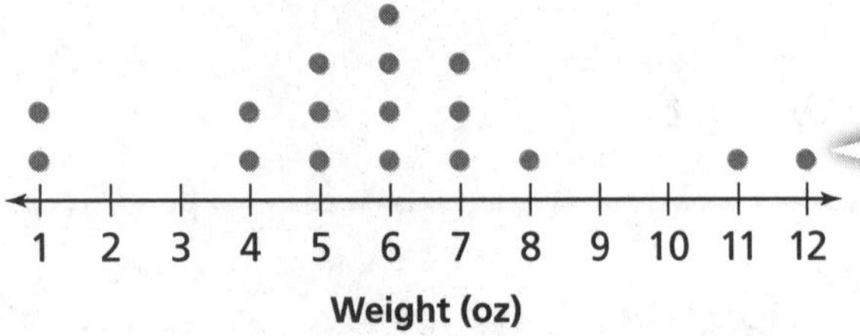

There are gaps between 1 and 4, and between 8 and 11. Most data points are grouped between 4 and 8.

Do You Understand?

1. **Essential Question** How can you summarize a data distribution?

2. **Reasoning** This data set has an outlier.

   0, 40, 50, 60, 60, 70, 80, 80

   How would the median and the mean be affected if the outlier was removed?

Do You Know How?

3. Five different students measured the length of a shadow in inches as follows: 38, $38\frac{1}{2}$, $37\frac{3}{4}$, 38, $38\frac{1}{4}$. Make a generalization about the data distribution of the shadow measurements.

4. What are the mean, the median, and the interquartile range of the data set in Exercise 3?

Name: ______________________

Practice & Problem Solving

PRACTICE TUTORIAL

Scan for Multimedia

In 5–8, use the data table.

Number of Home Runs Hit by Players on My Team									
Player Number	1	2	3	4	5	6	7	8	9
Home Runs	21	9	12	20	7	11	9	10	9

5. What are the mean and the median?

6. Draw a box plot of the data.

7. Describe the overall shape of the data.

8. Make a generalization about the data distribution.

9. Be Precise A doctor asked 15 people how many hours they spend exercising each week. The dot plot displays the data.

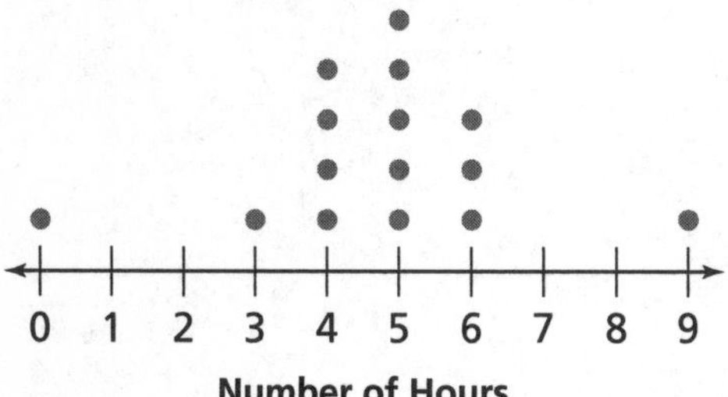

What do any clusters and gaps in the dot plot tell you about the exercise habits of these people?

10. Look for Relationships Describe the pattern in the dot plot. Then write about a situation that this data could represent. Explain why your situation has this pattern.

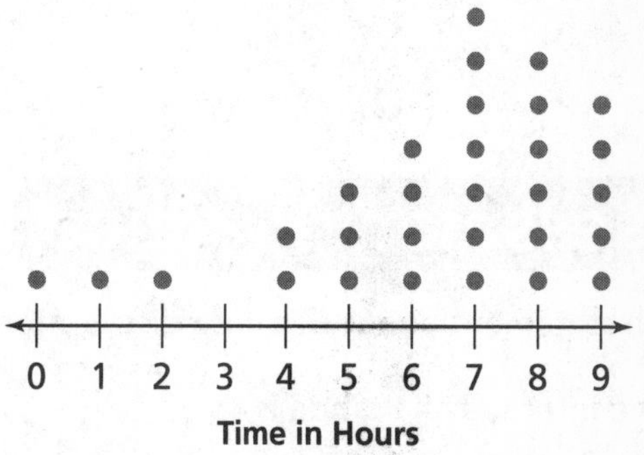

In 11 and 12, use the data in the table.

Adult	1	2	3	4	5
Salary	$35,000	$46,000	$38,000	$34,000	$52,000
Adult	6	7	8	9	10
Salary	$99,000	$64,000	$435,000	$22,000	$88,000

11. Model with Math Make a box plot for the data. What are the median, first quartile, third quartile, and interquartile range?

12. Higher Order Thinking Which data value most affects your choice of a measure of center to describe the data? Explain.

In 13–15, use the data in the dot plot.

13. Describe the shape of the data.

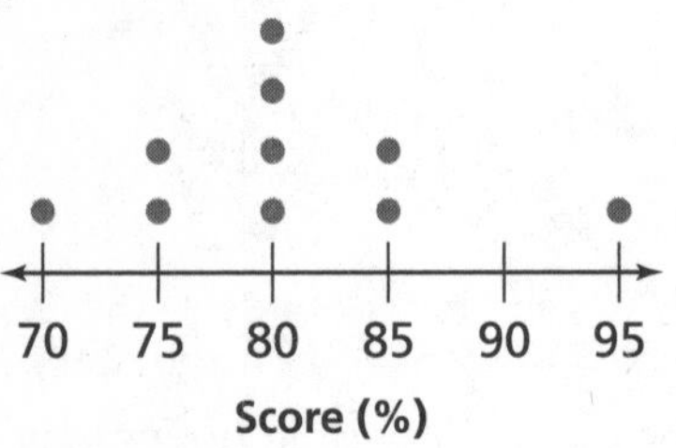

14. Describe the typical quiz scores of the students. Explain your choice of measure.

15. Describe the variability of the quiz scores.

Assessment Practice

16. Which statement about this data distribution is **NOT** true? 6.SP.1.2

Ⓐ The interquartile range is 4.

Ⓑ The median is the preferable measure of center.

Ⓒ The data cluster from 2 to 7.

Ⓓ The distribution is symmetrical.

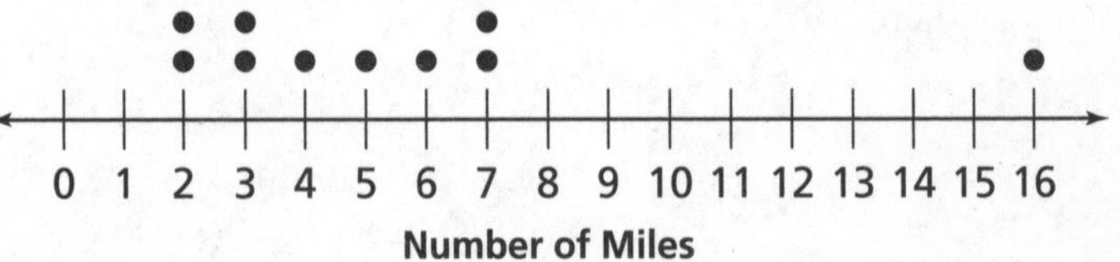

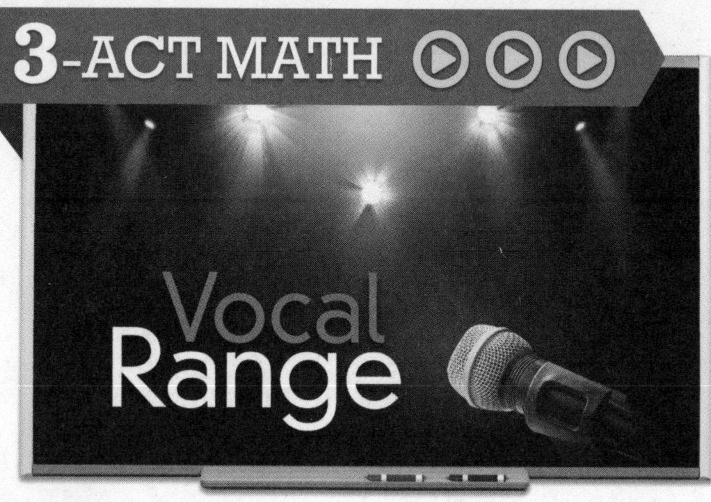

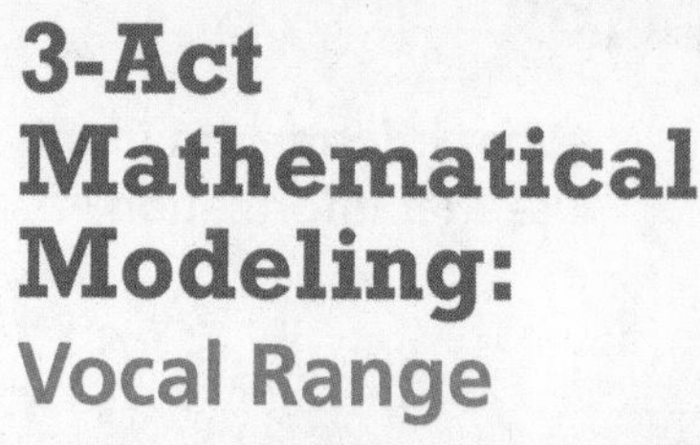

3-Act Mathematical Modeling: Vocal Range

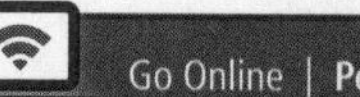

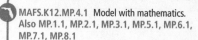

Go Online | PearsonRealize.com

MAFS.K12.MP.4.1 Model with mathematics. Also MP.1.1, MP.2.1, MP.3.1, MP.5.1, MP.6.1, MP.7.1, MP.8.1

MAFS.6.SP.1.2 Understand that a set of data collected to answer a statistical question has a distribution which can be described by its center, spread, and overall shape. Also 6.SP.1.3, 6.SP.2.5

ACT 1

1. After watching the video, what is the first question that comes to mind?

2. Write the Main Question you will answer.

3. Make a prediction to answer this Main Question.

   The person who should win the competition is ______.

4. **Construct Arguments** Explain how you arrived at your prediction.

ACT 2

5. What information in this situation would be helpful to know? How would you use that information?

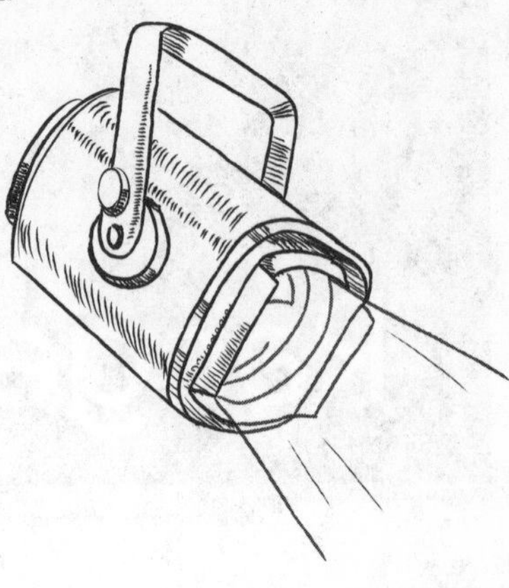

6. **Use Appropriate Tools** What tools can you use to get the information you need? Record the information as you find it.

7. **Model with Math** Represent the situation using the mathematical content, concepts, and skills from this topic. Use your representation to answer the Main Question.

8. What is your answer to the Main Question? Does it differ from your initial prediction? Explain.

ACT 3

9. Write the answer you saw in the video.

10. **Reasoning** Does your answer match the answer in the video? If not, what are some reasons that would explain the difference?

11. **Make Sense and Persevere** Would you change your model now that you know the answer? Explain.

ACT 3 Extension

Reflect

12. Model with Math Explain how you used a mathematical model to represent the situation. How did the model help you answer the Main Question?

13. Use Appropriate Tools What tools or technology did you use to answer the Main Question? What other tools did your classmates use?

SEQUEL

14. Be Precise Design your own singing competition. Explain how you would score each performance and how you would use those scores to choose a winner. Use a different method than you did to answer the Main Question.

LESSON 12-3 Display Data in Box Plots

Quick Review

Quartiles divide a data set into four equal groups. A box plot uses the minimum, first quartile, median, third quartile, and maximum values in a data set to show how the data are distributed.

Example

Make a box plot of the distances, in feet, that seven paper airplanes flew: 60, 75, 45, 55, 70, 40, 65.

40 (45) 55 (60) 65 (70) 75

First Quartile Median Third Quartile

Paper Airplane Distances

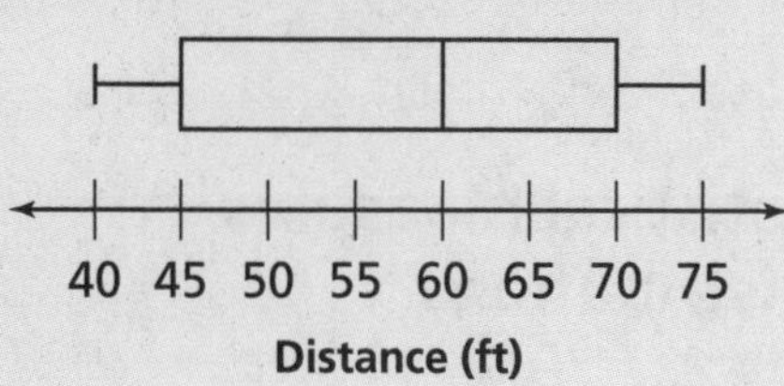

Practice

In 1 and 2, use the data to create a box plot.

1. 27, 31, 30, 33, 29, 25, 28

2. 3, 1, 3, 7, 5, 2, 3, 6, 3

LESSON 12-4 Display Data in Frequency Tables and Histograms

Quick Review

A frequency table shows the number of times a data value or a range of data values occurs in a data set. A histogram is a graph that uses bars to show the frequency of equal ranges or groups of data.

Example

Organize the ages of the campers listed below in a frequency table.

12, 14, 12, 14, 10, 11, 15, 13, 13, 11, 12, 12, 7, 14, 12

Divide the data into equal intervals and mark the frequency of the data using tally marks. Then write the frequency.

Ages of Campers	6–8	9–11	12–14	15–17
Tally	I	III	~~IIII~~ ~~IIII~~	I
Frequency	1	3	10	1

Practice

1. Represent the data in the frequency table on the left in a histogram.

LESSON 12-5 Summarize Data Using Measures of Variability

Quick Review

The mean absolute deviation (MAD) describes how spread out data values are from the mean. The interquartile range (IQR) describes the difference between the third quartile and the first quartile.

Example

Find the MAD of the data set.

6, 7, 8, 8, 8, 11

Mean = 8

The absolute deviations from the mean are 2, 1, 0, 0, 0, and 3, and their sum is 6.

So, MAD = $\frac{6}{6} = 1$.

Practice

In 1–3, find the mean and the MAD for each data set.

1. 5, 12, 0, 7

2. 8, 14, 22, 16

3. 1.25, 2.5, 3

In 4 and 5, find the median, first quartile, third quartile, and IQR for each data set.

4. 10, 20, 35, 45, 45, 50

5. 24, 12, 30, 17, 32, 13, 19

LESSONS 12-6 AND 12-7 Choose Appropriate Statistical Measures and Summarize Data Distributions

Quick Review

You can summarize data by finding the measure of center and the measure of variability. Use the IQR when the median is an appropriate measure of center, and the MAD when the mean is an appropriate measure of center.

Example

Use statistical measures to summarize the data set shown.

Test Scores

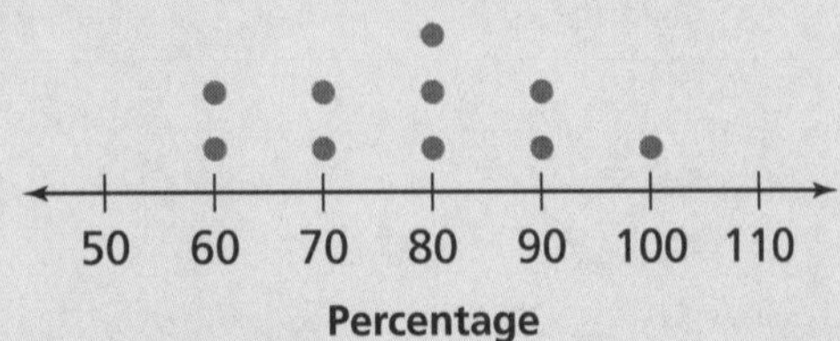

The mean and MAD are good measures to describe this data set.

The mean test score is 78 points. The MAD is 10.4, so most test scores are within 10.4 points of the mean.

Practice

In 1–3, use the data below.

Game Sales

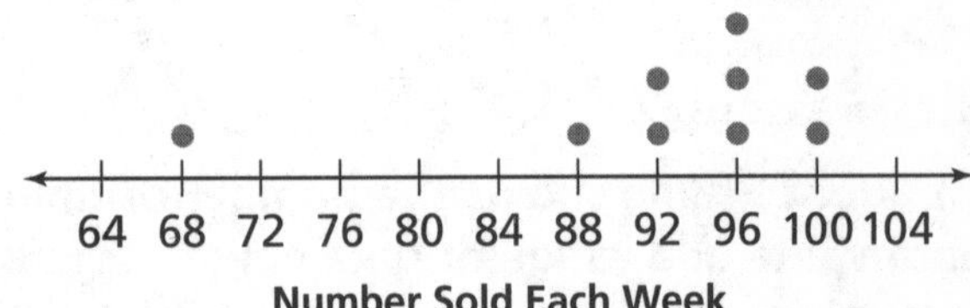

1. Describe the overall shape of the data. Include any outliers.

2. Which measure of center and measure of variability best describe the data set? Explain.

3. Summarize the data set.

Riddle Rearranging

Find each sum or difference. Then arrange the answers in order from least to greatest. The letters will spell out the answer to the riddle below.

I can...
add and subtract decimals.
6.NS.2.3, 6.NS.3.7

C	$14.56 + 9.471$
E	$33.582 - 2.8$
S	$8.999 + 2.3$
I	$45.74 - 22.08$
O	$1.43 + 12.89$
P	$20.4 - 11.81$
F	$25.35 - 2.5$
O	$2.456 + 7$
F	$7.074 + 12.75$
T	$80 - 66.7$

What place's name is only two words long but has hundreds of letters in it?

ACKNOWLEDGEMENTS

Photographs

CVR: fotorince/Shutterstock, grthirteen/Fotolia, Alfgar/Shutterstock, riccamal/Fotolia, Jusakas/Fotolia, Oksana Kuzmina/Fotolia; **409** (T) Mylisa/Shutterstock, (TC) Foonia/Shutterstcok; **410** (BCR) nito/Fotolia, (BR) yossarian6/Fotolia, (TR) Somchai Som/Shutterstock; **415** (C) Scattoselvaggio/Shutterstock, (R) Bernhard Richter/Shutterstock, (TCR) Javier Brosch/Shutterstock, (TR) Javier Brosch/Shutterstock; **417** (BCR) Alphalight Pro Stock/Shutterstock, (BR) Rawpixel/Shutterstock; **419** (Bkgrd) Sorapop Udomsri/Shutterstock, (BC) Takayuki/Shutterstock, (BCR) ChiccoDodiFC/Shutterstock, (BR) kak2s/Shutterstock, (C) kak2s/Shutterstock, (CL) Pete Pahham/Shutterstock, (CR) Leungchopan/Shutterstock, (TC) ChiccoDodiFC/Shutterstock; **420:** Technotr/E+/Getty Images; **425** (B) Khunaspix/123RF, (BL) Jiang Hongyan/Shutterstock, (BR) Eric Isselee/Shutterstock, (TL) Somchai Som/Shutterstock, (TR) Quaoar/Shutterstock; **427:** Kelly Nelson/123RF; **433** (T) Sergey Nivens/Fotolia, (TC) Blend Images Erik Isakson/Brand X Pictures/Getty Images; **443:** luanateutzi/Shutterstock; **444:** Maridav/Shutterstock; **449** (BCR) Arina P Habich/Shutterstock, (BR) Arina P Habich/Shutterstock; **451:** Purestock/Getty Images; **453:** Peter Anderson/Dorling Kindersley Limited; **461:** Vixit/Shutterstock; **462** (BCR) Yuriy Mazur/Fotolia, (BR) yossarian6/Fotolia, (C) tiero/Fotolia, (CR) kamonrat/Fotolia, (TC) Fenton/Fotolia, (TL) Kotomiti/Fotolia, (TR) Vladimir Melnik/Fotolia; **471** (TCL) jdoms/Fotolia, (TL) Sararoom/Fotolia; **476:** afxhome/Fotolia; **477:** Nattika/Shutterstock; **479:** susansantamaria/Fotolia; **481** (BCR) Jeffrey Kraker/Fotolia, (BR) Colette/Fotolia; **482:** PeterO/Fotolia; **485** (C) tigger11th/Fotolia, (CL) WavebreakmediaMicro/Fotolia; **490** (BCR) neuevector/Fotolia, (BR) Cla78/Fotolia; **491:** Lakov Filimonov/123RF; **493:** Belander/Shutterstock; **496** (BCR) vipman4/Fotolia, (BR) Elena Milevska/Fotolia, (CR) AlenKadr/Fotolia, (R) vipman4/Fotolia; **497:** Patrick Foto/Shutterstock; **498:** seanlockephotography/Fotolia; **499:** Bruce Shippee/Fotolia; **511:** RapidEye/iStock/Getty Images Plus/Getty Images; **543:** photastic/Shutterstock; **414** (BCR) Andrey Popov/Fotolia, (BR) yossarian6/Fotolia, (CL) Manaemedia/Fotolia, (CR) Lasse Kristensen/Fotolia, (R) Nikolai Tsvetkov/Fotolia, (TC) Tupungato/Fotolia, (TCL) lucadp/Fotolia, (TCR) Stephen VanHorn/Fotolia, (TR) Andrey Popov/Fotolia; **417** (Bkgrd) Sergey Yarochkin/Fotolia, (BL) Africa Studio/Fotolia, (BR) Denys Prykhodov/Fotolia, (C) Maxal Tamor/Fotolia, (TL) Leo Lintang/Fotolia, (TR) BillionPhotos.com/Fotolia; **429** (C) Sorapop Udomsri/Shutterstock, (CL) Semen Lixodeev/Shutterstock, (CR) Semen Lixodeev/Shutterstock; **430:** Iko/Shutterstock; **431:** Greiss Design/Shutterstock; **432** (CR) Anterovium/Fotolia, (R) LoopAll/Shutterstock; **438** (TCR) Adogslifephoto/Fotolia, (TR) adogslifephoto/Fotolia; **439:** juserdiuk/Fotolia; **547** (C) Verve/Fotolia, (CL) David Pereiras/Fotolia; **550:** Goir/Fotolia; **555** (TCR) Gennady Poddubny/Fotolia, (TR) Georgerudy/Fotolia; **565; 601:** Derek Hatfield/Shutterstock; **566** (BR) yossarian6/Fotolia, (CL) Macrovector/Fotolia, (CR) Stephen VanHorn/Fotolia; **575** (C) picsfive/Fotolia, (CL) kungverylucky/Fotolia, (CR) david_franklin/Fotolia, (L) kungverylucky/Fotolia, (R) yevgeniy11/Fotolia, (TCL) sripfoto/Fotolia, (TCR) gomolach/Fotolia; **581:** portokalis/Fotolia; **585** (BCR) nipaporn/Fotolia, (CR) Dmitriy Syechin/Fotolia, (R) Orlando Bellini/Fotolia; **587:** halfbottle/Fotolia; **593** (C) FreedomMan/Fotolia, (CL) Guzel Studio/Fotolia, (CR) Casejustin/Fotolia, (T) michaeljung/Fotolia, (TC) Elnur/Fotolia; **605** (Bkgrd) Beemar/Fotolia, (C) Determined/Fotolia, (CL) Altanaka/Fotolia, (CR) Davit85/Fotolia, (R) Mat Hayward/Fotolia; **606** (C) milphoto/Fotolia, (CR) .shock/Fotolia, (TC) tarapong/Fotolia; **610:** Sofya Apkalikova/Shutterstock; **611** (CL) Somjring34/Fotolia, (CR) Pixelrobot/Fotolia; **617:** Dmitriy Syechin/Fotolia; **239:** slava_samoilenko/Fotolia; **625:** Cottonfioc/Fotolia; **590** (B) yossarian6/Fotolia, (BCL) Roman Samokhin/Fotolia, (BCR) fotonen/Fotolia, (BL) vlorzor/Fotolia, (BR) Coprid/Fotolia, (C) bravissimos/Fotolia, (CL) monticellllo/Fotolia, (CR) nito/Fotolia, (TC) yvdavid/Fotolia, (TCR) Jaimie Duplass/Fotolia, (TL) viperagp/Fotolia, (TR) Carolyn Franks/Fotolia; **598** (B): eboss6/Fotolia; **647** (TCR) Budimir Jevtic/Fotolia, (TR) Roman_23203/Fotolia; **659:** Andreas Metz/Fotolia; **664:** Zudy/Shutterstock; **675** (C) dadoodas/Fotolia, (CL) Photocreo Bednarek/Fotolia, (CR) littlestocker/Fotolia; (TC) Steve Byland/Shutterstock; **681** (TC) Bogdan Florea/Shutterstock, (TL) Lovely Bird/Shutterstock; **685:** Pixelrobot/Fotolia; **693:** Ryan Burke/DigitalVision Vectors/Getty Images; **695:** Yongcharoen_kittiyaporn/Shutterstock; **696** (BR) yossarian6/Fotolia, (CL) puckillustrations/Fotolia, (CR) andresgarciam/Fotolia, (TR) Ig0rZh/Fotolia; (BCR) Pisaphotography/Shutterstock; **705** (CL) mouse_md/Fotolia, (TC) Ljupco Smokovski/Fotolia; **707:** Csak Istvan/123RF; **712:** 3drenderings/Fotolia; **713:** ki33/Fotolia; **714** (C) aleciccotelli/Fotolia, (T) Racobovt/Shutterstock; **719:** bluecherrygfx/Fotolia; **727:** Gleb Semenjuk/Fotolia; **738** (CR) pixelrobot/Fotolia, (TR) Natsmith1/Shutterstock; (R) BillionPhotos.com/Fotolia; **741:** OmniArt/Shutterstock; Amnachphoto/Fotolia; Bonzami Emmanuelle/123RF; Chaivit/Fotolia; Coprid/Fotolia; Pavlo Vakhrushev/Fotolia; **F16** (BL) Natis/Fotolia, (TR) Natis/Fotolia; **F17** (BL) mike166146/Fotolia, (BR) macrovector/Fotolia; **F18:** Gelpi/Fotolia; **F19** (T) blueringmedia/Fotolia, (TC) lukeruk/Fotolia; **F20** (C) piai/Fotolia, (CR) Fotolia, (CR) Natis/Fotolia; **F21:** Taras Livyy/Fotolia; **F22** (T): duke215/Fotolia; **F23** Fotolia, mike166146/Fotolia; Geargodz/Fotolia; GraphicCompressor/Fotolia; Koya979/Fotolia; Kurhan/Fotolia; Lars Christensen/Shutterstock; Popova Olga/Fotolia; Stephen VanHorn/Fotolia; Taras Livyy/Fotolia.